Le Cordon Bleu
AT HOME

HEARST BOOKS   NEW YORK

The publisher gratefully acknowledges the editorial contributions
of Stephanie Lyness and Dolores Simon.

Library of Congress Cataloging-in-Publication Data

Le Cordon Bleu at home.
p. cm.
Includes index.
ISBN 0-688-09750-2
1. Cookery, French. I. Cordon bleu (School: Paris, France)
TX719.C61123   1991
641.5944—dc20   90-27345
                                                        CIP

Printed in the United States of America

First Edition
1 2 3 4 5 6 7 8 9 10

BOOK DESIGNED BY JOEL AVIROM

CONTENTS

FOREWORD

*L*e Cordon Bleu is pleased to present its first complete English-language cookbook, *Le Cordon Bleu at Home*. Based on the same successful teaching methods of the world-famous cooking school in Paris, the book is designed to initiate the amateur chef in the fundamentals of classical French cuisine and guide the professional in advanced techniques of French cooking.

Le Cordon Bleu at Home seeks to pass on to the reader a solid understanding of the philosophy and skills taught in the school's Classic Cycle. Progressing through three stages, from basic to advanced techniques, it is an in-depth and professional approach to traditional French cuisine, presented in a series of easy-to-follow menus that correspond to actual classes at the school. Many of the recipes given here are taught at Le Cordon Bleu by a team of master chefs from France's various Michelin-star restaurants. Each year, these chefs train students from more than fifty different countries, combining time-honored traditions with the latest, most sophisticated techniques. It is this kind of outstanding training, together with the exceptional state-of-the-art equipment available to each student, that makes Le Cordon Bleu unique.

Nearing its one-hundredth birthday, Le Cordon Bleu is continuing its international expansion with new schools in Tokyo and London. It has also established academic ties with some of the finest universities in North America as well as countries throughout the world. Publication of *Le Cordon Bleu at Home* has been a labor of love for all of us, our way of safeguarding a culinary tradition unlike any other in the world.

ANDRÉ J. COINTREAU
President

INTRODUCTION

*I*n the course of its long history Le Cordon Bleu published not only its famous magazine but books as well. These books were often the work of chefs associated with the school and, as such, were a means of codifying and diffusing Le Cordon Bleu's approach to cuisine.

This book, however, is a landmark in the history of the school. It is the first time that recipes have been assembled with an international audience in mind (all previous books were published exclusively in French), and it is the first time in eighty years that *any* collection of Cordon Bleu recipes has appeared in book form. All the recipes included here are taught at the school; they were developed by the school chefs and tested with the home cook in mind, and will give the reader a wide-ranging and varied introduction to French cuisine.

France, French cuisine, and Le Cordon Bleu have evolved greatly over the last hundred years. Over the last decade, eighty different nationalities were represented at the school. Today, thousands of students are enrolled at Le Cordon Bleu, all having come to Paris for the same reasons: to work with French chefs and to learn from their skills. The reader is invited to join them via the recipes published here. Drawn mainly from the classic repertoire, they reflect the kind of cooking practiced by professional chefs in France today.

We divided this book into lessons that take the form of menus. These menus, identical to the ones we use to teach our classes in Paris, are designed to take you from the simplest task to the most complex, at each step building on the skills just learned. The menus are constructed for maximum teaching results, and as such they may require some rearranging before they suit your "real life" cooking needs.

Close your eyes, imagine you are in Paris on a street called Rue Léon Delhomme. You are entering the doors of a school whose very name evokes excellence in the culinary arts.

Welcome to Le Cordon Bleu.

A BRIEF HISTORY

Rue Léon Delhomme is a quiet street on the Left Bank in Paris, not far from the Eiffel Tower. Usually there is not much traffic, people stroll leisurely down the sidewalk, and children run next to buildings that have stood undisturbed for centuries. But on the eve of February 1, 1988, Rue Léon Delhomme was the scene of much excitement. Floodlights lit the facade of No. 8 and thousands of well-dressed people filled the street. Limousines with diplomatic plates brought ambassadors from twenty-four nations. Champagne corks popped and the sound of applause echoed down the street as the French Minister of Finance unveiled a bronze plaque to commemorate the building's inauguration.

What was going on? The next day French papers announced the news: The world's most famous cooking school had officially relocated. Le Cordon Bleu had moved, and Rue Léon Delhomme would never be the same again. In the weeks to come, curious neighbors got their first glimpse of the new school, examining brochures in French, English, Japanese, and Spanish neatly displayed in one window. By the time the year wore on, a visitor might notice that the students looked surprisingly tense; they were taking final exams. Beginning students, faced with a box full of fresh ingredients, had to prepare a dish named by the chef only minutes before; if they succeeded and the chef approved, they earned their first diploma. They could then go on and enroll in more advanced classes in hopes of one day winning the most coveted prize of all, *Le Grand Diplôme du Cordon Bleu*.

Though these sights and sounds were new to Rue Léon Delhomme, they were not new to Paris. Le Cordon Bleu is a well-established Parisian institution, as venerable as the Eiffel Tower, and almost as old. It dates back to 1895 when a woman named Marthe Distel formed a weekly publication called *La Cuisinière Cordon-bleu*, in which famous chefs gave courses via articles they wrote and in which she and others shared recipes, gave advice, and discussed the pleasures of the table.

The title had been carefully chosen. It derives from the sixteenth-century French knightly order, *Ordre du Saint Esprit*, the most exclusive in France, whose members—royalty included—were called *Cordons-bleus* after the broad blue ribbons they wore. Nothing was too good for a *Cordon-bleu*, and the dinners that accompanied their ceremonious meetings were legendary.

By the eighteenth century, the term *Cordon-bleu* was applied to anyone who excelled in a particular field. The term became chiefly associated with fine cooks. Some say this is because students at the school founded by Madame de Maintenon at Saint Cyr wore a blue sash during their last year of attendance, and that among the skills they mastered was cooking. Others claim this association arose after Louis XV bragged to his mistress, Madame du Barry, that only men made great chefs. The lady believed otherwise and invited the king to a meal prepared by her *cuisinière*. It was a great success and the king exclaimed, "Who is the new man you have cooking for you? He is as good as any cook in the royal household." "It's a woman cook, Your Majesty," Madame du Barry replied, "and I think you should honor her with nothing less than the *Cordon-bleu*."

In 1827 the first Cordon Bleu cookbook was published, called *Le Cordon bleu ou nouvelle cuisinière bourgeoise*. It would remain in print for fifty years, teaching the art of cooking through its recipes. Mademoiselle Distel realized that an even better way to teach cooking would be to organize classes where students could see the chef at work and practice under his trained eye. In December 1895 subscribers were informed that "the ever-growing popularity of *La Cuisinière Cordon-Bleu* makes the management feel that it has a duty to find new ways of satisfying those who have faithfully supported our enterprises; hence we have decided to offer free cooking classes to our subscribers and to publish the recipes taught in those classes in future issues of our magazine."

Professional chefs were invited to teach the newly announced classes; among those active in the early years were Chef Barthélémy, director of a professional pastry chefs' publication; Chef Charles Poulain, former director of one of Paris's most famous catering houses; and Chef August Colombié, whose cookbooks were extremely popular at the turn of the century.

The first Cordon Bleu cooking class was held on January 14, 1896, in Paris's Palais Royal. Its organizers proudly announced a glimpse of the latest in culinary technology—electricity was installed in one of the kitchens!

The cooking courses were a great success. At first the emphasis was on *La cuisine pratique* (practical cooking), although in September 1896 the magazine announced that courses would also be given in *haute cuisine classique*. These early courses were overseen by one of the most prominent chefs of the day, Charles Driessens. He would later become Directeur des Cours de Cuisine du Cordon-Bleu; Mademoiselle Distel remained director of the magazine, staying discreetly in the background until 1904, when she became head of the *cours de cuisine* as well.

Both the magazine and the classes attracted the attention of cooking professionals around the world, including Russia. By the time of Mademoiselle Distel's death in the late 1930s, the magazine had twenty-five thousand subscribers, and the school—begun as an "extra" offered to subscribers—had become a drawing card in its own right. Indeed, less than ten years after the first courses were offered, the magazine became dependent upon the school, existing simply as the official school publication. The importance of the magazine diminished until finally, in the 1960s, it was discontinued. In all, more than sixty volumes of recipes had been published by the school, and this ensemble stands as one of the most extensive collections of recipes ever printed in France.

By publishing the school recipes, the magazine contributed in a major way to the codification of French cuisine. In its pages definitions were furnished and examples given that provided form and substance to ideas that were sometimes expressed for the first time in print. Both the magazine and the school responded to the growing demand for a rigorous culinary education, as well as contributing to and reflecting the evolution of the art of cooking in France for more than half a century.

Le Cordon Bleu grew, changed, and flourished in the following decades. Originally a purely Parisian institution, the school quickly became international, and by 1905 students were coming from as far away as Japan to learn French cooking. An article in the London *Daily Mail*, dated November 16, 1927, described a visit to the school in Paris where, the author writes, "It is not unusual for as many as eight different nationalities to be represented in the classes. . . . The purposes of the students vary; some are instructors desiring to add further to their qualifications, while others are novices who intend to become chefs."

Those who attended courses in the early years of this century had the privilege of learning French cuisine from one of the great master chefs of the day, Henri-Paul Pellaprat. Born in 1869, he began cooking at the age of twelve. His talent was quickly recognized and he went on to direct some of the finest restaurant kitchens in France. As time passed, he realized that his real calling was teaching and he accepted a professorship at Le Cordon Bleu. He taught at the school for forty years, during which time he wrote his master work, *L'Art Culinaire Moderne*. It was translated into five languages, and when it appeared in English (as *The Great Book of French Cookery*), as it was hailed as "the most comprehensive, authoritative, and up-to-date book on French cooking and gastronomy ever written." As an author and teacher, Pellaprat did much to consolidate Le Cordon Bleu's position as the world's leading cooking school, and the tributes paid to his books echo the importance accorded the school, which was setting standards and teaching classic French cuisine to an ever-growing number of graduates.

After the Second World War, Le Cordon Bleu continued to prosper and grow under the direction of Madame Elisabeth Brassart. She would welcome two generations of cooks to Le Cordon Bleu, revise the curriculum, and see the school receive official recognition. One of the female students who was enrolled at Le Cordon Bleu did more than sense the trend toward "good cooking and eating," she made it a reality in millions of homes across the United States. That woman, a tall energetic American, to whom Madame Bressart awarded the *Grand Diplôme du Cordon Bleu*, was Julia Child.

By the 1950s Le Cordon Bleu represented not only the highest level of culinary training but was a symbol of Paris itself. It seemed only natural for Audrey Hepburn to attend a cooking school in the shadow of the Eiffel Tower when she played the role of Sabrina in the film of the same name. The reference to Le Cordon Bleu could hardly have been more explicit, and the scene in which she learns to make an omelet was yet another illustration of the growing interest in French cooking and Le Cordon Bleu in particular.

Le Cordon Bleu has not only set the standard for cooking schools around the world but has been innovative in more ways than one: It was the first school to organize demonstrations during which a chef made dishes and gave participants the chance to sample each one (on the following days students made the same dishes in practical classes themselves). Through a judicious mixture of practical classes and demonstrations, students learn French cuisine from French chefs "at the source."

When it comes to the teaching of French cuisine and pastry, Le Cordon Bleu is unrivaled. The school's reputation is based on the professional quality of the courses taught. Beginners are introduced to basic techniques and professionals improve their skills through contacts with awarding-winning French chefs who hail from Michelin-starred restaurants. *Le Grand Diplôme du Cordon Bleu* is recognized throughout the culinary world and opens the doors to the best kitchens in France and abroad.

Today, as in the past, courses are conducted entirely in French, though teaching assistants translate the chef's instructions into English. Students in all classes have their own work surface, fully equipped with refrigerator blocks, a professional oven, and a whole range of kitchen utensils. Special work areas are reserved for courses devoted to pastry, bread baking, and *sous-vide* (vacuum-packed) cuisine. Intensive sessions treat such specific aspects of French cuisine as pastry, chocolate, and regional cuisine.

Le Cordon Bleu also organizes workshops for groups visiting the school and those eager to get a glimpse of the famous kitchens. It has close academic ties with professional training institutions inside and outside of France, and in 1990 purchased Le Cordon Bleu London with which it had no previous affiliation. There, students will receive the same rigorous classical training in French cuisine as their counterparts in Paris, but will have the added benefit of being offered courses designed to exploit such fine British products as Scottish salmon or Welsh lamb and sampling traditional dishes from the British Isles.

With the publication of this book, cooks everywhere will be able to benefit from the years of experience that have made Le Cordon Blue *the* place to learn French cooking and to perfect culinary skills. No other school can claim a hundred years of experience in teaching French cuisine or boast a more qualified staff or well-furnished facilities.

Located in the culinary capital of Europe, in a city whose cultural and artistic importance never ceases to grow, Le Cordon Bleu is more than a cooking school. It is an institution devoted to promoting and preserving a fine art—French cooking. The school's name is synonymous with excellence, and it is easy to understand why there is a waiting list of cooks to be admitted and why each year enthusiastic men and women from fifty countries are so eager to cross the threshold at No. 8 Rue Léon Delhomme. These new students know they will be a part of a great tradition and that French cuisine will soon hold no mysteries for them. As time passes, they gain confidence in their skills and, if they apply themselves, they will be awarded one of the school's prestigious diplomas. Those who successfully pass their exams can rightfully feel proud; they are now members of a very special group—they are graduates of Le Cordon Bleu.

PART ONE

Pratique de Base

GETTING STARTED

*L*earning to cook, like learning to sing or dance, involves becoming proficient in a certain number of basic skills, and mastering the basics can be both a challenging and a creative experience. The recipes included in these first menus introduce techniques and procedures all French cooks must be familiar with and which are employed by them virtually every day. These techniques will be taught in recipes that evoke the gastronomic diversity of France and the simplicity of French home cooking, and should provide a first glimpse of the fireworks, precision, and polish so characteristic of *grande cuisine*.

What exactly can you expect to learn in the following pages? You will be taught how the French roast, poach, fry, sauté, braise, and stew. You will discover that scrambled eggs (made the French way) can be an elegant first course, that crêpes can be both desserts and starters, how egg whites can be combined with either chocolate (mousse) or cheese (soufflé), how to unlock the secrets of French sorbet and ice cream, and how a simple dough can be transformed into miniature swans with wings, graceful necks and a whipped cream filling.

Cooking methods will be given the attention they deserve. Indeed, though sauces are the hallmark of French cuisine, they cannot save poorly cooked dishes, and a cook who does not know the secrets of making a good sauté, poaching a fish, or roasting a chicken will never produce satisfying results. You will learn what utensils simplify each task, what cuts of meat are most appropriate for the different types of cooking described, what kinds of preliminary preparations might be required, and, most of all, what signs indicate that all is well.

The recipes chosen to illustrate techniques are those most commonly used in French homes—roast chicken, roast leg of lamb, poached trout, poached fruit, pan-fried sole, breaded veal, apple fritters, and so on. Some recipes are associated with a specific area (a beef stew from Provence and a fish stew from Brittany are cases in point), while others are simply classic preparations drawn from the extensive repertoire of dishes all French chefs know by heart (*sauté de veau marengo*, sautéed potatoes, *blanquette de veau*, to name a few). Each of these recipes, and indeed all of those in this book, will teach you more than one thing. In this first section, particular emphasis will be placed not only on the cooking methods but on two other building blocks of French cuisine directly related to them: sauces and stocks.

Classic French cuisine relies heavily on the use of basic stocks and sauces ("mother sauces") for flavoring and seasoning dishes. They are not difficult to make, and in the course of the menus that follow, you will discover how bones, water, and vegetables can be made into flavorful, richly colored stocks, how a simple mother sauce can be combined with vegetables, eggs, or fish to make a wide variety of dishes, and how, in all cases, each element is used to its best effect. You will be introduced to such favorites as mayonnaise, béchamel, and vinaigrette, and learn the Cordon Bleu's method for making each; once the basic sauce is mastered, you will learn how each can be transformed to create a host of other sauces simply by changing the seasoning or modifying a technique.

Thanks to the menu format adopted here, this first collection of recipes will also provide an occasion to introduce basic pastry preparations which, like their cuisine equivalents, are the easiest to learn but are by no means the least important in the book. Indeed, pastry, even more than cuisine, demands a perfect familiarity with the basics; and if French pastry was once said to be a branch of architecture it was not only because some desserts are "monumental" but because all involve assembling an array of elements with a final design in mind.

Starting with the dough most popular with French cooks at home, pâte brisée (short crust), you will learn the tricks that make doughs light, crumbly, and rich and how to create new doughs by changing a few elements in the basic preparation. Examples will demonstrate how the same dough can be used in various ways. Pâte brisée, for example, is used in making not only sweet tarts but also a savory onion tart, while choux pastry is baked and filled with chantilly cream on one occasion and deep fried on another to make two very different desserts. You will learn how sugar, water, and fruit combine to make delicious fruit sorbets and how a simple crème anglaise can be used as a sauce with desserts or become the starting point for numerous frozen creations.

In addition to the basic doughs and creams, traditional bistro specialties, such as *oeufs à la neige* (meringue "eggs" with caramel and custard cream sauce), and simple classics like *poires belle Hélène* (poached pears with vanilla ice cream and warm chocolate sauce) are also included to complete this first look at the way the French typically end a meal.

In short, those who master the recipes included in this chapter on getting started will be well versed in the techniques constantly drawn upon in the more advanced cooking chapters to come. In gaining this experience, they will become familiar with a rich and varied repertoire of dishes that will do them honor and rival the best home cooking in France.

LESSON 1

Concombre à la Menthe

CUCUMBER SALAD WITH MINT

———

Poulet Rôti

ROAST CHICKEN

———

Petits Pois à la Française

SPRING PEAS WITH LETTUCE, CHERVIL, AND ONIONS

———

Salade des Fruits

FRESH FRUIT SALAD WITH COINTREAU

Concombre à la Menthe

CUCUMBER SALAD WITH MINT

———

SERVES 6

Cucumber salad can be seasoned with either a classic vinaigrette or a cream-based dressing in which heavy cream is used rather than oil. This is a refreshing variation using yogurt instead of cream.

Note: In France, cucumbers are traditionally salted before serving in salads, which draws out natural moisture and heightens taste, but those who prefer crunchy cucumbers can omit this step if they like.

*2 pounds small pickling cucumbers
  or 2 medium European
  hothouse cucumbers*
2 teaspoons salt

YOGURT MINT DRESSING
3/4 cup plain yogurt
1 tablespoon red-wine vinegar
Freshly ground pepper
12 large fresh mint leaves

Peel the cucumbers and slice thin. Put the slices into a colander, sprinkle with the salt and let drain 30 minutes.

Prepare the dressing: In a serving bowl, stir together the yogurt, vinegar, and a pinch of pepper. Stack 8 mint leaves one on top of the other and roll them up tight into a cylinder. Then cut the cylinder crosswise into thin slivers. Stir the mint into the dressing.

Wrap the cucumber slices in a clean dish towel and squeeze gently to dry them. Add the cucumber to the dressing and toss. Let the salad stand 20 minutes before serving. Serve garnished with the remaining mint leaves.

Poulet Rôti
ROAST CHICKEN

SERVES 6

Not all chickens are equal in France. The famous white-feathered birds from Bresse, near Lyon, fetch the highest prices and are remarkably tender, plump, and tasty. Like wine, they are *appellation controlée* (quality controlled and protected by law). Ordinary free-range birds (*poulets fermier*) from other regions—particularly Périgord and the Loire Valley—can also be excellent; when perfectly roasted and served with a simple *jus*, or pan juices, a bird of this quality can turn a family meal into a memorable event.

5-pound chicken, giblets removed
Salt and freshly ground pepper
1 clove garlic, peeled
1 bay leaf
Several sprigs fresh thyme or
  1/2 teaspoon dried

2 tablespoons unsalted butter,
  softened
1 tablespoon vegetable oil

Preheat the oven to 425°. Rinse the chicken inside and out under cold running water. Dry with paper towels. Season the cavity with salt and pepper and then add the garlic and herbs.

Truss the chicken with kitchen twine (see technique photos on page 530): Place the chicken on its back on a work surface. Pass a long piece of kitchen twine underneath the tail. Bring the ends of the twine up around each leg and cross the ends over the top. Bring both ends of the twine under the tips of the legs and pull both ends of the twine to draw the legs together. Then draw the ends of the twine along either side of the chicken and over the wing joints. Turn the chicken over on its breast, cross the twine over the neck skin, and tighten to pull the wings to the body. Tie securely.

Rub the chicken with the butter and oil and season with salt and pepper. Place the chicken on its side in a roasting pan just large enough to hold it and roast 20 minutes. Turn the chicken on its other side and roast 20 minutes longer. Finally, turn the chicken breast side up, add 1/2 cup water to the pan, and continue roasting until the juices run clear when the thigh is pierced with a skewer, 20 to 30 minutes longer. Transfer the chicken to a platter and let rest for at least 15 minutes after removing from the oven, covered with aluminum foil. The juices will be absorbed into the meat and carving will be easier.

While the chicken is resting, spoon off the fat in the roasting pan. Bring the remaining juices to a boil on top of the stove, scraping with a whisk to release any cooked particles that adhere to the bottom of the pan. Reduce the heat to medium and simmer the juices until reduced by one-third; strain.

To serve, remove the trussing twine from the chicken. Pour some of the reduced juices over the chicken and serve the remainder in a sauceboat on the side.

ROASTING

Roasting is the technique of cooking meat, poultry, or fish with dry heat. A high heat is used to sear the roast, forming a crisp skin on fish and poultry and an attractive brown crust on meats. After cooking, the roast must rest for at least 15 minutes to allow the juices that have fled to the center to be reabsorbed into the flesh. This resting period also facilitates carving. A very old method of cooking, roasting was originally done on a rotating spit over an open fire. Now, of course, oven roasting is much commoner.

Roasting is ideal for poultry, especially fatty birds such as duck or goose, which benefit from a long cooking time to drain as much fat as possible from under the skin. (Leaner birds, on the other hand, such as quail, pheasant, and guinea hen, are often barded with strips of fat to keep their flesh from drying out during cooking.) The best meats for roasting are the tender, well-marbled, and more expensive cuts, such as beef filet and rack of lamb; very dry cuts or those that contain a great deal of connective tissue or gristle (such as shoulders or shanks) should be saved for the moist heat of braises or stews.

Meats and poultry are often trussed, both to provide a uniform shape for even cooking and to make an attractive table presentation. This is particularly useful if the meat has been boned and crucial if it has been stuffed.

Choose a roasting pan that is just slightly larger than the food to be cooked: If the pan is too small, the roast will stew in the pan juices; too large, and you risk burning the pan juices and ruining your sauce. Setting the roast on top of bones or vegetables in the pan will further discourage the meat from stewing, and will flavor the pan juices as well. Make sure your oven is well preheated and allow the roast to come to room temperature before cooking so that it will cook evenly.

Petits Pois à la Française

SPRING PEAS WITH LETTUCE, CHERVIL, AND ONIONS

SERVES 6

Peas should be small and squeaky fresh if you squeeze a handful of pods. In France, their season is short and demand is high. This traditional method of cooking them is by far the most popular: Peas are simmered with pearl onions and lettuce and perfumed with chervil, an herb with a mildly licorice taste.

1 small head leaf lettuce
5 tablespoons unsalted butter
3 cups shelled young peas
(or 2 pounds peas in the pod, shelled)

18 pearl onions, peeled
1 small bunch chervil or parsley
1½ tablespoons sugar
1 teaspoon salt

Cut the lettuce into chiffonade (see technique photo on page 520): Stack the lettuce leaves one on top of the other and roll them up tight into a cylinder. Then cut the cylinder crosswise into thin slices.

Heat the butter in a heavy saucepan over medium heat. Add the lettuce, peas, and onions to the pan and stir gently with a wooden spoon until the lettuce wilts. Tie the chervil into a bouquet with kitchen twine and add it to the pan along with ⅓ cup water, the sugar, and the salt. Cover and cook gently until the peas are tender, 15 to 25 minutes. Remove the chervil and serve.

Salade des Fruits

FRESH FRUIT SALAD WITH COINTREAU

SERVES 6

A fruit salad is as good as the fruit it is made from. Always choose perfectly ripe, unbruised fruit—better to use fewer fruits than fruits that are green or not in season. This particular salad has an orange-flavored base and, like any good fruit salad, provides an interesting mixture of colors, textures, and tastes.

¹/₂ pint basket strawberries
1 orange
1 peach
1 apple
1 pear
2 thick slices fresh pineapple,
* peeled and cored*

1 banana
Juice of one 1 lemon, strained
¹/₂ cup superfine sugar
1 tablespoon Cointreau
1 kiwifruit

Rinse the strawberries and pat them dry with paper towels. Hull and slice them.

Peel and section the orange: Cut a small slice off the top and bottom of the orange. Stand the orange upright on a work surface and, following the contours of the fruit, use a small paring knife to cut away the skin and bitter white pith to expose the flesh. Then, holding the orange in the palm of your hand over a large bowl to catch the sections and juice, slide the knife between the membrane and the flesh to release the orange sections. Squeeze the remaining membrane over the bowl to extract as much juice as possible and discard.

Skin the peach: Bring a small saucepan of water to a boil. Fill a bowl with cold water. Lower the peach into the boiling water and let it remain there for 20 to 30 seconds. Transfer to the bowl of cold water with a slotted spoon. Slip off the skin with a paring knife. Cut the peach in half, remove the pit, and then cut the flesh in thin, even slices.

Peel and core the apple and pear and cut each into thin slices. Cut the pineapple into small wedges. Peel and slice the banana.

Combine all of the fruit in the bowl with the orange sections and juice. Stir together the lemon juice, sugar and Cointreau and pour the mixture over the fruit. Let the salad stand 1 hour, stirring gently once or twice.

Just before serving peel the kiwifruit and slice it thin. Transfer the salad to a glass serving bowl and garnish with the kiwifruit.

PREPARING FRUITS

The recipe above for Salade des Fruits demonstrates two techniques for preparing fruits. That used to peel the orange is known as *peler à vif* and may be used for all citrus fruits. Be sure to remove as much of the white pith as possible, because it is very bitter. The technique used to skin the peach (a few seconds' immersion in boiling water and then a cold water bath) can be used for other similar fruits such as nectarines and for tomatoes (page 31). Do not let the fruit sit in the boiling water too long or you will cook the flesh.

LESSON 2

Soupe Villageoise
COUNTRY-STYLE VEGETABLE SOUP WITH NOODLES

—

Escalopes de Veau
Vallée d'Auge
VEAL SCALLOPS WITH APPLES AND CALVADOS

—

Crème Renversée au Caramel
CARAMEL CUSTARD

Soupe Villageoise
COUNTRY-STYLE VEGETABLE SOUP WITH NOODLES

—

SERVES 6

Country soups are filling and this one is no exception. Some use beans or potatoes while others, like the one described below, use pasta to complete the vegetable base. Leeks, cabbage, and parsley or chervil give the soup an attractive greenish tint and their flavors harmonize nicely in this hearty peasant dish.

1 small head green cabbage	Salt and freshly ground pepper
6 tablespoons unsalted butter	1 cup vermicelli pieces
2 pounds leeks	Chervil or parsley leaves
8 cups Chicken Stock (page 12)	for garnish

Prepare the cabbage: Bring a large saucepan of water to a boil. Remove and discard the large outer leaves of cabbage. Quarter the head and cut out and discard the hard central core. Rinse in cold water, drain, and slice fine. Add the cabbage to the boiling water, return the water to a boil, and blanch the cabbage 5 minutes. Drain, refresh under cold running water, and drain again. Heat 3 tablespoons of the butter in a large frying pan over low heat.

Add the cabbage and stir to coat with the butter. Cover and cook, stirring occasionally, until soft but not colored, about 15 minutes.

Meanwhile, prepare the leeks: Cut off the stringy roots at the base of each leek. Cut off the upper two thirds of the green tops. Starting about 1 inch from the root end, insert a knife through the white part of a leek and cut through to the top of the green. Rotate the leek and repeat the process so that the leek has been quartered lengthwise but is still connected at the root end. Repeat with remaining leeks. Rinse the leeks well in cold water. Drain and slice thin.

Melt the remaining 3 tablespoons butter in a large saucepan over low heat. Add the leeks, cover and cook, stirring occasionally, until soft but not colored. Add the cooked cabbage and stock. Bring to a boil and simmer over medium heat for about 40 minutes. Season to taste with salt and pepper.

Add the vermicelli to the soup, bring to a boil, and cook until tender, about 5 minutes. Pour the soup into a tureen and serve garnished with chervil or parsley leaves.

STOCKS

Without stocks there would be no French cuisine. Called *fonds de cuisine,* which translates literally as "foundations of cooking," they are a crucial element in soups, sauces, braises, and stews. Good stocks are made by simmering raw meat or fish, and bones, with aromatic vegetables and herbs, peppercorns, water, and a little salt. Richly colored brown stocks, made with beef and veal, are made by first browning the meat and bones in the oven before simmering them with the remaining ingredients; brown stocks are used in brown sauces and with red meats and game. Light-colored white stocks, made with veal, poultry, and fish, require no browning, and have a lighter flavor suitable for the delicate flavors of poultry, fish, and vegetables.

Stocks must be simmered long enough to extract the maximum flavor from the ingredients. For a veal stock, this means at least 3½ hours, while a chicken stock requires only 2½ hours and a fish stock just 20 minutes. The stock must be carefully skimmed after it is brought to a boil to remove any fat and gray scum that rise to the surface, but it must never be boiled during cooking, as this would make it cloudy.

Stocks may be refrigerated for several weeks provided they are brought to a boil every 2 to 3 days. Or they may be reduced to a thick, syrupy glaze, called a *glace,* that will set to a very firm consistency when chilled and may be refrigerated for several months (*glaces* are used as sauce bases of or to intensify the flavor of and give body to sauces). Stocks may also be frozen for several months; it makes good sense to freeze them in small quantities so that you need thaw only the amount necessary.

Chicken Stock
FOND DE VOLAILLE

8 CUPS

4-pound chicken
3 small onions
3 cloves
3 carrots
3 leeks
2 stalks celery
6 cloves garlic

4 large sprigs parsley
   (including stems)
2 branches thyme
1 bay leaf
1 teaspoon coarse salt
10 peppercorns
12 cups water

Rinse chicken inside and out. Cut off wing tips. Truss (see recipe on page 6 and technique photos on page 530).

Peel the onions. Press the cloves into 1 of the onions and cut the other 2 onions into quarters. Peel and trim carrots, leeks, celery, and garlic. Cut carrots and leeks in quarters. Tie leeks, celery, parsley, thyme, and bay leaf into a large bouquet with kitchen twine (see technique photo on page 520).

Put the chicken, the neck, wing tips, and gizzard into a soup kettle. Add the vegetables, garlic, salt, peppercorns, and water. Bring to a boil and skim off all the froth that rises to the surface. Reduce the heat and simmer for 1 hour, skimming off any froth or fat that floats to the surface during cooking. Remove the chicken and reserve for another use. Continue simmering the stock for another 1½ hours. Strain through a fine strainer. If necessary, continue cooking until reduced to 8 cups.

Cool the stock, uncovered, as quickly as possible. The stock will keep for 2 to 3 days in the refrigerator or several weeks if it is boiled every day; or it can be frozen. Bring to a boil before using.

Escalopes de Veau Vallée d'Auge
VEAL SCALLOPS WITH APPLES AND CALVADOS

SERVES 6

The Auge Valley in Normandy boasts three famous "C's"—Camembert, cream, and Calvados (apple brandy). The combination of the latter two with apples, another local specialty, characterizes this distinctive dish.

3/4 pound mushrooms
8 tablespoons unsalted butter
Salt and freshly ground pepper
1 cup crème frâiche
6 small Golden Delicious apples

6 veal scallops, 6 ounces each
1/4 cup vegetable oil
2 large shallots, chopped fine
2 tablespoons Calvados
1 tablespoon chopped parsley

Trim the bases of the mushroom stems. Rinse the mushrooms quickly in cold water, pat dry with paper towels and slice thin. Heat 2 tablespoons of the butter in a medium frying pan over high heat. Add the mushrooms and cook, stirring, until all the moisture has evaporated. Season to taste with salt and pepper. Stir in 3 tablespoons of the cream. Cover and set aside.

Preheat the oven to 450°. Melt 2 tablespoons of the butter. Peel and core the apples and trim to about 2 inches in diameter. Put the apples in an ovenproof pan just large enough to hold them and brush with the melted butter. Bake until tender but still firm, about 15 minutes. Set aside.

Flatten the veal scallops with the flat side of a large knife. Season both sides with salt and pepper. Heat 2 tablespoons of the oil and 2 tablespoons of the butter in a large frying pan over high heat. Add 3 of the scallops and sauté until golden brown on both sides. (Do not overcook or the veal will be tough.) Transfer to a serving platter; cover to keep warm. Discard the fat from the pan and sauté the remaining scallops in the remaining butter and oil. Transfer to the serving platter.

Add the shallots to the pan and cook over medium heat until tender but not colored. Remove the pan from the heat and spoon off the fat. Return the pan to the heat, add the Calvados or brandy, and light with a match. When the flames die, stir in the mushrooms and the remaining cream, bring to a boil, and boil 2 minutes until the sauce has reduced and thickened slightly. Taste and adjust seasonings.

To serve, spoon the mushrooms and sauce over the scallops and sprinkle with the parsley. Arrange the baked apples around the edge of the platter.

SAUTÉING AND DEGLAZING

Sautéing is the technique of browning foods quickly over high heat in a small amount of hot fat. When sautéing, it is important that (1) the fat be very hot so that the food browns well and doesn't absorb the fat; (2) the pan be low sided and large enough to hold the food without crowding so that the food browns quickly rather than stewing in its own juices; and (3) the food to be cooked be completely dry to prevent it from stewing (this last is particularly a consideration when sautéing foods that have been marinated).

In the recipe above for Escalopes de Veau Vallée d'Auge the veal is sautéed until completely cooked. Often, however, foods are sautéed just to brown the exterior, then finished in a simmering liquid, as in a sauté (Poulet Sauté Basquaise, page 59) or stews and braises (Éstouffade de Boeuf Provençale, page 139).

The sauce for the veal is made by deglazing—a useful technique by which a liquid is added to the pan to pick up the flavorful meat juices that have cooked onto the bottom. Deglazing is a basic step in the preparation of a variety of sauces and, depending on the desired result, may be accomplished with water, stock, cream, or an alcohol. A simple sauce for a roast can be made by deglazing the pan with water (Gigot d'Agneau, page 25).

Crème Renversée au Caramel

CARAMEL CUSTARD

SERVES 6

French children and their parents all love this eggy custard with its dark caramel sauce. It epitomizes the best of home cooking and simple bistro fare.

Note: A successful custard must be cooked through or the eggs will not set correctly and the custard will not be firm enough to unmold. Baking in a water bath (*bain marie*) keeps the custard from overheating and guarantees a perfectly smooth texture. However, great care must be taken that the water in the water bath never boils—otherwise the custard will be grainy.

CARAMEL
1/2 cup sugar
1/4 cup water

CUSTARD
2 cups milk
1 1/2 teaspoons vanilla extract
2 eggs
4 egg yolks
2/3 cup sugar

EQUIPMENT: 4-cup charlotte mold

Preheat the oven to 350°.

Prepare the caramel: Fill a bowl with cold water. Combine the sugar and the ¼ cup water in a small saucepan and bring to a boil over low heat, stirring to dissolve the sugar. Then raise the heat to high and cook, without stirring, until the syrup turns a light caramel color. Watch the caramel carefully—once it begins to color it will darken very quickly. Remove the saucepan from the heat and dip the bottom of it immediately into the cold water to stop the cooking. Pour the caramel into the charlotte mold and, working quickly before the caramel sets, tilt the mold so that the caramel coats the bottom and sides. Let the caramel cool.

Prepare the custard: Put the milk and vanilla into a saucepan and bring to a boil; remove from heat. Combine the eggs and egg yolks in a heatproof bowl and whisk to blend. Whisk in the sugar, then gradually add the hot milk, whisking constantly but gently so that the mixture does not become frothy.

Pour the custard mixture into the cooled mold. Put the mold into a deep baking or roasting pan and add hot water to come about two-thirds of the way up the sides of the mold (this is known as a *bain marie*). Bring the water to a simmer on top of the stove, transfer the pan to the oven, and bake until a knife inserted into the custard comes out clean, 40 to 50 minutes. The water should stay at a bare simmer at all times—if it boils or even comes to a hard simmer, lower the oven temperature. Remove from the pan and let cool.

To serve, run the tip of a small knife around the top of the custard to loosen it. Invert a serving platter over the mold and quickly reverse the two. Carefully remove the mold.

COOKING IN A WATER BATH

Crème Renversée au Caramel, above, is baked in a larger pan of barely simmering water known as a water bath, or *bain marie*; its purpose is to surround and protect delicate foods during cooking by maintaining an even, low, moist heat. A water bath is useful for baking many egg-based preparations (Oeufs Cocotte à la Crème, page 100) and Gâteau Blond de Foies de Volaille (page 348), because it ensures the low temperature necessary for perfect texture and because the moisture from the steaming liquid protects the egg from the harsh, dry heat of the oven so that it does not dry out during cooking. Terrines and pâtés are baked in water baths but at a higher heat, because they are less delicate.

A water bath may also be used on top of the stove to melt chocolate, which scorches easily, or to cook egg-yolk-based sauces (Sabayon, page 116) or the egg-sugar base for Génoise (page 177), both of which require a very low heat and slow cooking. Finally, a water bath is often used to hold hot preparations that cannot be rewarmed over direct heat; make sure that egg-based sauces are held off the heat in water that is just hot, not simmering.

Oeufs à la Tripe
GRATIN OF HARD-BOILED EGGS

Rouelles de Veau Bourgeoise
VEAL SHANKS WITH PEARL ONIONS AND MUSHROOMS

Mousse au Chocolat aux Noisettes et au Whisky
CHOCOLATE MOUSSE WITH HAZELNUTS AND WHISKY

Oeufs à la Tripe
GRATIN OF HARD-BOILED EGGS

SERVES 6

Literally "eggs cooked like tripe," this is one of the oldest dishes in the Cordon Bleu repertoire (we find recipes for it in French cookbooks going back to the seventeeth century). This version, developed in the nineteenth century, calls for coating the eggs with a sauce béchamel, one of the mother sauces most frequently encountered in classic French cuisine.

6 eggs
3 tablespoons unsalted butter
1 large onion, sliced thin

BÉCHAMEL SAUCE
3 tablespoons unsalted butter
5 tablespoons all-purpose flour
2 cups milk
1/8 teaspoon freshly grated nutmeg
Salt
White pepper

EQUIPMENT: 9-by-13-inch gratin dish

Hard-boil the eggs: Bring a saucepan of salted water to a boil. Add the eggs, reduce the heat, and simmer 10 minutes. Put into cold water until just cool enough to handle and then peel. (A trick for peeling hard-boiled

ROUX AND FLOUR-BOUND SAUCES

Roux, a combination of butter and flour cooked on top of the stove, is the thickening agent for many important French sauces, notably the *sauces mères* or mother sauces from which all flour-bound sauces derive. The *sauces mères* are classified by color—béchamel and velouté, which are white sauces, and sauce espagnole, a brown sauce. Béchamel is made by adding milk to a white roux (*roux blanc*), in which the flour and butter are cooked just long enough to eliminate the taste of raw flour without coloring the mixture. A velouté is made with a lightly colored roux (*roux blond*), to which a white stock (veal, chicken, or fish) is added. Sauce espagnole is made with a brown roux—in which the flour and butter are cooked until well browned—and a brown veal or beef stock. Nowadays, sauce espagnole is rarely used and brown sauces are more likely to be made without the roux; the sauce is thickened simply by the reduction of the stock.

The *sauces mères* are the basis for many variations: Béchamel with cheese becomes a sauce mornay (page 44). Velouté made with chicken stock and enriched with cream is a sauce suprême (page 175). A brown sauce with red wine, shallots, and herbs is called a sauce bordelaise (page 193); with the addition of port wine, cognac, truffles, and foie gras a brown sauce becomes a sauce Périgueux (page 493). Both béchamel and velouté sauces may be further thickened and enriched with a liaison (page 20) of egg yolk, or cream and egg yolk (Rouelles de Veau Bourgeoise, page 18). Brown sauces may be enriched with a small amount of butter for added flavor and sheen.

In any roux-bound sauce, care must be taken to avoid lumps. To this end it is necessary to add either a cold liquid to a hot roux or a hot liquid to a cold roux. (If both liquid and roux are hot, it suffices to remove the roux from the heat and let it cool a few minutes before adding the hot liquid.) The mixture must be whisked constantly while the liquid is added.

A béchamel sauce and its variations may be used to sauce or gratiné vegetables (Gratin de Blettes, page 26), egg dishes (Oeufs à la Tripe, page 16), fish or chicken. A béchamel is also used as a base for other preparations such as soufflés (page 83) or terrines (page 356). The thickness of the sauce may be adjusted to the dish. Velouté sauces are appropriate for vegetable, fish, veal, or chicken dishes. A velouté sauce may be made separately from the dish it embellishes (Fonds d'Artichauts Cussy, page 507) or it may be made with the liquid in which the food is cooked (Blanquette de Veau à l'Ancienne, page 55). Brown sauces are used to sauce red meat (Entrecôte Bordelaise, page 193) and game (Noisettes de Chevreuil, Grand Veneur, page 469).

Béchamel, velouté, and brown sauces may be made ahead and reserved in a water bath or reheated over low heat. (Do not boil if the sauce has been bound with egg yolk.) Rub the surface with a bit of butter to keep a skin from forming.

eggs is to roll them with the palm of your hand on a hard surface to break up the shell and then peel them under a slow stream of running water.) Reserve the eggs in a bowl of warm water.

Melt the butter in a saucepan or small frying pan over low heat. Add the onion and cook, stirring frequently, until tender but not colored.

Prepare the béchamel sauce: Melt the butter in a medium, heavy-bottomed saucepan over low heat. Add the flour and whisk about 2 minutes; do not allow it to color. Whisk in the milk and bring to a boil, whisking constantly to avoid lumps. Season with the nutmeg and salt and pepper to taste. Reduce the heat and simmer 10 minutes, whisking constantly and scraping the bottom and sides of the pan to prevent the sauce from sticking. Stir in the cooked onions and cook 5 more minutes.

Heat the broiler. Slice the eggs ¼ inch thick. Spread a thin layer of the béchamel over the bottom of the gratin dish. Layer the egg slices over the béchamel and cover with the remaining sauce. Broil, turning the dish if necessary to color evenly, until the top is golden brown. Serve immediately.

Rouelles de Veau Bourgeoise
VEAL SHANKS WITH PEARL ONIONS AND MUSHROOMS

6 SERVINGS

Veal shank is rarely cooked whole in France. It is often sliced and simmered slowly before being combined with a vegetable garnish that is prepared separately to preserve individual tastes. This recipe, with its pearl onions and mushrooms, is called "bourgeoise" because the garnish and the egg yolk and cream *liaison*, or thickener, are characteristic of family-style dishes, particularly in Paris and the surrounding Île de France.

3 pounds (approximately) veal shanks, sawed into 6 slices, each about 1½ inches thick
5 tablespoons unsalted butter
¼ cup all-purpose flour
1 Bouquet Garni (page 20)
Salt and freshly ground pepper

30 pearl onions, peeled
1 clove
¾ pound small button or quartered large mushrooms, trimmed and cleaned
2 egg yolks
Parsley leaves for garnish

Put the veal in a large saucepan and cover with cold water. Bring the water to a boil, reduce the heat, and simmer 15 minutes, skimming any impurities that rise to the surface. Remove the veal and set aside. Strain and reserve the cooking liquid.

Melt 4 tablespoons of the butter in a large, deep frying pan over low heat. Add the flour and whisk 2 minutes without coloring. Whisk in 2 cups of the strained cooking liquid. Arrange the veal in the pan and add more cooking liquid as necessary to just cover the veal. Bring the liquid slowly to a boil, scraping the bottom of the pan to make sure that the flour does not stick. Add the bouquet garni and season with salt and pepper. Reduce the heat, cover and simmer 45 minutes. Then stud one of the onions with the clove and add it along with the other onions to the stew. Continue cooking until the veal is tender when pierced with the point of a small knife, about 30 minutes longer.

While the stew is cooking, melt the remaining tablespoon of butter in a medium frying pan over high heat. Add the mushrooms and cook quickly until all the moisture has evaporated. Season with salt and pepper. Add the mushrooms to the stew about 5 minutes before the end of cooking time.

When tender, transfer the veal to a serving platter with a slotted spoon. Spoon the onions and mushrooms around it. Cover with aluminum foil to keep warm.

Whisk the egg yolks in a small bowl with a little of the hot cooking liquid. Return the mixture to the pan of cooking liquid and cook over medium heat, whisking constantly, until the sauce just comes to a boil. Remove from heat. Taste and adjust seasonings. Pour the sauce over the veal and garnish with parsley leaves.

LIAISONS

The sauce for the Rouelles de Veau Bourgeoise (page 18) is thickened and enriched with egg yolks just before serving. This final, lightly cooked thickening is known as a *liaison* (the meaning is the same as in English), and may also be achieved with cornstarch, arrowroot, or a flour and butter paste known as a *beurre manié* (page 205), all of which require only a brief cooking. If you are using an egg yolk liaison, temper the yolks first with a little of the hot cooking liquid to prevent them from graining. A flourless sauce bound with egg yolks must never be boiled.

Bouquet Garni

1 bay leaf
3 sprigs fresh thyme
4 large sprigs parsley
(including stems)

4-inch piece celery stalk
with leaves
2 4-inch pieces leek green

Lay the bay leaf, thyme, parsley, and celery on one piece of leek green. Cover with the remaining piece of leek green. Tie securely with kitchen twine, leaving a length of twine attached so that the bouquet garni can be easily retrieved. (See technique photo on page 520.)

Mousse au Chocolat aux Noisettes et au Whisky
CHOCOLATE MOUSSE WITH HAZELNUTS AND WHISKY

SERVES 6

This popular bistro dessert can be made up to two days in advance—indeed, it improves if left to mature before serving. Although chocolate mousse can be made plain, in France it is often flavored with candied orange peel, ginger, or coffee. Orange-flavored brandy, rum, and cognac are other additions used in small doses to complement the chocolate taste. Our recipe adds hazelnuts and Scotch to the basic mousse mixture, producing an excellent result.

Note: Although the mousse may be prepared well in advance, the Chantilly cream decoration should not be made and applied more than an hour before serving.

CHOCOLATE MOUSSE

2 ounces (1/2 cup) skinned
  hazelnuts, crushed
1 pound semisweet chocolate,
  cut into small pieces
2 tablespoons unsalted butter
1 cup sugar
6 egg yolks
6 tablespoons Scotch whisky
6 egg whites

CHANTILLY CREAM

1 cup heavy cream
1/2 teaspoon vanilla extract
2 tablespoons confectioner's sugar

EQUIPMENT: Pastry bag, large star pastry tip

Prepare the mousse: Preheat the oven to 400°. Spread the crushed hazelnuts on a baking sheet and toast until fragrant and golden brown. Bring about 1 inch of water just to a simmer in a saucepan. Combine the chocolate, butter and 1/2 cup of the sugar in a heatproof bowl and set the bowl over the simmering water. (The water must not touch the bottom of the bowl.)

Let stand without stirring until the chocolate has melted. (If you stir the chocolate it may stiffen or "seize" and become unworkable.) Remove the bowl from the heat and stir in the egg yolks. Stir in the hazelnuts and whisky.

Beat the egg whites with a whisk or electric mixer until stiff peaks form. Gradually beat in the remaining 1/2 cup sugar and continue beating until stiff peaks form again. Whisk about one-third of the egg whites into the chocolate mixture (it is fine to whisk vigorously—this step serves to lighten the chocolate mixture sufficiently that it may be folded into the remaining whites without diminishing their volume). Gently fold the chocolate mixture into the remaining whites with a wooden spoon. Pour the mousse into a serving bowl or individual dessert glasses. Refrigerate until firm, 2 to 3 hours.

Chill a mixing bowl for the Chantilly cream.

Not more than 1 hour before serving, prepare the Chantilly cream: Combine the cream and vanilla in the chilled bowl and beat with a whisk or electric beater until the cream begins to stiffen. Add the sugar and continue beating until stiff peaks form and the cream clings to the whisk or beater. Fit the pastry bag with the star tip and fill with the Chantilly cream. Refrigerate until serving time.

To serve, pipe rosettes of Chantilly cream on top of the mousse(s) and serve any remaining cream in a sauceboat on the side.

Crêpes au Saumon Fumé
SMOKED SALMON CRÊPES

Gigot d'Agneau
ROAST LEG OF LAMB

Gratin de Blettes
SWISS CHARD GRATIN

Ananas Givré
PINEAPPLE SORBET

Crêpes au Saumon Fumé
SMOKED SALMON CRÊPES

SERVES 6

Crêpes are made not only for dessert in France. Indeed, especially in Brittany, an entire meal can be composed of crêpes (savory dark buckwheat crêpes are served as a main course, sweet golden wheat crêpes for dessert). These particular crêpes are a French variation on a Baltic theme: blini with caviar and sour cream. They may be served as a first course or made into a light meal.

10 ounces smoked salmon,
  sliced thin
2 cups milk

SAVORY CRÊPE BATTER
3/4 cup all-purpose flour
Pinch salt
2 eggs
1 cup milk
3 tablespoons unsalted butter,
  melted and cooled

1³/4 cups crème fraîche or
  heavy cream
Salt
White pepper

Melted butter for crêpe pans
  and serving dish

EQUIPMENT: Two 5-inch crêpe pans

Arrange the salmon slices in an even layer in a shallow container. Cover with the milk and let stand in a cool place to macerate for at least 2 hours.

Prepare the crêpe batter: Sift the flour and salt into a bowl. Make a well in the center of the flour mixture. Break the eggs into the well and add one-third of the milk. Gradually whisk the flour mixture into the wet ingredients until very smooth. Then whisk in the butter and the remaining milk. Let the batter rest 30 minutes at room temperature.

Brush a crêpe pan with the melted butter and wipe out the excess with a paper towel. Heat the pan over medium heat until a drop of water will sizzle on it. Then pour in about 2 tablespoons of batter, tilting the pan to thinly coat the bottom. Cook the crêpe until golden brown (check the color by lifting the edges of the crêpe with a metal spatula). Then flip it with the spatula and cook the other side. Transfer to a heated plate and keep warm in a low oven. Repeat to cook all the crêpes, rebuttering the pan only if the batter begins to stick. Stack the crêpes as they are made.

Remove the salmon from the milk. Drain on paper towels and pat dry. Cut into 2-inch-long strips, about 1/8 inch wide.

Preheat the broiler. Brush an ovenproof serving dish with butter.

Lay the crêpes on a flat surface. Divide the strips of salmon between the crêpes, forming a line down the center of each. Roll the crêpes into cylinders and place seam side down, side by side in the dish. Season the crème fraîche with salt and pepper to taste and spoon over the crêpes. Broil until the top is golden brown, about 5 minutes. Serve immediately.

CRÊPES

Crêpes may be served hot or cold, rolled into cylinders, folded into triangle shapes, or even stacked one on top of another in a many-layered construction using a variety of fillings. Crêpes may be used to wrap savory fillings (Crêpes au Saumon Fumé, above) or, with the addition of a little sugar (page 77), they are appropriate for sweet fillings as well. Browning the butter very slightly to a golden brown (called a *beurre noisette*) before adding it to the batter will give the crêpes a distinctive, nutty flavor.

Crêpe batter is quick to prepare but it must rest for about 30 minutes after it is made; this is to allow the grains of starch in the flour to expand and the batter to thicken. Crêpes should be very light—coat the pan with a very thin layer of batter and use as little butter as possible for cooking. If you add the next batch of batter to the pan before returning it to the heat, it will not need to be rebuttered each time. Wipe the pan well with a paper towel or cloth after use and do not wash it unless absolutely necessary: you will be rewarded with a well-seasoned pan that does not stick. When you become proficient at crêpe making you may like to try using two pans to hasten the cooking. And don't worry if there are leftover crêpes—wrapped in plastic they freeze very well.

Gigot d'Agneau
ROAST LEG OF LAMB

———

SERVES 6

From Marseille to Lille, lamb is the most popular meat in France, and Sunday dinner often means leg of lamb, sparingly larded with slivers of garlic, roasted, and served with white beans or green beans depending on the season of the year. Like beef, lamb is served quite rare in France, and though an experienced cook can judge doneness by gently pressing the meat (it stiffens as it cooks) we recommend using a meat thermometer to monitor cooking. When inserted into the thickest part of the leg, it should register 130° when the leg is done.

Note: A shortened leg of lamb, called a *gigot raccourci* in French, is just the leg itself and does not include the pelvic bone or the muscles attached to it (the sirloin), often included on legs prepared in the United States.

3-pound shortened leg of lamb (see Note), trimmed of excess fat
3 cloves garlic, cut into slivers
3 tablespoons unsalted butter, softened
1 tablespoon vegetable oil

Salt and freshly ground pepper
1 medium onion, chopped coarse
1 medium carrot, chopped coarse
Several sprigs fresh thyme or ½ teaspoon dried
1 bay leaf
1 bunch watercress for garnish

Preheat the oven to 450°. With a sharp knife, remove the thin parchment-like outer skin, or fell, from the lamb.

Make several incisions about ¾ inch deep in the leg of lamb with the point of a knife and insert a garlic sliver into each. Place the lamb in a roasting pan. Rub with the butter and oil. Season with salt and pepper. Roast the lamb, turning it once, for 20 minutes. Then add the vegetables and herbs and continue roasting, turning once, until medium rare, about 20 more minutes.

Transfer the lamb to a serving platter and cover with aluminum foil to keep warm. Let rest at least 15 minutes.

Spoon off the fat in the pan. Set the pan over medium heat, add 1 cup water and whisk to deglaze, scraping the bottom of the pan to release any cooked particles. Reduce the heat to low and simmer until reduced and flavorful. Strain.

Arrange the watercress around the lamb on the platter and serve the juices in a sauceboat on the side. Serve with Gratin de Blettes (recipe follows).

Gratin de Blettes
SWISS CHARD GRATIN

SERVES 6

Swiss chard is particularly popular in the South of France. The green leafy part is often used in stuffings while the white stalks are cooked separately to make a vegetable dish. Here both leaves and stalks are combined, moistened with a cream-enriched béchamel, and baked with a topping of Gruyère cheese.

Salt
2 pounds Swiss chard
2 tablespoons unsalted butter
14 ounces mushrooms, sliced fine
Freshly ground pepper
1/4 cup crème fraîche

BÉCHAMEL SAUCE
2 tablespoons unsalted butter
1/4 cup all-purpose flour
1 3/4 cups milk
Pinch grated nutmeg
Salt
White pepper

1/2 cup crème fraîche
1/4 cup grated Gruyère cheese

EQUIPMENT: 10-by-15-inch gratin dish

Prepare the chard: Bring 2 large saucepans of salted water to a boil. Cut the chard stalks from the leaves. Peel the stalks with a vegetable peeler to remove the tough fibers. Cut the stalks into 2-inch lengths and rinse in cold water; drain. Add to one of the saucepans of boiling water, return to a boil, and cook until crisp-tender, about 10 minutes; drain and set aside. Meanwhile, rinse and drain the leaves and add them to the second saucepan. Return the water to a boil and blanch 2 to 3 minutes; drain.

Heat the butter in a frying pan over high heat. Add the sliced mushrooms and cook quickly until all the liquid has evaporated. Season to taste with salt and pepper. Add 1/4 cup of the crème fraîche and cook until slightly thickened. Remove from the heat and set aside.

Preheat the oven to 425°. Brush the gratin dish with butter.

Prepare the béchamel sauce: Use the butter, flour, milk, nutmeg, salt, and pepper and follow the directions on page 18. Remove from the heat and whisk in the remaining 1/2 cup of crème fraîche.

Squeeze the chard leaves well to remove as much water as possible. Roughly chop and transfer to a bowl. Stir in one-third of the béchamel sauce. Taste and adjust seasonings. Put the chard stalks into a second bowl and stir in one-half of the remaining béchamel. Taste and adjust seasonings.

Assemble the gratin: Spread half of the leaf mixture over the bottom of the gratin dish. Top with the mushrooms, followed by the remaining leaf mixture. Then spread the stalk mixture evenly over the leaves and top with the remaining béchamel. Sprinkle with the grated cheese and bake until the top is bubbling and golden brown, 10 to 15 minutes.

Ananas Givré
PINEAPPLE SORBET

SERVES 6

French sorbet is made from freezing a fresh fruit puree with sugar syrup. The result has a fruit flavor far more intense than that of any fruit ice cream. Sometimes, as in the following recipe, egg white is added to the sorbet to ensure a perfectly smooth end result.

Note: Fruits filled with a sorbet of the same fruit are called *fruits givrés* in French (literally, "frosted fruits"). The most common fruits served this way are oranges, lemons, and pineapple; to enjoy the freshest possible taste, they should be served within 24 hours of being made.

1¼ cups water	1 egg white, lightly beaten
1½ cups sugar	Confectioner's sugar for dusting
1 teaspoon vanilla extract	pineapple leaves
1 pineapple (about 2½ pounds)	

EQUIPMENT: Ice cream maker

Chill a mixing bowl in the freezer for the sorbet.

Prepare a sugar syrup: Combine the water, sugar, and vanilla in a saucepan and bring to a boil over low heat, stirring to dissolve the sugar. Boil 1 to 2 minutes, then remove from the heat and let cool.

Cut the top off the pineapple about ½ inch below the leaves. Freeze the top until serving time. Cut a thin slice off the base of the fruit (without exposing the flesh) so that the pineapple will stand upright.

Hollow out the pineapple (see technique photos on page 521): Stand the fruit upright. Insert a long thin sharp knife, vertically, ¼ inch in from the rind, through the top and just short of the base of the pineapple. Carefully cut all around the inside of the rind with an up-and-down sawing motion to release the flesh, without cutting through the base. Remove the knife and reinsert the blade horizontally into the base of the fruit, ½ inch from the bottom, pushing the knife tip almost through to the opposite side. Swivel the blade to the left to release one-half of the base of the pineapple. Remove the knife, turn it over so that the blade faces in the opposite direction, and reinsert it into the base of the fruit. Repeat the operation, swiveling the blade to the right, to release the other half of the base. The flesh should now be freed from the rind, and the rind intact. Insert a fork into the top of the core, and twist to pull out the flesh in one piece. If it sticks, repeat the above steps until it is freed.

Put the hollowed pineapple shell in the freezer. Cut the fruit lengthwise into quarters and remove and discard the core. Cut the fruit into chunks and puree in a food mill or food processor. Combine the syrup, pineapple puree, and egg white and mix well. Pour the mixture into an ice cream maker and freeze according to the manufacturer's instructions. Pack the sorbet into the chilled pineapple shell—it should extend above the rim. Freeze until firm, about 1 hour.

To serve, nestle the filled pineapple in a bowl of crushed ice. Dust the leaves of the pineapple top with confectioner's sugar and set it on top of the sorbet.

SUGAR SYRUPS

Simple sugar syrups, like the one used to make Ananas Givré (page 27), are made by heating a measured quantity of sugar and water to boiling to dissolve the sugar and then boiling very briefly until the syrup is clear. Cooked sugar syrups differ from simple syrups in that they are left to boil until the water evaporates and the sugar cooks to a higher temperature. (The quantity of water used to make a cooked sugar is not crucial because it will be completely boiled off; you need use only enough to dissolve the sugar and in fact, some professionals do without the water entirely.) Cooked sugars are categorized by different stages of cooking, from the soft ball stage at a temperature of about 240°, through hard ball, light crack, hard crack, and finally to caramel, which measures well over 300°, depending on the darkness of the color.

When preparing a cooked sugar, it is important that the sugar be completely dissolved before it comes to a boil. If not, you risk crystallizing and burning the sugar. To further prevent crystallization, use a pastry brush dipped in water to wash any sugar crystals down off the sides of the pan during cooking. Test the temperature of a cooked sugar either with a candy thermometer or by spooning a bit of the boiling syrup into ice water: At the soft ball stage it will form a very soft ball that will not hold its shape; at the hard ball stage it will form a hard but still pliable ball that will hold its shape; at light crack the sugar is becoming brittle but still pliable; at hard crack the sugar is brittle.

Sugar syrups are used in sorbets, to poach fruits (Poires Belle Hélène, page 107), and to soak certain cakes (Savarin aux Kiwis et aux Fraises, page 409). Sugar cooked to the soft ball stage is used to make Italian meringue (page 294), and sugar cooked to the hard crack stage is used to make masterpieces of pulled sugar. Caramel is used in a variety of preparations, from sauces to praline.

LESSON 5

Salade Messidor

SUMMER HARVEST SALAD

———

Cassoulet de Poissons

FISH AND WHITE-BEAN STEW

———

Biscuit de Savoie,
Crème Anglaise

SPONGE CAKE WITH CRÈME ANGLAISE

Salade Messidor
SUMMER HARVEST SALAD

———

SERVES 6

Messidor is the tenth month of the Republican calendar established at the time of the French Revolution. It corresponds to the period between the end of June and the end of July when artichokes are most abundant. Here, artichoke bottoms are stuffed with a mixture of green beans, cauliflower, and tomatoes seasoned with mayonnaise to make a colorful summertime first course.

ARTICHOKE BOTTOMS	MAYONNAISE
2 lemons	*2 egg yolks*
6 large artichokes	*1 tablespoon Dijon mustard*
Salt	*Salt and fresh ground pepper*
2 tablespoons vegetable oil	*1³/₄ cups vegetable oil*
	1 tablespoon wine vinegar
5 ounces green beans	
Salt	*1 small head curly endive*
4 stalks celery	*1 small bunch chives, chopped*
1 small cauliflower	
2 tablespoons white vinegar	
¹/₂ pound tomatoes	

Prepare the artichoke bottoms (see technique photos on pages 520–21): Fill a bowl with cold water. Cut one lemon in half. Squeeze the juice into the bowl of water and add the squeezed lemon halves; set aside. Snap off the stem of one of the artichokes (any tough fibers in the heart will be removed along with the stem). Cut off the outer leaves until you reach the soft, light-colored inner core. Cut a thin slice off the base of the artichoke so that it will stand upright. Cut off the top of the artichoke, leaving the bottom about 1 inch high. Trim the artichoke bottom to remove all the tough, outer green parts so that it has a round, regular shape and a smooth edge. Rub well with the cut edge of the lemon half to prevent discoloration and drop it into the bowl of cold water. Repeat for the remaining artichokes.

Bring a large saucepan of salted water to a boil. Add the juice of the remaining lemon, the oil, and the artichoke bottoms and cook until tender, about 30 minutes. Invert the bottoms on a rack to cool. When cool enough to handle, scoop out the chokes with a teaspoon; set the artichoke bottoms aside.

String the beans, if necessary, by snapping off the ends and pulling down the length of the bean to remove the string. Bring a saucepan of salted water to a boil. Add the beans and cook until crisp-tender, 8 to 10 minutes. Drain and refresh under cold running water; drain again. Cut into 1-inch lengths.

Peel the tough fibers from the celery with a vegetable peeler. Cut the stalks into thin matchstick pieces, about 1 inch long and ¹/₄ inch thick.

Remove the leaves from the cauliflower and divide the head into the smallest possible florets. Fill a large bowl with cold water, add the vinegar and soak the florets for about 5 minutes; drain well.

Peel, seed, and dice the tomatoes: Bring a saucepan of water to a boil. Fill a bowl with cold water and set aside. Remove the stems from the tomatoes and make a shallow, cross-shaped incision in the opposite ends. Gently lower the tomatoes into the boiling water for about 10 seconds. Remove with a slotted spoon and drop immediately into the bowl of cold water. Peel off the skins with a paring knife. Halve the tomatoes crosswise and squeeze gently to remove the seeds. Cut the flesh into ¼-inch dice (this is known as *tomate concassée)*.

Prepare the mayonnaise: Bring all the ingredients to room temperature. Combine the egg yolks, mustard, salt, and pepper in a bowl and beat well with a small whisk. Whisking continuously, add about ½ cup of the oil drop by drop until the mayonnaise has thickened and emulsified. Then whisk in the remaining oil in a thin, slow stream until the mayonnaise is smooth and thick. Whisk in the vinegar. Taste and adjust seasonings.

Combine the green beans, celery, cauliflower, and tomatoes in a large bowl along with two-thirds of the mayonnaise. Rinse and dry the endive.

To serve, line a serving platter with endive leaves. Fill each artichoke bottom with the vegetable salad, mounding it slightly. Coat the mounded filling with the remaining mayonnaise and arrange on the bed of greens Sprinkle with chives.

MAYONNAISE

Mayonnaise is very easy to make if you follow a few rules. First, have all the ingredients at room temperature before you begin. Add the oil very slowly, drop by drop, at the beginning until the sauce begins to emulsify; then you may add the remainder in a steady stream without risk of breaking the mayonnaise. If the sauce does separate, whisk in a teaspoon of cold water. If the mayonnaise remains broken, whisk 1 teaspoon of the broken mayonnaise into 1 teaspoon mustard in a warm, dry bowl until creamy (mustard helps to emulsify the sauce). Then gradually whisk in the remaining mayonnaise.

A simple mayonnaise is the foundation for a number of sauces. With the addition of pureed herbs and greens it becomes a Sauce Verte (page 84), flavored with pureed red pepper it becomes a Provençale Sauce Rouille (page 111), and with chopped capers, onions, gherkins, and hard-boiled eggs it becomes a spicy Sauce Tartare (page 163).

At Le Cordon Bleu, we never refrigerate mayonnaise; we make just what is needed and use it that day. But if you like, you may make mayonnaise in advance and store it in a cool place for a few hours or refrigerate it for 2 to 3 days. Bring it back to room temperature before stirring to prevent it from breaking.

Cassoulet de Poissons

FISH AND WHITE-BEAN STEW

SERVES 6

A new twist on the traditional white-bean stew of southwestern France, this cassoulet substitutes whiting and monkfish for the usual preserved goose (*confit d'oie*), sausages, pork, and bacon.

Like a meat-based cassoulet, this version is finished in the oven after being dusted with bread crumbs. The result is a crisp surface that contrasts nicely with the creamy bean and fish mixture.

3/4 pound dried white beans such
    as Great Northern
1 medium onion
1 clove
1 Bouquet Garni (page 20)
Salt
2 carrots, sliced thin
6 tablespoons vegetable oil
6 tablespoons unsalted butter
2 medium onions, chopped fine

2 cloves garlic, chopped fine
3/4 pound tomatoes, peeled, seeded,
    and chopped (page 31)
Freshly ground pepper
6 whiting, 5 ounces each, or
    2 trout, about 1 pound each
1 1/2 pounds monkfish fillets
6 sea scallops
3/4 cup dried bread crumbs

EQUIPMENT: 10-by-15-inch gratin dish

Soak the beans overnight in cold water to cover. Drain and rinse. Transfer to a large saucepan and cover with 4 to 5 inches of fresh cold water. Peel the whole onion and stud with the clove and add it to the pan along with the bouquet garni. Bring to a boil and skim the froth that rises to the surface. Reduce the heat and simmer for 1 1/2 hours. Season to taste with salt. Add the carrots and continue simmering until the carrots and beans are tender, about 30 minutes. Drain; discard the bouquet garni and the onion.

While the beans are cooking, heat 3 tablespoons oil and 2 tablespoons butter in a frying pan over low heat. Add the chopped onions and cook slowly, stirring occasionally, until tender but not colored. Add garlic and cook 1 minute. Add tomatoes, season with salt and pepper, and simmer for 15 minutes.

Clean the whiting (see technique photos on page 524): Cut off all of the fins except the tail fin with kitchen or fish scissors. Working from tail to head, against the direction in which the scales lie, scrape the back of a knife blade along the skin of the fish to remove the scales. Rinse the fish under cold running water to remove any scales that adhere. To gut the fish, make a small incision in the belly just behind the head and pull out the entrails. Pull or cut out the gills. Rinse the fish thoroughly under cold running water and dry well with paper towels inside and out. This is the basic technique for cleaning roundfish. In addition, if the fish is to be served whole the tail fin is trimmed for aesthetic reasons: The tail fin may either be cut straight across, so that it is about ½ inch long or it may be trimmed to a V shape.

With a heavy chef's knife, cut off the heads and tails of the whiting and cut the fish into 1-inch-thick slices (see technique photo on page 524). Cut the monkfish fillets into 1-inch-thick slices. Cut the scallops in half crosswise. Heat the remaining 3 tablespoons oil and 2 tablespoons of the butter in a large frying pan over high heat. Add the whiting slices and sauté until golden brown on both sides; set aside. Brown the monkfish and sliced scallops in the same way; set aside.

Preheat the oven to 450°.

Combine the tomato mixture and drained beans in a saucepan and simmer for 5 minutes. Taste and adjust seasonings. Spread one-half of the mixture over the bottom of the gratin dish. Arrange the fish and scallops on top and cover with the remaining bean mixture. Sprinkle with the bread crumbs and dot with the remaining 2 tablespoons of butter. Bake until the bread crumbs are golden brown, 10 to 15 minutes.

Biscuit de Savoie
SPONGE CAKE

MAKES 2 NINE-INCH CAKES

This light sponge cake has long been associated with the region of Savoy (an area touching the Swiss border in eastern France). It is served with a rich custard sauce, or crème anglaise; note that the sauce is served next to the cake and not spooned over it. If fresh raspberries, strawberries, or peaches are in season, use them to decorate each plate, adding a fresh taste and a dash of color to a classic dessert.

7 eggs, separated
1¼ cups sugar
1 teaspoon vanilla extract
¾ cup sifted all-purpose flour
¾ cup sifted potato flour

Confectioner's sugar for dusting

Unsalted butter, softened,
  for cake pans
All-purpose flour for cake pans

EQUIPMENT: Two 9-inch round cake pans

Preheat the oven to 350°. Cut 2 rounds of parchment paper to the diameter of the cake pans. Brush the pans evenly with the softened butter and line each with a round of paper. Brush the papers with butter. Dust the pans with flour and tap out the excess.

Combine the egg yolks, sugar, and vanilla in a bowl. Beat with a whisk, or an electric mixer, until the mixture is pale yellow and creamy. Combine the flours and fold into the egg mixture.

Beat the egg whites until stiff peaks form. Stir one-third of the beaten whites into the batter until thoroughly blended. Then gently fold in the remaining whites with a spatula. Divide the batter evenly between the 2 cake pans. Bake until the blade of a small knife inserted into the center of the cakes comes out clean and dry, about 25 minutes. Turn the cakes out onto a rack and let cool to room temperature.

To serve, sift confectioner's sugar over the top of the cakes and transfer to doily-lined cake plates. Serve Crème Anglaise (recipe follows) on the side.

CRÈME ANGLAISE

Crème anglaise, a lightly cooked milk and egg custard, is the basis for a multitude of desserts. Frozen, it is transformed into ice cream; bound with gelatin it becomes the base for bavarian creams. Or it may be served simply as a sauce with fruit or a charlotte or, as in this recipe, to dress up a sponge cake. It is most often flavored with vanilla, but chocolate, coffee, caramel, orange, and lemon flavors are not unusual.

As with all egg-based preparations, care must be taken not to curdle the eggs with too high a heat. As a precaution, the eggs are first tempered, or partially cooked, by the addition of the hot milk before the custard is cooked on top of the stove. Stir the crème anglaise constantly while cooking to avoid burning and do not allow it to boil or it will become grainy. Crème anglaise may be prepared in advance and refrigerated for up to 2 days, but at Le Cordon Bleu, we prefer to serve it the same day, at room temperature. (See technique photos on page 552.)

Crème Anglaise

CUSTARD SAUCE

SERVES 6

This "English cream," called custard sauce in England, has been thoroughly French since the nineteenth century. At first there was some resistance to the name—one chef suggested rechristening it *crème à glacer* (literally "cream for freezing") since it is the basic cream used for making ice creams, but the original name stuck.

Unlike some English custard sauces, which may use whole eggs, a French crème anglaise uses only egg yolks. It can be flavored with an endless variety of flavorings and is served either cold or at room temperature, spooned over or around almost any cakey dessert, or churned in an ice cream freezer to make delicious ice cream.

NOTE: When heating the cream, great care must be taken not to let it boil or it will curdle. When it has thickened enough to coat a spoon, it should immediately be removed from the heat and allowed to cool.

2 cups milk	*4 egg yolks*
1 teaspoon vanilla extract	*1/3 cup sugar*

Put the milk and vanilla into a heavy-bottomed saucepan and bring to a boil. Remove from heat. Combine the egg yolks and sugar in a heatproof bowl and whisk until thick and pale yellow; the mixture should form a ribbon when the whisk is lifted from the bowl. Gradually whisk in half of the hot milk. Then whisk in the remaining milk and return the mixture to the saucepan. Cook over low heat, stirring constantly with a wooden spoon, until the custard is thick enough to leave a clear trail when a finger is drawn across the back of the spoon. Do not boil. Test the consistency of the custard by drawing a finger across the back of the spoon; it should leave a clear trail. Remove the custard from the heat and strain it into a bowl; let cool, stirring occasionally to prevent a skin from forming. Serve at room temperature. (See technique photos on page 552.)

LESSON 6

Tarte à l'Oignon
ONION TART

Mouclade
MUSSELS WITH WINE AND CREAM SAUCE

Bavarois à la Vanille, Coulis de Framboise
VANILLA BAVARIAN CREAM
WITH RASPBERRY COULIS

Tarte à l'Oignon
ONION TART

SERVES 6

Onion tart is a specialty of Alsace. Several versions exist, some of which include bits of bacon, others a mixture of egg yolks and cream; still others are made with onions alone. Prepared as described here, the tart can be served as a starter or with a fresh green salad as a light luncheon or supper dish. It is delicious served either hot or at room temperature.

PÂTE BRISÉE
1 cup all-purpose flour
¹/₂ cup cake flour
1 egg
1 tablespoon water
Pinch salt
7 tablespoons unsalted butter, softened
1 egg, lightly beaten, for glazing

5 tablespoons unsalted butter
1 pound onions, sliced fine
Salt and freshly ground pepper
1 cup crème fraîche or heavy cream
3 egg yolks
Freshly grated nutmeg

EQUIPMENT: 9-inch fluted, removable-bottomed tart pan

Prepare the pâte brisée (see technique photos on page 540): Combine the flours in a mound on a cool work surface. Make a well in the center and put the egg, water, salt and butter into the well. Move the butter to one side and mix the egg, water and salt with the fingertips of one hand. Work the butter into the wet ingredients until well blended. Gradually cut in the flour with a plastic pastry scraper, until the dough holds together. Then use the heel of your hand to push bits of the dough away from you (about 2 tablespoons at a time), smearing it across the work surface to blend the butter and flour into a smooth dough. Repeat until the dough is very smooth. (This is known as *fraiser*.) Scrape into a ball, flatten into a disc, and dust with flour. Wrap in plastic wrap; refrigerate at least 30 minutes.

Preheat the oven to 400°.

Line the mold and blind bake the tart shell (see technique photos on page 541): Dust a work surface with flour. Roll out the dough to a round about ⅛ inch thick. Roll the dough up onto the rolling pin or fold it in half and then unroll or unfold loosely over the tart pan. Use your fingers or a small ball of dough dipped in flour to gently press the dough into the pan.

PÂTE BRISÉE AND PÂTE BRISÉE SUCRÉE

Pâte brisée is French short-crust pastry dough, generally used for savory preparations (Tarte à l'Oignon, above). Pâte brisée sucrée, a sweet dough (Tarte aux Pommes, page 61), is made exactly the same way as pâte brisée, with the addition of a little sugar and vanilla.

French chefs typically make doughs on a cold marble surface, but any kitchen counter top will do as long as it is cool. (If your kitchen is very warm you may cool the counter by setting a large pan filled with ice water on it for a few minutes.) The important point is to work quickly and handle the dough as little as possible; if overworked, it will become elastic and difficult to roll and the finished crust will be tough. So, when mixing the flour with the wet ingredients, work lightly with your fingertips or a pastry blender. Don't worry if the dough is not entirely smooth at this point; you will finish it with the French technique of *fraisage*, a pushing out of the dough with the heel of the hand, to ensure a thorough blending of the flour and butter. Then, to counteract elasticity, the dough is left to relax in the refrigerator for at least 30 minutes before rolling.

To ensure against a soggy crust, tart shells are prebaked, or blind baked, before they are filled: First the shell is baked weighted with metal pie weights or dried beans to keep the crust from puffing as it cooks. Then the weights are removed, the bottom of the shell is brushed with egg glaze to make it very resistant to liquid, and the crust is returned to the oven until dry and cooked through. Shells for fresh fruit tarts, or other tarts in which the fillings are not baked with the crust, are always blind baked.

The dough can be made 2 to 3 days in advance, wrapped tightly in plastic wrap and refrigerated, but let it soften slightly at room temperature before rolling it out. (See technique photos on page 540.)

With your thumb and index finger, mold a ¼-inch horizontal lip around the inside of the rim, then roll the rolling pin over the rim to cut off the excess dough. Push the lip up so that it extends about ¼ inch above the pan. Pinch the lip of dough into a decorative shape with pastry pinchers or your fingers. Prick the bottom of the tart shell all over with a fork and refrigerate for 10 minutes. Cut out a round of parchment paper several inches larger than the tart pan and fit it over the dough. Fill with pie weights or dried beans, and bake until the edges begin to brown, about 15 minutes. Remove the paper and pie weights, brush the interior of the shell with the egg glaze and bake until lightly browned and dry, 10 to 15 minutes longer. Remove the fluted rim of the tart pan and let the tart shell cool.

Reduce the oven temperature to 375°.

Melt the butter in a large frying pan over medium heat. Add the onions and cook, stirring frequently, until soft but not colored. Season with salt and pepper. Reduce heat to low and cook until tender and golden, about 40 minutes. Spread the onions over the cooked pastry shell. Whisk the cream with the yolks, season with salt, pepper and a pinch of nutmeg, and pour over the onions. If the border of the crust is well colored, place the fluted edge of the tart pan upside down over the rim of the tart to prevent from scorching. Bake until puffed and golden brown, 15 to 20 minutes.

Mouclade

MUSSELS WITH WINE AND CREAM SAUCE

SERVES 6

Mussels are popular throughout France but perhaps nowhere more than on the Atlantic coast above Bordeaux, where this delicious dish comes from.

Note: Mussels must always be purchased live, in tightly closed shells ("yawning" mussels should close tightly when gently pressed; if not, discard them). Avoid mussels with broken or cracked shells. Never beard or scrape them until just before cooking, and, though they may be refrigerated for several days, it is best to cook them the day they are purchased.

3 pounds mussels
6 tablespoons unsalted butter
1 large onion, chopped fine
1 large shallot, chopped fine
½ cup dry white wine
2 tablespoons chopped parsley

Freshly ground pepper
½ cup crème fraîche or
heavy cream
1 sprig fresh thyme or
¼ teaspoon dried

Clean the mussels: Scrape the shells of the mussels under running water with the back of a paring knife to remove any barnacles. Pull off the beards.

(continued)

Mouclade (continued)

Rinse the mussels in several changes of cold water and discard any that are not completely closed. Set aside in a colander.

Cook the mussels: Heat the butter in a large saucepan over low heat. Add the onion and shallot and cook until soft but not colored. Add the wine and 1 tablespoon of the parsley and bring to a boil. Add the mussels and season with pepper. Cover and cook, shaking the pot once or twice to rotate the mussels and ensure even cooking, until the shells open—about 6 minutes. Remove the mussels with a slotted spoon and set aside. Strain the cooking liquid through a fine strainer lined with a damp dish towel into a small saucepan to remove any sand.

Bring the cooking liquid to a boil and boil until slightly reduced to concentrate the flavors; set aside. When the mussels are cool enough to handle, pull off and discard one half of each shell, leaving the mussel in the remaining half shell. Arrange the mussels in their shells on a large deep platter or in an earthenware casserole.

Whisk the cream into the reduced cooking liquid. Add the thyme leaves, bring to a boil, and cook until reduced by one-third. Pour the sauce over the mussels and serve sprinkled with the remaining parsley.

Bavarois à la Vanille, Coulis de Framboise

VANILLA BAVARIAN CREAM WITH RASPBERRY COULIS

SERVES 6

Recipes for bavarian cream, or *bavarois*, do not appear in French cookbooks until the early nineteenth century. The preparation was popularized by Carême ("the king of chefs and the chef of kings") and is also used in making charlottes—another Carême contribution to the classic repertoire. The main difference between the two is that ladyfingers are used to line the mold before adding the bavarian cream for a charlotte, whereas for a *bavarois*, the cream is poured directly into the mold.

BAVARIAN CREAM
1/4 ounce powdered gelatin
    (about 1 tablespoon)
2 tablespoons cold water

CRÈME ANGLAISE:
    1 cup milk
    2 teaspoons vanilla extract
    3 egg yolks
    1/2 cup sugar
1 3/4 cups heavy cream

RASPBERRY COULIS
1 1/2 cups raspberries
1/2 cup confectioner's sugar
Juice of 1/2 lemon, strained

EQUIPMENT: 6-cup charlotte mold

Prepare the bavarian cream: Chill a mixing bowl for the whipped cream. Sprinkle the gelatin over the water and let stand until softened, about 5 minutes. Then make a crème anglaise: Use the milk, vanilla, egg yolks, and sugar and follow directions on page 35 and technique photos on page 552. Remove from the heat, add the softened gelatin, and stir to dissolve. Strain the mixture into a bowl and let cool, stirring occasionally, until it begins to thicken. (Do not allow to gel completely.)

Beat the cream in the chilled bowl with a whisk or electric mixer until stiff peaks form and the cream clings to the whisk or beater. When the crème anglaise mixture is cool and has begun to thicken, fold in the whipped cream. Rinse the charlotte mold with cold water and pour in the bavarian mixture. Level the surface with a spatula and refrigerate until completely set, at least 3 hours.

Prepare the coulis: Puree the raspberries in a food mill or food processor and then strain through a fine sieve to remove the seeds. Whisk with the sugar; add the lemon juice and refrigerate until cold.

To serve, dip the mold in hot water for a few seconds. Invert a serving platter over the mold and turn the bavarian out onto the platter. Pour a ring of the coulis around the bavarian and serve the remainder in a sauceboat on the side.

BAVARIAN CREAMS

A bavarian cream is traditionally a cold molded dessert based on a flavored crème anglaise that is set with gelatin and lightened with whipped cream. A lighter version (Charlotte aux Fraises, page 336) replaces the crème anglaise with a base of fruit puree or flavored syrup. Bavarians may be set in any mold and are often layered in bands of contrasting flavors. They may be served with fruit or a fruit sauce, or decorated with whipped cream. A bavarian mixture is the classic filling for charlottes (Charlotte aux Poires, page 309).

Once you have mastered a crème anglaise a bavarian mixture is not much more difficult. But timing is all important in this dessert: You must take care that the mixture is just on the point of setting (you'll see it begin to thicken) before you fold in the whipped cream. If you wait until the mixture has stiffened, it will lump. In that case, set it in a saucepan of hot water and stir until smooth. Then cool again and fold in the cream.

Profiteroles au Gruyère
CHOUX PUFFS WITH GRUYÈRE CHEESE

Pintadeaux au Chou
GUINEA HEN WITH CABBAGE

Crème Fraisalia
STRAWBERRY BAVARIAN CREAM

Profiteroles au Gruyère
CHOUX PUFFS WITH GRUYÈRE CHEESE

SERVES 6

Choux pastry is most frequently garnished with sweet fillings such as pastry cream (éclairs) or ice cream (profiteroles). Here, however, it is filled with a cheese-flavored béchamel called mornay sauce. These savory cheese pastries can be served either with drinks or as a first course.

Note: When making a mornay sauce it is most important to stir the cheese into the sauce away from the heat; otherwise it will become stringy.

CHOUX PASTRY
2/3 cup water
3 tablespoons unsalted butter
1/4 teaspoon salt
9 tablespoons sifted all-purpose flour
3 to 4 eggs
1 egg, lightly beaten, for glazing

2 ounces Gruyère cheese, grated (about 1/2 cup)

Unsalted butter, softened, for baking sheets

MORNAY SAUCE

Salt and white pepper

BÉCHAMEL SAUCE:

1/8 teaspoon freshly grated nutmeg

4 tablespoons unsalted butter

2 egg yolks

5 tablespoons all-purpose flour

4 ounces Gruyère cheese, grated

2 cups milk

(about 1 cup)

EQUIPMENT: Pastry bag, 1/2-inch plain pastry tip, small plain pastry tip

Preheat the oven to 425°. Brush two baking sheets with the softened butter.

Prepare the choux pastry (see technique photos on page 548): Combine the water, butter, and salt in a heavy-bottomed saucepan. Cook over medium heat until the butter melts and the water comes to a boil; remove from the heat and add the flour all at once. Beat vigorously with a wooden spoon until a thick, smooth dough forms. Reduce the heat to low and return the pan to the stove. Cook, stirring constantly, until the dough pulls away from the sides and bottom of the pan. Remove the pan from the heat and beat in 1 egg until thoroughly blended. Repeat with the second egg. Lightly beat the third egg in a small bowl and add it to the dough, a little at a time, until the dough is smooth, shiny, and falls slowly from the spoon in a point. (It may not be necessary to use all of the third egg, or it may be necessary to add all or part of a fourth egg in the same manner, depending on the size of the eggs and the quality of the flour.)

Pipe the choux pastry dough for profiteroles (see technique photos on page 548): Fit the pastry bag with the plain 1/2-inch tip and spoon in the dough (the bag will be easier to handle if it is not completely full). Pipe

CHOUX PASTRY

Choux pastry is perhaps the simplest of all doughs to make. The only challenge it presents to the cook is in determining the quantity of eggs to add—the number will vary depending on the size of the eggs, the quality of the flour, and how much you have dried out the dough on top of the stove. The ideal is to add as much egg as possible, to make the choux light and airy without making the dough runny. So, after the addition of the second egg, you'll need to add the remaining egg or eggs a little at a time until the dough is just right—glossy and just thick enough to pipe.

Choux pastry is employed just as commonly in sweet as in savory pastries, but a small amount of sugar is added to the dough when used in desserts (page 66). The most stunning example in the French repertoire of a choux pastry dessert is probably the croquembouche, in which choux puffs are filled with cream and glued into a pyramidal shape with caramel. This elaborate dessert is reserved for special occasions such as marriages, baptisms, and communions. (See technique photos on page 548.)

small mounds of dough, about 1 inch in diameter and ¹/₂ inch high, 1 to 2 inches apart on the baking sheet. Brush each choux with egg glaze, flatten slightly with the back of a fork dipped in water, and sprinkle with the cheese. Bake 15 minutes without opening the oven door. Then reduce the heat to 350° and continue baking until the choux are golden brown (including the interior of any small cracks) and sound hollow when tapped, about 10 minutes. The choux should have at least doubled in volume.

Prepare the mornay sauce: First make a béchamel sauce using the butter, flour, milk, salt, pepper, and nutmeg and following the directions on page 18. Then whisk the egg yolks with a little of the béchamel to temper them, and return the mixture to the pan. Bring to a boil over medium heat, whisking constantly, and cook 1 minute, still whisking. Remove from the heat and stir in the cheese. Taste and adjust seasonings.

Pierce the bottom of each chou with the point of the small plain pastry tip. Fit the pastry bag with the same tip, and fill with the mornay sauce. Fill each choux puff with the sauce. Arrange on a platter and serve hot.

Pintadeaux au Chou
GUINEA HEN WITH CABBAGE

SERVES 6

In France cabbage is a popular garnish not only for pork but also for game birds and dark-fleshed domestic fowl. Here guinea hens and sausages are served together on a bed of cabbage. Each of the three elements is cooked separately, then combined only for the final cooking. The result is a dish in which complementary tastes are juxtaposed, rather than blended together as in stews or one-pot meals.

Note: The taste of guinea hen, commonly available at French markets, is often compared to that of pheasant or partridge. Either of the latter or, in a pinch, Rock Cornish game hen may be used instead.

1 medium head green cabbage	*2 guinea hens, 2 pounds each*
2 tablespoons vegetable oil	*2 cloves garlic*
4 tablespoons unsalted butter	*2 sprigs fresh thyme or*
1 large onion, sliced	*¹/₄ teaspoon dried*
³/₄ pound carrots, sliced	*2 bay leaves*
1 Bouquet Garni (page 20)	*2 tablespoons softened butter*
Salt and freshly ground pepper	*³/₄ pound Polish sausage*
³/₄ pound slab bacon, sliced	
¹/₄ inch thick	

Prepare the cabbage: Bring a large saucepan of water to a boil. Remove and discard the large outer leaves of the cabbage. Quarter the head and cut

out and discard the hard central core. Rinse in cold water; drain. Add the cabbage to the boiling water and blanch until tender, 8 to 10 minutes. Drain, refresh under cold running water, and drain again; set aside.

Heat 1 tablespoon of the oil and 2 tablespoons of the butter in a large casserole over low heat. Add the sliced onion and cook until tender but not colored. Add the sliced carrots and cook 2 to 3 minutes. Add the cabbage and bouquet garni and season to taste with salt and pepper. Add 2½ cups water, bring to a boil, reduce the heat, and simmer for about 1 hour.

Meanwhile, prepare the lardons: Trim the rind from the bacon. Cut each slice lengthwise into 3 strips and then each strip into ¼-inch cubes, known as *lardons*. Put the lardons into a small saucepan and cover with cold water. Bring to a boil, reduce the heat, and simmer for 1 minute. Drain, refresh under cold running water, and drain again.

Preheat the oven to 425°.

While the cabbage is cooking, rinse the guinea hens inside and out with cold water. Pat dry with paper towels. Season the insides with salt and pepper and stuff each with half of the garlic, a sprig of thyme, and a bay leaf. Truss with kitchen twine, just as you would a chicken (see directions on page 6 and technique photos on page 530). Put the guinea hens into a roasting pan just large enough to hold them. Rub with the 2 tablespoons softened butter. Season with salt and pepper and roast about 30 minutes, turning occasionally for even browning.

When the cabbage is cooked, heat the remaining tablespoon of oil and 2 tablespoons butter in a frying pan over high heat. Add the lardons and sauté until golden. Drain, discard the fat, and add the lardons to the casserole with the cabbage. Prick the sausage all over with a fork and add it to the casserole, nestling it underneath the vegetables.

Transfer the guinea hens to the casserole. Discard the fat in the roasting pan and set the pan over high heat. Add ½ cup water and deglaze, scraping the pan with a wooden spoon to release any cooked particles. Add this liquid to the casserole. Cover and simmer gently over low heat until the hens and sausage are cooked, 20 to 30 minutes.

Remove the guinea hens from the casserole. Discard the trussing twine and cut each hen into 4 pieces: Cut each hen in half down the breast and back bones. Cut off the legs at the joint. Slice the sausage diagonally, about ¼ inch thick. Discard the bouquet garni.

To serve, taste the vegetables and adjust seasonings. Spoon onto a serving platter and arrange the guinea hen and sausage slices on top.

Crème Fraisalia

STRAWBERRY BAVARIAN CREAM

SERVES 6

Henri-Paul Pellaprat was one of France's most influential chefs in the early years of the twentieth century. He wrote books on cooking that are now classics, and for many years he taught at Le Cordon Bleu. One of his many creations was this dessert. Essentially a bavarian cream to which a fresh strawberry puree has been added, it is still as popular at the school today as it was when Pellaprat first invented it.

1 package powdered gelatin
   (¹/₄ ounce)
2 tablespoons cold water

CRÈME ANGLAISE
2 cups milk
1 teaspoon vanilla extract
4 egg yolks
1 cup sugar

³/₄ pint basket fresh
   strawberries
1 tablespoon lemon juice
2 teaspoons kirsch
1 cup heavy cream

Chill a mixing bowl for the whipped cream and a glass or crystal dessert bowl.

Sprinkle the gelatin over the water and let stand until softened, about 5 minutes. Prepare a crème anglaise, using the milk, vanilla, egg yolks, and sugar and following the directions on page 35. Remove from the heat. Add the softened gelatin and stir to dissolve. Strain the mixture into a bowl and let cool, stirring occasionally, until it begins to thicken. Do not allow to gel completely.

Meanwhile, rinse and pat the strawberries dry. Choose 6 perfect berries for decoration and refrigerate. Hull the remainder and puree in a food mill or food processor. Stir the puree into the cooled crème anglaise mixture along with the lemon juice and kirsch.

Beat the cream in the chilled bowl with a whisk or electric mixer until stiff peaks form and the cream clings to the whisk or beater. When the crème anglaise mixture has begun to thicken, fold in the whipped cream. Pour the bavarian mixture into the chilled dessert bowl and refrigerate until completely set, about 3 hours.

Serve decorated with the reserved strawberries.

Soupe à l'Oignon Gratinée
GRATINÉED ONION SOUP

Truite aux Amandes
TROUT WITH ALMONDS

Pommes à l'Anglaise
ENGLISH-STYLE BOILED POTATOES

Oeufs à la Neige
SNOW EGGS WITH CARAMEL
AND CRÈME ANGLAISE

Soupe à l'Oignon Gratinée
GRATINÉED ONION SOUP

SERVES 6

When Les Halles, the famous Paris food market, was in the center of the city, late-night merrymakers could be found sitting shoulder to shoulder with butchers eating onion soup from midnight to dawn in busy bistros. This combination of cheese, bread, and onions was said to restore strength. Today Les Halles is gone but *gratinée* lives on, no longer the midnight meal of yore but a popular first course during the winter months in Paris.

3 tablespoons unsalted butter
1¼ pounds onions, sliced thin
3 tablespoons all-purpose flour
1 cup dry white wine
6 cups water
1 Bouquet Garni (page 20)

Salt and freshly ground pepper
12 slices slender French baguette or
  6 slices French-style bread
3 ounces Gruyère cheese, grated
  (about ¾ cup)

EQUIPMENT: 6 ovenproof soup bowls

Heat the butter in a large saucepan over medium heat. Add the onions and cook until tender and golden, about 20 minutes. Add the flour and cook 2 minutes, stirring frequently. Add the wine, bring to a boil, reduce the heat and simmer 2 minutes. Gradually whisk in the water, add the bouquet garni and season to taste with salt and pepper. Bring to a boil, stirring constantly. Reduce the heat, cover, and simmer for 30 minutes.

Preheat the oven to 400°.

Put the bread slices in a single layer on a baking sheet and toast in the oven until golden.

To serve, preheat the broiler.

Ladle the soup into the soup bowls. Float the toasted bread on top of each and sprinkle with the cheese. Broil until the cheese melts. Serve very hot.

Truite aux Amandes
TROUT WITH ALMONDS

SERVES 6

This recipe is one of the rare French savory dishes that use almonds. It is, in fact, a variation on a classic *truite meunière* (trout with nut-brown butter)—the difference being the almonds. In both recipes the butter and oil used to cook the fish are discarded, and fresh butter is heated until nut brown and poured over the fish. As here, trout cooked this way is always served whole with lemon, boiled potatoes, and freshly chopped parsley.

6 trout, about 8 ounces each
1 lemon
Salt and freshly ground pepper
3/4 cup all-purpose flour
1/2 pound unsalted butter

2 tablespoons vegetable oil
6 ounces sliced almonds
1 tablespoon chopped parsley
Parsley for garnish

Clean the trout as you would any roundfish and trim the tails (see directions on page 32 and technique photos page 524) but do not scale the fish. (Trout have such small scales as to make scaling unnecessary.)

With a small sharp knife, cut a slice off the top and bottom of the lemon. Stand the fruit upright on a work surface and, following the contours of the fruit, use a small paring knife to cut away the skin and bitter white pith. Cut crosswise into 6 slices 1/4 inch thick; set aside.

Season the trout, inside and out, with salt and pepper. Dip the trout in flour to coat completely and shake off the excess. Heat 3 tablespoons of the butter and 1 tablespoon of the oil in a large frying pan over medium heat. Add 3 trout and cook until golden brown on one side, 5 to 8 minutes. Turn and continue cooking until golden brown and tender when the flesh is pierced with the point of a knife, 5 to 8 minutes longer. Transfer to a platter and cover to keep warm. Repeat to cook the 3 remaining trout.

Discard the butter and oil in the pan. Heat the remaining 10 tablespoons butter in the same pan over medium heat. Add the almonds and sauté until golden brown. Remove the foil from the trout, and pour the almonds and butter over. Place 1 slice of lemon on each trout. Sprinkle with the chopped parsley. Decorate the platter with small bunches of parsley.

Pommes à l'Anglaise
ENGLISH-STYLE BOILED POTATOES

SERVES 6

In France, anything that is simply boiled is said to be *à l'anglaise*, English-style. Unlike their English counterparts, however, French chefs typically "turn" their vegetables before boiling them to ensure even cooking (see box below).

18 small waxy potatoes	*Salt*
(red or white)	*1 tablespoon chopped parsley*

"Turn" the potatoes (see technique photo on page 520): Fill a bowl with cold water. Use a paring knife to cut the potatoes into chunks about 2½ inches long and 1½ inches thick. Cut off both ends of the chunks and then pare down the sides, shaping or "turning" them into small barrel shapes with 7 faces. To prevent discoloration, hold the finished turned potatoes in the bowl of cold water while you are working.

Drain the potatoes and put them into a saucepan with cold salted water to cover. Bring to a boil, reduce heat to medium and cook until tender when pierced with the point of a knife, about 10 minutes. Let the potatoes stand in the cooking liquid to keep warm until serving time.

Drain the potatoes. Serve in a vegetable dish, sprinkled with the parsley.

TURNED VEGETABLES

Almost any firm vegetable may be turned in the same manner as for Pommes à l'Anglaise. This technique serves a dual purpose—the vegetables will cook evenly and the presentation is elegant. You will need a sharp paring knife and, in the beginning, a little patience! Use the vegetable parings in soups or stocks.

Turned potatoes occupy such an important role in French cuisine that they have been codified by size, each bearing a unique name: À l'anglaise refers to potatoes which are 2 inches long and 1 inch thick; "cocotte" identifies those that are slightly shorter and more olive shaped; and "château" refers to those that are about ½ inch longer and thicker than pommes à l'anglaise.

Oeufs à la Neige

SNOW EGGS WITH CARAMEL AND CRÈME ANGLAISE

SERVES 6

Sometimes called "snow eggs" (a literal translation of the French), this dessert is standard bistro fare. It calls for three basic preparations: crème anglaise, French meringue, and caramel. Don't confuse it with a similar dessert, Île Flottante, or floating island (see page 259) in which the meringue "eggs" are replaced by a large, molded "island" of meringue.

Note: Use two large spoons or an oval ice cream scoop to shape the meringue—the scoop is the easiest solution. You may prepare the dessert in advance but the caramel should be drizzled over it only just before serving.

CRÈME ANGLAISE
2 cups milk
1 teaspoon vanilla extract
4 egg yolks
¹/₃ cup sugar

FRENCH MERINGUE
4 egg whites
4 tablespoons sugar

CARAMEL
¹/₂ cup sugar
¹/₂ cup water

Prepare the crème anglaise: Use the milk, vanilla, egg yolks, and sugar and follow the directions on page 35 and technique photos page 552. Refrigerate until serving time.

(continued)

Oeufs à la Neige (continued)

Prepare the French meringue: Beat the egg whites with a whisk or electric mixer until stiff. Gradually beat in the sugar, then continue beating until stiff peaks form again; the meringue will be glossy and smooth.

Shape the meringue "eggs": Fill a large shallow frying pan with water and bring just to a boil. Reduce the heat to maintain a low simmer. Dip an ice cream scoop or two large spoons in cold water to keep the meringue from sticking, then scoop out an evenly shaped mound of meringue. Slide the meringue "egg" off the scoop (or use the second spoon to push it off the first) into the simmering water. Poach 3 minutes, then turn with a slotted spoon and poach until firm, about 3 minutes longer. Repeat to make as many meringue "eggs" as will fit into the pan without crowding. Transfer to a dish towel to drain. Repeat until all the meringue is poached.

Prepare the caramel: In a small saucepan combine the sugar and ¼ cup of the water. Bring to a boil over low heat, stirring to dissolve the sugar. Then raise the heat to medium and cook, without stirring, until the syrup turns a rich caramel color. Remove from the heat and carefully add the remaining ¼ cup water. When the liquid stops sputtering, set over low heat and cook until the caramel redissolves and is syrupy.

To serve, pour the crème anglaise into a shallow dessert bowl and arrange the meringue eggs on top. Drizzle a little caramel over the meringue eggs and serve with the remaining caramel in a sauceboat on the side. (For a more elaborate presentation, Oeufs à la Neige is sometimes served with a spun caramel topping as shown in the photo on page 51.)

FRENCH MERINGUE

Oeufs à la Neige (above) is made with a French meringue, the simplest of the three types of meringues found in French cooking (see Italian meringue, page 294, and Swiss meringue, page 417). French meringue is made by whipping egg whites until stiff and then beating in sugar until stiff peaks form again, the meringue is shiny, and the sugar has dissolved. It is crucial that the egg whites be beaten stiff and to maximum volume, just as for a soufflé (see tips on beating egg whites on page 83).

French meringue may be poached, as for Oeufs à la Neige, or baked until crisp and dry to make a base or container for fillings (Vacherin, page 428, and technique photos page 551). French meringue is also used in some mousse mixtures (Nougat Glacé, page 392).

LESSON 9

Salade de Pissenlits aux Lardons
WILTED DANDELION SALAD WITH BACON

Blanquette de Veau
à l'Ancienne
WHITE VEAL STEW WITH ONIONS AND MUSHROOMS

Ananas à la Ninon
FRUIT SALAD WITH A RED BERRY COULIS

GETTING STARTED

Salade de Pissenlits aux Lardons
WILTED DANDELION SALAD WITH BACON

SERVES 6

Dandelions grow wild along roadsides in France and, although they are considered weeds in flower gardens, when properly prepared the greens make a delicious salad. Their pleasant bitterness contrasts nicely with the sweetness of the bacon and the lightly poached eggs.

1 pound dandelion greens
  or chicory
6 ounces slab bacon, sliced
  1/4 inch thick

VINAIGRETTE
3 tablespoons sherry vinegar
1/2 teaspoon salt
Freshly ground pepper
6 tablespoons vegetable oil

1/2 cup white vinegar
6 eggs

CROUTONS
3 slices firm white bread,
  crusts removed
2 cloves garlic

Vegetable oil for frying croutons

Remove and discard wilted leaves and roots from the dandelion greens. Rinse, drain, and spin the greens dry; set aside.

Cut the bacon into lardons (see page 46). Blanch and drain.

Prepare the vinaigrette: Combine 2 tablespoons of the vinegar, the salt, and the pepper in a small bowl; whisk in the oil. Set aside.

Poach the eggs: Put 8 cups water in a large frying pan. Bring to a boil, add the white vinegar, and reduce the heat to maintain a slow simmer. Fill a bowl with cold water. Break an egg into a cup and slide it gently into the pan, gathering the white around the yolk with a slotted spoon. Poach until the white is cooked through and the yolk is still soft to the touch, about 3 minutes. Transfer the poached egg to the bowl of cold water with a slotted spoon. Repeat until all eggs are poached. (You may poach 2 or 3 eggs at the same time but it is important to keep the water simmering.) Drain the poached eggs on paper towels. Trim the whites to uniform oval shapes with a small knife.

Prepare the croutons: Preheat the oven to 400°. Put the bread on a baking sheet and bake until dry but not colored. Cut the garlic in half and rub over both sides of the dried bread, then cut the bread into 1/2-inch cubes. Heat a little oil in a large frying pan (just enough to film the bottom of the pan) over medium heat. Add the diced bread and fry until golden on all sides. Drain on paper towels. Add the blanched lardons to the skillet and fry until crisp and golden, 3 to 5 minutes.

To serve, combine the vinaigrette, dandelion greens, and croutons in a large salad bowl. Transfer the lardons to the bowl with a slotted spoon. Discard the fat in the pan. Return the pan to the heat, deglaze with the remaining tablespoon of sherry vinegar, and pour over the salad. Toss well. Place the poached eggs on top of the salad and serve.

VINAIGRETTES

The standard proportions for a French vinaigrette are 3 parts oil to 1 part vinegar. Mustard is often added as well, both for flavoring and to make a thicker, more emulsified vinaigrette. The type of oil and vinegar used depends upon the ingredients in the salad; the tart, slightly bitter flavor of dandelion greens is well served by a mixture of sherry wine vinegar and vegetable oil, while a salad of spinach and marinated sardines (page 197) is perfectly balanced by a cider vinegar and olive oil vinaigrette. At Le Cordon Bleu the chefs insist on using peanut oil for their vinaigrettes, and often use it in combination with olive oil. In America, however, we use vegetable instead of peanut oil in vinaigrettes because American peanut oil has a substantially stronger flavor than its tasteless French counterpart.

To make a vinaigrette, first whisk together the vinegar, salt, pepper, and mustard, if using. Then whisk in the oil in a thin, steady stream. Additional flavorings are added at the end.

Blanquette de Veau
à l'Ancienne
WHITE VEAL STEW WITH ONIONS AND MUSHROOMS

SERVES 6

This old-fashioned stew is an excellent way to use inexpensive cuts of veal. Boned shoulder or breast of veal is preferred.

2 onions, peeled and quartered
1 clove
2 carrots, chopped coarse
1 stalk celery, chopped coarse
10 parsley stems
1 sprig thyme or 1/4 teaspoon dried
1 bay leaf
20 peppercorns, crushed
3 1/2 pounds boned shoulder or breast of veal, trimmed of excess fat and connective tissue

5 tablespoons unsalted butter
1/4 cup all-purpose flour
Salt and freshly ground pepper
10 ounces pearl onions
1 tablespoon sugar
12 ounces button mushrooms or quartered large mushrooms

1 egg yolk
Juice of 1/2 lemon
1/4 cup crème fraîche

Put 8 cups water in a large saucepan. Stud one of the onion quarters with the clove and add it to the pan along with the remaining quartered onions, the carrots, celery, parsley stems, thyme, bay leaf, and crushed pepper-corns. Bring to a boil and boil 15 minutes.

Cut the meat into 2-inch cubes and add it to the saucepan with the boiled vegetables. Reduce the heat and simmer for about 45 minutes, skimming any impurities that rise to the surface. Remove the meat from the saucepan with a slotted spoon; set aside. Strain and reserve the cooking liquid. Discard the vegetables.

Melt 3 tablespoons of the butter in a heatproof casserole over low heat. Whisk in the flour and cook 2 to 3 minutes without coloring. Add the hot cooking liquid, whisking constantly to avoid lumps. Add the veal and, if necessary, enough water to just cover the veal. Season with a pinch of salt. Bring to a simmer and cook over low heat until the veal is tender when pierced with the point of a knife, 1 hour to 1 hour and 15 minutes.

While the veal is cooking, prepare the garnish: Peel the pearl onions (to avoid tears, put the onions in a bowl of warm water with a teaspoon of vinegar before peeling). Put the onions in a low-sided saucepan or frying pan large enough to hold them in a single layer, if possible, and add water to barely cover. Season with salt and pepper and add the sugar and 1 tablespoon of the butter. Bring to a boil. Cover with buttered parchment paper, reduce the heat, and simmer for 8 to 10 minutes. Remove the paper and continue cooking, shaking the pan occasionally, until the liquid evaporates and the onions are lightly glazed. Do not allow to color. Set aside.

Put the mushrooms in a low-sided saucepan and add water to barely cover. Season with salt and pepper and add the remaining 1 tablespoon butter. Bring to a boil. Cover with buttered parchment paper, lower the heat, and simmer until just tender, 5 to 8 minutes. Remove the paper and cook, shaking the pan occasionally, until the liquid evaporates. Do not allow to color; set aside.

When the veal is tender, add the mushrooms and onions and cook 5 minutes longer.

To serve, transfer the veal and vegetables to a serving platter with a slotted spoon. If the cooking liquid is thin, reduce over high heat until it is thick enough to lightly coat the back of a spoon (it should measure about 4 cups). Whisk together the egg yolk, lemon juice, and cream in a small bowl. Add a little of the hot cooking liquid and whisk until smooth. Return the mixture to the saucepan and heat gently, whisking constantly, until the sauce just comes to a boil. Remove from heat. Taste and adjust seasoning. Spoon the sauce over the meat and vegetables. Serve with rice.

Ananas à la Ninon
FRUIT SALAD WITH A RED BERRY COULIS

SERVES 6

This salad combines fresh pineapple and bananas with a dark red sauce made from raspberries and strawberries. The pineapple must be perfectly ripe; it should have a uniformly golden exterior and smell sweet and delicious even before being cut into.

FRUIT SALAD
1 large pineapple
3 tablespoons kirsch
3 bananas
Juice of 1/2 lemon, strained
2 tablespoons confectioner's sugar
1/2 pint basket strawberries

RED BERRY COULIS
1/2 pint basket strawberries
1 cup raspberries
6 tablespoons confectioner's sugar
1 tablespoon kirsch
Juice of 1/2 lemon, strained

Confectioner's sugar for dusting

Cut off the top of the pineapple 1/2 inch below the leaves and freeze the top until serving time. Cut a thin slice off the base of the pineapple without exposing the flesh so that it will stand upright. Remove the flesh of the pineapple, leaving the shell whole (see directions on page 27 and technique photos page 521). Freeze the shell until serving time.

Slice the pineapple flesh into rounds 1/8 inch thick. Cut out the hard central core of each slice with a small cookie cutter. Put the slices into a container and sprinkle with 1 tablespoon of the kirsch. Cover and let macerate in the refrigerator.

Peel the bananas and slice into rounds 1/8 inch thick. Put the slices into a bowl and sprinkle with the lemon juice, 1 tablespoon of the sugar, and 1 tablespoon of the kirsch. Cover and let macerate in the refrigerator.

Rinse, drain, pat dry, and hull the strawberries for the fruit salad. Set aside 6 perfect berries for decoration. Slice the remainder and put them in a bowl. Sprinkle with the remaining tablespoon of sugar and kirsch. Cover and let macerate in the refrigerator.

Prepare the coulis: Clean the strawberries for the coulis, then puree with the raspberries in a food mill or food processor. Strain through a fine strainer into a bowl and add the sugar. Whisk in the kirsch and the lemon juice. Cover and refrigerate until serving time.

To serve, cut 3 pineapple slices in half and reserve for decoration. Dice the remainder. Combine the macerated bananas and strawberries and carefully mix in the diced pineapple. Place the pineapple shell on a platter and mound the mixed fruit salad in it. Dust the pineapple leaves with confectioner's sugar and place the pineapple top carefully on top of the mixed fruit. Arrange the halved pineapple slices around the pineapple and top each with a strawberry. Serve the coulis in a sauceboat on the side.

LESSON 10

Crème Vichyssoise

CHILLED CREAM OF POTATO AND LEEK SOUP

Poulet Sauté Basquaise

CHICKEN BASQUE STYLE

Riz Pilaf

RICE PILAF

Tarte aux Pommes

APPLE TART

Crème Vichyssoise

CHILLED CREAM OF POTATO AND LEEK SOUP

SERVES 6

Though Vichy is a city in central France, this chilled leek and potato soup is said to be the creation of a French chef working in the United States in the early years of this century. It has since returned to France, where the term *vichyssoise* is occasionally applied to cold soups in general. At Le Cordon Bleu, only the whites of the leeks are used in making the soup and they are mixed with only a small amount of potato to produce a creamy texture and refreshing taste.

Note: Cold soups require more seasoning than hot; taste the soup after chilling and add extra salt and pepper as needed.

3 tablespoons unsalted butter
4 leeks (white part only), trimmed and sliced thin
2 medium onions, sliced thin
10 ounces baking potatoes, diced

6 cups Chicken Stock (page 12)
Salt and freshly ground pepper
1 cup crème fraîche or heavy cream
1 tablespoon minced fresh chives

Heat the butter in a large saucepan over medium heat. Add the leeks and onions and cook until tender but not colored. Add the potatoes and stock and season to taste with salt and pepper. Bring to a boil, reduce the heat, cover, and simmer until the potatoes are tender, about 20 to 30 minutes.

Puree the soup in a food mill or food processor. Then strain it back into the saucepan, pressing down on the solids to extract all of the liquid; discard the solids. Bring the soup to a boil.

Whisk the cream with a little of the hot soup in a small bowl. Return the mixture to the saucepan and whisk until smooth. Taste and adjust seasonings. Refrigerate until cold, 3 to 4 hours.

To serve, pour into a soup tureen and sprinkle with minced chives.

Poulet Sauté Basquaise
CHICKEN BASQUE STYLE

SERVES 6

Dishes in the Basque style typically contain bell peppers, onions, tomatoes, garlic, and ham—and this one is no exception. Basque dishes can also be quite spicy (especially when they are seasoned with a local chili called *piment d'espelette* instead of pepper). At Le Cordon Bleu, a French version of the classic Turkish *pilāv* (*pilaf* in French) accompanies the sauté.

Note: Though this particular recipe is for chicken, veal or even fresh tuna can be prepared in exactly the same way and served with the same rice garnish.

4½-pound chicken
Salt and freshly ground pepper
2 tablespoons vegetable oil
2 tablespoons unsalted butter
4 cloves garlic, chopped fine
2 medium onions, sliced thin
1½ pounds green bell peppers, seeded and sliced thin
⅔ cup dry white wine
½ pound tomatoes, peeled, seeded, and diced (page 31)
1 Bouquet Garni (page 20)

RICE PILAF

3 tablespoons unsalted butter
1 medium onion, chopped fine
2 cups long-grain rice
Salt and freshly ground pepper
4 cups water
1 Bouquet Garni

1 tablespoon vegetable oil
5 ounces dry-cured ham such as Bayonne or Parma ham, sliced thin
1 tablespoon chopped parsley

Cut the chicken into 6 serving pieces (see technique photos on pages 530–531): Lay the chicken flat on its back on a work surface. To remove the legs, pull 1 leg away from the body. Cut through the skin between the leg and the body and then through the flesh and down to the leg joint. Twist the leg to break the joint and cut through the joint to separate the leg from the body. Cut off the small bit of leg remaining below the drumstick at the joint. (French butchers leave this bit of leg when they cut off the feet, but you will not find it on most American chickens.) Cut the leg into 2 pieces at the joint between the thigh and drumstick. Repeat for the other leg. Then cut the breast in half lengthwise through the breastbone and backbone. Cut the ribs and backbones from the 2 halves of the breast. Repeat for the other breast. Cut off and discard the end two sections of the wings at the joints.

Season the chicken pieces on both sides with salt and pepper. Heat the oil and the butter in a large frying pan over high heat. Brown the chicken on all sides and then remove it from the pan. Add the garlic, onions, and peppers to the pan, cover, and cook over low heat, stirring occasionally, until the vegetables are soft but not colored. Return the chicken to the pan and add the wine, tomatoes, and bouquet garni. Season with salt and pepper. Bring to a boil, cover, reduce the heat, and simmer until the chicken is tender, about 30 minutes.

When the chicken is tender, remove from the pan; cover and keep warm. Bring the cooking liquid to a boil and reduce it until it is thick enough to lightly coat the back of a spoon. Taste and adjust seasonings.

Heat the remaining 1 tablespoon of oil in a frying pan over high heat. Add the ham and sauté about 10 seconds on each side.

To serve, arrange the sliced ham on an oval serving platter. Top with the chicken and spoon the sauce over. Sprinkle with the chopped parsley. Serve with Riz Pilaf (below).

Riz Pilaf

RICE PILAF

SERVES 6

3 tablespoons unsalted butter	*Salt and fresly ground pepper*
1 medium onion, chopped	*4 cups water*
2 cups long-grain rice	*Bouquet Garni (page 20)*

Preheat the oven to 400°. Heat the butter in an ovenproof frying pan over medium heat. Add the chopped onion and cook until tender but not colored. Add the rice and cook, stirring frequently, until translucent. Season with salt and pepper, add the water and the bouquet garni, and bring to a boil. Cover with a tight-fitting lid, transfer to the oven, and cook 17 minutes. Remove from the oven and let stand, covered, for 5 to 10 minutes. Remove the bouquet garni and separate the grains with a fork.

SAUTÉS

Poulet Sauté Basquaise is an example of a traditional French preparation called a *sauté*. A sauté is classically made from meat or poultry, cut into even-sized pieces for uniform cooking, that is first sautéed and then cooked gently on top of the stove or in the oven with just enough liquid to cover (usually wine, water or stock). A vegetable garnish may be cooked along with the meat or poultry to add flavor. The cooking liquid may then be served as is or creamed. If this sounds like a stew to you, you're not far wrong: A sauté differs from a stew (page 140) in that it cooks much faster and uses less liquid. (See Poulet Sauté à la Grecque, page 116, for a variation on a chicken sauté.)

Tarte aux Pommes
APPLE TART

—

SERVES 6

An apple tart can be as simple or as complicated as you like. At home in France, it is often made by layering thin-sliced apples over pie dough, dotting them with butter, sprinkling with sugar, and baking—that's it. This Cordon Bleu apple tart is slightly more elaborate, but baking the dough blind and giving it an egg glaze before garnishing it ensures that the crust will never be soggy.

PÂTE BRISÉE SUCRÉE
1 cup all-purpose flour
1/2 cup cake flour
1 egg
1 tablespoon water
Pinch salt
3 tablespoons sugar
1 teaspoon vanilla extract
7 tablespoons softened butter
1 egg, slightly beaten, for glazing

APPLESAUCE
6 Golden Delicious apples
3 tablespoons unsalted butter
1/4 cup sugar
1 teaspoon vanilla extract

APRICOT GLAZE
3/4 cup apricot jam
1 tablespoon kirsch

EQUIPMENT: 9-inch fluted removable-bottomed tart pan

Make the pâte brisée sucrée just as you would a pâte brisée (see directions on pages 37–38 and technique photos page 540), but add the sugar and vanilla to the well along with the egg, water, and salt.

(continued)

Peel and core 3 of the apples. Cut into quarters and roughly chop. Melt the butter without coloring in a nonstick or heavy-bottomed saucepan over medium heat. Add the chopped apples and cook, shaking the pan frequently or stirring with a wooden spoon, until the apples reduce to a puree. Do not let the apples color. Add the sugar and vanilla and cook until all the liquid evaporates. (The puree must be dry so as not to soak the pastry crust.) Remove from the heat and let cool to room temperature.

Preheat the oven to 400°. Roll out the dough and blind bake the tart shell (see directions on pages 38–39 and technique photos on page 541).

Peel and core the remaining 3 apples. Cut each in half. Lay each half flat on a work surface and cut crosswise into slices ⅛ inch thick.

Fill the cooked tart shell with the cold apple puree. Starting at the outside edge and working inward toward the center, arrange the apple slices in overlapping circles on top of the puree. Finish with a small "rose" of slices in the center (see photo below). Bake the tart until the apples are tender and golden brown, about 25 minutes. If necessary, place the fluted edge of a second tart pan upside down over the rim of the tart to prevent the edges of the pastry from scorching. Remove from the oven and let cool slightly on a rack, to allow air to circulate around it.

Prepare the apricot glaze: Work the jam through a fine sieve into a heavy-bottomed saucepan. Whisk in 1 to 2 tablespoons of water to thin jam, then cook over low heat until the glaze is smooth and syrupy. Remove from the heat and stir in the kirsch. Dip a pastry brush into the warm glaze and pat it gently over the surface of the tart to coat it completely with the glaze. If the glaze becomes too thick to work with, add a little water and reheat. Serve warm or cold.

LESSON 11

Petits Légumes à la Grecque

MARINATED VEGETABLES WITH
LEMON AND CORIANDER

———

Sole Belle Meunière

PAN-FRIED SOLE WITH NUT-BROWN
BUTTER AND MUSHROOMS

———

Cygnes Chantilly

CHOUX PASTRY SWANS

Petits Légumes à la Grecque
MARINATED VEGETABLES WITH LEMON AND CORIANDER

———

SERVES 6

French salads are typically seasoned with a vinaigrette—this one is an exception. Vegetables or mushrooms prepared *à la grecque* are marinated in olive oil, lemon juice, and white wine; they can be refrigerated up to two days in advance.

30 coriander seeds
30 black peppercorns
2¼ cups olive oil
5 cups dry white wine
Juice of 4 lemons, strained
4 teaspoons salt
2 bay leaves

ARTICHOKE BOTTOMS
6 small artichokes
1 lemon

¾ pound tomatoes, peeled, seeded,
    and diced (page 31)
30 pearl onions
1½ pounds carrots
1 cauliflower, about 1½ pounds
2 tablespoons white vinegar
1¾ pounds button mushrooms or
    quartered, large mushrooms
10 medium leeks (white part only)
Salt

In a large saucepan, combine the coriander, peppercorns, olive oil, wine, lemon juice, salt, bay leaves, and 5 cups water. Bring to a boil and remove from the heat; reserve. (This cooking liquid will be used to cook and marinate all of the vegetables.)

Prepare the artichoke bottoms (see directions on page 30 and technique photos pages 520–21) but do not cook them. Remove the chokes with a small spoon. Cut the artichoke bottoms into sixths and put them into a saucepan. Add one-sixth of the tomatoes and enough of the reserved cooking liquid to just cover the vegetables. Bring to a boil, reduce the heat to low, and cook until the artichokes are crisp-tender. Let cool in the cooking liquid.

Divide the diced tomatoes into 6 equal portions.

Peel the onions. (To avoid tears, put the onions in a bowl of warm water with a teaspoon of vinegar before peeling.) Put the onions into a small saucepan. Add one-sixth of the tomatoes and enough of the reserved cooking liquid to just cover the vegetables. Bring to a boil, reduce the heat to low, and cook until the onions are crisp-tender. Let cool in the cooking liquid.

Peel and cut the carrots into bâtonnets about 2 inches long and $3/16$ inch thick. Cook as described above with one-sixth of the tomatoes and enough cooking liquid to just cover the vegetables. Let cool in the cooking liquid.

Trim the outer leaves from the cauliflower. Break the head into small florets and soak for 5 minutes in a large bowl of water with the vinegar added. Then drain and cook as described above with one-sixth of the tomatoes and enough cooking liquid to just cover the vegetables. Let cool in the cooking liquid.

Trim and rinse the mushrooms. Cook as described above with one-sixth of the tomatoes and a very little cooking liquid; the mushrooms will release some water. Let cool in the cooking liquid.

Remove the tough outer leaves from the leeks and trim off the root ends at the bases. Cut each leek on the diagonal into chunks about 2 inches long. Rinse carefully in cold water to remove any sand. Bring a large saucepan of salted water to a boil. Add the leeks and blanch for 3 minutes. Drain, refresh under cold running water and drain again. Put the leeks in a saucepan. Cook as described above with one-sixth of the tomatoes and cooking liquid to just cover the vegetables; set aside to cool.

Refrigerate all the vegetables separately in their cooking liquid. Serve chilled in separate serving dishes.

Sole Belle Meunière

PAN-FRIED SOLE WITH NUT-BROWN BUTTER AND MUSHROOMS

SERVES 6

A *meunier* is someone who mills wheat and makes flour; a *meunière* is a miller's wife. The name of this dish might literally be translated as "sole cooked the way the beautiful miller's wife cooks it." More prosaically, the fish is simply floured and fried.

Note: Though sole is used at Le Cordon Bleu, fillets taken from any flatfish, such as flounder, or any small fish, such as trout, may be prepared in exactly the same way.

Before serving any fish *meunière*, fresh butter is heated until it turns a light brown color (*beurre noisette*), which gives it a slightly nutty flavor. Be careful not to let the butter darken too much and burn or else it will spoil the delicate flavor of this dish.

2 lemons	12 large mushrooms, sliced
6 whole sole, ½ pound each (see Note)	Salt and freshly ground pepper
4 tablespoons vegetable oil	¾ cup all-purpose flour
15 tablespoons unsalted butter	Juice of ½ lemon, strained
	2 tablespoons chopped parsley

Prepare fluted lemon slices: Cut a small slice off the top and bottom of each lemon. Using a zester, score the lemons lengthwise at ¼-inch intervals. Slice the lemons crosswise into thin slices. Set aside 6 whole lemon slices for the garnish. Stack the remaining slices and cut in half; reserve.

Clean the sole (see technique photos on page 527): Cut the tail fin of one fish straight across with kitchen or fish scissors, leaving it about ½ inch long. Cut along both sides of the fish to remove all the remaining fins. Lay the sole flat, black side up, on a work surface. Make a shallow cut across the tail fin and scrape up about ¼ inch of skin. With one hand on the tail to hold the fish steady, grasp the detached bit of skin in the other hand, using a piece of paper towel to hold it firmly. Pull the skin sharply toward the head of the fish; the skin will pull away from the flesh in one piece. Turn the fish over, white side up. Working from tail to head, against the direction in which the scales lie, scrape the back of a knife blade along the skin of the fish to remove the scales. Rinse under cold running water. To gut the fish, lay it skin side down on a work surface, with the tail toward you. Starting behind the head and about ½ inch in from the edge, make a 3-inch incision along the length of the right-hand side of the fish. Pull out the entrails and gills. Cut away any stained flesh. Cut out the gills with kitchen scissors. Rinse the sole well under cold running water, inside and out. Pat dry with paper towels. Repeat with the remaining sole; set aside.

Heat 1 tablespoon each of the oil and butter in a large frying pan over high heat. Add the mushrooms and cook quickly until all moisture has evaporated. Season to taste with salt and pepper. Remove from the heat; cover to keep warm.

Season the sole on both sides with salt and pepper. Dredge in the flour and shake off the excess.

Heat 1 tablespoon oil and 2 tablespoons butter in a large frying pan over high heat. (If the pan is not hot enough, the fish will stick.) Put 2 sole in the pan and sauté until golden brown and the flesh is tender when tested with the point of a knife, about 3 minutes on each side. Arrange on a long platter so that they overlap slightly; cover to keep warm. Discard the fat in the pan. Repeat twice more to cook all 6 sole.

Melt the remaining ¼ pound butter in the pan over medium heat. Season to taste with salt and pepper and cook until nut-brown in color. Remove from the heat and immediately whisk in the lemon juice to stop the cooking. Pour over the sole and sprinkle with parsley. Spoon the mushrooms around the sole. Put a whole lemon slice on the head of each fish and decorate the edge of the platter with the half slices. Serve with Pommes à l'Anglaise (page 50).

Cygnes Chantilly
CHOUX PASTRY SWANS

SERVES 6

Making choux pastry and Chantilly cream look like miniature swans may seem like no simple feat but it's all a matter of cleverly piping the dough and neatly assembling the pieces. The fainthearted might want to begin by making round choux pastries and filling them with cream, but once you are comfortable handling the pastry bag, swans and constructions of your own invention will crown dessert platters delighting children and grownups alike.

CHOUX PASTRY
⅔ cup water
3 tablespoons unsalted butter
Pinch salt
1 tablespoon sugar
⅔ cup sifted all-purpose flour
3 to 4 eggs
1 egg, slightly beaten, for glazing

CHANTILLY CREAM
1¼ cups heavy cream
2 tablespoons confectioner's sugar
1 teaspoon vanilla extract

Unsalted butter, softened, for baking sheets
Confectioner's sugar for dusting

EQUIPMENT: Pastry bags, small and medium plain tips, medium stars tip

Preheat the oven to 400°. Brush 2 baking sheets with the softened butter. Prepare the choux pastry, using the above ingredients and following the directions on page 43 and technique photos on page 548, but add the sugar to the water along with the butter and salt.

Pipe the choux pastry dough to make the swans' bodies (see technique photo page 548): Fit a pastry bag with the medium plain tip and fill with dough. (Do not overfill or it will be difficult to handle.) Pipe 18 teardrop shapes (about 1 inch wide by 1½ inches long) approximately 2 inches apart on the baking sheets: These will be the bodies. Brush with egg glaze and bake 15 minutes without opening the oven door. Reduce the oven temperature to 350° and continue baking until choux puffs are golden, including the interior of any small cracks, and sound hollow when tapped, 5 to 10 minutes longer. Cool on a rack.

Increase the oven temperature to 400°. Brush another baking sheet with the softened butter.

Pipe the choux pastry dough to make the swans' necks (see technique photo): Fit a pastry bag with the small plain tip and fill it with the remaining dough. Pipe 18 S-shaped figures, each about 2 inches long, on the baking sheet: These will be the heads and necks. Bake, unglazed, for about 8 minutes without opening the oven door. Reduce the heat to 350° and continue baking until golden, about 4 to 7 minutes. Cool on a rack.

Not more than 1 hour before serving, prepare the Chantilly cream (page 21). Fit a pastry bag with the medium star tip and fill with the Chantilly cream; refrigerate until serving time.

Assemble the swans: Slice the top one-third off each body with a serrated knife. Cut each top in half, lengthwise, to make wings; set aside. Pipe a continuous figure 8 of Chantilly cream into the cavities of each body, finishing about 2 inches above the top of the pastry. Sift confectioner's sugar over the outsides of the wings. Insert 2 wings, rounded edges down, into the center of each Chantilly cream body so that they form a V shape, with the rounded edges meeting in the cream and the pointed tips standing out like uplifted wings. Insert an S-shaped neck into the cream at the narrow end of each body. Pipe a small point of Chantilly cream at the wide end to represent the tail. Serve on a platter.

LESSON 12

Oeufs Mollets Florentine
SOFT-BOILED EGGS WITH SPINACH
AND MORNAY SAUCE

—

Fricassée de Veau aux Poivrons Rouges
FRICASSEE OF VEAL WITH SWEET PEPPERS,
TOMATOES, AND OLIVES

—

Riz à l'Impératrice
EMPRESS RICE PUDDING

Oeufs Mollets Florentine

SOFT-BOILED EGGS WITH SPINACH AND MORNAY SAUCE

SERVES 6

In France, any dish *à la florentine* is made with spinach. Here, soft-boiled eggs are baked on a bed of spinach covered with a cheese-rich béchamel. If the eggs are omitted and a little less sauce is used, the spinach can easily serve as a vegetable garnish for roast meat or fish.

12 eggs
Salt
2 pounds spinach

MORNAY SAUCE
BÉCHAMEL SAUCE:
    1 tablespoon unsalted butter
    2 tablespoons all-purpose flour
    1 cup cold milk
    Salt
    White pepper
    1/8 teaspoon freshly grated
       nutmeg
1 egg yolk
1/3 cup crème fraîche or
   heavy cream
1 ounce Gruyère cheese, grated
   (about 1/4 cup)

5 tablespoons unsalted butter
1 1/2 ounces Gruyère cheese,
   grated (about 6 tablespoons)

Unsalted butter, softened, for
   gratin dish

EQUIPMENT: 9-by-13-inch oval gratin dish

Put the eggs into a large saucepan and cover with cold, salted water. Bring to a boil, reduce the heat, and simmer for 5 minutes. Transfer to a bowl of cold water. Peel the cooled eggs under warm running water and set aside in a bowl of salted lukewarm water.

Stem the spinach and discard any wilted leaves. Rinse the spinach in several changes of cold water until the spinach and water are free of sand and dirt. Drain. Bring a large saucepan of salted water to a boil. Add the spinach and return the water to a boil. Immediately drain the spinach and let cool. Then squeeze well to remove as much water as possible.

Prepare the mornay sauce: First make a béchamel sauce using the butter, flour, milk, salt, pepper, and nutmeg and following the directions on page 18. Then whisk the egg yolk with the cream and add it to the sauce. Bring to a boil over medium heat, whisking constantly, and cook for 1 minute, still whisking. Remove from the heat and stir in the cheese. Taste and adjust seasonings. Keep the sauce hot in a saucepan set over simmering water.

Preheat the broiler. Brush the gratin dish with the softened butter.

(continued)

Oeufs Mollets Florentine (continued)

Heat 5 tablespoons of butter in a large frying pan over medium heat. Add the spinach, season to taste with salt and pepper, and cook, stirring, until heated through. Transfer the hot spinach to the gratin dish and smooth the surface with a spatula. Nestle the eggs in a circle on the spinach, and top with the mornay sauce. Sprinkle with the cheese and the bread crumbs. Broil, turning the dish if necessary, until the surface is golden brown. (For individual serving, see photo on page 68.)

Fricassée de Veau aux Poivrons Rouges

FRICASSEE OF VEAL WITH SWEET PEPPERS, TOMATOES, AND OLIVES

SERVES 6

This is a summertime fricassee whose olive oil, peppers, tomatoes, and olives give it a particularly southern flavor. Though the dish could be cooked entirely on top of the stove, chefs at Le Cordon Bleu prefer finishing it in the oven because the even heat ensures perfect results.

Note: *Quatre épices*, or four-spice mixture, is sold in groceries throughout France. It can be found in specialty stores elsewhere and is generally a mixture of ground pepper, nutmeg, cinnamon, and cloves.

3 pounds boned veal shoulder, trimmed of excess fat and connective tissue

Salt and freshly ground pepper

3 tablespoons olive oil

1 medium onion, chopped fine

10 cloves garlic, chopped fine

1 medium red bell pepper, diced fine

1 medium green bell pepper, diced fine

3/4 pound tomatoes, peeled, seeded, and diced (page 31)

3 sprigs fresh thyme or 1/2 teaspoon dried

1 small bay leaf

Pinch cayenne pepper

Pinch four-spice mixture, or mixed spices

1 1/2 cups rosé wine

1 cup Brown Veal Stock (opposite page)

1 bunch basil, stemmed

4 ounces black and green olives, pitted

Unsalted butter for parchment paper

Preheat the oven to 400°.

Cut the veal into 2-inch cubes. Season with salt and pepper. Heat the olive oil in a large frying pan over high heat. Add the veal and brown quickly on all sides. Reduce the heat to low, add the chopped onion, garlic, and peppers, and cook, stirring occasionally, until soft but not colored, 5 to 8 minutes.

Add the tomatoes, thyme, bay leaf, cayenne pepper, and four-spice mixture to the pan. Cook, stirring, until the tomatoes soften, about 5 minutes. Add the wine and stock and bring to a boil. Skim any froth that rises to the surface. Cover the pan with a round of buttered parchment paper and then the lid. Reduce the oven heat to 350° and cook the veal until the meat is tender when pierced with the tip of a knife, 1 hour and 15 minutes to 1½ hours. Meanwhile, stack the basil leaves into manageable piles, roll them into cylinders and slice thin. Add the olives and three quarters of the basil to the veal during the last 10 minutes of cooking time. Taste and adjust seasonings.

To serve, transfer the fricassee to a serving platter. Sprinkle with the remaining basil. Serve with Pâtes Fraîches (page 199) tossed with butter, basil and grated Parmesan cheese, if desired.

Fond de Veau Brun

BROWN VEAL STOCK

---

12 CUPS

6 pounds veal bones, sawed
   in pieces
2 pounds meaty veal knuckle
6 quarts water
3 medium carrots, chopped coarse

3 onions, quartered
4 tablespoons tomato paste
Salt
12 peppercorns
1 Bouquet Garni (page 20)

EQUIPMENT: 3-gallon stockpot

Preheat the oven to 500°.

Put the bones and the knuckle in a roasting pan and roast, turning occasionally, until browned on all sides, about 40 minutes.

Discard the fat and transfer the bones to the stockpot. Cover with the water. Add the chopped carrots, onions, tomato paste, a pinch of salt, peppercorns, and bouquet garni. Bring to a boil and skim off all froth that rises to the surface. Then reduce the heat and simmer for 3½ hours, skimming off any froth and fat that floats to the surface during cooking. Strain the stock into a large bowl. Remove the last drops of fat by skimming the surface of the stock with paper toweling.

Cool the stock, uncovered, as quickly as possible. The stock will keep for 2 or 3 days in the refrigerator (or for several weeks if it is boiled every day), or it can be frozen. Bring to a boil before using.

Riz à l'Impératrice
EMPRESS RICE PUDDING

SERVES 6

The empress who loved rice pudding is said to be Empress Eugénie (1826–1920), the wife of Napoleon III. Candied fruit, kirsch, and egg yolks enrich an otherwise humble mixture and a red current glaze adds color and luster to give this dessert an imperial look and taste.

At Le Cordon Bleu, Riz à l'Impératrice is made by combining a bavarian cream with the cooked rice and chilling for several hours before serving.

½ cup diced candied fruit

3 tablespoons kirsch

⅔ cup short-grain white rice

3 cups milk

1 teaspoon vanilla extract

1 package (¼ ounce) powdered gelatin

2 tablespoons cold water

BAVARIAN CREAM
CRÈME ANGLAISE:

   2 cups milk

   2 teaspoons vanilla extract

   4 egg yolks

   ¾ cup sugar

⅔ cup heavy cream

RED CURRANT GLAZE
½ teaspoon powdered gelatin

1 tablespoon cold water

2 tablespoons red currant jelly

Unsalted butter, softened, for charlotte mold

EQUIPMENT: 6-cup charlotte mold

Brush the charlotte mold with the softened butter.

Chill a mixing bowl for the whipped cream.

Combine the diced candied fruit and the kirsch and let macerate until required.

Put the rice in a saucepan, cover with cold water, and bring it to a boil. Boil for 4 minutes; drain well.

Combine the milk and the vanilla in the same saucepan and bring to a boil. Add the partially cooked rice, reduce the heat and simmer until the rice has absorbed most of the milk and the mixture becomes very thick, 20 to 30 minutes. Set aside to cool.

Sprinkle the gelatin over the water and let stand until softened, about 5 minutes.

Prepare bavarian cream: First make a crème anglaise, using the milk, vanilla, yolks, and sugar and following the directions on page 35 and technique photos page 552. Remove from the heat. Add the softened gelatin and stir to dissolve. Strain the mixture into a bowl and let cool, stirring occasionally. (Do not allow it to gel completely.) Add the candied fruit and the kirsch. Beat the cream in the chilled mixing bowl, with a whisk or electric mixer until stiff peaks form and the cream clings to the whisk or beater. When the crème anglaise mixture is cool and has begun to thicken, fold in the whipped cream and then the rice. Pour the mixture into the prepared charlotte mold and refrigerate until firm, about 2 hours.

Just before unmolding the pudding, prepare the glaze: Sprinkle the gelatin over the water and let stand until softened, about 5 minutes. Heat the jelly in a small saucepan over low heat until liquid. Remove the pan from the heat and whisk in the softened gelatin until smooth.

To serve, dip the mold in hot water for a few seconds. Invert a serving platter over the mold and turn the pudding out onto the platter. Drizzle the jelly over the pudding and chill until serving time.

LESSON 13

Daurade Crue à l'Aneth
MARINATED SEA BREAM WITH FRESH DILL

———

Canard à la Niçoise
DUCK WITH GARLIC, TOMATOES, AND OLIVES

———

Crêpes à la Gelée de Groseilles
CRÊPES WITH RED CURRANT JELLY

Daurade Crue à l'Aneth
MARINATED SEA BREAM WITH FRESH DILL

SERVES 6

In recent years, certain raw fish dishes have been appearing on menus throughout France. In fact, the fish is rarely served raw since, as in this recipe, it is usually left to marinate several hours in lime or lemon juice before serving (the marinade is said to cook the fish).

3¹/₂-pound sea bream
2 large shallots, chopped fine
3 tablespoons chopped fresh dill
Juice of 2 limes, strained
Juice of 1 lemon, strained
Salt and freshly ground pepper
¹/₄ cup olive oil

AVOCADO SALAD

2 avocados
Juice of 1 lemon, strained
Salt and freshly ground pepper
2 tablespoons olive oil

4 medium tomatoes, peeled,
*   seeded, and chopped (page 31)*
Fresh dill for garnish
1 head leaf lettuce

Clean the sea bream as you would any roundfish (see directions on page 32 and technique photos 1 to 6 on page 524). Then fillet the sea bream (technique photos page 525): Lay the fish on a flat work surface with the tail toward you. Place your free hand on the fish to steady it and, using a sharp filleting knife with a thin flexible blade, cut along the length of the backbone from head to tail. Then cut crosswise down to the bone, above the tail. Holding the blade of the knife flat, slide it along the length of the backbone and ribs to detach the fillet in 1 piece.

Make a curved cut down to the bone behind the head to release the fillet.

To remove the second fillet, turn the fish over so that the tail is turned away from you. Make a curved cut down to the bone behind the head. Then cut crosswise, down to the bone, above the tail and cut along the length of the backbone from tail to head. Finally, slide the knife along the backbone and ribs to release the fillet.

Skin the fillets (see technique photo page 525): Lay one fillet, skin side down, on the work surface. Grasp the fillet firmly at the tail end. Holding the knife blade flat, work it in between the flesh and skin and slide it down the length of the fillet to remove skin. Rinse the fillet under cold running water and dry well with paper towels.

Working from tail to head, run your fingers over the surface of the fillets to locate any small bones; remove them.

Cut the skinned fillets into escalopes (see technique photo on page 525): Starting at the tail end and holding the blade of the knife at a slight angle, cut the fillets diagonally into very thin slices. Sprinkle the bottom of a platter with one-half of the shallots and 1¹/₂ tablespoons dill. Combine the lime and lemon juices and pour one-half of the juice mixture over the shallots and dill. Season with salt and pepper. Lay the sliced fish in a single layer on top. Sprinkle with the remaining shallots and 1 1/2 tablespoons dill. Whisk the remaining lemon and lime juices with the oil and pour over the fish. Cover and let marinate at least 2 to 3 hours.

Prepare the avocado salad: Halve, seed and peel the avocados. Dice the flesh and sprinkle with the lemon juice. Season to taste with salt and pepper. Sprinkle with the oil and mix carefully; set aside in a cool place.

To serve, use a slotted spoon to mound the avocado salad in the center of a serving platter. Season the chopped tomatoes with salt and pepper and place small mounds of tomato around the avocado salad. Sprinkle with chopped dill. Garnish each mound of tomato with a sprig of dill. Decorate the edge of the platter with lettuce leaves. Serve the fish in its marinade on a separate platter. A simplified presentation is pictured on page 74.

Canard à la Niçoise
DUCK WITH GARLIC, TOMATOES, AND OLIVES

SERVES 4

The olives, thyme, tomatoes, and garlic are culinary allusions to the Mediterranean port of Nice. This *grande cuisine* version of a peasant dish uses butter instead of olive oil and stock instead of water but retains the flavors typical of the south. Note that the cooking liquids are carefully skimmed to remove all fat before serving.

5-pound duck
Salt and freshly ground pepper
1 bay leaf
2 sprigs thyme
2 cloves garlic
3 tablespoons butter
3 tablespoons cognac

3 tablespoons dry white wine
2 pounds tomatoes, peeled, seeded (page 31), and quartered
1/4 cup Chicken Stock (page 12)
6 ounces pitted green olives
Parsley leaves for garnish

Prepare the duck: Cut off the wing tips and discard along with the neck. Cut out the fat glands at the base of the tail with the point of a small knife. Cut out the wishbone to facilitate carving (see technique photos 1 and 2 on page 531): Lay the duck breast side up on a work surface. Pull up the skin around the opening of the cavity at the neck and scrape along both sides of the opening to expose the V-shaped wishbone. Hook your finger behind the bone and give it a sharp tug to remove it in one piece. Rinse the duck inside and out with cold water; dry well with paper towels.

Season the cavity of the duck with salt and pepper and add the bay leaf, 1 sprig thyme and 1 garlic clove. Truss the duck just as you would a chicken (see directions on page 6 and technique photos on page 530) and sprinkle all over with salt and pepper.

Heat the butter in a deep ovenproof casserole over high heat. Add the duck and brown well on all sides. Remove the duck from the casserole and discard the fat. Deglaze the pan with the cognac and wine over medium heat, scraping the bottom of the casserole with a wooden spoon to detach any cooked particles. Return the duck to the casserole, breast side up. Add the leaves from the remaining sprig of thyme, the remaining garlic clove, the tomatoes and chicken stock. Bring to a boil, reduce the heat, cover and simmer gently until the duck is tender, and the legs move easily at the joints, about 1 hour and 20 minutes to 1 hour and 30 minutes.

Meanwhile, put the olives in a small saucepan with cold water to cover. Boil 2 minutes. Drain and rinse with cold water. Add the olives to the casserole after the duck has cooked 1 hour.

When the duck is tender transfer it to a serving platter. Remove the trussing twine. Remove and discard the garlic clove from the sauce. Spoon the olives and tomatoes around the duck with a slotted spoon. Skim as much fat as possible from the sauce and then spoon it over the duck. Garnish with parsley leaves.

Crêpes à la Gelée de Groseilles
CRÊPES WITH RED CURRANT JELLY

SERVES 6

One can buy crêpes on many a Paris street corner, and one of the most popular garnishes is simply jam or jelly. At Le Cordon Bleu the chefs often use red currant jelly, but any jelly, jam, or marmalade could be used.

Note: The crêpes can be cooked in advance, stacked on a plate, and reheated quickly in the oven as described, or a crêpe "cake" can be made by stacking the garnished crêpes on top of each other, reheating in the oven, and slicing into wedges to serve.

SWEET CRÊPE BATTER
3/4 cup all-purpose flour
Pinch salt
2 tablespoons sugar
1/2 teaspoon vanilla extract
2 eggs
1 cup milk
3 tablespoons unsalted butter,
  melted and cooled

1 1/4 cups red currant jelly
1/4 cup confectioner's sugar

Unsalted butter, melted,
  for crêpe pans and
  serving platter

Prepare the crêpe batter (page 23), adding the sugar and vanilla to the bowl along with the flour and salt, and cook the crêpes.

Brush an oval serving platter with butter. Preheat the oven to 450°.

Place 1 tablespoon of red currant jelly in the center of each crêpe. Roll up the crêpes and place them, seam side down, on the platter.

Warm in the oven until hot, about 2 minutes. Sift confectioner's sugar over the crêpes and serve immediately.

Coquilles Saint Jacques Dieppoise
SCALLOPS WITH MUSSELS AND
SHRIMP IN CREAM SAUCE

—

Foie de Veau au Vinaigre et aux Deux Pommes
SAUTÉED CALF'S LIVER WITH ROASTED
APPLES AND POTATOES

—

Soupe de Fraises Cécile
FRESH ORANGE ICE CREAM
WITH STRAWBERRY SAUCE

Coquilles Saint Jacques Dieppoise
SCALLOPS WITH MUSSELS AND SHRIMP IN CREAM SAUCE

SERVES 6

Dieppe is the Monte Carlo of Normandy, a glamorous resort with beautiful beaches, grand hotels, and casinos. As it is on the coast, sea scallops, mussels, and shrimp are also plentiful and here, combined with cream, this trio harmonizes in a classic dish *à la Dieppoise*.

MUSSELS
2 pounds mussels
2 tablespoons unsalted butter
2 large shallots, chopped fine
1/2 cup dry white wine
1 tablespoon chopped parsley
Freshly ground pepper
2 tablespoons unsalted butter

1 pound mushrooms, trimmed,
   cleaned, dried, and sliced fine
Salt
10 ounces medium-size shrimp,
   cooked and peeled
18 large sea scallops
1/2 cup crème fraîche or
   heavy cream
1 tablespoon chopped parsley

First clean the mussels (pages 39–40). Then heat the butter in a large saucepan over medium heat. Add the shallots and cook until soft but not colored. Add the wine and parsley and bring to a boil. Add the mussels and season with pepper. Cover and cook, shaking the pan once or twice to rotate the mussels and ensure even cooking, until the shells open, about 6 minutes. Remove the mussels with a slotted spoon and set aside. Strain the cooking liquid into a large saucepan through a fine strainer lined with a damp dish towel. When the mussels are cool enough to handle, shell them and discard the shells.

Heat 2 tablespoons butter in a large frying pan over high heat. Add the mushrooms and cook quickly until the moisture has evaporated. Season to taste with salt and pepper and stir in the shrimp and mussels. Set the pan aside.

Cut the scallops in half crosswise and add to the saucepan with the mussel cooking liquid. Bring to a boil over high heat. Immediately reduce the heat and simmer 3 minutes. Remove the scallops with a slotted spoon and add them to the pan with the mushrooms, shrimp and mussels. Strain the cooking liquid into another saucepan, bring to a boil and cook over high heat until reduced by half. Stir in the cream and add to the pan with the mushrooms and shellfish. Bring to a boil over high heat, then immediately lower the heat and simmer for about 2 minutes.

To serve, remove the mushrooms and shellfish from the pan with a slotted spoon and mound in the center of a serving platter. Spoon the sauce over and sprinkle with the chopped parsley.

Foie de Veau au Vinaigre et aux Deux Pommes
SAUTÉED CALF'S LIVER WITH ROASTED APPLES AND POTATOES

SERVES 6

Several French dishes combine *les deux pommes*—literally "the two apples" ("apples of the earth," or potatoes, and the fruit, sometimes called "apples of the air"). Often when apples are used, another apple product is added to heighten their taste. In this case apple cider vinegar is boiled with veal stock to make a sauce both for the calf's liver and the two *pommes*.

2 pounds waxy potatoes (red or white)
Salt
4 tablespoons vegetable oil
8 tablespoons unsalted butter
6 Golden Delicious apples

6 slices calf's liver, 6 ounces each
Freshly ground pepper
1/4 cup apple cider vinegar
1/2 cup Brown Veal Stock (page 71)
Chervil or parsley for garnish

Preheat the oven to 450°. "Turn" the potatoes into small ovals, about 2 inches long and 3/4 inch thick, known as "pommes cocotte" (see directions on page 50 and technique photos page 520). Put the potatoes in a saucepan with cold salted water to cover and bring to a boil. Boil 2 minutes; drain. Heat 1 tablespoon of the oil and 2 tablespoons of the butter in an ovenproof frying pan over medium heat. Add the potatoes and shake the pan to coat them well with the fat. Season with salt. Transfer to the oven and roast, shaking the pan occasionally, until the potatoes are tender and golden on all sides, about 20 minutes. Remove and keep warm.

Peel, core and cut the apples into quarters. "Turn" the quarters, then "turn" them into the same shape as the potatoes. Heat 1 tablespoon of the oil and 2 tablespoons of the butter in a large frying pan. Add the apples and shake the pan to coat them with the fat. Season with salt. Transfer to the oven and roast, shaking the pan occasionally so that they color evenly, until the apples are tender and golden about 15 minutes. Remove and keep warm.

Trim the calf's liver of any membrane. Season both sides of each slice with salt and pepper. Heat the tablespoon oil and 2 tablespoons butter in a large frying pan over high heat. Add 3 slices of liver and brown 2 to 3 minutes on one side. Turn and cook 1 more minute. The interior should still be slightly pink; do not overcook. Transfer the liver to a platter; cover to keep warm. Repeat with the remaining liver, oil, and butter. Pour off the fat from the pan. Add vinegar and veal stock and cook over high heat until thickened, about 2 minutes. Season to taste.

To serve, pour the sauce over the liver. Garnish each slice with a sprig of chervil. Surround with alternating mounds of apples and potatoes.

Soupe de Fraises Cécile
FRESH ORANGE ICE CREAM WITH STRAWBERRY SAUCE

SERVES 6

The word *soupe* is used to describe this creation because it is served in flat soup plates; an intense strawberry sauce is topped with scoops of orange ice cream, producing a dramatic contrast in both color and taste.

But who is Cécile? The inventor of this dessert won't say. Only mysterious Cécile (and the chef) knows who is being honored.

ORANGE ICE CREAM
3 ounces candied orange peel, diced fine
1/4 cup Cointreau
4 egg yolks
1 cup sugar
2 cups fresh orange juice
1 teaspoon vanilla extract

1 1/2 pint baskets strawberries
1/2 cup confectioner's sugar
Mint leaves for garnish

EQUIPMENT: Ice cream maker

Chill a mixing bowl in the freezer for the ice cream.

Prepare the ice cream: Put the candied orange peel into a bowl. Sprinkle with the Cointreau and let macerate for at least 1 hour. Combine the egg yolks and sugar in a bowl. Whisk until thick and pale yellow in color. Bring the orange juice and vanilla to a boil in a medium saucepan. Whisk half of the hot orange juice mixture into the egg-sugar mixture and return to the saucepan. Cook over low heat, stirring constantly with a wooden spoon, until the mixture thickens enough to coat the back of the spoon. Do not boil. Test the consistency of the mixture by drawing a finger across the back of the spoon; it should leave a clear trail. Strain into a bowl and let cool, stirring occasionally. Transfer to an ice cream maker and freeze according to the manufacturer's instructions. Transfer the ice cream to the chilled bowl and freeze until firm, about 1 hour.

Rinse, drain and pat the strawberries dry. Set aside 12 small perfect whole strawberries for decoration; hull the remainder. Puree one-half of the hulled strawberries in a food mill or food processor. Strain through a fine sieve to remove the seeds. Stir in the confectioner's sugar. Cut the remaining hulled strawberries into quarters and then each quarter in half. Carefully stir the strawberry pieces into the puree; refrigerate until serving time.

To serve, spoon a little strawberry puree onto each of 6 dessert plates. Top each with a scoop of ice cream and decorate with fresh mint leaves and reserved strawberries.

LESSON 15

Soufflé au Comté

CHEESE SOUFFLÉ

———

Truite de Mer, Sauce Verte

WHOLE POACHED SALMON TROUT
WITH HERBED MAYONNAISE

———

Clafoutis aux Cerises

CHERRY FLAN

Soufflé au Comté

CHEESE SOUFFLÉ

———

SERVES 6

Soufflés are among the most dramatic dishes in the French culinary repertoire but are neither difficult nor complicated to make. This cheese soufflé is simply a cheese-and-egg-yolk–rich béchamel with beaten egg whites folded in. It may be served as a first course or entree and makes a particularly good luncheon dish served with a green salad and a dry white wine.

NOTE: Comté is a hard cheese similar to Gruyère, made primarily in the eastern provinces of France near Switzerland.

*1¼ cups grated Comté or other
    imported Swiss cheese such
    as Gruyère or Emmenthal*
1¼ cups milk
3 tablespoons unsalted butter
¼ cup all-purpose flour
Salt

White pepper
Freshly grated nutmeg
4 eggs, separated

*Unsalted butter, softened,
    for soufflé mold*

EQUIPMENT: 6-cup soufflé mold

Preheat the oven to 425°.

Brush the interior of the soufflé mold with the softened butter. Coat with ¼ cup of the grated cheese; refrigerate.

Bring the milk to a boil; set aside. In a medium heavy-bottomed sauce-pan, heat the butter over medium heat. Stir in the flour and cook 3 minutes, whisking constantly to prevent coloring. Remove from the heat and whisk in the hot milk. Bring to a boil over medium heat and season to taste with salt, pepper, and nutmeg. Reduce the heat and simmer 10 minutes, whisking constantly to avoid lumps. (Be careful to reach all parts of the pan with the whisk as this preparation sticks to the pan and burns easily.) Remove from the heat and whisk in the egg yolks one by one, mixing well after each addition. Stir in the remaining cup of cheese. Transfer to a large bowl; set aside. Cover to keep hot.

Beat the egg whites with a whisk or electric beater until stiff peaks form. Whisk one-third of the egg whites into the hot soufflé mixture. Gently fold in the remainder with a spatula. Pour the soufflé mixture into the prepared mold; it should come to within ¼ inch of the rim. Bake 15 minutes, then reduce the heat to 375° and bake until puffed and golden, about 15 minutes longer. Do not open the oven for the first 25 minutes or the soufflé will not rise correctly. Serve immediately.

SOUFFLÉS

The key to a successful soufflé is properly beaten egg whites and a good folding technique.

Perfectly beaten egg whites are smooth and shiny, not dry, and hold a stiff peak when the whisk or beater is raised from the bowl; a separated or grainy look indicates that the whites have been overbeaten. Make sure that the whites, as well as the bowl and whisk, are absolutely clean; any trace of yolk or grease will lessen the volume of the beaten whites. Traditionally, egg whites are beaten in a dome-shaped copper bowl: The copper reacts chemically with the whites to produce a very stable foam that is not easily overbeaten. A glass or stainless steel bowl is preferable to plastic.

The purpose of folding is to incorporate the beaten whites into the soufflé base while losing as little volume as possible. Always stir a little of the beaten whites into the soufflé base before folding in order to loosen the mixture and to make it more nearly the same consistency as the whites. Then add the remaining egg whites and fold them in: Cut straight down to the bottom of the bowl with a spatula or wooden spoon, then lift up the contents of the bowl while giving the bowl a quarter turn. Continue this motion until the whites and the soufflé mixture are well blended.

Soufflés are essentially last-minute preparations because the egg whites must be beaten and folded in just before baking. You may, however, make the base several hours ahead; when you are ready to bake the soufflé, reheat the base and then fold in the egg whites.

Traditional high, straight-sided molds are used for baking soufflés, to ensure even rising. Butter the mold well.

Truite de Mer, Sauce Verte

WHOLE POACHED SALMON TROUT WITH HERBED MAYONNAISE

SERVES 6

This might be called "fish disguised as fish." Whole trout (or salmon) is poached, then decorated with slices of cucumber that imitate its scales. It makes for a stunning presentation and can be prepared well in advance. At Le Cordon Bleu, the trout is served with "Green Sauce"—a sauce which, in one form or another, has been served in France since the early thirteenth century.

COURT BOUILLON

1 carrot, chopped coarse
1 onion, chopped coarse
1 stalk celery, chopped coarse
Bouquet Garni (page 20)
1 lemon, quartered
1 cup white vinegar
4 cups dry white wine
3 cups water
Salt

3½-pound salmon trout or salmon

SAUCE VERTE

MAYONNAISE:
2 egg yolks
1 teaspoon Dijon mustard
Juice of ½ lemon
Salt and freshly ground pepper
1⅓ cups vegetable oil

10 ounces spinach
4 ounces watercress
1 tablespoon each chopped fresh
    tarragon, chervil, and parsley

3 eggs, hard-boiled (page 16)
1 cucumber
2 lemons

EQUIPMENT: Fish poacher

Prepare the court bouillon: Combine the carrot, onion, celery, bouquet garni, lemon, vinegar, wine, water, and salt to taste in a large saucepan. Bring to a boil, reduce the heat and simmer for 20 minutes. Let cool to room temperature.

Clean the salmon trout as you would any roundfish and trim the tail (see directions on page 32 and technique photos page 524). Roll the fish in a clean dish towel. Lay it on the rack of the fish poacher and cover with the cooled court bouillon. Add water as needed to barely cover the fish. Bring just to a simmer over medium heat and poach for 6 to 8 minutes. Remove the pan from the heat. Let the pan stand for 10 minutes; then remove the fish from the court bouillon and let it cool in the towel.

Prepare the sauce verte: First make a mayonnaise. Use the above ingredients and follow the directions on page 31. Stem, rinse and drain the spinach and watercress. Blanch the spinach and watercress in a large saucepan of boiling salted water for 2 minutes; drain and refresh under cold running water. Squeeze out as much water as possible. Puree in a food mill or food processor and add to the mayonnaise along with the chopped herbs. Mix well; set aside.

Shell the hard-boiled eggs and cut in half. Separate the whites from the yolks. Push the whites through a fine sieve with the back of a spoon. Repeat with the yolks and set both aside separately.

Rinse and pat the cucumber dry. Slice the unpeeled cucumber into paper-thin rounds.

Prepare fluted lemon slices (page 65) and cut the slices in half.

When the trout is cool, unroll carefully onto a long platter. Scrape off the skin with a small sharp knife. With a spatula, spread a thin coating of sauce verte over just the body of the fish, leaving the head and tail uncoated. Starting at the tail end, cover the fish with overlapping cucumber slices, to resemble fish scales. Sprinkle a band of sieved egg yolk around the fish and then sprinkle another band of the sieved egg white outside the border of yolk. Decorate the edge of the platter with the fluted lemon slices (see photo for a variation of this presentation). Serve the remaining sauce verte in a sauceboat on the side.

POACHING

Poaching is the technique of cooking foods over low heat in a gently simmering liquid. It is particularly appropriate for cooking fragile foods such as fish, lean poultry and meat, or fruit, that may fall apart, or dry out and toughen over a higher heat. It is also a good way to cook foods that are to be served cold. Depending on the food to be cooked, the liquid used may simply be water or a highly seasoned liquid known as a *court bouillon,* a flavorful stock or wine, or a sweet syrup.

The temperature of the poaching liquid is all-important. It must be maintained at a bare simmer (the French say it must just *frissonne,* or shiver)—a more vigorous simmer may cause the food to fall apart or cook unevenly. A favorite method for poaching fish at Le Cordon Bleu is to bring the cool poaching liquid to a simmer with the fish, then remove the pan from the heat and let the fish continue cooking in the hot liquid (page 84); this technique ensures that the fish is gently cooked and is never overdone.

The choice of poaching liquid depends on the desired result. If you plan to serve the liquid as a broth or to make a rich sauce, a well-flavored stock is indicated (Saumon au Champagne, page 486). For dishes that do not make use of the poaching liquid, it is appropriate to use a court bouillon, made by simmering water and wine and/or lemon juice with aromatic herbs and vegetables for 20 minutes (page 84). For poached fruits (Pêches, Poires, et Pruneaux au Vin Rouge, page 90), a sugar syrup and sweetened, spiced wine are common poaching mediums; both may be reduced to make a sauce.

Poaching is ideal for cooking whole fish (Truite de Mer, page 84). Make sure that the poaching liquid is cold when you add the fish or the outside flesh will be too cooked before the inside is cooked through. It is helpful to wrap the fish in a dish towel before cooking to help hold its shape and make it easier to handle (poultry and large pieces of meat are usually trussed before poaching for the same reason). A fish poacher, a long narrow kettle with a removable rack, is a perfect vessel for poaching a whole fish, but you may also use a large deep pan such as a roasting pan.

Clafoutis aux Cerises

CHERRY FLAN

SERVES 6

The Limousin district in central France is famous for its beef—and for its cherry flan. There, unpitted cherries are placed in a dish and a liquid batter is poured over before baking. The Cordon Bleu recipe is much like the original but the cherries are pitted and a little kirsch is added to bring out their taste.

1 cup all-purpose flour
3/4 cup sugar
5 eggs
1 teaspoon vanilla extract
1 cup milk
1 cup heavy cream

Pinch salt
2 tablespoons kirsch
1 pound cherries, pitted
Confectioner's sugar for dusting

*Unsalted butter, softened,
    for gratin dish*

EQUIPMENT: 9-by-13-inch gratin dish

Preheat the oven to 350°. Brush the gratin dish with the softened butter.

Combine the flour and sugar in a bowl. Add the eggs and vanilla and whisk until blended. Gradually add the milk and cream, whisking constantly to avoid lumps. Whisk in the salt and kirsch.

Spread the cherries over the bottom of the gratin dish. Pour the batter over the fruit. Bake until the clafoutis is lightly browned and a knife inserted into the custard comes out clean, 35 to 45 minutes. Cool completely. Sift confectioner's sugar over the top and serve the clafoutis directly from the gratin dish.

LESSON 16

Potage Crécy
CARROT SOUP

—

Escalopes de Veau à la Milanaise
BREADED VEAL SCALLOPS WITH
MILANAISE SAUCE AND SPAGHETTI

—

Pêches, Poires, et Pruneaux
au Vin Rouge
POACHED FRUIT IN RED WINE

—

Madeleines de Commercy
MADELEINES

Potage Crécy
CARROT SOUP

—

SERVES 6

Two cities called Crécy (one near Paris, the other in Picardy) were once famous for their carrots; today any dish with Crécy in its name necessarily contains this much neglected vegetable.

2¹/₂ tablespoons unsalted butter
1 large onion, sliced thin
2 pounds carrots, sliced thin
8 cups water

Salt and freshly ground pepper
3 tablespoons heavy cream
Chervil or parsley leaves
*   for garnish*

Heat the butter in a large saucepan over low heat. Add the onion and cook, stirring frequently, until tender but not colored. Add the carrots and stir to coat with butter. Add the water and a pinch of salt and bring to a boil. Reduce the heat, cover and cook at a low boil until the carrots are very tender, about 1 hour. Puree in a food mill or food processor and return the soup to the saucepan. If the soup is very thin, boil, uncovered, until reduced to the consistency of heavy cream. Season to taste with salt and pepper. Stir in the heavy cream. Serve hot, garnished with a few leaves of chervil or parsley.

Escalopes de Veau à la Milanaise
BREADED VEAL SCALLOPS WITH
MILANAISE SAUCE AND SPAGHETTI

SERVES 6

Veal scallops are so lean that they can easily dry out and toughen when cooked. To keep them moist and tender, they are often breaded before cooking, but properly breaded veal scallops require care and attention. The veal is floured, then dipped in egg, then breaded. Even with this protective coating, veal should never be overcooked—once the scallops are golden brown they are ready to serve.

Though veal scallops are popular today in France they are a relatively recent addition to the French repertoire—they were first mentioned in the early 1800s but almost a century passed before they won the favor of French chefs. To this day, they are prepared in ways which evoke their "foreign" origin: *à la milanaise*, as here, or *à la viennoise* (Vienna style), a translation of *Wiener Schnitzel*.

MILANAISE SAUCE
3 ounces mushrooms, trimmed, rinsed, dried, and sliced 1/8 inch thick
3 ounces cooked ham, sliced 1/8 inch thick
3 ounces cured beef tongue, sliced 1/8 inch thick
1 tablespoon unsalted butter
3 tablespoons Madeira
1 1/3 cups Brown Veal Stock (page 71)

TOMATO SAUCE
2 tablespoons unsalted butter
1 tablespoon fine-chopped shallots
1 clove garlic, chopped fine
1 pound tomatoes, peeled, seeded, and diced (page 31)
1 small Bouquet Garni (page 20)
Salt and freshly ground pepper

ANGLAISE BREADING
3/4 cup all-purpose flour
2 eggs
2 tablespoons vegetable oil
1 tablespoon water
Salt and freshly ground pepper
2 cups fresh bread crumbs
1/2 cup grated Parmesan

6 veal scallops, 6 ounces each, about 1/4 inch thick
3/4 pound spaghetti
8 tablespoons unsalted butter
4 tablespoons vegetable oil
3/4 cup grated Parmesan

Prepare the Milanaise sauce: Cut the sliced mushrooms, ham and tongue into a julienne about 2 inches long and 1/8 inch wide (see technique photo on page 519). Heat the butter in a small saucepan. Add mushrooms, ham, and tongue and cook until mushrooms are tender, 4 to 5 minutes. Add Madeira and cook 2 minutes longer. Add veal stock and simmer the sauce until reduced by half. Taste and adjust seasonings; cover to keep warm.

(continued)

Escalopes de Veau à la Milanaise (continued)

Prepare the tomato sauce: Heat the butter in a small saucepan over low heat. Add the chopped shallots and cook until tender but not colored. Add the garlic and cook 1 minute. Add the tomatoes and bouquet garni, and season to taste with salt and pepper. Simmer until the tomatoes are cooked, 15 to 20 minutes. Remove and discard the bouquet garni; cover to keep warm.

Prepare the anglaise breading: Put the flour on a large plate. In a shallow dish, beat the eggs with the oil and water; season with salt and pepper. Combine the bread crumbs and the cheese on another large plate.

Sandwich the veal scallops between two sheets of parchment paper and flatten with a mallet or the flat side of a very large knife until thin.

Bring a large saucepan of salted water to the boil. Add the spaghetti and cook until just tender, 8 to 10 minutes. Drain well and return to the saucepan. Toss with 4 tablespoons of the butter; cover and keep warm.

Dredge the veal scallops in the flour and shake off the excess. Then dip them in the egg mixture and finally in the bread crumb mixture. (Make the coating as even as possible on both sides.) Gently press the bread crumbs onto the scallops to be sure they adhere.

In a large frying pan, heat 2 tablespoons of butter and 2 tablespoons of the oil over high heat. Add 3 of the breaded scallops and sauté until golden on both sides. Transfer the veal to a serving platter. Cover with aluminum foil to keep warm. Cook the remaining veal scallops in the remaining 2 tablespoons of butter and oil.

To serve, spoon the Milanaise sauce around the edges of the platter. Transfer the spaghetti to a serving bowl and top with the tomato sauce. Sprinkle with the Parmesan cheese and serve alongside the veal.

Pêches, Poires, et Pruneaux au Vin Rouge
POACHED FRUIT IN RED WINE

———

SERVES 6

Prunes, pears, and peaches each can be poached individually in red wine or in combination to make this elegant dessert. At Le Cordon Bleu we sweeten the wine with red currant jelly instead of sugar, and use whole cinnamon sticks and peppercorns (neither should be ground) to give the syrup a pleasantly aromatic taste.

Note: Served warm or chilled, this dessert is excellent accompanied by Madeleines (page 92), Almond Tiles (page 125), or a simple sponge cake such as a Biscuit de Savoie (page 33). If available, fresh cherries, raspberries, or strawberries can be added to the cooked fruits just before serving.

24 pitted prunes

6 small peaches

6 small pears

¹/₂ lemon

1 bottle dry red wine, preferably
   Burgundy

12 ounces red currant jelly

12 peppercorns

1 stick cinnamon

1 teaspoon vanilla extract

Mint leaves for garnish
   (optional)

Soak the prunes in cold water to cover for 20 minutes.

Peel the peaches (see directions on page 9).

Peel the pears, leaving the stems intact. Insert a vegetable peeler into the base of the pears, and work it in to a depth of about 1 inch. Twist and pull out the cores. Rub with lemon to avoid darkening.

Combine the wine, jelly, peppercorns, cinnamon stick, and vanilla in a large saucepan. Bring to a boil and boil 5 minutes. Add the prunes, reduce the heat and simmer very gently for 20 minutes. Add the peaches and pears and simmer until tender, about 15 minutes longer. Remove the pan from the heat and let the fruit cool to room temperature in the poaching liquid. When cool, transfer with a slotted spoon to a dessert bowl. Strain the syrup over the fruit and refrigerate. Serve chilled, decorated with mint leaves, if desired.

Madeleines de Commercy

MADELEINES

SERVES 6

Madeleines, a specialty of the town of Commercy in northeastern France, are small cakes baked in special shell-shaped molds. They are often served in late afternoon with tea or to accompany certain somewhat liquid desserts such as the poached fruit mixture described in the preceding recipe.

1 cup sugar
3 eggs
Grated zest of 1 lemon
2¼ cups cake flour
1¾ teaspoons baking powder
1 teaspoon vanilla extract

5 ounces unsalted butter,
 softened
⅓ cup milk

Softened butter and flour for
 madeleine molds

EQUIPMENT: Madeleine mold(s), pastry bag, medium plain pastry tip

Heavily brush the madeleine mold(s) with the softened butter. Dust with flour, then invert the mold(s) and tap out excess.

Combine the sugar and eggs in a bowl and beat with a whisk or electric beater until pale yellow and creamy. Add the zest, flour, baking powder, and vanilla and beat until blended. Beat in the softened butter and then the milk. Set aside to rest for 15 minutes.

Preheat the oven to 400°.

Fit the pastry bag with the medium plain tip and fill with the madeleine batter. Pipe the batter into the molds, filling each indentation to the rim. Bake the madeleines until golden, 12 to 15 minutes. Unmold the madeleines immediately onto a cake rack and let cool completely. (Madeleines can be stored for up to one week in an airtight container.)

LESSON 17

Fondants de Poisson au Beurre de Citron

SALMON CROQUETTES WITH LEMON-CHIVE SAUCE

———

Magrets de Canard aux Poires

DUCK BREASTS WITH PEARS

———

Petits Pots de Crème

VANILLA, CHOCOLATE, AND COFFEE CUSTARDS

Fondants de Poisson au Beurre de Citron

SALMON CROQUETTES WITH LEMON-CHIVE SAUCE

———

SERVES 6

These salmon croquettes are more elegantly called *fondants* in French—literally "melting" or "moist" tidbits. Indeed, the mixture of poached fish and béchamel creates a dish with a meltingly creamy interior and a light, crisp crust. At Le Cordon Bleu we poach salmon especially for making these croquettes, but leftover fish may also be used. Indeed, any cooked vegetable or meat can be prepared in exactly the same way.

Note: The butter used to make the sauce served with the croquettes is clarified to remove milk solids. This technique produces a perfectly transparent liquid that can also be used as a cooking fat. Clarified butter can be heated to very high temperatures without breaking down and gives a delicious flavor to foods cooked in it. Butter loses up to 25 percent of its weight (in water and milk solids) when clarified.

(continued)

Fondants de Poisson au Beurre de Citron (continued)

COURT BOUILLON

6 cups water

1/4 cup white vinegar

Large pinch coarse salt

2 carrots, sliced thin

2 onions, sliced thin

2 sprigs fresh thyme or
   1/4 teaspoon dried

1 small bay leaf

10 peppercorns, crushed

1 pound salmon fillet, skinned

BÉCHAMEL SAUCE

3 tablespoons unsalted butter

1/3 cup all-purpose flour

1 cup milk

Salt

White pepper

Pinch freshly grated nutmeg

3 egg yolks

LEMON-CHIVE SAUCE

12 tablespoons unsalted butter

Juice of 1 lemon, strained

3 tablespoons chopped chives

Salt and freshly ground pepper

ANGLAISE BREADING

3/4 cup all-purpose flour

2 eggs

2 tablespoons vegetable oil

2 tablespoons water

Salt and freshly ground pepper

2 cups fresh white bread crumbs

1 bunch parsley for garnish

Unsalted butter for croquette
   mixture

Oil for deep-fat frying

Prepare the court bouillon in a large shallow saucepan, using the above ingredients and following the directions on page 84. Let cool to room temperature.

Add the salmon to the saucepan with the cooled court bouillon and bring to a boil. Remove the pan from the heat and let stand until cool. Remove the fish from the poaching liquid and drain well on a wire rack.

Prepare the béchamel sauce: Use the above ingredients and follow the directions on page 18. Whisk the egg yolks with a little of the hot sauce and return to the pan. Return the sauce to the heat and cook 1 minute.

Flake the drained salmon and stir into the béchamel sauce. Spread the mixture out on a dish. Pat the surface with butter to prevent a crust from forming. Refrigerate until cold, about 1 hour.

Meanwhile, prepare a clarified butter: Melt the butter in a saucepan over very low heat, without stirring. Skim the foam from the surface. Remove from the heat and let stand a few minutes until the milk solids settle to the bottom. Carefully pour the clear yellow liquid (the clarified butter) into a container, leaving the milk solids in the bottom of the saucepan; discard the solids.

Prepare the lemon-chive sauce: Whisk the lemon juice into the clarified butter. Add the chives and season to taste with salt and pepper. Keep the sauce warm over a saucepan of hot water.

Fill a large saucepan or deep-fat fryer about one-third full with the oil and heat to a temperature of about 360°.

Prepare the anglaise breading: Put the flour on a large plate. In a shallow dish, beat the eggs with the oil and water. Season with salt and pepper. Put the bread crumbs on another large plate.

Shape the croquettes: Dip two tablespoons in cold water to keep the croquette mixture from sticking. Scoop out a mound of the cooled fish mixture with one of the spoons. Invert the second spoon over the top of the mound to smooth the croquette into an oval shape. Then slide the top spoon under the croquette and transfer it to the plate with the flour. Dredge it in the flour and shake off the excess. Gently pinch one end of the croquette to form it into a pear shape. Dip it in the egg mixture, then roll it in the bread crumbs. Repeat with the remaining fish mixture.

Gently lower the croquettes into the hot oil, frying no more than three at a time. Fry until golden, about 3 minutes. Drain on paper towels.

To serve, line a serving platter with a white napkin and stand the croquettes on the platter. Insert a small piece of parsley stem in the top of each to represent the stems of the pears. Decorate the platter with parsley sprigs. Serve the sauce in a sauceboat on the side.

DEEP-FAT FRYING

Success in deep-fat frying depends in large part on the temperature of the cooking oil—it must be hot enough so that the food doesn't absorb the oil and become greasy but not so hot that the outside burns before the interior is fully cooked. The optimal cooking temperature may vary from between 350° and 400°, depending on the size of the food being cooked (larger foods requiring a slightly lower temperature). An accurate deep-fat thermometer will take the guesswork out of frying.

Use a large, deep saucepan to deep-fry and never fill it more than one third full with the oil, which may bubble up when the food is added. At Le Cordon Bleu, we always use peanut oil for deep-fat frying because it does not burn easily at high temperatures. Vegetable or corn oil also works well. To maintain the oil at a constant temperature, always deep-fry in small batches—frying too much at a time will cause the oil to cool off.

Magrets de Canard aux Poires
DUCK BREASTS WITH PEARS

SERVES 6

A true *magret de canard* is the breast meat of force-fed ducks raised to produce *foie gras*. The breasts are extremely thick and have a much beefier taste than ordinary duck breasts. Long a specialty of the southwestern provinces of France, today *magrets* are served in restaurants throughout the country. Like steaks in France, they are served rare, but unlike beef they are often served with a slightly sweet and sour sauce and/or fruit, all said to counteract the natural fattiness of the meat.

Note: At Le Cordon Bleu real *magrets* are used, but since they are rarely available outside of France, this recipe substitutes ordinary duck breasts with excellent results.

12 small pears
3 cups dry red wine
20 peppercorns
3 tablespoons sugar
3 tablespoons red-wine vinegar
1 cup Brown Veal Stock
    (page 71)
3 tablespoons unsalted butter,
    softened
Salt and freshly ground pepper

3 whole boneless duck breasts,
    split and trimmed of excess fat
    and nerve tissue
3 tablespoons unsalted butter,
    melted
Chervil or parsley for garnish

Unsalted butter, softened, for
    parchment paper and
    baking sheet

Peel the pears, leaving the stems intact. Insert a vegetable peeler into the base of the pears and work it in to the depth of about 1 inch. Twist and pull out the cores. Put the pears into a bowl, and add the red wine and peppercorns. Let macerate 30 minutes. Transfer to a medium-sized saucepan and cover with a buttered round of parchment paper. Cover the saucepan with a lid. Bring to a boil, reduce the heat and simmer until the pears are just tender when pierced with the point of a knife, 15 to 20 minutes. Remove the pan from the heat and let the pears cool in the cooking liquid. Transfer the pears to a rack with a slotted spoon and let drain. Reserve 2 cups of the cooking liquid for the sauce; discard the remainder or refrigerate for another use (such as other poached fruits).

Combine the sugar and vinegar in a small heavy-bottomed saucepan. Cook over low heat, stirring to dissolve the sugar. Then raise the heat to medium and cook until the mixture turns a light caramel color. Remove from the heat and immediately add the stock to stop the caramel from cooking. Be careful, as the caramel will sputter. When it stops sputtering, add the reserved pear cooking liquid and simmer over low heat until the liquid reduces and becomes slightly syrupy. Remove from the heat and season to taste with salt and pepper. Set aside.

Lightly score the skin of the duck breasts with criss-cross incisions. Rub both sides with salt and pepper. Heat a large frying pan over high heat until hot. Add the duck breasts, skin side down (the fat released from the skin will be sufficient to cook the breasts), and cook until the skin is browned and crisp, 2 to 3 minutes. Turn the breasts and continue cooking until medium rare, about 6 minutes longer. Remove from the pan and wrap in aluminum foil to keep warm; set aside. Discard the fat from the pan. Add the sauce and deglaze the pan, scraping the bottom with a wooden spoon to release the cooked particles. Cook for 1 minute, strain and return to the pan. Off the heat, whisk in the butter, bit by bit. Adjust seasonings.

Preheat the broiler. Brush a baking sheet with softened butter. Arrange the pears upright on the baking sheet. Brush with the melted butter and rewarm for a few minutes under the broiler.

To serve, cut the duck breasts into thin, diagonal slices and arrange in the center of a large serving platter. Spoon over a little sauce. Garnish with chervil or parsley leaves. Arrange the pears around the duck breasts. Serve the remaining sauce in a sauceboat on the side. (For individual serving, see photo.)

Petits Pots de Crème

VANILLA, CHOCOLATE, AND COFFEE CUSTARDS

———

SERVES 6

Flavored custards, traditionally baked and served in small, decorative porcelain pots, differ from molded custards such as the Crème Renversée au Caramel (page 14) in that they are not turned out, but rather served in the pots in which they are baked. Like other custards, they must be cooked in a water bath and allowed to cool completely before serving.

3¼ cups milk
¾ cup sugar
2 teaspoons vanilla extract
1 teaspoon instant coffee

2 tablespoons unsweetened
   cocoa powder
3 whole eggs
3 egg yolks

EQUIPMENT: Twelve ½-cup ramekins or custard cups

Preheat oven to 400°.

Combine the milk, sugar, and 1 teaspoon of the vanilla in a medium saucepan and bring to a boil; remove from the heat.

Put the instant coffee, the cocoa powder, and the remaining vanilla in separate heatproof bowls.

Combine the whole eggs and egg yolks in a bowl and whisk to blend. Whisk in the hot milk. Strain and divide the mixture equally between the three bowls. Whisk to dissolve the flavorings. Fill four of the custard cups with the coffee mixture, four with the chocolate, and the remaining four with the vanilla. Skim off any bubbles or froth on the surface with a spoon.

Line the bottom of a roasting pan with parchment paper. Set the custard cups in the pan without touching one another. Pour hot water into the pan to come halfway up the sides of the custard cups. Bring the water to a simmer over medium heat and transfer the pan to the oven. Reduce the oven heat to 375° and bake until the blade of a knife or wooden pick inserted in the center of the custards comes out clean, 15 to 20 minutes. Remove from the roasting pan. Let cool and refrigerate. Serve chilled.

LESSON 18

Oeufs Cocotte à la Crème
BAKED EGGS WITH CREAM

———

Paupiettes de Veau
STUFFED VEAL ROLLS

———

Carottes Vichy
VICHY CARROTS

———

Tarte aux Agrumes
CITRUS TART

Oeufs Cocotte à la Crème
BAKED EGGS WITH CREAM

—

SERVES 6

Cocotte usually designates a rather large stew pot (or a woman with questionable morals) in French; here, the *cocottes* are actually individual porcelain dishes—ramekins or custard cups. Eggs are baked in these dishes until the yolks are warm and the whites have lost their transparency. The cream is heated separately and simply poured over the eggs just before serving.

12 eggs
1¼ cups crème fraîche or
    heavy cream
Salt and freshly ground pepper

Parsley sprigs for garnish

Unsalted butter, softened,
    for ramekins

EQUIPMENT: Twelve ½-cup ramekins or custard cups

Preheat the oven to 325°. Brush the interior of each ramekin with the softened butter.

Break an egg into a saucer and then slide it, without breaking the yolk, into a buttered ramekin. Repeat with the remaining eggs and ramekins. Set the ramekins in a roasting pan and fill the pan with hot water to come halfway up the sides of the ramekins. Bring the water to a boil over high heat. Transfer the pan to the oven and bake until the egg whites have set but the yolks are still soft, about 5 minutes.

Meanwhile, bring the cream to a boil in a small saucepan. Cook over a medium heat until reduced by one-third. Season to taste with salt and pepper.

When the eggs are cooked, remove the ramekins from the pan. Spoon some of the reduced cream over each egg. Garnish each ramekin with a sprig of parsley and serve immediately.

Paupiettes de Veau
STUFFED VEAL ROLLS

—

SERVES 6

This is French family cooking at its best (and an inexpensive way to serve costly veal scallops to a large family). Not only does the stuffing turn a pound and a half of veal into a dinner for six, but it keeps the scallops from drying out as they are gently braised with stock and vegetables.

6 veal scallops, 4 ounces each

STUFFING

2 tablespoons unsalted butter

2 large shallots, chopped fine

1 pound ground pork

1 egg

1 tablespoon chopped parsley

Salt and freshly ground pepper

12 slices bacon

3 tablespoons unsalted butter

6 ounces carrots (about 2 large),
    chopped fine

6 ounces onions (about 1 large),
    chopped fine

1 stalk celery, chopped fine

1 leek (white part only),
    chopped fine

2 cloves garlic, chopped fine

1/2 cup dry white wine

1 1/4 cups Brown Veal Stock
    (page 71)

Several sprigs fresh thyme or
    1/4 teaspoon dried

1 bay leaf

Sandwich the veal scallops between 2 sheets of parchment or waxed paper. Gently flatten the scallops with a wooden mallet or the wide flat part of a large knife to about 3/8 inch thick.

Prepare the stuffing: Heat the butter in a small frying pan over medium heat. Add the shallots and cook until soft but not colored. Scrape the shallots into a large bowl. Add the ground pork, the egg, and parsley and season with salt and pepper. Test the seasoning by frying a small patty of the stuffing; taste and adjust seasonings if necessary. Divide the stuffing into 6 equal portions.

Arrange the veal scallops on a flat work surface with the long sides facing you. Put 1 portion of the stuffing in the center of each and fold the long sides of the scallops up over the stuffing. Then fold the ends in toward the middle and roll the scallops over once so that the seams are on the bottom. Wrap 2 pieces of bacon lengthwise around each veal package. Tie each package with kitchen twine.

Preheat the oven to 350°. Heat the butter in an ovenproof pan over high heat. Add the veal packages and brown on all sides. Remove from the pan and set aside. Add the chopped vegetables and garlic to the pan and cook over medium heat until soft. Add the white wine and deglaze the pan, scraping the bottom to release any cooked particles. Add the veal stock and bring to a boil. Arrange the veal packages in the pan. Add the thyme and bay leaf and season with salt and pepper. Cover and bake until the veal is tender, about 45 minutes.

When the veal is tender, remove and discard the twine and arrange on a serving platter. Cover to keep warm. Strain the cooking liquid into a saucepan, pressing down on the solids to extract all of the juices; discard the solids. Skim as much fat as possible from the surface of the cooking liquid. Bring to a boil, reduce the heat and simmer over medium heat until reduced by half. Season to taste with salt and pepper. Spoon the reduced cooking liquid over the veal. Serve with Carottes Vichy (page 102).

Carottes Vichy
VICHY CARROTS

SERVES 6

At Le Cordon Bleu stuffed veal rolls are served with a dish of Vichy carrots. Tradition would have the carrots cooked in the bubbly mineral water from Vichy but, with or without Vichy water, carrots cooked this way make an excellent garnish for many meat dishes.

3 pounds carrots
6 tablespoons unsalted butter
Salt and freshly ground pepper

1 tablespoon chopped parsley (optional)

Peel and slice the carrots ⅛ inch thick. Put the carrots into a low-sided saucepan with the butter, 1 cup water, and salt and pepper. Bring to a boil, cover, reduce the heat and simmer slowly over low heat until tender, about 25 minutes. Taste and adjust seasonings. Spoon into a serving bowl and, if desired, sprinkle with parsley.

Tarte aux Agrumes
CITRUS TART

SERVES 6

A variation on the classic fresh fruit tart, this decorative dessert combines a sweet pastry crust with orange-flavored pastry cream and tart-sweet candied slices of orange and lemon. All of the components may be made a day ahead (the lemon and orange slices should be stored in the syrup); the tart can be assembled at any time but must not be served until the glaze has had time to cool and set.

1½ cups sugar
1½ cups water
2 teaspoons vanilla extract
2 small oranges, unpeeled and sliced thin
2 lemons, unpeeled and sliced thin

PÂTE BRISÉE SUCRÉE
1 cup all-purpose flour
½ cup cake flour
1 egg
1 tablespoon water
Pinch salt
3 tablespoons sugar
1 teaspoon vanilla extract
7 tablespoons unsalted butter, softened
1 egg, lightly beaten, for glazing

ORANGE PASTRY CREAM I
1 cup orange juice, strained
3 egg yolks
3 tablespoons sugar
1 tablespoon all-purpose flour
1 tablespoon cornstarch
1 tablespoon Cointreau

ORANGE GLAZE
Juice of 3 oranges, strained
*1/2 cup apricot jam or jelly,
  strained*

Fresh mint for garnish

Unsalted butter for pastry cream

EQUIPMENT: 9-inch fluted, removable-bottomed tart pan

Combine 3/4 cup of the sugar, 3/4 cup of the water, and 1 teaspoon of the vanilla in a heavy-bottomed saucepan. Bring to a boil over low heat, stirring to dissolve the sugar. Boil 1 to 2 minutes. Add the orange slices, lower the heat and simmer gently for 10 minutes. Remove from heat and let cool in the syrup. Cook the lemon slices in the same manner, using the remaining 3/4 cup sugar, 3/4 cup water, and 1 teaspoon vanilla. Let the orange and lemon slices stand in the syrup for at least 3 to 4 hours or overnight to allow the fruit to absorb the syrup and soften.

Prepare the pâte brisée sucrée just as you would a pâte brisée (see directions on pages 37–38 and technique photos on page 540), using the above ingredients, but add the sugar and vanilla to the well along with the egg, water, and salt. Chill.

Prepare the pastry cream: Bring the orange juice to a boil in a heavy-bottomed saucepan. Whisk the egg yolks and sugar in a bowl until thick and pale yellow. Combine the flour and cornstarch and whisk into the egg-sugar mixture. Whisk in one-half of the orange juice and then whisk in the remaining juice. Return the mixture to the saucepan and bring to a boil over medium heat, whisking constantly. Reduce the heat and simmer gently for 5 minutes, whisking constantly to reach all parts of the pan; the cream burns easily. Spread the cream in an even layer in a long shallow dish. Lightly pat the surface with the butter to prevent a skin from forming. Let cool.

Preheat the oven to 400°. Roll out the dough, line the pan and blind bake the crust, following the directions on pages 38–39 and technique photos on page 541. Let cool.

Remove the orange and lemon slices from the syrups with a slotted spoon. Drain on a rack.

Prepare the glaze: Bring the orange juice to a boil. Reduce the heat and simmer until reduced by three quarters. Add the strained apricot jam or jelly and mix well. Remove from the heat.

Add the Cointreau to the cold pastry cream and whisk until smooth. Spread evenly over the cooled tart shell with a spatula. Arrange a circle of overlapping orange slices around the outside edge of the tart. Then make a second circle of overlapping lemon slices, just inside of and overlapping the orange slices. Continue with circles of orange and lemon slices until the top of the tart is completely covered. Lightly brush the fruit with the warm glaze (the glaze will not spread evenly if it has cooled; gently reheat it if necessary). Arrange a bouquet of fresh mint in the center of the tart. Serve chilled.

PASTRY CREAM

Pastry cream is a stiff egg-yolk–based cream cooked on top of the stove. Traditionally pastry cream is made with a flavored milk (Crêpes Soufflées au Cointreau, page 182), but other liquids, such as orange juice (Tarte aux Agrumes, page 102), are occasionally used. As a matter of personal preference the cream may be bound with either flour or cornstarch. At Le Cordon Bleu we use a combination of the two when a lighter cream is desirable, and flour alone when we want something sturdier (Mille-feuilles, page 321). Pastry cream is a favorite filling for choux pastries or fresh fruit tarts, and it is often used as the base for dessert soufflés (page 365).

The technique for making a pastry cream is much the same as that for making a crème anglaise (page 35). The egg yolks, sugar, flour, and/or cornstarch are whisked together, the hot liquid is added, and then the mixture is cooked until thickened. Because the cream is bound with flour, however, it may be boiled, and it must be cooked for several minutes to remove the flour's raw taste. And because the cream burns easily, it should be made in a heavy-bottomed saucepan and whisked constantly during cooking, taking care to reach all parts of the saucepan.

Pastry cream may be lightened with whipped cream or enriched with butter (Paris-Brest, page 369). And the famous crème Chiboust used to fill the Saint-Honoré (page 510) is a unique variation on pastry cream—lightened with beaten egg whites and stiffened with gelatin. Pastry cream may be covered with plastic wrap and refrigerated overnight; rub the surface with butter to prevent a skin from forming as the cream cools.

LESSON 19

Oeufs Brouillés aux Foies de Volailles
SCRAMBLED EGGS WITH SAUTÉED CHICKEN LIVERS

Côtes de Porc Flamande
BAKED PORK CHOPS WITH POTATOES AND THYME

Poires Belle Hélène
POACHED PEARS WITH VANILLA ICE CREAM AND WARM CHOCOLATE SAUCE

Oeufs Brouillés aux Foies de Volailles
SCRAMBLED EGGS WITH SAUTÉED CHICKEN LIVERS

SERVES 6

Scrambled eggs are served as a first course in France. They can be eaten plain, but are more often seasoned or garnished with fresh herbs (parsley, chervil, or chives, for example), sautéed wild mushrooms or truffles, or a variety of other elements that include chicken livers, cooked lightly as described here.

10 ounces chicken livers, trimmed of fat and connective tissue
5 tablespoons unsalted butter
1 large shallot, chopped fine
Salt and freshly ground pepper
2 tablespoons port wine

1/4 cup Brown Veal Stock (page 71)
12 eggs
1/4 cup heavy cream
2 tablespoons chopped fresh chervil or parsley

Cut the chicken livers on an angle into thin slices. (This is known as *escaloper.*)

(continued)

Oeufs Brouillés aux Foies de Volailles (continued)

Melt 2 tablespoons of the butter in a large frying pan over low heat. Add the shallot and cook until soft but not colored. Season the livers with salt and pepper. Increase the heat to high, add the livers to the pan and cook quickly until browned on all sides and light pink in the interior. Add the port and stock and simmer for 1 minute. Remove from the heat; cover to keep warm.

Prepare the scrambled eggs (see technique photos on page 522): Break the eggs into a bowl. Add the cream and whisk until blended. Season with salt and pepper. Heat the remaining 3 tablespoons butter in a frying pan over low heat. Add the egg mixture and cook, stirring constantly with a wooden spoon or whisk, until the eggs have thickened but are very creamy and smooth.

Transfer the eggs to a serving platter and spoon the livers and sauce over the center. Sprinkle with chopped chervil or parsley and serve immediately.

FRENCH SCRAMBLED EGGS

Enriched with cream and butter and enhanced by a variety of garnishes from smoked salmon to asparagus to truffles, French scrambled eggs have very little in common with their American counterpart. Correctly cooked, they have almost the consistency of thickened cream and are absolutely never dry. Cook scrambled eggs in a heavy-bottomed pan over very low heat, stirring constantly so that they thicken gently into small, creamy curds. (Some cooks find that a water bath gives a more reliable result, but if you are careful and patient you should have success over direct heat.) French scrambled eggs must be eaten immediately. (See technique photos on page 522.)

Côtes de Porc Flamande
BAKED PORK CHOPS WITH POTATOES AND THYME

SERVES 6

In many regional recipes, vegetables and meat are prepared and served in the same dish. Flemish-style dishes *(à la Flamande)* often include potatoes, as here, or braised red cabbage, another favorite food from the north of France.

Note: Lamb chops (shoulder chops in particular) can be prepared as described here but they should be browned more quickly than the pork chops and placed in the oven for only 10 to 15 minutes to finish cooking.

6 pork chops, 6 to 8 ounces each   *1 tablespoon vegetable oil*
Salt and freshly ground pepper   *2 pounds baking potatoes*
¼ pound unsalted butter   *Several sprigs fresh thyme*

EQUIPMENT: 9-by-13-inch gratin dish

Preheat the oven to 400°. Season the pork chops on both sides with salt and pepper. Heat 2 tablespoons of the butter and the oil in a large frying pan over high heat. Add the chops and cook until golden on each side. Remove from the heat; cover to keep warm.

Peel, rinse and slice the potatoes ⅛ inch thick. Brush the gratin dish with 1 tablespoon of the butter. Spread a layer of potatoes over the bottom of the dish and season with salt and pepper. Place the chops on top in a single layer and cover with the remaining potatoes. Season with salt and pepper and then sprinkle with the thyme leaves. Melt the remaining 2 tablespoons butter and drizzle over the potatoes. Bake until the potatoes are tender, about 40 minutes. If the potatoes brown too quickly, cover with foil to prevent scorching. Serve hot.

Poires Belle Hélène
POACHED PEARS WITH VANILLA ICE CREAM
AND WARM CHOCOLATE SAUCE

SERVES 6

French chefs have frequently named their creations after celebrities or noteworthy events; this dessert is said to have been created in honor of Offenbach's operetta *La Belle Hélène*, an instant success from its first performance.

6 small pears
½ lemon

SUGAR SYRUP
1½ cups sugar
3 cups water
1 teaspoon vanilla extract

VANILLA ICE CREAM
2 cups milk
1 teaspoon vanilla extract
4 egg yolks
½ cup sugar

CHOCOLATE SAUCE
6 ounces semisweet chocolate,
   broken up
2 tablespoons unsalted butter
2 tablespoons heavy cream

Fresh mint leaves for garnish

EQUIPMENT: Ice cream maker

Chill a large mixing bowl and 6 dessert plates in the freezer for the ice cream.

Peel the pears, leaving the stems intact. Insert a vegetable peeler into the base of the pears and work it in to the depth of about 1 inch. Twist and pull out the cores. Rub the pears with the lemon to avoid darkening.

Prepare the sugar syrup: Combine the sugar, water and vanilla in a medium saucepan and bring to a boil over low heat, stirring to dissolve the sugar. Boil 1 to 2 minutes. Add the pears; reduce the heat and simmer over low heat until the pears are tender when pierced with a knife, about 20 minutes. Transfer the pears and the syrup to a bowl and let cool. Refrigerate until chilled.

Prepare the ice cream: First, make a crème anglaise. Use the above ingredients and follow the directions on page 35. Cool and pour into an ice cream maker; freeze according to the manufacturer's instructions. Transfer the ice cream to the chilled bowl and freeze until firm, about 1 hour.

Prepare the chocolate sauce: Bring 1 to 2 inches of water to a simmer in a medium saucepan. Combine the chocolate, butter and cream in a medium heatproof bowl and set it over the saucepan. Let stand, without stirring, until the chocolate has completely melted. Then whisk the sauce gently until blended. Add a little water if too thick. Keep the sauce warm over the simmering water.

To serve, scoop the ice cream into each of the chilled dessert plates. Place a pear on top and spoon the warm chocolate sauce over the pears. Decorate with mint leaves and serve immediately.

LESSON 20

Crudités et Leurs Sauces

RAW VEGETABLES WITH THREE DIPS

———

Cotriade

BRITTANY FISH STEW

———

Sorbet aux Fruits de la Passion

PASSION FRUIT SORBET

Crudités et Leurs Sauces
RAW VEGETABLES WITH THREE DIPS

SERVES 6

Raw vegetables *(crudités)* are a favorite first course in France, most often served grated or sliced with a simple vinaigrette. At Le Cordon Bleu whole fresh vegetables are served with three different sauces or dips.

ROUILLE DIP
1 small waxy potato
   (red or white)
Salt
1 to 2 pinches saffron threads
1/2 red bell pepper
3 cloves garlic, chopped
Coarse salt
1 egg yolk
Pinch cayenne pepper
1/2 cup vegetable oil
1/2 cup olive oil
1/2 teaspoon tomato paste

VEGETABLES
8 small carrots
2 stalks celery
1 cauliflower, about 1 1/4 pounds
Dash white vinegar
4 medium tomatoes
1 bulb fennel
1 small bunch scallions
1 bunch radishes

AVOCADO DIP
MAYONNAISE:
   1 egg yolk
   Salt and freshly ground pepper
   1/2 teaspoon Dijon mustard
   Juice of 1/2 lemon, strained
   1/2 cup vegetable oil
1 medium avocado
Juice of 1 lemon, strained
2 tablespoons chopped watercress
2 tablespoons chopped parsley
2 tablespoons chopped fresh
   tarragon
2 shallots, chopped fine
1 clove garlic, chopped fine
Pinch cayenne pepper

CREAMED HORSERADISH DIP
5 teaspoons grated horseradish
1 teaspoon lemon juice
1 teaspoon sugar
Salt and freshly ground pepper
2 tablespoons fresh bread crumbs
1/2 cup heavy cream

Make the rouille dip: Preheat the oven to 350°. Peel and quarter the potato and put it into a saucepan with cold, salted water to cover. Bring to a boil, reduce the heat and simmer until tender, about 20 minutes. Drain and mash while still hot. Stir in a pinch of saffron. Roast the red bell pepper until the skin blackens slightly and wrinkles, about 15 minutes. Remove the pepper from the oven and cover with a dish towel to allow steam to loosen the skin from the flesh. When cool, peel the skin under cold running water. Finely chop the pepper and puree in a food processor or work it through a fine sieve; set aside.

Combine the garlic and a pinch of coarse salt on a cutting board and crush to a paste with the flat side of a knife blade. Put the garlic paste into a bowl along with the pureed pepper, the egg yolk, and cayenne pepper. Gradually whisk in the oils as if making a mayonnaise. Add the potato puree and tomato paste and mix well. Taste and adjust seasoning; the dip should be spicy.

Chill a mixing bowl for the whipped cream.

Prepare the horseradish dip: Combine the horseradish, lemon juice, and sugar in a small bowl. Season to taste with salt and pepper. Add the bread crumbs and mix well to form a smooth paste. Whisk the cream in the chilled bowl until soft peaks form. Fold in the horseradish mixture. Taste and adjust seasonings. Refrigerate until serving time.

Prepare the avocado dip: First make a mayonnaise, using the egg yolk, salt, pepper, mustard, juice of ½ lemon, and the oil (follow the directions on page 31); set aside. Halve the avocado. Remove and discard the pit. Scoop out the flesh with a teaspoon and puree in a food processor, or pass it through a fine sieve. Add the lemon juice to prevent discoloration. Whisk in the chopped watercress, parsley, tarragon, shallots, and garlic. Whisk the avocado mixture into the mayonnaise and season with cayenne.

Prepare the vegetables: Peel the carrots and celery. Cut into *bâtonnets* 2 inches long by ¼ inch square. Remove the leaves from the cauliflower and cut out the core. Divide the head into small florets and soak in a bowl of cold water with the vinegar. Cut the tomatoes into wedges. Peel the fennel with a vegetable peeler and cut it lengthwise into about 8 wedges. Trim and wash the scallions and radishes. Drain and rinse the cauliflower in cold water; drain again.

To serve, arrange all the vegetables decoratively on a round serving platter. Serve the dips alongside.

Cotriade

BRITTANY FISH STEW

SERVES 6

Brittany juts out into the Atlantic on the northwest corner of France. Its sardines and lobsters are famous, and in recent years inland farmers have made Brittany synonymous with cauliflower and artichokes of spectacular quality. *Cotriade* is another pride of the region. The fish and potatoes can be served in the broth, as described here, or separately, in which case the broth is generally served first, with fried croutons.

1 porgy (1¼ pounds)	*Salt and freshly ground pepper*
2 mackerel or trout,	*6 tablespoons unsalted butter*
7 ounces each	*2 medium onions, sliced thin*
1 sea robin (¾ pound)	*6 large baking potatoes,*
(or snapper or monkfish)	*sliced ¼ inch thick*
3 perch, 4 ounces each	*1 Bouquet Garni (page 20)*

Clean the fish as you would any roundfish (see directions on page 32 and technique photos 1–6 on page 524). Cut off and discard the heads and tails. Cut the fish into 1-inch-thick slices and put into a bowl. Sprinkle with salt and pepper and let stand 30 minutes.

Heat the butter in a large saucepan over low heat. Add the onions and cook until tender but not colored. Remove from the heat, layer the potatoes on top of the onions, and season with salt and pepper. Add the bouquet garni and enough water to cover the potatoes. Cover and cook over low heat until the potatoes are tender. Arrange the fish pieces on top of the potatoes. Cover and simmer gently, so the fish will not break apart, until the fish is tender when pierced with a knife. Serve in a soup tureen.

Sorbet aux Fruits de la Passion
PASSION FRUIT SORBET

SERVES 6

Once a rarity in France, passion fruit is now easy to come by and often used to flavor sorbets and mousses. The bright color of the juice—a deep saffron yellow—its exotic flavor, and its romantic name all contribute to its success. At Le Cordon Bleu this sorbet is served with slices of green kiwifruit and sprigs of fresh mint, which heighten its refreshing appearance and taste.

SUGAR SYRUP
1 cup water
1/2 cup sugar
1 teaspoon vanilla extract

4 pounds fresh passion fruit or 2 cups canned passion fruit juice
2/3 cup water
Juice of 1 lemon, strained
2 kiwifruit
Mint leaves for garnish

EQUIPMENT: Ice cream maker

Chill a mixing bowl and 6 dessert glasses in the freezer.

Prepare the sugar syrup: Combine the water, sugar and vanilla in a saucepan. Bring to a boil over low heat, stirring to dissolve the sugar. Boil 1 to 2 minutes. Cool over ice.

Cut the passion fruit in half. Remove the pulp and seeds with a teaspoon. Strain, pressing hard on the solids to extract the juice. (You should have about 2 cups of juice.)

Whisk the water, lemon juice, and cooled syrup with the fruit juice. Transfer to an ice cream maker and freeze according to the manufacturer's instructions. Transfer to the chilled bowl and freeze until firm, about 1 hour.

Peel the kiwifruit and slice 1/8 inch thick.

To serve, put 2 or 3 scoops of sorbet in each chilled dessert glass. Garnish with 2 kiwifruit slices and 1 or 2 mint leaves.

LESSON 21

Gratin de Langoustines
LANGOUSTINE GRATIN

———

Poulet Sauté à la Grecque
SAUTÉED CHICKEN, GREEK STYLE

———

*Pudding Diplomate,
Crème Anglaise*
LADYFINGER PUDDING WITH CRÈME ANGLAISE

Gratin de Langoustines
LANGOUSTINE GRATIN

———

SERVES 6

Langoustines are exceptionally delicious little crustaceans that look something like small lobsters and are found both in the Mediterranean and in the waters of Northern Europe. Only the tail meat is eaten. Fresh langoustines are, unfortunately, not widely available in America. Although the result will taste different, large shrimp or lobster may be substituted in many recipes that call for langoustines.

*3¹/₂ pounds unshelled langoustines
  or large shrimp*
6 tablespoons unsalted butter
1 small carrot, diced fine
1 small onion, diced fine
4 shallots, chopped fine
1 stalk celery, diced fine
1 sprig parsley
*1 sprig fresh thyme or
  ¹/₄ teaspoon dried*
1 bay leaf

6 tablespoons cognac
¹/₂ cup dry white wine
Salt and freshly ground pepper
2 pounds mushrooms, sliced thin
*1 cup crème fraîche or
  heavy cream*
3 egg yolks
¹/₄ cup water

*Unsalted butter, softened,
  for gratin dish*

EQUIPMENT: Large gratin dish

Rinse the langoustines. Twist off the tails, peel off the shells (see technique photos on page 523) and set the tails aside. (Or shell the shrimp.) Put the heads and shells into a large saucepan and crush with a pestle. (Or, coarsely grind the heads and shells in a food processor and then transfer to a large saucepan.) Add 2 tablespoons of butter to the pan and melt over low heat. Add the carrot, onion, 1 of the shallots, the celery, parsley, thyme, and bay leaf and cook over low heat until the vegetables are tender but not colored, 5 to 6 minutes. Add 3 tablespoons of the cognac and carefully light it with a match. When the flames die, add the white wine. Cover and cook over low heat for about 10 minutes, stirring occasionally. Strain into a small saucepan, pressing down on the solids to extract all of the liquid; set the strained cooking liquid aside.

Melt 2 tablespoons butter in a large frying pan over low heat. Add 2 of the shallots and cook until soft but not colored. Raise the heat to high, stirring constantly to avoid burning the shallots. When the butter is hot, add the langoustine tails, season with salt and pepper, and cook quickly, stirring, for 1 minute. Add the 3 remaining tablespoons of cognac and carefully light it with a match. When the flames die, remove the langoustine tails with a slotted spoon; set aside. Strain the contents of the pan into the saucepan with the strained cooking liquid.

Melt the remaining 2 tablespoons butter in the same frying pan over low heat. Add the remaining shallot and cook 2 to 3 minutes. Raise the heat to high, stirring constantly to avoid burning the shallot. When the butter is hot, add the mushrooms, season with salt and pepper, and cook quickly for about 5 minutes. Strain any juices given out into the saucepan with the strained cooking liquid.

Brush the gratin dish with the softened butter. Spread the mushrooms over the bottom of the gratin dish and arrange the langoustine tails on top. Set aside while you prepare the sauce.

Prepare the sauce: First, stir the cream into the strained cooking liquid. Cook over medium heat until reduced by about one-third. Remove from heat and let cool to lukewarm.

Then, prepare a sabayon: Bring a saucepan of water to a simmer. Combine the egg yolks and water in a heatproof bowl and beat with a whisk or electric mixer until pale yellow and foamy. Set the bowl over the simmering water without allowing the bottom of the bowl to touch the water. Continue beating until the mixture becomes thick and creamy and increases in volume, and the whisk or beater leaves a clear trail on the bottom of the bowl. Test the temperature of the sabayon occasionally with a finger: If it feels hotter than just tepid (the temperature should not exceed 80°), remove from the heat and beat until slightly cooled. Return to the heat and finish cooking as described, then gradually whisk in the lukewarm cream mixture.

Preheat the broiler.

Spoon the sauce over the langoustine tails in the gratin dish and broil until the surface is lightly colored. Serve hot.

SABAYON

The sauce for the Gratin de Langoustines on the preceding page is based on a foamy mixture called a sabayon (a cousin of the light, egg-based Italian dessert *zabaglione*). A sabayon is made by beating egg yolks with a liquid over simmering water until thickened and increased in volume. (In Gratin de Langoustines the liquid is water, but champagne or wine is often used for a savory sabayon.) The sabayon must not get too hot during cooking or it will become grainy: If it begins to feel warmer than body temperature, remove the pan briefly from the heat, beating continuously, until the mixture cools. Then return the pan to the heat and continue cooking. Sabayon may be served warm or cold; a cold sabayon is beaten off the heat until cooled.

Sabayons may be sweet or savory. They may be served simply as a sauce (Feuilletés aux Poires Chauds au Sabayon, page 499), often flavored with an alcohol, or they may form the base of some mousse mixtures (Mousse Créole, page 417). They may also be used to gratiné sweet or savory dishes. Cornstarch is sometimes added for stability.

Poulet Sauté à la Grecque
SAUTÉED CHICKEN, GREEK STYLE

SERVES 6

Greece was traditionally France's supplier of raisins and currants. Their combination here with hot chili peppers gives this dish an exotic flavor rarely encountered in French recipes.

1/3 cup golden raisins
1/3 cup currants or dark raisins
4 1/2-pound chicken
5 tablespoons unsalted butter
2 tablespoons vegetable oil
Salt and freshly ground pepper
1 large onion, chopped fine
1 small hot green chili pepper,
 such as jalapeño, chopped
3 tablespoons all-purpose flour
2 cloves garlic, crushed
4 cups Chicken Stock (page 12)

RICE PILAF

3 tablespoons unsalted butter
1 medium onion, chopped fine
2 cups long-grain rice
Salt and freshly ground pepper
4 cups Chicken Stock
1 Bouquet Garni (page 20)
3 cloves garlic, crushed

Chopped parsley for garnish

Unsalted butter, softened,
 for parchment paper

Put the raisins in a small bowl and cover with lukewarm water: set aside.

Preheat the oven to 425°.

Cut the chicken into 6 pieces (see directions on pages 59–60 and technique photos pages 530–31). (Reserve the carcass, giblets, neck, and wing tips for chicken stock, if desired.)

Heat 3 tablespoons butter and 1 tablespoon oil in a large frying pan over high heat. Sprinkle the chicken pieces with salt and pepper and add them, skin side down, to the pan. Cook until the skin is golden brown, then turn and brown the other side. Remove the chicken pieces from the pan and discard the fat. Put 1 tablespoon oil and 2 tablespoons butter in the pan. Add the chopped onion and the chili pepper, and cook over medium heat until soft but not colored. Whisk in the flour and cook 2 minutes. Add the crushed garlic and chicken stock and stir well. Return the chicken to the pan and add water as necessary to just cover the chicken. Bring to a boil. Cover with a round of buttered parchment paper and then a lid, transfer to the oven, and cook until tender, 20 to 25 minutes.

While the chicken is cooking, prepare the pilaf: Use the above ingredients and follow the directions on page 60, using chicken stock instead of water. Crush the garlic with the back of a heavy knife and add it to the pan along with the bouquet garni.

When the chicken is tender, remove it from the pan and arrange it on a long serving platter; cover with aluminum foil to keep warm.

Strain the chicken cooking liquid into a small saucepan and add the raisins. Cook over medium heat until the sauce reduces and thickens slightly.

To serve, spoon a little of the sauce over the chicken and top each piece with a spoonful of raisins. Sprinkle with parsley. Remove the bouquet garni and the garlic from the rice and separate the grains with a fork. Transfer to a serving dish. Serve the remaining sauce in a sauceboat on the side.

Pudding Diplomate, Crème Anglaise

LADYFINGER PUDDING WITH CRÈME ANGLAISE

———

SERVES 6

*P*udding (like *parking* and *steak)* is now a French word. Indeed, it entered the language in the seventeenth century, and almost every bakery in Paris sells its version of what was originally a simple English bread pudding. The Pudding Diplomate made at Le Cordon Bleu is one of the more elaborate French interpretations; it is prepared with ladyfingers in place of the traditional bread, while candied fruits and raisins lend a festive air.

Note: Leftover sponge cake, brioche, or génoise may be used instead of ladyfingers. At Le Cordon Bleu, ladyfingers are baked especially for this and other desserts that call for them. Ladyfinger batter is fragile, based as it is on a meringue (the flour and yolks must be carefully folded in so that the whites do not lose volume). The finished ladyfingers may be stored in an airtight container for up to one week, or frozen.

2 tablespoons mixed candied
    fruits
2 tablespoons golden raisins
2 tablespoons kirsch

LADYFINGERS
3 eggs, separated
6 tablespoons granulated sugar
3/4 cup sifted cake flour
6 tablespoons confectioner's sugar

CUSTARD
2 cups milk
1 teaspoon vanilla extract
6 egg yolks
1/2 cup sugar

CRÈME ANGLAISE
1 cup milk
1 teaspoon vanilla extract
5 tablespoons sugar
2 egg yolks
1/4 cup kirsch

Unsalted butter, softened,
    for baking sheet and mold

EQUIPMENT: 8-inch round straight-sided mold, 3 inches deep; pastry bag; large plain pastry tip

Macerate the candied fruit and raisins in the kirsch for at least 1 hour.

Prepare the ladyfingers: Preheat the oven to 350°. Brush 2 baking sheets with the softened butter and line with parchment paper.

Beat the egg whites with a whisk or electric mixer until stiff peaks form. Gradually beat in the granulated sugar and continue beating until stiff peaks form again; the meringue will be glossy and smooth. Lightly beat the egg yolks with a fork and fold into the meringue with a wooden spoon. Sift the flour over the mixture and fold in gently.

Pipe the ladyfingers (see technique photos on page 549): Fit the pastry bag with the large plain tip and fill with the ladyfinger batter. Pipe strips of batter 5 inches long and ¾ inch wide diagonally onto the baking sheets, leaving 1 to 2 inches between each strip. Sprinkle half of the confectioner's sugar over the ladyfingers; wait 5 minutes and sprinkle with the remaining sugar.

Holding the parchment paper in place with your thumb, lift one side of the baking sheet and gently tap it on the work surface to remove excess confectioner's sugar. Bake without opening the oven door for 10 minutes. Then rotate the baking sheet so the ladyfingers color evenly, and cook until lightly golden, about 5 more minutes. Remove the ladyfingers from the baking sheet with a metal spatula while still hot and let cool on a rack. Reserve 15 to 20 ladyfingers for the pudding and store the remainder in an airtight container for another use.

Make a custard: Bring the milk and vanilla to a boil in a small saucepan; remove from heat. Beat the egg yolks with the sugar in a heatproof bowl until thick and pale yellow in color. Gradually whisk in the boiling milk; set aside.

Assemble the pudding: Brush the mold with the softened butter. Line the bottom with a round of parchment paper and butter the paper. Arrange a layer of ladyfingers, halving them as necessary to fit into the mold, on the bottom of the mold and sprinkle with some of the macerated candied fruit and raisins. Repeat, arranging each layer of ladyfingers at right angles to the preceding one, to make a lattice, until all the ladyfingers, candied fruit, and raisins have been used. Pour in the custard mixture.

Put the filled mold into a large baking dish and add hot water to the pan to come halfway up the sides of the mold. Bring to a simmer on top of the stove and then bake at 350° until a knife inserted into the center of the pudding comes out clean, about 25 minutes. Remove the mold from the pan and cool completely before unmolding.

Prepare the crème anglaise: Use the above ingredients and follow the directions on page 35. Add the kirsch when the crème has cooled.

To serve, invert a round serving platter on top of the mold and quickly reverse the two. Carefully remove the mold from the pudding and then peel off the paper. Spoon a little crème anglaise around the base of the pudding. Serve the remaining sauce in a sauceboat on the side.

LESSON 22

Flamiche
LEEK PIE

—

Longe de Porc aux Pruneaux
ROAST PORK LOIN WITH PRUNES

—

Mousseline de Céleri Rave
CREAMED CELERY ROOT PUREE

—

Poires à la Diable
FLAMED POACHED PEARS

—

Tuiles aux Amandes
ALMOND TILE COOKIES

Flamiche
LEEK PIE

S E R V E S 6

In northwest France, near the Belgian border, *flamiche* is as popular as pizza in the south. Indeed, like pizza, a *flamiche* can be garnished with almost anything (though the classic filling is made with leeks). At Le Cordon Bleu the *flamiche* is made using a double crust of short pastry, but topless versions can be made, pizza fashion, and sometimes either bread dough or even puff pastry is used.

PÂTE BRISÉE
1½ cups all-purpose flour
¾ cup cake flour
2 eggs
1 tablespoon water
½ teaspoon salt
10 tablespoons unsalted butter,
  softened
1 egg, lightly beaten, for glazing

3 pounds leeks
3 tablespoons unsalted butter
3 egg yolks
¼ cup heavy cream
Salt and freshly ground pepper

EQUIPMENT: 9-inch fluted, removable-bottomed tart pan

Prepare the pâte brisée, using the above ingredients and following the directions on pages 37–38 (see technique photos on page 540). Roll out two-thirds of the dough. Line the tart pan with it, and blind bake (see recipe on pages 38–39 and technique photos on page 541). Reserve the remaining dough and egg glaze.

Cut off and discard the green tops and the root ends of the leeks. Slice the remaining white parts about ¼ inch thick. Rinse well in cold water to remove any sand; drain. Melt the butter in a large frying pan over low heat. Add the leeks. Cover and cook, stirring frequently, until soft, about 20 minutes.

Meanwhile, preheat the oven to 450°. Whisk the egg yolks and cream in a small bowl until blended. Stir in the leeks and season to taste with salt and pepper; set aside.

Roll out the remaining dough into a 10-inch round, ⅛ inch thick. Pour the leek mixture into the cooked pastry shell. Brush the rim of the shell with the reserved egg glaze and cover the pie with the dough round. Press down gently around the edges to seal the top crust and sides. Trim off the excess.

Brush the top of the pie with egg glaze. Cut a small hole in the center for the steam to escape. With the tip of the knife, cut a shallow design on the surface or use the dough scraps to decorate (see photo opposite). Brush again with egg glaze and bake until the crust is golden brown, about 30 minutes.

Remove the tart from the oven and let cool for 10 minutes. Unmold, transfer to a platter, and serve warm.

Longe de Porc aux Pruneaux
ROAST PORK LOIN WITH PRUNES

SERVES 6

Prunes are cooked with both rabbit and pork in France. This pork recipe uses them not only dried as a stuffing, but also simmered in water with a pinch of tea as a garnish. A sauce made from pan juices accompanies this roast; its goodness depends on the coarsely chopped vegetables and fresh herbs left to caramelize underneath the meat and the addition of a slightly sweet and sour *sauce gastrique* (boiled vinegar and sugar) that completes its complex array of tastes.

3-pound boneless pork loin roast, trimmed of excess fat

Salt and fresh ground pepper

1½ pounds prunes, pitted

1 tablespoon vegetable oil

1 tablespoon unsalted butter

1 carrot, chopped coarse

1 onion, chopped coarse

1 teaspoon fresh rosemary leaves or ¼ teaspoon dried

1 teaspoon fresh thyme leaves or ¼ teaspoon dried

1 bay leaf, crushed

2 cloves garlic

Large pinch Ceylon tea

¼ cup sugar

¼ cup vinegar

Small bunch watercress for garnish

Trim the pork of any nerves and connective tissue. Set the trimmings aside. Butterfly the pork loin: Cut horizontally along the length of the loin to within 1 inch of the opposite side, as if you were going to cut it in half. Open up the loin like a book and flatten it into a rectangular shape. Season with salt and pepper. Arrange a row of 12 to 15 overlapping prunes about 2 inches in from one of the short sides of the rectangle. Fold the 2-inch border of meat over the prunes and roll the loin up tightly. Tie securely in 4 or 5 places with kitchen twine. Rub with salt and pepper.

Preheat the oven to 400°.

Heat the oil and butter in a roasting pan over high heat. Add the pork and trimmings, chopped carrot and onion and brown the pork quickly on all sides. Sprinkle with the herbs and add the garlic cloves. Push the vegetables underneath the roast. Reduce the oven temperature to 375° and roast the pork, basting frequently with the pan juices, until cooked to medium (about 145° on a meat thermometer), about 50 minutes.

Meanwhile, bring a medium saucepan of water to a boil; remove from the heat. Add the tea and let stand for 10 minutes to infuse; strain and then return to the saucepan along with the remaining prunes. Bring to a simmer and poach until the prunes are plump, 10 to 15 minutes. Remove from the heat and set aside in the cooking liquid.

When the roast is cooked, remove from the pan and wrap in foil to keep warm. Spoon off the fat from the roasting pan and deglaze with ½ cup water, scraping the bottom with a wooden spoon to release the cooked particles. Simmer for 15 minutes; strain.

Combine the sugar and vinegar in a small heavy-bottomed saucepan. Bring to a boil over low heat, stirring to dissolve the sugar. Then raise the heat and boil without stirring until the mixture turns a rich caramel color. Immediately remove from the heat and add the juices from the roasting pan. Be careful: this will cause the mixture to sputter. When the sputtering stops, return the pan to the heat and skim any fat from the surface; keep warm over low heat.

To serve, rewarm the prunes in the tea; drain. Remove the twine and slice the pork ¼ inch thick. Overlap the slices on a serving platter and arrange the watercress at one end. Spoon a little of the sauce over the meat and spoon the prunes around the pork. Serve the remaining sauce in a sauceboat on the side. Serve with Mousseline de Céleri Rave, below.

Mousseline de Céleri Rave
CREAMED CELERY ROOT PUREE

SERVES 6

Celery root is an autumn and winter root vegetable that has a wonderfully mellow celery taste. It can be served pureed, gratinéed, in soups, or raw in salads. Pureed and enriched with cream, this mousseline goes perfectly with pork, duck, game, or any other fatty meat.

1¼ pounds celery root
Salt
4 tablespoons unsalted butter

¼ cup crème fraîche or
   heavy cream
Freshly ground pepper

Peel the tough, brown exterior from the celery root with a vegetable peeler and cut the bulb(s) into uniform pieces. Put the pieces in a saucepan, and cover with cold salted water. Bring to a boil, reduce the heat and simmer until tender; drain. Puree in a food mill or food processor. Stir in the butter and cream and season to taste with salt and pepper.

Poires à la Diable
FLAMED POACHED PEARS

———

SERVES 6

Why are these perfectly poached pears said to be "diabolical"? Because they come to the table in flames, of course. They are, however, served with Chantilly cream and several spoonfuls of a lightly flavored vanilla sugar syrup; a heavenly trio if ever there was one.

12 small pears
1 lemon, halved

SUGAR SYRUP
4 cups water
2²/3 cups granulated sugar
1 teaspoon vanilla extract
Juice of ¹/2 lemon, strained

CHANTILLY CREAM
1¹/2 cups heavy cream
¹/3 cup confectioner's sugar
1 teaspoon vanilla extract

¹/4 cup Poire William liqueur
or kirsch

EQUIPMENT: Pastry bag, medium star pastry tip

Peel the pears, leaving the stems intact. Insert a vegetable peeler into the base of the pears to the depth of about 1 inch. Gently twist and pull out the cores. Cut a thin slice off the base of each pear so they will stand upright. Rub with the cut lemon to prevent darkening.

Prepare the syrup: Combine the water, sugar, vanilla and lemon juice in a large saucepan. Bring to a boil over low heat, stirring to dissolve the sugar. Boil 1 to 2 minutes. Add the pears, reduce the heat to medium, and cover with a round of parchment paper. Poach until tender when pierced with the point of a knife, 15 to 20 minutes. Cool to room temperature in the poaching liquid. Remove with a slotted spoon and drain on paper towels. Measure 2¹/2 cups liquid (discard the remainder or reserve to poach other fruit). Cook over medium heat until reduced by one-third and slightly syrupy.

Up to 1 hour before serving, prepare the Chantilly cream. Use the above ingredients and follow the directions on page 21. Fit the pastry bag with the medium star tip and fill it with the Chantilly cream; refrigerate until serving time.

To serve, stand the pears on a serving platter and spoon a little warmed syrup around them. Pipe the Chantilly cream into a serving bowl. Just before serving, heat the Poire William or kirsch in a small saucepan. Flame it at the table and pour it, flaming, over the pears.

Serve with Tuiles aux Amandes, opposite page.

Tuiles aux Amandes
ALMOND TILE COOKIES

SERVES 6

Traditional roof tiles in France are arched like these crisp almond cookies—hence their name. They must be quickly and gently pressed around a rolling pin as they come from the oven; otherwise they become too brittle to shape. Handle them carefully once they have cooled (they break very easily) and bake only small quantities at a time; they do not keep well and are always best the day they are baked.

2/3 cup sugar
1 egg
3 egg whites
4 ounces sliced almonds

1/3 cup sifted all-purpose flour
1 teaspoon vanilla extract

Unsalted butter, softened,
 for baking sheets

Combine the sugar, egg, and egg whites in a bowl and whisk well. Fold in the almonds. Let the mixture rest 15 minutes to soften the almonds. Gently stir in the flour and vanilla so as not to break the almonds. Refrigerate the batter for 2 to 3 hours.

Preheat the oven to 400°. Brush several baking sheets with the softened butter.

Spoon 6 small spoonfuls of batter about 4 inches apart on a baking sheet. With the back of a fork dipped in cold water, flatten each mound to a 2-inch round (see technique photo on page 551). (Dip the fork in the water before flattening each cookie to prevent it from sticking to the batter.)

Transfer the baking sheet to the oven and immediately reduce the temperature to 350°.

Bake the tiles until evenly golden, 5 to 10 minutes.

Shape the cooked tiles while still warm (see technique photo): Open the oven door and pull the baking sheet halfway out. Starting with the most colored, remove the tiles one at a time with a metal spatula and drape them over a rolling pin. Press gently to shape the cookies to the pin. If the tiles cool and become too brittle to shape, return them to the oven for about 30 seconds to soften. Repeat with the remaining batter. Scrape and rebutter the baking sheets in between each batch so that the tiles don't stick. While preparing each subsequent batch, increase the oven temperature to 400°, reducing it immediately to 350° as you put each new batch into the oven.

Let the tiles cool completely and store them in an airtight tin.

Omelette aux Fines Herbes
FRESH HERB OMELET

Pavés de Rumsteak au Poivre Vert
SIRLOIN STEAKS WITH GREEN PEPPERCORNS

Pommes Sautées à Cru
SAUTÉED POTATOES

Pets de Nonnes
CHOUX PASTRY FRITTERS WITH APRICOT SAUCE

Omelette aux Fines Herbes
FRESH HERB OMELET

SERVES 6

No French cook has completed his apprenticeship until he can make a perfect omelet. It's not as easy as it seems. Moist inside (not runny) and lightly brown outside (not dry), it should be rolled onto the plate from the pan and served seam side down.

Note: This is one of the most popular French omelets, flavored simply with freshly chopped herbs. Dried herbs are no substitute. If all those listed are not available, use fewer herbs, different herbs, or no herbs at all (if no herbs are added the result will be a delicious *omelette nature*).

18 eggs
Salt and freshly ground pepper
2 tablespoons chopped fresh chives
2 tablespoons chopped fresh
   chervil
2 teaspoons chopped parsley

9 tablespoons unsalted butter
Several sprigs parsley for garnish

Unsalted butter, softened,
   for platter

EQUIPMENT: 6-inch frying pan (preferably nonstick)

Lightly butter a serving platter with the softened butter.

Break the eggs into a bowl. Add salt and pepper and the fresh herbs. Beat lightly with a fork to blend. Let the mixture rest for at least 30 minutes to allow the herbs to flavor the eggs.

Prepare six omelets (see technique photos on page 522): Heat 1 tablespoon of butter in the frying pan over medium heat until hot; do not let the butter brown. Pour in about one-sixth of the egg mixture and cook gently, stirring constantly with a wooden spoon. When the eggs begin to set but are still soft on top, use a spatula to fold the edge of the omelet that is closest to the handle in towards the center (ideally you will fold the omelet into thirds). Lift up the folded edge and slide about ½ tablespoon butter under it. Then, with your free hand, tap the handle of the pan sharply, so that the far edge of the omelet slides up the side of the pan. Fold this edge in towards the center and continue cooking until the omelet is very lightly golden on the bottom, about 2 minutes.

Holding the buttered platter with one hand, grasp the handle of the pan in the palm of the other hand, and turn the omelet out, seam side down, onto the platter. If necessary, shape the omelet into an even form with a wooden spoon. Pour any butter remaining in the pan over the omelet. Cover the platter with aluminum foil to keep warm. Repeat for the remaining five omelets.

Serve garnished with sprigs of parsley.

Pavés de Rumsteak au Poivre Vert
SIRLOIN STEAKS WITH GREEN PEPPERCORNS

———

SERVES 6

Pepper steak has long been part of the classic French repertoire. This is a modern variation on that theme. It substitutes green peppercorns ("fresh" peppercorns sold bottled or canned) for the traditional black (dried) peppercorns used to season the steak in the past. Green peppercorns are not as hot as black peppercorns and have a fruitier taste.

2 tablespoons green peppercorns	3 tablespoons cognac
6 sirloin steaks, about 6 ounces each	¾ cup Brown Veal Stock (page 71)
Salt	¾ cup heavy cream
1 tablespoon vegetable oil	Watercress for garnish
2 tablespoons unsalted butter	

Coarsely crush the peppercorns with the bottom of a small heavy saucepan. Season the steaks on both sides with salt and then sprinkle with the peppercorns, pressing them onto the surface of the steaks.

(continued)

Pavés de Rumsteak au Poivre Vert (continued)

Heat ½ tablespoon of the oil and 1 tablespoon of the butter in a large frying pan over high heat. Add three steaks, brown on both sides and then continue to cook until done as desired (see opposite page). Remove to a serving platter; cover to keep warm. Discard the fat from the pan and repeat with the remaining oil and butter to cook the remaining steaks.

Return all the steaks to the pan, add the cognac and carefully light with a match. When the flames die, transfer the steaks to a platter. Add the stock and cream to the pan and deglaze over high heat, scraping the bottom of the pan with a wooden spoon to release any cooked particles. Cook until the liquid has reduced by one-half and season to taste with salt and pepper; strain.

To serve, arrange the steaks in the center of the platter and spoon the sauce over. Decorate the platter with watercress. Serve the remaining sauce in a sauceboat on the side. Accompany with Pommes Sautées à Cru (page 130).

HOW TO DETERMINE WHEN
A STEAK IS DONE

When demonstrating the technique for cooking a steak, the chefs at Le Cordon Bleu hesitate to give students an exact cooking time because there are so many variables to consider. Obviously the thickness of the steak and the degree to which it is to be cooked (very rare, rare, medium, or well done) will have a considerable effect on the timing. The temperature of the meat before cooking (if you like your steak rare or medium rare it must be at room temperature before cooking), the presence of a bone, the method of cooking (sautéing, broiling, or grilling), and the heat of the stove, broiler, or coals will also affect the cooking time. The best way to gauge the doneness of the meat is by touch and sight as well as by the clock: As a steak cooks, the meat becomes firmer and the interior color lightens from a dark purple-red to pink. With experience you will be able to determine when all meats, poultry, and even fish are done, merely by touch.

Here are guidelines for cooking steaks to the desired degree of doneness (approximate times are given for ¾- to 1-inch-thick steaks):

VERY RARE (called *bleu* in French): Sear both sides just until browned (about 1 minute each side) in very hot oil and butter. The steak will feel very soft when touched; interior color will not have changed from the purple-red color of raw meat.

RARE *(saignant)*: Sear 2 minutes each side and 1 minute on the edge in very hot oil and butter. The steak will still feel soft when touched; interior color will be red.

MEDIUM *(à point)*: Sear 3 minutes each side and 1 minute on the edge in very hot oil and butter. The steak will offer resistance when touched; interior color will be pink, and pink juices will bead on the surface of the seared side of the steak when turned.

WELL DONE *(bien cuit)*: Sear both sides just until browned (about 1 minute each side) and then cook about 15 minutes in a 325° oven. The steak will be very firm when touched; interior color will no longer be at all pink.

Pommes Sautées à Cru
SAUTÉED POTATOES

SERVES 6

Sautéed potatoes should be nicely brown, moist inside, and never oily or greasy when served. The trick is to wash the raw potatoes after slicing and pat them dry before cooking (this removes much of their starch and keeps them from sticking together). Their cooking fat should be discarded and the potatoes finished in a little fresh butter just before serving.

2 pounds waxy potatoes (red or white)	*Salt and freshly ground pepper*
4 tablespoons vegetable oil	*2 tablespoons unsalted butter*
	1 tablespoon chopped parsley

Peel and slice the potatoes into ⅛-inch rounds. Rinse quickly in cold water, drain, and pat dry with paper towels. Heat the oil in a large frying pan over high heat. Add the potatoes, season with salt and pepper, and sauté, tossing the potatoes frequently by pulling the pan toward you with the jerk of the wrist, until the potatoes are lightly browned and crisp on the outside, and tender inside. Remove from the pan with a slotted spoon and drain on paper towels. Discard the oil.

To serve, add the butter to the pan and melt over high heat. Add the potatoes and sauté until golden brown. Taste and adjust seasonings. Serve sprinkled with parsley.

Pets de Nonnes
CHOUX PASTRY FRITTERS WITH APRICOT SAUCE

SERVES 6

These deep-fried pastries were already popular in France in the eighteenth century. At that time, vanilla was not yet commonly available, and either orange flower water or grated lemon zest was used to flavor the dough.

This is an unusual use of choux pastry. Normally piped out and baked, here it is deep fried. The batter differs slightly from classic choux pastry in that milk rather than water is used, but the procedure for making it is the same.

Note: Pay special attention to the temperature of the oil during frying. If it is not hot enough, the fritters will be soggy, but if it is too hot, they will brown before they expand and puff.

CHOUX PASTRY

1¹/₄ cups milk
4 tablespoons unsalted butter
1 tablespoon sugar
Salt
1 teaspoon vanilla extract
1¹/₄ cups sifted all-purpose flour
¹/₃ cup cake flour
4 eggs

APRICOT SAUCE

1¹/₂ pounds pitted fresh apricots
 or canned apricot halves
¹/₄ cup sugar (optional)
Juice of ¹/₂ lemon, strained
¹/₃ cup water
2 tablespoons kirsch

Confectioner's sugar for dusting
Oil for deep-fat frying

Prepare the choux pastry: Use the above ingredients and follow the directions on page 43, using the milk instead of water, and adding the sugar and vanilla to the milk before stirring in the flour (see technique photos on page 548).

Prepare the sauce: Puree the apricots in a food mill or food processor. (If using a food processor, pass the puree through a sieve to remove the skins.) Taste the puree, then whisk in the sugar, if needed, and then the lemon juice, water, and kirsch. Refrigerate until serving time.

Heat the oil to 360° in a deep saucepan or deep-fat fryer. (It is important that the pan be no more than one-third full of oil.)

Dip two teaspoons in cold water to keep the dough from sticking. Scoop up a mound of dough with one spoon. Invert the second spoon over the top of the mound to smooth the dough to an even, rounded oval shape. Then slide the top spoon under the dough to push it off the spoon into the hot oil. Repeat to form five or six more fritters (the exact number will depend on the size of your pan—if you cook too many at once the temperature of the oil will drop and the fritters will not color properly). As the fritters rise to the surface, flip them over to color the other side. Continue to fry until uniformly golden and at least doubled in volume. Drain on a rack covered with paper towels. Repeat to fry the remaining batter.

To serve, arrange the fritters in a pyramid shape on a doily-lined platter. Sift confectioner's sugar generously over the top. Serve hot or lukewarm, accompanied by the apricot sauce.

LESSON 24

Julienne Darblay
CREAMED LEEK AND POTATO SOUP WITH
JULIENNED VEGETABLES

Émincés de Rognons de Veau à la Graine de Moutarde
SLICED VEAL KIDNEYS WITH MUSTARD SAUCE

Pommes Parisiennes
PARISIAN POTATOES

Gâteau de Riz Autrichien
AUSTRIAN RICE PUDDING

Julienne Darblay
CREAMED LEEK AND POTATO SOUP WITH JULIENNED VEGETABLES

SERVES 6

Said to have been invented at Versailles, this soup is an elegant variation on the simple leek and potato soup all French housewives know. What makes it special is the colorful mixture of vegetable matchsticks (*julienne*) that are added to the soup just before serving.

2 leeks
4 tablespoons unsalted butter
1½ pounds baking potatoes, diced
1 Bouquet Garni (page 20)
6 cups Chicken Stock (page 12) or water
Salt

White pepper
2 medium carrots
2 medium turnips
1 cup crème fraîche or heavy cream
Chervil or parsley leaves for garnish

Cut off the root ends of the leeks. Cut off the green tops and cut them into julienne (see technique photo on page 519). Slice the white parts into thin rounds. Rinse the greens and whites of the leeks separately in cold water to remove all of the sand; drain. Set the julienned leek greens aside.

(continued)

Julienne Darblay (continued)

Heat the butter in a large saucepan over medium heat. Add the sliced leek whites and cook until soft but not colored. Add the potatoes, bouquet garni, and stock. Season with salt and pepper, bring to a boil, reduce the heat, cover, and simmer about 30 minutes.

Meanwhile, peel and cut the carrots and turnips into julienne. Put the carrots in a saucepan with cold salted water to cover. Bring to a boil and cook 1 minute. Add the turnips and cook 2 minutes; drain and set aside. Refill the saucepan with salted water and bring to a boil. Add the reserved leek greens and cook for 2 minutes; drain.

Puree the potato/leek mixture in a food mill or food processor. Strain, pressing down on the solids to extract all of the liquid. Discard the solids. Return the soup to the saucepan.

Whisk the cream with a little of the hot soup in a small bowl. Return the mixture to the pan with the soup. Bring just to a simmer over low heat.

To serve, put the julienned vegetables into a soup tureen and pour the soup over. Garnish with chervil leaves.

Émincés de Rognons de Veau à la Graine de Moutarde
SLICED VEAL KIDNEYS WITH MUSTARD SAUCE

SERVES 6

The delicate taste of properly cooked calf's kidneys has nothing in common with the taste of lamb, pork, or beef kidneys. Indeed, only calf's kidneys are served in the best restaurants in France. They must be served pink; if overcooked they become chewy and lose their subtle flavor. At Le Cordon Bleu whole-grain mustard, a specialty of the town of Meaux, not far from Paris, is added to the sauce made from pan juices, cream, and Armagnac. The resulting combination of tastes should persuade even those unfamiliar with kidneys that they merit the place of honor they have earned in the eyes of all French chefs.

2 pounds veal kidneys
Salt and freshly ground pepper
3 tablespoons vegetable oil
3 tablespoons unsalted butter
1 large shallot, chopped fine
1 pound mushrooms, trimmed,
  rinsed, dried, and sliced fine

3 tablespoons Armagnac or cognac
6 tablespoons whole-grain mustard
1/2 cup Brown Veal Stock
  (page 71)
5 tablespoons heavy cream
1 tablespoon chopped parsley

Remove the outer membrane from the kidneys with the point of a small knife. Cut away the fat from the interior. Season with salt and pepper. Heat the oil in a large frying pan over high heat. Add the kidneys and brown quickly on all sides, then reduce heat and cook 10 to 15 minutes; the interior should remain slightly pink. Remove from the pan; cover to keep warm.

Discard the oil from the pan, add the butter and melt over low heat. Add the shallot and cook until soft but not colored. Raise the heat to high and, stirring constantly, add the sliced mushrooms. Cook quickly until all moisture evaporates. Add the Armagnac and carefully light it with a match. When the flames die, add the mustard, stock and cream. Cook over high heat until the sauce reduces by one-half. Taste and adjust the seasonings.

To serve, discard any juices that have accumulated around the kidneys. Slice the kidneys thin and arrange them, overlapping, on a serving platter. Spoon the sauce over the kidneys and sprinkle with chopped parsley. Serve with Pommes Parisiennes, below.

Pommes Parisiennes
PARISIAN POTATOES

SERVES 6

A melon ball scooper is sometimes called a *cuiller parisienne* (a Parisian spoon), no doubt because this particular type of sautéed potatoes cannot be made without one. Unlike most sautéed potatoes, these are blanched and drained before being browned in hot fat. They can be finished either on top of the stove or in the oven; in either case, the initial blanching guarantees that the inside will be tender and moist when the outside has finished browning.

3 pounds large waxy potatoes (red or white)
Salt

3 tablespoons vegetable oil
3 tablespoons unsalted butter

Peel the potatoes and put them into a bowl of cold water. Scoop out potato balls with a medium-size melon baller, removing as many balls as possible from each potato (see technique photo on page 520). Keep the finished balls in the bowl of cold water while you work, to prevent discoloration. Drain and put the potato balls into a saucepan. Cover with cold salted water, bring to a boil, and blanch for about 3 minutes; drain well.

Preheat the oven to 450°. Heat the oil and butter in an ovenproof frying pan over high heat. Add the blanched potatoes and toss until well coated with the fat. Season with salt and bake, shaking the pan from time to time for even browning, until the potatoes are golden brown, about 25 minutes. Transfer to a serving bowl and serve.

Gâteau de Riz Autrichien
AUSTRIAN RICE PUDDING

SERVES 6

The presence of apples and cinnamon in this rich rice pudding is a culinary allusion to the cuisine of Austria (and Eastern Europe in general). Home-made applesauce is spread over egg yolk–enriched rice, baked, then topped with French meringue and returned to the oven to brown. Served warm or cold, this is a substantial fall or winter dessert that will particularly delight young appetites.

2¼ cups milk	⅔ cup granulated sugar
1 teaspoon vanilla extract	3 egg yolks
½ cup short-grain rice	3 egg whites
2 tablespoons unsalted butter	¼ cup confectioner's sugar
3 large Golden Delicious apples, peeled, cored, and chopped	Unsalted butter, softened, for gratin dish
½ teaspoon cinnamon	

EQUIPMENT: Large gratin dish, pastry bag, ⅜-inch star pastry tip

Brush the gratin dish with the softened butter.

Combine the milk and the vanilla in a saucepan and bring to a boil. Add the rice, and return the mixture to a boil. Reduce the heat and simmer, stirring occasionally, until most of the milk is absorbed by the rice and the mixture is quite thick, about 20 minutes.

Meanwhile, prepare an apple puree: Heat the butter in a large saucepan over low heat. Add the apples, cinnamon, and ⅓ cup of the granulated sugar and cook, stirring frequently, until the apples are reduced to a coarse puree, about 20 minutes.

Stir the remaining ⅓ cup of granulated sugar into the cooked rice mixture and simmer 5 minutes. Remove the pan from the heat. Stir in the egg yolks quickly so that they will not grain. Spread the mixture evenly in the gratin dish and let cool. Then spread the apple puree evenly over the rice mixture.

Preheat the oven to 425°.

Prepare a French meringue: Beat the egg whites with a whisk or electric mixer until stiff peaks form. Gradually beat in the confectioner's sugar and continue beating until stiff peaks form again and the meringue is glossy and smooth.

Fit the pastry bag with the star tip and fill with the meringue. Pipe the meringue in a lattice design, on top of the apple puree. Bake until the meringue is lightly browned, about 15 minutes. Serve warm or cold.

Salade Hermine

CHICKEN SALAD WITH ENDIVE, CELERY, AND TRUFFLE

———

Éstouffade de Bœuf Provençale

BRAISED BEEF CASSEROLE, PROVENCE STYLE

———

Melon Majestic

CANTALOUPE SORBET

Salade Hermine

CHICKEN SALAD WITH ENDIVE, CELERY, AND TRUFFLE

SERVES 6

The black and white color of this salad evokes the appearance of an ermine coat (and the precious truffle its cost). One might simply call it the ultimate chicken salad—strips of white meat are combined with homemade mayonnaise, served on a bed of Belgian endive, and garnished with black truffle. Though this Cordon Bleu salad is at its best when prepared as described here, a family-style version might be made with leftover chicken, the same mayonnaise, endive . . . and black olives instead of truffles.

3½-pound chicken
1 carrot, chopped coarse
2 leeks, chopped coarse
1 stalk celery, chopped coarse
*1 large onion, studded with
    a whole clove*
1 Bouquet Garni (page 20)
Salt
1 tablespoon peppercorns, crushed
1 pound small new potatoes
6 Belgian endives
1 tablespoon strained lemon juice
¾ pound celery hearts

MAYONNAISE
2 egg yolks
1 tablespoon Dijon mustard
Freshly ground pepper
1 cup vegetable oil
Juice of ½ lemon, strained

2 tablespoons chopped parsley
1 black truffle, sliced

Combine the chicken, carrot, leeks, celery, studded onion, bouquet garni, salt to taste, and crushed peppercorns in a large saucepan. Add water to cover. Cover the saucepan and bring to a boil. Reduce the heat and poach the chicken until the juices run clear when the thigh is pierced with a knife, about 1 hour.

Meanwhile, rinse the potatoes but do not peel. Put them in a saucepan and add cold salted water to cover. Bring to a boil, reduce the heat and simmer until tender, 20 to 30 minutes. Drain and let cool.

When it is cooked, remove the chicken from the pan and drain. Remove and discard the skin. Cover the chicken with a clean damp dish towel and let cool. When cool enough to handle, remove the breasts and slice crosswise about ⅛ inch thick. Cut the slices into julienne (see technique photo on page 519) and set aside. Refrigerate the remaining chicken and the stock for another use (such as croquettes or soup).

Peel the potatoes and slice lengthwise ⅛ inch thick. Reserve enough slices to decorate the serving platter (see serving instructions). Cut the remaining slices into ⅛-inch-thick julienne.

Rinse and drain the endives. Reserve 3 whole endives to garnish the serving platter. Remove the cores from the remaining endives with the point of a vegetable peeler. Trim the leaves to approximately the same size and then cut into julienne. Toss with the lemon juice.

Cut the celery hearts into ⅛-inch-thick julienne.

Prepare the mayonnaise: Use the above ingredients and follow the directions on page 31, using the lemon juice instead of vinegar.

To serve, combine the chicken, potatoes, endives, and celery in a bowl. Add the mayonnaise and toss carefully to mix. Cut the leaves from the reserved endives and trim to 2-inch lengths; discard the cores. Arrange the endive leaves in a ring around the rim of a serving platter, with the base of each leaf toward the center. Arrange the reserved potato slices in a second ring at the base of the endive leaves. Mound the mixed salad in the center of the platter. Sprinkle the endive leaves with chopped parsley. Arrange the truffle slices in a row down the center of the salad.

Éstouffade de Boeuf Provençale
BRAISED BEEF CASSEROLE, PROVENCE STYLE

SERVES 6

This is a wonderful Sunday-family-supper sort of dish. The meat is larded with strips of fatback to keep it from becoming dry and stringy when stewed, then marinated overnight in red wine before cooking. Serve the beef as it comes bubbling from the oven (the leftover meat is also delicious served cold the next day with a simple green salad).

Note: If fatback is not available, substitute fat salt pork that has been blanched 10 minutes in water to cover, rinsed in cold water, dried with paper towels, and chilled.

5 ounces pork fatback, sliced ⅛ inch thick (see Note)
2½ pounds beef chuck roast

MARINADE
2 onions, sliced
2 carrots, sliced
1 tomato, quartered
4 cloves garlic, crushed
1 Bouquet Garni (page 20)
20 peppercorns, crushed
4 cups dry red wine

3 tablespoons cognac
3 tablespoons olive oil

3 tablespoons vegetable oil
5 ounces bacon rind, diced
3 tablespoons all-purpose flour
1 pound tomatoes, peeled, seeded, and chopped (page 31)
Salt
6 ounces black olives, preferably Niçoise or Kalamata, pitted

Cut the fatback into small strips ⅛ inch wide and 1 inch long. Make 1-inch-deep incisions all over the surface of the beef and insert the fatback strips.

Prepare the marinade: Combine all of the ingredients except the olive oil in a nonaluminum container. Immerse the beef in the liquid and drizzle the oil over the surface. Let marinate for at least 12 hours.

(continued)

Éstouffade de Boeuf Provençale (continued)

Preheat the oven to 375°.

Remove the beef from the marinade and pat dry with paper towels. Strain the marinade, reserving the vegetables and bouquet garni; drain well. Reserve the marinade. Heat the oil in an ovenproof casserole over high heat. Add the meat and brown on all sides. Remove the meat from the pan; set aside. Add the diced bacon rind to the pan and brown it. Then add the reserved vegetables and cook until golden. Sprinkle with the flour and cook, stirring, 2 minutes. Add the marinade and stir to blend. Return the meat to the pan, along with the tomatoes, the bouquet garni, and a pinch of salt. Add a little water if necessary to cover the meat. Bring to a boil, reduce the heat, cover and simmer very gently, turning the meat every hour, until it is very tender when pierced with the point of a knife, at least 3 hours. Do not allow the liquid to boil.

If the olives are very salty, simmer them in water to cover for 2 minutes. Drain and refresh under cold running water.

When the meat is tender, remove it from the pan and cover with a warm damp dish towel, to prevent it from drying out. Discard bouquet garni. Skim the fat from the cooking liquid. Add the olives to the pan and reduce over medium heat until the sauce thickens slightly. Adjust seasonings.

To serve, carve the beef into thin slices. Arrange overlapping slices on a deep serving platter. Spoon the vegetables and sauce over the beef.

BRAISING AND STEWING

Braising is the technique of cooking large cuts of meat, poultry, or vegetables in flavored liquid to partially cover over a very low heat. The food may be lightly browned before the liquid is added (this makes for a brown braise; the food is not browned for a white braise), and a *mirepoix* of roughly cut vegetables is often included for flavoring. The pot is tightly covered so that the food cooks slowly in the liquid and steam until very tender. The resulting braising liquid is exceptionally flavorful and is served as a sauce, either as is or reduced. Stewing (Blanquette de Veau à l'Ancienne, page 55) is much the same as braising except that the food is cut into regular pieces, may or may not be browned, and is cooked in enough liquid to cover.

Braises and stews are an opportunity to use flavorful but tough and gelatinous cuts of meat, such as shank and shoulder, and tough, old poultry; save the tender cuts for roasting and sautéing. (Mature poultry is, unfortunately, uncommon in American supermarkets; younger birds really don't have the flavor to do these long-cooked dishes justice.) Meat is often larded (*larder* in French) with thin strips of fatback to keep it from drying out during its long cooking. You may cook braises and stews on an even low heat either on top of the stove or in the oven; if cooked too fast they will be dry and stringy, despite the fatback. When browning the meat, respect the caveats for sautéing (page 13).

Melon Majestic
CANTALOUPE SORBET

———

SERVES 6

This fragrant sorbet is served in hollowed-out melons garnished with raspberries and elegant chocolate curls. Its name is somewhat of a mystery but most probably comes from the Hôtel Majestic in Monte Carlo. Musk melon or cantaloupe is recommended, but if neither is available, other melon varieties may be used; adjust the sugar depending on the sweetness of the melon. Chocolate curls can also be made with milk or white chocolate.

SUGAR SYRUP
2 cups sugar
1³/4 cups water

2 cantaloupes, 1¹/2 pounds each
6 ounces semisweet chocolate,
    cut into small pieces
1 cup raspberries

EQUIPMENT: Ice cream maker

Chill a mixing bowl in the freezer for the sorbet.

Prepare the syrup: Combine sugar and water in a small saucepan. Bring to a boil over low heat, stirring. Boil 1 to 2 minutes. Cool over ice.

To steady the melons while cutting them, fit each into a bowl or charlotte mold, leaving the top half of the melon protruding above the top of the bowl. Then, cutting deep into the melons in a zigzag pattern, cut all the way around with a paring knife so that you can remove the top halves. (See photo on page 137.) Scrape out and discard the seeds and fibers from both halves of the melons. Scoop out the flesh with a spoon. Puree the flesh and juice in a food mill or food processor. Freeze the shells.

Whisk the melon puree with the cooled syrup. Transfer to the ice cream maker and freeze according to the manufacturer's instructions. Transfer the sorbet to the chilled bowl and freeze until firm, about 1 hour.

Prepare the chocolate curls (see technique photo on page 552): Bring 1 to 2 inches of water to a simmer in a medium saucepan. Put the chocolate into a medium, heatproof bowl and set it over the pan of simmering water. Let stand without stirring until the chocolate has completely melted. (If stirred, the chocolate will become stiff and unworkable.) Remove the bowl from the simmering water and beat the chocolate vigorously with a wooden spoon until smooth and shiny. With a metal spatula, spread the chocolate ¹/8 inch thick on a marble surface or a baking sheet. When the chocolate is firm but not brittle, hold a metal spatula or the blade of a large knife at an angle and scrape it away from you along the surface of the chocolate to make curls of chocolate. (If the chocolate becomes too hard to curl, scrape it off the surface and melt it again over the simmering water. Beat well and repeat the process.) Set the curls aside.

To serve, place the frozen melon shells on a serving platter. Fill with scoops of the sorbet, mounding the scoops well above the sides of the melons. Decorate the sorbet with raspberries and chocolate curls.

LESSON 26

Potage Santé

POTATO AND LEEK SOUP WITH SORREL

---

*Noisettes d'Agneau à la
Crème d'Ail*

MEDALLIONS OF LAMB WITH GARLIC CREAM SAUCE

Gratin de Courgettes

ZUCCHINI GRATIN

Tarte aux Poires Alsacienne

ALSATIAN PEAR TART

Potage Santé
POTATO AND LEEK SOUP WITH SORREL

———

SERVES 6

Sorrel gives this leek and potato soup a lemony tang that makes it equally attractive hot or cold. If serving cold, simply omit the croutons and cool over ice or refrigerate for 3 to 4 hours before serving.

4 tablespoons unsalted butter

2 medium leeks (white part only), sliced thin

1 medium onion, sliced thin

1½ pounds baking potatoes, diced

6 cups Chicken Stock (page 12) or water

Salt

White pepper

5 ounces sorrel, stemmed, rinsed, and cut into chiffonade (see directions on page 8 and technique photo on page 520)

6 slices slender French baguette or 3 slices French-style bread

½ cup crème fraîche or heavy cream

Chervil or parsley leaves for garnish

Heat 2 tablespoons of the butter in a large saucepan over medium heat. Add the leeks and onions and cook until soft but not colored. Add the potatoes and stock and season with salt and pepper. Bring to a boil, reduce the heat, cover and simmer for about 25 minutes.

Puree the mixture in a food mill or food processor. Strain through a sieve, pressing down on the solids to extract all of the liquid; discard the solids. Return to the saucepan; cover to keep warm.

Preheat the oven to 425°.

Heat the remaining 2 tablespoons of butter in a medium frying pan over high heat. Add the sorrel and cook, stirring frequently, until the moisture has evaporated. Season to taste with salt.

Prepare the croutons: If using baguette, leave it in slices. If using French-style bread, remove the crusts and cut it into ¼-inch cubes. Arrange the bread on a baking sheet and toast in the oven until golden, 5 to 10 minutes.

Whisk the cream with a little of the hot soup in a small bowl. Return the mixture to the soup and bring to a boil. Add the sorrel and remove from the heat.

To serve, pour the soup into a tureen and sprinkle with chervil leaves. Serve the croutons separately.

Noisettes d'Agneau à la Crème d'Ail

MEDALLIONS OF LAMB WITH GARLIC CREAM SAUCE

SERVES 6

A *noisette* or "medallion," a term originally used exclusively for lamb, is a thick (1¼- to 1½-inch) boneless slice cut from the loin; now the term is also used for similar cuts of veal, beef, and venison.

Lamb is frequently flavored with garlic in France (a leg of lamb is traditionally larded with garlic before being roasted). Here garlic is thoroughly cooked before its soft pulp is worked though a sieve to both thicken and flavor the sauce.

*1 small saddle of lamb, boned and
    split to yield 2 loins and
    2 tenderloins (see technique
    photos 1–4 on page 538),
    about 2½ to 3 pounds
    clean meat*
Freshly ground pepper
*2 sprigs fresh thyme or
    ¼ teaspoon dried*

5 tablespoons vegetable oil
18 cloves garlic, unpeeled
⅔ cup heavy cream
Salt
Watercress for garnish

Prepare the medallions (see technique photos 5–7 on page 538): Use a large knife to slice each loin into 6 rounds (or medallions), each about 1¼ inches thick. Flatten each medallion slightly with the side of the knife. Slice each medallion into 3 equal pieces or tie the 2 tenderloins together in 4 places with kitchen twine and then cut into 3 or 4 slices approximately the same thickness. Put the meat into a dish and sprinkle with pepper and thyme leaves; set aside.

Combine 2 tablespoons of the oil and the garlic in a saucepan. Cook over low heat, stirring frequently, for 10 minutes without browning. Add the cream, ⅔ cup water and salt and pepper, and simmer gently for 20 minutes. Strain the mixture into a saucepan, pushing the garlic cloves through the strainer with a wooden spoon to extract as much of the pulp as possible; discard the skins. Bring the sauce to a boil, reduce the heat and simmer until thickened enough to coat the back of a spoon. Cover to keep warm.

Season the lamb with salt. Heat the remaining 3 tablespoons oil in a large frying pan over high heat. Add the lamb medallions and sauté until browned on both sides and medium rare, about 2 minutes each side. Transfer to a round serving platter and arrange in a ring around the edge. Garnish the center of the platter with watercress. Spoon the sauce over the lamb and serve with Gratin de Courgettes, opposite page. For individual serving suggestion, see photo on page 142.

Gratin de Courgettes
ZUCCHINI GRATIN

SERVES 6

Though you can buy zucchini in any Paris market they still evoke the sunny south. Here they are cooked with tomatoes to make a colorful gratin. By carefully laying the vegetables across the dish in alternating rows, tastes are juxtaposed and intensified rather than being merged as when vegetables are mixed and stewed.

4 tablespoons olive oil
1 medium onion, chopped fine
2 cloves garlic, chopped fine
1 pound tomatoes, peeled, seeded, and diced (page 31)
Salt and freshly ground pepper
2 1/2 pounds zucchini, sliced 1/4 inch thick

4 medium tomatoes, sliced
2 sprigs fresh thyme or 1/4 teaspoon dried
1/2 cup grated Gruyère cheese
1 tablespoon chopped parsley

EQUIPMENT: 9-by-13-inch gratin dish

Heat 2 tablespoons of the oil in a medium frying pan over low heat. Add the onion and cook until soft but not colored. Add the chopped garlic and diced tomatoes, and season with salt and pepper. Cook, uncovered, until the tomatoes are almost in puree, about 15 minutes. Spread over the bottom of a gratin dish.

Preheat the oven to 375°. Arrange the sliced zucchini and tomatoes in alternating rows on top of the tomato sauce. Sprinkle with thyme leaves and drizzle with the remaining 2 tablespoons of oil. Sprinkle with the cheese. Bake until the cheese is lightly browned, 20 to 25 minutes. Sprinkle with parsley and serve in the gratin dish.

Tarte aux Poires Alsacienne
ALSATIAN PEAR TART

SERVES 6

Typically, Alsatians fill their fruit tarts with a mixture of egg yolks, sugar, and cream. Not only pears, but apples and even blueberries are treated this way, and the resulting desserts, served hot or cold, are the pride of the region.

PÂTE BRISÉE SUCRÉE
1 cup all-purpose flour
1/2 cup cake flour
1 egg
Pinch salt
1 tablespoon water
3 tablespoons sugar
1 teaspoon vanilla extract
7 tablespoons unsalted butter, softened
1 egg, lightly beaten for glazing

3 small pears
2/3 cup heavy cream
2 eggs
3 tablespoons granulated sugar
1/8 teaspoon vanilla extract
1/2 cup confectioner's sugar
2/3 cup slivered almonds
2 egg whites, lightly beaten
Confectioner's sugar for dusting

EQUIPMENT: 8-inch fluted removable-bottomed tart pan

Prepare the pâte brisée sucrée just as you would a pâte brisée (see directions on pages 37–38 and technique photos on page 540), using the ingredients above, but add the sugar and the vanilla to the well along with the egg, salt and water. Line the tart pan and blind bake the shell (pages 38–39 and technique photos on page 541).

Preheat the oven to 350°.

Peel and core the pears and halve lengthwise. Starting about 1/2 inch below the stem end, cut down the length of each pear half as if you would cut each into six slices, but leave the slices connected at the stem end. Flatten each pear half slightly with the palm of your hand to fan the slices. Arrange the fanned halves in the tart shell with the stem ends facing toward the center. Beat together the cream, eggs, granulated sugar and vanilla and pour the mixture over the pears. Bake until the filling is puffed and golden, about 35 minutes. Stir together the confectioner's sugar, the almonds and egg whites and spread the mixture over the surface of the tart. Bake until the almonds are lightly browned, about 12 more minutes. Let the tart cool to room temperature and sift confectioner's sugar evenly over the surface.

LESSON 27

Salade Caprice de la Reine
ENDIVE, CELERY, APPLE, AND TRUFFLE SALAD

Thon Basquaise
FRESH TUNA, BASQUE STYLE

Sorbet au Sauternes
SAUTERNES SORBET

Salade Caprice de la Reine
ENDIVE, CELERY, APPLE, AND TRUFFLE SALAD

SERVES 6

Belgian endive can be eaten both raw in salads and cooked. In a salad, its slight bitterness combines well with mayonnaise and, as in this recipe, is often countered by the natural sweetness of apples. Be sure to cut and add the apples only just before serving so that they don't discolor.

The "Queen's caprice" alluded to in this recipe's French title refers both to the idea of enriching the mayonnaise with heavy cream and of sprinkling truffles over all—an undeniably royal whim.

MAYONNAISE
1 egg yolk
2 teaspoons Dijon mustard
Salt and freshly ground pepper
1 cup vegetable oil
1 tablespoon wine vinegar
1/3 cup heavy cream

2 large Belgian endives
1 celery heart
1 black truffle
2 large Red Delicious apples
*Chervil or parsley sprigs
  for garnish*

Prepare the mayonnaise: Use the above ingredients and follow the directions on page 31. Whisk in the heavy cream at the end. Adjust seasonings.

(continued)

Salade Caprice de la Reine (continued)

Separate the endive leaves. Rinse in cold water to remove any sand: discard the cores. Stack the leaves and cut them lengthwise into julienne (see technique photo on page 519). Cut the celery heart into julienne. Slice the truffle thin and cut the slices into thin strips.

Just before serving, rinse, stem, and core the apples and slice them fine. Stack the slices and cut them into 1/8-inch-thick julienne.

To serve, arrange the endive leaves on each of six salad plates like the spokes of a wheel with the bases meeting in the center. Gently toss the celery and apple with the mayonnaise. Place a mound in the center of each plate. Sprinkle the truffle over the top and garnish with chervil.

Thon Basquaise
FRESH TUNA, BASQUE STYLE

SERVES 6

Tuna is abundant in the waters off the Basque coast and plays a prominent role in the local cuisine. As in many Basque-style recipes, it is prepared with bell peppers, tomatoes, and garlic. Great care should be taken not to overcook tuna; in this recipe it is simmered only 15 minutes.

Note: Swordfish is a good substitute if fresh tuna is unavailable.

*2 1/2 pounds fresh tuna, sliced
1 inch thick, skin removed*
*2 cloves garlic, quartered, plus
2 cloves garlic, chopped fine*
Salt and freshly ground pepper
1/2 cup olive oil
1 large onion, chopped fine
*1 medium red bell pepper,
cut into julienne (see technique
photo on page 519)*
*1 medium green bell pepper,
cut into julienne*
*3/4 pound tomatoes, peeled,
seeded and diced (page 31)*
*1 tablespoon tomato paste
(optional)*
*3 sprigs fresh thyme or
1/2 teaspoon dried*
1 bay leaf

RICE PILAF
3 tablespoons olive oil
1/2 red bell pepper, diced fine
1/2 green bell pepper, diced fine
2 cloves garlic, chopped fine
1 1/2 cups long-grain rice
Salt and freshly ground pepper
3 cups water
1 Bouquet Garni (page 20)
1 tablespoon chopped parsley

Make shallow incisions in the tuna and insert the garlic quarters into the incisions. Sprinkle the tuna with salt and pepper.

Heat ¼ cup of the oil in a large frying pan over high heat. Add the tuna and cook until lightly browned on both sides. Remove from the pan; set aside.

Heat the remaining ¼ cup oil in a large frying pan over medium heat. Add the onion and julienned peppers and cook, stirring frequently, until soft, about 10 minutes. Add the chopped garlic and cook 1 minute. Add the tomatoes, tomato paste, thyme, and bay leaf and cook for 15 minutes. Add the tuna and season with salt and pepper. Cover with a buttered round of parchment paper and cook over low heat for 15 minutes.

While the tuna is cooking, prepare the rice pilaf: Preheat the oven to 375°. Heat the olive oil in an ovenproof frying pan over medium heat. Add the diced peppers and cook, stirring frequently, until soft, about 10 minutes. Add the garlic and cook 1 minute. Stir in the rice and cook until translucent, 3 to 4 minutes. Sprinkle with salt and pepper and add the water along with the bouquet garni. Bring to a boil, cover with a tight-fitting lid, transfer to the oven and cook 17 minutes. Remove from the oven and let stand, covered, for about 5 minutes. Discard the bouquet garni. Separate the grains of rice with a fork. Transfer to a serving dish.

To serve, arrange the tuna on a serving platter. Spoon the sauce around it and sprinkle with parsley. Serve with the rice pilaf. (For individual servings see photo.)

Sorbet au Sauternes

SAUTERNES SORBET

SERVES 6

Sauternes is France's (the world's?) most famous sweet wine. It can be served chilled with foie gras or, at the end of a meal, with Roquefort cheese. At Le Cordon Bleu, Sauternes is used to make this intensely aromatic sorbet; serve it with strawberries and a glass of Sauternes for a taste you'll never forget.

1³/4 cups water
1 cup sugar
Juice of 1 lemon, strained
2 cups Sauternes or other
 sweet dessert wine

6 small strawberries, rinsed
 and dried

EQUIPMENT: Ice cream maker

Chill a mixing bowl and 6 dessert glasses in the freezer for the sorbet.

Combine 1 cup of the water, the sugar and lemon juice in a saucepan. Bring to a boil over low heat, stirring to dissolve the sugar; boil 1 to 2 minutes and then let cool. Add the Sauternes and the remaining ³/4 cup water. Pour into the ice cream maker and freeze according to the manufacturer's instructions. Transfer to the chilled bowl and freeze until firm, about 1 hour.

To serve, put 2 or 3 scoops of sorbet into each chilled dessert glass. Garnish each with a strawberry and serve immediately.

LESSON 28

Garbure
FARMER'S VEGETABLE SOUP

———

Escalopes de Veau Viennoise
BREADED VEAL SCALLOPS

———

Pommes Allemandes
SAUTÉED POTATOES, GERMAN STYLE

———

Oranges et Citrons Givrés
FROSTED ORANGE AND LEMON SORBETS

Garbure
FARMER'S VEGETABLE SOUP

SERVES 6

Depending on the season of the year and the income of the family, the elements combine to make this hearty soup in southwest France form either a meal, when it might include preserved goose or duck (*confit*), or a starter; it was even served for breakfast in peasant homes not that long ago. In any case, it always contains cabbage and white beans (a local variety from the town of Tarbes is particularly sought after), but otherwise its composition can vary from home to home.

1/3 cup dried white beans,
*   such as Great Northern*

4 tablespoons unsalted butter

2 cloves garlic, chopped

2 medium carrots, chopped

2 medium turnips, chopped

4 medium waxy potatoes
*   (red or white), chopped*

2 medium tomatoes, peeled,
*   seeded, and chopped (page 31)*

3/4 pound green cabbage,
*   sliced fine*

8 cups water

10 ounces slab bacon or Parma
*   ham, sliced 1/4 inch thick,*
*   blanched, and drained (page 46)*

1 Bouquet Garni (page 20)

Salt and freshly ground pepper

CHEESE CROUTONS

1 egg

2 ounces Gruyère cheese, grated
*   (about 1/2 cup)*

12 1/4-inch-thick slices slender
*   French baguette, or 6 slices*
*   firm white bread, halved*

Soak the beans overnight in 1 cup cold water; drain. (Three parts water to 1 part beans is the standard proportion for soaking dried beans.)

Heat the butter in a large saucepan over low heat. Add all of the vegetables except the beans. Cover and cook, stirring occasionally, until the vegetables are soft but not colored, about 5 minutes. Add the water along with the drained beans, the slab bacon, and the bouquet garni. Bring to a boil, reduce the heat and simmer 1 hour. Season to taste with salt and pepper and continue cooking until the beans are tender, about 30 minutes longer.

Prepare the croutons: Preheat the oven to 425°. Stir together the egg and cheese and spread the mixture on each bread slice. Transfer the slices to a baking sheet and bake until golden brown, 5 to 10 minutes.

To serve, cut the slab bacon into small pieces and return it to the soup. Serve the garbure in a soup tureen, accompanied by the croutons.

Escalopes de Veau Viennoise
BREADED VEAL SCALLOPS

SERVES 6

In France, when veal scallops are breaded, fried, and served with hard-boiled egg and lemon they are said to be Viennese style. At Le Cordon Bleu anchovies, black olives, and capers also accompany the veal. This multicolored collection of condiments is placed on a serving platter with the veal and guests create their own garnish using as many, or as few, of the provided elements as they desire.

6 veal scallops, 4 ounces each
3 hard-boiled eggs, peeled
 (page 16)
6 oil-packed anchovy fillets
6 pitted green or black olives

ANGLAISE BREADING
³/₄ cup all-purpose flour
2 eggs
2 tablespoons vegetable oil
1 tablespoon water
Salt and freshly ground pepper
2 cups fresh bread crumbs

5 tablespoons clarified butter
 (page 94)
3 tablespoons vegetable oil
2 lemons, fluted (page 65)
 and sliced
3 tablespoons capers
3 tablespoons chopped parsley
Juice of ¹/₂ lemon, strained

Sandwich the scallops between two sheets of parchment paper and flatten with a mallet or the flat side of a large knife; set aside.

Cut the hard-boiled eggs in half and separate the whites from the yolks. Press the whites through a fine sieve with the back of a spoon. Repeat with the yolks; set the whites and yolks aside separately.

Roll an anchovy around each olive and set aside.

Bread the scallops using the above ingredients and following the directions on page 90. Set aside. (If this is done too far in advance, the breading will become soggy.)

Heat 1¹/₂ tablespoons of clarified butter and 1¹/₂ tablespoons of the oil in a large frying pan over high heat. Add 3 of the veal scallops and brown quickly on both sides, then lower the heat and cook 3 to 4 minutes on each side, until just cooked through, basting constantly with the fat. Transfer to a serving platter. Repeat with the remaining oil and 1¹/₂ tablespoons of the clarified butter to cook the remaining scallops. Garnish each scallop with a fluted lemon slice (reserve the remaining lemon slices) and an anchovy-wrapped olive. Decorate each end of the platter with a triangle of capers, egg yolk, parsley and egg whites, as shown in the photo. Cut the reserved lemon slices in half and place around the rim of the platter. Heat the remaining clarified butter and the lemon juice in the pan. Strain over the veal scallops. For individual servings, see photo on page 151.

Serve accompanied by Pommes Allemandes, page 154.

Pommes Allemandes
SAUTÉED POTATOES, GERMAN STYLE

SERVES 6

At Le Cordon Bleu, this particular version of sautéed potatoes is tradi-tionally served with breaded veal scallops. The potatoes are boiled in their skins before being peeled, sliced, and sautéed in a mixture of oil and clar-ified butter to give them a buttery taste and crisp appearance. Because of this two-step cooking method, the potatoes can be boiled well in advance and simply finished quickly in the oil and butter just before serving.

*1¹/₄ pounds waxy potatoes
(red or white), unpeeled
1 tablespoon vegetable oil
3 tablespoons clarified butter
(page 94)*

*Salt and freshly ground pepper
1 tablespoon chopped parsley*

Put the potatoes in a saucepan with cold, salted water to cover. Bring to a boil, reduce the heat and simmer until tender. Drain and let cool.

Peel and slice the potatoes into rounds about ¹/₄ inch thick. Heat the oil and the clarified butter in a large frying pan over medium heat. Add the potatoes and sauté, turning often, until golden brown. Season to taste with salt and pepper. Transfer to a serving bowl and serve sprinkled with parsley.

Oranges et Citrons Givrés
FROSTED ORANGE AND LEMON SORBETS

SERVES 6

Almost every Parisian café offers oranges and lemons filled with sorbet—unfortunately their taste is rather uniform and disappointing (they are in-dustrially produced and distributed). At Le Cordon Bleu, lemons and oranges are filled with freshly frozen sorbet and the resulting taste is far superior to that of their commercial counterparts; the sorbets have an in-tense fruit flavor that makes them a refreshingly tart finish to almost any meal.

ORANGE SORBET
*6 oranges
1 cup sugar cubes
¹/₂ cup water
1 tablespoon lemon juice, strained*

LEMON SORBET
*1³/₄ cups water
1 cup granulated sugar
6 large lemons*

EQUIPMENT: Ice cream maker

Prepare the orange sorbet: Rinse and dry the oranges. Rub the skins of the oranges with the sugar cubes so that the cubes absorb the strongly flavored orange oil. Combine the sugar cubes and the water in a heavy-bottomed saucepan. Bring to a boil over low heat, stirring to dissolve the sugar. Boil 1 to 2 minutes. Remove from the heat and let the syrup cool slightly.

Cut thin slices off the bases of the oranges so they will stand upright. Slice the top third off each orange and reserve. (These will serve as caps for the filled oranges.) Carefully squeeze the juice from the oranges, taking care not to break the skins; set aside. Then, with a small spoon or knife, remove and discard the pulp and membranes inside the oranges and the reserved caps. Freeze the shells and caps.

Strain the orange juice into the cooled syrup. Add the lemon juice and refrigerate until chilled. Transfer to the ice cream maker and freeze according to the manufacturer's instructions. Fill the frozen orange shells with the sorbet, mounding it about 1½ inches above the rims of the oranges. (Or if the sorbet is soft enough, you may pipe it into the frozen shells, using a pastry bag fitted with a medium star tip.) Top each gently with a cap and freeze until firm, about 1 hour.

Prepare the lemon sorbet: Combine the water and sugar in a heavy-bottomed saucepan. Bring to a boil over low heat, stirring to dissolve the sugar. Boil 1 to 2 minutes. Remove from the heat and let cool slightly. Cut thin slices off the bases of the lemons so they will stand upright, then proceed exactly as described for the oranges.

Serve on a doily-lined platter.

LESSON 29

Omelette aux Pointes d'Asperges
OMELET WITH ASPARAGUS TIPS

—

Entrecôte Lyonnaise
STEAK, LYONNAISE STYLE

—

Beignets aux Pommes, Sauce Abricot
APPLE FRITTERS WITH APRICOT SAUCE

Omelette aux Pointes d'Asperges
OMELET WITH ASPARAGUS TIPS

—

SERVES 6

Though thick white asparagus is the pride of France, some classic preparations are made only with the thin green variety common in the rest of the world. Indeed, when a French chef refers to *pointes d'asperges* (literally, asparagus tips), he means green asparagus, not white. The term can be doubly confusing since the *pointes* in question are in fact not just the tips but the tips plus several inches of the stalk. In any case, asparagus omelets are almost systematically made with *pointes d'asperges*, whose green herbal taste makes a nice counterpoint to the rich creamy flavor of the eggs.

2 pounds green asparagus
Salt
6 tablespoons unsalted butter
12 eggs
Freshly ground pepper

Chervil or parsley sprigs
*   for garnish*

Unsalted butter, softened,
*   for serving platter*

EQUIPMENT: 8-inch frying pan (preferably nonstick)

Prepare the asparagus: Snap off and discard the tough ends. Then, starting 1 inch below the tip, peel each stalk with a vegetable peeler. Tie the asparagus in several even bundles with kitchen twine. Bring a large saucepan of salted water to a boil. Add the asparagus and simmer until tender, 12 to 15 minutes. Drain.

Cut off the asparagus tips, leaving them about 2 inches long; reserve and keep warm. Cut the asparagus stalks into 1/2-inch lengths. Melt 1 tablespoon of the butter in the frying pan over low heat. Add the asparagus stalk pieces and reheat until warmed through. Remove from the heat; cover to keep warm.

Butter an oval platter with the softened butter.

Prepare the omelets (see technique photos on page 522): Break the eggs into a bowl. Season with salt and pepper and blend lightly with a fork. Heat 2 tablespoons of the butter in the frying pan over medium heat until hot; do not let the butter brown. When hot, pour in one-half of the egg mixture and cook gently, stirring constantly with a wooden spoon. When the eggs begin to set but are still soft on top, spread about one half of the asparagus stalk pieces over the center third of the omelet. With a spatula, fold the edge of the omelet that is closest to the handle in towards the center (ideally you will fold the omelet into thirds). Lift up the folded edge and slide about 1/2 tablespoon of butter under it. Then, with your free hand, tap the handle of the pan sharply so that the far edge of the omelet slides up the side of the pan. Fold this edge in towards the center and continue cooking until the omelet is very lightly browned on the bottom, about 2 minutes.

Holding the buttered serving platter with one hand, grasp the handle of the pan in the palm of the other hand, and turn the omelet out, seam-side down, onto the platter. If necessary, shape the omelet into an even form, with a wooden spoon. Repeat with the remaining eggs and asparagus pieces to make another omelet.

To serve, surround the omelets with the asparagus tips (rewarm them, if necessary, over low heat). Spoon over any butter remaining in the skillet. Garnish with sprigs of chervil.

Entrecôte Lyonnaise
STEAK, LYONNAISE STYLE

SERVES 6

Lyon calls itself the gastronomic capital of the world, and indeed, the city and the area surrounding it have long been the home of some of the best restaurants in France. Lyonnaise cooking, however, is not pretentious; it is simple bistro fare at its best.

Lyonnaise-style dishes, like the steak and potatoes described below, typically contain a noticeable quantity of thin-sliced onions. In this case, the onions are cooked separately from the meat, seasoned with vinegar, wine, and stock, then finished with fresh butter to make a tasty garnish/sauce.

Like German-style sautéed potatoes, lyonnaise potatoes are first boiled in their skins, cooled, peeled, and then sautéed, but the addition of the onions totally transforms both the taste and the appearance. Potatoes cooked this way also make an excellent garnish for pork chops, lamb chops, and roasts in general.

LYONNAISE POTATOES
2 pounds medium waxy potatoes
   (red or white), unpeeled
6 tablespoons unsalted butter
2 tablespoons vegetable oil
2 medium onions, sliced fine
Salt and freshly ground pepper

1 tablespoon vegetable oil
3 sirloin steaks, 14 ounces each
Salt and freshly ground pepper
6 tablespoons unsalted butter
6 medium onions, sliced fine
1/2 cup dry white wine
1 1/2 tablespoons red-wine vinegar
1 cup Brown Veal Stock
   (page 71)
1 tablespoon chopped parsley
1/2 bunch watercress for garnish

Prepare the potatoes: Put the potatoes in a saucepan with cold water to cover. Bring to a boil, reduce the heat and simmer until tender. Drain and let cool. Peel the cooled potatoes and slice 1/4 inch thick. Divide the butter and oil between two large frying pans and heat over high heat until foamy. Add the potatoes to one of the pans and the sliced onions to the other. Season to taste with salt and pepper and sauté, turning frequently, until both the potatoes and onions are golden brown. Toss together the potatoes and the onions. Keep warm.

Heat the oil in a large frying pan over high heat. Season the steaks on both sides with salt and pepper. Place in the pan and brown each side. Continue cooking over high heat until cooked as desired (page 129). Transfer to a serving platter; cover to keep warm.

Heat 2 tablespoons of butter in the same pan over medium heat. Add the onions and cook, stirring frequently, until golden brown. Season to taste with salt and pepper. Stir in the wine, vinegar, and stock, and cook until the liquid has evaporated. Whisk in the remaining 4 tablespoons butter and taste and adjust seasonings. Spread the onion mixture over the steaks and sprinkle with chopped parsley. Surround the steaks with potatoes and garnish with watercress.

Beignets aux Pommes, Sauce Abricot

APPLE FRITTERS WITH APRICOT SAUCE

SERVES 6

Deep-fried desserts are fewer and fewer these days, though there is a long tradition of making fruit-filled fritters in almost every province of France. The batter used for fruits often includes beer or wine in addition to (or instead of) yeast, since it must ferment and rise if the fritters are to be light and crisp. At Le Cordon Bleu, beaten egg whites are added to the batter to the ensure the best possible results.

SWEET FRITTER BATTER
1/4 cup milk

1 cup all-purpose flour

1 teaspoon fresh yeast or
   3/4 teaspoon active dry yeast

1 1/2 teaspoons sugar

1/2 teaspoon salt

2 tablespoons unsalted butter,
   melted

1/3 cup beer, lukewarm

1 tablespoon vegetable oil

3 egg whites

SUGAR SYRUP
1/2 cup water

2 tablespoons sugar

1/3 cup Calvados or domestic
   apple brandy

Juice of 1 lemon, strained

3 large Golden Delicious apples

1 cup apricot jam

Oil for deep-fat frying

Confectioner's sugar for dusting

Prepare the batter: Heat the milk to lukewarm. Put the flour into a large bowl and make a well in the center. Dissolve the yeast in the lukewarm milk and add it to the well. Whisk in the sugar, salt, and melted butter and then gradually whisk in the flour until smooth. Whisk in the beer. Drizzle the oil onto the surface of the batter to prevent a crust from forming. Cover with a clean dish towel or plastic wrap and let the batter rise in a warm, draft-free place for 45 minutes. Reserve the egg whites to be beaten and added to the batter just before frying.

Prepare the syrup: Combine the water and sugar in a saucepan and bring to a boil over low heat, stirring to dissolve the sugar. Boil 1 to 2 minutes. Remove from the heat and let cool to room temperature. Add the Calvados and the lemon juice; set aside.

Peel, core and slice the apples into rounds 1/8 inch thick. Put the apple slices into a shallow dish. Pour the sugar syrup over and let macerate, turning occasionally, for 30 minutes. Remove the apple slices from the syrup. Drain and pat dry with paper towels. Reserve the syrup.

Prepare the apricot sauce: Puree the apricot jam in a food mill or food processor. Transfer to a saucepan and stir in ½ cup of the reserved syrup. (Refrigerate the remaining syrup for another use, such as poaching fruit.) Bring to a boil and cook 3 minutes. Remove from the heat; cover to keep warm.

Preheat the oven to 350°.

Heat the oil to 350° in a deep-fat fryer or deep, heavy-bottomed saucepan (the fryer or pan should be no more than one-third full of oil).

When the fritter batter has risen, beat the egg whites until stiff peaks form. Whisk one-third of the beaten whites into the batter to loosen it and then fold in the remainder with a wooden spoon or spatula. Dip an apple slice into the batter and then slide it into the oil, holding it carefully (use tongs if you like) until it is halfway in so as not to splatter. Repeat with a second slice. The fritters should fall to the bottom of the fryer and then slowly rise. If they remain at the bottom, the oil is not hot enough. Fry until golden brown, turning with a wooden spoon so that they color evenly. Do not fry more than 2 at a time. Drain well on paper towels; keep warm in the oven with the door ajar while you fry the remaining fritters.

To serve, arrange the fritters on a platter and sift confectioner's sugar over them just before serving. Serve the apricot sauce in a sauceboat on the side.

Beignets de Langoustines, Sauce Tartare

LANGOUSTINE FRITTERS WITH TARTAR SAUCE

Sauté de Veau Marengo

VEAL STEW WITH WHITE WINE AND TOMATOES

Miroir aux Kiwis

VANILLA BAVARIAN CREAM WITH KIWIFRUIT

Beignets de Langoustines, Sauce Tartare

LANGOUSTINE FRITTERS WITH TARTAR SAUCE

SERVES 6

Shellfish are particularly well suited for deep frying: They make nice individual mouthfuls. They can be served with a sauce or simply with salt and lemon juice. At Le Cordon Bleu, langoustines are a favorite choice when deep frying. They are dipped in a batter lightened with baking powder and potato starch for browner results, and served with an egg, gherkin, and caper-flavored mayonnaise—a true tartar sauce, with a small amount of onions and chives to give it a savory bite.

36 langoustines, in the shells,
  if possible (see page 114),
  or 36 large shrimp
  (about 2 pounds)
Salt and freshly ground pepper
Juice of 1 lemon, strained
1 tablespoon chopped parsley
Olive oil

SAVORY FRITTER BATTER
1¼ cups all-purpose flour
1¼ cups potato flour
1 tablespoon baking powder
Salt
¼ cup olive oil
1 cup cold water
3 egg whites

TARTAR SAUCE
MAYONNAISE:
2 egg yolks
1 tablespoon Dijon mustard
2 tablespoons white-wine vinegar
Salt and freshly ground pepper
1¼ cups vegetable oil
2 hard-boiled eggs (page 16)
2 tablespoons fine-chopped gherkins
2 tablespoons fine-chopped capers
1 tablespoon fine-chopped onion
1 tablespoon chopped parsley
1 tablespoon chopped fresh chives

Parsley sprigs for garnish
3 lemons, cut into wedges

Vegetable oil for frying

Shell the langoustines, leaving the tail fins attached (see directions on page 115 and technique photos on page 523), or shell the shrimp in the same manner. Remove and discard the heads, if attached.

Arrange the langoustines or shrimp in a single layer in a nonaluminum container. Season with salt and pepper, and then sprinkle with lemon juice and parsley. Add just enough oil to cover and let marinate for at least 1 hour.

Prepare the batter: Sift the flours and baking powder into a large bowl and make a well in the center. Add the salt and 3 tablespoons of the oil to the well. Add the water and then gradually whisk in the flour until smooth. Drizzle the remaining oil onto the surface of the batter to prevent a crust from forming. Cover with a clean dish towel or plastic wrap and let the batter rest in a warm, draft-free place for about 45 minutes. (Reserve the egg whites to be beaten and added to the batter just before frying.)

Prepare the tartar sauce: First, make a mayonnaise using the above ingredients and following the directions on page 31. Remove and discard the whites from the hard-boiled eggs. Mash the yolks and whisk into the mayonnaise along with the remaining ingredients. Taste and adjust the seasonings. Transfer to a sauceboat and set aside.

Heat the oil to 350° in a large heavy-bottomed saucepan or deep-fat fryer (the fryer or pan should be no more than one-third full of oil).

When the fritter batter has rested, beat the egg whites until stiff peaks form. Whisk one-third of the beaten whites into the batter to loosen it and then gently fold in the remainder with a wooden spoon.

Hold the langoustines by the tail fins and dip into the batter, leaving the tail fins uncoated. Lower gently into the hot oil, holding them carefully until they are halfway in so as not to splatter. Do not cook more than 3 or 4 at a time or the oil will cool and the langoustines will not color. The langoustines should fall to the bottom of the fryer and slowly rise; if they remain at the bottom, the oil is not hot enough. Fry until golden brown, turning with a slotted spoon as they rise to the surface so that they color evenly. Remove with a slotted spoon and drain on paper towels; keep warm in a 350° oven with the door ajar while you fry the remaining langoustines.

To serve, arrange the langoustines on a serving platter and surround with parsley sprigs. Garnish with lemon wedges. Serve the tartar sauce on the side.

Sauté de Veau Marengo
VEAL STEW WITH WHITE WINE AND TOMATOES

SERVES 6

This is a legendary dish. It is said to have been created by Napoleon's chef with the elements he could assemble on the spot to celebrate the emperor's victory at the battle of Marengo. Although it was originally made with chicken, many versions of this dish exist (some include fried egg and crayfish in addition to the obligatory tomatoes, garlic, and mushrooms cited below). Today, veal or chicken is used and the dish has been simplified to suit modern taste.

2¹/₂ pounds lean boneless veal, trimmed of excess fat

Salt and freshly ground pepper

2 tablespoons vegetable oil

7 tablespoons unsalted butter

2 medium onions, sliced fine

2 carrots, sliced fine

2 tablespoons tomato paste

2 tablespoons all-purpose flour

²/₃ cup dry white wine

1¹/₃ cups Veal Stock (page 71) or water

2 cloves garlic, crushed

1 Bouquet Garni (page 20)

24 pearl onions, peeled

1 tablespoon sugar

¹/₂ pound button or quartered large mushrooms, trimmed, rinsed, and patted dry

1 pound tomatoes, peeled, seeded, and chopped (page 31)

HEART-SHAPED CROUTONS

6 slices firm white bread, crusts removed

3 tablespoons unsalted butter, melted

¹/₄ cup chopped parsley

All-purpose flour for dusting veal

Preheat the oven to 350°. Cut the veal into 2-inch cubes. Season with salt and pepper. Dust lightly with flour and shake off the excess. Heat 1 tablespoon of oil and 1 tablespoon of butter in a large frying pan over high heat. Add the cubed veal and brown quickly on all sides, shaking the pan so that the meat colors evenly. Remove the meat from the pan and discard the fat.

Reduce the heat to medium. Add 2 more tablespoons butter to the pan and melt. Add the sliced onions and carrots and cook until tender but not colored. Stir in the tomato paste and return the veal to the pan. Sprinkle with the 2 tablespoons flour and cook, stirring, until the flour is well blended, about 2 minutes. Add the wine, bring to a boil, and cook about 2 minutes. Add the stock or water as necessary to just cover the veal.

Season with salt and pepper. Add the garlic and bouquet garni. Bring to a boil, stirring and scraping the bottom of the pan to lift any flour stuck to the bottom. Cover with a round of buttered parchment paper and a lid. Transfer to the oven and cook until the meat is tender when pierced with the point of a knife, about 1½ hours.

Glaze the pearl onions: Put the pearl onions in a low-sided saucepan or frying pan large enough to hold them in a single layer, if possible, and add water to barely cover. Season with salt and pepper, and add 1 tablespoon of the butter and the sugar. Bring to a boil. Cover with a round of buttered parchment paper, reduce the heat and simmer for 8 to 10 minutes. Remove the paper and continue cooking until the liquid evaporates. (Watch carefully here because the onions will burn easily.) Then continue cooking the onions in the butter remaining in the pan, until golden brown. Shake the pan frequently to color the onions evenly. Set the onions aside.

Heat the remaining 1 tablespoon of oil and 1 tablespoon of the butter in a medium saucepan over high heat. Add the mushrooms and cook quickly without coloring until all the liquid evaporates, 5 to 10 minutes. Season to taste with salt and pepper. Remove from the heat; set aside.

Heat 2 tablespoons of butter in a large saucepan or frying pan over medium heat. Add the diced tomato, season with salt and pepper, and cook quickly until all liquid has evaporated. Remove from the heat and set aside.

When the veal is tender, remove it from the pan with a slotted spoon and set aside. Strain the sauce into a saucepan, pressing down on the solids to extract as much liquid as possible; discard the solids. Return the veal to the sauce along with the pearl onions, mushrooms, and tomatoes. Bring to a boil over medium heat and simmer for about 5 minutes. Taste and adjust seasonings.

Prepare the croutons: Raise the oven heat to 425°. Cut the bread in half diagonally, to make triangles. With a small knife, round off the shortest sides of the triangles. Cut a V-shaped incision in the center of the long edges to make a heart shape; trim the heart to even it. Or, cut the bread into heart shapes with a cookie cutter. Brush both sides of the hearts with the melted butter and transfer to a baking sheet. Bake until golden, about 8 minutes.

To serve, spoon the veal and sauce onto a serving platter. Dip the point of each heart crouton into the sauce, then into the chopped parsley. Place the croutons around the platter, parsley-dipped ends pointing outward. Sprinkle the veal lightly with the remaining chopped parsley.

Miroir aux Kiwis

VANILLA BAVARIAN CREAM WITH KIWIFRUIT

SERVES 6

Chilled dessert cakes are relative newcomers to French pastry shops, but in recent years those shopwindows have been crowded with *miroirs* (literally "mirrors") of different types. A *miroir* is essentially a bavarian cream that has been molded, like a cake, turned out, and topped with a shiny mirror-like glaze. This particular *miroir* is decorated with kiwifruit and strawberries—a colorful combination as pleasing to the eye as to the palate.

BAVARIAN CREAM
1 package gelatin (1/4 ounce)
2 tablespoons cold water

CRÈME ANGLAISE:
2 cups milk
1 teaspoon vanilla extract
4 egg yolks
1/2 cup granulated sugar
1/2 cup heavy cream

ORANGE COULIS
Juice of 4 large oranges strained
6 tablespoons confectioner's sugar

3 kiwifruit
5 large strawberries
1/4 cup Apricot Glaze (page 62)
12 mint leaves for garnish

EQUIPMENT: 8-inch round cake pan

Prepare the bavarian cream: Chill a mixing bowl for the whipped cream. Sprinkle the gelatin over the water and let stand until softened, about 5 minutes. Then make a crème anglaise, using the above ingredients and following the directions on page 35 and technique photos page 552. Remove from the heat. Add the softened gelatin and stir to dissolve. Strain the mixture into a bowl and let cool, stirring occasionally, until it begins to thicken. (Do not allow to gel completely.)

Beat the cream in the chilled bowl with a whisk or electric mixer until it forms stiff peaks. When the crème anglaise mixture is cool and has begun to thicken, carefully fold in the whipped cream. Rinse the cake pan with cold water. Pour in the bavarian cream and level the surface with a spatula. Refrigerate until firm, about 3 hours.

Prepare the coulis: Combine the orange juice and sugar in a saucepan. Bring to a boil over medium heat and cook until reduced by one-half. Remove from the heat and chill.

Peel the kiwifruit and cut into thin slices. Rinse and hull the strawberries. Reserve one whole strawberry and cut the remainder in half lengthwise.

Heat the apricot glaze in a small saucepan over low heat until liquid. If too thick add a little water.

To serve, unmold the bavarian cream: Dip the mold into hot water for a few seconds to loosen the bavarian from the mold. Cover the mold with a dessert platter and carefully invert the two. Remove the mold. To decorate, arrange overlapping slices of kiwifruit around the sides of the bavarian. Place a strawberry in the center and surround it with a ring of kiwifruit slices. Brush the kiwifruit with the apricot glaze. Pour a ribbon of orange coulis around the base of the bavarian. Decorate the rim of the platter with the strawberry halves and mint leaves. Serve the remaining orange coulis in a sauceboat on the side. The bavarian is pictured on page 166 without the orange coulis and garnishes.

PART TWO

Intermédiaire

PERFECTING SKILLS

*M*ost cooks have specialties, and everyone enjoys serving a dish that is a proven success. But once a few preparations have been mastered, some cooks easily fall into routines that exploit only a limited repertoire and essentially lose interest in learning more about cuisine. Le Cordon Bleu was created not just to teach beginners how to make good meals but to encourage all cooks, regardless of their knowledge and experience, to improve their cooking and to learn new skills, always keeping in mind that learning to cook is an orderly process and that students must acquire a certain number of fundamental skills before attempting to learn more demanding techniques.

For example, all cooks must be able to make at least one pie dough. In France, this generally means mastering short pastry (pâte brisée); and making it, or a similar simple dough, must have become second nature to Cordon Bleu students before they experiment with the intricacies of puff pastry. The time finally comes, however, when the mysteries of wrapping a brick of butter in a sheet of dough are demonstrated for the first time. Students generally watch with astonishment as the rolling pin flattens this pliable package into a long rectangular slab. The dough is folded and rolled again and the process repeated until hundreds of paper-thin layers of butter are sandwiched between equally thin layers of dough. When baked, the dough rises to flaky heights, and few can resist wanting to substitute it for the simpler pastry doughs they used prior to its discovery.

Similarly, all students at Le Cordon Bleu learn how to beat egg whites to make a fluffy white meringue. Many think this simple meringue (French meringue) is versatile enough to be used on all occasions. While there is no substitute when it comes to making hot soufflés, more advanced students discover that certain desserts are improved (or indeed can only be made) with a close cousin, Italian meringue, which involves pouring hot sugar syrup onto stiffly beaten egg whites. Many a novice has found this as daunting an operation as rolling puff pastry or making mayonnaise for the first time but, guided by experienced teachers, those who dare to try find that patience and scrupulous attention to detail are all it takes to master the new procedure.

This section of the book is primarily devoted to providing experiences like those described above. That is, to perfecting skills and to learning more demanding techniques. Some of the recipes may appear complicated at first, but who can resist learning how a béarnaise sauce is made, how a French chef makes French fries, how chicken stock is transformed into a crystal-clear consommé . . . and more?

As is the case throughout this book, recipes are not learned in a vacuum. Each one is part of a menu, each menu being divided into courses. By choosing from the menus and dishes that follow, the reader, like a student at Le Cordon Bleu, will discover how familiar foods are transformed into a variety of elegant dishes. Indeed, variety is the keyword in these recipes; they illustrate not only how courses can be varied but how the same foods can be used in different ways and at different times. Starters, for example, are made with seafood, meat, eggs, or vegetables. Of the seafood starters, some are pâtés (mackerel rillettes), some soups (made with oysters, mussels, or scampi), some salads (calling for herring, fresh sardines, or scallops), and so on. Among the meat starters is a warm chicken liver salad, among the eggs are both omelets and poached egg dishes, whereas vegetables appear in salads, pastries, soufflés, and soups.

When it comes to main dishes, recipes illustrate varied approaches to preparing and serving specific foods. For instance, of the three lamb dishes, one calls for roasting the lamb, as dictated by French tradition (rack of lamb), one for braising it, as is done in a regional preparation from the city of Avignon *(daube d'agneau avignonnaise)*, and, finally, one demonstrates how lamb can be turned into an exotic curry following the Cordon Bleu's own recipe for this popular dish. Poultry recipes are equally varied: Among them is not only a simple home-style pot-roasted bird with its bacon and vegetable garnish *(poulet cocotte grand-mère)*, but a classic *coq au vin* and a dish created by Henri-Paul Pellaprat, one of the school's most famous instructors (a Turkish-style pilaf with zucchini and oranges). In short, a full range of new tastes, consistencies, and techniques will be explored in the course of the recipes to come.

Learning to cook at Le Cordon Bleu means constant exposure to an ever-growing range of preparations and methods. As weeks pass, students cook better and better meals; more important, they learn to diversify menus and exploit more demanding procedures. Skills learned when getting started are heavily drawn upon as they progress; some are simply given a new twist while others become the starting point for learning new skills. In short, Cordon Bleu students are taught that no one ever "finishes" learning to cook; after mastering the basics, they are constantly perfecting their skills, increasing their knowledge, and enlarging the repertoire of dishes they can call their own.

LESSON 31

Salade Alice
APPLE AND RED CURRANT SALAD

———

*Poularde au Riz,
Sauce Suprême*
CHICKEN WITH SUPRÊME SAUCE

———

Ananas Princesse
FRESH PINEAPPLE WITH
STRAWBERRY SORBET AND GÉNOISE

Salade Alice
APPLE AND RED CURRANT SALAD

———

SERVES 6

This is what the French call a *salade composée*, that is, a "mixed salad." In France, however, mixed salads are not always served in bowls; indeed, this particular salad (part of the classic repertoire since the turn of the century) is a mixture of apples, cream, almonds, and red currants served in the hollowed-out apples themselves.

6 large red apples with stems
¼ cup lemon juice, strained
½ cup heavy cream
1½ cups slivered almonds

Salt and freshly ground pepper
1 cup fresh red currants
1 small head leaf lettuce
Mint leaves for garnish

Slice the top quarter off each apple. Brush the flesh with the lemon juice to prevent darkening and set aside. Cut a wafer-thin slice from the base of each apple so that the apple will stand upright. With a melon baller, scoop out balls of the flesh of the apple, leaving the shell about ¼ inch thick and taking care not to pierce the skin. Discard the pieces of core and scrape the inside wall to smooth it. Brush the inside of the apples with a little of the lemon juice; refrigerate until serving time.

(continued)

Salade Alice (continued)

Put the apple balls in a bowl and toss with the remaining lemon juice. Then add the cream, slivered almonds, and salt and pepper to taste and gently fold together. Fold in the red currants. Refrigerate until serving time.

Rinse and spin the lettuce dry. Stack the leaves one on top of the other, roll up tight and cut into a chiffonade (see directions on page 8 and technique photo page 520).

To serve, make a bed of the lettuce on a serving platter. Fill the apple shells with the chilled apple mixture. Nestle the apples in the bed of lettuce and cap each with an apple top. Garnish with mint leaves.

Poularde au Riz, Sauce Suprême
CHICKEN WITH SUPRÊME SAUCE

SERVES 6

A *poularde* is a specially fattened pullet that has never laid eggs. These birds, which are a particularly tender delicacy in France, are served only in the finest restaurants or sometimes in homes on festive occasions. The finest *poulardes* come from the region of Bresse near Lyon. They are sold wrapped in a white linen cloth with only their heads and feathery necks protruding.

Note: *Poulardes* are often poached in France. This does not mean that they are tough old birds—quite the contrary!—so if substituting chicken be sure to choose a tender roasting fowl (cooking times, though short, will vary depending on the size of the bird).

4¹/₂-pound chicken
2 medium onions
2 whole cloves
1 Bouquet Garni (page 20)
2 medium carrots, chopped coarse
Salt
White pepper

RICE PILAF
3 tablespoons unsalted butter
1 medium onion, chopped fine
2 cups long-grain rice
Salt and freshly ground pepper
*4 cups chicken stock
   (use the poaching liquid
   from the chicken)*
1 Bouquet Garni

SUPRÊME SAUCE
2 tablespoons unsalted butter
¹/₄ cup all-purpose flour
2¹/₂ cups chicken stock
*1 cup crème fraîche or
   heavy cream*
Salt and freshly ground pepper

Prepare and truss the chicken for cooking (see directions on page 6 and technique photos page 530).

Stud each onion with a clove. Put the chicken in a soup kettle with the bouquet garni, the carrots, and the studded onions. Season with salt and pepper. Add 8 cups cold water, or as needed to cover the chicken, and bring to a boil. Skim the froth that rises to the surface, reduce the heat, and simmer the chicken until the juices run clear when the thigh is pierced with the tip of a knife, 1 hour and 20 minutes to 1½ hours. Transfer the chicken to a platter and cover with a dish towel so that it will not dry out; cover with aluminum foil to keep warm. Strain the poaching liquid and skim as much fat from the surface as possible; reserve 2½ cups for the sauce and 4 cups for the pilaf.

Prepare a rice pilaf: Use the above ingredients and follow the directions on page 60.

Prepare the suprême sauce: Melt the butter in a heavy-bottomed sauce-pan over low heat. Whisk in the flour and cook 2 minutes without coloring. Remove the pan from the heat and let cool slightly. Add 2½ cups of the stock, whisking constantly to avoid lumps. Whisk until smooth. Return to the heat, bring to a boil, reduce the heat and simmer 15 minutes. Add the cream and simmer 10 minutes longer. Season to taste with salt and pepper.

To serve, remove the skin from the chicken, if you wish. Place the chicken on a serving platter and spoon a small amount of the sauce over it. Serve the remaining sauce in a sauceboat on the side, and the rice in a vegetable dish.

Ananas Princesse
FRESH PINEAPPLE WITH STRAWBERRY SORBET AND GÉNOISE

SERVES 6

Génoise is the cake most frequently used by French pastry chefs. It is generally cut horizontally into two, three, or four slices, a technique that requires considerable skill and a steady hand.

In the following recipe, the *génoise* is sliced into three layers and two disks are cut from each layer. They are then topped with a slice of pineapple, an intense strawberry sorbet, and Chantilly cream. All of the components of this dessert, with the exception of the Chantilly, may be prepared several hours in advance but should not be assembled until just before serving (the Chantilly should be made no more than an hour ahead of time).

(continued)

Ananas Princesse (continued)

GÉNOISE

3 eggs (room temperature)

1/2 cup sugar

3/4 cup sifted all-purpose flour

1 teaspoon vanilla extract

STRAWBERRY SORBET

1 cup water

1 1/3 cups sugar

1 teaspoon vanilla extract

1 3/4 pint baskets strawberries

Juice of 1/2 lemon, strained

6 slices fresh pineapple,
 1/2 inch thick

2 tablespoons kirsch

CHANTILLY CREAM

2/3 cup heavy cream

2 tablespoons confectioner's sugar

1 teaspoon vanilla extract

Unsalted butter, softened,
 for cake pan

All-purpose flour, for cake pan

EQUIPMENT: 8-inch round cake pan, ice cream maker, pastry bag, small star pastry tip

Preheat the oven to 375°. Chill a mixing bowl in the freezer for the sorbet.

Prepare the génoise: Cut a round of parchment paper the diameter of the bottom of the cake pan. Brush the pan evenly with the softened butter. Put the round of parchment paper in the pan and brush with butter. Refrigerate until the butter hardens. Dust the pan with flour and tap out the excess.

Half-fill a deep saucepan with water. Bring it just to a boil and then reduce the heat to maintain the water at a simmer. Combine the eggs and sugar in a large heatproof bowl. Beat with a large whisk or electric mixer until foamy, about 1 minute. Set the bowl over the simmering water (the bottom of the bowl must not touch the water) and continue beating until the batter turns pale yellow and at least doubles in volume, about 8 minutes. (If the batter becomes hotter than body temperature, take it off the heat, and beat until it cools slightly.) Remove the batter from the heat, add the vanilla and continue beating off the heat until the batter is completely cool, thick and glossy, and falls in a ribbon from the whisk or beater. Fold in the sifted flour with a wooden spoon or spatula in 2 or 3 batches, turning the bowl with your free hand as you fold.

Pour the batter into the cake pan and tap the pan lightly on the work surface to remove any air pockets. Bake until a knife inserted into the center of the cake comes out clean and dry, and a finger lightly pressed onto the surface leaves no mark, 20 to 25 minutes. Unmold onto a rack, remove the paper and let cool.

Prepare the sorbet: Combine the water, sugar and vanilla in a saucepan. Bring to a boil over low heat, stirring to dissolve the sugar. Boil 1 to 2 minutes. Remove from the heat and cool the syrup over crushed ice. Rinse and dry the strawberries. Reserve 6 small perfect strawberries for decoration and hull the remainder. Combine the hulled strawberries and the lemon juice in a food mill or food processor and puree. Stir in the chilled syrup. Pour the mixture into an ice cream maker and freeze according to the manufacturer's instructions. Transfer to the chilled bowl and freeze until firm, at least 1 hour.

With a cookie cutter, cut the pineapple slices into 3½-inch rounds. Remove the hard central core with a small round cookie cutter and discard. Transfer the slices to a container. Sprinkle with kirsch and let macerate at least ½ hour.

Up to 1 hour before serving time prepare the Chantilly cream: Use the above ingredients and follow the directions on page 21. Fit the pastry bag with the small star tip and fill with the cream. Refrigerate until serving time.

To serve, cut the cooled génoise horizontally into three even layers with a serrated knife. Cut out two 3½-inch rounds from each layer with a cookie cutter. Put the rounds of génoise on a serving platter and top each with a slice of pineapple. Put a scoop of sorbet in the center of each pineapple slice. Pipe rosettes of cream around the base of the sorbet and decorate the tops with a rosette of cream and a reserved strawberry. Serve immediately.

GÉNOISE

Génoise is an all-purpose sponge cake used in literally hundreds of French desserts (a listing of petits fours variations alone would be a project). It is made by beating whole eggs and sugar over low heat until thickened and increased in volume, and then quickly folding in the flour and melted butter. (The amount of butter varies depending on how rich a cake is desired and is by no means mandatory—the génoise used in Ananas Princesse, above, is made with none at all.) Don't confuse génoise with a similar French sponge cake called a *biscuit* (page 33), which is made with separated eggs; the yolks are beaten with the sugar and then the whites are beaten separately and folded in at the end to make a drier, less airy cake. (A variation on the *biscuit* mixture is also used for ladyfingers, page 118.)

Because génoise is somewhat dry, it is often soaked with a sugar syrup or liquor; in the case of Ananas Princesse, the macerated pineapples will soak the cake adequately.

LESSON 32

Quiche aux Épinards
SPINACH AND HAM QUICHE

Bar à la Normande
SEA BASS WITH MUSHROOMS AND CREAM

Crêpes Soufflées au Cointreau
SOUFFLÉED CRÊPES FLAMED WITH COINTREAU

Quiche aux Épinards
SPINACH AND HAM QUICHE

SERVES 6

Quiche, a specialty of Lorraine, originally was made with bacon and an egg-cream custard. Today, virtually any pielike creation whose filling includes a custard can be called a quiche.

PÂTE BRISÉE
1 cup all-purpose flour
1/2 cup cake flour
1 egg
1 tablespoon water
Pinch salt
7 tablespoons unsalted butter
1 egg, lightly beaten,
  for glazing

3/4 pound spinach
1/4 pound sliced ham
2 tablespoons unsalted butter
2 egg yolks
1/2 cup heavy cream
2 ounces grated Gruyère cheese
Freshly ground pepper
Pinch freshly grated nutmeg
Salt

EQUIPMENT: 9-inch fluted, removable-bottomed tart pan

Prepare pâte brisée; line the pan, and blind bake. Use above ingredients and follow directions on pages 37–38 and technique photos on pages 540–41.

(continued)

Quiche aux Épinards (continued)

Preheat the oven to 375°.

Strip off and discard the stems from the spinach. Rinse the leaves well in several changes of water; drain and chop.

Cut the ham into strips ½ inch wide and 1½ inches long. Heat 1 tablespoon of the butter in a frying pan over medium heat. Add the ham and cook until golden. Discard the fat.

Combine the egg yolks and cream in a bowl. Stir in the cheese. Season with pepper and nutmeg. Stir in the ham.

Heat the remaining tablespoon of butter in a large saucepan over medium heat. Add the spinach and cook, stirring frequently, until all the moisture has evaporated. Season to taste with salt and pepper.

Spread the spinach in an even layer over the bottom of the cooked pastry shell. Pour the egg and ham mixture over the spinach and bake until a knife inserted into the center of the quiche comes out clean, about 25 minutes. Cool on a rack for 10 minutes. To serve, remove the rim from the pan. Transfer the quiche to a round serving platter and serve warm.

Bar à la Normande
SEA BASS WITH MUSHROOMS AND CREAM

SERVES 6

As might be expected, sea bass *à la Normande* is served with a cream sauce. The fish is baked on a bed of shallots moistened with white wine and fish stock (or water); once the fish is cooked, it is removed from the pan, then cream is added to the strained cooking liquids and boiled down to make a sauce.

Note: Sea bass is a delicate, firm-fleshed fish found in the Mediterranean. Although you will not find the same fish in American markets, striped bass or any whole white-fleshed fish may be cooked and served like the bass described here.

3-pound sea bass or striped bass
5 tablespoons unsalted butter
2 shallots, chopped fine
Salt
White pepper
1 cup dry white wine

1 cup Fish Stock (opposite page)
or water
1 pound mushrooms, sliced fine
1¼ cups crème fraîche

Unsalted butter, softened,
for parchment paper

Preheat the oven to 400°.

Clean the bass as you would any roundfish and trim the tail straight across (see directions on page 32 and technique photos page 524). Score the skin with a sharp knife.

Butter a roasting pan or baking dish just large enough to hold the fish with 3 tablespoons butter. Sprinkle with the shallots and salt and pepper. Put the fish in the roasting pan and add the wine and fish stock. Butter a piece of parchment paper and place it, buttered side down, over the fish. Bring to a boil over high heat, then transfer to the oven and bake until a knife penetrates the flesh easily, 20 to 25 minutes.

Heat the remaining 2 tablespoons of butter in a medium frying pan over high heat. Add the mushrooms and cook, stirring frequently, until all the moisture has evaporated. Season to taste with salt and pepper.

When the fish is cooked, transfer it carefully to a serving platter with two spatulas. Carefully scrape off the skin with a small sharp knife. (It is important to do this while the fish is still warm as the skin becomes difficult to remove once the fish cools.) Cover the fish to keep warm.

Strain the cooking liquid into a small, heavy-bottomed saucepan and cook over medium heat until the liquid has reduced by half. Add the cream and continue to cook, whisking frequently, until the sauce thickens and coats the back of a spoon. Taste and adjust seasonings.

To serve, reheat the mushrooms. Uncover the fish and blot up any liquid on the platter with paper towels. Surround the fish with the mushrooms. Spoon the sauce over the body of the fish only, leaving the head unsauced. Serve any remaining sauce in a sauceboat on the side.

Fumet de Poissons

BASIC FISH STOCK

MAKES 4 CUPS

Fish stock is always made with white-fleshed fish or fish bones. When butter is used, as described below, the resulting stock flavors soups and sauces; butter is omitted in aspics and consommés.

Note: No salt is used in a fish stock if it is to be boiled down to make a fish glaze (*glace de poisson*) but a small amount can be added on other occasions.

2 whole whiting, 8 ounces each,
or 1 pound other lean white fish
with bones, or 1 pound fish
bones (except salmon, tuna,
and mackerel)
3 tablespoons unsalted butter
2 medium onions, chopped

4 shallots, chopped
2 leeks (white part only), chopped
1 Bouquet Garni (page 20)
10 peppercorns
1½ cups dry white wine
3 cups water

If using whole fish, clean and scale it as you would any roundfish (see page 32). Then cut the fish, with the heads, into large pieces. If using fish bones, rinse and chop into several pieces.

(continued)

Fumet de Poissons (continued)

Melt the butter in a large saucepan over medium heat. Add the fish and the vegetables, and cook until the vegetables are soft but not colored, about 2 minutes. Add the bouquet garni, peppercorns and wine and bring to the boil. Cook until reduced by about one half. Then, stir in the water and return to a boil, skimming off any froth that rises to the surface. Lower the heat and simmer slowly for 20 minutes. Strain the stock through a fine strainer lined with cheesecloth, pressing down on the solids to extract all the liquid. The final yield should be about 4 cups; if necessary, return the stock to the saucepan and simmer over medium heat until reduced to 4 cups.

Crêpes Soufflées au Cointreau
SOUFFLÉED CRÊPES FLAMED WITH COINTREAU

SERVES 6

Few desserts are as spectacular as these flaming crêpes with their souffléed filling. The trick is to make the crêpes and the pastry cream well in advance. Add the egg whites to the pastry cream just before filling the crêpes and baking. The crêpes must be served and flamed as soon they come from the oven since, like all soufflés, they fall as quickly and as dramatically as they rise.

SWEET CRÊPE BATTER
1 cup all-purpose flour
2 eggs
Pinch salt
2 tablespoons sugar
1 cup milk
5 tablespoons unsalted butter, melted
Grated zest of 1 orange

PASTRY CREAM
1 cup milk
1 teaspoon vanilla extract
2 egg yolks
$^1/_3$ cup sugar
2 tablespoons all-purpose flour
2 tablespoons cornstarch

$^1/_4$ cup Cointreau plus 3 tablespoons for flaming the crêpes
1 egg, separated
3 egg whites
Confectioner's sugar for dusting

Unsalted butter, melted, for crêpe pans
Softened unsalted butter for pastry cream and baking sheet

EQUIPMENT: Two 5-inch crêpe pans

Prepare the sweet crêpe batter just as you would a savory crêpe batter, using the above ingredients and following the directions on page 23, but

add the sugar to the flour and the orange zest along with the eggs. Let the batter rest for ½ hour.

Meanwhile, prepare the pastry cream: Put the milk and vanilla in a heavy-bottomed saucepan and bring to a boil. Combine the egg yolks and sugar in a heatproof bowl and beat until thick and pale yellow. Whisk in the flour and cornstarch. Whisk in the hot milk and return the mixture to the saucepan. Bring to a boil over medium heat, whisking constantly. Reduce the heat and simmer 5 minutes, whisking constantly to reach all parts of the pan; the cream burns easily. Spread the cream in a shallow dish and pat with butter to prevent a crust from forming. Let cool.

Cook 12 crêpes following the directions on page 23.

Preheat the oven to 350°. Brush a baking sheet with the softened butter.

Put the cooled pastry cream in a large bowl and blend in ¼ cup of Cointreau and the egg yolk. Beat the egg whites with a whisk or electric mixer until stiff peaks form. Whisk one-third of the egg whites into the pastry cream mixture to loosen it; lightly fold in the remainder with a wooden spoon.

Transfer 1 crêpe to the baking sheet. Spoon a small mound of the soufflé filling on one-half of the crêpe and fold the opposite side over it. Repeat for the remaining crêpes. Bake until the crêpes have risen, about 20 minutes.

To serve, transfer the crêpes to a long oval platter with a wide spatula. Warm 3 tablespoons Cointreau in a small saucepan. Sift confectioner's sugar over the crêpes. Carefully light the warmed Cointreau and pour it, flaming, over the crêpes at the table. Serve immediately.

LESSON 33

Bisque de Langoustines
LANGOUSTINE BISQUE

———

Pintade à la Cévenole
GUINEA HEN WITH MUSHROOMS AND CHESTNUTS

———

Mousse à l'Orange
ORANGE MOUSSE

INTERMÉDIAIRE

Bisque de Langoustines
LANGOUSTINE BISQUE

SERVES 6

Bisques are creamy, shellfish-based soups, but when they first became popular in France, during the seventeenth century, they were quite different from what they are today. At that time there were various kinds of bisque, all of them extremely elaborate dishes (generally made with meat and/or fowl), but by the early nineteenth century only one bisque remained—crayfish bisque. This is a Cordon Bleu version of that now classic preparation; it substitutes langoustines for crayfish and, unlike its ancestor, uses the langoustine tail meat to make a delicate mousseline forcemeat which is shaped and poached at the last minute to garnish this most elegant of soups.

*18 unshelled langoustines
  (see page 114)
  or 1½ pounds shrimp
12 tablespoons unsalted butter
6 tablespoons fine-chopped shallots
6 tablespoons fine-chopped leek
  (white part only)
1 medium carrot, diced fine
2 tablespoons chopped fresh
  tarragon or 2 teaspoons dried
1½ tablespoons chopped parsley
1 cup cognac
3 cups dry white wine
1 tablespoon tomato paste*

*Salt
White pepper
1 cup crème fraîche or
  heavy cream
2 cups water
¼ cup rice flour
1 egg, separated
4 sprigs chervil or parsley,
  chopped fine
1 egg yolk
Chervil or parsley leaves
  for garnish

Unsalted butter for frying pan
  and parchment paper*

Chill a mixing bowl for the mousseline.

Shell the langoustines (see directions on page 115 and technique photos page 523). Set aside the tail meat. Put the heads and shells in a large saucepan and crush with a pestle. (Or, coarsely grind in a processor and then transfer to a saucepan.)

Add 6 tablespoons of the butter to the saucepan and melt over low heat. Add the shallots, leek, carrot, tarragon and parsley and stir well to coat with the butter. Cover and cook gently for a few minutes until the vegetables are tender. Add the cognac and carefully light with a match. When the flames die, add the wine, the tomato paste, a pinch of salt, pepper, ½ cup of the cream, and the water. Bring to a boil, reduce the heat, and simmer 45 minutes. Strain the broth through a fine sieve; discard the solids. Add water as needed to measure 6 cups.

Heat the remaining 6 tablespoons butter in the saucepan and whisk in the rice flour. Gradually whisk in the strained broth until smooth and slightly thickened. If the bisque is too thick, thin with a bit of water. Season to taste with salt and pepper and simmer very gently for 20 minutes; set aside.

Prepare a mousseline: Work the langoustine tails or shrimp through a sieve, or process briefly to make a fine puree. Transfer to the chilled bowl and set over crushed ice. Season with salt and pepper. Beat egg white until just foamy and add it gradually to the puree, beating vigorously until well blended and thickened. Add 2 tablespoons of cream little by little in the same way; stir in the chervil.

Prepare the quenelles: Brush a large frying pan with the softened butter. Dip 2 teaspoons in cold water to keep the mousseline from sticking. Scoop out a mound of the mousseline with 1 of the spoons. Invert the second spoon over the top of the mound to smooth it into an oval shape, known as a "quenelle." Slide the top spoon under the quenelle and transfer it to the frying pan. Repeat to form all of the mousseline mixture into quenelles. Add enough bisque to just cover the quenelles. Butter a piece of parchment paper and lay it, buttered side down, over the quenelles. Poach gently in the simmering broth over low heat until firm, about 10 minutes. Remove the quenelles with a slotted spoon and set aside; cover to keep warm. Return the poaching liquid to the pan of bisque.

Whisk the egg yolks with the remaining 6 tablespoons cream in a small bowl. Whisk in a little of the hot bisque and then return the mixture to the saucepan. Bring to a boil, reduce heat and simmer 2 minutes.

To serve, pour the bisque into a soup tureen and add the quenelles. Garnish with chervil leaves and serve very hot.

MOUSSELINES

Mousseline is a term used to describe any number of delicate, airy, sweet or savory preparations containing egg whites and/or cream. One common savory mousseline preparation is that used to make quenelles (Bisque de Langoustines, above) and terrines (Mousseline de Saint Jacques au Concombre, page 244); it is made with any pureed raw lean fish, meat, or poultry and bound with cream and eggs or egg white. The amount of egg white is crucial to the mixture; there must be just enough to bind it adequately but not so much that it becomes tough. The mixture is beaten over ice so that it stays firm and to ensure that it does not separate. The egg and cream are added little by little and the mousseline must be well chilled before the next addition. A mousseline may also be cooked in small, individual molds called *dariole* molds (Mousseline de Merlans aux Champignons Sauvages, page 343). Mousselines require delicate cooking—poaching for quenelles and a water bath for those cooked in terrine and dariole molds. The mousseline mixture may be prepared a few hours ahead and refrigerated.

Mousseline is also used as an adjective to describe sauces into which whipped cream has been folded (as in a mayonnaise mousseline or hollandaise mousseline) or vegetable purees enriched with whipped cream (Mousseline de Carottes, page 331).

Pintade à la Cévenole
GUINEA HEN WITH MUSHROOMS AND CHESTNUTS

SERVES 6

The Cévennes is an arid, rough region of central France bordering on the Massif Centrale mountain range; chestnuts are one of this area's natural resources and dishes said to be *à la Cévenole* often contain them. Like many a country preparation, this dish also contains bacon and mushrooms. At Le Cordon Bleu, oyster mushrooms are used (they are cultivated on a large scale in France), but button mushrooms or wild mushrooms, particularly chanterelles, would be equally appropriate.

*¾ pound slab bacon, sliced
¼ inch thick
12 tablespoons unsalted butter
½ pound pearl onions, peeled
1 pound oyster mushrooms,
trimmed, rinsed, and dried
¾ pound button or quartered
large mushrooms, trimmed,
rinsed and dried
Salt and freshly ground pepper
2 guinea hens, 2 pounds each*

*1 tablespoon vegetable oil
2 cups red wine
1 Bouquet Garni (page 20)
¾ pound whole shelled chestnuts
3 shallots, chopped fine
1 tablespoon chopped parsley

Flour for guinea hens
Unsalted butter, softened,
for parchment paper*

Cut the bacon into lardons; blanch and drain (page 46).

Melt 1 tablespoon butter in a large frying pan over high heat. Add the blanched lardons and sauté until golden. Remove with a slotted spoon and set aside; discard the fat. Melt 1 tablespoon of butter in the same pan over medium heat. Add the onions and cook until colored, about 3 minutes. Add another tablespoon of butter to the pan, increase the heat to high and add all of the mushrooms. Season with salt and pepper and cook quickly until all the liquid has evaporated, 5 to 8 minutes. Remove from the heat and return the lardons to the pan; set aside.

Preheat the oven to 375°. Cut each guinea hen into 4 pieces each, just as you would a chicken, leaving the legs whole (see directions on pages 59–60 and technique photos page 530). Trim off and discard the wing tips. Heat 1 tablespoon of butter and the oil in a large ovenproof casserole over medium heat. Dredge the guinea hens in the flour and shake off the excess. Season with salt and pepper and add, skin side down, to the casserole; brown on both sides. Discard the fat from the pan and then add 1 cup of the wine to deglaze. Bring to a boil, scraping the bottom of the pan to release any cooked particles that adhere. Add the bouquet garni, the lardons, pearl onions and mushrooms. Butter a piece of parchment paper and lay it, buttered side down, over the guinea hens. Cover with a lid and bake until the juices run clear when the thigh is pierced with the tip of a knife, 30 to 40 minutes.

(continued)

Melt 1 tablespoon of butter in a saucepan over medium heat. Add the chestnuts and cook gently for about 2 minutes, then transfer to a large baking dish or ovenproof serving dish. Remove the lardons, pearl onions and mushrooms from the casserole with a slotted spoon and spread over the chestnuts. Arrange the pieces of guinea hen on top. Reserve the cooking liquid. Cover the dish with foil and bake for about 8 minutes to allow the chestnuts to absorb the flavors of the other ingredients.

Meanwhile, prepare the sauce: Cut 6 tablespoons butter into ½-inch pieces; set aside. Heat the remaining tablespoon of butter in a saucepan over low heat. Add the shallots and cook until tender but not colored. Add the remaining cup of red wine and the reserved cooking liquid. Increase the heat to high and cook until the liquid reduces by about half. Remove from the heat and whisk in the butter, piece by piece. Taste and adjust seasonings.

To serve, spoon the sauce over the guinea hens in the baking dish. Sprinkle with chopped parsley.

Mousse à l'Orange
ORANGE MOUSSE

SERVES 6

A sabayon made from fresh orange juice and stiffened with a small amount of gelatin is the base for this mousse. The mousse is served in hollowed-out oranges and, like a frozen soufflé, it is collared to rise above the orange skin just as a hot soufflé rises up above the soufflé mold. Any citrus fruit can be prepared like the oranges described here or, for that matter, a combination of citrus fruit juices can be used to make the sabayon, which can be used to fill the skin of your choice.

Note: The fruit skins may be filled up to 24 hours in advance.

7 oranges
1 cup heavy cream

SABAYON
1 package powdered gelatin
  (¹/4 ounce)
2 tablespoons cold water
4 egg yolks
¹/4 cup sugar

CHANTILLY CREAM
1 cup heavy cream
1 tablespoon confectioner's sugar
¹/2 teaspoon vanilla extract

6 cherries, bottled in liqueur
  or syrup, for garnish
6 mint leaves for garnish

EQUIPMENT: Pastry bag, small star pastry tip

Chill a mixing bowl for the whipped cream. Grate the zest from one of the oranges; set the zest aside.

Slice the top third off all of the oranges. With a small spoon, scoop out the pulp from the bases and tops into a bowl; set aside. Discard all of the orange tops and the shell of just the grated orange. Cut out 6 bands of flexible cardboard 1½ inches wide and about 8 inches long. Fit the bands into the reserved orange shells so that they extend about 1 inch above the top edges of the orange skins; freeze.

Puree the pulp in a food mill or processor and strain (you should have about 2 cups juice). Put the juice in a medium saucepan, bring to a boil and then cook over medium heat until reduced to 1 cup; set the reduced juice aside.

Beat the cream in the chilled bowl with a whisk or electric mixer until stiff peaks form and the cream clings to the whisk or beater; refrigerate.

Prepare the sabayon: Half-fill a large saucepan with water and bring it to a simmer. Sprinkle the gelatin over the 2 tablespoons of cold water and let stand until softened, about 5 minutes. Combine the reduced orange juice, the softened gelatin, the egg yolks, reserved orange zest and the sugar in a heatproof bowl and beat with a large whisk or electric mixer until foamy. Set the bowl over the simmering water (the bottom of the bowl must not touch the water). Continue beating until the mixture becomes thick and creamy and increases in volume, and the whisk or beater leaves a clear trail on the bottom of the bowl. Test the temperature of the sabayon occasionally with a finger: If it feels hotter than just tepid (the temperature should not exceed 80°), remove from the heat and beat until slightly cooled. Then return to the heat and finish cooking. When the sabayon is thickened and fully cooked, remove from the heat and beat until cool.

Fold the whipped cream into the cooled sabayon. Fill the frozen orange shells with the mixture, all the way to the top of the cardboard collars. Smooth the tops with a metal spatula. Refrigerate until firm, 3 to 4 hours.

Not more than 1 hour before serving, prepare the Chantilly cream: Use the above ingredients and follow the directions on page 21. Fit the pastry bag with the small star tip. Fill it with the cream; refrigerate.

To serve, dip a knife blade into hot water and dry it. Slide the blade around the inside of each cardboard collar and then carefully remove the collars. Put the mousse-filled oranges on a doily-lined platter. Pipe a Chantilly cream rosette in the center of each orange mousse. Top each with a cherry and decorate with a mint leaf.

LESSON 34

Éffeuillé de Saint Jacques et Petits Légumes au Safran
SEA SCALLOPS AND SPRING VEGETABLES WITH SAFFRON

Entrecôte Bordelaise
RIB-EYE STEAK WITH BORDELAISE SAUCE

Pommes Anna
POTATOES ANNA

Café Liégeois
COFFEE ICE CREAM SUNDAE

Éffeuillé de Saint Jacques et Petits Légumes au Safran
SEA SCALLOPS AND SPRING VEGETABLES WITH SAFFRON

SERVES 6

This is a particularly beautiful dish: Thinly sliced sea scallop petals are served with a brightly colored vegetable garnish and a saffron-flavored sauce. Neither the scallops nor the vegetables should be overcooked; taste both periodically and adjust the cooking times if necessary.

Note: The most exotic element in this dish is the saffron, made by drying the tiny stigmas of the saffron crocus. More than 100,000 crocus flowers must be picked and sorted to produce one pound of this precious spice. Because of saffron's high price, powdered saffron is sometimes adulterated, but if you purchase saffron threads, you can be sure to have bought the real thing.

In France, scallops are usually sold alive, in the shell. In the United States, however, you will almost invariably find them sold out of the shell, without their bright orange roe (which is completely edible and delicious). Fresh scallops should smell very fresh (bad scallops have an uncontestably "off" odor) and should look firm and plump, not flabby.

12 sea scallops
10 ounces carrots (about 3 large)
7 ounces turnips (about 2 medium)
Salt
1/2 pound string beans,
    cut in 1-inch lengths
1/4 pound green peas, shelled
3 tablespoons unsalted butter
White pepper

SAFFRON SAUCE

2 shallots, chopped fine
3/4 cup dry white wine
1 teaspoon white-wine vinegar
3/4 cup crème fraîche or
    heavy cream
12 tablespoons unsalted butter,
    softened
Salt and freshly ground pepper
1/4 teaspoon saffron threads

1 small head red leaf lettuce
Chervil or parsley leaves
    for garnish

Rinse the scallops in cold water and drain. Remove the orange roe, if any, and set aside. Pull off and discard the small hard muscle on the side of each scallop. Cut the scallops horizontally into slices about 1/8 inch thick; set aside.

Peel and cut the carrots and turnips into *bâtonnets* 1 inch long and 3/8 inch wide. (Or you may prefer to turn the vegetables as in the photo below; see directions on page 50 and technique photo on page 520.)

Bring a large saucepan of salted water to a boil. Add the beans and cook until crisp-tender, about 10 minutes; drain. Refresh under cold water and

drain again. Cook the peas in the same way.

Heat the butter in a medium frying pan over medium heat. Add the carrots and cook for 7 minutes. Add the turnips and cook until the vegetables are crisp-tender, about 6 more minutes. Season to taste with salt and pepper. Remove the pan from the heat. Stir in the cooked beans and peas. Cover and set aside.

Preheat the oven to 475°.

Prepare the saffron sauce: Combine the shallots, white wine and vinegar in a small heavy-bottomed saucepan. Cook over medium heat until the liquid has evaporated. Whisk in the cream, lower the heat and simmer until reduced by one-half. Remove the pan from heat and whisk in the softened butter, little by little. Season to taste with salt and pepper and stir in the saffron. Keep the sauce warm off the heat over a saucepan of hot water.

Season the sliced scallops and roe, if using, with salt and pepper. Arrange on top of the mixed vegetables and bake until the scallops are just opaque, about 4 minutes.

To serve, arrange a crown of lettuce leaves on a serving platter. Mound the vegetables in the center of the platter and arrange the scallops and coral, if using, on top. Spoon the sauce over and garnish with chervil leaves. (For an alternative presentation, see photo on page 191.)

BEURRE BLANC SAUCE AND VARIATIONS

Beurre blanc is a delicate hot butter sauce flavored with a reduction of white wine, vinegar, herbs, and shallot. The reduction is made by cooking the mixture over a low heat (to extract maximum flavor from the aromatics) until it is reduced to a thick glaze. Then at Cordon Bleu we add a little cream to stabilize the sauce (a classic beurre blanc is made without cream) and softened butter is whisked in bit by bit—off the heat so the butter does not melt completely but emulsifies into the reduction, giving the sauce a thick, creamy consistency.

Many variations on beurre blanc exist in French cooking. The technique is always the same but the reduction is made from another wine or vinegar, lemon juice, or from a stock. Or the sauce may be flavored with any number of ingredients such as saffron, as in the recipe above, or even sea urchin roe.

Unlike flour-bound sauces, hot butter sauces are too delicate to reheat (if the sauce is placed over direct heat the butter will melt and the sauce will separate) but they may be held off the heat for ten to fifteen minutes over a saucepan of hot water. If your sauce should separate while you are adding the butter (because the saucepan is too hot), you may retrieve it by adding a teaspoon of cold water. If this is not successful, make a second reduction in another pan and then slowly whisk in the separated sauce, drop by drop at first and then in a steady steam as the sauce begins to emulsify.

Beurre blanc sauce is served with fish and shellfish or with vegetables.

Entrecôte Bordelaise
RIB-EYE STEAK WITH BORDELAISE SAUCE

SERVES 6

Arguments rage about this recipe. Some chefs make the sauce with white wine, others with red; some use garlic, others only shallots. All seem to agree that the steaks should be served rare with beef marrow.

Cooking the marrow is perhaps the trickiest part of this recipe; be careful to poach it gently and only for a short time—otherwise it will dissolve.

Note: Marrow is found in beef leg bones, which may be ordered at many butcher shops. Purchase it sawed crosswise into 3-inch pieces to facilitate removal of the marrow. Place the bones in hot water for 2 or 3 minutes or until marrow just begins to loosen. Drain; using a small knife, loosen and push marrow from the bones in 1 piece.

12 slices beef marrow, about ³/₄ inch thick (4 bones)

BORDELAISE SAUCE
³/₄ cup dry red wine (preferably Bordeaux)
2 shallots, chopped fine
1 sprig fresh thyme or ¹/₄ teaspoon dried
1 bay leaf
2 cups Brown Veal Stock (page 71)

Salt and freshly ground pepper
1 tablespoon unsalted butter

2 tablespoons unsalted butter
2 tablespoons vegetable oil
6 rib-eye steaks, about 8 ounces each
Salt and freshly ground pepper

Soak the sliced beef marrow in cold water to remove any impurities.

Prepare the sauce: Combine the wine, shallots, thyme and bay leaf in a small heavy-bottomed saucepan. Bring to a boil over medium heat; then lower the heat and simmer until the liquid has almost evaporated. Add the stock, return to a boil and skim the froth from the surface. Reduce the heat and simmer until the mixture thickens enough to coat the back of a spoon, about 20 minutes. Strain. Season to taste with salt and pepper and rub the butter over the surface to prevent a skin from forming. Keep warm.

Heat 1 tablespoon each of the butter and oil in a large frying pan over high heat. Season 3 of the steaks on both sides with salt and pepper and brown for 3 minutes on each side. Reduce the heat and continue cooking as desired (page 129). Transfer to a serving platter and cover to keep warm. Discard fat in pan. Repeat to cook the remaining steaks.

Bring 2 cups salted water to a gentle simmer. Lift the marrow from the cold water with a slotted spoon to a plate. Carefully slide the marrow from the plate into the gently simmering water and poach for 15 to 30 seconds.

To serve, place 2 slices of marrow on each steak and spoon over the Bordelaise sauce. Accompany with Pommes Anna (page 194).

Pommes Anna

POTATOES ANNA

———

S E R V E S 6

This golden, soft-centered cake of thin-sliced potatoes is said to have been named for Anna Deslions, a prominent figure in the artistic community of nineteenth-century France.

Though potatoes Anna can be prepared in a cake pan, many elegant French kitchens have a special high-sided copper pan fitted with a deep lid designed expressly for making this dish.

Note: Only clarified butter should be brushed on the potatoes before they are baked. Ordinary butter would overheat and burn.

3¹/₂ pounds waxy potatoes (red or white)	*7 tablespoons clarified butter (page 94)*
6 tablespoons vegetable oil	*Salt and fresh ground pepper*
6 tablespoons unsalted butter	*Unsalted butter for aluminum foil*

EQUIPMENT: 8-inch round cake pan

Peel the potatoes and pare slightly to shape roughly into cylinders, about 2 inches in diameter. Slice ¹/₁₆ inch thick with a mandoline or in a food processor. Put the slices in a bowl of cold water, to remove as much starch as possible. Remove from the water with a slotted spoon and drain well on paper towels. Pat dry.

Heat 2 tablespoons each oil and butter in a large frying pan over high heat until butter starts to sizzle. Add about one-third of the potato slices and sauté, tossing the potatoes frequently by pulling the pan toward you with a jerk of the wrist, until the potatoes are slightly stiffened and lightly golden on the outside, but still raw on the inside. Transfer to a colander to drain. Discard the fat and repeat twice more until all the potatoes are golden.

Preheat the oven to 400°. Brush the cake pan with clarified butter. Line the side of the cake pan with overlapping potato slices. Then, starting at the outside and working toward the center, line the bottom with circles of overlapping slices. Brush the potatoes with clarified butter and sprinkle with salt and pepper. Make a second layer of slices in the same way, brush with the clarified butter, and sprinkle with salt and pepper. Continue the layering process until all of the potato slices are used. Press down on the finished cake with a metal spatula to compact the slices, gently folding the slices lining the sides in toward the center. Drizzle with any remaining clarified butter.

Brush a round of aluminum foil with the softened butter and place it, buttered side down, over the potato cake. Transfer to the oven and bake until the potatoes are soft when pierced with a knife, 30 to 40 minutes.

Unmold the potatoes: Set the pan over medium heat and shake gently to release any slices of potato that have stuck to the pan. Remove the pan from the heat. Invert a round serving platter over the top and carefully reverse the two. Wait 1 minute to allow excess butter to escape before removing the pan. Blot up any excess butter on the platter with paper towels. (If the cake is not colored evenly, return it to the hot oven or broiler, and cook until evenly browned.)

Café Liégeois
COFFEE ICE CREAM SUNDAE

SERVES 6

This coffee ice cream confection was originally called Café Viennois; then, at the outbreak of the First World War, it was diplomatically rechristened. Like any ice cream sundae, it can be served either as a dessert or between meals; in fact, Café Liégeois can be ordered at almost any hour in most large Parisian cafés.

COFFEE ICE CREAM
CRÈME ANGLAISE:
- 1 cup milk
- 1 cup heavy cream
- 1 teaspoon vanilla extract
- 4 egg yolks
- 1/2 cup sugar
- 1 tablespoon instant coffee granules

CHANTILLY CREAM
- 1 cup heavy cream
- 1 teaspoon vanilla extract
- 2 tablespoons confectioner's sugar
- 3/4 cup strong black coffee, chilled
- 24 candied coffee beans

EQUIPMENT: Ice cream maker, pastry bag, small star pastry tip

Chill a mixing bowl and 6 dessert glasses in the freezer for the ice cream.

Prepare the ice cream: First make a crème anglaise (see directions on page 35 and technique photos page 552), using the above ingredients and combining the milk and cream. In a bowl, dissolve the coffee in a little of the hot crème anglaise. Return the mixture to the rest of the anglaise and stir to blend. Let cool. Pour into an ice cream maker and freeze according to the manufacturer's instructions. Transfer to the chilled mixing bowl and freeze until firm, at least 1 hour.

Not more than 1 hour before serving, prepare the Chantilly cream: Use the above ingredients and follow directions on page 21. Fit a pastry bag with a small star tip and fill with the Chantilly cream; refrigerate until serving time.

To serve, place 2 scoops of ice cream in each chilled dessert glass. Spoon 2 tablespoons of chilled coffee over each. Decorate with rosettes of Chantilly cream and top with candied liqueur coffee beans. Serve immediately.

LESSON 35

Salade de Sardines Crues aux Épinards

SPINACH SALAD WITH FRESH SARDINES

—

Lapin à la Graine de Moutarde

RABBIT IN MUSTARD CREAM SAUCE

—

Pâtes Fraîches

FRESH PASTA

—

Tarte Bourdaloue

PEAR AND ALMOND CREAM TART

Salade de Sardines Crues aux Épinards

SPINACH SALAD WITH FRESH SARDINES

SERVES 6

Fresh sardines are a favorite for outdoor barbecues in France. These little fish are carefully arranged in special racks that can hold twenty or more; with a flick of the wrist, a whole colony can be rotated over hot coals.

This Cordon Bleu recipe adopts a different approach. Sardine fillets are "cooked" in lime juice and served with a light vinaigrette on a bed of raw spinach—perfect for campers who prefer to keep away from the fire!

12 fresh sardines
Salt and freshly ground pepper
1 shallot, chopped fine
Juice of 3 limes, strained

VINAIGRETTE
1/4 cup cider vinegar
Salt and freshly ground pepper
1 tablespoon chopped fresh chives
3/4 cup olive oil

5 ounces mushrooms, trimmed, rinsed, dried and sliced thin
14 ounces spinach
1/4 red bell pepper, diced fine
1 tablespoon chopped fresh chives
2 limes, sliced crosswise into thin rounds

Cut the fins and tails off the sardines. Working from tail to head, scale with the blunt edge of a small knife. Cut off the heads. Run a small sharp knife down each side of the backbone of one of the fish. Then, steady the fish with your free hand and, holding the knife blade flat against the backbone, slide the knife along the ribs from head to tail without cutting through the skin of the stomach, to free the flesh. Turn the fish over and repeat for the other side. Remove the backbone and innards. Repeat with the remaining sardines. Rinse well under cold running water and pat dry with paper towels.

Open the sardines like a book and lay skin side down in a nonaluminum container. Sprinkle generously with salt and pepper, then with the chopped shallot. Sprinkle with the lime juice. Cover with parchment paper and let marinate 3 hours in the refrigerator.

Make the vinaigrette: Combine the vinegar, salt, pepper, and chives in a bowl. Whisk in the olive oil.

Toss the mushrooms gently with half the vinaigrette. Let marinate at room temperature for at least 1 hour.

Stem the spinach and rinse it in several changes of water; dry well. Stack, roll, and cut the leaves into a chiffonade (see directions on page 8 and technique photo page 520).

To serve, toss the spinach in a bowl with the remaining vinaigrette. Arrange the mushrooms in a line down the middle of a long serving platter. Arrange the spinach on either side of the mushrooms. Drain the sardines and place them on top of the spinach, fanning them outward from the mushrooms and alternating them, one skin side up, and then one skin side down. Sprinkle the sardines with diced red pepper. Sprinkle the mushrooms with chives. Garnish the platter with the lime slices. (For individual servings, see photo on page 196.)

Lapin à la Graine de Moutarde
RABBIT IN MUSTARD CREAM SAUCE

SERVES 6

Rabbits are farmed on large scale in France and are generally sold by butchers or shops that specialize in poultry *(volaillers)*. The legs and saddle (below the ribs) are the meatiest parts and are sometimes sold separately for this very reason.

Of all the rabbit dishes in France, *lapin à la moutarde* (rabbit with mustard sauce) is undoubtedly the most universally appreciated and practiced. This Cordon Bleu recipe is a particularly refined version of a classic preparation.

Note: At the school, whole-grain mustard is used to flavor the rabbit rather than Dijon mustard, because it has a milder, fruity flavor.

3-pound rabbit
Salt and freshly ground pepper
Whole-grain mustard for coating rabbit
2 large shallots, chopped fine

1/2 cup dry white wine
3/4 cup crème fraîche or heavy cream

Unsalted butter, softened, for serving dish

Preheat the oven to 450°. Brush an ovenproof serving dish with the softened butter.

Cut the rabbit into serving pieces (see technique photos on page 534): With a large heavy knife, trim the ends of the front and hind legs and then cut off the front and hind leg sections. Cut the hind legs into 2 pieces at the joint and the saddle into 3 equal sections. Cut the rib section in half through the breast and back bones and then cut each half into half again. Season lightly with salt and pepper, then use a small pastry brush to coat the pieces all over with a thin layer of mustard. Put the rabbit in the serving dish and roast for 35 minutes. Add the chopped shallots to the dish and roast 5 more minutes.

Remove the dish from the oven and spoon off any fat. Add the white wine and continue roasting for 10 minutes. Then add the cream and roast 5 minutes longer. Taste the sauce and adjust seasoning.

Serve the rabbit very hot in its baking dish, accompanied by fresh pasta (opposite page).

Pâtes Fraîches

FRESH PASTA

—

SERVES 6

2 cups all-purpose flour
3 egg yolks
3 tablespoons vegetable oil

Salt
5 to 6 tablespoons cold water

2 tablespoons unsalted butter

Put the flour on a work surface or in a large bowl and make a well in the center. Add the egg yolks, oil, ¼ teaspoon salt, and 5 tablespoons water to the well and mix with one hand to blend. Then, slowly draw in the flour with a pastry scraper and mix until the dough comes together, adding the last tablespoon of water if the dough is dry. With the palm of your hand, work the dough until it forms a smooth elastic ball by slapping it on the work surface, until it no longer sticks to your fingers or the work surface. Cover with plastic wrap and refrigerate for at least 30 minutes.

Lightly dust the work surface with flour. Roll out the pasta dough ¹/₁₆ inch thick. Use the edge of the rolling pin or a ruler as a guide and cut the dough into long strips, ¼ inch wide. Lay 2 or 3 dish towels on the work surface, dust lightly with flour and dry the noodles in a single layer on them for at least 30 minutes before cooking.

Bring a large saucepan of salted water to a boil. Add the pasta and cook until tender, about 3 to 5 minutes. Drain well. To serve, melt 2 tablespoons butter in same saucepan. Add the drained pasta and toss until coated with the butter. Transfer to a platter or serving bowl.

FRESH PASTA

Fresh pasta, made with all-purpose flour, egg yolk, oil, salt, and water, is a completely different food from commercial dried pasta or macaroni which, excellent in its own right, is made with semolina flour and water. Fresh pasta is very easy to make: The ingredients are mixed into a rough dough that is worked by being slapped down on a work surface until it becomes very smooth and elastic. After resting, it is rolled out very thin, cut into noodles, and then left to dry for a short time so that the noodles don't stick together. The dough may be refrigerated for up to 1 day.

At Le Cordon Bleu we always roll pasta by hand, but a hand-crank pasta machine (there are many brands on the market) will also yield a fine result. If you use a machine, you will see that it has two attachments—one for rolling the dough and one for cutting the pasta. First work the dough through the machine using successively smaller settings, until it is $1/16$ inch thick. Then, with the other attachment, cut it to the desired shape.

Cook fresh pasta in lots of water and be sure to time the cooking carefully; if you haven't made fresh pasta before you will be surprised at how fast it cooks. Fresh pasta is delicious tossed in butter; for variation, add fresh herbs to the butter.

Tarte Bourdaloue
PEAR AND ALMOND CREAM TART

SERVES 6

Once a specialty of a small pastry shop in Paris, this pear tart with its almond filling is now to be had throughout the country. Those interested in sampling the original still make pilgrimages to 7 rue Bourdaloue, where the dessert was created over a century ago.

PÂTE BRISÉE SUCRÉE
1 cup all-purpose flour
1/2 cup cake flour
1 egg
1 tablespoon water
Pinch of salt
3 tablespoons sugar
1 teaspoon vanilla extract
7 tablespoons unsalted butter, softened
1 egg, lightly beaten, for glazing

3 fresh pears or 5 canned pear halves
1/2 lemon

SUGAR SYRUP
2 cups water
1 1/4 cups sugar
1 teaspoon vanilla extract
1/2 lemon

ALMOND PASTRY CREAM

1 cup milk

1 teaspoon vanilla extract

2 egg yolks

1/3 cup sugar

3 tablespoons cornstarch

2 ounces almonds, ground fine
   (about 1/2 cup)

1 tablespoon kirsch

2 tablespoons unsalted butter,
   softened

APRICOT GLAZE

1/2 cup apricot jam

1 tablespoon kirsch

EQUIPMENT: 8-inch fluted removable-bottomed tart pan, pastry bag, medium star pastry tip

Prepare the pâte brisée sucrée just as you would a pâte brisée, but add the sugar and vanilla to the well along with the egg, water, and salt; line the pan and blind bake the tart shell (see directions on pages 38–39 and technique photos pages 540–41). Let cool.

Peel the fresh pears and cut in half. Remove the cores and stems. Rub with lemon; set aside.

Poach the pears: Combine the water, sugar and vanilla in a medium saucepan. Bring to a boil over low heat, stirring to dissolve the sugar. Boil 1 to 2 minutes. Reduce the heat to medium and add the lemon and pears. Simmer until tender when pierced with the point of a knife, 10 to 15 minutes. Do not allow to boil. Remove the pears from the syrup with a slotted spoon and drain on a rack. (If using canned pears, drain well.)

Prepare the pastry cream: Use the above ingredients and follow the directions on page 183. Add the ground almonds along with the cornstarch, instead of the flour. Let cool to room temperature. Transfer the cooled pastry cream to a bowl. Add the kirsch and whisk until smooth. Add the softened butter, little by little, whisking after each addition.

Fit a pastry bag with a medium star tip and fill it with the pastry cream. Starting at the center and working in a spiral pattern, pipe the pastry cream over the bottom of the cooked tart shell. Reserve a little pastry cream for final decoration. Cut the pear halves crosswise into thin slices, but keep the slices together. Gently press down on each sliced half with a metal spatula or the palm of your hand to spread the slices. Lift the pear halves onto the pastry cream with the spatula and arrange them in a circle so that the stem ends meet in the center. Pipe the remaining pastry cream decoratively in between each pear and around the inside edge of the tart. Pipe a rosette of pastry cream in the center of the tart.

Prepare the apricot glaze: Work the apricot jam through a fine sieve with the back of a spoon into a heavy-bottomed saucepan. Whisk in 1 to 2 tablespoons of water as needed to thin the jam. Cook over low heat until smooth and liquid. Remove from heat and add the kirsch. Using a pastry brush, pat the pears and pastry cream lightly with the glaze. Refrigerate and serve cold on a doily-lined platter.

LESSON 36

Pain de Petits Pois Frais à la Crème de Cives
TERRINE OF FRESH GREEN PEAS WITH CHIVE CREAM SAUCE

Sole Bercy
SOLE BAKED IN WHITE WINE

Pêches Flambées
FLAMBÉED PEACHES IN MERINGUE SHELLS

Pain de Petits Pois Frais à la Crème de Cives
TERRINE OF FRESH GREEN PEAS WITH CHIVE CREAM SAUCE

SERVES 6

This fresh pea loaf is a modern alternative to classic meat pâtés. Made with cooked, pureed vegetables and egg-enriched béchamel, it can be served either hot or cold. The loaf is garnished with miniature bouquets made of string beans tied with a "ribbon" of bell pepper. The result is a stunningly colorful display and a subtle symphony of tastes.

Other vegetables could be prepared exactly like the peas described here. An equal weight of cauliflower could be used to make an ivory-colored loaf or carrots could be cooked and pureed to make a spectacular orange terrine.

The same herb-flavored sauce used with the peas can be served with almost any vegetable-based terrine. Only fresh herbs should be used and, though a little fresh tarragon is added at Le Cordon Bleu, if this is unavailable, we recommend omitting the tarragon completely and increasing the amount of chives rather than using a dehydrated substitute.

Note: The terrine may be made and refrigerated for 1 to 2 days before serving.

(continued)

Pain de Petits Pois Frais à la Crème de Cives (continued)

Salt

2¹/₂ pounds green peas, shelled,
about 3¹/₂ cups or
2 ten-ounce frozen packages

1 cup fresh bread crumbs

BÉCHAMEL

1¹/₂ tablespoons unsalted butter

3 tablespoons all-purpose flour

²/₃ cup milk

Pinch freshly grated nutmeg

Salt and white pepper

3 egg yolks

2 egg whites

¹/₂ pound green beans

1 small red bell pepper,
cut into ¹/₈-inch julienne
(technique photo page 519)

CHIVE CREAM SAUCE

1¹/₄ cups crème fraîche or
heavy cream

Salt and freshly ground pepper

Juice of ¹/₂ lemon, strained

1 tablespoon chopped fresh chives

1 tablespoon chopped fresh
chervil or parsley

1 tablespoon chopped fresh
tarragon

Chopped chives for garnish

Unsalted butter, melted,
for loaf pans and
parchment paper

EQUIPMENT: 2 loaf pans, 7 by 2³/₄ by 2¹/₂ inches

Bring a large saucepan of salted water to a boil. Add the peas, return to a boil, and cook until tender, 8 to 10 minutes; drain. Puree in a food mill or food processor; set aside.

Preheat the oven to 450°. Brush the pans with the melted butter. Line the bottoms with parchment paper and brush the paper well with butter. Coat the insides of both pans with bread crumbs; tap out the excess.

Make a béchamel, using the above ingredients and following the directions on page 18. Remove the béchamel from the heat and stir in the egg yolks, one at a time. Return the pan to the heat and bring to a boil, stirring. Remove from the heat and stir in the puree of peas; set aside.

Beat the egg whites with a whisk or electric mixer until stiff peaks form. Whisk about one-third of the beaten whites into the hot puree mixture. Gently fold in the remainder with a wooden spoon or spatula.

Fill the loaf pans to within ¹/₂ inch of the tops with the mixture. Set the pans in a roasting pan and pour in hot water to come about halfway up the sides of the loaf pans. Bring to a simmer on top of the stove. Cut 2 strips of parchment paper. Butter them and lay them over the pans. Lower the oven temperature to 400° and bake the terrines until the blade of a knife inserted into the centers comes out clean and hot to the touch, 40 to 45 minutes. Cool on a rack for about 15 minutes.

Meanwhile, snap the ends off the green beans and cut into pieces about 2 inches long. Bring a saucepan of salted water to a boil. Add the beans, return to a boil, and cook until crisp-tender, 8 to 10 minutes. Drain, refresh under cold water and drain again. Set aside. Cook the julienned red peppers the same way.

Prepare the chive sauce: Bring the cream to a simmer in a small saucepan over medium heat. Season to taste with salt and pepper. Stir in the lemon juice. Bring to a boil and cook 3 to 4 minutes. Remove from the heat and stir in the herbs. Cover to keep warm.

To serve, unmold the terrine: Slide the blade of a knife around the edge of each loaf pan. Invert onto a long platter so that the terrines lie diagonally on the platter. Tap the bottom of each pan to release the terrine, then remove the pans and peel off the papers. Spoon a little sauce around the terrines. Sprinkle the tops with chopped chives and garnish the platter with small, evenly sized bundles of green beans. Place a strip of red bell pepper around the middle of each bundle, to "tie" them. Serve the remaining sauce in a sauceboat on the side. (For individual serving, see photo on page 202.)

Sole Bercy
SOLE BAKED IN WHITE WINE

SERVES 6

Most of the wine sold in Paris once passed through the warehouses in the neighborhood called Bercy; hence certain wine-based sauces or dishes using wine as a cooking medium are called Bercy. In this Cordon Bleu recipe, sole is baked with white wine, then removed from the pan, and the juices that remain are turned into a light sauce. Any small flatfish or firm white-fleshed fish, such as snapper or grouper, can be cooked like the sole.

6 whole sole, 8 ounces each
2 large shallots, chopped fine
1 tablespoon chopped parsley
Salt and freshly ground pepper
1 cup dry white wine
3/4 cup Fish Stock (page 181)
2 tablespoons unsalted butter, softened

1/4 cup all-purpose flour
1 lemon, fluted (page 65), halved lengthwise, and sliced

Unsalted butter, softened, for pan and parchment paper

Clean the sole (see directions on page 65 and technique photos on page 527). Preheat the oven to 425°. Brush a large ovenproof pan with the softened butter and sprinkle with the shallots, parsley, salt and pepper. Place the fish in the pan, white-skin side down, and season with salt and pepper. Add the wine and fish stock. Cover with a buttered piece of parchment paper, buttered side down. Bake until the point of a knife pierces the flesh easily, 12 to 15 minutes.

When tender, carefully transfer the fish to a work surface; reserve the cooking liquid. With the point of a knife, remove the small bones that run around the edge of each sole. Arrange the fish on a serving platter. Cover with aluminum foil to keep warm.

Mash the butter and flour to a paste. (This is known as *beurre manié* or kneaded butter.) Strain the reserved cooking liquid into a small saucepan and bring to a boil. Whisk in one-half of the beurre manié, bit by bit, until smooth. Cook, whisking, until the sauce boils and is thick enough to coat the back of a spoon. If it needs further thickening, add beurre manié until the sauce reaches the desired consistency. Adjust seasonings.

To serve, spoon the sauce over the fish and garnish with the fluted half-slices of lemon. Serve with boiled potatoes or rice.

Pêches Flambées
FLAMBÉED PEACHES IN MERINGUE SHELLS

SERVES 6

Meringue is not simply a topping for pies. In France it is often piped into various shapes, baked, and used for making layer cakes or, as in this recipe, edible baskets in which a variety of desserts can be served.

This recipe includes descriptions of several important techniques and demonstrates how nougatine, an element found in many desserts, is made and used.

FRENCH MERINGUE

3 egg whites

1/2 cup granulated sugar

1 cup confectioner's sugar, plus additional for dusting

3 ripe medium peaches

1/4 cup cognac

NOUGATINE

1 cup sugar

1/2 cup water

1/2 teaspoon lemon juice

5 ounces almonds, chopped coarsely

1 teaspoon unsalted butter

CHANTILLY CREAM

2 cups heavy cream

5 tablespoons confectioner's sugar

1 teaspoon vanilla extract

Vegetable oil for baking sheet and spatula

Unsalted butter, softened, for baking sheets

EQUIPMENT: Pastry bags, medium plain pastry tip

Chill a mixing bowl for the Chantilly cream.

Brush a baking sheet lightly with the softened butter. Cover with parchment paper. Cut a circle about 4 inches in diameter from a thin piece of cardboard and use it to trace 6 circles on the parchment paper.

Prepare the meringue: Beat the egg whites with a whisk or electric mixer until fluffy but not stiff. Gradually beat in the granulated sugar and then continue beating until stiff peaks form again and the meringue is glossy and smooth. Fold in the 1 cup confectioner's sugar with a wooden spoon. Fit a pastry bag with the medium plain tip and fill with two-thirds of the meringue. Set the remainder aside.

Prepare the meringue baskets (see technique photo on page 551): Heat the oven to 200°. Starting at the center of each circle and working outward in a spiral fashion, pipe the meringue to fill each circle on the baking sheet. Fit a second pastry bag with the medium star tip and fill with the remaining meringue. Pipe a raised border around the edge of each meringue round. Dust generously with confectioner's sugar. Transfer to the oven and bake the meringues until dry, 4 to 6 hours. (The meringue may be prepared in advance and kept in an airtight container for several days.)

Skin the peaches (page 9). Cut them in half and remove the pits.

Put the peach halves in a heatproof container. Heat the cognac in a small saucepan, then light it with a match and pour it flaming over the peaches. Let cool to room temperature. Refrigerate until serving time.

Prepare the nougatine: Brush a baking sheet and a metal spatula generously with oil. Combine the sugar, water and lemon juice in a small saucepan. Bring to a boil over low heat, stirring to dissolve the sugar. Then boil, without stirring, until the sugar caramelizes to a golden brown. Remove from the heat, add the almonds and stir in the butter. Pour immediately onto the oiled baking sheet and spread evenly in a thin layer over the sheet with the oiled metal spatula. Let cool until hardened. Wrap in a dish towel and crush coarsely with a rolling pin, or coarsely grind in a food processor. Do not reduce to a powder.

Not more than 1 hour before serving, prepare the Chantilly cream: Use the above ingredients and follow the directions on page 21. Fit a pastry bag with the medium star tip and fill with cream; refrigerate until serving time.

To serve, transfer the meringues to a doily-lined platter. Pipe a bed of Chantilly cream rosettes into each meringue and sprinkle with 1 teaspoon of crushed nougatine. Top each with a peach half, round side up. Pipe a rosette of Chantilly cream on top of each peach and sprinkle with nougatine.

NOUGATINE

Nougatine, made with caramel and chopped nuts, is tremendously versatile. It may be crushed for use as a topping (Pêches Flambées, above), cut into shapes, or, in the hands of a skilled pastry chef, it may be worked while still warm to form decorative shapes or containers for dessert fillings.

When working with nougatine, make sure that your baking sheet and knives, if you will be cutting the nougatine, are well coated with oil to prevent it from sticking. If you plan to cut or mold the nougatine you must work quickly to shape it before it hardens; if it does harden, simply return it to the pan briefly to remelt it.

(See also Praline, page 371.)

LESSON 37

*Feuilletés de Poireaux à la
Confiture d'Oignon*

PUFF PASTRIES WITH LEEKS AND ONION RELISH

—

Cailles à la Normande

QUAIL WITH CREAM AND APPLES

—

Soufflé au Chocolat

CHOCOLATE SOUFFLÉ

Feuilletés de Poireaux à la Confiture d'Oignon

PUFF PASTRIES WITH LEEKS AND ONION RELISH

SERVES 6

Puff pastry is a magical dough. A flour-water dough is combined with butter in an unusual way to produce countless paper-thin, buttery layers of the flakiest pastry imaginable. Few people succeed in making puff pastry on their first attempt, but once the method of rolling and folding the dough has been mastered, it quickly becomes second nature.

In France, puff pastry has traditionally been used for sweet desserts but, especially in recent years, chefs have taken to serving puff pastry rectangles *(feuilletés)* filled with vegetables or fish as starters. This Cordon Bleu recipe illustrates one such use of this very special dough.

PUFF PASTRY
1 1/2 cups all-purpose flour
3/4 cup cake flour
1 teaspoon salt
2/3 to 3/4 cup cold water
2 tablespoons melted
unsalted butter
14 tablespoons unsalted butter
1 egg, slightly beaten, for glazing

6 tablespoons unsalted butter
1 pound onions, sliced thin
1/2 cup red-wine vinegar
1/4 cup sugar
Salt and freshly ground pepper
2 pounds leeks
1/2 cup heavy cream
Chervil or parsley leaves
(optional), for garnish

Unsalted butter, softened
for baking sheet

Prepare the pastry (see technique photos on pages 542–43): Combine the flours in a mound on a cool work surface. Make a well in the center. Add the salt, 2/3 cup water, and melted butter to the well and mix with your fingertips, until the salt dissolves. Then use a plastic pastry scraper to pull the flour little by little into the well, and mix until blended, adding the remaining water if the dough is dry. Work the dough quickly into a ball with the pastry scraper (the dough will be slightly sticky). Make an X-shaped incision on top of the dough, wrap in a lightly floured dish towel or parchment paper, and refrigerate for about 30 minutes. (This is the *détrempe*.)

Sandwich the remaining 14 tablespoons butter between 2 sheets of parchment or waxed paper and tap with a rolling pin until softened to the same consistency as the *détrempe*. Form the butter into a square about 3/4 inch thick.

Set the chilled ball of dough on a lightly floured work surface and flatten slightly with the palm of your hand. Then press the rolling pin into the top edge of the dough and roll out an "arm." Give the dough a quarter turn and roll out another arm. Continue to turn and roll twice more until the dough is in the shape of a cross. It should be mounded in the center, tapering out to the four arms. Place the square of butter on the mounded center and fold in the arms, stretching the dough slightly as needed, to completely seal in the butter. (The four thicknesses of dough on the top should be approximately the same thickness as the mound of dough under the butter.) Lightly tap the top of the dough with a rolling pin to seal the edges and to enlarge and flatten the square a little. (This is the *pâton*.)

Roll out the pâton to a long rectangle about 7 inches wide and 21 inches long. Fold the bottom third of the rectangle up toward the center, carefully aligning the edges, and brush off any flour. Fold the top third down to make a neat square, and brush off any flour. Give the square a quarter turn to the left so that the folds are at the sides. Always rotate the dough in the same direction so that the seam is always on the same side. Roll the dough out again to a long rectangle, and fold again into thirds. Gently press two fingertips into the dough to indicate that 2 turns have been completed, wrap in a lightly floured dish towel, or parchment paper, and refrigerate 30 minutes.

Give the dough 2 more turns. Then mark it with 4 fingerprints to indicate that a total of four turns have been completed. Rewrap the dough and return it to the refrigerator for another 30 minutes. (After 4 turns the dough may be refrigerated for 2 days or frozen.)

Give the dough another 2 turns and mark it with 6 fingerprints. Then wrap and refrigerate it for 10 more minutes before rolling out for shaping and baking.

Heat the oven to 400°. Brush a baking sheet with the softened butter and sprinkle it with cold water.

Prepare the feuilletés (see technique photos on page 544): Dust a work surface with flour. Roll out the dough to a thickness of ⅛ inch and cut it into six 6-by-3-inch rectangles. Transfer the rectangles to the baking sheet with a metal spatula. Brush with the egg glaze but do not let the glaze run over the edges of the dough or it will not rise evenly. Bake until crisp and golden, about 30 minutes. Let cool on a rack.

Prepare the fillings: Heat 3 tablespoons of butter in a large frying pan over low heat. Add the onions, cover and cook until golden. Add the vinegar, sugar, and salt and pepper to taste, and cook, uncovered, until the onions are reduced to a puree; set aside.

Cut the green tops off the leeks and discard. Cut off and discard the stringy root ends. Rinse the white of the leek carefully to remove any sand and slice into a fine julienne about 2 inches long (see technique photo on page 519). Heat the remaining 3 tablespoons butter in a large frying pan over low heat. Add the leeks and stir to coat with the butter and then cook until tender but not colored. Add the cream, season to taste with salt and pepper and cook until the cream has thickened, about 5 more minutes.

To serve, cut each feuilleté rectangle in half horizontally. Spread the bottom half with a layer of onions and then with a layer of leeks. Cover with the pastry tops. Transfer to a serving platter and garnish with chervil leaves, if desired.

PÂTE FEUILLETÉE

A well-made puff pastry is one of the great delights of the French kitchen. Buttery, flaky, and rich without being heavy, it is hardly more difficult than simple shortcrust pastry but always impressive.

The principle behind the pastry is to create many (several hundred, actually) layers of dough and butter by folding or turning the two together. (Unlike short pastry, the butter is not incorporated into the dough but rather folded into it in layers.) You start by mixing flour, water, salt, and a very little butter to make the *détrempe*. Then an amount of butter equal to the weight of the *détrempe* is pounded and softened (not melted) to the same consistency so that when the two are rolled together the butter will not tear the dough. The softened butter is encased in the *détrempe* and then the resulting dough, called a *pâton,* is rolled out to a long rectangle, folded in thirds, turned one-quarter turn, then rolled and folded again. These double turns are performed twice more, with time in between for the dough to rest and lose the elasticity which would make it tough. For maximum rising, it is important always to rotate the dough in the same direction each time you turn it; the seam must be on the same side each time. Finally the dough is rolled out to a thin sheet (a thick dough will not rise well and will be heavy) and cut into rounds or rectangles for the specific recipe.

It is crucial that the butter not melt while the dough is worked. Therefore, you must work as quickly as possible (particularly if your kitchen is hot) and on as cold a surface as possible. Professional pastry chefs use a refrigerated marble. You need not go that far, but if it is a warm day you may want to cool the surface periodically with a large container of ice. And since you want an evenly layered pastry, it is important that you always roll it to the same thickness and that the edges be very straight and even (admittedly this will take some practice!).

Puff pastry dough is best stored after 4 turns. Wrap it carefully and refrigerate for up to 2 days (or freeze it). When you are ready to use the dough, let it sit briefly at room temperature to warm it slightly, then complete the last 2 turns and roll it out to the desired shape. (See technique photos on pages 542-43.)

Cailles à la Normande
QUAIL WITH CREAM AND APPLES

SERVES 6

Originally game birds, quail are now farmed and available the year round in France. Here, each bird is wrapped in a thin strip of pork fat to keep the delicate breast meat from drying out during roasting. The quail are presented on individual croutons, garnished with apples, and served with a typically Norman cream sauce flavored with a dash of apple brandy.

*6 quail, necks removed
    and reserved
Salt and freshly ground pepper
1 thin slice fatback, 12 by
    5 inches (see Note, page 139)
6 small Golden Delicious apples
1/2 lemon
5 tablespoons unsalted butter,
    melted
6 slices firm white bread*

*3 tablespoons unsalted butter
2 tablespoons Calvados or
    domestic apple brandy
1/2 cup crème fraîche or
    heavy cream
1/4 cup Brown Veal Stock
    (page 71)
1 tablespoon sugar
1 tablespoon chopped parsley*

Prepare the quail: Season the cavities of the quail with salt and pepper. Cut the fatback into six 2-by-5-inch rectangles. Place the quail, breast side up, on a work surface. Wrap a piece of fatback around each breast and tie with kitchen twine.

Preheat the oven to 400°.

Peel and core the apples. Pare down to about 2 inches in diameter with a small knife. Rub the apples with the cut side of the lemon to prevent darkening. Brush with 2 tablespoons of the melted butter and transfer to a baking sheet. Bake until tender and lightly golden, about 15 minutes. Remove from the oven and set aside.

Reduce the oven heat to 375°.

Prepare the croutons: Cut the bread slices into rounds with a 4-inch cookie cutter. Brush both sides with the remaining 3 tablespoons melted butter. Transfer to a baking sheet and bake until golden brown, 10 to 15 minutes. Set aside.

Heat 3 tablespoons butter in a roasting pan over high heat. Add the quail and the necks and cook, turning occasionally, until the quail are lightly browned. Set the quail on their backs, slide a neck under each quail, and season with salt and pepper. Transfer to the oven and roast for 20 to 25 minutes. Remove the quail from the roasting pan to a warm platter. Cover with aluminum foil to keep warm.

Discard the fat from the roasting pan. Add the Calvados and carefully light with a match. When the flames die, whisk in the crème fraîche and the stock. Cook over medium heat until the sauce thickens and coats the back of a spoon. Remove the necks from the sauce.

To serve, heat the broiler. Sprinkle the apples with the sugar and broil for about 2 minutes until slightly caramelized. Remove the twine and the fat from the quail. Place the croutons on a serving platter and place a quail on top of each. Spoon a little of the sauce over the quail. Arrange the apples around the quail and sprinkle with chopped parsley. Serve the remaining sauce in a sauceboat on the side.

Soufflé au Chocolat
CHOCOLATE SOUFFLÉ

———

SERVES 6

Invented in France in the eighteenth century, soufflés of all kinds were served in restaurants and described in cookbooks in the century that followed. They quickly became a culinary emblem of France.

In recent years their popularity has declined, and though there is still one restaurant in Paris that serves only soufflés, they tend to be made more in homes nowadays and are limited to a few favorite flavors—like the ever popular chocolate soufflé students learn to make at Le Cordon Bleu.

CHOCOLATE PASTRY CREAM
*4 ounces semisweet chocolate,
  chopped into small pieces*
2 cups milk
1 teaspoon vanilla extract
4 egg yolks
1/2 cup sugar
7 tablespoons all-purpose flour

6 egg whites
Confectioner's sugar for dusting

*Unsalted butter, softened, and
  sugar for soufflé mold*

EQUIPMENT: 9-inch or 6-cup soufflé mold

Brush the soufflé mold generously with the softened butter and coat with sugar; tap out the excess. Refrigerate until needed.

Preheat the oven to 425°.

Prepare the chocolate pastry cream: Bring 1 to 2 inches of water just to a simmer in a saucepan. Put the chocolate in a heatproof bowl and set it over the pan of simmering water. Let stand, without stirring, until the chocolate has completely melted. While the chocolate is melting, prepare a classic pastry cream, using the above ingredients and following the directions on page 183. Whisk the melted chocolate into the hot pastry cream; keep warm.

Beat the egg whites with a whisk or electric mixer until stiff peaks form. Stir one-third into the hot pastry cream to lighten it and then gently fold in the remainder with a spatula. Pour into the prepared soufflé mold and bake 15 minutes. Reduce the heat to 375° and bake until the soufflé is puffed and firm to the touch, about 15 minutes longer.

Sift confectioner's sugar over the top and serve immediately.

Cocktail d'Avocat et de Langoustines

LANGOUSTINE AND AVOCADO SALAD

———

Colombo de Porc Frais

CURRIED PORK WITH BANANAS AND COCONUT

———

Coupe Glacée Créole

LIME SORBET WITH FRESH PINEAPPLE

INTERMÉDIAIRE

Cocktail d'Avocat et de Langoustines

LANGOUSTINE AND AVOCADO SALAD

SERVES 6

A cocktail, be it a drink or a salad, is generally a mixture of colorful elements. In this case a slightly tart avocado puree surrounds a mound of peeled and seeded tomatoes topped with freshly cooked langoustines and carefully cut grapefruit wedges. This pleasing juxtaposition of tastes is a refined French cousin of the familiar shrimp cocktail so popular in the U.S.

Note: At Le Cordon Bleu students cook fresh langoustines when making this salad, but large boiled shrimp could be used instead.

COURT BOUILLON
1 carrot, chopped coarse
1 onion, chopped coarse
1 clove garlic, crushed
1 Bouquet Garni (page 20)
10 peppercorns
Salt
1/2 cup white-wine vinegar
8 cups water

24 whole, unpeeled langoustines
    (see page 114)
    or large shrimp
3 grapefruit
8 avocados
1 teaspoon white-wine vinegar
Salt and freshly ground pepper
3 medium tomatoes, peeled,
    seeded, and diced (page 31)
Chervil or parsley sprigs,
    for garnish

Prepare the court bouillon: Combine all of the ingredients in a large saucepan. Bring to a boil and boil 5 minutes. Reduce the heat, add the langoustines or shrimp and simmer 3 minutes. Remove the pan from the heat and let the langoustines cool in the court bouillon.

Peel and section 2 of the grapefruit (page 9). Squeeze the juice from the third grapefruit into a small bowl.

Peel, pit, and puree 2 of the avocados in a food mill or food processor. Transfer the puree to a bowl and slowly whisk in the grapefruit juice and vinegar. Season to taste with salt and pepper.

Put the diced tomato into a bowl and season with salt and pepper.

Carefully peel the langoustine tails, leaving the heads attached (see technique photos on page 523).

To serve, peel, halve and pit the 6 remaining avocados. Slice each half into long thin sections. Counting one avocado per plate, arrange the slices like the spokes of a wheel, with the ends meeting in the center, on each of 6 plates. Spoon a thin ring of avocado puree around the edge of the plate and place a small mound of diced tomato in the center. Place 2 grapefruit sections on each mound of tomatoes. Arrange 4 langoustines on top of the avocado and garnish each plate with a sprig of chervil.

Colombo de Porc Frais

CURRIED PORK WITH BANANAS AND COCONUT

SERVES 6

France not only exported its cuisine to its colonies but imported a number of dishes in return. This Caribbean dish is a standard in Parisian restaurants specializing in the cooking of the French West Indies. The name of the dish, "colombo," is also the name of the spice mixture (similar to curry powder) used to give this dish its characteristic taste.

1/4 cup vegetable oil
3 1/2 pounds lean, boneless pork,
    cut into 1-inch cubes
1 pound onions, diced fine
2 medium red bell peppers,
    diced fine
5 tablespoons curry powder
2 sprigs thyme or 1/4 teaspoon
    dried
1 bay leaf
2 tablespoons chopped fresh ginger
4 cloves garlic, chopped
Salt and freshly ground pepper
1/2 cup flaked coconut
4 bananas, cut into chunks

RICE PILAF

3 tablespoons unsalted butter
1 onion, chopped fine
1 red bell pepper, chopped fine
1 1/2 cups long-grain rice
1/4 cup flaked coconut
3 cups water
1 clove garlic, crushed
1 Bouquet Garni (page 20)

Salt and freshly ground pepper

Heat the oil in a large flameproof casserole over high heat. Add the pork and cook until browned. Add the diced onions and red peppers and cook, stirring frequently, until the onions are soft but not colored, about 10 minutes. Stir in the curry powder, thyme, bay leaf, ginger, chopped garlic, salt and pepper, and the flaked coconut. Add water to cover and bring to a boil. Reduce the heat, cover and simmer, stirring occasionally, for 1 hour. Stir in the bananas, and cook until the pork is tender, about 30 minutes longer.

Prepare a rice pilaf: Preheat the oven to 375°. Heat the butter in an ovenproof frying pan over medium heat. Add the onion and red pepper and cook, stirring frequently, until the vegetables are soft but not colored. Stir in the rice and cook, stirring frequently, until translucent. Stir in the coconut, the water, the crushed garlic clove and the bouquet garni. Season with salt and pepper. Bring to a boil, cover with a tight-fitting lid, transfer to the oven and cook 17 minutes. Let stand, covered, about 5 minutes.

To serve, remove the bouquet garni, separate the grains of rice with a fork, and transfer to a serving dish. Spoon the pork onto a deep platter and serve with the pilaf.

Coupe Glacée Créole
LIME SORBET WITH FRESH PINEAPPLE

SERVES 6

Any dessert labeled *Créole* or *à la Créole* in France contains rum. In this case, fresh pineapple is marinated in white rum, then used to decorate scoops of lime sorbet served in the hollowed-out pineapple shell. It is a particularly refreshing tropical conclusion to this sunny Caribbean meal.

SUGAR SYRUP
1¹/₂ cups water
1¹/₂ cups sugar
¹/₂ teaspoon vanilla extract

³/₄ cup lime juice, strained
1 egg white, lightly beaten
1 pineapple (about 1³/₄ pounds)
¹/₄ cup white rum
Zest of 1 lime, cut into julienne
   (see technique photo 519)

EQUIPMENT: Ice cream maker

Chill a mixing bowl in the freezer for the sorbet.

Prepare the sugar syrup: Combine the water, sugar, and vanilla in a small saucepan. Bring to a boil over low heat, stirring to dissolve the sugar. Boil 1 to 2 minutes. Cool the syrup over crushed ice.

Add the lime juice to the cooled sugar syrup. Transfer to an ice cream maker and freeze according to the manufacturer's instructions for about 15 minutes. Add the egg white and continue freezing until firm. Transfer to the chilled bowl and freeze, at least 1 hour.

Meanwhile, trim the brown tips off the pineapple leaves with scissors, if necessary. Then hollow out the pineapple: Cut the pineapple in half lengthwise with a serrated knife. Cut down the length of the central core of one half of the pineapple, without cutting through the rind. Then, insert the knife between the rind and the flesh and cut around the inside of the rind to release the flesh in two pieces. Repeat for the other half of the fruit. Dry the insides of the pineapple shells with paper towels. Invert on a rack and freeze until serving time.

Cut the hard central core from the pineapple flesh. Slice the pineapple quarters crosswise ¹/₈ inch thick, and then cut the slices into thirds to make small triangles. Put the fruit into a container and add the rum. Let macerate for about 1 hour in the refrigerator.

To serve, place the frozen pineapple shells on a platter. Mound scoops of the sorbet into the shells. Spike the sorbet with the pineapple triangles and sprinkle with the julienned lime zests. Serve any remaining pineapple in a dish on the side.

LESSON 39

Salade Niçoise

NIÇOISE SALAD

———

Pigeonneaux en Papillote

SQUAB COOKED IN PAPILLOTES

———

Tarte Tatin

CARAMELIZED APPLE TART

Salade Niçoise

NIÇOISE SALAD

———

SERVES 6

There are probably as many versions of salade Niçoise as there are cooks in Nice. Most include hard-boiled egg, lettuce, canned tuna, tomatoes, olives, and olive oil, but insofar as the other ingredients go, few cooks agree. Some will include artichokes, cucumber, sweet peppers, or fresh fava beans (or all four) in their salade Niçoise. Here is the Cordon Bleu recipe for this summertime favorite—as popular in Paris as on the Côte d'Azur.

4 small new potatoes
Salt
¼ pound green beans
3 medium tomatoes,
*   peeled (page 31)*
3 eggs, hard-boiled (page 16)

VINAIGRETTE
3 tablespoons white-wine vinegar
Salt and freshly ground pepper
3 tablespoons olive oil
6 tablespoons vegetable oil

*¹/₂ green bell pepper,
    cut into julienne
    (see technique photo 519)*
*¹/₂ red bell pepper,
    cut into julienne*
1 head butter lettuce

7-ounce can tuna fish, drained
*8 oil-packed anchovy fillets,
    drained*
1 red onion, sliced thin
*8 black olives (preferably Niçoise
    or Kalamata), pitted*

Rinse the potatoes but do not peel them. Put them in a saucepan with cold salted water to cover. Bring to a boil, reduce the heat and simmer until just tender when pierced with the point of a knife, about 15 minutes. Drain and refresh under cold running water. Let the potatoes cool to room temperature and then peel and slice them into thin rounds.

Snap the ends off the beans and cut them in half crosswise. Cook in boiling salted water until crisp-tender, about 10 minutes.

Cut the tomatoes and eggs into quarters.

Prepare the vinaigrette: Combine the vinegar, salt, and pepper in a small bowl and whisk to blend in the oils.

To serve, combine the potatoes, beans and peppers in a bowl. Toss with half the vinaigrette. Make a bed of lettuce on a serving platter and mound the mixed vegetables in the center. Flake the tuna fish over the vegetables. Cut the anchovy fillets in half lengthwise and arrange them in a lattice design on top of the tuna. Arrange the onion in rings around the base of the vegetables. Alternate tomato wedges and egg sections around the base of the salad. Garnish with the black olives. Spoon the remaining vinaigrette over the salad just before serving.

Pigeonneaux en Papillote
SQUAB COOKED IN PAPILLOTES

SERVES 6

Wrapping food in a parchment paper *papillote* is a very old cooking method in France. The flavors and aromas are intensified and kept intact until the papillotes are served and the seal is broken.

3 squab (about 1 pound each)
Salt and freshly ground pepper
4 tablespoons unsalted butter
1 tablespoon vegetable oil
1 shallot, chopped fine
14 ounces mushrooms, chopped fine

6 ounces cooked ham, chopped fine
1 egg white, beaten
*7 tablespoons unsalted butter,
    melted*

*Unsalted butter, softened,
    for baking sheet*

Prepare the squab (see technique photos on page 532): Cut off and reserve the neck and wing tips. Cut each squab in half lengthwise through the breastbone and backbone. Season both sides with salt and pepper. Heat 2 tablespoons butter and ½ tablespoon oil in a large frying pan over medium heat. Add the squab, skin side down, and cook, covered, for 10 minutes. Turn the squab over and continue cooking 2 to 3 more minutes. Remove the squab from the pan and set aside.

Prepare the sauce: Discard the fat from the pan. Add ½ cup water and bring it to a boil, scraping the bottom of the pan with a whisk to release any cooked particles. Reduce the heat to low and cook 2 to 3 minutes. Strain into a small saucepan and skim the fat. Set the sauce aside.

Preheat the oven to 400°. Brush a baking sheet with the softened butter.

Heat the remaining 2 tablespoons butter and ½ tablespoon oil in the same pan over medium heat. Add the shallot and cook until soft but not colored. Add the chopped mushrooms and cook, stirring occasionally, until all the moisture has evaporated. (This is known as a *duxelles*.) Stir in the ham and cook over low heat for 15 minutes. Season to taste with salt and pepper; set aside.

Prepare the papillotes (see technique photos on page 532): Cut out six 12-by-10-inch rectangles of parchment paper. Place each squab half, cut side down, on the lower half of each rectangle. Spoon 2 tablespoons of the duxelles mixture on top of each squab. Brush a ¼-inch border of beaten egg white along the edges of the lower half of the rectangle. Fold the upper half of the paper rectangle over the squab and align the edges. Brush all but the folded edge with a ¼-inch border of beaten egg white. Then fold up the border in 2-inch sections, incorporating the preceding fold into each new fold to make a strong seal. Brush the surface of the papillotes with melted butter. Brush the folded edges a second time with the egg white. Transfer to the baking sheet and bake until the packages are puffed and brown, about 15 minutes.

To serve, arrange the papillotes on a long serving platter. Reheat the sauce and serve it in a sauceboat on the side.

COOKING ''EN PAPILLOTE''

"En papillote" is a technique whereby the food is enclosed and cooked (often along with some liquid and an accompanying garnish) in a paper or foil package so that it steams gently in its own juices. It is a wonderful way to cook delicate foods (fish, poultry, and veal are especially good this way). And it is a treat for your guests, each of whom is greeted by the aroma of the captured juices when he opens his individual package at the table.

Either parchment paper or aluminum foil may be used for cooking en papillote, but the parchment makes a much nicer presentation at the table. It is important to seal the package tight so that the steam does not escape: Make sure that each fold incorporates the preceding one so that there are no gaps. Egg white brushed over the edges further helps the seal. (See technique photos on page 532.)

Tarte Tatin

CARAMELIZED APPLE TART

—

SERVES 6

This legendary apple pie, baked upside down but served downside up, was created around the turn of the century by the Demoiselles Tatin in their hotel-restaurant in Sologne. It has become so popular that special high-sided heavy copper *Tatin* pans are now sold especially for making this dessert.

At Le Cordon Bleu, caramel is poured into the cake pan before the apples are put into place, and the finished tart is coated with a little extra caramel to give it a candied look and ensure perfectly delicious results.

PÂTE BRISÉE SUCRÉE

1 cup all-purpose flour

1/2 cup cake flour

1 egg

1 1/2 teaspoons cold water

Pinch salt

2 tablespoons sugar

1 teaspoon vanilla extract

6 tablespoons softened butter

*2 1/2 pounds Pippin or
   Golden Delicious apples
   (about 7 apples)*

Juice of 1 lemon, strained

CARAMEL BUTTER

1/3 cup sugar

1 tablespoon water

*4 tablespoons unsalted butter,
   softened*

1/2 cup sugar

1/4 cup water

*Unsalted butter, softened,
   for cake pan*

EQUIPMENT: 9-inch round cake pan, 2 to 3 inches deep

Prepare the pâte brisée sucrée just as you would a pâte brisée: Use the above ingredients and follow the directions on pages 37–38 and technique photos on page 540, but add the sugar and the vanilla to the well along with the egg, water, and salt. Chill.

Peel and core the apples and cut them into halves or quarters, depending on the size of the fruit. Brush with lemon juice to prevent darkening.

Preheat the oven to 400°. Brush the cake pan with the softened butter.

Prepare the caramel butter: Combine the sugar and water in a small heavy-bottomed saucepan. Bring to a boil over low heat, stirring to dissolve the sugar. Then boil, without stirring, until caramelized to a golden brown color. Remove from the heat and add the butter (this will cause the caramel to foam). Stir until blended and pour into the cake pan. Rotate the pan to coat the bottom evenly with the caramel. Put two apple halves, upright, in the center of the cake pan. Arrange the remaining apple halves, upright, in a circle around them (see photo on page 221).

Roll out the dough 1/8 inch thick. Cut out a round of dough 9 1/2 inches in diameter and drape it over the apples, leaving a gap of about 1/2 to 1 inch between the edge of the dough and the edge of the cake pan to allow the steam to escape. Bake until the crust is golden brown and the apples are tender when pierced with a knife, about 35 minutes. Let cool on a rack for 10 to 15 minutes.

To unmold, invert a shallow round dessert platter over the crust. Carefully; tilt the pan to pour out any liquid into a bowl set the liquid aside. Carefully reverse the pan and dessert platter and then lift off the pan. If the apples are not evenly caramelized, broil for a few minutes, being careful not to burn the crust.

Combine the sugar and the water in a small saucepan. Bring to a boil over low heat, stirring to dissolve the sugar, then boil, without stirring, until caramelized to a golden brown color. Remove from the heat and carefully add the reserved cooking liquid from the apples (this will cause the caramel to foam). Return the mixture to a low heat and simmer, stirring, until syrupy. Pour over the tart.

Serve warm, accompanied by a bowl of crème fraîche, if you wish.

LESSON 40

Soufflé aux Épinards

SPINACH SOUFFLÉ

———

Coq au Vin

CHICKEN STEWED IN RED WINE

———

Sorbet aux Poires

PEAR SORBET

Soufflé aux Épinards

SPINACH SOUFFLÉ

———

SERVES 6

Spinach makes a delicious soufflé for the fall or winter months; traditionally it is flavored only with a little salt, pepper, and nutmeg, but some people like to coat the inside of the mold with grated Parmesan along with the butter since it combines nicely with this vegetable's earthy taste.

4 tablespoons unsalted butter
1 pound spinach, stemmed, rinsed,
*   and chopped coarse*
Salt
2 tablespoons all-purpose flour
1 cup cold milk

Freshly ground pepper
1/4 teaspoon freshly grated nutmeg
3 eggs, separated

Unsalted butter, softened,
*   for soufflé mold*

EQUIPMENT: 9-inch soufflé mold

Brush the interior of the soufflé mold with the softened butter. Refrigerate for at least 20 minutes.

Heat 2 tablespoons of butter in a large frying pan over high heat. Add the spinach and cook, stirring frequently, until the moisture has evaporated. Season to taste with salt.

(continued)

Soufflé aux Épinards (continued)

Heat the oven to 425°.

In a medium, heavy-bottomed saucepan heat the remaining 2 tablespoons of butter over low heat. Whisk in the flour and cook, whisking, for 2 minutes without coloring. Remove from the heat and add the milk, whisking constantly to avoid lumps. Return the pan to the heat and bring to a boil. Season to taste with salt, pepper and nutmeg.

Reduce the heat and simmer for 10 minutes, whisking constantly and scraping the bottom and sides of the pan to prevent the mixture from burning, until thick and smooth. Stir in the cooked spinach and cook 1 minute. Whisk in the egg yolks off the heat.

Beat the egg whites with a whisk or electric mixer until stiff peaks form. Stir one-third of the beaten whites into the hot spinach mixture and then gently fold in the remaining whites with a wooden spoon or spatula.

Remove the soufflé mold from the refrigerator and brush it with a second layer of butter. Pour in the soufflé mixture to within 1/4 inch of the top of the mold. Bake 15 minutes, reduce the oven heat to 375° and bake until the soufflé is puffed and firm to the touch, about 15 minutes longer. Serve immediately.

Coq au Vin

CHICKEN STEWED IN RED WINE

SERVES 6

Coq au vin literally means "rooster in wine," but tough old roosters have given way to tender roasting chickens in most French homes today. The bird is marinated overnight, then cooked in an aromatic mixture of red wine, onions, carrots, crushed peppercorns, and thyme. Country cooks would add pearl onions, bacon, and mushrooms directly to the pot with the chicken, but at Le Cordon Bleu we prefer to cook the garnish separately so that each element retains more of its individual taste. Onions, mushrooms, and bacon are simmered in the strained cooking liquid for only 5 minutes before serving.

Note: Like many red-wine stews, *Coq au Vin* can be prepared ahead of time; kept refrigerated after serving, any left over will be even better the next day.

5-pound chicken

MARINADE
2 carrots, sliced
2 onions, sliced
1 tomato, quartered
2 cloves garlic, crushed
3 sprigs fresh thyme or
    ½ teaspoon dried
1 bay leaf
10 sprigs parsley
1 stalk celery, sliced
20 peppercorns, crushed
6 cups dry red wine
    (preferably Bordeaux)
¼ cup cognac
¼ cup vegetable oil

8 tablespoons unsalted butter
6 tablespoons vegetable oil
⅓ cup all-purpose flour
Salt
9 ounces pearl onions, peeled
Freshly ground pepper
1 tablespoon sugar
10 ounces mushrooms, trimmed,
    rinsed, dried, and sliced thin
9 ounces slab bacon, sliced
    ¼ inch thick

HEART-SHAPED CROUTONS
8 slices firm white bread, crusts
    removed
4 tablespoons unsalted butter,
    melted
2 tablespoons chopped parsley

Unsalted butter, softened,
    for parchment paper

Cut the chicken into 6 serving pieces (see directions on pages 59–60 and technique photos on pages 530–31).

Prepare the marinade: Put the chicken pieces in a large, nonaluminum bowl together with the carrots, onions, tomato, garlic, thyme, bay leaf, parsley sprigs, celery, and peppercorns. Add the wine and cognac and drizzle the oil over the surface. Refrigerate and let marinate for 12 hours.

Preheat the oven to 425°.

Remove the chicken from the marinade and pat dry with paper towels; reserve the marinade and vegetables. Heat 3 tablespoons of the butter and ¼ cup of the oil in a large, ovenproof casserole over high heat. Add the chicken pieces, skin side down, and brown on both sides. Drain the vegetables and herbs from the marinade (reserve the liquid) and add to the pan with the chicken. Cook, stirring, until softened, about 5 minutes. Stir in the flour and cook 2 to 3 minutes. Add the reserved marinating liquid, season with salt and bring to a boil. Cover the casserole with a round of buttered parchment paper, buttered side down, and a lid. Transfer to the oven and cook until the chicken is tender, 30 to 40 minutes.

While the chicken is cooking, glaze the pearl onions: Put the pearl onions in a low-sided saucepan that will hold them in one layer, if possible, and add water to barely cover. Season with salt and pepper, 1 tablespoon butter, and the sugar and bring to a boil. Cover with a round of buttered parchment paper, buttered side down, reduce the heat, and simmer until barely tender, 8 to 10 minutes. Remove the paper and continue cooking until the liquid evaporates, about 10 more minutes. (Watch carefully here because the onions will burn easily.) Then lightly glaze the onions in the butter remaining in the pan, shaking the pan frequently. Set aside.

Heat 2 tablespoons of butter in a large frying pan over a high heat. Add the mushrooms and cook quickly until all the moisture has evaporated. Season to taste with salt and pepper. Add to the pan with the onions.

Cut the bacon into lardons; blanch and drain (page 46). Heat the remaining 2 tablespoons of oil and butter in a frying pan over high heat. Add the lardons and sauté until crisp and golden. Remove with a slotted spoon and add to the pan with the onions and mushrooms.

Prepare heart-shaped croutons from the bread slices, following the directions on page 165.

When the chicken is tender, remove from the casserole with a slotted spoon; set aside. Strain the cooking liquid, pressing down on the solids with the back of a wooden spoon or ladle to extract all of the liquid. Discard the solids. Return the strained liquid to the casserole, bring to a boil and skim off the fat. Return the chicken to the casserole along with the pearl onions, mushrooms and lardons and simmer gently for 5 minutes.

To serve, arrange the chicken pieces on a deep serving platter. Spoon the sauce over the onions, mushrooms and lardons. Dip the pointed end of the croutons first in the sauce and then in the chopped parsley. Arrange around the platter, parsley-dipped ends pointing outward (or serve as shown in the photo on page 225). Serve with Pommes à l'Anglaise (page 50) or Pâtes Fraîches (page 199), if desired.

Sorbet aux Poires

PEAR SORBET

SERVES 6

Pears are always poached before being turned into sorbet; nonetheless, only perfectly ripe fruit should be used. In France, a little lemon juice and pear brandy are added to the pears before freezing; giving the resulting sorbet a pleasantly grainy texture and an intense pear taste.

1 lemon
1¼ pounds ripe pears
1¾ cups water
1 cup sugar
1 teaspoon vanilla extract
Juice of 1 lemon, strained

3 tablespoons Poire William or domestic pear brandy
Mint sprigs for garnish
Fresh raspberries or red currants for garnish

EQUIPMENT: Ice cream maker

Chill a mixing bowl and 6 dessert glasses in the freezer for the sorbet.

Strip off an inch-wide length of lemon zest; set aside. Halve the lemon and reserve. Peel and quarter the pears. Cut out and discard the central cores. Rub with the reserved lemon to prevent darkening.

In a heavy-bottomed saucepan, combine the water, sugar, vanilla and the reserved strip of lemon zest. Bring to a boil over low heat, stirring to dissolve the sugar. Boil 1 to 2 minutes, then add the pears, reduce the heat, and simmer until the pears are tender when pierced with the point of a knife, about 20 minutes. Let the pears cool in the poaching liquid, then remove with a slotted spoon and puree in a food mill or food processor. Transfer the puree to a bowl and stir in 1 cup of the poaching liquid, the lemon juice, and the Poire William. Cool over ice. Transfer the mixture to an ice cream maker and freeze according to the manufacturer's instructions.

Transfer the sorbet to the chilled bowl and freeze until firm, at least 1 hour.

To serve, put 2 scoops of sorbet into each chilled dessert glass. Garnish each with a small branch of mint and a few raspberries or a small bunch of red currants. Serve immediately.

INTERMÉDIAIRE

LESSON 41

Omelette Portugaise
PORTUGUESE OMELET WITH TOMATOES AND ONIONS

———

Sauté de Veau Catalan
SAUTÉED VEAL WITH CHIPOLATAS,
OLIVES, AND CHESTNUTS

———

Pithiviers
ALMOND CREAM-FILLED PASTRY

Omelette Portugaise
PORTUGUESE OMELET WITH TOMATOES AND ONIONS

———

SERVES 6

A *sauce portugaise* is a tomato sauce that includes onions and garlic. Here the sauce is used both as filling for omelets and as a sauce to be served around them.

TOMATO SAUCE
1/4 cup olive oil
1 medium onion, chopped fine
2 cloves garlic, chopped fine
1 1/2 pounds tomatoes, peeled,
   seeded, and diced (page 31)
Several sprigs fresh thyme or
   1/2 teaspoon dried
Salt and freshly ground pepper

12 eggs
5 tablespoons unsalted butter
2 tablespoons chopped parsley

Unsalted butter, softened,
   for serving platter

EQUIPMENT: 8-inch frying pan (preferably nonstick)

Prepare the sauce: Heat the oil in a saucepan over low heat. Add the onion and cook until soft but not colored. Add the garlic and cook 1 minute. Stir in the tomatoes and thyme and season to taste with salt and pepper. Simmer, stirring occasionally, until most of the moisture has evaporated, about 15 minutes. Puree one half of the sauce in a food mill or food processor and reserve in a small saucepan. Set aside the other half of the sauce for the omelet filling; cover to keep warm. Butter an oval serving platter.

Prepare the omelet (see technique photos on page 522): Break the eggs into a bowl. Season with salt and pepper and blend lightly with a fork. Heat 2 tablespoons of the butter in the frying pan over medium heat until hot; do not let the butter brown. Pour in half the eggs and cook gently, stirring constantly with a wooden spoon. When the eggs begin to set but are still soft on top, spoon half of the tomato filling over the center of the omelet. Then, use a spatula to fold the edge of the omelet that is closest to the handle in toward the center (ideally you will fold the omelet into thirds). Lift up the folded edge of the omelet and slide ½ tablespoon of butter under it. Then, with your free hand, tap the handle of the pan sharply so that the far edge of the omelet slides up the side of the pan. Fold this edge in toward the center and continue cooking until the omelet is very lightly browned on the bottom, about 2 minutes.

Hold the buttered serving platter with one hand. Grasp the handle of the pan in the palm of the other hand, and turn the omelet out, seam side down, onto the platter. If necessary, shape the omelet into an even form.

Repeat to make a second omelet.

Rewarm the reserved tomato sauce and pour a ring around the omelets. Sprinkle each omelet with parsley.

Sauté de Veau Catalan
SAUTÉED VEAL WITH CHIPOLATAS, OLIVES, AND CHESTNUTS

SERVES 6-8

The former kingdom of Catalonia is now partially in France and partially in Spain. Barcelona is its capital on the Spanish side, Perpignon on the French. This hearty country dish evokes flavors typical of Catalan cooking.

Note: Chipolatas are small fresh finger-shaped pork sausages flavored with chives, coriander, and thyme.

4 pounds lean veal (preferably center roast), trimmed of fat and connective tissue
Salt and freshly ground pepper
¼ cup all-purpose flour
10 tablespoons unsalted butter
2 tablespoons vegetable oil

1 large onion, chopped
1 tablespoon tomato paste
1 cup dry white wine
1¾ cups Brown Veal Stock (page 71)
2 cloves garlic, crushed
1 Bouquet Garni (page 20)

*1 pound chipolatas or other
mild fresh pork sausages*

*1½ pounds tomatoes, peeled,
seeded, and diced (page 31)*

½ pound pitted green olives

*1¼ pounds whole, canned
unsweetened chestnuts*

HEART-SHAPED CROUTONS

*4 slices firm white bread,
crusts removed*

*3 tablespoons unsalted butter,
melted*

3 tablespoons chopped parsley

*Unsalted butter, melted,
for parchment paper*

Preheat the oven to 400°. Cut the veal into pieces about 1½ inches square. Season with salt and pepper. Flour lightly and shake off the excess.

Heat 3 tablespoons of the butter and 1 tablespoon of the oil in a large ovenproof frying pan over high heat. Add the veal cubes and brown quickly on all sides. Remove the meat from the pan and discard the fat. Reduce the heat to low. Add 3 tablespoons of the butter and 1 tablespoon oil. Add the onion and cook until soft but not colored. Return the veal to the pan along with the tomato paste and stir to blend. Add the wine, bring to a boil, and cook for 3 to 4 minutes. Add the stock, garlic, and bouquet garni and return to a boil. Cover the pan with a round of buttered parchment paper and a lid. Transfer to the oven and cook until the veal is tender when pierced with the point of a small knife, at least 1 hour. Remove the pan from the oven; set aside.

Meanwhile, heat 2 tablespoons of the butter in a large frying pan over medium heat. Add the sausages and cook, turning occasionally, until evenly browned, 5 to 10 minutes. Remove with a slotted spoon. Discard the fat. Put the remaining 2 tablespoons of butter into the same pan. Add the tomatoes and cook 3 to 4 minutes. Return the sausages to the pan along with the olives. Reduce the heat to low and cook 10 minutes. Add the chestnuts and cook for 10 to 15 minutes; set aside.

Prepare the croutons: Preheat the oven to 425°. Cut the bread in half, diagonally, to make triangles. With a small knife, round off the shortest sides of the triangles. Then, make V-shaped incisions midway between the rounded edges to make heart shapes; trim the hearts to even them. Or, cut the bread into heart shapes with a cookie cutter. Brush the hearts on both sides with melted butter and transfer to a baking sheet. Bake until golden, about 8 minutes.

When the veal is tender, remove and discard the garlic and the bouquet garni. The sauce should be just thick enough to coat the back of a spoon. If it is too thin, remove the veal with a slotted spoon and reduce the sauce over medium heat until it thickens. Return the veal to the pan. Carefully stir in the tomatoes, sausages, olives and chestnuts.

To serve, reheat the sauté if necessary. Spoon onto a long serving platter and sprinkle with parsley. Dip the pointed end of each crouton into the sauce and then into the chopped parsley. Surround the meat with the croutons, parsleyed ends pointing outward.

Pithiviers

ALMOND CREAM-FILLED PASTRY

SERVES 6

Pithiviers is a town not far from Orléans, but today most people think of it as the name of a famous cake. Made from two rounds of puff pastry with a rum-flavored almond cream filling, it has become a Parisian favorite.

PUFF PASTRY
1½ cups all-purpose flour
¾ cup cake flour
Salt
⅔ to ¾ cup cold water
2 tablespoons unsalted butter, melted
14 tablespoons unsalted butter
1 egg, lightly beaten, for glazing

ALMOND CREAM
6 tablespoons unsalted butter, softened
⅓ cup sugar
2 eggs
⅔ cup fine-ground almonds
1 teaspoon vanilla extract
2 tablespoons rum

Confectioner's sugar for glazing
Unsalted butter, softened, for baking sheet

Prepare the puff pastry: Use the above ingredients and follow the directions on pages 209–10 and technique photos on pages 542–43.

Prepare the almond cream: Combine the butter and sugar in a mixing bowl and beat until creamy. Beat in the eggs. Add the almonds, vanilla, and rum and beat until well blended. Refrigerate for 30 minutes.

Lightly butter a baking sheet with the softened butter and sprinkle with cold water.

Prepare the pithiviers (see technique photos on page 546): Divide the puff pastry dough in half. On a lightly floured surface, roll out one half about ⅛ inch thick; set aside. Roll out the remaining dough ⅛ inch thick and place it in the center of the baking sheet. Brush the dough with a 2-inch border of egg glaze.

Remove the almond cream from the refrigerator and whisk briefly to soften. Mound the cream in the center of the sheet of dough on the baking sheet to within ¼ inch of the glaze (or pipe the cream using a pastry bag with a plain round tip). Cover with the reserved sheet of dough. Press the edges together carefully to seal. Refrigerate for 20 minutes.

Preheat the oven to 425°.

Remove the pithiviers from the refrigerator. Using an 8-inch vol-au-vent cutter (or an 8-inch plate or cake pan) as a guide, cut a scalloped edge with the point of a small knife. Discard the trimmings. Brush the surface with egg glaze but do not let the glaze run over the sides or the pastry will rise unevenly. Use a knife to trace shallow, curved lines radiating from the center of the pastry out to the edge, like the spokes of a wheel.

Bake the pithiviers for 20 minutes. Then sift confectioner's sugar over the top and bake until the crust is glazed and golden brown, about 10 minutes longer. Transfer to a rack to cool slightly. Serve warm.

LESSON 42

Salade Croquante aux Oeufs de Caille
SPRING SALAD WITH QUAIL EGGS AND ASPARAGUS

———

Truites à l'Oseille
TROUT STUFFED WITH SORREL

———

Clafoutis Normand
APPLE AND CREAM TART

Salade Croquante aux Oeufs de Caille
SPRING SALAD WITH QUAIL EGGS AND ASPARAGUS

———

SERVES 6

Quail eggs are about the same size as walnuts, and their appeal lies more in their miniature appearance than their taste (they taste like ordinary eggs). Here they are served with green asparagus, tomatoes, cucumbers, and a delicate hazelnut oil vinaigrette. The same salad could be made on other occasions with six ordinary hard-boiled eggs, quartered before being served and seasoned as described here.

Note: Hazelnut oil is very perishable; buy it in small quantities, keep it out of the light, or store it in the refrigerator.

Sherry vinegar, here combined with the hazelnut oil, has become readily available in France in recent years. It is much stronger and more aromatic than red wine vinegar, but if none is available, ordinary wine vinegar may be used instead.

(continued)

Salade Croquante aux Oeufs de Caille (continued)

18 quail eggs

Salt

36 stalks green asparagus

1 bunch watercress

1 head red leaf lettuce

Freshly ground pepper

1/4 cup sherry vinegar

3/4 cup hazelnut oil

3 medium tomatoes, peeled,
    seeded, and diced (page 31)

1 medium cucumber, peeled,
    seeded, and diced

1/2 bunch whole chives

Cook the eggs in simmering salted water for 7 minutes. Drain and refresh under cold running water; drain again. Peel and set aside in a bowl of salted lukewarm water.

Snap the tough ends off the asparagus stalks. Trim the ends so that the stalks are all the same length. Tie in 6 even bundles with kitchen twine. Bring a large saucepan of salted water to a boil. Add the asparagus bundles and return the water to a boil. Cook until the asparagus is crisp-tender, about 12 minutes. Drain and refresh in cold water; drain again. Remove the twine and spread the asparagus on a rack lined with paper towels; set aside.

Soak the watercress in cold water to remove any grit; drain well and spin dry. Trim off the tough stems. Rinse, drain and spin the red lettuce dry.

Prepare a vinaigrette: Whisk together the salt, pepper, and vinegar in a small bowl. Whisk in the oil. Taste and adjust seasonings.

Combine the tomatoes and cucumber in a bowl. Add one-quarter of the vinaigrette and stir gently.

To serve, put the watercress in a bowl and toss with one-half of the remaining vinaigrette. Do the same with the red lettuce, in a separate bowl. Make a mound of watercress in the center of 6 large plates. Surround the watercress with red lettuce, then arrange 6 asparagus spears on each salad, on top of the red lettuce and radiating out like the spokes of a wheel. Sprinkle the watercress with the tomato-cucumber mixture. Drain the quail eggs and cut each in half lengthwise. Arrange an egg half, yolk side up, between each asparagus stalk and sprinkle with chives.

Truites à l'Oseille
TROUT STUFFED WITH SORREL

SERVES 6

Sorrel's tart, lemony taste was long associated in France with that of veal in a dish called *fricandeau,* but today it is more likely to be served with fish—particularly salmon or shad.

6 trout, about 8 ounces each	*2 shallots, chopped fine*
Salt and freshly ground pepper	*1¼ cups dry white wine*
4 tablespoons unsalted butter	*1¼ cups crème fraîche or*
5 ounces sorrel, rinsed, trimmed,	* heavy cream*
* and cut into chiffonade*	*2 egg yolks*
* (technique photo page 520)*	*1 tablespoon chopped parsley*
18 small waxy potatoes (red or	
* white), "turned" (page 50)*	*Unsalted butter, softened,*
3 tablespoons unsalted butter	* for serving platter and*
	* parchment paper*

Clean the trout: With kitchen or fish scissors, cut the tail of each fish straight across, leaving it ½ inch long. Make a V-shaped cut in the center of the trimmed tail. Cut off all of the fins (see technique photos 1, 2, and 3 on page 524). Place the fish on a work surface and pull or cut out the gills (see technique photo 5). It is not necessary to scale trout.

Bone the trout (see technique photos on page 526): Lay the fish flat on a work surface with the tail toward you. Using a sharp filleting knife with a thin flexible blade, make a shallow incision down the length of both sides of the backbone. Holding the blade against one side of the backbone, insert the blade down into the body, being careful not to pierce the skin of the stomach. Then, working from head to tail, slide the blade along the rib bones to lift the flesh. Do not cut through the head or tail end of the fish. Turn the fish over and repeat the process on the other side. To remove the backbone, cut it twice, just behind the head and as close to the tail as possible. Pull out the backbone and the entrails. Rinse the fish inside and out under cold running water. Dry well with paper towels. Season the insides with salt and pepper.

Heat 1 tablespoon of the butter in a medium frying pan over medium heat. Set aside 1 ounce of the shredded sorrel for the sauce. Add the remaining sorrel to the pan and cook until all moisture has evaporated. Cool to room temperature.

Prepare the potatoes: Fill a large saucepan with cold salted water. Add the potatoes, bring to a boil, and cook until tender when pierced with the point of a knife, about 10 minutes. Set aside in the cooking liquid.

Preheat the oven to 400°.

Stuff each trout with 1 tablespoon of cooked sorrel. Gently press the two sides of the fish together to close the opening. Butter the bottom of a roasting pan with the remaining 3 tablespoons of butter. Sprinkle with shallots and salt and pepper. Arrange the trout in a single layer in the pan. Pour in the wine and cover with a piece of buttered parchment paper. Bring quickly to a boil over high heat on top of the stove. Then transfer to the oven and cook until the point of a knife easily enters the flesh, 12 to 15 minutes, depending on the size of the fish.

Lightly brush a long serving platter with the softened butter and transfer the trout to the platter. Scrape off the skin gently on the upturned side with a small knife. Blot up any liquid on the platter with paper towels. Cover the trout to keep warm.

Strain the trout cooking liquid into a small saucepan. Cook over high heat until reduced by one-third. Whisk the cream and yolks together in a small bowl. Whisk in some of the reduced cooking liquid and then return the mixture to the saucepan. Cook gently over medium heat, stirring constantly, until warm. Do not allow the sauce to boil or it will separate. Taste and adjust seasonings. Stir in the reserved ounce of shredded sorrel.

Drain the potatoes. Heat 3 tablespoons of butter in a large frying pan over medium heat. Add the potatoes and shake the pan to coat them with butter. Put the potatoes into a vegetable dish and sprinkle with the chopped parsley. To serve, spoon a little sauce over only the body of each fish (do not coat the heads). Serve the remaining sauce in a sauceboat.

Clafoutis Normand

APPLE AND CREAM TART

SERVES 6

This is a variant on the classic cherry *clafoutis* described earlier in the book. It was created by one of the chefs at Le Cordon Bleu and differs from the traditional dessert in that it is made with apples instead of cherries and its filling is spiked with a tablespoon of Calvados (apple brandy).

PÂTE BRISÉE SUCRÉE
1 cup all-purpose flour
1/2 cup cake flour
1 egg
1 tablespoon water
Pinch of salt
1 tablespoon sugar
1 teaspoon vanilla extract
7 tablespoons unsalted butter
1 egg, *lightly beaten, for glazing*

BAKED APPLES
3 apples (preferably
    Golden Delicious)
1 lemon, halved
4 tablespoons melted butter
1 tablespoon Calvados
1 tablespoon sugar

1 egg yolk
2 eggs
1/4 cup sugar
1 ounce fine-ground almonds
    (about 1/4 cup)
1 teaspoon vanilla extract
2/3 cup crème fraîche or
    heavy cream

Unsalted butter, softened,
    for baking sheet

EQUIPMENT: 9-inch fluted, removable-bottomed tart pan

Prepare the pâte brisée sucrée just as you would pâte brisée, but add the sugar and vanilla to the well along with the eggs, water, and salt; line the pan and blind bake (see directions on pages 37–39 and technique photos pages 540–41).

Preheat the oven to 375°.

Brush a baking sheet with the softened butter. Peel and core the apples and rub them with lemon. Cut each apple in half through the stem end and then thinly slice each half crosswise, keeping the shape of each half intact. Transfer the sliced apple halves to the baking sheet with a wide spatula. Brush with the melted butter. Flatten slightly with the spatula. Sprinkle with Calvados and sugar and bake until golden, 15 to 20 minutes.

Whisk the egg yolk with the whole eggs in a small bowl. Add the sugar, almonds, vanilla and cream, and whisk well to blend.

Arrange the baked apple halves like the spokes of a wheel in the cooked pastry shell. Pour over the egg-cream mixture. Bake until firm, about 30 minutes. If necessary, remove the fluted edge of the tart pan and put it upside down over the rim of the tart to prevent the edges from scorching.

Serve warm or cold on a doily-lined platter.

LESSON 43

Brochettes de Langoustines,
Sauce Mousquetaire

SKEWERED LANGOUSTINES WITH MUSKETEER SAUCE

Pilaf de Volaille à la Turque

TURKISH-STYLE CHICKEN PILAF
WITH ZUCCHINI AND ORANGES

Abricots à la Royale

ALMOND GÉNOISE FILLED WITH
APRICOTS AND CREAM

Brochettes de Langoustines, Sauce Mousquetaire

SKEWERED LANGOUSTINES WITH MUSKETEER SAUCE

SERVES 6

No one knows why this shallot-and-herb-flavored mayonnaise is called a musketeer sauce. Early versions of the recipe included cayenne pepper, and some authorities have suggested that its spiciness can be read as a culinary allusion to the flamboyant personalities of Alexandre Dumas' musketeers. It provides a perfect complement to the taste and texture of breaded and broiled langoustines as well as an excellent demonstration of the versatility of mayonnaise.

36 langoustines
  (see page 114) or
  large shrimp on the shell
Salt and freshly ground pepper
Juice of 1 lemon, strained
1 tablespoon chopped parsley
2 cups milk

MUSKETEER SAUCE
MAYONNAISE:
  2 egg yolks
  1 tablespoon Dijon mustard
  2 tablespoons white-wine vinegar
  Salt and freshly ground pepper
  1 1/2 cups vegetable oil
2 tablespoons unsalted butter
2 large shallots, chopped fine
1/2 cup dry white wine
1 Bouquet Garni (page 20)
Freshly ground pepper
2 tablespoons chopped chives
1 tablespoon chopped chervil
1 tablespoon chopped parsley

ANGLAISE BREADING
1 1/2 cups all-purpose flour
2 eggs
3 tablespoons vegetable oil
2 tablespoons water
Salt and freshly ground pepper
2 cups fresh white bread crumbs

3 lemons, cut in wedges

Unsalted butter, softened,
  for baking sheet

EQUIPMENT: 6 skewers

Shell the langoustines (see directions on page 115 and technique photos page 523) and discard the shells. Arrange in a single layer in a nonaluminum container. Season with salt and pepper. Sprinkle with lemon juice and parsley. Pour in the milk and marinate at room temperature for at least 1 hour.

Prepare the sauce: First, make a mayonnaise. Use the above ingredients and follow the directions on page 31. Next, make a white wine reduction: Melt the butter in a small saucepan over low heat. Add the shallots and cook until soft but not colored. Add the wine, the bouquet garni and pepper to taste. Raise the heat to medium and simmer until the liquid has reduced by three-quarters. Cool to lukewarm and remove the bouquet garni. Whisk the wine reduction into the mayonnaise and add the chopped herbs. Set aside at room temperature.

Preheat the broiler.

Drain the langoustines on paper towels and pat dry.

Prepare the breading: Spread the flour on a large plate. In a shallow dish, beat the eggs, oil, water, salt, and pepper with a fork. Spread the bread crumbs out on another large plate. Roll the langoustines in the flour and shake off the excess. Dip them in the egg mixture and then roll them in the bread crumbs, patting gently so the crumbs will adhere.

Thread 6 langoustines onto each skewer (see photo). Refrigerate for ½ hour.

Brush a baking sheet well with the softened butter and heat it under the broiler. Put the filled skewers on the baking sheet in a single layer and turn to coat both sides evenly with butter. Broil until golden, about 2 minutes on each side.

To serve, remove from skewers and transfer langoustines to a serving platter. Garnish with lemon wedges and serve hot, accompanied by a sauce-boat of the musketeer sauce.

Pilaf de Volaille à la Turque
TURKISH-STYLE CHICKEN PILAF
WITH ZUCCHINI AND ORANGES

———

SERVES 6

This preparation was created at Le Cordon Bleu in the first half of this century by one of the school's most famous chefs—Henri-Paul Pellaprat. The combination of oranges, lemons, garlic, and zucchini with a classic chicken sauté lent his dish an exotic touch, prompting him to name it *"à la turque."* It has been a favorite with our students for more than fifty years.

4½-pound chicken
9 oranges
1 lemon
¼ cup olive oil
Salt and freshly ground pepper
1 teaspoon paprika
⅔ cup dry white wine
1 bay leaf

1 sprig fresh thyme or
  ¼ teaspoon dried
⅔ cup Brown Veal Stock
  (page 71)
1½ pounds zucchini
2 cloves garlic, peeled
1 tablespoon chopped parsley

Cut the chicken into 6 serving pieces (see directions on pages 59–60 and technique photos on pages 530–31).

Use a vegetable peeler to remove the zest from 2 of the oranges and the lemon. Slice the zests into very thin julienne strips (see technique photo on page 519). Bring a small saucepan of water to the boil and add the julienned zests. Blanch for 2 minutes; drain, refresh under cold running water, and drain again. Squeeze the juice from 5 of the oranges and the lemon. Strain the juice; reserve.

Heat 2 tablespoons of the oil in a large frying pan over high heat. Season the chicken with salt, pepper and paprika and add to the pan, skin side down. Sauté on both sides until golden brown. Discard the fat from the pan. Add the wine, reserved citrus juice, bay leaf, thyme, salt, pepper and stock. Bring to a boil, reduce the heat, cover and cook for 15 minutes. Add the blanched orange and lemon zests and simmer, covered, 20 minutes longer.

Prepare the zucchini: Cut the zucchini into small sticks (bâtonnets). Heat the remaining 2 tablespoons oil in a large frying pan over high heat. Add the garlic and the zucchini, and sauté, stirring frequently, until the zucchini is crisp-tender. Season to taste with salt and pepper. Discard the garlic; cover the zucchini to keep warm.

Peel and section the 4 remaining oranges (page 9).

When the chicken is tender, remove from the pan and arrange in the center of a large serving platter. Reduce the cooking liquid by one-half over medium heat; add the orange sections and taste and adjust seasonings. Pour the sauce over the chicken and surround with the zucchini. Sprinkle the zucchini with the parsley.

Abricots à la Royale

ALMOND GÉNOISE FILLED WITH APRICOTS AND CREAM

SERVES 6

A classic French layer cake is made by carefully slicing a génoise horizontally into two, three, or even four layers. To cut the cake properly, a long serrated knife must be used (the knife should be several inches longer than the cake is wide). The layers are generally garnished with a butter cream, a mousse, or a fruit-based filling and either iced or topped with a decorative display of fruit and cream. French layer cakes can be served alone, with a fruit-flavored sauce (fruit coulis) or with a crème anglaise.

This apricot-flavored layer cake is made by cutting an almond génoise into two layers, garnishing simply with Chantilly cream and apricots, then decorating the top of the cake with another spiral of Chantilly and apricots surrounded by a jewel-like crown of bright red candied cherries and green pistachios. Need we explain why it is called "à la royale"?

(continued)

Abricots à la Royale (continued)

ALMOND GÉNOISE

3 eggs (room temperature)

¹/₂ cup sugar

¹/₂ cup sifted all-purpose flour

6 tablespoons fine-ground almonds

3 tablespoons unsalted butter, melted and cooled

SUGAR SYRUP

¹/₃ cup sugar

¹/₃ cup water

1¹/₂ tablespoons kirsch

¹/₂ teaspoon vanilla extract

32-ounce can apricot halves in syrup

CHANTILLY CREAM

1³/₄ cups heavy cream

¹/₄ cup confectioner's sugar

1 teaspoon vanilla extract

3 tablespoons Apricot Glaze (page 62)

8 candied cherries, halved

16 pistachios, shelled, peeled, and halved

Unsalted butter, softened, for mold

All-purpose flour for mold

EQUIPMENT: 8-inch round cake pan for génoise, pastry bag, medium star pastry tip

Brush the ring mold with the softened butter and dust with flour.

Prepare the almond génoise just as you would the basic génoise, following the directions on page 176, but add the ground almonds along with the flour, and fold in the melted butter at the end. Let cool.

Prepare the sugar syrup: Combine the sugar and water in a small saucepan. Bring to a boil over low heat, stirring to dissolve the sugar. Boil 1 to 2 minutes, remove from the heat and add the kirsch and vanilla; set aside.

Drain the apricots and place them, cut side down, on a rack to drain. Discard the canned syrup.

Slice the cooled cake in half horizontally with a large serrated knife. Put the bottom half, cut side up, on a serving platter. Brush it with half of the sugar syrup.

Prepare the Chantilly cream (page 21): Fit a pastry bag with the medium star tip and fill it with the cream. Pipe an even layer of cream over the bottom half of the génoise. Reserve several apricot halves for final decoration and arrange the remainder in overlapping circles on top of the cream. Pipe another layer of cream on top of the apricots and top with the other half of the génoise, cut side down. Brush the top with the remaining syrup.

Heat the apricot glaze and add a little water if it is too thick. Brush the top of the génoise with the glaze. Arrange the cherries in a large circle on top of the cake. Place 1 pistachio half on either side of each cherry. Pipe the remaining cream in a spiral over the top of the cake and garnish with the remaining apricots. Chill for 1 hour and serve cold.

LESSON 44

Mousseline de Saint Jacques au Concombre
SCALLOP TERRINE WITH SHRIMP AND CUCUMBERS

Carré d'Agneau
RACK OF LAMB

Ratatouille Niçoise
NICE-STYLE RATATOUILLE

Fondant Sévigné, Sauce Café
CHOCOLATE FONDANT WITH COFFEE SAUCE

PERFECTING SKILLS

Mousseline de Saint Jacques au Concombre

SCALLOP TERRINE WITH SHRIMP AND CUCUMBERS

SERVES 6

Everything in this seafood starter is white, or almost (with one exception). The pastel colors of the scallops, cauliflower, cucumbers, cream, and shrimp contrast strikingly with the flaming color of a delicious mayonnaise reddened with a bell-pepper puree. This cooling combination is pleasing to both eye and palate and provides a perfect beginning to an elegant meal.

SCALLOP MOUSSELINE
2 tablespoons fine-diced red
    bell pepper
2 tablespoons fine-diced green
    bell pepper
14 ounces sea scallops
2 eggs
1/2 cup crème fraîche or
    heavy cream
Salt and freshly ground pepper
Cayenne pepper

RED PEPPER MAYONNAISE
1 egg yolk
1 tablespoon Dijon mustard
Salt and freshly ground pepper
1/2 teaspoon lime juice
1/3 cup olive oil
1/3 cup vegetable oil
2 bottled roasted red bell peppers
Pinch of cayenne pepper

1 cucumber
1/4 head cauliflower
1/4 pound small cooked and
    peeled shrimp

VINAIGRETTE
Juice of 2 limes, strained
1/2 cup olive oil
3 sprigs fresh dill, chopped
Salt and freshly ground pepper
Pinch of saffron
1 teaspoon chopped fresh mint

Unsalted butter, softened,
    for loaf pan and
    parchment paper

EQUIPMENT: 8-by-3 1/2-inch loaf pan, pastry bag, medium star pastry tip

Preheat the oven to 450°. Brush the loaf pan with the softened butter. Line the bottom with parchment paper. Brush the paper with butter.

Prepare the mousseline: Chill a mixing bowl. Bring a small saucepan of salted water to a boil. Add the diced peppers and blanch for 3 minutes. Drain, refresh under cold running water and drain again.

Cut off and discard the small muscle from each scallop. Pat the scallops dry with paper towels. Pass the scallops twice through a meat grinder using the finest disc, or puree in a food processor. Transfer the puree to the chilled bowl and set it over a larger bowl filled with crushed ice. Add the eggs one at a time, beating vigorously after each addition with a wooden spoon in a forward-to-backward motion, until the mixture is well blended and slightly thickened. Beat until the mixture is completely chilled after each egg is added. Add the cream little by little, beating well after each addition. (The mousseline will be fairly liquid.) Add the blanched peppers and season to taste with salt, pepper and cayenne. Pour the mousseline into the loaf pan and cover with buttered parchment paper. Put the loaf pan into a roasting pan and pour in hot water to come halfway up the sides of the loaf pan. Bring to a simmer on top of the stove. Then transfer to the oven and cook until a knife inserted into the center is warm to the touch and clean when withdrawn, 35 to 40 minutes. Let cool to room temperature before unmolding.

Prepare the mayonnaise: Use the above ingredients and follow the directions on page 31. After the oil has been incorporated, puree the bell peppers and add along with the cayenne pepper.

Peel the cucumber lengthwise; reserve the peel. Cut the cucumber in half lengthwise and scrape out the seeds with the handle of a spoon. Cut each cucumber half lengthwise into 3 strips and then cut the strips into 4 or 5 even pieces. Set aside in a small bowl.

Separate the cauliflower into the smallest possible florets. Bring a saucepan of salted water to a boil. Add the florets and blanch 2 to 3 minutes. Drain; refresh under cold running water and drain again. Combine the cauliflower and the shrimp in a small bowl.

Prepare the vinaigrette: Whisk together all of the ingredients. Toss half of the vinaigrette with the cucumbers and half with the cauliflower and shrimp. Marinate until serving time, or at least 1 hour.

Bring a saucepan of salted water to a boil. Cut the cucumber skin into long, thin strips. Blanch for a few seconds. Drain, refresh under cold running water and drain again on paper towels.

To serve, unmold the scallop mousseline: Slide the blade of a knife around the edge of the mousseline. Invert a long serving platter over the loaf pan and quickly reverse the two. Blot up any liquid on the platter with a paper towel. Peel off the parchment paper. Slice the mousseline about ½ inch thick. Overlap the slices on the platter. Drain the cucumbers and toss with the cauliflower and shrimp. Remove from the vinaigrette with a slotted spoon and arrange around the edge of the platter. Fit the pastry bag with the medium star tip and fill with the mayonnaise. Pipe rosettes in between the shrimp-vegetable mixture and the sliced mousseline. Scatter the strips of cucumber skin over the mounds of mayonnaise and serve immediately.

Carré d'Agneau
RACK OF LAMB

———

SERVES 6

Rack of lamb, like leg of lamb, is served rare in France. But rare doesn't mean raw; the trick is to leave the meat to rest after roasting so that the juices in the center have time to flow back toward the skin, making the lamb an even pink color throughout.

The fat that covers the rack should be lightly scored before roasting; it will run off the meat more readily and baste the rack as it cooks.

2 racks of lamb with 6 ribs each	*1 medium carrot, cut into chunks*
Salt and freshly ground pepper	*1 medium onion, quartered*
3 tablespoons vegetable oil	*Bunch of watercress for garnish*

Preheat the oven to 450°. Prepare the racks (see technique photos on page 539): Use a boning knife to remove the flat, semicircular pieces of cartilage that lie at one end of each of the racks. Remove the skin and trim all but ½ inch of fat from the meat. Lay the racks fat side down on the work surface and cut off the yellow strips of connective tissue that lie underneath the backbones. Set the racks on one end and cut off the chine bones (backbones) with a cleaver. Place each rack fat side down on the work surface and score a line along the rib bones, about 2 inches in from the tips. Then cut along the edge of each rib, down to the scored line, to cut out the meat between the bones. Turn the racks over, fat side up, and score a line down to the rib bones, about 2 inches in from the tips. Remove the fat and meat above the line, in one piece, to expose the rib bones. Scrape carefully around the exposed rib bones to clean them of all meat and connective tissue. Score the fat lightly and season with salt and pepper. Reserve bones and all trimmings except fat and skin.

Heat the oil in a roasting pan over high heat. Add the carrot, onion, trimmings and the racks of lamb, fat side down, and cook, turning, until golden brown on all sides. Transfer to the oven and roast for about 12 minutes. Turn the meat over and roast until medium rare, about 12 minutes longer.

Remove the lamb from the roasting pan and wrap in aluminum foil to keep warm. Discard the fat from the pan. Place the pan over medium heat, add 2 cups of water and deglaze, scraping the bottom of the pan to release the cooked particles. Bring the water to a boil and reduce for a few minutes to concentrate the flavor of the juices. Taste and adjust seasonings. Strain into a saucepan and keep warm over low heat until serving time.

To serve, stand the racks of lamb on a serving platter and spoon a little of the sauce over them. Decorate the platter with the watercress and serve the remaining sauce in a sauceboat on the side. Serve with Ratatouille Niçoise (opposite page). (For individual serving, see photo on page 243.)

Ratatouille Niçoise
NICE-STYLE RATATOUILLE

SERVES 6

Though ratatouille can be found all over Provence it is, above all, a specialty of Nice. In its most primitive form, vegetables are all tossed together in a large pot and cooked for a very long time with olive oil and garlic to make a thick vegetable stew. In its most refined form, the vegetables are cooked separately to soften, then simmered together for a relatively short time simply to combine tastes.

Ratatouille can be served hot as a vegetable garnish or cold as a refreshing summertime first course.

1 pound eggplant	1 sprig fresh thyme or
1 pound small zucchini	1/4 teaspoon dried
1 medium green bell pepper	2 tablespoons chopped fresh basil
1 medium red bell pepper	1 tablespoon rosemary leaves
9 tablespoons olive oil	1 pound tomatoes, peeled, seeded,
2 large onions, sliced	and diced (page 31)
3 cloves garlic, chopped fine	1 tablespoon tomato paste
1 bay leaf	Salt and freshly ground pepper

Peel the eggplant and cut into bâtonnets, 1½ inches long and ¼ inch wide. Cut the zucchini into bâtonnets of the same size. Slice off each end of the peppers; remove and discard the seeds and ribs. Then cut into bâtonnets of the same size as the other vegetables.

Heat 3 tablespoons of the olive oil in a large frying pan over high heat until very hot. Add the eggplant and zucchini and sauté until golden brown. Remove from the pan with a slotted spoon and drain on paper towels to remove excess oil.

Heat the remaining 6 tablespoons of olive oil in a large saucepan over low heat. Add the onions and peppers and cook until soft but not colored. Add the garlic, herbs, tomatoes, tomato paste, and the sautéed zucchini and eggplant. Season to taste with salt and pepper. Simmer over low heat, without stirring, for about 20 minutes. Taste and adjust seasonings.

Fondant Sévigné, Sauce Café

CHOCOLATE FONDANT WITH COFFEE SAUCE

SERVES 6

Madame de Sévigné was a seventeenth-century lady and patron of the arts whose many letters provide insights into the Parisian society of her day. Chocolate was a novelty then, and she raves about the pleasures of consuming it. This Cordon Bleu chocolate dessert was named in her honor; it also contains coffee, another now-familiar item introduced to France in Madame de Sévigné's day and used here to make a sauce that heightens the chocolate flavor.

9 ounces semisweet chocolate,
  cut into small pieces
4 eggs, separated
11 tablespoons unsalted butter,
  softened
4 tablespoons superfine sugar

COFFEE SAUCE
1 cup milk
1 teaspoon vanilla extract
1 teaspoon dry instant coffee
3 egg yolks
¼ cup sugar

Unsalted butter, melted, for mold

EQUIPMENT: 3-cup round mold

Brush the mold with melted butter.

Bring 1 to 2 inches of water to a simmer in a saucepan. Put the chocolate in a heatproof bowl and set it over the pan of simmering water. Let stand, without stirring, until completely melted. Remove from the heat and whisk in the egg yolks, one at a time. Whisk in the softened butter, little by little.

Beat the egg whites with a whisk or electric mixer until stiff peaks form. Stir one-third of the whites into the chocolate mixture. Fold in the remaining whites carefully with a wooden spoon. Then carefully fold in the sugar. Pour into the prepared mold and refrigerate until firm, 4 to 5 hours.

Prepare the coffee sauce just as you would a crème anglaise (page 35), but dissolve the instant coffee in the milk as it is heating. Cool and refrigerate.

To serve, unmold the fondant: Dip the mold into hot water for 5 seconds. Invert a glass serving dish or platter over the mold and quickly reverse the two. Serve the coffee sauce in a sauceboat on the side. Serve with Almond Tile Cookies (page 125), if you like.

Salade de Choux Panachés aux Pommes Reinettes
RED AND GREEN CABBAGE SALAD WITH APPLES

Coeur de Filet Henri IV
FILET MIGNONS WITH ARTICHOKES
AND BÉARNAISE SAUCE

Pommes Pont Neuf
PONT NEUF POTATOES

Gâteau Basque
ALMOND-FILLED BASQUE CAKE

Salade de Choux Panachés aux Pommes Reinettes
RED AND GREEN CABBAGE SALAD WITH APPLES

SERVES 6

Red cabbage and green cabbage are commonly served as salads in France. Here both are artistically arranged around a mound of apples and cream to make a simple but elegant first course.

Note: At Le Cordon Bleu, rather than cooking the cabbage or serving it entirely raw, hot vinegar is poured over it to wilt and season it at the same time. Though the vinegar is later discarded, the cabbage retains its tart taste and is of a perfect consistency for salads of all kinds.

3/4 pound green cabbage, shredded
3/4 pound red cabbage, shredded
1 1/4 cups red- or white-wine vinegar
1/2 cup vegetable oil

Salt and freshly ground pepper
1/2 cup crème fraîche or heavy cream
2 Granny Smith apples
2 tablespoons chopped fresh chives

Put the green cabbage into a bowl and the red into another. Bring 1 cup plus 2 tablespoons of the vinegar to a boil in a small saucepan. Add the hot vinegar to the green cabbage and stir well; let stand for 10 minutes. Strain the vinegar back into the saucepan and return it to a boil. Add the reheated vinegar to the red cabbage and stir well; let stand for 30 minutes. Drain the cabbage; discard the vinegar.

Stir ¼ cup oil into each bowl of cabbage. Season to taste with salt and pepper. Let stand 10 minutes.

In a large bowl, whisk together the cream and the remaining 2 tablespoons of vinegar. Season to taste with salt and pepper. Peel, core and cut the apples into julienne (see technique photo on page 519). Immediately toss them with the cream mixture to prevent discoloring.

To serve, arrange the red and green cabbage in 12 equal mounds in a ring on a serving platter, alternating the colors. Put the apple and cream salad into the middle and sprinkle with chives.

Coeur de Filet Henri IV
FILET MIGNONS WITH ARTICHOKES AND BÉARNAISE SAUCE

SERVES 6

If anything might be called a steak sauce in France it would have to be sauce béarnaise, a thick creamy sauce served almost exclusively with beef. It is made by whisking butter into warm egg yolks seasoned with a spicy mixture of shallots, white wine, pepper, and tarragon.

6 center-cut tenderloin steaks, about 7 ounces each

ARTICHOKE BOTTOMS
6 large artichokes
2 lemons
Salt
2 tablespoons vegetable oil

BÉARNAISE SAUCE
4 peppercorns, crushed
1 large shallot, chopped fine
3 tablespoons chopped fresh tarragon
2 tablespoons white-wine vinegar
¼ cup white wine
2 egg yolks
2 tablespoons water
8 ounces clarified butter (page 94)
1 tablespoon chopped fresh chervil
Salt
Cayenne pepper

2 tablespoons vegetable oil
Freshly ground pepper
Small bunch watercress

Bring the steaks to room temperature. (This will allow them to be cooked rare or medium rare.)

(continued)

Coeur de Filet Henri IV (continued)

Prepare and cook the artichoke bottoms (see directions on page 30 and technique photos on pages 520–21).

Prepare the béarnaise sauce: Combine the crushed peppercorns, the shallot, 2 tablespoons of the tarragon, the vinegar and wine in a small heavy-bottomed saucepan. Bring to a boil and cook over low heat until all the liquid has evaporated. Remove from the heat and let cool. Add the egg yolks and the water to the saucepan. Whisk over very low heat until the mixture becomes foamy and thickens and the whisk leaves a clear trail on the bottom of the pan. Do not let the mixture boil. Remove from the heat. Whisking constantly, add the clarified butter, drop by drop, until the mixture starts to emulsify. Then whisk in the remaining butter in a slow steady stream until the sauce is thick and creamy. Whisk in the chopped chervil and the remaining tablespoon of tarragon. Season to taste with salt and cayenne pepper. Set aside, off the heat, in a pan of warm water.

Tie a length of kitchen twine around each beef tenderloin steak to hold its shape during cooking. Preheat an open grill or a grill pan over high heat, or heat a little oil in a heavy frying pan over high heat. Brush the steaks with oil and season with salt and pepper. Sear the steaks about 3 minutes on each side. (If using a grill pan, make the traditional lattice design by giving the steak a 90° turn after 1 or 2 minutes of cooking time.) Turn the steaks with a spatula or tongs rather than with a fork, which would pierce the meat and allow the juices to escape. Continue cooking until done as desired; remove twine (see page 129).

To serve, arrange the steaks in the center of a serving platter. Fill the artichoke bottoms with béarnaise sauce and arrange around the edge of the platter. Decorate the platter with watercress. Serve with Pommes Pont Neuf, opposite page.

TWO-STEP DEEP FRYING

To ensure that deep-fried thick-cut potatoes such as Pommes Pont Neuf are both crisp on the outside and completely cooked through on the inside, they are fried twice: once at a low heat (350°) to cook them completely without browning (this is known as "blanching") and then again at a higher heat (355 to 375°) for just a few minutes to crisp the outside. You may blanch the potatoes several hours ahead of time and then brown them just before serving.

Pommes Pont Neuf
PONT NEUF POTATOES

SERVES 6

Le Pont Neuf (literally, the New Bridge) was built at the end of the sixteenth century. Today, ironically, it is the oldest bridge in Paris. At the beginning of the nineteenth century, street vendors wandered across the bridge selling a new street food—French fries! To this day thickly cut French fries are still called "Pommes Pont Neuf."

Note: At Le Cordon Bleu, potatoes are fried in the two-step method French professionals prefer (see opposite page). This guarantees potatoes with a moist, tender inside and a brown, crisp outside and allows for their being finished at the last minute and in the shortest possible time.

2 pounds large baking potatoes   *Oil for deep-fat frying*
Salt

Peel the potatoes. Trim the ends and sides of each potato to form rectangular blocks. Cut each block of potato into slices about 3/8 inch thick. Stack the slices and cut into sticks 3/8 inch wide (see technique photo on page 520). Soak in a bowl of cold water for 5 to 10 minutes to remove excess starch. Fill a large saucepan or deep fryer no more than one-third full with oil and heat oil to 350°. Lift the potatoes out of the bowl into a colander. (This will leave the excess starch in the bottom of the bowl.) Drain and pat dry with paper towels. Working in batches so as not to crowd the pan, lower the potatoes slowly into the hot oil and fry for 7 minutes without coloring. (This is known as blanching.) Reduce the temperature of the oil if they begin to brown. Drain on paper towels.

Just before serving, heat the oil to 375°. Working in batches, return the blanched potatoes to the hot oil and fry until golden brown. Remove from the oil and drain on paper towels. Season with salt. Arrange the potatoes in a pyramid on a doily-lined platter.

ALMOND-FILLED BASQUE CAKE

SERVES 8

This rich cake filled with almond cream is a sophisticated version of a simple country dessert. In the Basque region near the Spanish border, either a local black cherry or plum jam is used as a filling. This Cordon Bleu recipe is similar to the one now used by pastry chefs throughout France.

(continued)

Gâteau Basque (continued)

1 1/2 *cups sifted all-purpose flour*
3/4 *cup sifted cake flour*
1 *cup sugar*
Pinch salt
Grated zest of 1 lemon
12 *tablespoons unsalted*
butter, cut into small
pieces and softened
1 *whole egg*
2 *egg yolks*

ALMOND PASTRY CREAM
1 *cup milk*
1 *teaspoon vanilla extract*
2 *egg yolks*
1/4 *cup sugar*
1/4 *cup sifted all-purpose flour*
1 *ounce fine-ground almonds*
(about 1/4 cup)

1 *egg, lightly beaten, for glazing*
Unsalted butter for pastry cream
and tart pan

EQUIPMENT: 1 removable-bottomed 9-inch tart pan

Combine the flours, sugar, salt, and grated lemon zest in a large bowl. Make a well in the center. Add the butter to the well along with the whole egg and 2 egg yolks. Mix the butter and eggs with fingertips, and then gradually incorporate the dry ingredients until the dough just comes together. Do not overwork. Shape the dough into a ball and sprinkle lightly with flour. Wrap in parchment paper. Refrigerate for about 2 hours.

Prepare the almond pastry cream just as you would a basic pastry cream (page 183), but add the ground almonds after the flour.

Preheat the oven to 400°. Brush the tart pan with the softened butter.

Lightly flour a work surface. Cut off one-third of the dough and set it aside. Roll out the remaining dough into a 1/4-inch-thick round. Cut a circle about 10 1/2 inches in diameter. Fold the round of dough in half, and then in half again. Transfer to the tart pan and open it out. Press the dough evenly into the pan. The edge should be 1/4 inch higher than the rim of the pan.

Put the almond pastry cream in a bowl. Whisk until smooth and then spread it over the bottom of the dough-lined tart pan. Brush the exposed wall of dough with some of the egg glaze. Roll out the remaining dough into a round 1/4 inch thick and about 9 1/2 inches in diameter. Lay it on top of the almond cream. Press the edges of the dough together and then trim the edges level with the rim of the pan. Brush the dough with egg glaze. Lightly score a criss-cross pattern on the top. Brush again with the egg glaze and transfer to the oven. Reduce the temperature to 350° and bake until the top is golden brown, 50 to 60 minutes. Let cool 10 to 15 minutes before removing from the tart pan. Serve warm or cold.

LESSON 46

Aubergines Bayildi
GRATIN OF STUFFED EGGPLANT

Canard aux Navets
ROAST DUCK WITH GLAZED TURNIPS

Île Flottante aux Pralines Roses
FLOATING ISLAND WITH CANDIED ALMONDS

Aubergines Bayildi
GRATIN OF STUFFED EGGPLANT

SERVES 6

This is a French adaptation of a Turkish dish called *Imam Bayildi*, literally "The Imam fainted." Stories diverge as to whether it was the delicious taste of the dish or the expense of the olive oil used that caused the Imam to lose his senses. The Cordon Bleu version is faithful to the original except that the amount of olive oil is reduced.

3 small eggplants
Salt
5 tablespoons olive oil
3 shallots, chopped fine
4 cloves garlic, chopped fine
1 tablespoon tomato paste
1³/₄ pounds tomatoes, peeled, seeded, and diced (page 31)
Freshly ground pepper

3 tablespoons finely sliced basil leaves
2 tomatoes
4 ounces grated Gruyère cheese (about 1 cup)
3 tablespoons unsalted butter
Basil leaves for garnish

Vegetable oil for baking sheet

Remove and discard the stems from the eggplants and then cut the eggplants in half lengthwise. Score the cut side of the eggplants and sprinkle with salt. Cover a rack with a dish towel or paper towels. Arrange the eggplant halves, in a single layer and cut sides down, on the towel to drain.

Heat 1/4 cup of the olive oil in a frying pan over medium heat. Add the shallots and cook until soft but not colored. Add the garlic and cook 1 minute. Then stir in the tomato paste and chopped tomatoes. Season with salt and pepper and cook over medium heat until the liquid has evaporated. Remove about two-thirds of the tomato mixture from the pan and reserve for the sauce. Continue cooking the remaining tomato mixture until it is completely dry; remove from the heat and set aside.

Preheat the oven to 400°. Lightly brush a baking sheet with the oil.

Scrape the salt from the eggplant halves with the blade of a small knife and blot any moisture with paper towels. Put the eggplant halves on the baking sheet, in a single layer and cut sides down. Transfer the eggplants to the oven, lower the oven temperature to 350° and cook until soft, 15 to 20 minutes. Then scrape out the pulp, leaving the wall of each eggplant half about 1/4 inch thick; set the eggplant shells aside. Chop the pulp roughly.

Heat the remaining tablespoon of olive oil in a frying pan over low heat. Add the eggplant pulp and cook for a few minutes until dry. Add the tomato mixture that was cooked until dry. Stir in 2 tablespoons of the finely sliced basil leaves and cook 1 minute.

Slice the 3 tomatoes about 1/4 inch thick. Brush the baking sheet again with oil.

Fill each eggplant shell with the eggplant mixture. Top each with 2 or 3 overlapping slices of tomato and then sprinkle generously with the grated cheese. Dot each with 1/2 tablespoon of butter. Arrange the stuffed eggplants on the baking sheet and bake until browned, 10 to 12 minutes.

Meanwhile puree the tomato mixture reserved for sauce in a food mill or food processor. Transfer to a frying pan and cook over medium heat for several seconds to rewarm. If the mixture is too thick, thin with a little water. Remove from the heat and stir in the remaining tablespoon of sliced basil.

To serve, spoon a small amount of the sauce over the bottom of a serving platter to cover. Place the stuffed eggplant halves on top of the sauce and serve garnished with a few basil leaves.

Canard aux Navets

ROAST DUCK WITH GLAZED TURNIPS

———

SERVES 6

In French cuisine, turnips frequently accompany fatty meats such as duck and lamb. They were commonly used in stews of all kinds before the potato became popular in the latter half of the eighteenth century.

In this and other recipes where turnips are served as a garnish, only very young, tender ones should be used. Their sweet, delicate taste is accented here by the shiny sugar-butter coating they acquire during the glazing.

2 ducks, 4 to 5 pounds each
Salt and freshly ground pepper
2 bay leaves
2 sprigs thyme
2¹/2 cups Brown Veal Stock
  (page 71)
3 tablespoons unsalted butter
2 carrots, chopped coarse
2 onions, chopped coarse

GLAZED TURNIPS
3 pounds small white turnips
Salt
2 tablespoons unsalted butter
1 tablespoon sugar
2 tablespoons Brown Veal Stock

¹/2 cup dry white wine
1 Bouquet Garni (page 20)
1 tablespoon chopped parsley
¹/2 bunch watercress or parsley
  for garnish

Preheat the oven to 425°. Prepare the ducks and remove the wishbones (see technique photos 1 and 2 on page 531): Cut off the wing tips and set them aside with the necks. Cut out the fat glands at the base of the tails with a small knife. Rinse the ducks inside and out with cold water; dry with paper towels. Season the cavities of the ducks with salt and pepper and add a bay leaf and a sprig of thyme to each. Truss the ducks just as you would a chicken (page 6 and technique photos on page 530) and sprinkle all over with salt and pepper.

Reduce the stock by one-half over medium heat. Set aside; cover to keep warm. Heat the butter in a roasting pan over high heat. Add the ducks, necks and wing tips and brown quickly, turning, until evenly colored. Turn the ducks onto one side and add the carrots and onions to the pan. Transfer to the oven and roast 20 minutes, basting frequently. Then turn onto the other side and roast 20 minutes longer, continuing to baste.

Remove the roasting pan from the oven. Remove the ducks and pour the juices into a bowl. Skim off the fat and return the juices to the pan. Return the ducks to the pan, this time on their backs, and baste with about one-third of the reduced veal stock and the pan juices. Roast until the legs move easily at the joints, 30 to 40 minutes longer, basting frequently with the remaining reduced stock.

Prepare the turnips: Turn the turnips into small ovals (page 50 and technique photo on page 520) and put them in a large saucepan with cold salted water to cover. Bring to a boil, and then cook over medium heat until crisp-tender, about 8 minutes; drain. Heat the butter in a frying pan over medium heat. Add the turnips and shake the pan to rotate and coat the turnips evenly with butter. Add the sugar and cook, shaking the pan frequently, until the turnips caramelize slightly. Add the stock. Remove from the heat. Cover to keep warm.

When the ducks are cooked, transfer to a serving platter. Remove and discard the trussing twine; cover the ducks with aluminum foil to keep warm.

Pour the contents of the roasting pan into a small saucepan. Add the wine to the roasting pan and deglaze: Bring to a boil and cook over medium heat for 2 minutes, scraping the bottom of the pan with a wooden spoon to release any cooked particles. Whisk in $1/2$ cup water and then pour into the saucepan. Add the bouquet garni and cook over medium heat for 15 minutes. Strain the sauce, pressing down on the solids to extract as much of the liquid as possible. Discard the solids. Skim any fat on the surface of sauce.

To serve, spoon a little sauce over the ducks. Spoon a few of the turnips around the ducks and serve the remainder in a bowl, sprinkled with the chopped parsley. Decorate the platter with the watercress or parsley. Serve the remaining sauce in a sauceboat on the side.

Île Flottante aux Pralines Roses
FLOATING ISLAND WITH CANDIED ALMONDS

SERVES 6

Few people can resist a white island of meringue floating on a sea of vanilla custard. At Le Cordon Bleu, crushed rose-colored candied almonds are added to the meringue and sprinkled in the cream.

Note: If the colorful candied almonds are unavailable, crushed nut brittle or nougatine (see page 207) may be used instead.

4 ounces pink candied almonds, crushed (see Note)

FRENCH MERINGUE

4 egg whites

1/2 cup sugar

Unsalted butter, softened, for mold and parchment paper

CRÈME ANGLAISE

2 cups milk

4 egg yolks

1 teaspoon vanilla extract

1/2 cup sugar

Whole pink candied almonds for garnish

Mint leaves for garnish

EQUIPMENT: 6-cup charlotte mold

Brush the mold with the softened butter. Cut out a round of parchment paper to the diameter of the bottom of the mold. Line the mold with it and brush with butter. Sprinkle about three-quarters of the crushed candied almonds over the bottom of the mold. Preheat the oven to 275°.

Prepare the meringue: Beat the egg whites with a whisk or electric mixer until fluffy but not stiff. Gradually beat in the sugar and then continue beating until stiff peaks form and the meringue is glossy and smooth. Fold in the remaining crushed candied almonds with a wooden spoon. Pour the mixture into the mold and tap it on the work surface to eliminate any air pockets. Smooth the top with a spatula and cover with a piece of buttered parchment paper. Put the filled mold into an ovenproof pan. Pour hot water into the pan to come halfway up the sides of the charlotte mold. Bring to a boil on the stove and then transfer to the oven and cook until the blade of a knife inserted in the center of the meringue comes out clean, about 40 minutes. Remove the mold from the pan and let cool to room temperature.

Prepare the crème anglaise: Use the above ingredients and follow the directions on page 35.

To serve, pour the crème anglaise into a shallow, wide serving bowl. Remove the buttered paper from the top of the meringue. Invert a plate on top of the mold and quickly reverse the two. Remove the mold and peel off the paper. Gently slide the meringue off the plate into the bowl with the crème anglaise. Decorate the edge of the meringue with a few whole candied almonds and fresh mint leaves. Serve immediately.

Salade Danicheff
ARTICHOKE, ASPARAGUS, AND LANGOUSTINE SALAD

———

Fricassée de Ris de Veau aux Pleurotes
FRICASSEED SWEETBREADS WITH OYSTER MUSHROOMS

———

Tarte Soufflée
SOUFFLÉED TART

Salade Danicheff
ARTICHOKE, ASPARAGUS, AND LANGOUSTINE SALAD

———

SERVES 6

Prince Danicheff was a Russian aristocrat and a well-known figure in Paris at the turn of the century. This salad was named in his honor. Noble asparagus, artichokes, and langoustines are combined with homely potatoes, mushrooms, and celery root in a mayonnaise lightened by whipped cream and seasoned with chives just before serving.

Note: Cut down on last-minute work by preparing the langoustines and vegetables several hours ahead of time and refrigerating; make the mayonnaise and assemble the salad at the last moment.

ARTICHOKE BOTTOMS
2 lemons
3 artichokes
Salt
2 tablespoons vegetable oil

1/2 pound waxy potatoes (red or white)

30 stalks green asparagus
6 large mushrooms, trimmed, rinsed and dried
Juice of 1 1/2 lemons, strained
3/4 pound celery root
24 langoustines in the shell (see page 114) or large shrimp
1/4 cup vegetable oil

CREAMED MAYONNAISE
2 egg yolks
1 tablespoon Dijon mustard
Salt and freshly ground pepper
1³/4 cups vegetable oil
Juice of ¹/2 lemon, strained

¹/2 cup heavy cream or
    crème fraîche
1 tablespoon chopped chives

1 head butter lettuce
¹/2 bunch chives for garnish

Prepare and cook the artichoke bottoms: Follow the directions on page 30 and technique photos on pages 520–21.

Rinse the unpeeled potatoes and put into a saucepan with cold salted water to cover. Bring to a boil and cook until tender when pierced with the point of a knife. Drain and let cool. Peel and slice ¹/8 inch thick.

Prepare the asparagus: Snap the tough ends off the asparagus. Trim the ends so that the stalks are all the same length. Tie into 3 equal bunches with kitchen twine. Bring a saucepan of salted water to a boil. Add the asparagus bundles and return the water to a boil. Cook until crisp-tender, 10 to 12 minutes. Drain and refresh in cold water; drain again. Remove the twine and spread the asparagus on a rack lined with paper towels to cool.

Remove the stems from the mushrooms and slice lengthwise into julienne (see technique photo on page 519). Slice the caps into rounds and discard the dark parts. Then cut the white rounds into julienne. Toss with a little lemon juice to prevent darkening.

Peel the celery root and cut into thin round slices. Cut into julienne approximately the same size as the mushrooms. Toss with lemon juice and cover with parchment or waxed paper to avoid darkening.

Shell the langoustines (see directions on page 115 and technique photos on page 523) or shrimp. Heat the oil in the frying pan until very hot. Add the langoustines and cook until pink, about 2 minutes. (If necessary, cook them in two batches; do not crowd the pan.) Set aside.

Slice the artichoke bottoms into rounds and then cut the rounds into julienne the same size as the mushrooms and the celery root. Sprinkle with lemon juice; set aside.

Prepare a mayonnaise using the above ingredients and following the directions on page 31 but use lemon juice instead of vinegar. When the mayonnaise is smooth and thick, whisk in the cream and add the chopped chives.

Toss the sliced potatoes with one-third of the mayonnaise. Combine the artichokes, celery root and mushrooms and gently toss with the remaining mayonnaise.

(continued)

Salade Danicheff (continued)

To serve, rinse, drain, and spin the lettuce dry. Arrange the leaves around the rim of a long serving platter, with the base of each leaf pointing toward the center. Arrange a bed of potatoes down the center of the platter. Mound the mixed salad of artichokes, celery root and mushrooms on top of the potatoes. Decorate the top with the whole chives, arranged in a lattice design. Arrange the asparagus spears, in pairs, on the lettuce leaves around the platter. Arrange the shelled langoustine tails around the mixed salad. (For individual plate presentation, see photo.)

Fricassée de Ris de Veau aux Pleurotes

FRICASSEED SWEETBREADS WITH OYSTER MUSHROOMS

SERVES 6

Veal sweetbreads are a delicacy on a par with the finest cuts of meat. They have no "tripe" taste; indeed, they are often compared to veal scallops and, like scallops, are frequently served with a creamy sauce.

Sweetbreads should be soaked in cold water to draw out any blood they might contain; they are parboiled before cooking to firm them up and make it easier to remove the thin membrane that surrounds each one.

NOTE: At Le Cordon Bleu, oyster mushrooms are used as a garnish for this fricassee. Other flavorful wild mushrooms, particularly chanterelles, may be used as well, or (in a pinch) fresh button mushrooms could take their place.

3 veal sweetbreads, approximately 12 ounces each
Salt and freshly ground pepper
6 tablespoons unsalted butter
1 large carrot, diced
1 large onion, diced
1 stalk celery, diced
1 medium leek (white part only), diced
2 cloves garlic, diced fine
3/4 cup Brown Veal Stock (page 71)

1/2 cup dry white wine
1 bay leaf
1 sprig thyme
1 medium shallot, chopped fine
1 pound oyster mushrooms, chopped coarse (see Note)
2/3 cup heavy cream
2 tablespoons chopped chervil or parsley

Unsalted butter, softened, for parchment paper

Prepare the sweetbreads (see technique photos on page 534): Soak the sweetbreads in cold water for about 4 hours to remove any impurities; drain. Put the sweetbreads into a large saucepan with cold water to cover. Bring to a boil, reduce the heat and simmer 2 minutes. Drain and refresh under cold running water; drain again. Carefully pull off the ducts and fat. Then remove the thin outer membrane with the point of a small knife. Reserve these trimmings.

Preheat the oven to 400°.

Season the sweetbreads with salt and pepper. Heat 3 tablespoons of the butter in a large ovenproof frying pan over high heat. Add the sweetbreads and cook until golden brown on both sides. Remove and set aside. Add the diced vegetables and garlic to the pan. Stir to coat well with butter. Reduce the heat to low and cook until tender but not colored. Add the stock, wine, bay leaf and thyme, along with the trimmings from the sweetbreads. Place the sweetbreads on top of the vegetables and season with salt and pepper. Bring to a boil, cover with a round of buttered parchment paper, and transfer to the oven. Cook, basting occasionally with the cooking liquid, until very tender, about 40 minutes.

While the sweetbreads are cooking, prepare the mushrooms: Heat the remaining 3 tablespoons of butter in a large frying pan over low heat. Add the shallot and cook until tender but not colored. Increase the heat to high and add the mushrooms. Cook, stirring constantly, until all liquid has evaporated. Season to taste with salt and pepper and stir in the cream. Bring to a boil and then remove from the heat; set aside. Cover to keep warm.

When the sweetbreads are tender, transfer from the pan to a container; cover to keep warm. Strain the cooking liquid into a small saucepan and reduce over medium heat by three-quarters; the liquid should become thick and syrupy. Add to the mushroom mixture.

To serve, cut the sweetbreads diagonally into slices about ½ inch thick and arrange on a serving platter. Spoon the mushroom sauce over and sprinkle with chervil.

Tarte Soufflée

SOUFFLÉED TART

SERVES 6

Two desserts in one: a soufflé flavored with candied fruit is baked in a tart shell rather than in a traditional mold. Remember that this is a soufflé and that the proverb that applies to other soufflés applies here: "Everyone waits for a soufflé, but a soufflé waits for no one."

¹/₄ cup mixed candied fruit, diced
3 tablespoons kirsch

PÂTE BRISÉE SUCRÉE
1 cup all-purpose flour
¹/₂ cup cake flour
1 egg
Pinch of salt
1 tablespoon water
3 tablespoons sugar
1 teaspoon vanilla extract
7 tablespoons unsalted butter
1 egg, lightly beaten, for glazing

PASTRY CREAM
1 cup milk
1 teaspoon vanilla extract
2 egg yolks
¹/₃ cup sugar
2 tablespoons all-purpose flour
2 tablespoons cornstarch

1 egg yolk
2 egg whites
Confectioner's sugar for dusting
1 whole candied cherry

EQUIPMENT: 8-inch fluted, removable-bottomed tart pan

Macerate the candied fruits in kirsch; set aside.

Prepare the pâte brisée sucrée just as you would a pâte brisée, using the above ingredients and following the directions on pages 37–38 and technique photos on page 540. Put the sugar and the vanilla into the well along with the egg, salt and water; line the tart pan with the dough and blind bake it (pages 38–39 and technique photos on page 541).

Preheat the oven to 400°.

Prepare the pastry cream: Use the above ingredients. Follow the directions on page 183, but do not cool: Stir in the candied fruit and kirsch, and the egg yolk while the cream is still warm. Blend well.

Beat the egg whites with a whisk, or electric mixer, until stiff peaks form. Fold gently into the warm pastry cream. Pour into the cooked pastry shell and smooth the top. Bake until the top is puffed and golden and a knife inserted into the center of the tart comes out clean, 15 to 20 minutes. Sift confectioner's sugar over the top and decorate the center of the tart with the candied cherry. Serve immediately.

LESSON 48

Consommé Madrilène

CHILLED CONSOMMÉ WITH RED PEPPERS
AND TOMATOES

—

Boeuf Bourguignon

BEEF STEW, BURGUNDY STYLE

—

Fraises Margot

STRAWBERRY MOUSSE WITH PISTACHIOS
AND STRAWBERRY COULIS

INTERMÉDIAIRE

Consommé Madrilène

CHILLED CONSOMMÉ WITH RED PEPPERS AND TOMATOES

SERVES 6

Though any dish containing tomatoes can be called "Madrilène" or "Madrid-style," the term is almost exclusively used to designate this particular chilled consommé, perhaps because the golden consommé and the red garnish echo the colors of the Spanish flag.

Note: The method used to clarify chicken stock in this recipe can be applied to any stock to make consommé.

CLARIFICATION
10 cups Chicken Stock (page 12),
    well skimmed of fat
Salt
12 ounces very lean ground beef
1 leek (green part only),
    chopped fine
1/2 stalk celery, chopped fine
2 carrots, chopped fine
3 medium tomatoes, chopped
2 tablespoons fine-chopped
    fresh herbs (parsley,
    chervil, and tarragon)

1 teaspoon fresh thyme leaves or
    1/4 teaspoon dried
1/2 bay leaf
2 egg whites
30 peppercorns, crushed

8 ounces red bell pepper, diced fine
1 small tomato, peeled, seeded,
    and diced (page 31)
Chervil or parsley leaves
    for garnish

Prepare the clarification: Season the stock with salt and bring to a boil in a large saucepan. Combine the beef, vegetables, herbs, egg whites, and peppercorns in a large bowl and mix well. Add 1/4 cup water and a little of the hot stock. Stir well and pour the mixture into the saucepan of hot stock. Return the mixture to a boil over medium heat, whisking and scraping the bottom of the pan to make sure that nothing sticks. Do not whisk or stir after the mixture boils. Reduce the heat and simmer 45 to 60 minutes. As the mixture simmers, the egg white mixture will form a soft crust on top of the stock through which the impurities will rise and be filtered. (If there is no natural break in the crust through which the stock can bubble up, gently clear a hole or "chimney" with a ladle.)

Rinse a clean dish towel in water and wring it out to remove the excess moisture. Line a fine strainer with the dish towel and set it over a bowl. Slowly pour the clarified stock through the strainer, being careful not to disturb the crust. Do not squeeze or press down on the contents of the strainer, or the stock will become cloudy; leave it to filter through the dish towel and strainer. Remove the strainer carefully and discard the contents. Degrease the stock by pulling strips of paper towels across the surface. Let cool and then chill the clarified consommé in the refrigerator.

(continued)

Consommé Madrilène (continued)

Put the diced red pepper in a small saucepan with cold salted water to cover. Bring to a boil and blanch for 10 minutes; drain. Refresh under cold running water and drain again.

To serve, ladle a serving of cold consommé into each of 6 soup bowls. Add a little diced tomato and red pepper to each. Garnish with chervil.

CONSOMMÉ

A consommé is a crystal-clear, flavorful broth made from a stock (most commonly beef, veal, or poultry, although one occasionally sees a fish consommé as well) that has been "clarified" of all cloudiness and impurities. It may be served as a soup, with or without a garnish, or, if the stock is naturally gelatinous or has gelatin added, as aspic.

The clarification process is accomplished by simmering a well-defatted stock through a crust of congealed egg whites. First, the whites are stirred into the stock along with a mixture of lean beef, vegetables, and aromatic herbs to enrich its flavor (in the Consommé Madrilène above, tomatoes are added to give the consommé its amber color). The mixture is brought slowly to a boil—it must be stirred constantly during this time to keep the whites from sticking and burning on the bottom of the pan—and then simmered. Once the mixture has come to the boil, the egg whites will solidify into a soft crust on top of the stock and the mixture must not be stirred at all; stirring will cause the clarification to become cloudy. Any fats and solid impurities in the stock will attach to the whites as the stock filters through and the stock will be left beautifully transparent.

After the consommé has been clarified, it is strained through a damp-towel-lined strainer. Do not press down on the solids at all or you will return the impurities to the stock; it is better to forfeit a tiny amount of liquid than to lose the results of your work.

Boeuf Bourguignon
BEEF STEW, BURGUNDY STYLE

SERVES 6

French butchers tend to call any stewing cut of beef *bourguignon* not because it comes from Burgundy but because they assume most people making a beef stew will be making this one. They are probably right, for this once regional specialty is now a standard preparation on national (if not to say international) tables.

MARINADE

2 garlic cloves, crushed

2 onions, sliced

2 carrots, sliced

10 parsley stems

Bouquet Garni (page 20)

20 peppercorns, crushed

Salt

3 tablespoons cognac

*1 bottle dry red wine, preferably
    Burgundy*

2 tablespoons vegetable oil

*3 pounds lean stewing beef
    (preferably chuck), trimmed
    of excess fat and cut into
    1½-to-2-inch cubes*

Salt and freshly ground pepper

6 tablespoons vegetable oil

2 tablespoons all-purpose flour

1 tablespoon tomato paste

3 tomatoes, quartered

GARNISH

*½ pound slab bacon, sliced
    ¼ inch thick*

4 tablespoons vegetable oil

30 pearl onions

3 tablespoons unsalted butter

1 tablespoon sugar

*¾ pound button or quartered
    large mushrooms, trimmed,
    rinsed, and dried*

HEART-SHAPED CROUTONS

*6 slices firm white bread,
    crusts removed*

*3 tablespoons unsalted butter,
    melted*

2 tablespoons chopped parsley

*Unsalted butter for
    parchment paper*

Prepare the marinade: Combine all of the ingredients except the oil in a large, nonaluminum container. Add the meat (it must be totally submerged in the liquid) and sprinkle the surface with the oil. Cover and marinate for 12 hours.

Preheat the oven to 400°.

Remove the beef from the marinade and drain well on paper towels. Remove the garlic and bouquet garni; set aside. Strain and reserve the marinating liquid. Drain the marinated vegetables on paper towels; set aside.

Heat ¼ cup of the oil in a large frying pan over high heat until very hot. Season the beef with salt and pepper and add to the pan, a few pieces at a time. Sauté, turning frequently, until evenly browned. Remove the beef from the pan and discard the oil. Add the remaining 2 tablespoons of oil to the pan. Reduce the heat to medium, add the marinated vegetables, and cook until lightly colored. Add the beef, sprinkle with flour and stir well. Stir in the tomato paste and cook 1 minute. Add the reserved marinating liquid along with the garlic, bouquet garni and the quartered tomatoes. Add water as needed to cover all of the ingredients. Bring to a boil and cover with a buttered round of parchment paper and then with a lid. Transfer to the oven, reduce the oven heat to 375° and cook until the beef is tender when pierced with the point of a knife, about 2½ hours.

Prepare the garnish: Cut the bacon into lardons; blanch and drain (page 46). Heat 2 tablespoons of the oil in a small frying pan over high heat. Add the lardons and sauté until golden brown. Drain and set aside.

Prepare and glaze the onions (page 165), using 1 tablespoon of the butter and the sugar.

(continued)

Boeuf Bourguignon (continued)

Heat the remaining 2 tablespoons oil and 2 tablespoons butter in a large frying pan over high heat. Add the mushrooms and cook quickly until all moisture has evaporated, about 5 minutes. Season to taste with salt and pepper; set aside.

When the beef is tender, remove from the cooking liquid with a slotted spoon; set aside. Strain the cooking liquid, pressing down on the vegetables with the back of a spoon to extract all of the liquid; discard the solids. Skim any fat from the surface of the cooking liquid and return it to the pan along with the beef. Add the lardons, onions and mushrooms and cook over medium heat for 15 minutes.

Prepare the croutons: Preheat the oven to 425°. Cut the bread in half, diagonally, to make triangles. With a small knife, round off the shortest sides of the triangles. Then, make a V-shaped incision midway along the rounded edges to make heart shapes; trim the hearts to even them. Or, cut the bread into heart shapes with a cookie cutter. Brush both sides with melted butter and transfer to a baking sheet. Bake until golden, about 8 minutes.

To serve, transfer the beef, lardons, onions and mushrooms to a large platter with a slotted spoon. Dip the pointed end of the croutons first in the sauce and then in chopped parsley. Arrange around the stew with the parsley-dipped ends pointing outward. Spoon the sauce over the beef and sprinkle the meat with the remaining parsley. Accompany with Pommes à l'Anglaise (page 50), if desired, or Pâtes Fraîches (page 199).

Fraises Margot

STRAWBERRY MOUSSE WITH PISTACHIOS
AND STRAWBERRY COULIS

———

SERVES 6

This mousse is a quick, lightened version of a bavarian cream (page 41). Instead of using a crème anglaise, it is made by simply combining softened gelatin and whipped cream with a strawberry puree.

The pink color of the mousse, the dark red of the fresh strawberry sauce, and the bright green of the pistachios make this a beautiful end to any meal.

2 pint baskets strawberries
1 cup confectioner's sugar
Juice of 1 lemon, strained
1¹/₂ envelopes powdered gelatin
  (³/₄ ounce)
3 tablespoons cold water
1¹/₂ cups heavy cream

STRAWBERRY COULIS
Strawberry puree (see above)
³/₄ cup confectioner's sugar
Juice of ¹/₂ lemon, strained

2 tablespoons shelled pistachios

CHANTILLY CREAM
1 cup heavy cream
2 tablespoons confectioner's sugar
1 teaspoon vanilla extract

EQUIPMENT: 6-cup charlotte mold, pastry bag, medium star pastry tip

Chill a mixing bowl for the whipped cream.

Rinse and dry the strawberries. Set aside about 10 small, perfect strawberries for garnish, hull the remainder, and puree in a food processor or pass through a food mill. Reserve half for the strawberry coulis. Add the 1 cup sugar and the lemon juice to the remaining puree.

Sprinkle the gelatin over the water in a heatproof container and let stand until softened, about 5 minutes.

Bring 2 to 3 inches of water to a simmer in a small saucepan. Set the container of softened gelatin in it and let stand until liquid. Whisk the liquified gelatin into the sweetened strawberry puree.

Beat the cream with a whisk or electric mixer in the chilled bowl until stiff peaks form and the cream clings to the whisk. Fold in the strawberry mixture with a wooden spoon.

Sprinkle the inside of a charlotte mold with cold water; invert and tap out excess. Cut out a round of parchment paper to the diameter of the bottom of the mold and line the mold with it. Pour in the strawberry-cream mixture and smooth the surface with a metal spatula. Refrigerate until firm, 4 to 5 hours.

Prepare the strawberry coulis: Pass the reserved puree through a fine sieve to remove the seeds. Whisk in the sugar and lemon juice; refrigerate.

Bring a saucepan of water to a boil. Add the pistachios, and then immediately remove the pan from the heat. Let stand for 10 minutes. Drain the pistachios and rinse in cold water. Peel and chop coarse; set aside.

Not more than 1 hour before serving, prepare the Chantilly cream (page 21). Fit a pastry bag with the medium star tip and fill it with the Chantilly cream; refrigerate until serving time.

Unmold the dessert: Dip the mold into hot water for a few seconds. Then dip a knife blade in cold water and slide it all around the inside of the mold. Invert a dessert platter over the mold and quickly reverse the two. Peel off and discard the parchment paper.

To serve, spoon a little of the strawberry coulis around the base of the mousse. Decorate the top with a circle of Chantilly cream rosettes and a smaller circle of strawberries enclosing a central rosette sprinkled with the chopped pistachios. (See photo on page 266.) Serve the remaining coulis and Chantilly cream in sauceboats on the side.

LESSON 49

Salade Gourmande

GOURMET SALAD OF GREEN BEANS, MUSHROOMS,
FOIE GRAS, AND LANGOUSTINES

———

Turbot, Sauce Hollandaise

TURBOT WITH HOLLANDAISE SAUCE

———

Charlotte au Chocolat

CHOCOLATE CHARLOTTE

Salade Gourmande

GOURMET SALAD OF GREEN BEANS, MUSHROOMS, FOIE GRAS, AND LANGOUSTINES

SERVES 6

Foie gras is the buttery liver of a specially fattened (force-fed) goose or duck. Up until recently, it was most often encountered in Alsace and south-western France, its chief centers of production, but today chefs throughout the country have foie gras on their menus.

ARTICHOKE BOTTOMS
6 artichokes
2 lemons
Salt
2 tablespoons vegetable oil

3/4 pound green beans
1/2 pound mushrooms, trimmed, rinsed, and dried
18 langoustines (see page 114) or large shrimp, in the shell
2 tablespoons olive oil
1 head red leaf lettuce

VINAIGRETTE
1/4 cup sherry vinegar
1 shallot, chopped fine
Salt and freshly ground pepper
1/4 cup walnut oil
1/2 cup vegetable oil
1 tablespoon chopped fresh chervil or parsley
6 slices rye bread

1/2 pound prepared foie gras, chilled
Chervil for garnish

Prepare and cook the artichoke bottoms. Follow the directions on page 30 and technique photos on pages 520–21.

Snap the ends off the green beans. Bring a large saucepan of salted water to a boil and add the beans. Return the water to a boil and cook until the beans are crisp-tender, 8 to 10 minutes. Drain and refresh under cold running water; drain again. Transfer to a large bowl; set aside.

Remove the mushroom stems and refrigerate for another use (soups, fish stock, or salads). Cut the caps into julienne (technique photo on page 519).

Shell the langoustines (see directions on page 115 and technique photos on page 523). Heat the olive oil in a large nonstick frying pan over high heat. Add the langoustines and cook until pink, 2 to 3 minutes; set aside.

Rinse, drain, and spin the lettuce dry; set aside.

Prepare the vinaigrette: Combine the vinegar, chopped shallot, salt and pepper in a bowl. Whisk in the oils. Add the chopped chervil.

Slice the artichoke bottoms thin, slightly on the bias. Add to the bowl with the green beans. Add the mushroom slices and the vinaigrette. Toss carefully.

Toast the bread.

To serve, arrange the lettuce leaves around the outside of a round serving platter. Mound the mixed vegetable salad in the center. Shave off strips of the chilled foie gras with a vegetable peeler and carefully arrange on the mounded vegetables. Put a sprig of chervil on each shaving. Garnish the salad with the langoustines and serve with the toast.

Turbot, Sauce Hollandaise
TURBOT WITH HOLLANDAISE SAUCE

SERVES 6

Turbot is a European flatfish that can grow to a gigantic size. Up until this century, a whole turbot was considered a mandatory pièce de résistance in well-to-do homes, and a special turbot-shaped pot *(turbotière)* was invented for cooking the fish. Today, turbot remains highly esteemed though one is more likely to encounter it *en filets* than whole, at least at the dinner table. Then as now, its classic accompaniment remains a buttery hollandaise and parsley-flecked boiled or steamed potatoes.

Note: As turbot is not often available in the United States, halibut or flounder fillets may be used instead.

2 pounds small waxy potatoes (red or white)
6 turbot fillets, 8 ounces each
2/3 cup milk
Salt
6 peppercorns
Several sprigs thyme or 1/2 teaspoon dried
1 bay leaf

HOLLANDAISE SAUCE
3 egg yolks
1/4 cup water
1/2 pound unsalted butter, clarified (page 94) and cooled to lukewarm
Salt
Cayenne pepper
Juice of 1/2 lemon, strained

2 tablespoons chopped parsley
Parsley sprigs for garnish

Turn and cook the potatoes following the directions for pommes à l'anglaise (see recipe on page 50 and technique photo page 520). Keep warm in cooking liquid.

Put the fish fillets in a large shallow pan. Add the milk, salt, peppercorns, thyme, bay leaf and enough water to just cover the fillets. Bring to a boil, immediately reduce the heat and simmer gently for 5 minutes or until tender. Remove from the heat and let stand in the cooking liquid.

Prepare the hollandaise sauce: Combine the egg yolks and water in a medium, heavy-bottomed saucepan and whisk continuously over very low heat until the mixture becomes frothy and thickens, and the whisk leaves a clear trail on the bottom of the pan. Do not let the mixture boil. Remove from the heat. Whisk in the clarified butter drop by drop until the mixture starts to emulsify. Then, whisk in the remaining butter in a slow steady stream until the sauce thickens. Season to taste with salt, cayenne pepper and lemon juice. Set aside, off the heat, in a pan of warm water.

To serve, remove the fillets from the pan with a slotted spoon. Drain on a dish towel or paper towels. Arrange the fillets in the center of a serving platter. Drain the potatoes, dip one end in the chopped parsley and arrange a few around the fish, parsley-dipped ends pointing outward. Decorate the platter with sprigs of parsley. Serve the remaining potatoes in a serving dish and the hollandaise in a sauceboat on the side.

HOLLANDAISE AND RELATED SAUCES

A hollandaise sauce, like a mayonnaise (page 31), is a creamy emulsification of fat and egg yolk. A hollandaise differs from a mayonnaise, however, in a number of ways: A hollandaise is served hot, it is made with melted butter rather than oil, and it has a lighter, airier consistency than mayonnaise because the egg yolks are whipped to a foamy consistency over heat before the butter is added.

A hollandaise is not particularly complicated but, as always, the egg yolks are a bit tricky. They must be cooked slowly over a low heat, whisking constantly, to prevent graining. Then the melted butter, cooled to lukewarm (again, in consideration of the delicate eggs), is whisked in off the heat, drop by drop until the mixture begins to thicken, and then in a steady stream, just like a mayonnaise.

There are various ways to "fix" a broken hollandaise. If the sauce separates, it may be too hot: Try whisking in a tablespoon of cold water or an ice cube to cool it. If the sauce won't thicken, you may have added the butter too quickly: Whisk a little of the sauce with a tablespoon of cold water or lemon juice in a clean pan until thickened and then whisk in the remaining sauce in a steady stream. If, however, you overcook your eggs and they become grainy, your sauce is ruined—you must start over again.

Variations on the hollandaise are made with the addition of flavorings such as orange (sauce maltaise), mustard (sauce moutarde), brown butter (sauce noisette), or whipped cream (sauce mousseline). Also in the same family but made a little differently is the béarnaise sauce and its derivatives; these sauces start with a reduction of wine, vinegar, and aromatics and finish just like a hollandaise.

Hollandaise and its variations are delicious served with vegetables, eggs, and fish dishes.

Charlotte au Chocolat
CHOCOLATE CHARLOTTE

SERVES 6

When Antonin Carême lined a high-sided mold with ladyfingers and filled it with a bavarian cream he called his creation a *charlotte à la Parisienne*. This was in the early years of the nineteenth century. Later called a *charlotte russe* and then, finally, simply a *charlotte*, this dessert is now made around the world and in as many flavors and sizes as one can imagine. At Le Cordon Bleu this is our favorite. A rich chocolate filling is surrounded with homemade ladyfingers and served with a cool vanilla sauce—superb!

(continued)

Charlotte au Chocolat (continued)

LADYFINGERS

3 eggs, separated

6 tablespoons granulated sugar

3/4 cup cake flour

6 tablespoons confectioner's sugar

2 tablespoons rum

2 tablespoons water

9 ounces semisweet chocolate,
  cut into small pieces

1/2 pound unsalted butter,
  softened

2 egg yolks

2 egg whites

CRÈME ANGLAISE

2 cups milk

1 teaspoon vanilla extract

4 egg yolks

1/3 cup sugar

EQUIPMENT: Pastry bag, large plain pastry tip, 6-cup charlotte mold

Prepare the ladyfingers: Use the above ingredients and follow the directions on page 118 and technique photos on page 549.

Line the charlotte mold with ladyfingers (see technique photos on page 549): First, line the bottom of the mold: Cut 6 to 8 ladyfingers in half crosswise and trim the cut end of each to a V shape. (Each piece will resemble a daisy petal.) Turn mold upside down and arrange the shaped ladyfingers on the bottom to form a flower pattern. Do not leave any space between pieces. If necessary, trim again to fit tight. Use a small round cookie cutter to cut a circle in the center of the flower; discard the loose pieces. Use the same cutter to cut a neat round piece from another ladyfinger. Place in the center of the flower. Invert a plate on top of mold and reverse the two. Re-form the flower, rounded side facing down, in bottom of mold.

Second, line the sides of the mold: Square off one end each of about 14 ladyfingers, leaving them long enough to extend above the rim of the mold. Trim the sides slightly and fit tightly around the inside of mold, rounded ends up. Trim again, if necessary, and fill any spaces.

Mix the rum and water in a small bowl. Brush the ladyfingers with the rum mixture, starting with the sides of the mold and then brushing the base.

Bring 1 to 2 inches of water just to a simmer in a saucepan. Put the pieces of chocolate in a heatproof bowl and set it over the simmering water. Let stand, without stirring, until the chocolate melts completely. Remove from heat. Gradually whisk the softened butter into the melted chocolate. Stir in the egg yolks one by one with a wooden spoon until well blended.

Beat the egg whites with a whisk or electric mixer until stiff peaks form. Whisk one-third of the whites into the chocolate mixture to loosen it, then fold the mixture carefully into the remaining egg whites with a wooden spoon. Pour into the lined charlotte mold, up to the rim. Refrigerate until firm, 4 to 5 hours.

Prepare the crème anglaise: Use the above ingredients and follow the directions on page 35. Chill.

To serve, remove the charlotte from the refrigerator. Use a small sharp knife to trim the ladyfingers to the level of the filling. Invert a round platter over the charlotte. Quickly reverse the two and slide the charlotte mold off. Serve the chilled crème anglaise in a sauceboat on the side.

Pain de Poisson, Sauce Crevette
WARM FISH TERRINE WITH SHRIMP SAUCE

———

Tournedos Baltimore
TENDERLOIN STEAKS WITH CHÂTEAUBRIAND SAUCE

———

Pêches Melba
PEACH MELBA

Pain de Poisson, Sauce Crevette
WARM FISH TERRINE WITH SHRIMP SAUCE

———

SERVES 6

A terrine is an oval or rectangular dish used for baking an aromatic mixture of ingredients, generally chopped; by extension, the preparation that fills the dish is also called a terrine. It can also be referred to as a *pâté* and, occasionally, as a *pain*. Technically speaking, however, a *pain* (literally a "loaf") is unlike a classic terrine in several respects: it is generally turned out after baking and served warm with a sauce, whereas terrines are typically served cold in the mold they baked in and without a sauce.

Though French chefs have recently begun experimenting with new types of terrines made with vegetables, fruit, or fish, traditional terrines are generally made with meat. *Pains*, on the other hand, have long been made from a wide variety of ingredients, and classic French cookbooks contain numerous recipes for *pains* made of game, fish, shellfish, poultry, vegetables, and even eggs. Indeed, this very recipe can be found in cookbooks written over a hundred years ago—the only difference being that, in the older versions, chefs decorated their *pains de poisson* with thin slices of fresh black truffle to make them "richer," creating a sensational contrast of colors and tastes.

Note: At Le Cordon Bleu either white-fleshed fish (hake or pike) or pink-fleshed salmon is used when making this *pain;* it is always served with a shrimp and garlic-flavored sauce. In France, shrimp are almost systematically sold boiled and ready to eat. Chefs at Le Cordon Bleu prefer using a popular, inexpensive variety of small gray shrimp known as *crevettes grises* when making this shrimp sauce, but an equal weight of ordinary shrimp could be used instead.

FISH MOUSSELINE

1 pound salmon, pike,
  or hake fillet, skinned
Salt and freshly ground pepper
1/2 cup crème fraîche or
  heavy cream
3/4 cup fresh white bread crumbs
  for loaf pan

BÉCHAMEL SAUCE

2 tablespoons unsalted butter
3 tablespoons all-purpose flour
1 cup milk
Salt and freshly ground pepper

1/4 cup crème fraîche or
  heavy cream
2 eggs
2 egg yolks
Pinch cayenne pepper

SHRIMP SAUCE

3 tablespoons unsalted butter
1 medium onion, chopped fine
1 carrot, diced fine
1 stalk celery, diced fine
1 leek (white part only),
  chopped fine
3 cloves garlic, crushed
1 tablespoon tomato paste
6 ounces small shrimp (preferably
  the tiny brown shrimp known in
  France as "crevettes grises"),
  shelled and chopped coarse
1/4 cup cognac
1 cup dry white wine
3 tomatoes, quartered
1 Bouquet Garni (page 20)
Salt and freshly ground pepper
1/2 cup crème fraîche or
  heavy cream

3 ounces cooked shrimp, shelled
1 tablespoon unsalted butter
Pinch of paprika
Fresh chervil or parsley, chopped
  fine, for garnish

Unsalted butter, softened, for
  loaf pans and parchment paper

EQUIPMENT: Two 7-by-2 3/4-by-2 1/2-inch loaf pans

Prepare the mousseline: Chill a mixing bowl. Working from tail to head, run your fingers over the surface of the fish fillet to detect any small bones; remove them. Pass the fish through a meat grinder fitted with the finest disc, or puree in a food processor. Work the puree through a fine sieve to eliminate any remaining bones. Transfer the puree to the chilled bowl and set it over a larger bowl of crushed ice. Season with salt and pepper. Add the cream little by little, beating vigorously with a wooden spoon in a forward-to-backward motion until the mixture is well blended and smooth. Taste and adjust seasonings; refrigerate.

Brush the loaf pans with the softened butter. Coat with the bread crumbs and tap out the excess.

Preheat the oven to 400°.

Prepare the béchamel sauce. Use the above ingredients and follow the directions on page 18. Remove from the heat.

Stir together the cream, whole eggs, egg yolks, and cayenne pepper until blended. Gradually whisk into the béchamel. Return the mixture to the heat, and cook for a few minutes, stirring constantly. Do not allow to boil. Remove from the heat and fold in the chilled fish mixture.

Pour the fish mixture into the loaf pans and tap on a flat surface to remove any air bubbles. Put the loaf pans into a roasting pan and pour in hot water to come halfway up the loaf pans. Bring to a simmer on top of the stove over medium heat. Then transfer to the oven and cook until a knife inserted into the center is warm to the touch and clean when withdrawn, 20 to 25 minutes.

While the terrines are cooking, prepare the sauce: Melt the butter in a large skillet over medium heat. Add the onion, carrot, celery and leek and cook, stirring frequently with a wooden spoon, until tender but not colored, 5 to 10 minutes. Stir in the garlic and tomato paste. Then stir in the chopped shrimp and cook 1 to 2 minutes. Add the cognac and carefully light with a match. When the flames die, add the wine, quartered tomatoes and bouquet garni. Season to taste with salt and pepper. Cover with a round of buttered parchment paper. Reduce the heat and simmer gently for 25 minutes. Stir in the cream, then bring to a boil over high heat and cook for 1 minute. Strain through a fine sieve, pressing down on the solids to extract as much liquid as possible; discard the solids. The sauce should be just thick enough to coat the back of a spoon. If it is too thin, return it to the saucepan and reduce over medium heat until thickened.

Put the cooked shrimp in a saucepan with the butter. Heat gently over medium heat until warmed through, about 2 minutes.

To serve, remove the terrines from the oven. Let cool for about 5 minutes. Slide a knife around each terrine, then invert onto an oval platter to unmold. Arrange the terrines diagonally on the platter and spoon some sauce around the base of each. Garnish with the shrimp. Sprinkle a little paprika over the terrines and garnish the centers with a little chopped chervil. Serve the remaining sauce in a sauceboat on the side.

Tournedos Baltimore
TENDERLOIN STEAKS WITH CHÂTEAUBRIAND SAUCE

SERVES 6

Few American cities can claim the honor of having a French dish named after them. Baltimore is an exception. At the turn of the century, Escoffier included this recipe in his famous *Guide Culinaire* and it has been part of the classic repertoire ever since.

(continued)

Tournedos Baltimore (continued)

Like most dishes that evoke the New World, this recipe includes corn (an oddity in France) but, otherwise, it has little or nothing to do with the way steaks are cooked and served in Baltimore or elsewhere in the U.S.

PÂTE BRISÉE
1 cup all-purpose flour
1/2 cup cake flour
1 egg
1 tablespoon water
Pinch of salt
7 tablespoons unsalted butter
1 egg, lightly beaten, for glazing

CHÂTEAUBRIAND SAUCE
15 tablespoons unsalted butter
3 shallots, chopped fine
5 ounces mushrooms, trimmed, rinsed, dried, and chopped fine
1 bay leaf
1 sprig fresh thyme or 1/4 teaspoon dried
3/4 cup dry white wine
1 cup Brown Veal Stock (page 71)
1 tablespoon chopped fresh tarragon or 1 teaspoon dried
1 tablespoon chopped parsley
Salt and freshly ground pepper

1 green bell pepper, cut into julienne (see technique photo on page 519)
1 can (16-ounce) corn kernels
1 tablespoon unsalted butter
Salt and freshly ground pepper
2 tomatoes
2 tablespoons vegetable oil
6 beef tenderloin steaks, 7 ounces each
Watercress for garnish

EQUIPMENT: Six 3-inch tartlet molds

Prepare the pâte brisée, using the above ingredients and following the directions on pages 37–38 and technique photos on page 540.

Line and bake the tartlet molds (see technique photos on page 541): On a lightly floured work surface, roll out the pâte brisée dough about 1/8 inch thick and then cut out 6 rounds with a 4-inch fluted cookie cutter. Gently press the dough onto the bottom and sides of the molds; the dough should extend slightly above the rims. Refrigerate for 30 minutes. Meantime, preheat the oven to 400°.

Lightly prick the bottom of each tartlet shell with a fork. Put a smaller mold inside each to prevent the pastry from rising and deforming during cooking (or line with a round of parchment paper and dried beans as described in technique photo 6 on page 541). Bake for 10 minutes. Remove the smaller molds (or the parchment paper and beans). Brush the interior of each tartlet shell with egg glaze and bake until golden brown, about 5 minutes longer. Let cool slightly and then remove the tartlet shells from the molds; set aside.

Prepare the châteaubriand sauce: Heat 3 tablespoons of butter in a medium frying pan over medium heat. Add the shallots and cook until soft but not colored. Stir in the mushrooms and cook for a few minutes. Add the bay leaf, thyme and white wine. Bring to a boil, reduce the heat and simmer until the liquid has evaporated. Remove the bay leaf and thyme sprig. Add the stock, tarragon and parsley and season to taste with salt and pepper. Bring to a boil, remove from the heat and whisk in the remaining butter, bit by bit. Taste and adjust seasonings. Set aside off the heat in a pan of warm water.

Bring a small saucepan of salted water to a boil. Add the julienned green peppers and blanch 5 minutes. Drain; cover to keep warm,

Drain the corn. Heat 1 tablespoon of the butter in a skillet over low heat. Add the corn and cook until warmed through and coated with the butter. Season to taste with salt and pepper. Cover to keep warm.

Preheat the oven to 400°.

Slice the top and bottom off each tomato and discard. Cut each tomato crosswise into three equal slices. Put the slices in a single layer on a baking sheet. Season with salt and pepper and drizzle with 1 tablespoon of the oil. Bake 3 to 5 minutes.

Tie a length of kitchen twine around each beef tenderloin steak to hold its shape during cooking. Heat the remaining tablespoon oil in a large frying pan until very hot. Season the steaks on both sides with salt and pepper. Add to the pan and sear on both sides. (Use a spatula or tongs rather than a fork to turn the steaks; a fork would pierce the meat, allowing the juices to escape.) Continue cooking until done as desired (see page 129).

To serve, rewarm the tart shells in the hot oven. Arrange the steaks down the center of a serving platter. Place a baked tomato slice on each and top with strips of green pepper. Fill the tartlets with corn and arrange on both sides of the steaks. Put 2 small bouquets of watercress at both ends of the platter. Spoon a little châteaubriand sauce around the steaks; serve the remainder in a sauceboat on the side. (For individual plate servings, see photo on page 280.)

Pêches Melba
PEACH MELBA

—

SERVES 6

Like the previous dish, this is an Escoffier creation. He invented it while chef at the Savoy restaurant in London and named it in honor of the famous opera singer Nellie Melba. Originally it was served without a sauce, in a silver bowl hidden between the wings of a swan carved in ice. Escoffier later simplified its presentation and added the raspberry sauce; this final version of his recipe is the one served throughout the world and taught to students at Le Cordon Bleu today.

6 small ripe yellow peaches

SUGAR SYRUP
1¹/₄ cups water
³/₄ cup sugar
Juice of ¹/₂ lemon

VANILLA ICE CREAM
CRÈME ANGLAISE:
2 cups milk
1 teaspoon vanilla extract
4 egg yolks
¹/₂ cup sugar

RASPBERRY COULIS
1³/₄ cups raspberries
3 tablespoons confectioner's sugar
¹/₂ cup sliced almonds

2 tablespoons confectioner's sugar

EQUIPMENT: Ice cream maker

Peel the peaches (page 9).

Prepare the syrup: Combine the water, sugar and lemon juice in a heavy bottomed saucepan. Bring to a boil over low heat, stirring to dissolve the sugar. Boil 1 to 2 minutes. Add the peaches, return the syrup to a boil and then simmer until the peaches are tender when pierced with the point of a knife, 7 to 8 minutes. Remove the pan from the heat and let the peaches cool in the syrup. Refrigerate the peaches in the syrup.

Chill a bowl and 6 dessert glasses in the freezer.

Prepare the ice cream: First make a crème anglaise. Use the milk, vanilla, egg yolks, and sugar and follow the directions on page 81. Let cool and then transfer to an ice cream maker and freeze according to the manufacturer's instructions. Transfer to the chilled bowl and freeze until firm, at least 1 hour.

Make a raspberry coulis: Puree the raspberries in a food mill or food processor. Strain through a fine strainer to remove the seeds. Whisk in the confectioner's sugar and chill.

Preheat the broiler.

Spread the almonds on a baking sheet and sprinkle with a little of the peach syrup and the confectioner's sugar. Broil until lightly browned; let cool.

Remove the chilled peaches from the syrup. Cut into halves and discard the stones.

To serve, place a scoop of ice cream in each chilled dessert glass. Top each with 2 peach halves. Spoon 1 tablespoon of raspberry coulis over. Sprinkle with the broiled almonds and serve immediately. Serve the remaining raspberry coulis in a sauceboat on the side.

LESSON 51

*Croustades d'Oeufs Pochés,
Sauce Hollandaise*

EGG TARTLETS WITH HOLLANDAISE SAUCE

———

Rôti de Veau Nivernaise

ROAST LOIN OF VEAL WITH ROOT
VEGETABLES AND BRAISED LETTUCE

———

Coupe Dijonnaise

RED-WINE–POACHED PEARS WITH
BLACKBERRY SORBET

INTERMÉDIAIRE

Croustades d'Oeufs Pochés, Sauce Hollandaise

EGG TARTLETS WITH HOLLANDAISE SAUCE

SERVES 6

A *croustade* is a small pastry shell made of short crust or puff pastry, baked, and allowed to cool before being filled with a garnish. *Croustades* were once baked in extremely ornate molds and filled with such delicacies as lobsters and truffles. At Le Cordon Bleu a simple egg *croustade* provides an occasion for students to practice three techniques: baking blind, poaching eggs, and making the delicate hollandaise emulsion.

Note: The three elements combined to make this dish are prepared separately: the pastry can be baked well in advance but the eggs and hollandaise should be prepared only at the last minute.

PÂTE BRISÉE
1 cup all-purpose flour
1/2 cup cake flour
1 egg
1 tablespoon water
Pinch of salt
7 tablespoons unsalted butter, softened
1 egg, slightly beaten, for glazing

HOLLANDAISE SAUCE
3 egg yolks
1/4 cup cold water
1/2 pound unsalted butter, clarified (page 94) and cooled to lukewarm
Salt
Cayenne pepper
Juice of 1/2 lemon, strained

1/2 cup vinegar
6 eggs
1 tablespoon each chopped fresh tarragon and chervil, or whole parsley leaves

EQUIPMENT: Six 3-inch tartlet molds

Prepare the pâte brisée: Use the above ingredients and follow the directions on pages 37–38 and technique photos on page 540.

Roll out the dough about 1/8 inch thick and cut out 6 rounds with a 4-inch fluted cookie cutter (see technique photo 1 for lining tartlet molds on page 541). Gently press the dough onto the bottom and sides of the molds; the dough should extend slightly above the rims. Refrigerate for 30 minutes.

Preheat the oven to 400°.

Lightly prick the bottom of each tartlet shell with a fork. Put a smaller mold inside each to prevent the pastry from rising and deforming during cooking (see technique photo 2 on page 541) or line with a round of parchment paper and dried beans as described on page 39 and in technique photo 6 on page 541. Bake for 10 minutes. Remove the smaller molds or the parchment paper and beans. Brush the interior of each tartlet shell with egg glaze and bake until golden brown, about 5 minutes longer. Let cool slightly and then remove the tartlet shells from the molds. Keep warm.

Prepare the hollandaise sauce: Use the above ingredients and follow the directions on page 274. Set aside, off the heat, in a pan of warm water.

Poach the eggs: Bring 8 cups water to a boil in a large frying pan. Add the vinegar and then reduce the heat to maintain the water at a slow simmer. Fill a bowl with warm water. Break an egg into a cup and slide it gently into the pan, gathering the white around the yolk with a slotted spoon. Repeat with 1 to 2 more eggs, depending on the size of your pan (the eggs must not be crowded and the water must maintain a gentle simmer). Poach until the whites are firm and the yolks are still soft to the touch, about 3 minutes.

Transfer the poached eggs to the bowl of warm water. Repeat to poach all of the eggs. Remove the eggs from the water and drain on paper towels. Trim the whites to uniform oval shapes with a small knife.

To serve, arrange the tartlet shells on a platter and spoon a little of the hollandaise sauce onto each. Place a poached egg on top and coat with the sauce. Sprinkle with chopped herbs or garnish with parsley leaves.

Rôti de Veau Nivernaise
ROAST LOIN OF VEAL WITH ROOT VEGETABLES AND BRAISED LETTUCE

SERVES 6

The Nivernais is a small, largely agricultural province to the west of Burgundy, and several country-style meat dishes (generally veal or beef) served with mixed vegetables are said to be *à la Nivernaise*.

In typical Nivernaise fashion, the recipe below has the meat and vegetables prepared separately. And is the case of this roast loin of veal, lettuce is braised and served with the root vegetables that garnish the meat.

3-pound boneless veal loin roast
2 medium onions, chopped coarse
2 medium carrots, chopped coarse
2 cloves garlic, chopped
Several sprigs fresh thyme or
  1/2 teaspoon dried

1 bay leaf
Salt and freshly ground pepper
3 tablespoons unsalted butter
1/3 cup Brown Veal Stock
  (page 71)

VEGETABLE GARNISH
*1 pound waxy potatoes
    (red or white)*
1 pound turnips
1 pound carrots
Salt
3 tablespoons unsalted butter
36 pearl onions
1 tablespoon sugar

3 heads Boston lettuce
*1/3 cup Brown Veal Stock
    (page 71)*
1 tablespoon chopped parsley

*Unsalted butter, softened,
    for baking dish and
    parchment paper*

Preheat the oven to 425°. Tie the veal loin roast with several lengths of kitchen twine into a regular compact package that will hold its shape during cooking. Place the veal in a roasting pan and scatter the chopped onions, carrots and garlic, thyme and bay leaf around it. Season with salt and pepper. Dot the vegetables with the butter and roast for 30 minutes. Add the stock and 1/3 cup of water to the pan and roast 30 minutes longer, basting with the pan juices every 10 minutes.

While the roast is cooking, prepare the vegetable garnish: Turn the potatoes, turnips, and carrots into small ovals (see directions on page 50 and technique photo on page 520). Put the potatoes in a saucepan with cold salted water to cover. Bring to a boil, reduce the heat to medium and cook until just tender when pierced with the point of a knife, about 10 minutes. Set aside in the cooking liquid to keep warm.

Put the turnips and carrots into 2 separate saucepans, each with 1 tablespoon butter, and a little salt. Add water to barely cover, bring to a boil, reduce the heat and simmer until the water evaporates. Then continue cooking until the vegetables are lightly browned. Remove from the heat; cover to keep warm.

Peel and glaze the pearl onions, using 1 tablespoon butter, the sugar and a little salt (page 165). Keep warm.

Braise the lettuce: Bring a large saucepan of salted water to a boil. Fill another container with cold water. Blanch the lettuce in the boiling water for 1 minute. Transfer to the cold water to cool. Drain well on paper towels. Cut each head in half lengthwise. Fold in the sides and bottom of each half to make a neat bundle. Brush an ovenproof baking dish well with the softened butter. Arrange the lettuce in the dish and add the stock. Season with salt. Cover the lettuce with a piece of buttered parchment paper, buttered side down. Bake in the 425° oven until the liquid has evaporated, 15 to 20 minutes.

Transfer the veal to a platter. Remove the trussing twine and cover the veal with aluminum foil to keep warm. Strain the cooking juices through a fine strainer into a small saucepan; discard the solids. Bring the juices to a boil and skim as much fat as possible from the surface. Season to taste with salt and pepper.

To serve, arrange the vegetables in small, alternating mounds around the veal. Spoon some of the juices over the veal. Sprinkle the potatoes with parsley. Serve the remaining juices in a sauceboat on the side.

Coupe Dijonnaise

RED-WINE–POACHED PEARS WITH BLACKBERRY SORBET

SERVES 6

Dijon is as well known for its local black currant liqueur, *cassis*, as for its mustard; indeed, desserts *à la Dijonnaise* are often made with black currants, although blackberries are sometimes used instead.

In this recipe, a classic preparation made by stewing pears in red wine is served with a rich blackberry sorbet and Chantilly cream.

6 pears
1 bottle dry red wine
 (preferably Burgundy)
1 cup sugar
1 teaspoon vanilla extract
1/2 teaspoon cinnamon

BLACKBERRY SORBET
3/4 cup water
3/4 cup sugar
1 teaspoon vanilla extract
3 cups blackberries

CHANTILLY CREAM
3/4 cup heavy cream
1/4 cup sugar
1 teaspoon vanilla extract

EQUIPMENT: Ice cream maker, pastry bag, medium star pastry tip

Chill a mixing bowl and 6 dessert glasses in the freezer.

Peel the pears, leaving the stems intact. Insert a vegetable peeler into the base of the pears and work it in to the depth of 1 inch. Twist and pull out the cores. Cut a thin slice off the base of each pear, so they will stand upright. Put the pears into a bowl and pour in the wine. Marinate at room temperature for at least 1 hour. Transfer pears and wine to a large saucepan. Add sugar, vanilla and cinnamon. Bring to a boil. Cover with a round of parchment paper, reduce heat and poach until the pears are tender when pierced with the point of a knife, 15 to 20 minutes. Transfer pears and poaching liquid to a heatproof bowl and cool over crushed ice.

Prepare the sorbet: Combine the water, sugar and vanilla in a saucepan. Bring to a boil over low heat, stirring to dissolve the sugar. Boil 1 to 2 minutes. Remove from the heat and let cool. Reserve 6 perfect blackberries for garnish; refrigerate. Put the remaining blackberries through a food mill or puree in a food processor; strain through a fine strainer to remove the seeds. Mix the puree with the cooled syrup. Transfer to an ice cream maker and freeze according to the manufacturer's instructions. Transfer to the chilled bowl and freeze until firm, about 1 hour.

Not more than 1 hour before serving, prepare the Chantilly cream: Use the above ingredients and follow the directions on page 21. Fit the pastry bag with the medium star tip and fill with the cream; refrigerate.

To serve, put a large scoop of sorbet into each dessert glass. Place a pear right beside it. Pipe a swirl of cream on each scoop of sorbet and top with a reserved blackberry. Serve immediately.

LESSON 52

Tourte aux Artichauts
COUNTRY-STYLE ARTICHOKE PIE

Merlans Colbert
DEEP-FRIED WHITING WITH TARTAR SAUCE

Crème Mousseuse au Café
COFFEE MOUSSE

Tourte aux Artichauts
COUNTRY-STYLE ARTICHOKE PIE

SERVES 6

A *tourte* is a double-crusted pie made with short crust or puff pastry. It may be savory or sweet and is almost always a rustic or regional dish. This *tourte* is filled with small spring artichokes and a quiche mixture. Large artichoke bottoms may be substituted for the smaller artichokes; cook (page 30) and slice them before adding to the quiche mixture.

PÂTE BRISÉE
1½ cups all-purpose flour
¾ cup cake flour
2 eggs
½ teaspoon salt
10 tablespoons unsalted butter
1 egg, slightly beaten, for glazing

2 pounds small artichokes
1 lemon, halved
4 tablespoons unsalted butter
½ cup heavy cream or
    crème fraîche
3 egg yolks
Salt and freshly ground pepper

EQUIPMENT: 8-inch fluted, removable-bottomed tart pan

Prepare the pâte brisée: Use the above ingredients and follow the directions on pages 37–38 and technique photos on page 540.

(continued)

Tourte aux Artichauts (continued)

Snap off the stems of the artichokes (any tough fibers in the hearts will be removed along with the stems). Trim a thin slice off the base of each artichoke with a sharp knife. Cut off all the outer leaves, leaving the tender, yellow leaves. Cut off the tops of the leaves, leaving them about 1 inch high. Cut the artichokes in half vertically and remove and discard the fibers from the center with a small spoon. Rub with the cut side of the lemon to prevent darkening and then finely slice. Heat the butter in a frying pan over low heat. Add the sliced artichokes, cover and cook, stirring frequently, until tender but not colored. Set aside. Meantime, preheat oven to 400°.

Cut off two-thirds of the dough; refrigerate the remaining third. Line the tart pan with the dough and blind bake it following the directions on pages 38–39 and technique photos on page 541.

Raise the oven temperature to 425°.

Lightly beat the cream and egg yolks in a bowl. Add the cooked artichokes, season with salt and pepper, and pour into the cooked pastry shell.

Roll out the remaining third of the dough to a ⅛-inch-thick round. Paint the exposed edge of the cooked pastry shell with the egg glaze. Loosely roll the dough up onto the rolling pin and then unroll it over the tart. Press the edges together and trim off the excess dough with a knife. Make a small round hole in the top of the pie with the point of a knife for the steam to escape. Brush the top with egg glaze. Bake until golden brown, about 25 minutes. Serve hot on a round platter, lined with a paper doily.

Merlans Colbert

DEEP-FRIED WHITING WITH TARTAR SAUCE

———

SERVES 6

In this popular recipe, named after an influential finance minister of Louis XIV, the soft, delicate flesh of the whiting is coated with a protective anglaise breading and then deep-fried to a crunchy, golden brown. A lively tartar sauce is the classic accompaniment, but the whiting could also be served simply with wedges of lemon.

TARTAR SAUCE
MAYONNAISE:
  2 egg yolks
  1 tablespoon Dijon mustard
  Salt and freshly ground pepper
  1¼ cups vegetable oil
  *2 tablespoons white-wine
    vinegar*

*2 tablespoons chopped gherkins
  or French cornichons*
2 tablespoons capers, chopped fine
1 tablespoon fine-chopped onion
1 tablespoon chopped parsley
1 tablespoon chopped fresh chives
2 hard-boiled egg yolks, mashed

*6 whole whiting or trout,
  8 ounces each*

ANGLAISE BREADING

1 cup all-purpose flour

2 eggs

2 tablespoons vegetable oil

1 tablespoon water

Salt and freshly ground pepper

2 cups fresh bread crumbs

2 lemons, cut into wedges

Parsley sprigs for garnish

Oil for deep-fat frying

Prepare the tartar sauce: First, make a mayonnaise. Use the above ingredients and follow the directions on page 31. Then whisk in the chopped gherkins, capers, onion, parsley, chives, and mashed egg yolks. Taste and adjust seasonings. Set aside in a sauceboat.

Clean the whiting and trim the tails straight across, but do not gut it (see directions on page 32 and technique photos 1 to 5 on page 524). Bone the whiting, leaving the fish whole (see directions on page 236 and technique photos on page 526).

(continued)

Merlans Colbert (continued)

Heat the oil to 350° in a deep fryer or large saucepan (the fryer or pan should be no more than one-third full of oil).

Prepare the breading: Spread the flour out on a large plate. In a shallow dish, lightly beat the eggs, oil, water, salt and pepper. Spread out the bread crumbs on another large plate.

Preheat the oven to 200°.

Use the flat side of a large knife to gently open out and flatten each fish. Dip both sides first in the flour, then in the egg mixture and finally in the bread crumbs. Gently press each fish again to make sure that the breading sticks well and to ensure that the fish will lie open while it cooks. Fry the fish, two at a time, until golden brown, 7 to 8 minutes. Drain on paper towels and keep hot in the oven with the door ajar until all the fish are cooked.

To serve, arrange the fish on a large serving platter. Garnish with lemon wedges and sprigs of parsley and serve with the tartar sauce.

Crème Mousseuse au Café

COFFEE MOUSSE

SERVES 6

Any airy dessert can be called a mousse. This is a *haute cuisine* version of a familiar dessert. Based on a sabayon, with body supplied by Italian meringue and a small amount of gelatin, it can easily be refrigerated for 24 hours and even improves if allowed to mature overnight before serving.

Note: Chocolate-coated coffee beans or liquor-filled candies in the shape of coffee beans make an attractive decoration.

ITALIAN MERINGUE
3 egg whites (room temperature)
3/4 cup plus 1 tablespoon sugar
1/4 cup water
A few drops lemon juice

1 envelope powdered gelatin
(1/4 ounce)
2 tablespoons water

SABAYON
2 tablespoons instant coffee granules
6 tablespoons water
6 egg yolks
3 tablespoons sugar

1 cup heavy cream

CHANTILLY CREAM
2/3 cup heavy cream
1 tablespoon confectioner's sugar
1 teaspoon vanilla extract

Chocolate-coated coffee beans or
coffee candy for garnish

EQUIPMENT: Pastry bag, medium star pastry tip, ice cream maker

Chill a mixing bowl for the whipped cream.

Prepare the Italian meringue: This is done in 3 steps:

First: Put the egg whites in a mixing bowl and set aside. Then, cook the sugar: In a heavy-bottomed saucepan, combine the ¾ cup sugar, the water and the lemon juice. Bring just to a boil over low heat, stirring to dissolve the sugar. Then cook over medium heat without stirring until the syrup reaches the soft ball stage (239° on a candy thermometer). This will take about 5 minutes. To test, dip the point of a knife into the syrup, then quickly into cold water. If the syrup forms a soft ball when pressed between two fingers, it is ready.

Second: As soon as the syrup is on the heat, start beating the egg whites with a whisk or electric mixer until firm, but not stiff. Add the 1 tablespoon sugar and continue beating until stiff peaks form. (These two operations, making the syrup and beating the egg whites, must be completed at the same time.)

Third: Beating continuously, pour the boiling syrup in a thin stream over the egg whites. (The syrup must be beaten into the egg whites fast enough so that it does not collect in the bottom of the mixing bowl.) Continue beating the Italian meringue until it is thick, glossy, and cool.

Sprinkle the gelatin over the water in a small heatproof bowl and let stand until softened, about 5 minutes.

Prepare the sabayon: Bring 2 to 3 inches of water to a simmer in a large saucepan. Combine the coffee and the water in a large heatproof bowl and whisk to dissolve. Add the egg yolks and sugar and beat with a whisk or electric mixer until foamy. Set the bowl over the simmering water (the bottom should not touch the water). Continue beating until the mixture becomes thick and creamy and increases in volume, and the whisk leaves a clear trail on the bottom of the bowl. Test the temperature of the sabayon occasionally with a finger: If it feels hotter than just tepid (the temperature should not exceed 80°), remove from the heat and beat until slightly cooled. Then return to the heat and finish cooking as described. Remove from the heat and beat until cool.

Meanwhile, set the bowl of gelatin over the simmering water and let stand until just liquid. (Do not allow it to become hot.) Pour into the sabayon and continue to beat until cool. The cooled sabayon should be thick and form a ribbon when it falls from the whisk. Fold the sabayon carefully into the Italian meringue with a wooden spoon.

Beat the 1 cup cream in the chilled bowl with a whisk or electric mixer until stiff peaks form and the cream clings to the whisk or beater. Fold the whipped cream into the sabayon mixture. Mound the mousse in a decorative serving bowl and smooth the surface with a spatula. To decorate, use the tip of a vegetable peeler to trace thin curved lines on the surface, starting at the center of the mousse and radiating out to the edge like the spokes of a wheel. Refrigerate until very firm, at least 3 hours.

Just before serving, prepare the Chantilly cream: Use the remaining cream, confectioner's sugar, and vanilla and follow the directions on page 21. Fit the pastry bag with the medium star tip. Fill it with the cream and pipe rosettes onto the mousse. Top each with a chocolate-coated coffee bean.

ITALIAN MERINGUE

An Italian meringue is made by beating cooked sugar (239° on a candy thermometer—the soft ball stage) into stiffly beaten egg whites. The result is a meringue that is less dry and more velvety than the simpler French meringue (page 52) and much more stable; it may be stored for a few days without separating or losing volume.

The secret to an Italian meringue is twofold: First, the whites must be correctly beaten so that they are stiff and dry and have maximum volume (see page 83 for a discussion of beating egg whites). And second, you must carefully time the process so that the cooked sugar and beaten whites are ready at the same time. Start the sugar cooking before you begin beating the whites; your sugar should just have reached the soft ball stage by the time the whites are stiff. Then carefully pour the hot syrup into the whites, beating constantly, and continue beating until the meringue is cool (a standing mixer is ideal for this).

Italian meringues are typically used in mousses (Crème Mousseuse au Café, page 292) and cold soufflés (Petits Soufflés Glacés aux Abricots, page 381), as a baked meringue topping (Gâteau à l'Ananas Singapour, page 397), in bombes (frozen, molded desserts composed of layers of ice cream or sorbet and bombe mixture, made from a whole egg or egg yolk mousse, or Italian meringue, into which whipped cream is folded), and to lighten buttercreams.

LESSON 53

Soupe Jeannette

MIXED VEGETABLE SOUP JEANNETTE

———

Poulet en Cocotte Grand-Mère

BRAISED CHICKEN CASSEROLE WITH BACON,
MUSHROOMS, POTATOES, AND ONIONS

———

Beignets Soufflés à l'Orange

ORANGE CREAM–FILLED FRITTERS

Soupe Jeannette

MIXED VEGETABLE SOUP JEANNETTE

———

SERVES 6

Jeannette was a popular name for working-class girls in France at the turn of the century. Many such women were employed as cooks in middle-class households and, indeed, we might suppose that this hearty soup was created by just such a Jeannette. It is unusual in that it contains a healthy amount of fresh sorrel as well as milk: two inexpensive ingredients in France that might be a clue to Jeannette's humble origins.

3 medium carrots, quartered
2 medium white turnips, quartered
3 leeks (white part only),
  quartered
3 large baking potatoes, quartered
8 cups Chicken Stock (page 12)
Salt
6 ounces green beans

3/4 cup shelled green peas
3 tablespoons unsalted butter
1 pound sorrel, sliced fine
3/4 cup milk
Freshly ground pepper
Chervil leaves for garnish

Put the quartered carrots, turnips, leeks, and potatoes into a saucepan with the chicken stock and add a little salt. Bring to a boil, reduce the heat, and simmer gently for about 40 minutes.

Snap the ends off of the green beans and cut into ½-inch lengths. Cook in boiling salted water for 10 minutes. Add the peas and cook until tender, about 5 more minutes. Drain the beans and peas and refresh under cold running water; set aside.

Heat 1 tablespoon of the butter in a saucepan over medium heat. Add the sorrel and cook until soft; set aside.

Pass the cooked carrots, turnips, leeks, potatoes, and the broth through a food mill, or puree in a food processor. Return to the saucepan and stir in the milk and the remaining 2 tablespoons butter. Season to taste with salt and pepper. Add the green beans, peas, and sorrel to the soup and reheat for a few minutes.

Pour the soup into a tureen. Serve sprinkled with chervil leaves.

Poulet en Cocotte Grand-Mère
BRAISED CHICKEN CASSEROLE WITH BACON, MUSHROOMS, POTATOES, AND ONIONS

SERVES 6

Grandmothers are often associated with slowly simmered one-pot meals, and the most popular *grand-mère* dish in France is this one. Granny would undoubtedly have cooked everything in the same pot, but professionals cook the vegetables separately to perfection and then simmer them with the chicken for only a short time before serving. A bit complicated for Granny, perhaps, but she would most certainly have approved of the taste.

4½-pound chicken
Salt and freshly ground pepper
1 sprig thyme or ¼ teaspoon dried
1 bay leaf
8 tablespoons unsalted butter
2 tablespoons vegetable oil
24 pearl onions
2½ pounds waxy potatoes (red or white)

1 pound button or quartered large mushrooms, trimmed, rinsed, and dried
10 ounces slab bacon, sliced ¼ inch thick
1 tablespoon chopped parsley

Prepare, season, and truss the chicken as described on page 6 (omitting the garlic) and in technique photos on page 530. Rub the breast with 1½ tablespoons butter and ½ tablespoon oil. Sprinkle the outside with salt and pepper. Heat 1½ tablespoons butter and ½ tablespoon oil in a heatproof casserole over high heat. Add the chicken and brown well on all sides. Reduce the heat to low, cover, and cook for 45 minutes (or bake it in a 350° oven).

While the chicken is cooking, prepare the garnish: Peel the onions (to avoid tears, put them in a bowl of warm water with 1 teaspoon of vinegar before peeling). Put them into a low-sided pan large enough to hold them in a single layer if possible, and add water to barely cover. Add a pinch of salt and 1 tablespoon butter and cook over high heat until the water has evaporated. Then continue cooking the onions in the butter remaining in the pan until golden brown and crisp-tender. Remove from the heat. Cover to keep warm.

Peel and turn the potatoes into small ovals 2 inches by ¾ inch as described for pommes cocotte on page 50 and technique photos on page 520. Put the potatoes in a saucepan with cold salted water to cover and bring to a boil. Blanch for 3 minutes; drain. Heat the remaining tablespoon oil and 2 tablespoons of the butter in a frying pan over high heat until foamy. Add the potatoes and sauté until golden brown, but not completely cooked through (they will be cooked further with the chicken). Remove from the pan; set aside.

Heat 2 tablespoons butter in the same pan over high heat. Add the mushrooms and cook quickly until all the moisture has evaporated. Season to taste with salt and pepper. Remove from the heat; cover to keep warm.

Cut the bacon into lardons; blanch and drain (page 46). Then, when the chicken has cooked for 45 minutes, add the lardons to the casserole, and cook stirring occasionally, until crisp and golden, about 10 minutes.

Remove the chicken from the casserole; cover with aluminum foil to keep warm. Pour off and discard any fat in the casserole. Stir in ¼ cup water, scraping the bottom of the pan to deglaze. Add the chicken, onions and mushrooms and cook 15 minutes. Add the potatoes and cook 10 minutes longer.

To serve, remove and discard the trussing twine from the chicken and transfer it to a serving platter. Spoon the vegetables and the sauce around the chicken and sprinkle with chopped parsley.

Beignets Soufflés à l'Orange
ORANGE CREAM–FILLED FRITTERS

SERVES 6

These cream-filled fritters make an elegant dessert when presented piled high, pyramid-style, on a large platter and served with an apricot-orange sauce. The cream, the fritters, and even the sauce can be prepared in advance but the fritters should not be filled until shortly before serving.

(continued)

Beignets Soufflés à l'Orange (continued)

ORANGE PASTRY CREAM

2 cups milk

1 teaspoon vanilla extract

Grated zest of 1 orange

4 egg yolks

3/4 cup sugar

1/2 cup sifted all-purpose flour

1/2 cup fresh orange juice

ORANGE COULIS

6 ounces canned apricots

Juice of 6 oranges, strained

Juice of 1/2 lemon, strained

2 tablespoons Cointreau

CHOUX PASTRY

1 cup water

8 tablespoons unsalted butter

Pinch salt

1 tablespoon sugar

1 1/4 cups sifted all-purpose flour

4 eggs

Grated zest of 1 orange

Confectioner's sugar for dusting

*2 oranges, fluted and sliced
  (page 65) and cut in half,
  for garnish*

Oil for deep-fat frying

EQUIPMENT: Pastry bag, medium plain pastry tip, small plain pastry tip

Prepare the pastry cream: Put the milk, vanilla and orange zest in a heavy-bottomed saucepan and bring to a boil. Combine the egg yolks and sugar in a heatproof bowl and whisk until thickened and pale yellow. Whisk in the flour. Whisk in the hot milk and return the mixture to the saucepan. Bring to a boil over medium heat, whisking constantly. Reduce the heat and simmer for 5 minutes, whisking constantly to reach all parts of the pan; the cream burns easily. Whisk in the orange juice, return to a boil and remove from the heat. Spread in an even layer on a platter or in a shallow dish. Pat the surface with butter to prevent a skin from forming; let cool.

Prepare the orange coulis: Puree the apricots in a food mill or food processor. Combine the pureed apricots with the strained citrus juices and the Cointreau in a medium saucepan. Cook over low heat until the mixture reduces and becomes syrupy. Remove from heat and let cool to room temperature.

Prepare the choux pastry: Use the above ingredients and follow the directions on page 43, adding the grated orange zest to the saucepan along with the water, butter, salt, and sugar.

Heat the oil to 360° in a large saucepan or deep-fat fryer (the pan or fryer must be no more than one-third full of oil).

Shape the fritters: Dip 2 teaspoons in cold water to keep the dough from sticking. Scoop out a spoonful of choux dough with one of the spoons. Invert the second spoon over the top to smooth the dough into a ball, about 1 inch in diameter. Then push the ball of dough off the spoon into the hot oil. Repeat to make 3 or 4 more fritters. (Do not cook more than 4 or 5 at one time or the oil will cool too much to properly color the fritters.) As the fritters rise to the surface, turn them frequently so that they color evenly. Cook until the fritters double in size and crack open slightly, 4 to 5 minutes; then continue cooking until golden brown, about 5 minutes longer. (If fritters become too colored and do not puff, lower the temperature of the oil.) Drain on a rack covered with paper towels.

Fill the fritters: Put the pastry cream in a bowl and whisk until smooth. Fit the pastry bag with the small round tip and fill with the pastry cream. Make a small hole in each fritter with the pastry tip and fill with the cream.

To serve, arrange the fritters in a pyramid shape on a doily-lined serving platter, so that the holes for the filling are out of sight. Sift confectioner's sugar generously over the fritters. Decorate the platter with the halved orange slices. Serve the orange coulis in a sauceboat on the side. Serve hot or warm.

LESSON 54

Omelette de la Mère Poulard
LA MÈRE POULARD'S SOUFFLÉED OMELET

Côtes de Veau Maintenon
VEAL CHOPS WITH HAM, MUSHROOMS,
AND MORNAY SAUCE

Profiteroles au Chocolat
PROFITEROLES WITH VANILLA ICE CREAM
AND HOT CHOCOLATE SAUCE

Omelette de la Mère Poulard
LA MÈRE POULARD'S SOUFFLÉED OMELET

SERVES 6

In the 1870s, "Mère Poulard" (Mother Poulard) ran a country inn on one of France's most famous sites—Mont Saint-Michel. Her omelets, cooked in a long-handled pan directly in the fireplace, were famous. Her recipe remains a secret but this omelet, developed by chefs at Le Cordon Bleu, comes as close as possible to duplicating the original.

10 large eggs
¼ cup heavy cream
Salt and freshly ground pepper
5 tablespoons unsalted butter

Unsalted butter, softened,
for serving platter

EQUIPMENT: 10-inch frying pan (preferably nonstick)

Butter an oval serving platter with the softened butter.

Separate 5 of the eggs into 2 large bowls; set the whites aside. Break the remaining 5 eggs into the bowl with the egg yolks. Add the cream to the whole-egg mixture. Season with salt and pepper and whisk to combine.

(continued)

Omelette de la Mère Poulard (continued)

Beat the egg whites with a whisk or electric mixer until stiff peaks form. Fold gently into the whole-egg mixture.

Prepare the omelet (see technique photos on page 522): Melt 4 tablespoons butter in the frying pan over medium heat. Pour in the egg mixture and cook gently, stirring constantly with a wooden spoon. When the eggs begin to set, use a spatula to fold the edge of the omelet that is closest to the handle in toward the center (ideally you will fold the omelet into thirds). Lift up the folded edge and slide 1 tablespoon of butter under it. Then, with your free hand, tap the handle of the pan sharply so that the far edge of the omelet slides up the side of the pan. Fold this edge in toward the center and continue cooking for a few minutes until the omelet rises.

Hold the buttered platter with one hand, grasp the handle of the pan in the palm of your other hand, and turn the omelet, seam side down, out onto the platter. Serve immediately.

Côtes de Veau Maintenon
VEAL CHOPS WITH HAM, MUSHROOMS, AND MORNAY SAUCE

SERVES 6

This is a classic chef's dish that involves coating veal chops with a cooked mixture of mushrooms, truffles, and ham called a *salpicon* in French. It is an aromatic garnish created in the eighteenth century which, when combined with a rich béchamel, characterizes dishes *"à la Maintenon."* Veal chops Maintenon are a challenge for Cordon Bleu students but an aid in mastering several useful techniques.

SALPICON

1½ tablespoons unsalted butter
¼ pound mushrooms, trimmed, rinsed, dried, and diced fine
½ cup dry white wine
3 ounces cooked ham, diced fine
1 black truffle (⅔ ounce), diced fine
¼ cup Brown Veal Stock (page 71)

MORNAY SAUCE
BÉCHAMEL SAUCE:
2 tablespoons unsalted butter
3 tablespoons all-purpose flour
1 cup milk
Salt and freshly ground pepper
Pinch freshly grated nutmeg
½ cup crème fraîche or heavy cream
2 egg yolks
1 ounce Gruyère cheese, grated (about ¼ cup)

TOMATO SAUCE
2 tablespoons unsalted butter
1 small onion, chopped fine
2 cloves garlic, chopped fine
*1 1/2 pounds tomatoes, peeled,
  seeded, and diced (page 31)*
*1 sprig fresh thyme or
  1/4 teaspoon dried*
Salt and freshly ground pepper

*6 trimmed veal chops,
  6 ounces each*
2 tablespoons vegetable oil
1 tablespoon unsalted butter
*2 ounces Gruyère cheese, grated
  (about 1/2 cup)*

Prepare the salpicon: Heat the butter in a small frying pan over high heat. Add the mushrooms and sauté until almost dry. Add the wine, bring to a boil, reduce the heat to medium and cook until the liquid is reduced by one-half. Add the ham, truffle and stock and continue to cook until almost dry. Remove from the heat; cover to keep warm.

Prepare the mornay sauce: First make a béchamel, using the butter, flour, milk, salt, pepper, and nutmeg, and following the directions on page 18. Then whisk together the cream and egg yolks in a small bowl and stir into the sauce. Bring the sauce to a boil over medium heat, whisking constantly, and cook for 1 minute. Remove from the heat and stir in the cheese. Taste and adjust seasonings; keep warm over a saucepan of hot water.

Prepare the tomato sauce: Melt the butter in a frying pan over low heat. Add the onion and cook until tender but not colored. Add the garlic and cook for 1 minute. Stir in the tomatoes and thyme. Season with salt and pepper and simmer 15 minutes. Puree the sauce in food mill fitted with the finest disc or in a food processor. Return to the pan and simmer gently until slightly thickened. Remove from the heat; cover to keep warm.

Preheat the oven to 450°.

Season both sides of the veal chops with salt and pepper. Heat the oil and butter in a large frying pan over high heat. Add the chops and brown lightly on both sides. Remove from the pan; drain and pat dry with paper towels. Arrange the chops on a large baking sheet. Spread the salpicon over the chops and coat with a layer of mornay sauce. Sprinkle with the cheese and bake in the upper part of the oven until the chops are cooked through and the cheese is golden brown, about 10 minutes. If necessary, brown the cheese a few minutes under the broiler.

To serve, arrange the chops on a large platter and spoon the tomato sauce around them.

Profiteroles au Chocolat

PROFITEROLES WITH VANILLA ICE CREAM
AND HOT CHOCOLATE SAUCE

———

SERVES 6

Good profiteroles are hard to find. Even in Paris, few restaurants make them with homemade ice cream and freshly baked pastry and fewer still serve them with the boiling chocolate sauce tradition demands.

The temperature of the sauce is crucial; it must not be simply hot but boiling as it is poured over the ice cream–filled pastries seconds before serving.

VANILLA ICE CREAM
2 cups milk
1 teaspoon vanilla extract
4 egg yolks
1/2 cup sugar

CHOUX PASTRY
1/2 cup water
4 tablespoons unsalted butter
Pinch salt
1 tablespoon sugar
2/3 cup sifted all-purpose flour
2 eggs
1 egg, slightly beaten, for glazing

CHOCOLATE SAUCE
7 ounces semisweet chocolate,
  cut into pieces
1/2 cup milk
4 tablespoons unsalted butter

Unsalted butter for baking sheets

EQUIPMENT: Ice cream maker, pastry bag, plain 1/2-inch pastry tip

Chill a mixing bowl in the freezer for the ice cream.

Prepare the vanilla ice cream: First, use the milk, vanilla, egg yolks, and sugar and make a crème anglaise, following the directions on page 35; let cool. Pour the cooled custard into the ice cream maker and freeze according to the manufacturer's instructions. Transfer to the chilled bowl. Freeze until firm, at least 1 hour.

Preheat the oven to 425°. Brush the baking sheets with the softened butter.

Prepare and bake the choux pastry: Use the above ingredients and follow the directions on page 43 and technique photos on page 548, adding the sugar to the saucepan with the water, butter and salt. You will need 18 puffs. Freeze the choux puffs for about 30 minutes, before filling with the ice cream.

Prepare the chocolate sauce: Bring 1 to 2 inches of water to a simmer in a saucepan. Combine the chocolate, milk and butter in a heatproof bowl and set it over the pan of simmering water. Let stand, without stirring, until the chocolate has melted. Then, whisk to combine and keep warm off the heat over the hot water.

Fill the choux puffs: Cut off the top third of each puff with a serrated knife; reserve these caps. Spoon the vanilla ice cream into the base of each puff with a teaspoon. Top each with a cap and transfer to the freezer.

To serve, place 3 filled puffs on each of 6 dessert plates, or make a large pyramid in a stemmed glass bowl. Heat the chocolate sauce over medium heat for 30 seconds, whisking constantly to avoid sticking. Pour it over the puffs and serve immediately.

LESSON 55

Salade de Foies de Volailles Tièdes

SALAD OF WARM SAUTÉED
CHICKEN LIVERS

Brochet au Beurre Blanc

WHOLE POACHED PIKE WITH
WHITE BUTTER SAUCE

---

*Charlotte aux Poires,
Coulis de Framboise*

PEAR CHARLOTTE WITH
RASPBERRY COULIS

Salade de Foies de Volailles Tièdes

SALAD OF WARM SAUTÉED CHICKEN LIVERS

SERVES 6

Salads made with quickly sautéed chicken livers have long been a specialty of Lyon. In recent years the idea has spread, and warm salads are almost as popular today as the cold salads of yore. This Cordon Bleu recipe calls for slicing the chicken livers before cooking them, which makes for a most attractive salad; however, great care must be taken not to overcook them.

1 head escarole
1 head red leaf lettuce

VINAIGRETTE
1/4 cup sherry vinegar
Salt and freshly ground pepper
3/4 cup vegetable oil
2 tablespoons chopped fresh chives
*1 tablespoon chopped fresh chervil
   or parsley*

1 pound chicken livers
Salt and freshly ground pepper
2 tablespoons unsalted butter
1 shallot, chopped fine
1/2 cup port wine
*3/4 cup crème fraîche or
   heavy cream*
*1 tablespoon chopped chervil
   or parsley*

Rinse, drain and spin the lettuce dry. Using the crispest and most colorful leaves, decorate the edge of a large serving platter with alternating leaves of red lettuce and escarole. Set the remaining lettuce leaves aside in a bowl.

Prepare the vinaigrette: Combine the vinegar, salt, and pepper. Whisk in the oil. Whisk in the herbs; set aside.

Trim the chicken livers of any fat or connective tissues. Remove the green bile ducts. Rinse in cold water and pat dry. Cut on an angle into thin slices (*escalopes*). Season with salt and pepper. Melt the butter in a frying pan over medium heat. Add the shallot and cook until soft but not colored. Increase the heat to high, stirring constantly. When the pan is hot, add the chicken livers and sauté, stirring frequently, until seared on all sides and slightly pink in the interior, 2 to 3 minutes. Stir in the port and then the cream. Reduce the heat and simmer for 2 minutes.

To serve, toss the mixed lettuce in the bowl with the vinaigrette. Arrange in the center of the platter. Remove the chicken livers from the sauce and arrange on the lettuce. Spoon a little of the sauce over the livers. Sprinkle with chervil. Serve any remaining sauce on the side.

Brochet au Beurre Blanc
WHOLE POACHED PIKE WITH WHITE BUTTER SAUCE

SERVES 6

Freshwater fish, including pike, were once prominent on princely tables throughout France, but they are rarely served in fine restaurants today. They are still encountered in regional recipes, however, such as this one from the western end of the Loire Valley near Nantes, an area said to be the birthplace of the famous beurre blanc sauce.

COURT BOUILLON
1 bunch parsley
1/2 cup dry white wine
1 pound onions, chopped coarse
1 stalk celery, chopped coarse
1 leek, chopped coarse
1 sprig fresh thyme or
　1/4 teaspoon dried
1 bay leaf
Coarse salt
20 peppercorns

31/2-pound pike

BEURRE BLANC SAUCE I
2 shallots, chopped fine
3/4 cup dry white wine
2 tablespoons white-wine vinegar
1 sprig fresh thyme or
　1/4 teaspoon dried
1 bay leaf
1/2 cup crème fraîche
1/2 pound softened butter
A few drops lemon juice
Salt and freshly ground pepper

2 lemons, fluted, thinly sliced
　(page 65), and halved

EQUIPMENT: Fish poacher

Prepare the court bouillon: Cut the stems off the parsley; reserve the tops. Combine the stems with the remaining ingredients in a fish poacher. Bring to a boil, reduce the heat and simmer for 15 to 20 minutes; let cool to room temperature.

Clean the pike as you would any roundfish and trim the tail to a V shape (see directions on page 32 and technique photos on page 524). Roll the fish in a clean dish towel, so it will hold its shape during poaching. Lay it on the rack of the fish poacher, and lower it into the cooled court bouillon. Add water as needed to barely cover the fish. Cover and bring to a boil over medium heat. Remove immediately from the heat and set aside to cook slowly in the hot court bouillon for about 30 minutes.

Prepare the beurre blanc sauce: Combine the shallots, wine, vinegar, thyme and bay leaf in a small, heavy-bottomed saucepan. Cook over medium heat until the liquid has evaporated. Remove the thyme sprig and bay leaf. Whisk in the cream, reduce the heat to low and cook until reduced by one-half. Remove the pan from the heat and whisk in the softened butter, little by little. Add a few drops of lemon juice and season to taste. Keep the sauce warm off the heat over a saucepan of hot water.

To serve, remove the fish from the fish poacher and carefully unroll it onto a serving platter. Peel off the skin with a small knife while the fish is still warm. Blot up any liquid on the platter with paper towels. Spoon a little sauce over only the body of the fish, leaving the head unsauced. Garnish the platter with the fluted lemon slices and the reserved parsley tops. Serve the remaining sauce in a sauceboat on the side. Serve with Pommes à l'Anglaise (page 50), if desired.

Charlotte aux Poires, Coulis de Framboise

PEAR CHARLOTTE WITH RASPBERRY COULIS

SERVES 6

Pears can be delicious eaten raw, but they are rarely used in desserts without first being poached. This not only softens them but prevents them from discoloring or giving out too much juice. In this charlotte, half the pears are pureed and mixed with the creamy filling and the rest are diced and marinated in pear brandy before being stirred into the cream as well. Served with a dark red sauce of fresh raspberries, the resulting dessert has both a striking appearance and an unforgettable taste.

LADYFINGERS
3 eggs, separated
6 tablespoons granulated sugar
3/4 cup cake flour
Confectioner's sugar, sifted
Unsalted butter, softened,
    for baking sheet

PEAR BAVARIAN CREAM
1 pound pears
3/4 cup sugar
1 teaspoon vanilla extract
1/4 ounce powdered gelatin
    (about 1 tablespoon)
2 tablespoons cold water

CRÈME ANGLAISE
1 cup milk
1 teaspoon vanilla extract
2 egg yolks
¹/₄ cup sugar

*¹/₄ cup Poire William or domestic
    pear brandy*
¹/₂ cup heavy cream

RASPBERRY COULIS
1¹/₂ cups raspberries
¹/₂ cup confectioner's sugar
Juice of ¹/₂ lemon, strained

EQUIPMENT: 4-cup charlotte or soufflé mold

Chill a small mixing bowl for the whipped cream.

Prepare the ladyfingers: Use the above ingredients and follow the instructions on page 118 and technique photos on page 549. Line the bottom and sides of the charlotte mold with the ladyfingers (see the directions on pages 352–53 and technique photos on page 549).

Prepare the pear bavarian: First, peel, halve, and core the pears. Put them into a saucepan with water to cover, the sugar and the vanilla. Bring to a boil to dissolve the sugar, then reduce the heat and poach the pears until tender when pierced with the point of a knife, about 10 minutes. Let the pears cool in the syrup.

Sprinkle the gelatin over the water and let stand until softened, about 5 minutes.

Make a crème anglaise: Use the milk, vanilla, egg yolks, and sugar and follow the directions on page 35. Add the softened gelatin off the heat and stir to dissolve. Strain into a bowl and let cool, stirring occasionally. Do not allow to jell.

Meanwhile, drain the cooled pears well and reserve the syrup. Puree half of the pears in a food processor or a food mill. Finely dice the remaining pears and sprinkle with pear brandy; set aside. Whisk the pureed pears into the crème anglaise mixture. Beat the cream in the chilled bowl with a whisk or electric mixer until stiff peaks form and the cream clings to the whisk or beater. Fold into the crème anglaise mixture. Stir in the diced pears and brandy.

Assemble the charlotte: Brush the ladyfingers lining the mold with the reserved pear cooking syrup. (Brush first the sides and then the bottom until the ladyfingers are well saturated but not soggy.) Pour the pear bavarian cream mixture into the prepared mold and refrigerate until firm, 4 to 5 hours.

Prepare the raspberry coulis: Set aside 10 perfect raspberries for the decoration. Puree the remaining raspberries in a food mill or food processor; strain through a fine sieve to remove the seeds. Whisk the puree with the sugar. Add the lemon juice and refrigerate.

Unmold the charlotte: Use a small sharp knife to trim the ladyfingers to the level of the filling. Invert a round platter over the mold and quickly reverse the two. Slide the mold off carefully.

To serve, decorate the top of the charlotte with the reserved raspberries. Ladle a ring of the coulis around the charlotte and serve the remaining coulis in a sauceboat on the side. (For an alternate presentation, see photo on page 309.)

LESSON 56

Billy Bi aux Paillettes
MUSSEL SOUP WITH CHEESE STRAWS

Magrets de Canard aux Trois Poivres
**DUCK BREASTS WITH GREEN, PINK,
AND BLACK PEPPERCORNS**

Pommes Sarladaises
SAUTÉED POTATOES WITH TRUFFLES

Poires Impériales
IMPERIAL PEARS

Billy Bi aux Paillettes
MUSSEL SOUP WITH CHEESE STRAWS

SERVES 6

This dish is a relatively recent addition to the list of French classic recipes. It is thought to have been created in the 1950s by Louis Barthe, who was then chef at Maxim's in Paris. The soup must have shocked some of the restaurant's wealthy clientele since mussels, being plentiful and cheap, were rarely served on fashionable tables. One client, William Brand (known as "Billy"), heartily congratulated the chef and sang the praises of his creation; in return the dish was christened in his honor ("Billy B."). The humble mollusk has been served this way at Maxim's ever since. At Le Cordon Bleu, the soup is garnished with cheese-flavored "straws" made by sprinkling Parmesan on puff pastry before baking.

Note: Mussels must always be purchased live, that is, in their shells and tightly closed. If their shells are open and do not close tightly when lightly tapped, the mussel should be discarded.

In France mussels called *moules de bouchot* are considered the best. They are farmed mainly along the Atlantic coast and, though rarely more than 3 inches long, are very plump. They can be purchased all year round but are at their best from July to January (although tradition dictates that they be served only during months with an "r" in them, just like oysters).

(continued)

Billy Bi aux Paillettes (continued)

CHEESE STRAWS

PUFF PASTRY:

1¹/₂ cups all-purpose flour

³/₄ cup cake flour

1 teaspoon salt

²/₃ to ³/₄ cup cold water

2 tablespoons unsalted butter,
     melted

14 tablespoons unsalted butter

1 egg, slightly beaten,
     for glazing

2 ounces Parmesan cheese,
     grated (¹/₂ cup)

MUSSEL SOUP

2 pounds mussels

3 tablespoons unsalted butter

2 medium shallots, chopped fine

1 cup dry white wine

8 cups water

1 stalk celery, chopped coarse

Freshly ground pepper

2 tablespoons all-purpose flour

²/₃ cup heavy cream

2 tablespoons coarse-chopped
     fresh chives

Unsalted butter, softened,
     for baking sheet

Prepare the cheese straws: First, use the above ingredients and make a puff pastry, following the directions on pages 209–10 and technique photos on pages 542–43.

Preheat the oven to 450°. Brush a baking sheet lightly with the softened butter and sprinkle with cold water.

Roll out the dough ¹/₈ inch thick and ¹/₂ inch longer and wider than the baking sheet. Loosely roll up the dough onto the rolling pin and then unroll it over the baking sheet. Trim the edges to the size of the baking sheet. Brush with the egg glaze and prick the surface all over with a fork. Sprinkle with the cheese, pressing it gently into the pastry. Refrigerate 20 minutes.

When it is chilled, cut the dough on the baking sheet into strips ¹/₂ inch wide and 3 inches long. Bake until puffed and golden, about 15 minutes. Remove the pastry from the oven and carefully break apart any strips that are still attached to one another. Cool the cheese straws on a rack.

Prepare the mussel soup: First clean the mussels following the directions on pages 39–40. Then heat 1 tablespoon of the butter in a large saucepan over medium heat. Add the shallots and cook until soft but not colored. Add the wine, water and celery and bring to a boil. Add the mussels and season with pepper. Cover and cook, shaking the pot once or twice to rotate the mussels and ensure even cooking, until the shells open, about 6 minutes. Remove the mussels with a slotted spoon and set aside. Strain the cooking liquid through a fine strainer, lined with a damp kitchen towel, into a medium saucepan to remove the sand.

Remove the mussels from the shells; discard the shells. Set half the mussels aside. Put the remaining half in the saucepan along with the strained cooking liquid. Bring to a boil and then reduce over medium heat until it measures about 6 cups. Strain the liquid again, pressing down on the mussels to extract as much liquid as possible. Discard the crushed mussels.

Heat the remaining 2 tablespoons of butter in a saucepan over medium heat. Whisk in the flour and cook 2 minutes. Add the strained cooking liquid and whisk well to prevent lumps from forming. Cook over medium heat for 20 minutes. Add the cream and bring to a boil. Remove from the heat, add the reserved mussels, and wait 5 minutes for the mussels to reheat gently before serving. Taste and adjust seasonings.

Serve the soup in a tureen or in individual bowls, sprinkled with chives. Serve the cheese straws on the side.

Magrets de Canard aux Trois Poivres

DUCK BREASTS WITH GREEN, PINK, AND BLACK PEPPERCORNS

SERVES 6

The use of thick duck steaks instead of beef and a mixture of black, green, and pink peppercorns impart a fanciful, exotic touch to this colorful modern version of a classic steak au poivre.

Note: This recipe has been adapted to use ordinary duck breasts, but at Le Cordon Bleu the breasts of the specially fattened ducks that produce foie gras are used. They are very thick, weighing up to a pound each, and are called *magrets* in French.

3 whole duck breasts, split and trimmed of excess fat and nerve tissue
Salt and freshly ground black pepper
30 pink peppercorns
20 green peppercorns

¹/₄ cup cognac
1 cup Brown Veal Stock (page 71)
3 tablespoons unsalted butter, softened
¹/₂ bunch watercress for garnish

Score the skin of the duck breasts lightly with criss-cross incisions. Rub both sides with salt and pepper; set aside.

Heat a large frying pan over medium heat until hot. Put in the duck breasts, skin side down (the fat released from the skin will be sufficient to cook the breasts), and cook until the skin is browned and crisp, 2 to 3 minutes. Add the peppercorns. Turn the breasts and continue cooking until medium rare, about 6 minutes longer. Pour off and discard all the fat from the pan. Add the cognac. Carefully light it with a match. When the flames die, remove the breasts; cover with aluminum foil to keep warm. Add the stock to the pan and deglaze, scraping the bottom of the pan with a wooden spoon to release the cooked particles. Cook over medium heat until the liquid has reduced by half. Remove from the heat and whisk in the softened butter, little by little, shifting the pan on and off the heat as necessary so that the sauce thickens and emulsifies.

To serve, slice the duck breasts diagonally and arrange on a serving platter. Spoon the sauce over and garnish with small bunches of watercress. Serve with Pommes Sarladaises, below.

Pommes Sarladaises
SAUTÉED POTATOES WITH TRUFFLES

———

SERVES 6

Rich foie gras and preserved duck *(confit)* are not the only specialties of southwest France, where even humble potatoes are transformed into a gastronomic treat. This recipe, from the picturesque town of Sarlat, calls for cooking them in goose or duck fat with another precious resource found in the region—pungent black truffles.

2 pounds waxy potatoes
 (red or white)
5 ounces goose or duck fat

Salt and freshly ground pepper
1 black truffle, sliced thin

EQUIPMENT: Large gratin dish

Preheat the oven to 500°.

Peel the potatoes and slice into ⅛-inch-thick rounds. Put the slices into a bowl of cold water to remove as much starch as possible. Remove from the water with a slotted spoon; drain and repeat. Pat dry with paper towels. Heat the fat in a medium frying pan over high heat. Add the potatoes and sauté for a few minutes until lightly colored, turning gently. Season with salt and pepper. Layer half of the potatoes in the gratin dish. Scatter the slices of truffle over. Cover with the remaining potatoes. Transfer to the oven and bake until golden, about 20 minutes. Serve hot from the gratin dish.

Poires Impériales
IMPERIAL PEARS

SERVES 6

This is a pear-flavored version of the classic Riz à l'Impératrice created in honor of Napoleon III's Caribbean bride, Eugénie. Both imperial desserts include rice and a rich combination of egg yolks and cream. In this case, some of the poached pears are embedded in the rice and others are sliced and artistically arranged on top. An apricot glaze and whipped cream rosettes complete the decoration and create a jewel-like effect.

8 small pears, preferably Bartlett
1 lemon, halved

SUGAR SYRUP
4 cups water
2¹/₂ cups sugar
1 teaspoon vanilla extract

¹/₄ cup Poire William liqueur,
  or domestic pear brandy
¹/₂ cup short-grain rice
2¹/₄ cups milk
1 teaspoon vanilla extract
1¹/₂ envelopes powdered gelatin
  (³/₈ ounce)
3 tablespoons cold water

CRÈME ANGLAISE
1¹/₂ cups milk
1 teaspoon vanilla extract
¹/₂ cup sugar
3 egg yolks

1¹/₂ cups heavy cream
1 tablespoon confectioner's sugar
1 teaspoon vanilla extract
¹/₂ cup Apricot Glaze (page 62)

EQUIPMENT: 9-inch springform pan, pastry bag, medium star pastry tip

Chill a mixing bowl for the whipped cream.

Peel and stem the pears. Insert the point of a vegetable peeler into the base of the pears and work it in to the depth of about 1 inch. Twist and pull out the cores. Rub the pears with lemon to prevent darkening; reserve the lemon for the sugar syrup.

Prepare the syrup: Combine the water, sugar and vanilla in a large saucepan. Add the reserved lemon. Bring to a boil over low heat, stirring to dissolve the sugar. Boil 1 to 2 minutes. Add the pears, and return to a boil. Reduce the heat, cover with a round of parchment paper, and poach until the pears are tender when pierced with the point of a knife, 15 to 20 minutes. Remove the pears from the poaching syrup with a slotted spoon. Drain on a rack; let cool.

Set the poaching syrup over high heat and cook until reduced to a very thick, syrupy consistency. Cut the cooled pears in half lengthwise. Set 12 pear halves aside. Cut the 4 remaining halves into ¹/₄-inch dice and add to the thick syrup. Cook over low heat (so that the liquid barely simmers) until the liquid has almost evaporated and the pears are translucent, golden, and lightly candied. Drain the pears and discard the syrup. Put the diced pears into a small bowl and sprinkle with the liqueur. Macerate in a cool place until needed.

Put the rice in a medium saucepan with cold water to cover. Bring to a boil and cook 4 minutes, stirring occasionally to avoid sticking. Drain well. Combine the milk and the vanilla in the same saucepan and bring to a boil. Return the rice to the pan and cook over medium heat, stirring frequently, until the rice absorbs most of the milk and the mixture is thick and creamy, about 20 minutes. Remove from the heat and let cool.

Sprinkle the gelatin over the water and let stand until softened, about 5 minutes.

Prepare the crème anglaise, using the milk, vanilla, sugar, and egg yolks and following the directions on page 35. Add the softened gelatin to the hot crème anglaise and let cool, stirring occasionally. (Do not allow the mixture to gel completely.) When cool, stir in the candied, diced pears and the macerating liquid.

Beat the cream in the chilled bowl with a whisk or electric mixer until stiff peaks form and it clings to the whisk or beater. When the crème anglaise mixture is cool and has begun to thicken, stir in the cooled cooked rice and then fold in 1 cup of the whipped cream. (Refrigerate the remaining whipped cream to be used for the Chantilly cream.)

Assemble the dessert: Put the metal ring from the springform pan on a round serving platter. Line the inside of the ring with 8 of the pear halves, stem ends up and round sides against the inside of the ring. Spoon the custard-rice mixture into the ring and smooth the top.

Slice each of the remaining 4 pear halves lengthwise into thin slices, cutting from the bottoms up to about ½ inch from the tops, leaving the slices attached at the stem ends. Flatten each pear half slightly with a spatula or the palm of your hand to fan out the slices. Transfer the pears with a spatula to the top of the rice mixture and arrange in a circular fashion with the stem ends pointing toward the center. Chill until firm, about 3 hours.

No more than 1 hour before serving, prepare the Chantilly cream: Give the reserved cream a couple of turns with the whisk to stiffen it again. Fold in the sugar and vanilla and whisk lightly. Fit the pastry bag with the medium star tip and fill with the Chantilly cream. Refrigerate until serving time.

To serve, unmold the dessert: Dip the blade of a knife into hot water and then slide it carefully around the inside of the ring. Slide the ring carefully off the dessert. Pat the pears lightly with a brush soaked in apricot glaze. Pipe rosettes of Chantilly cream between the pears.

LESSON 57

Sardines en Escabèche
FRESH SARDINES IN ESCABÈCHE

Daube d'Agneau Avignonnaise
BRAISED LAMB WITH TOMATO SAUCE

Mille-feuilles
NAPOLEONS

Sardines en Escabèche
FRESH SARDINES IN ESCABÈCHE

SERVES 6

Dishes made from fish or meat and flavored with a spicy vinegar marinade are found in France and Spain. Such foods are said to be *en escabèche*.

In southern France, fresh whole sardines are frequently prepared this way and served as a first course; they can even be eaten bones and all.

24 fresh sardines
1 cup olive oil
1 carrot, diced fine
*1 leek (white part only),
  chopped fine*
1 stalk celery, diced fine
2 cloves garlic
2 shallots, chopped fine
1 large pinch dried rosemary
1 large pinch dried thyme

½ bay leaf
Salt and freshly ground pepper
Pinch of allspice
Grated zest of 1 lemon
*2 small hot green chili peppers,
  seeded and chopped fine*
1 cup dry white wine
¼ cup white vinegar
*2 lemons, fluted, halved,
  and sliced thin (page 65)*

Cut the fins and tails off the sardines. Working from tail to head, scale with the blunt side of a small knife. Cut off the heads and remove the entrails.

(continued)

Sardines en Escabèche (continued)

Rinse under cold running water. Dry carefully with paper towels.

Heat ½ cup of the oil in a large frying pan over high heat until sizzling hot. Add the sardines and lightly brown on one side only. Remove from the pan and drain on paper towels. Then transfer to a deep, nonaluminum container, browned side up. Discard the oil in the pan.

Add the remaining ½ cup oil to the pan. Add the diced carrot, leek and celery and cook over medium heat until soft but not colored. Crush the garlic with the flat side of a knife blade and add to the pan along with the shallots, rosemary, thyme and bay leaf. Season to taste with salt and pepper and the allspice. Add the lemon zest and peppers. Reduce the heat to low and cook 2 minutes, stirring. Add the wine and vinegar and bring to a boil. Reduce the heat to medium and simmer about 10 minutes. (If the mixture looks dry, add ½ cup water and cook for 1 to 2 minutes longer.) Remove and discard the garlic. With a slotted spoon, spread the vegetables over the fish. Bring the liquid back to a boil and pour it over the fish. Cover and refrigerate 24 hours.

To serve, transfer the sardines and vegetables to a serving platter and arrange the fluted lemon slices around the edge.

Daube d'Agneau Avignonnaise
BRAISED LAMB WITH TOMATO SAUCE

SERVES 6

A daube generally consists of beef stewed in red wine. Various daubes are made throughout France but this one, a specialty of Avignon, is unlike all others because it is made with lamb. At Le Cordon Bleu it is served with eggplant, the southern vegetable most frequently associated with lamb. The meat and vegetables are prepared separately and served with a fresh tomato sauce.

Note: Eggplant, cooked as described below, is also an excellent garnish for roast lamb or pork.

*5-pound shortened leg of lamb
(see Note, page 25)*
13 cloves garlic
1 large onion, chopped
1 Bouquet Garni (page 20)
1 bottle dry red wine
¾ cup olive oil
Salt and freshly ground pepper
2 cups Brown Veal Stock (page 71)

TOMATO SAUCE
2 tablespoons olive oil
2 shallots, chopped fine
*¾ pound tomatoes, peeled,
seeded, and diced (page 31)*
30 green olives, pitted
Salt and freshly ground pepper

2 pounds eggplant

1 pound tomatoes, peeled, seeded, and diced

3 sprigs fresh thyme or ¹/₂ teaspoon dried

2 tablespoons chopped parsley

Unsalted butter for parchment paper

Bone the leg of lamb (see technique photos on page 535): Trim the skin, fat, and connective tissue from the meat. Then lay the leg, skinned side down, on the work surface. Make a cut down the length of the upper leg to expose the bone. Cut and scrape around the bone to free it from the meat. Then cut from the joint down the shank bone to expose the bone; cut and scrape to free the meat. Remove the bones in one piece and reserve them. Cut the meat into 1¹/₂-inch cubes. Crush 8 of the garlic cloves; set the remaining 5 garlic cloves aside. Combine the lamb and its bones, the crushed garlic, the onion, bouquet garni, and wine in a large nonaluminum container. Sprinkle with 2 tablespoons of the oil. Let marinate for 12 hours, turning the meat occasionally.

Remove the meat from the marinade: pat dry with paper towels. Strain the marinating liquid and reserve. Reserve the vegetables, bouquet garni, and bones.

Preheat the oven to 425°.

Heat ¹/₄ cup of the oil in an ovenproof frying pan over high heat. Season the lamb cubes with salt and pepper and brown on all sides. Remove with a slotted spoon. Discard the oil. Reduce the heat to medium and add 2 tablespoons oil to the pan. Add the marinated onions and cook until soft but not colored. Return the lamb to the pan along with the garlic, bouquet garni and marinating liquid. Stir in the stock, season with salt and pepper and bring to a boil. Cover with a round of buttered parchment paper and then a lid. Reduce the oven heat to 400°. Transfer the pan to the oven and cook until the lamb is tender when pierced with a knife, 1 hour to 1 hour and 20 minutes.

Meanwhile, prepare the tomato sauce: Heat the oil in a large frying pan over medium heat. Add the shallots and cook until soft but not colored. Add the tomatoes and cook for about 20 minutes. Reduce the heat to low, add the olives, and cook 10 minutes longer. Season to taste with salt and pepper. Remove from the heat; set aside.

Peel the eggplant and cut it lengthwise into ³/₈-inch-thick slices. Cut each slice in "bâtonnets" ³/₈ inch wide and 2 inches long. Finely chop the reserved 5 garlic cloves. Heat ¹/₄ cup oil in a large frying pan over high heat until very hot. Add the eggplant and sauté, stirring frequently, until golden brown. Reduce the heat, add the chopped garlic, tomatoes, thyme, and salt and pepper and cook 20 to 25 minutes.

When the lamb is tender, transfer it to a long serving platter with a slotted spoon; cover with aluminum foil to keep warm. Set the pan over high heat and cook to reduce and thicken the cooking liquid; skim off any fat. Taste and adjust seasonings.

To serve, spoon the reduced cooking liquid over the lamb. Spoon a ribbon of tomato sauce and olives down the center of the lamb and sprinkle with chopped parsley. Serve the eggplant in a vegetable dish, sprinkled with chopped parsley.

Mille-feuilles
NAPOLEONS

---

6 SERVINGS

Called *mille-feuilles* in French (literally "a thousand leaves"), this pastry is one of the most popular in France. It can be found in shops throughout the country and is eaten either as a late-afternoon snack or a dessert.

The dough is deliberately pricked to keep it from rising too high. Although a perfect *mille-feuilles* is made of pastry no more than a half inch thick, the leaves are nevertheless perfectly visible.

Note· This classic *mille-feuilles* has a pastry cream filling, but whipped cream and fresh fruit can be substituted to make a light and colorful dessert.

PUFF PASTRY	PASTRY CREAM
1½ cups all-purpose flour	1 cup milk
¾ cup cake flour	2 teaspoons vanilla extract
1 teaspoon salt	3 egg yolks
⅔ to ¾ cup water	⅓ cup sugar
2 tablespoons melted butter	⅓ cup all-purpose flour
14 tablespoons unsalted butter	
	2 tablespoons kirsch
Unsalted butter, softened, for baking sheet	Confectioner's sugar for dusting
	Chopped nuts, raspberries, and mint leaves for garnish

Prepare the puff pastry: Use the above ingredients and follow the directions on pages 209–10 and technique photos on pages 542–43.

Prepare the pastry cream: Use the above ingredients and follow the directions on page 183.

Preheat the oven to 450°. Lightly brush a baking sheet with the softened butter and sprinkle with water.

Roll out the dough to a rectangle about ⅛ inch thick, just slightly larger than the baking sheet. Loosely roll up the dough on the rolling pin and then unroll it over the baking sheet. Trim the edges with a sharp knife. Prick the surface of the dough all over with a fork to prevent it from rising too much. Bake until golden brown and crisp, about 25 minutes. Let cool.

Whisk the pastry cream until smooth. Whisk in the kirsch.

Assemble the napoleon: Trim the edges of the pastry with a serrated knife. Cut lengthwise into 3 equal strips. Spread 1 strip with one-half of the pastry cream. Cover with a second strip of pastry and spread with the remaining pastry cream. Place the remaining strip, upside down (so that the top is flat), on top of the final layer of pastry cream. Smooth off any pastry cream on the sides with a spatula.

Sift confectioner's sugar liberally over the pastry. Lightly press chopped nuts to the sides. Garnish with raspberries and mint leaves.

LESSON 58

Rillettes de Maquereaux

MACKEREL RILLETTES

—

Cake de Légumes

VEGETABLE BREAD

—

Fricassée de Poulet à l'Ail et à la Sauge

CHICKEN FRICASSEE WITH GARLIC AND SAGE

—

Gratin d'Aubergines

EGGPLANT GRATIN

—

Glace à la Noix de Coco

COCONUT ICE CREAM

INTERMÉDIAIRE

LESSON 59

Salade Polonaise

POLISH SALAD OF POTATOES, BEETS,
EGG, AND HERRING

---

*Grenadins de Veau au
Coulis de Céleri-Rave*

VEAL WITH CELERY ROOT CREAM SAUCE

Mousseline de Carottes

CARROT MOUSSELINE

Tarte aux Mirabelles

PLUM TART

Salade Polonaise
POLISH SALAD OF POTATOES, BEETS, EGG, AND HERRING

SERVES 6

According to the strictly codified language of French cuisine, it is neither the herring, the beets, nor the potatoes that make this salad "Polish" but the hard-boiled egg yolks that are crushed and stuffed back into the whites to garnish the plate.

Note: Served with a dark rye bread and a glass of beer, this colorful cold platter could easily be turned into a simple meal.

$^1/_2$ pound waxy potatoes
  (red or white), unpeeled
Salt
6 eggs
$^1/_2$ pound cooked beets
$^1/_2$ pound carrots
$^1/_2$ pound turnips
1 European hothouse cucumber
  (see Note, page 5)
5 herring fillets, packed in oil,
  drained

VINAIGRETTE
2 teaspoons Dijon mustard
Pinch of salt
Freshly ground pepper
$^1/_4$ cup white-wine vinegar
$^3/_4$ cup vegetable oil
1 tablespoon each chopped fresh
  chervil, tarragon, and parsley

MAYONNAISE
1 teaspoon Dijon mustard
1 egg yolk
Salt and freshly ground pepper
$^3/_4$ cup vegetable oil
Juice of $^1/_2$ lemon, strained

6 small gherkins

EQUIPMENT: Pastry bag, medium star pastry tip, small star pastry tip

Rinse the potatoes and put them in a large saucepan with cold salted water to cover. Bring to a boil, reduce the heat and simmer until tender when pierced with the point of a knife. Drain and cool.

Hard-boil the eggs; cool and shell them (page 16). Set aside.

Peel the beets, carrots, and turnips and slice about $^1/_2$ inch thick. Cut each slice into strips $^1/_2$ inch wide and then cut the strips into $^1/_2$-inch dice.

Put the diced carrots in a saucepan with cold salted water to cover. Bring to a boil, reduce the heat and simmer until crisp-tender, about 5 minutes. Drain, refresh under cold running water, and drain again; set aside.

Cook the turnips as described above until crisp-tender, about 3 minutes. Drain, refresh under cold running water, and drain again; set aside.

Peel and seed the cucumber and cut it into ½-inch dice; set aside.

Cut half of the herring fillets into ½-inch dice. Cut the other half into small strips about ¼ inch wide and 3 inches long; set aside.

Prepare the vinaigrette: Combine the mustard, salt, pepper and vinegar in a small bowl and whisk to blend. Whisk in the oil. Add half of the chopped herbs. (Set the remaining herbs aside for garnish.) Pour half of the vinaigrette into a sauceboat and set aside. Reserve the remainder.

Prepare the mayonnaise, using the above ingredients and following the directions on page 31.

Cut the eggs in half lengthwise. Mash the yolks in a small bowl with a fork. Mix in two-thirds of the mayonnaise. Fit the pastry bag with the medium star tip and fill with the egg yolk mixture. Pipe the mixture into the egg halves.

Fan the gherkins: Thinly slice each gherkin lengthwise, cutting from the bottom up to about ¼ inch from the stem end, leaving the slices attached at the stem end. Gently press down on the gherkin to fan it out; set aside.

Peel the potatoes and cut into ½-inch dice.

Assemble the salad: Combine the diced potatoes, herring, and one-third of the carrots in a bowl. Toss with a little of the reserved vinaigrette. Arrange in a long dome down the center of an oval serving platter.

Toss the beets, the remaining carrots and the turnips separately with the remaining vinaigrette. Arrange the beets at each end of the platter. Arrange the egg halves around the dome of mixed salad. Divide both the carrots and turnips into 6 equal portions. Alternate mounds of carrots and turnips between the egg halves. Sprinkle the reserved chopped herbs over the mixed salad and arrange the herring strips in a lattice design on top. Fit the pastry bag with the small star tip and fill it with the remaining mayonnaise. Pipe the mayonnaise to fill each lattice diamond. Place the cucumber around the base of the mixed salad. Put a fanned gherkin on each mound of turnips.

Serve cool but not chilled, along with the vinaigrette in the sauceboat on the side.

Grenadins de Veau au Coulis de Céleri-Rave

VEAL WITH CELERY ROOT CREAM SAUCE

SERVES 6

The main ingredient in this recipe, veal steaks cut from the loin like beef filet mignons, is prepared as tradition dictates. The veal is larded with strips of fatback to keep it from drying out as it cooks. A modern touch comes from the use of a root vegetable, celery root, to thicken and flavor the sauce. The result is an elegant dish that combines classic techniques and modern tastes.

CELERY ROOT CREAM
3/4 pound celery root, peeled and
   cut into chunks
Salt
1/3 cup heavy cream or
   crème fraîche

6 boneless veal loin steaks
   (1 1/4 inches thick), 5 ounces each
5 ounces pork fatback (see Note,
   page 139)
Salt and freshly ground pepper
3 tablespoons unsalted butter

2 tablespoons vegetable oil
2 medium carrots, diced fine
2 medium onions, diced fine
1 clove garlic, diced
1 sprig thyme or 1/4 teaspoon dried
1 bay leaf, crumbled
1/3 cup Brown Veal Stock
   (page 71)
1/3 cup dry white wine

Chervil or parsley sprigs,
   for garnish

EQUIPMENT: Small larding needle (available in specialty cookware stores)

Prepare the celery root cream: Put the celery root into a saucepan with cold salted water to cover. Bring to a boil, reduce the heat and simmer until tender; drain well. Pass through a food mill fitted with the finest disc, or puree in a food processor. Stir in the cream; set aside.

Lard the veal steaks: Slice the fatback about 1/16 inch thick. Cut the slices into strips about 1/4 inch wide and 3/4 inch long. Use the small larding needle to insert four or five strips of the pork fat into each side of the meat. Or, make small slits in the steaks with the point of a knife and insert the pork fat.

Preheat the oven to 425°.

Season both sides of the meat with salt and pepper. Heat the butter and oil in a large ovenproof frying pan over high heat. Add the veal and brown on all sides. Remove the veal from the pan. Add the diced carrots, onions, and garlic and stir to coat well with the fat. Add the thyme and bay leaf and cook until the vegetables are tender but not colored, about 5 minutes. Add the stock and the wine and season to taste with salt and pepper.

Arrange the veal in a single layer on top of the vegetables. Bring to a boil, cover, transfer to the oven, and cook 25 minutes.

To serve, gently reheat the celery root cream over low heat. Transfer the veal to a serving platter and cover with aluminum foil to keep warm. Strain the cooking vegetables and juices through a fine strainer, pressing down on the vegetables with a wooden spoon to extract as much liquid as possible. Stir this liquid into the celery root cream. Season to taste with salt and pepper and spoon over the veal steaks. Garnish with the chervil. Serve with Mousseline de Carottes, below.

Mousseline de Carottes
CARROT MOUSSELINE

SERVES 6

Particularly light, creamy, and delicate sauces, desserts, or purees are often called *mousselines*. In France, the most frequently served vegetable mousseline is made with potatoes; at Le Cordon Bleu we find that this carrot mousseline makes for a colorful change of pace.

Salt	*4 tablespoons butter*
2¹/₂ pounds carrots, peeled and	*²/₃ cup heavy cream*
chopped coarse	*Freshly ground pepper*

Chill a bowl for the whipped cream. Bring a large saucepan of salted water to the boil. Add the carrots and cook until tender; drain. Pass through a food mill fitted with the finest disc or puree in a food processor. Stir in the butter. Beat the cream in the chilled bowl with a whisk or electric beater until stiff peaks form and the cream clings to the whisk or beater. Gently fold into the carrot mixture with a wooden spoon. Season to taste with salt and pepper. Transfer to a serving dish.

Tarte aux Mirabelles
PLUM TART

SERVES 6

Small yellow plums, known as *mirabelles*, are considered not only the best in France for making tarts but the best for making brandy as well. Both the tart and the brandy are specialties of the eastern province of Lorraine.

This Cordon Bleu version of a famous regional dessert calls for assembling three separately prepared elements: puff pastry, pastry cream, and the poached plums. The tart is served at room temperature, so each element has to be made in advance, but for best results they should not be combined until the last minute.

PUFF PASTRY

1½ cups all-purpose flour
¾ cup cake flour
1 teaspoon salt
⅔ to ¾ cup water
2 tablespoons melted butter
14 tablespoons unsalted butter
1 egg, lightly beaten, for glazing

PASTRY CREAM

1 cup milk
1 teaspoon vanilla extract
3 egg yolks
6 tablespoons sugar
2 tablespoons all-purpose flour
2 tablespoons cornstarch

SUGAR SYRUP

4 cups water
1 cup sugar
1 teaspoon vanilla extract
1 tablespoon kirsch

2 pounds small yellow plums, pitted
1 tablespoon kirsch
½ cup Apricot Glaze (page 62)

Unsalted butter, softened for baking sheet and pastry cream

Prepare the puff pastry: Use the above ingredients and follow the directions on pages 209–10 and technique photos on pages 542–43.

Prepare the pastry cream: Use the above ingredients and follow the directions on page 183. Refrigerate.

Prepare the syrup: Combine water, sugar, vanilla and kirsch in a large saucepan and bring to a boil over low heat, stirring to dissolve sugar. Boil 1 to 2 minutes. Add the plums, reduce heat, and simmer, uncovered, until plums are soft, about 15 minutes. Drain plums well; set aside to cool.

Preheat the oven to 450°. Lightly brush a baking sheet with the softened butter and sprinkle with cold water.

Prepare the pastry "bande" (see technique photos on page 544): On a lightly floured work surface, roll out the puff pastry dough ⅛ inch thick. Trim the edges. Then cut a 12-by-5½-inch-rectangle and 2 strips of pastry, each 12 inches long and ½ inch wide. Transfer the rectangle to the baking sheet and prick all over with a fork. Brush a ½-inch-wide border of egg glaze along the 2 long edges of the rectangle (be careful not to let the egg glaze run down the sides of the dough or it will rise unevenly), and then lay the pastry strips over the glazed borders, about 1/16 inch in from the edges. Press down gently to ensure that the pastry strips adhere, then use the back of a paring knife to make shallow indentations at ¼-inch intervals along the sides of the dough for decoration. (This is known as *chiqueter*.) Brush the pastry strips with the egg glaze and bake until the pastry is crisp and golden brown, about 30 minutes. Let cool.

Put the pastry cream in a bowl and whisk until smooth. Whisk in the kirsch. Spread the pastry cream down the center of the cooled puff pastry shell. Arrange the plums on the pastry cream in tightly packed rows.

Heat the apricot glaze, adding water as needed to thin it. Pat the glaze on the plums with a pastry brush. Serve at room temperature.

LESSON 60

*Potage aux Huîtres
à la Crème*
OYSTER SOUP

—

Épaule d'Agneau au Curry
CURRIED LAMB STEW

—

Charlotte aux Fraises
STRAWBERRY CHARLOTTE

Potage aux Huîtres à la Crème

OYSTER SOUP

SERVES 6

Oysters are always sold in their shells in France and if unopened may be stored (curved shell down) for up to a week in the refrigerator. They are normally eaten raw on the half shell, but for centuries French chefs have also served them warm as starters.

Today, when they are cooked they are often lightly poached. They should be heated just long enough to plump up and become slightly opaque; otherwise they will toughen and lose all of their natural juices. This soup is a simple and elegant way to serve oysters as a warm first course.

Note: Live oysters may be stored for up to 1 week in the refrigerator.

36 small oysters	1$^1/_2$ cups crème fraîche or
6 tablespoons unsalted butter,	heavy cream
softened	Cayenne pepper
2 shallots, chopped fine	Salt
1$^1/_2$ cups dry white wine	Parsley for garnish
3 tablespoons all-purpose flour	

Shuck the oysters (see technique photos on page 523): Fold a dish towel in half twice so that it covers the inside of your hand. Cushion an oyster in the center of your hand with the rounded shell in your palm and the pointed, hinged end of the oyster toward you. Work over a small bowl to catch the liquor. Insert a small knife between the 2 shells near the hinge and twist the knife slightly to open the shells. Slide the knife along the upper shell to sever the small muscle that connects the oyster to it. Remove the oyster and set aside. Repeat with the remaining oysters. Strain the oyster liquor carefully to remove sand or bits of shell.

Heat 4 tablespoons of the butter in a medium saucepan over low heat. Add the shallots and cook until soft but not colored. Add the wine and oyster liquor and bring to a boil. Reduce the heat, add the oysters and simmer 1 minute. Remove the oysters with a slotted spoon and drain. With a paring knife, trim and discard the fringe from the edges of the oysters. Set the oysters aside; cover with aluminum foil to keep warm.

Strain the cooking liquid and return to the saucepan. Make a beurre manié by mashing together the remaining 2 tablespoons butter and the flour. Add the cream to the saucepan and bring to a boil. Whisk about half of the beurre manié, little by little, into the cooking liquid until it starts to thicken. Then, cook until the liquid thickens enough to barely coat the back of a spoon. If the liquid does not thicken adequately, add more beurre manié. Season to taste with cayenne and salt, if needed.

To serve, place 6 oysters in the bottom of each of 6 soup bowls. Pour the thickened liquid over the oysters and garnish with parsley leaves.

Épaule d'Agneau au Curry
CURRIED LAMB STEW

SERVES 6

Few people realize that French colonies once extended to India (Pondicherry) and that curry powder is no modern addition to the French chef's spice shelf. Indeed, curries of different kinds were being served by French chefs in Paris in the early nineteenth century, but it is only in recent years that Indian restaurants have appeared on the Parisian scene.

This Cordon Bleu curry recipe is more authentic than most since it completes the basic curry powder with a mixture of fresh spices and calls for serving the curry Indian-style with a refreshing accompaniment of yogurt, bananas, raisins, and cashews.

3 pounds boneless lamb shoulder,
   trimmed of excess skin, fat,
   and connective tissue
1 bay leaf
2 sprigs thyme or
   1/2 teaspoon dried
2 tablespoons vegetable oil
2 medium carrots, diced fine
2 medium red bell peppers,
   diced fine
2 medium onions, diced fine
6 cloves garlic, diced fine
1 teaspoon ground ginger
8 cardamom pods
1 teaspoon turmeric
2 teaspoons curry powder
1/2 cinnamon stick or 1/2 teaspoon
   ground cinnamon
1/2 cup coconut milk or whole milk
2 apples, diced fine
Salt
Cayenne pepper

RICE PILAF
2 tablespoons butter
1 medium onion, chopped fine
1 clove garlic, chopped fine
Salt and freshly ground pepper
1 1/4 cups long-grain rice
2 1/2 cups water

1 Bouquet Garni (page 20)

GARNISH
1/2 small red bell pepper,
   cut into julienne
   (see technique photo
   on page 519)
1/2 small green bell pepper,
   cut into julienne

ACCOMPANIMENTS
2 bananas
Juice of 1/2 lemon, strained
4 ounces raisins (about 3/4 cup)
1 cup plain yogurt
4 ounces cashews (about 3/4 cup)

Cut the lamb into 1 1/2-inch cubes. Chop the bay leaf and strip the leaves from the thyme sprigs. Mix the herbs together in a bowl. Roll the lamb in the herbs and let stand for 1 hour.

Heat the oil in a large frying pan over medium heat. Add the carrots, peppers, onions and garlic, and stir to coat with the oil. Cook gently, stirring occasionally, until tender but not colored. Stir in the ginger, cardamom, turmeric, curry powder, cinnamon, and then the lamb. Add the milk and enough water to cover the mixture by about 1/2 inch. Bring to a boil. Add the apples and season to taste with salt and cayenne. Reduce the heat, cover and simmer until the lamb is tender when pierced with the point of a knife, about 1 hour to 1 hour and 20 minutes.

Prepare the rice pilaf: Use the above ingredients and follow the directions on page 60, adding the chopped garlic to the pan along with the onion.

Prepare the garnish: Blanch the julienned peppers in boiling salted water to cover for 3 to 4 minutes. Drain, refresh under cold running water, and drain again; set aside.

Prepare the accompaniments: Dice the bananas and sprinkle with lemon juice. Put the bananas, raisins, yogurt, and cashews in separate serving bowls.

When the lamb is tender, its sauce should be just thick enough to barely coat the back of a spoon; if too thin, remove the lamb from the sauce and reduce the sauce over a high heat until slightly thickened. Remove and discard the cinnamon stick. Return the lamb to the sauce and simmer a few minutes. Taste and adjust seasonings.

To serve, transfer the curried lamb to a deep dish and sprinkle with the blanched peppers. Serve the rice in a separate serving dish and the accompaniments on the side.

Charlotte aux Fraises
STRAWBERRY CHARLOTTE

SERVES 6

This might be called the most refined way imaginable to eat strawberries and cream. The taste of the strawberries in the charlotte is echoed and enhanced by a fresh strawberry sauce spooned around, not over, the pastry. A final sprinkling of confectioner's sugar is the crowning touch, providing a snowy contrast to the crimson sauce and the golden ladyfingers that surround this creamy dessert.

LADYFINGERS
1/2 cup granulated sugar
3 eggs, separated
3/4 cup all-purpose flour
Confectioner's sugar for dusting
Unsalted butter for baking sheet

1 1/2 envelopes powdered gelatin
  (3/8 ounce)
3 tablespoons cold water
2 pint baskets strawberries
1 cup confectioner's sugar
2 cups heavy cream
Juice of 1/2 lemon

Confectioner's sugar for dusting

EQUIPMENT: 6-cup charlotte mold

Chill a mixing bowl for the whipped cream.

Prepare the ladyfingers: Use the above ingredients and follow the directions on page 118 and technique photos on page 549.

Line the bottom and sides of the charlotte mold with the ladyfingers (pages 352–53 and technique photos on page 549).

Sprinkle the gelatin over the water in a heatproof container and let stand until softened, about 5 minutes.

Reserve 3 perfect strawberries for decoration. Rinse, dry, and hull the remaining strawberries and puree them in a food mill or food processor. Reserve 1 cup of the puree for a coulis.

Bring 2 to 3 inches of water to a simmer in a small saucepan. Set the container of softened gelatin in it and let stand until liquid. Whisk into the remaining strawberry puree along with 3/4 cup sugar.

Beat the cream in the chilled bowl with a whisk or electric mixer until stiff peaks form and the cream clings to the whisk or beater. Fold into the strawberry mixture. Pour the mixture into the mold, smooth the top and cover with a piece of parchment paper. Refrigerate until firm, at least 4 to 5 hours.

Prepare the coulis: Whisk the remaining 1/4 cup confectioner's sugar and the lemon juice into the 1 cup of reserved strawberry puree; set aside.

To serve, remove the charlotte from the refrigerator. Use a small sharp knife to trim the ladyfingers to the level of the cream filling. To unmold, invert a platter over the charlotte and quickly reverse the two. Carefully remove the mold. Sift confectioner's sugar over the top and spoon some of the strawberry coulis around the base of the charlotte. Garnish the top with the 3 reserved strawberries. Serve the remaining coulis in a sauceboat on the side.

PART THREE

Supérieure

PROFESSIONAL TOUCHES

*T*he best chefs in France are not chopping vegetables or stirring soups. Apprentices and subordinates do most of the work, but nothing leaves the kitchen without the chef's approval. The chef inspects every dish before it is served: discreetly tasting a sauce, gently pressing a chicken breast, or making last-minute adjustments in a presentation. Someone watching might think his only concern is the way a dish looks. This is, of course, not true. The chef generally conceived the dish, tested it innumerable times, and trained his staff until they could reproduce it to his specifications. It took him years to master the skills he draws upon daily and to develop a repertoire of dishes he calls his own. He holds himself responsible for every dish he serves, and only his expert eye can detect flaws in the hundreds of dishes presented for his approval. Cooking is no longer a matter of technique for him; it is a question of ideas and of finishing touches.

The recipes in this last section of the book concentrate on these last aspects of cooking. They illustrate a creative approach to French cuisine and emphasize the kind of attention to detail that is the hallmark of an experienced chef. As in the previous chapters, recipes are drawn from all realms of the French repertoire: regional, classic, traditional, and modern.

Menus in this chapter include examples of fine home cooking and complex festive fare. Good cooks should be able to prepare both. Through attention to detail and by using only the best fresh ingredients, talented cooks will turn simple meals into delightful occasions. What could be simpler, for example, than an applesauce and bread dessert? A French *charlotte aux pommes* (apple charlotte) is essentially that. But when the applesauce is homemade, properly flavored with butter, vanilla, and a hint of rum, then baked in a mold lined with buttered rectangles of bread and served with a rich custard sauce, this humble dish becomes a memorable dessert.

When is a steak more than a steak? When it is a *steak mirabeau,* crisscrossed with anchovy fillets and served with an anchovy butter. Simple? Absolutely. Little touches, like the anchovies, transform a familiar dish into a symphony of tastes, and as the following recipes illustrate, a Cordon Bleu cook will vary menus in other ways as well.

Pastry, for example, will be used not only for desserts but for elegant savory turnovers (like the crayfish-filled *chausson* in this chapter), for wrapping meat or fish to concentrate flavor; or to create pastry shells in which to serve a wide variety of preparations from scrambled eggs *(feuilletés d'oeufs brouillés aux asperges)* or shrimp *(bouchées de crevettes)* to pears with a sabayon sauce *(feuilletés aux poires chauds au sabayon)*.

Familiar techniques will also be put to new uses in these recipes and exploited in almost every conceivable way. A simple technique such as stuffing, for example, will be used to produce radically different results: tomatoes and zucchini will be stuffed and served as a starter *(petits farcis niçois)* while cabbage is stuffed and braised to make a hearty country meal *(chou farci);* rabbit will be totally boned and stuffed to make a traditional main dish *(lapin farci ménagère);* and a goose recipe will describe how to make the chestnut dressing served at Christmas throughout France *(oie farcie aux marrons et aux pommes)*. In the course of this chapter the full potential of simple techniques will be explored to demonstrate how versatile they can be in the hands of a chef.

More than in any other part of this book the recipes that follow will also stimulate your imagination. Some illustrate the innovative cuisine one encounters in better restaurants today while others evoke the rich regional heritage that continues to inspire French chefs.

Among the more creative recipes that illustrate a resolutely modern approach to cuisine, one could cite the *terrine de mer à la gelée de safran* or the *blanquette de lotte aux petits légumes*. The former is made from ingredients traditionally associated with Marseille's famous *bouillabaisse* (firm-fleshed fish, saffron, and a spicy rust-colored sauce) but combines them to produce a colorful cold fish terrine. The latter calls for serving monkfish with baby vegetables in a creamy white sauce which is reminiscent of a classic veal *blanquette*.

From the vast regional repertoire, several well-known dishes are presented in the following pages to round out the collection of country-style recipes found throughout this book (recipes for *gratin dauphinois* and *tian provençal* are included here). In addition to these favorites, several less well-known but equally enticing dishes are also described in this chapter (such as the *beuchelle angevine*, which combines delicate calf's sweetbreads and kidneys in the same dish). Chefs use these traditional recipes as a means of varying the classic repertoire and of reviving flavors from the past.

Lastly, this chapter includes a collection of what might be called showpieces. That is, stunning dishes which display the chef's talent and mastery of the culinary arts. The *barbue soufflée Aïda*, for example, calls for boning and stuffing a flounder with an airy soufflé mixture and serving the fish with little puff pastry shells filled with oysters and spinach. This chapter ends with what must be one of the most spectacular desserts of all—a classic baked Alaska, whose contrast of hot and cold delights even the most jaded palate and brings any meal to a festive end.

Above all, these recipes are addressed to those who have absorbed the lessons taught in previous chapters and who now view their cooking with a chef's critical eye.

LESSON 61

Mousseline de Merlans aux Champignons Sauvages

MOUSSELINE OF WHITING WITH
WILD MUSHROOMS

—

Chou Farci

STUFFED CABBAGE

—

Glace au Miel

HONEY ICE CREAM

Mousseline de Merlans aux Champignons Sauvages

MOUSSELINE OF WHITING WITH WILD MUSHROOMS

—

SERVES 6

Whiting is often used as a base for mousselines because it is very lean and has a mild flavor (it is also very reasonably priced). Its flesh, enriched with cream and eggs, contrasts nicely with the earthy taste of the wild mushrooms discreetly tucked inside each individual mousseline made here.

In this recipe, the bones are almost as important as the fish itself, since they are simmered with white wine and vegetables to make a rich stock that is later transformed into an elegant sauce by boiling it down to concentrate flavor, whisking in butter, and garnishing with thin strips of carrot and zucchini to add both color and taste.

Note: Bones from any white-fleshed fish can be used for making the stock if whiting fillets are purchased (never use the bones of a fatty fish such as mackerel or bluefish in making a fish stock as they can give it an oily taste).

At Le Cordon Bleu only wild mushrooms are used in this mousseline, but fresh button mushrooms may be cooked and seasoned in the same way if neither fresh nor dried wild mushrooms are available.

(continued)

Mousseline de Merlans aux Champignons Sauvages (continued)

4 whole whiting, or 1¹/₂ to 2
 pounds whiting or hake fillet
 with 1¹/₂ pounds bones for stock

FISH STOCK

Bones from whiting (see above),
 chopped coarse
1 leek, chopped coarse
1 stalk celery, chopped coarse
1 onion, chopped coarse
2 cloves garlic, chopped
1 cup dry white wine
Parsley stems
4 sprigs thyme or
 ¹/₂ teaspoon dried
1 bay leaf
Water

1 tablespoon unsalted butter
1 shallot, chopped fine
2 cloves garlic, chopped fine
6 ounces fresh wild mushrooms
 (chanterelles or morels), or
 1 ounce dried wild mushrooms,
 soaked overnight in cold water
 to cover and drained
1 tablespoon cognac
¹/₄ cup crème fraîche
2 teaspoons chopped parsley
2 teaspoons chopped fresh chives
Salt and freshly ground pepper

MOUSSELINE

Whiting puree (see above)
Salt
3 eggs
³/₄ cup crème fraîche or
 heavy cream
Freshly grated nutmeg
Cayenne pepper

1 small carrot, cut into julienne
 (see technique photo
 on page 519)
1 small zucchini, cut into julienne
7 tablespoons unsalted butter,
 softened
Chervil or parsley leaves
 for garnish

Unsalted butter, softened, for
 molds and parchment paper

EQUIPMENT: Six ¹/₂-cup molds or rámekins

If using whole whiting, clean the fish (see directions on page 32 and technique photos on page 524) and then fillet and skin them (page 75 and technique photos on page 525), reserving the bones for the stock. Dry the fillets well and run your finger along the flesh from tail to head to detect any small bones; remove them. Pass the fillets through a meat grinder fitted with the finest disc or puree in a food processor. Work the puree through a fine sieve to remove any remaining bones or skin. Transfer the puree to a large bowl and refrigerate for 2 hours, or until very cold.

Prepare the fish stock: Rinse the fish bones under cold running water and drain. Cut the backbones into several pieces. Combine the bones and vegetables in a large saucepan and heat 2 to 3 minutes over low heat, stirring constantly. Add the wine and herbs, bring to a boil, and cook until reduced by about one-third. Then add water as necessary to cover the contents of the pot and bring to a boil, skimming off any froth that rises to the surface. Lower the heat and simmer 20 minutes. Strain the stock into a medium saucepan and reduce over medium heat until the stock is thick and syrupy and measures just under ⅓ cup. Remove from the heat and set aside.

While the stock is cooking, melt the butter in a medium frying pan over low heat. Add the shallot and garlic and cook until tender but not colored. Raise the heat to medium, add the fresh or dried mushrooms, and cook quickly until all the moisture has evaporated. Add the cognac and cook 2 minutes. Stir in the cream, parsley and chives, season with salt and pepper and cook until all moisture has evaporated, 3 to 5 minutes. Let cool.

Preheat the oven to 375°.

Prepare the mousseline: Set the bowl with the whiting puree over a bowl of crushed ice. Season with salt. Beat the eggs until blended and add them little by little to the puree, beating vigorously in a backward to forward motion until well blended and thickened. Add the cream in the same way, beating well after each addition. Season with nutmeg and cayenne.

Brush the molds with the softened butter. Line the bottoms with rounds of parchment paper and brush the paper with butter. Half-fill each mold with mousseline. Make an indentation in the center of the mousseline with the back of a spoon and fill with a large tablespoon of the mushroom mixture. Then add mousseline to completely fill the molds and smooth the tops with a spatula. Tap the molds on a hard surface to remove any air bubbles. Put the molds in a roasting pan and pour hot water into the pan to come halfway up the sides of the molds. Bring to a simmer on top of the stove. Cover the molds with a piece of buttered parchment paper. Transfer to the oven and cook until a knife inserted into the centers is warm to the touch and clean when withdrawn, 25 to 30 minutes.

While the mousselines are cooking, bring a saucepan of salted water to a boil. Add the julienned carrots and zucchini and boil 1 minute. Drain, refresh under cold running water, and drain again. Set aside.

To serve, unmold the mousselines onto 6 serving plates. Rewarm the reduced stock, if necessary, and whisk in the softened butter off the heat, little by little. Spoon a little sauce over each mousseline and sprinkle the tops with the julienne of vegetables. Garnish with chervil leaves. Serve warm.

Chou Farci

STUFFED CABBAGE

SERVES 6

Stuffed cabbage is farmhouse fare in France as in so many other countries, but as demonstrated here, it can be quite an elegant dish as well. After the leaves are separated from a head of cabbage, the cabbage is reconstructed using alternating layers of leaves and stuffing. It is then braised with white wine, veal stock, and vegetables, to be served whole and carved at the table.

(continued)

Chou Farci (continued)

1 head green cabbage (about
    4 pounds), preferably Savoy
White vinegar

STUFFING

2 tablespoons unsalted butter
1 onion, chopped
1 clove garlic, chopped fine
14 ounces pork sausage meat
1½ cups fresh white bread crumbs
Salt and freshly ground pepper
Pinch quatre épice (see Note,
    page 70) or freshly grated
    nutmeg
1 tablespoon fine chopped parsley
1 egg

Thin sheet of fresh pork fat
    or 3 slices bacon
2 tablespoons unsalted butter
2 medium carrots, diced fine
1 medium onion, chopped fine
1 stalk celery, diced fine
½ cup dry white wine
1 cup Brown Veal Stock
    (page 71) or Chicken Stock
    (page 12)
Bouquet Garni (page 20)

Unsalted butter for
    parchment paper

Separate the cabbage leaves. Cut out the hard central vein from each leaf. Add a little vinegar to a container of cold water and rinse the leaves well. Bring a large saucepan of cold salted water to a boil. Add 6 to 7 cabbage leaves and blanch until tender, 3 to 8 minutes. (The blanching time will depend on the quality of the cabbage: If it is a young or spring cabbage, the time will be shorter.) Refresh the leaves under cold running water; drain. Repeat to blanch all the leaves. Reserve 6 or 7 of the largest and greenest leaves and spread them out on a dish towel to dry. Squeeze out the remaining leaves by hand and set them aside.

Prepare the stuffing: Heat the butter in a large frying pan over medium heat. Add the onion and cook until tender but not colored. Add the garlic and sausage meat and cook, stirring frequently, for 5 minutes without browning. Transfer to a bowl, add the bread crumbs and mix well. Season to taste with salt and pepper. Add the quatre épices or nutmeg, the parsley and egg. Mix thoroughly.

Stuff the cabbage: On a flat work surface, arrange 4 or 5 of the reserved, large leaves in a circle, overlapping them slightly. Place 4 or 5 of the smaller leaves over the center of the circle. Spread one-quarter of the stuffing over the smaller leaves. Add another layer of cabbage and then a second quarter of the stuffing, and continue alternating layers until all of the small cabbage leaves and stuffing have been used. Cover the final layer of stuffing with the remaining large leaves. Fold the outer leaves in toward the center to reshape the head of cabbage. Wrap the cabbage with the pork fat or bacon slices, and overlap the ends. Tie with kitchen twine to secure the fat or bacon, and then cross the twine over and under the cabbage two or three times to hold the shape of the head. Do not tie the twine too tightly or the cabbage will deform during cooking.

Preheat the oven to 425°.

Heat the butter in a casserole over medium heat. Add the vegetables and cook until soft but not colored, about 5 minutes. Add the wine, bring to a boil, and cook 2 minutes. Add the stock and bouquet garni. Place the stuffed cabbage in the center of the bed of vegetables. Cover with a round of buttered parchment paper and a lid. Transfer to the oven and cook, basting from time to time, until a knife inserted into the center of the cabbage comes out hot, 50 to 60 minutes.

To serve, transfer the cabbage to a round serving platter. Remove and discard the twine and pork fat or bacon. Strain the cooking liquid into a saucepan and arrange the chopped vegetables around the cabbage. Skim off the fat from the cooking liquid and reduce by half over medium heat. Pour a little sauce over the cabbage and serve the remainder in a sauceboat on the side.

Glace au Miel
HONEY ICE CREAM

SERVES 6

Honey is rarely used in French pastries, desserts, or, for that matter, cuisine (a notable exception being a popular honey-based gingerbread called *pain d'épices*). The French normally consume their honey at breakfast with fresh bread and butter, but honey ice cream has gained popularity in recent years thanks to a new generation of chefs who regularly serve it in their restaurants.

Note: When making honey ice cream, strong fragrant varieties such as orange blossom, rosemary, or thyme honey are preferred.

2 cups milk	*1/3 cup honey*
6 egg yolks	*1 cup heavy cream*
3/4 cup sugar	

EQUIPMENT: Ice cream maker

Chill a mixing bowl and a decorative serving bowl in the freezer.

Bring the milk to a boil in a medium heavy-bottomed saucepan; remove from heat. Combine the egg yolks and sugar in a heatproof bowl and beat until thickened and pale yellow. Add all but 2 tablespoons of the honey to the hot milk and stir until dissolved. Whisk the milk mixture into the eggs and sugar and then return the mixture to the saucepan. Cook over low heat, stirring constantly with a wooden spoon, until the custard is thick enough to coat the back of the spoon. Do not boil. Test the consistency of the custard by drawing a finger across the back of the spoon; it should leave a clear trail. Strain the custard into a bowl and let cool, stirring occasionally to prevent a skin from forming. Stir in the heavy cream. Pour into an ice cream maker and freeze according to the manufacturer's instructions. Transfer to the chilled bowl and freeze until firm, about 1 hour. To serve, drizzle the remaining 2 tablespoons honey over the top.

LESSON 62

Gâteau Blond de Foies de Volaille, Coulis de Tomates
CHICKEN LIVER FLAN WITH TOMATO SAUCE

Navarin d'Agneau Printanier
LAMB STEW WITH SPRING VEGETABLES

Charlotte aux Pommes, Crème Anglaise au Rhum
APPLE CHARLOTTE WITH
RUM-FLAVORED CRÈME ANGLAISE

Gâteau Blond de Foies de Volaille, Coulis de Tomates
CHICKEN LIVER FLAN WITH TOMATO SAUCE

SERVES 6

These delicate liver flans are a specialty of Lyon. There, chicken livers are pureed, mixed with eggs and cream, and baked in a bain-marie. At Le Cordon Bleu, added richness and a velvety texture are given by adding beef marrow to the livers before baking.

In Lyon, chicken liver flan is frequently served with a light crayfish sauce; it is equally delicious hot or cold with a simple fresh tomato sauce like the one described below.

CHICKEN LIVER FLAN

³/₄ pound large chicken livers

3 ounces beef marrow (see Note on page 193)

5 tablespoons all-purpose flour

4 egg yolks

4 whole eggs

¹/₄ cup milk

¹/₄ cup heavy cream

¹/₂ clove garlic, chopped fine

1 teaspoon chopped parsley

Salt and fresh ground pepper

¹/₈ teaspoon freshly grated nutmeg

TOMATO SAUCE

2 tablespoons unsalted butter

1 onion, chopped fine

1 clove garlic, chopped fine

³/₄ pound tomatoes, peeled, seeded, and diced (page 31)

1 sprig fresh thyme or ¹/₄ teaspoon dried

Salt and freshly ground pepper

Several sprigs parsley for garnish

Unsalted butter, softened, for ring mold or cake pan and parchment paper

EQUIPMENT: 8-inch ring mold or 8-inch round cake pan

Preheat the oven to 400°.

Brush the ring mold or cake pan with the softened butter. If using a cake pan, line the bottom with a round of parchment paper and brush the paper with butter.

Pass the livers and the marrow twice through a meat grinder fitted with the finest disc, or puree in a food processor. Work the puree through a fine strainer into a bowl to remove any filaments and to obtain a very fine puree.

Whisk the flour and egg yolks until smooth. Stir in the whole eggs and then gradually stir in the milk and the cream. Strain into the bowl with the liver-marrow puree. Add the garlic and parsley and season with salt, pepper, and nutmeg. Mix well and pour into the ring mold or cake pan.

Put the filled mold into a large pan. Add enough hot water to the pan to come halfway up the sides of the mold. Transfer to the oven and bake until the flan is firm and a knife inserted in the center comes out clean, about 30 minutes.

Prepare the tomato sauce: Melt the butter in a heavy-bottomed saucepan over low heat. Add the onion and cook until tender but not colored. Add the garlic and cook 1 minute. Stir in the tomatoes, thyme, salt and pepper. Bring to a boil, reduce the heat and simmer for about 20 minutes. Remove the thyme sprig and pass the sauce through a food mill fitted with the finest disc or puree in a food processor. Taste and adjust seasonings.

To serve, unmold the flan on a round serving platter. Spoon a little tomato sauce over the center and in a ring around the flan. Garnish with parsley. Serve any remaining sauce in a sauceboat on the side.

Navarin d'Agneau Printanier
LAMB STEW WITH SPRING VEGETABLES

SERVES 6

A navarin is a stew made with lamb and one or more vegetables. Originally turnips (*navets* in French) were included in every navarin but by the turn of the century potatoes began taking their place. Today, a navarin is frequently made with a mixture of fresh vegetables—particularly baby spring vegetables—including turnips, which once again find their place in the garnish of this popular dish.

3 pounds boneless lamb shoulder, trimmed of excess fat

2 tablespoons vegetable oil

1 tablespoon unsalted butter

2 medium onions, chopped fine

3 cloves garlic, chopped fine

2 tablespoons all-purpose flour

1 tablespoon tomato paste

3 medium tomatoes, peeled, seeded, and diced (page 31)

Several sprigs fresh thyme or 1/2 teaspoon dried

1 bay leaf

Salt and freshly ground pepper

VEGETABLE GARNISH

18 pearl onions

1 1/2 pounds small waxy potatoes (red or white)

1 1/4 pounds carrots

1 1/4 pounds turnips

3 tablespoons unsalted butter

Salt

3/4 cup shelled green peas (fresh or frozen)

1/4 pound green beans, trimmed

Cut the lamb into 1 1/2-inch cubes. Heat the oil in a deep, heavy-bottomed frying pan over high heat. Working in batches if necessary, add the meat and brown on all sides; remove the meat from the pan. Add the butter, onions and garlic to the pan, sprinkle with the flour and cook, stirring frequently, 1 to 2 minutes until lightly browned. Return the lamb to the pan and add hot water to barely cover. Add the tomato paste, tomatoes, thyme, bay leaf, salt and pepper. Bring to a boil, reduce the heat and simmer gently for 25 minutes.

While the lamb is cooking, prepare the garnish: Peel the pearl onions. (To avoid tears, put them in a bowl of warm water, with a little vinegar, before peeling.) Turn the potatoes, carrots, and turnips (see directions on page 50 and technique photo on page 520); set the potatoes aside in a bowl of cold water. Put the carrots, turnips and onions into three small, low-sided saucepans. Add 1 tablespoon of butter to each along with salt and cold water to barely cover. Bring to a boil, reduce the heat to medium and simmer until the water has evaporated and the vegetables are tender; set aside. Cook the peas and beans separately in saucepans of boiling salted water until crisp-tender. Drain, refresh under cold running water, and drain again.

When the lamb has cooked for 25 minutes, drain and add the potatoes. Continue cooking until the lamb is tender when pierced with the point of a knife, 25 to 30 minutes longer. Skim any fat from the surface of the stew. Gently fold in the other vegetables and cook 10 minutes longer. Taste and adjust seasonings. Serve the stew on a deep platter.

Charlotte aux Pommes, Crème Anglaise au Rhum

APPLE CHARLOTTE WITH RUM-FLAVORED CRÈME ANGLAISE

SERVES 6

This is the original charlotte—the one still to be found in many French homes today. It is a humble dish made with applesauce and bread and served with a custard sauce (quite different from the ladyfinger/bavarian cream creation popular with chefs). Like so many simple desserts, it is rarely seen on restaurant menus, but children love it and adults never tire of its taste.

APPLE COMPOTE

3 pounds apples (preferably
    Golden Delicious), peeled,
    cored, and diced
1/4 cup water
1/4 cup sugar
2 tablespoons unsalted butter
1/4 cup apricot jam
2 tablespoons dark rum
1 teaspoon vanilla extract

9 to 10 slices firm white bread
1/2 cup clarified butter (page 94)

RUM CRÈME ANGLAISE

1 cup milk
1 teaspoon vanilla extract
3 egg yolks
1/3 cup sugar
2 tablespoons dark rum

1/3 cup Apricot Glaze (page 62)

Unsalted butter, softened,
    for charlotte mold

EQUIPMENT: 6-cup charlotte mold

Brush the charlotte mold well with the softened butter.

Prepare the apple compote: Combine the diced apples and the water in a saucepan. Cover and cook over low heat for about 20 minutes, stirring occasionally with a wooden spoon to keep the apples from sticking to the pan. Stir in the sugar, butter, jam, rum, and vanilla. Raise the heat to medium and continue cooking, uncovered, until all the moisture has evaporated and the compote is thick and stiff, about 20 minutes.

Preheat the oven to 375°.

Remove the crusts from the bread and trim the bread to 4-inch squares. Cut 6 of the slices in half to make 12 rectangles; set aside. Cut the remaining slices in half diagonally and then in half again to make small triangles.

Line the charlotte mold (see technique photos on page 550): Turn the mold upside down and arrange the triangles of bread on it, like pieces of a pie, to cover the bottom. The pieces must fit tight; trim the bread as necessary so as not to leave any spaces. Remove the bread, and turn the mold over. Brush both sides of all of the bread pieces with the clarified butter. Fit the triangles into the bottom of the mold, and then arrange the rectangles around the inside of the mold so that they overlap generously. The bread should extend slightly above the rim of the mold. Fill the lined mold with the apple compote, mounding it in the center. (This is important because the compote tends to sink in the middle when cooking.)

Bake the charlotte 15 minutes, then cover with parchment paper to keep the exposed ends of bread from burning. Continue baking until the bread is golden, about 20 minutes longer.

Prepare the rum crème anglaise: First make a crème anglaise; use the milk, vanilla, egg yolks, and sugar and follow the directions on page 35. Cool and then add the rum. Refrigerate.

Remove the charlotte from the oven and cool for about 30 minutes. With a very sharp knife, trim the bread showing above the level of the filling. Invert a serving platter over the top of the mold and quickly reverse the two. Gently slide the mold off. (If the charlotte begins to collapse, replace the mold and let cool a little longer.) Heat the apricot glaze and brush it over the outside of the charlotte.

Pour a ring of rum crème anglaise around the base of the charlotte. Serve warm, with the remaining crème anglaise in a sauceboat on the side.

Pâté de Lapin aux Noisettes
RABBIT PÂTÉ WITH HAZELNUTS

———

Barbue Soufflée Aïda
SALMON-STUFFED FLOUNDER WITH
OYSTERS AND SPINACH

———

Sorbet au Champagne
CHAMPAGNE SORBET

Pâté de Lapin aux Noisettes
RABBIT PÂTÉ WITH HAZELNUTS

———

SERVES 6

Rabbit is one of the most popular meats used in making pâtés. Since its flesh is particularly lean, it is never used alone but always combined with pork and occasionally with veal. At Le Cordon Bleu, the meatiest parts of the rabbit and whole hazelnuts are marinated overnight in a little Armagnac before being layered into the pâté and baked.

Note: Like all pâtés, this one should be allowed to cool completely and then refrigerated for at least 24 hours before serving to allow the different flavors to mingle. It can be kept refrigerated for a week or more before serving and gets better the longer it sits.

3½-pound rabbit
Salt and freshly ground pepper
¼ pound shelled hazelnuts
1 ounce pork fat, cut into
    small cubes
6 tablespoons Armagnac
¼ cup vegetable oil
½ pound ground lean veal
10 ounces ground lean pork

Pinch allspice or freshly grated
    nutmeg
1 egg
2 sprigs fresh thyme or
    ½ teaspoon dried
1 bay leaf, crushed
1 sheet fresh pork fat,
    ⅛ inch thick

EQUIPMENT: 11-by-4¼-by-3¼-inch rectangular terrine mold with lid

Cut the hind and front legs from the rabbit. Remove the loin fillets. Bone the legs. Cut the meat into ¾-inch cubes and put it, in a single layer, in a long flat container. Season with salt and pepper; set aside. Cut all the remaining meat from the carcass and put into a separate container; refrigerate until required.

Skin the hazelnuts: Put the nuts into a small saucepan with cold water to cover and bring to a boil. Blanch for 3 minutes. Drain, refresh under cold running water, and remove the skins. Add the skinned hazelnuts and pork fat to the cubed rabbit meat. Sprinkle with 4 tablespoons Armagnac and the oil. Mix well to coat the rabbit. Cover and marinate overnight, or for about 12 hours.

Preheat the oven to 350°.

Pass the reserved rabbit meat from the carcass through a meat grinder fitted with the medium disk and put it in a bowl with the veal and pork. Add salt, pepper, 2 tablespoons Armagnac, the allspice or nutmeg, the egg, thyme leaves, and bay leaf. Mix well.

Assemble the pâté: Line the bottom and sides of the terrine mold with the sheet of pork fat, leaving 1 to 1½ inches of fat draped over the sides of the terrine. Spread a layer of the ground meat mixture over the bottom of the terrine. Cover with a layer of the marinated rabbit mixture. Fill the terrine with alternating layers of the 2 mixtures, pressing down on each layer to pack it well. Finish with a layer of the ground meat. Bring the overhanging edges of pork fat up over the top of the terrine to enclose the pâté. Cover the terrine with the lid and stand it in a roasting pan. Pour hot water into the pan to come halfway up the sides of the terrine. Bring to a simmer over medium heat and then transfer to the oven and cook for 1½ hours.

Remove the terrine from the roasting pan and let cool. Remove the pork fat that covers the top of the pâté. Serve the pâté in the terrine mold.

PÂTÉS AND TERRINES

The word *pâté* comes from the French *pâte,* or "pastry," and technically means a sort of pie filled with a chopped stuffing, or forcemeat, that is baked freeform or in a mold. Now, however, the meaning has been blurred to include terrines, which are, technically, meat, fish, or vegetable mixtures baked in a terrine mold rather than in pastry. A pastry-wrapped pâté may also be called a *pâté en croûte.*

Forcemeats for pâtés and terrines are usually made from pork or a combination of pork and veal, chicken, or game. They must include some fat (the usual proportion is two to one, lean to fat) to keep them moist, and may be bound with egg or bread crumbs. Forcemeats are ground or chopped to a variety of textures, from very smooth (as in a liver terrine) to quite rough. Pâtés and terrines often combine forcemeats layered with strips or cubes of a compatible meat (often marinated in alcohol) in the interests of texture and presentation. Nuts such as hazelnuts or pistachios are also common additions. Forcemeat mixtures must be highly seasoned because foods lose flavor when chilled; to test the seasoning, sauté or bake a small patty of the forcemeat and then taste it.

The pastry used to wrap pâtés must be flexible and sturdy. It can vary from a rough dough made simply with flour, water, lard, and salt, to a pâte à pâté dough (page 412)—similar to a pâte brisée but made with whole eggs and oil for added flexibility—to an elegant puff pastry dough (page 209).

For terrines, the mold (most commonly made of glazed earthenware, porcelain, or enameled cast iron) is usually lined, or barded, with a thin layer of pork fat or bacon to keep the meat moist during cooking. Then the terrine is cooked in a low oven in a water bath (page 15) to ensure even cooking and texture. (The exception is a country terrine, baked without a water bath to produce a crusty exterior.) Dough-covered pâtés are baked without a water bath and a hole is pierced in the top crust to let the moisture escape. After cooking, aspic is often added to pâtés through this hole (Pâté en Croûte, page 412) to fill the space between meat and crust.

Vegetable terrines may be made with almost any vegetable. The vegetables may be pureed and bound with egg, béchamel (Pain de Petits Pois Frais à la Crème de Cives, page 203) or bread crumbs (Terrine d'Aubergines, page 388) or the vegetables may be cooked separately and arranged in whole or large pieces in the terrine and bound with a mousseline.

For best flavor, pâtés and terrines should be served at room temperature rather than chilled.

Barbue Soufflée Aïda

SALMON-STUFFED FLOUNDER WITH OYSTERS AND SPINACH

SERVES 6

This dish, originally conceived for turbot or brill, can be made equally well using flounder. The fish is boned through a slit and stuffed with a delicate salmon mousseline. It is served surrounded by little pastry shells *(bouchées)* filled with fresh spinach and lightly poached oysters. In all, it is a spectacular dish which requires patience and skill—a worthy homage to Verdi and the famous opera for which it was named.

PUFF PASTRY
1 1/2 cups all-purpose flour
3/4 cup cake flour
1 teaspoon salt
2/3 to 3/4 cup water
2 tablespoons melted unsalted butter
14 tablespoons unsalted butter
1 egg, lightly beaten, for glazing

3 1/2-pound flounder

SALMON MOUSSELINE
6 ounces salmon fillets, skinned
Salt and freshly ground pepper
1 egg white
1/2 cup crème fraîche or heavy cream

2 tablespoons unsalted butter, softened
3 shallots, chopped fine
Salt
White pepper

1 1/4 cups dry white wine
2 pounds spinach, stemmed and rinsed
1 cup crème fraîche or heavy cream
12 medium oysters
1 egg yolk

Unsalted butter, softened, for baking sheet, ovenproof bowl, and parchment paper

Prepare the puff pastry: Use the above ingredients and follow the directions on pages 209–10 and technique photos on pages 542–43.

Prepare the bouchées (see technique photos on page 545): Preheat the oven to 400°. Lightly brush a baking sheet with the softened butter and sprinkle it with cold water. Dust a work surface with flour. Roll out the puff pastry dough about 1/8 inch thick. Use a fluted, 3-inch round cookie cutter to stamp out 12 rounds. Transfer 6 of the pastry rounds to the baking sheet. Prick all over with a fork and brush lightly with a little egg glaze. Be careful not to let the egg glaze run over the edges of the dough or it will not rise evenly. Cut out and discard the centers of the remaining 6 rounds using a 2-inch round cookie cutter. Place the rings on top of the glazed rounds, pressing gently to adhere. Brush the tops lightly with egg glaze and bake until puffed and golden, about 30 minutes.

Transfer the bouchées to a rack to cool. Cut and lift out the small caps that have formed in the centers and set aside. Use a teaspoon to remove the soft pastry from the center of each shell and discard. Set the bouchées and their caps aside.

Prepare the flounder for stuffing (see technique photos on page 528): Cut along both sides of the flounder with kitchen or fish scissors to remove all of the fins. Cut the tail straight across, leaving it about ½ inch long. Remove the dark skin: Place the flounder, dark skin facing up, on a work surface. Slide a filleting knife under the skin just behind the head and free a flap of skin across the width of the fish. Lift the flap with your free hand and gently pull it at the same time that you scrape the underside to completely remove the skin from the flesh. Then turn the fish over and scale the white skin, working from tail to head, against the direction in which the scales lie.

Then bone the flounder whole: Place the flounder, white-skin side down, on the work surface, with the tail facing toward you. With a flexible filleting knife, cut down the length of the backbone from head to tail. Then, holding the knife almost flat, insert the blade between the flesh and rib bones on the left side of the backbone. Slide the blade along the length of the fillet to lift it from the rib bones without cutting completely through the outer edge of the fish. Hold the blade flat against the bones so that you lose as little flesh as possible. Repeat on the right side. To remove the backbone and ribs, gently lift up the fillets to expose the ribs and slide the knife under ribs and backbone below the head of the fish to begin to detach them from the flesh. Cut the backbone just behind the head with kitchen scissors. Then cut all the way around the outer edges of the ribs with the scissors. Slide the knife blade underneath ribs and backbone to free them completely from the flesh. Cut the backbone again at the tail end and remove it. (You have now created a boneless pocket for the stuffing.) Remove the entrails and gills. Rinse the fish well under cold running water and pat dry with paper towels; set aside.

Prepare the mousseline: Chill a mixing bowl. Run your fingers along the surface of the salmon, from tail to head, to detect any small bones; remove them. Pass the salmon through a meat grinder fitted with the finest disc, or puree it in a food processor. Work the puree through a fine sieve to eliminate any bones. Transfer the puree to the chilled bowl and set it over a larger bowl of crushed ice. Season with salt and pepper. Beat the egg white until foamy and then add it gradually to the puree, beating vigorously with a wooden spoon in a forward to backward motion until the mixture is well blended and slightly thickened. Add the cream little by little in the same way, beating well after each addition.

Raise the oven temperature to 425°. Butter a large ovenproof pan with the softened butter. Sprinkle with two-thirds of the chopped shallots and the salt and pepper. Place the fish, white-skin side down, in the pan and season the pocket with salt and pepper. Fill the pocket with the salmon mousseline. Add the white wine to the pan and water as needed to come just to the top of the fish. Cover the fish with a buttered piece of parchment paper, buttered side down, and bake for 25 minutes.

While the fish is cooking, cook the spinach in a saucepan of boiling salted water until tender. Drain and refresh under cold running water. Squeeze to remove as much moisture as possible. Put the spinach in a lightly buttered bowl; cover to keep warm.

Bring ½ cup of the cream to a boil in a saucepan. Reduce until thickened; cover to keep warm. (This will be used to coat the oysters.)

Shuck the oysters over a bowl to catch the liquor (see directions on page 334 and technique photos on page 523). Strain the liquor and put it in a small saucepan with the oysters, remaining shallot, and a little pepper. Bring to a boil over high heat. Immediately remove the oysters with a slotted spoon; cover to keep warm. Set the flavored liquor aside.

Remove the fish from the oven. Use 2 spatulas to transfer to an oval serving platter. Pat the fish dry with paper towels. Cover with aluminum foil to keep warm.

Prepare the sauce: Strain the fish cooking liquid into the pan with the oyster liquor. Bring to a boil and whisk in the remaining ½ cup cream. Cook for 2 minutes. Whisk a little of this cream mixture with the egg yolk, and then return to the pan. Warm gently over low heat. (Do not allow the mixture to boil or the egg will curdle.) Season to taste with salt and pepper.

To serve, arrange the bouchées on the platter around the fish. Put a little warm spinach in the bottom of each bouchée and place 2 oysters on top. Spoon the reduced cream over the oysters. Spoon the sauce evenly over the fish and serve the remainder in a sauceboat on the side.

Sorbet au Champagne

CHAMPAGNE SORBET

SERVES 6

At Le Cordon Bleu, champagne sorbet is made with pink champagne and a little orange juice, which adds an interesting note of both taste and color. A garnish of raspberries enhances its pinkness, and the crisp almond tile cookies served with it provide a wonderful contrast of textures. For a really festive air, a glass of pink champagne is the perfect accompaniment.

2 cups pink champagne
²/₃ cup still mineral water
¹/₃ cup fresh orange juice
1 cup confectioner's sugar

ALMOND TILE COOKIES
²/₃ cup sugar
1 egg
3 egg whites
4 ounces sliced almonds
¹/₃ cup sifted all-purpose flour
1 teaspoon vanilla extract

¹/₂ cup fresh raspberries

Unsalted butter for baking sheets

EQUIPMENT: Ice cream maker

Chill a bowl and 6 champagne glasses in the freezer.

Combine the champagne, water, orange juice, and sugar and stir to dissolve the sugar. Pour into an ice cream maker and freeze according to the manufacturer's instructions. Transfer the sorbet to the chilled bowl. Freeze until firm, about 1 hour.

Prepare the cookies: Use the above ingredients and follow instructions on page 125 and technique photos on page 551.

To serve, place a scoop of sorbet in each chilled champagne glass. Top each with a few raspberries and serve with an almond tile cookie.

Rillettes de Saumon, Blinis

SALMON RILLETTES WITH BUCKWHEAT BLINI

———

Cailles à la Géorgienne

QUAIL WITH GRAPES AND WALNUTS

———

Soufflé Rothschild

ROTHSCHILD SOUFFLÉ

Rillettes de Saumon, Blinis
SALMON RILLETTES WITH BUCKWHEAT BLINI

SERVES 6

Miniature pancakes (blini) and smoked fish are a classic Slavic combination. This French adaptation pairs a rich pâté, made from both fresh and smoked salmon, with buckwheat blini. Served simply with a wedge of lemon and a little cream, these rillettes make either an elegant first course or a stunning addition to any buffet.

Note: Blini are made in miniature crêpe pans with sides about ½ inch high. The rillettes will keep, covered, in the refrigerator for up to 1 week.

SALMON RILLETTES

1 sprig fresh thyme or
  ¼ teaspoon dried
1 bay leaf
9 ounces fresh salmon or sea trout
  fillet, skinned (page 75)
4 ounces smoked salmon
10 ounces unsalted butter,
  softened
Juice of ½ lemon
Salt and freshly ground pepper
Cayenne pepper

BLINI

1½ cups milk
2 teaspoons fresh yeast or
  1½ teaspoons active dry yeast
1 cup sifted all-purpose flour
1 cup buckwheat flour
Salt
2 egg yolks
2 egg whites

3 tablespoons unsalted butter,
  melted
Parsley sprigs for garnish
2 lemons, cut in wedges
1 cup crème fraîche or sour cream

Unsalted butter, melted,
  for blini pans

EQUIPMENT: 10½-by-3-by-4-inch rectangular terrine mold, 2 blini pans

Prepare the rillettes: Put the terrine mold in the refrigerator or freezer to chill. Bring a large frying pan of water to a simmer with the thyme and bay leaf. Add the fresh salmon and poach 2 to 3 minutes. Remove with a slotted spoon and drain on paper towels. Let cool to room temperature and then crumble into a bowl. Chop the smoked salmon and add to the bowl; mix thoroughly. Beat in the softened butter with a wooden spoon. Add the lemon juice and season to taste with salt, pepper and cayenne. Pack the rillettes into the chilled terrine and smooth the surface with a metal spatula dipped in hot water. Refrigerate for about 2 hours.

Prepare the blini: Heat 1 cup of the milk to lukewarm. Pour over the yeast in a small bowl and let stand to dissolve. In a large mixing bowl, sift together the all-purpose flour, 1/2 cup of the buckwheat flour, and 1/2 teaspoon salt. Make a well in the center of the dry ingredients. Add the milk-and-yeast mixture and whisk to a smooth paste. Cover the bowl with a cloth and let the batter rise in a warm, draft-free place until nearly doubled in bulk, 1 to 1 1/2 hours.

After it has risen, push down the batter. Add the remaining 1/2 cup milk and the egg yolks and beat until smooth. Beat in the remaining 1/2 cup buckwheat flour. Cover and let rise again until nearly doubled in bulk, about 1 hour.

Preheat the oven to 450°. When you are ready to cook the blini, beat the egg whites with a pinch of salt until stiff peaks form. Fold into the batter.

Heat 2 blini pans over medium heat until hot. Brush with the melted butter. Pour 1/4 cup batter into each and cook until the blini are lightly browned on one side. Transfer the pans to the oven and cook until the blini have risen, and the tops are firm. Turn, adding a little more butter to the pan, and cook in the oven until browned on the other side. Remove from the oven and transfer to a plate; cover with aluminum foil to keep warm. Repeat to make about 10 more blini.

To serve, place the terrine of rillettes on a large serving platter. Brush the blini with the melted butter and arrange around the platter. Garnish the platter with parsley sprigs. Serve with lemon wedges and crème fraîche or sour cream.

Cailles à la Géorgienne
QUAIL WITH GRAPES AND WALNUTS

SERVES 6

This recipe has been taught at Le Cordon Bleu for the last eighty years. It calls for both quails and grapes (a classic combination in France) but combines them in a rather unusual way: part of the grapes are pureed to make the sauce and the rest are served whole as a garnish.

This dish is said to be Georgian style *(à la Géorgienne)* because two of its most characteristic ingredients, tea and grapes, are found in the Russian province of Georgia.

(continued)

Cailles à la Géorgienne (continued)

6 quail
Salt and freshly ground pepper
10 walnut halves
Pinch green tea leaves
3/4 cup water
1 pound white grapes, preferably
 Muscat

1 cup dry white wine
3 tablespoons unsalted butter
Juice of 2 oranges, strained
1 cup Brown Veal Stock
 (page 71)

Unsalted butter for
 parchment paper

Truss the quail just as you would truss a chicken (see directions on page 6 and technique photos on page 530). Reserve the necks and wing tips. Season with salt and pepper.

Bring a small saucepan of water to a boil. Add the walnuts and boil 2 to 3 minutes. Remove the pan from the heat and let stand for about 10 minutes. Drain the walnuts, then peel them and set aside.

Bring the tea leaves to a boil in a small saucepan with the water. Remove the saucepan from the heat and let the tea infuse for 3 to 4 minutes. Strain and set aside.

Preheat the oven to 375°.

Peel 40 of the grapes with a small knife and put them in a bowl with ½ cup of the wine; set aside to macerate. Puree the remaining grapes in a food mill. Strain the juice to remove the seeds and skin; set aside.

Heat the butter in a large ovenproof frying pan over high heat. Add the quail, necks and wing tips and sauté until golden brown on all sides. Discard the fat from the pan. Add the orange juice, the remaining ½ cup wine, the tea and grape juice and bring to a boil. Cover with buttered parchment paper and a lid. Transfer to the oven and cook for 25 to 30 minutes.

Remove the quail from the pan. Remove and discard the twine. Cover with aluminum foil to keep warm. Reduce the cooking liquid by half over medium heat, skimming any fat from the surface. Add the brown veal stock and cook until the sauce is reduced and thickened. Taste and adjust seasonings.

To serve, strain the peeled grapes and add to the sauce along with the walnuts. Reheat gently; do not boil. With a slotted spoon, mound the grapes and walnuts in the center of a serving platter. Arrange the quail in a circle around the edge. Spoon a little sauce over the quail, and serve the remainder in a sauceboat on the side.

Soufflé Rothschild
ROTHSCHILD SOUFFLÉ

SERVES 6

The French branch of the Rothschild family are bankers, wine growers, art collectors, and philanthropists. This soufflé, created in their honor at the turn of the century, was originally made with candied fruit macerated in a brandy containing specks of real gold (Goldwasser). At Le Cordon Bleu it is still prepared in the classic manner but using more affordable kirsch.

1/2 cup mixed candied fruit, diced
3 tablespoons kirsch

PASTRY CREAM
1 cup milk
1 teaspoon vanilla extract
2 egg yolks
1/3 cup sugar
2 tablespoons all-purpose flour
2 tablespoons cornstarch

1 egg yolk
4 egg whites
1 tablespoon granulated sugar
Confectioner's sugar for dusting

Unsalted butter for soufflé mold
Granulated sugar for soufflé mold

EQUIPMENT: 6-cup soufflé mold

Macerate the candied fruit in the kirsch for at least 1 hour.

Brush the interior of the soufflé mold with butter and coat lightly with the sugar; tap out excess. Refrigerate until required.

Prepare the pastry cream: Use the above ingredients and follow the directions on page 183. Let cool.

Preheat the oven to 425°. Put the cooled pastry cream in a bowl and whisk until smooth. Stir in the egg yolk, kirsch, and candied fruit.

Beat the egg whites with a whisk or electric mixer until stiff peaks form. Add the sugar and beat 1 minute. Whisk a third of the beaten egg whites into the pastry cream mixture to loosen it. Fold in the remainder with a wooden spoon. Pour into the prepared soufflé mold (the mixture should come to 1/4 inch below the rim). Bake 15 minutes, then reduce the heat to 375° and continue baking until the soufflé is puffed, golden, and firm to the touch, about 15 minutes longer. Remove from the oven and sift confectioner's sugar over the top. Serve immediately.

LESSON 65

Talmouses en Tricorne
CHEESE-FILLED PUFF PASTRIES

Mignons de Porc Arlonaise
PORK TENDERLOINS WITH BEER

Paris-Brest
**CHOUX PASTRY CROWN WITH
PRALINE CREAM**

Talmouses en Tricorne
CHEESE-FILLED PUFF PASTRIES

SERVES 6

Recipes for these cheese-filled pastries can be found in medieval French cookery manuscripts. They are made by sealing the dough around a cheese filling in the shape of little three-cornered hats. Though the dough and the cheese have changed, today's *talmouses* are strikingly similar to those described in texts written over four hundred years ago.

PUFF PASTRY
1¹/₂ cups all-purpose flour
3/4 cup cake flour
2/3 to 3/4 cup cold water
1 teaspoon salt
*2 tablespoons unsalted butter,
  melted*
14 tablespoons unsalted butter
1 egg, lightly beaten, for glazing

CHEESE FILLING
2 tablespoons unsalted butter
3 tablespoons all-purpose flour
1 cup cold milk
Salt and freshly ground pepper
Freshly grated nutmeg
1 egg yolk
*2 ounces Gruyère cheese, grated
  (about 1/2 cup)*

*Unsalted butter, softened,
  for baking sheet*

EQUIPMENT: 7-inch round fluted cookie cutter, 1 1/4-inch round, fluted cookie cutter, Pastry bag, Large plain pastry tip

Prepare the puff pastry: Use the above ingredients and follow the directions on pages 209–10 and technique photos on pages 542–43.

Prepare the cheese filling: Melt the butter in a medium, heavy-bottomed saucepan over low heat. Stir in the flour and cook for 2 minutes without coloring. Add the cold milk and whisk until smooth. Bring to a boil and season to taste with salt, pepper, and nutmeg. Reduce the heat and simmer for about 5 minutes, whisking constantly, until the sauce is smooth and thick. Remove from heat. Whisk a little sauce with the egg yolk in a small bowl and return to the pan. Cook 5 minutes, whisking constantly. Remove the sauce from the heat and whisk in the cheese. Taste and adjust seasonings. Let cool completely.

Preheat the oven to 425°. Brush a baking sheet lightly with the softened butter and sprinkle with cold water.

Dust a work surface with flour. Roll out the dough about 1/8 inch thick. Use the 7-inch round fluted cookie cutter to cut out 6 rounds of dough. Transfer the dough rounds to the baking sheet. Reserve the remaining dough.

Fit a pastry bag with the large plain tip and spoon the cheese filling into it. Pipe a small mound of filling in the center of each dough round. Brush the exposed surface of the rounds with cold water and fold up the edges to form a triangle, or a three-cornered hat. Press the edges together to seal. Brush the pastries with the egg glaze. Cut out six 1 1/4-inch rounds from the reserved dough and place one on top of each filled pastry using egg glaze, if necessary, to attach. Brush the rounds with egg glaze and bake until the pastries are golden brown, 20 to 25 minutes.

Serve hot on a doily-lined serving dish.

Mignons de Porc Arlonaise
PORK TENDERLOINS WITH BEER

SERVES 6

This dish is a specialty of the Belgian town of Arlon. There, dark beer is more likely to be used in cooking than wine, and people have a tendency to combine sweet and sour tastes as in this dish, where beer is flavored with a mixture of sugar and vinegar to make the sauce.

At Le Cordon Bleu this simple pork and potato dinner is given an elegantly modern look by simmering a colorful mixture of carrots, celery, leeks, mushrooms, and turnips in the sauce before serving.

(continued)

Mignons de Porc Arlonaise (continued)

18 *small waxy potatoes*
  (red or white)

Salt

2 *pork tenderloins, 1¹/₂ pounds*
  each, trimmed of fat

Freshly ground pepper

6 *tablespoons unsalted butter*

SAUCE

2 *tablespoons sugar*

¹/₄ *cup wine vinegar*

³/₄ *cup dark beer*

1¹/₄ *cups Brown Veal Stock*
  (page 71)

¹/₄ *pound carrots, cut into julienne*
  (see technique photo page 519)

¹/₄ *pound celery, cut into julienne*

¹/₄ *pound leeks (white part only),*
  cut into julienne

¹/₄ *pound mushrooms, trimmed,*
  rinsed, dried, and
  cut into julienne

¹/₄ *pound turnips, cut into julienne*

Turn the potatoes, as for Pommes à l'Anglaise (see directions on page 50 and technique photo on page 520). Put the potatoes into a saucepan with cold salted water to cover. Bring to a boil and cook until just tender, about 10 minutes. Let the potatoes stand in the cooking water until needed.

Preheat the oven to 425°.

Season the pork tenderloins with salt and pepper. Heat 2 tablespoons of the butter in a large ovenproof pan over high heat. Add the pork and brown on all sides. Transfer to the oven and roast 15 minutes.

While the pork is cooking, prepare the sauce: Combine the sugar and vinegar in a small heavy-bottomed saucepan. Cook over medium heat until the mixture caramelizes to a light amber color. Remove from the heat and immediately add the beer. (Be careful; the mixture will sputter.) When the sputtering stops, return the pan to the heat and stir to blend. Then cook over medium heat until reduced by two-thirds. Stir in the stock and reduce by about one-half.

Remove the pork from the oven, transfer to a shallow dish and cover with aluminum foil to keep warm. Discard the fat from the pan. Add the remaining 4 tablespoons butter to the pan and melt over medium heat. Add the julienned vegetables and stir until well coated with butter. Season with salt and pepper. Cover and cook, stirring occasionally, until the vegetables are crisp-tender. Return the pork to the pan, stir in the sauce and simmer 5 minutes.

To serve, slice the pork into ³/₈-inch-thick rounds and arrange down the center of a serving platter. Drain the potatoes and arrange around the meat along with the julienned vegetables. Spoon the sauce over the meat.

Paris-Brest

CHOUX PASTRY CROWN WITH PRALINE CREAM

SERVES 6 TO 8

Many French dishes are named after famous people or famous events. It's no surprise, therefore, that around the turn of the century an ingenious pastry chef decided to name one of his creations after a bicycle race. Indeed, the race from Paris to Brest was a major event, and this wheel-shaped pastry was an immediate success. Today it can be found in pastry shops all over France and is as famous as the race for which it was named.

Note: The praline powder and the pastry cream used to make the filling may be made up to 24 hours ahead of time and kept refrigerated in separate containers until needed.

(continued)

Paris-Brest (continued)

PRALINE POWDER

1¹/₂ *ounces finely ground almonds*
   (about 6 tablespoons)
¹/₂ *cup sugar*
3 *tablespoons water*
1 *teaspoon vanilla extract*

CHOUX PASTRY

1 *cup water*
7 *tablespoons unsalted butter*
Pinch salt
2 *tablespoons sugar*
1¹/₃ *cups sifted all-purpose flour*
4 *eggs*
1 *egg, slightly beaten, for glazing*

2 *ounces sliced almonds*

PRALINE PASTRY CREAM

PASTRY CREAM:
  1 *cup milk*
  1 *teaspoon vanilla extract*
  2 *egg yolks*
  ¹/₄ *cup sugar*
  2 *tablespoons all-purpose flour*
  2 *tablespoons cornstarch*
Praline powder (see above)
1 *tablespoon rum*
10 *tablespoons unsalted butter,*
  softened

Confectioner's sugar for dusting
Oil for baking sheet
Unsalted butter for baking
  sheet and pastry cream

EQUIPMENT: Pastry bag, large plain pastry tip, medium star pastry tip

Prepare the praline powder: Brush a baking sheet lightly with the oil. Toast the ground almonds in a nonstick frying pan over medium heat until golden and fragrant; set aside. Combine the sugar, water and vanilla in a small heavy-bottomed saucepan. Bring to a boil over low heat, stirring to dissolve the sugar. Then cook over medium heat, without stirring, until the mixture caramelizes to a golden brown. (Watch carefully because caramel burns very quickly.) Remove from the heat and immediately add the toasted ground almonds. Pour the mixture onto the oiled baking sheet and cool until hardened. Remove from the baking sheet and grind to a powder in a food processor or mortar. Set the praline powder aside.

Preheat the oven to 400°. Brush a baking sheet with the softened butter. Prepare the choux pastry: Use the above ingredients and follow the directions on page 43 and technique photos on page 548.

Trace a 9-inch circle onto the baking sheet. Fit the pastry bag with the large round tip and fill with the dough. Following the 9-inch guide, pipe a circle of dough about ³/₄-inch wide onto the baking sheet. Pipe another circle just inside and touching the first. Brush both with egg glaze. Finally, pipe a third circle on top of the first two, along the line where the two bottom circles meet. Brush with egg glaze and sprinkle with the sliced almonds. Bake for 10 minutes without opening the oven door. Then lower the oven temperature to 350° and continue to bake until the pastry is well risen and golden all over, including the interior of any small cracks that have formed on the surface, 15 to 20 minutes longer. Let cool on a raised cake rack to allow the air to circulate around the pastry so that it does not become soggy.

Prepare the praline pastry cream: First, make a pastry cream, using the milk, vanilla, egg yolks, sugar, flour, and cornstarch and following the directions on page 183. Remove from the heat but do not cool. Whisk the praline powder with a little of the hot pastry cream in a large bowl until smooth. Whisk in the remaining pastry cream. Spread on a platter and pat the surface with butter to prevent a skin from forming; let cool. When cool, return the praline pastry cream to a bowl and whisk in the rum until smooth. Then gradually whisk in the softened butter. Fit a pastry bag with the medium star tip. Fill with the praline pastry cream and refrigerate until firm.

Assemble the Paris-Brest: Slice the cooled choux pastry ring in half horizontally. Pipe all of the pastry cream onto the bottom half. Gently top with the other half and dust with confectioner's sugar (see photo on page 369). Transfer to a serving platter and refrigerate until serving time, or up to 4 or 5 hours.

PRALINE

Praline is a mixture of toasted ground almonds and caramel used to flavor ice creams, mousse and bavarois mixtures, and pastry creams. It is made by stirring toasted almonds into hot caramel, letting the mixture cool and harden, and then grinding it to a powder. Praline is available in the form of an already prepared paste in France and in some specialty food stores in the United States.

LESSON 66

Petits Farcis Niçois

STUFFED VEGETABLES, NICE STYLE

———

Escalopes de Saumon Gigondas

SAUTÉED SALMON WITH CRAYFISH
AND RED WINE SAUCE

———

Gratin de Fruits au Marasquin

FRUIT GRATIN WITH MARASCHINO LIQUEUR

Petits Farcis Niçois

STUFFED VEGETABLES, NICE STYLE

———

SERVES 6

In Nice everyone loves *lu farçun*, literally "stuffed things." The term is almost exclusively applied to vegetables that are stuffed, baked, and served hot or cold at the beginning of a meal. In addition to the vegetables cited below, stuffed tomatoes, eggplant, and bell peppers can also be prepared to complete this vegetable platter and the stuffing can be flavored with freshly grated Parmesan and/or fresh basil depending on personal taste.

3 medium zucchini
6 small turnips
6 medium red onions
Salt

STUFFING
4 slices firm white bread,
  crusts removed
1¹/₂ cups milk
1 tablespoon olive oil

¹/₂ pound lean ground veal
¹/₂ pound lean ground pork
6 cloves garlic, chopped fine
1 egg, lightly beaten
1 tablespoon chopped parsley
Salt and freshly ground pepper

Olive oil for roasting pan
  and vegetables

Cut the zucchini into 2½-inch lengths. Scoop out and discard the flesh with a melon baller or small spoon, leaving the walls of the hollowed cylinders about ⅜ inch thick.

Slice the top third from each turnip, leaving, if possible, ¾ inch of the green stems attached; reserve the tops. Scoop out and discard the flesh with a melon baller, leaving the turnip walls about ⅜ inch thick.

Prepare the onions in the same manner as the turnips.

Blanch the turnips and their caps for 2 minutes in a saucepan of boiling salted water. Place upside down on a rack to drain.

Preheat the oven to 400°.

Prepare the stuffing: Soak the bread slices in the milk; set aside. Heat the olive oil in a large frying pan over medium heat. Add the ground veal, pork and garlic and cook 5 minutes. Remove from the heat. Squeeze out the bread and stir into the meat mixture along with the egg, parsley, and salt and pepper to taste.

Season the interiors of the vegetables with salt and pepper. Mound the stuffing into the vegetables.

Brush a roasting pan with the olive oil. Arrange the vegetables in the pan and brush them with the oil. Reduce the oven heat to 375° and bake the vegetables until just tender, 40 to 45 minutes. Place the tops on the turnips 10 minutes before the end of cooking time. Serve hot or cold.

Escalopes de Saumon Gigondas
SAUTÉED SALMON WITH CRAYFISH
AND RED WINE SAUCE

SERVES 6

Red wine sauces are used almost exclusively with meat or poultry in France; this recipe is an exception. Here Gigondas, a full-bodied red wine from the Rhône valley, adds its taste and color to a dark crayfish-flavored sauce. The sauce is served with sautéed salmon fillets; the overall effect is stunning and the taste of the wine perfectly complements that of the fish.

As is the rule with other dishes that emphasize the taste of a specific wine, the wine used for making the sauce should also be served to accompany the fish.

Note: This recipe calls for freshwater crayfish, which are used in the sauce and as a garnish. Live crayfish may be stored in the refrigerator for up to 3 or 4 days. If purchased frozen, they must be used immediately upon defrosting.

(continued)

Escalopes de Saumon Gigondas (continued)

FISH STOCK

1 whiting or 1 pound lean white
   fish with bones and/or heads

1 leek, chopped coarse

1 stalk celery, chopped coarse

1 onion, chopped coarse

1 clove garlic

Parsley stems

1 sprig fresh thyme
   or ¼ teaspoon dried

1 bay leaf

1⅓ cups dry white wine

2⅔ cups water

2½ pounds salmon fillet,
   skinned (page 75)

2 pounds live freshwater crayfish
   or whole frozen crayfish, defrosted

Salt and freshly ground pepper

11 tablespoons unsalted butter

2 shallots, chopped fine

3 cups red wine from the
   Côtes-du-Rhône,
   preferably Gigondas

1 tomato, chopped coarse

BEURRE MANIÉ

1 tablespoon all-purpose flour

1 tablespoon unsalted butter,
   softened

6 large mushrooms, trimmed,
   cleaned, and cut into julienne
   (see technique photo
   on page 519)

½ pound scallions

1 tablespoon vegetable oil

Chervil or parsley sprigs
   for garnish

Prepare the fish stock: Use the above ingredients and follow the directions on page 181. Strain.

Cut the salmon into scallops, or *escalopes* (see technique photo on page 525): Use a small knife to remove the dark flesh from the fillets. Rinse quickly under cold running water and dry well with paper towels. Starting at the tail end and holding the knife at an angle, cut the fillets diagonally into thin scallops about 3 inches long; set aside.

Reserve 6 whole crayfish for garnish. Plunge the remainder into a large pot of boiling salted water. Boil for 1 minute; drain. Twist the middle tail fins and pull sharply to remove the intestines. Remove and reserve the shells. Season the shelled tails with salt and pepper; set aside.

Prepare the sauce: Melt 2 tablespoons of the butter in a large frying pan over medium heat. Add the crayfish shells and shallots and cook until the shallots are soft but not colored, about 5 minutes. Crush the shells in the pan with a wooden pestle or mallet. Add the wine and bring to a boil. Add the strained fish stock and tomato. Season with salt and pepper, and cook over medium heat until reduced by about one-third. Strain, pressing down on the solids to extract all of the liquid; discard the solids. Return to the heat and simmer until the sauce is reduced by one-third. Mash the flour and softened butter with a fork to make a beurre manié. Bring the sauce to a boil and whisk in the beurre manié little by little until the sauce reaches the consistency of heavy cream. (You may not need to add all of the beurre manié.) Set the sauce aside.

Heat 2 tablespoons of the butter in a frying pan over high heat. Add the mushrooms and cook quickly, without coloring, until all the moisture has evaporated. Season to taste with salt and pepper. Remove from the pan and set aside.

Trim the root ends from the scallions. Then, starting about 1 inch from the root ends, cut through the length of the scallions; rotate the scallions and repeat so that the scallions are quartered but still attached.

Heat 3 more tablespoons butter in the same pan over medium heat. Add the scallions and cook until soft but not colored. Remove from the pan and set aside.

Heat 1 tablespoon oil in the same pan over high heat until sizzling hot. Add the shelled crayfish tails and sauté 1 to 2 minutes, shaking the pan often; set aside.

Prepare the whole crayfish garnish: Insert the claws of the reserved whole crayfish into the base of the tails (see photo) and cook in boiling salted water 1 minute. Remove with a slotted spoon and set aside.

Sauté the salmon: Heat 2 tablespoons of the butter in a large frying pan over high heat. Season the salmon scallops with salt and pepper and add half of them to the pan. Sauté 2 minutes on each side. Remove from the pan and cover with aluminum foil to keep warm. Discard the fat in the pan. Add the 2 remaining tablespoons butter and repeat to cook the remaining scallops.

To serve, reheat the scallions, mushrooms, and sauce, if necessary. Spoon a shallow pool of sauce onto a serving platter. Arrange overlapping scallops of salmon on the sauce. Fold the scallions in halves and arrange around the salmon and top with crayfish tails. Scatter the mushrooms around the salmon scallops. Garnish with the whole crayfish and small sprigs of chervil. Serve any remaining sauce in a sauceboat on the side. (For individual servings, see photo.)

Gratin de Fruits au Marasquin

FRUIT GRATIN WITH MARASCHINO LIQUEUR

SERVES 6

Fruit gratins are now as common in France as their vegetable-based ancestors. Typically, fresh fruit is layered into individual dishes or arranged on plates, covered with a foamy sabayon, and browned under the broiler. A perfect gratin demands a great deal of attention; the sabayon cannot be made in advance and the gratin can easily burn, rather than brown, under the heat of the broiler.

3 mangoes	SABAYON
6 figs	2 egg yolks
2 tablespoons maraschino liqueur	1/2 cup confectioner's sugar
	2/3 cup dry white wine
	2 tablespoons maraschino liqueur

EQUIPMENT: 6 large, ovenproof plates

Peel and cut the mangoes into thin slices. Peel the figs and cut each lengthwise into 6 slices. Combine the fruit in a shallow container and sprinkle with the liqueur. Let the fruit macerate at room temperature for at least 20 minutes.

Prepare the sabayon: Bring 2 to 3 inches of water to a simmer in a large saucepan. Combine the egg yolks, sugar, wine, and liqueur in a large, heatproof bowl and beat with a whisk or electric mixer until pale yellow and foamy. Set the bowl over the simmering water (the bottom of the bowl must not touch the water) and continue beating until the mixture becomes thick and creamy and increases in volume, and the whisk or beater leaves a clear trail on the bottom of the bowl. Test the temperature of the sabayon occasionally with a finger: If it feels hotter than just tepid (the temperature should not exceed 80°) remove from the heat and beat until slightly cooled. Then return to the heat and finish cooking as described.

To serve, preheat the broiler. Arrange the mango slices in a fan shape in the center of each of the 6 ovenproof plates. Surround with the fig sections. Cover the fruit with the sabayon and broil for a few minutes until lightly browned. Watch carefully because the sabayon will color quickly. Serve hot.

LESSON 67

Artichauts à la Menthe
ROASTED SPRING ARTICHOKES STUFFED WITH GARLIC AND FRESH MINT

———

Lapin Farci Ménagère
STUFFED RABBIT

———

Petits Soufflés Glacés aux Abricots
FROZEN APRICOT SOUFFLÉS

Artichauts à la Menthe
ROASTED SPRING ARTICHOKES STUFFED WITH GARLIC AND FRESH MINT

———

SERVES 6

When they are in season, boiled artichokes can be seen piled high in front of many Parisian caterers' shops. Most people are happy to consume them this way with a little homemade mayonnaise or vinaigrette. A welcome alternative was devised by one of the chefs at Le Cordon Bleu. He decided to bake whole baby artichokes with a delicate filling made from freshly chopped mint and garlic. The result was an immediate success.

1 lemon, cut in half
6 small artichokes
6 cloves garlic, chopped fine
3 tablespoons chopped mint

Salt and freshly ground pepper
2 tablespoons olive oil

Olive oil for roasting pan
Unsalted butter for
  parchment paper

Prepare the artichokes: Fill a bowl with cold water and add the lemon halves. Leave the stem intact but snap off and discard the tough outer leaves of each artichoke until only the inner, pale yellow leaves remain. Trim the sides of the bases with a small knife to a round, smooth shape.

(continued)

Artichauts à la Menthe (continued)

Cut off the tops of the leaves, leaving the artichokes 1½ to 2 inches high, not including the stems. Insert the handle of a teaspoon into the center of the artichokes and scrape out the chokes. Peel the stems with a vegetable peeler and cut to a length of about 1½ inches. Rub the artichokes with the cut side of the lemon and put them into the bowl of water.

Preheat the oven to 375°. Brush a small roasting pan with the olive oil.

Combine the mint, garlic, salt and pepper on a cutting board. Crush to a paste with the flat side of a large knife.

Drain the artichokes. Spoon 2 teaspoons of the mint-garlic paste into each heart. Arrange the artichokes, stem sides up, in the roasting pan. Brush with oil. Season with salt and pepper and bake until tender when pierced with the point of a knife, 30 to 40 minutes. (Cooking time will vary depending on the quality of the artichokes.) Towards the end of cooking, add a little water to the pan and cover with a round of buttered parchment paper to prevent the artichokes from drying out and browning. Serve warm or cold.

Lapin Farci Ménagère
STUFFED RABBIT

———

SERVES 6

Rabbits have meaty hind legs but the upper half of the animal is bony indeed. Many a clever French *ménagère* (housewife) has turned a rabbit for four into a rabbit for six by boning and stuffing the little animal. The stuffing not only flavors the flesh but also keeps the lean rabbit meat from drying out when baked. Any leftover rabbit will be excellent cold; sliced and served with a little green salad, it makes for a nice lunch or a first course of another meal.

3¾-pound rabbit, head removed

STUFFING
2 tablespoons unsalted butter
1 medium onion, chopped fine
1 clove garlic, chopped fine
1 sprig fresh thyme or
  ¼ teaspoon dried
1 tablespoon chopped parsley
14 ounces lean ground pork
1 cup fresh bread crumbs

Salt and freshly ground pepper
4 tablespoons unsalted butter
1 medium onion, chopped
1 carrot, chopped
1 clove garlic
¾ cup dry white wine
¾ cup Brown Veal Stock
  (page 71)
1 bay leaf

Lay the rabbit on its back on a work surface. Cut off the tips of the fore and hind legs and remove the kidneys and liver. Remove the forelegs by cutting through the shoulder joints with a boning knife. Then, working on

the inside of the forelegs where the bones are most visible, cut along the length of the bones to expose them; scrape the bones free of the flesh and remove them; set the meat aside.

Then bone the rest of the rabbit whole (see technique photos on page 533): Working on the inside of a leg, cut along the length of the thigh and leg bones to expose them. Scrape around the bones to release them. Cut through the hip joints and remove the leg bones. Cut along the length of one side of the backbone to release the fillet; repeat with the fillet on the other side. Then, working at the tail end, carefully cut underneath the backbone to release it from the flesh. Moving toward the ribcage and taking care not to pierce the thin skin, continue to cut and shape the flesh from the backbone, cut and scrape the flesh away from around and underneath the ribcage; remove the backbone and ribs in 1 piece.

Preheat the oven to 400°. Prepare the stuffing: Melt the butter in a frying pan over medium heat. Add the onion and garlic and cook until soft but not colored. Remove from the heat, and transfer to a bowl. Add the thyme leaves, parsley, and the ground pork. Add the bread crumbs and mix well. Season to taste with salt and pepper.

Stuff the rabbit: Season the rabbit all over with salt and pepper. Spread it flat on a work surface, on its back, overlapping the legs slightly to hold the stuffing. Spoon the stuffing down the center of the rabbit. Put the 2 pieces of boned foreleg meat in a strip on top of the stuffing. Fold the sides of the rabbit up to enclose the stuffing and form a cylinder. Tie with kitchen twine in about 5 places along the length of the body and then once around the entire length. This will secure the stuffing and hold the shape of the rabbit during cooking.

Melt 2 tablespoons of the butter in a roasting pan. Add the chopped onion, carrot and garlic. Stir to coat with the butter. Put the rabbit on top of the vegetables and rub it with the remaining 2 tablespoons butter. Season with salt and pepper. Transfer to the oven and roast 10 to 15 minutes, until you see that the rabbit is beginning to brown. Then add the wine, stock and bay leaf and continue cooking, basting every 15 minutes with the pan juices, until a skewer or trussing needle inserted into the thickest part of the rabbit is warm to the touch, about 1 hour and 15 minutes longer. Turn the rabbit once during cooking and if it browns too much, cover with a piece of aluminum foil.

Transfer the rabbit to a serving platter. Remove and discard the twine. Strain the contents of the roasting pan, pressing down on the solids to extract all the liquid. Skim the fat from the surface. Spoon a little juice over the rabbit and serve the remainder in a sauceboat on the side.

Petits Soufflés Glacés aux Abricots
FROZEN APRICOT SOUFFLÉS

SERVES 6

Frozen soufflés? French chefs have been making them for more than a hundred years, but they still come as a surprise. They mimic their hot cousins in appearance and texture but are actually something of a cross between a classic parfait and a frozen mousse. Made from a combination of Italian meringue and whipped cream, the mixture is poured into soufflé molds rimmed with high cardboard collars. Before serving, the collars are removed, making the frozen desserts look as though they had risen several inches above the edges of the molds. *Voilà!*

11 ounces strained canned apricots (about 12 halves)

ITALIAN MERINGUE
5 egg whites
1 1/4 cups sugar
1/4 cup water

1 3/4 cups heavy cream

CHANTILLY CREAM
1 cup heavy cream
1 tablespoon confectioner's sugar
1 teaspoon vanilla extract

6 candied violets

EQUIPMENT: Six 1/2-cup ramekins or soufflé dishes, pastry bag, medium star pastry tip

Chill a mixing bowl for the whipped cream.

Cut 6 bands of flexible cardboard about 3 inches wide and 12 inches long. Tape a cardboard band around the outside of each ramekin to make a collar that extends 2 inches above the rim of the ramekin. Secure each with a rubber band. Chill in the refrigerator.

Puree the apricots in a food mill or food processor; set aside.

Prepare the Italian meringue: Use the above ingredients and follow the directions on pages 293–94. Set aside.

Beat the cream in the chilled bowl with a whisk or electric mixer until stiff peaks form and the cream clings to the whisk or beater. Carefully fold the cream into the Italian meringue and then fold in the apricot puree.

Fill the ramekins with the apricot mixture to the top of the cardboard collars. Smooth off the surfaces with a metal spatula. Freeze until firm, at least 2 hours.

Not more than 1 hour before serving, prepare the Chantilly cream (page 21): Fit the pastry bag with the medium star tip and fill it with the Chantilly cream. Refrigerate until serving time.

To serve, dip the blade of a knife in hot water and run it around the inside of each cardboard collar. Carefully remove the collars. Pipe a Chantilly cream rosette in the center top of each soufflé. Top each rosette with a candied violet.

SUPÉRIEURE

Huîtres Chaudes au Muscadet
POACHED OYSTERS WITH MUSCADET
SABAYON SAUCE

Canard à l'Orange
ROAST DUCK WITH ORANGE SAUCE

Charlotte Malakoff
ALMOND CREAM CHARLOTTE

Huîtres Chaudes au Muscadet
POACHED OYSTERS WITH MUSCADET SABAYON SAUCE

SERVES 6

Muscadet is a fruity, dry white wine from the western end of the Loire valley. The vineyards are not far from the coast where some of the finest oysters in France are harvested. Indeed, raw oysters from there and elsewhere are often served in France with a glass of cold Muscadet.

At Le Cordon Bleu, this classic combination sparked the creative inspiration of one of our chefs. Oysters are lightly poached, served in their shells on a bed of fresh spinach, and sauced with a foamy sabayon that includes a little of the oysters' own liquid and Muscadet.

Note: Though both the oysters and spinach can be cooked ahead of time, the sauce must be made at the last minute and everything quickly browned under the broiler just before serving.

(continued)

Huîtres Chaudes au Muscadet (continued)

24 oysters

2 pounds spinach, stemmed
and rinsed

Salt

MUSCADET SABAYON SAUCE

2 tablespoons unsalted butter

2 shallots, chopped fine

²/₃ cup dry white wine,
preferably Muscadet

²/₃ cup crème fraîche or
heavy cream

Freshly ground pepper

4 egg yolks

¼ cup water

½ pound unsalted butter, clarified
(page 94) and cooled
to lukewarm

4 tablespoons unsalted butter

Freshly ground pepper

Coarse salt for platter

Shuck the oysters over a bowl to collect the liquor (see directions on page 334 and technique photos on page 523). Discard the flat halves of the shells. Wash and dry the curved halves and set aside. Put the oysters in a small frying pan and strain the liquor through a fine strainer over them. Bring just to a boil over high heat and then immediately remove the pan from the heat. Let the oysters cool in the liquor.

Cook the spinach, uncovered, in a large saucepan of boiling salted water for about 3 minutes. Drain; refresh under cold running water and drain again. Squeeze well to remove as much water as possible; set aside.

Prepare the sauce: Heat the 2 tablespoons butter in a small heavy-bottomed saucepan over medium heat. Add the shallots and cook until soft but not colored. Add the Muscadet and most of the oyster liquor (leave a little in the pan to keep the oysters moist). Cook over medium heat until reduced and syrupy. Stir in the cream. Reduce the heat to low and cook until reduced by one half. Season to taste with pepper. Cover to keep warm and set aside.

Then make a sabayon: Bring 2 to 3 inches of water to a simmer in a saucepan. Combine the yolks and water in a heatproof bowl and beat with a whisk or electric mixer until foamy. Set the bowl over the simmering water (the bottom of the bowl must not touch the water) and beat until the mixture becomes thick and creamy and increases in volume, and the whisk or beater leaves a clear trail on the bottom of the bowl. Test the temperature of the sabayon occasionally with a finger: If it feels hotter than just tepid (the temperature should not exceed 80°) remove from the heat and beat until slightly cooled. Then return to the heat and finish cooking as described. Remove from the heat and whisk in the clarified butter in a slow steady stream. Whisk in the wine-oyster liquor reduction. Taste and adjust seasoning. Keep the sauce warm off the heat over a pan of hot water.

Heat the butter in a frying pan over high heat. Add the spinach and cook, stirring often, until all the moisture has evaporated. Season to taste with salt and pepper.

To serve, line the bottom of a serving platter with the coarse salt. (This will help to keep the oyster shells stable.) Put a little spinach in the bottom of each oyster shell and top each with an oyster. Spoon a little sauce over both and arrange on the platter. Or, if you like, pass the filled shells rapidly under a preheated broiler to gratinée them just before serving.

Canard à l'Orange
ROAST DUCK WITH ORANGE SAUCE

SERVES 6

For centuries, elaborate dinners in France included courses of both roast and stewed meats. Roasts were always served separately and almost systematically seasoned with a little orange juice (just as we season fish with a little lemon juice today). The oranges used were always bitter Seville oranges (bigarades), and this famous duck dish is a direct descendant of the traditional roasted fowl of yore.

Though it is often made with ordinary oranges today, if Seville oranges are available they should be substituted—their tartness makes a perfect counterpoint to the sweet elements in the sauce.

5-pound duck	**BIGARADE SAUCE**
Salt and freshly ground pepper	*1 lemon*
1 sprig fresh thyme or	*7 oranges*
¼ teaspoon dried	*3 tablespoons sugar*
1 bay leaf	*⅓ cup red-wine vinegar*
2 tablespoons unsalted butter,	*2 cups Brown Veal Stock*
softened	*(page 71)*
1 medium carrot, diced	*2 tablespoons Cointreau*
1 medium onion, diced	
1 stalk celery, diced	*Small bunch watercress*
1 leek (white part only), diced	*for garnish*

Preheat the oven to 400°.

Prepare the duck: Cut off the wing tips and set aside with the neck. Cut out the fat glands at the base of the tail with the point of a small knife. Cut out the wishbone to facilitate carving (see directions on page 76 and technique photos 1 and 2 on page 531). Rinse the duck inside and out with cold water; dry well with paper towels. Season the cavity with salt and pepper and add the thyme and bay leaf. Truss just as you would a chicken (page 6 and technique photos on page 530). Rub the skin all over with the softened butter and season with salt and pepper.

Put the duck on one side in a roasting pan, along with the reserved wing tips and neck. Roast 25 minutes. Then turn the duck onto the other side, add the diced vegetables, and roast 25 minutes longer. Finally, turn the duck breast side up and roast until the juices run clear when the thigh is pierced with the point of a knife, 25 to 35 minutes longer.

Prepare the bigarade sauce: First, remove the zest in thin strips from the lemon and 3 of the oranges with a vegetable peeler. (Be careful not to remove the bitter white pith.) Cut the zests into thin julienne strips. Bring a small saucepan of water to a boil. Add the julienned zests and boil 5 minutes. Drain, refresh under cold running water and drain again; set aside. Squeeze and strain the juice from the 3 peeled oranges into a bowl; set aside. Peel and section the 4 remaining oranges (page 9); set aside. Strain their juice into the bowl of orange juice.

Then, combine the sugar and vinegar in a small heavy-bottomed saucepan. Cook over medium heat until the mixture caramelizes to a light amber color. (Watch carefully because caramel burns very quickly.) Remove from the heat and immediately add the orange juice. Be careful; the sauce will sputter vigorously. When the sputtering stops, return the saucepan to the heat and whisk well to blend. Stir in the veal stock and simmer for about 10 minutes. Skim the surface to remove any fat and impurities.

Transfer the duck to a large serving platter. Remove the twine and cover the duck with aluminum foil to keep warm. Discard all the fat in the roasting pan. Set the pan over high heat, add the sauce, and deglaze, scraping the bottom of the pan with a wooden spoon to release any cooked particles. Cook over high heat until reduced and thickened, about 5 minutes. Strain the sauce into a small saucepan; taste and adjust seasonings. Add the blanched zests and Cointreau. Pour the sauce over the duck and scatter the orange sections around. Garnish the platter with small bouquets of watercress.

Charlotte Malakoff
ALMOND CREAM CHARLOTTE

SERVES 6

Only two charlottes were taught at Le Cordon Bleu at the turn of the century—the classic *charlotte russe* and this *charlotte malakoff*. They illustrate different approaches to making the cream used to fill the ladyfinger-lined charlotte mold. Unlike most charlottes, a *charlotte malakoff* does not use bavarian cream but rather an almond-flavored pastry cream, into which the Chantilly cream is folded as usual.

Both charlottes contain allusions to Russia in their names: Malakoff was the site of a fortress near the Ukrainian town of Sebastopol, captured by the French in 1855—this dessert commemorates that victory.

LADYFINGERS
3 eggs, separated
6 tablespoons granulated sugar
3/4 cup sifted cake flour
6 tablespoons confectioner's sugar

SUGAR SYRUP
2 tablespoons cold water
2 tablespoons kirsch
2 tablespoons confectioner's sugar

ALMOND CREAM

¼ pound unsalted butter

½ cup confectioner's sugar

4 ounces finely ground almonds (about 1 cup)

3 tablespoons kirsch

¾ cup heavy cream

CHANTILLY CREAM

¾ cup heavy cream

1 teaspoon vanilla extract

1 tablespoon confectioner's sugar

EQUIPMENT: 6-cup charlotte mold, pastry bag, small star pastry tip

Prepare the ladyfingers (use the above ingredients and follow the directions on page 118 and technique photos on page 549) and use them to line the bottom and sides of the charlotte mold (pages 352–53 and technique photos on page 549).

Chill a mixing bowl for the whipped cream.

Prepare the syrup: Combine the water, kirsch and confectioner's sugar in a small bowl. Whisk to dissolve the sugar. Brush the ladyfingers with the syrup, starting with the sides of the mold and then brushing the base; the ladyfingers should be well saturated but not soggy.

Prepare the almond cream: Work the butter with the heel of your hand to soften. Warm a heatproof bowl in a low oven or under hot, running water. Add the softened butter and beat with a whisk or electric mixer until creamy. Add the confectioner's sugar, ground almonds and kirsch and continue to beat until the mixture is light and creamy.

Beat the heavy cream in the chilled bowl with a whisk or electric mixer until stiff peaks form and the cream clings to the whisk or beater. Whisk about one-third of whipped cream into the almond cream mixture. Fold in the remainder with a wooden spoon. Pour the almond cream into the prepared mold and pack it down well with the back of the wooden spoon. Refrigerate until firm, at least 3 hours.

Not more than 1 hour before serving, prepare the Chantilly cream (page 21). Fit the pastry bag with the small star tip and fill with the Chantilly cream. Refrigerate until serving time.

To serve, unmold the charlotte: Use a small sharp knife to trim the ladyfingers to the level of the cream filling. Invert a round platter over the mold and quickly reverse the two. Decorate the center top and base of the charlotte with rosettes of Chantilly cream. Serve chilled.

Terrine d'Aubergines
EGGPLANT TERRINE

Filet de Veau en Croûte
LOIN OF VEAL IN PUFF PASTRY

Nougat Glacé
CHILLED NOUGAT MOUSSE

Terrine d'Aubergines
EGGPLANT TERRINE

SERVES 6 - 8

Eggplant can be purchased in markets throughout France but it is still an exotic food to many people. Some will buy the vegetable to make ever-popular *ratatouille* but most French people north of the Loire have little idea of what else to do with it.

This terrine demonstrates a thoroughly modern and creative use of eggplant. It is delicious either hot or cold.

4 large eggplants
3 tablespoons olive oil
3 onions, chopped
1 red bell pepper, diced fine
1 green bell pepper, diced fine
4 zucchini, peeled and diced

3 tomatoes, peeled, seeded,
* and diced (page 31)*
5 garlic cloves, chopped
Salt and fresh ground black pepper
Cayenne pepper
2 ounces fresh bread crumbs
* (about 1 cup)*

TOMATO COULIS

*1 pound tomatoes, peeled,
 seeded, and diced*

*Salt and freshly ground black
 pepper*

Cayenne pepper

1/2 bunch fresh basil

*1 small can oil-packed
 anchovy fillets*

*6 black olives, pitted
 and cut in half*

*Unsalted butter, softened,
 for loaf pan and
 parchment paper*

EQUIPMENT: 5-by-9-inch loaf pan

Preheat the oven to 450°.

Brush the loaf pan with the softened butter. Line the bottom with parchment paper and brush the paper with butter.

Peel the eggplants in wide lengthwise strips with a vegetable peeler. Trim the strips to even the edges; reserve. Put the whole peeled eggplants in a roasting pan, and bake until soft, about 40 minutes. Let cool slightly. Cut the eggplants in half lengthwise and scoop out the pulp. Discard the hard outside crusts. Chop the pulp coarsely and drain in a colander.

Blanch the reserved strips of eggplant skin in boiling water to cover for about 2 minutes until slightly softened. Drain and dry with paper towels. Line the bottom and sides of the loaf pan with the strips, shiny purple side against the pan.

Heat the oil in a large frying pan over medium heat. Add the onions and peppers. Cover and cook, stirring occasionally, until soft. Add the zucchini and cook 5 minutes. Add the diced tomatoes, the garlic and chopped eggplant pulp and season with salt, black pepper, and cayenne pepper. Cook until all the liquid has evaporated. Add the bread crumbs and mix well. Taste and adjust seasonings. Tightly pack the mixture into the loaf pan. Place the loaf pan in a roasting pan and add hot water to reach halfway up the loaf pan. Bring to a simmer on top of stove, then transfer to the oven and cook for 20 or 25 minutes.

Prepare the tomato coulis: Put the tomatoes in a saucepan and season with salt, black pepper, and cayenne pepper. Cook over medium heat until the tomatoes are very soft, 15 to 20 minutes. Puree in a food mill or food processor and then return to the saucepan; cover to keep warm. Stem the basil; stack and roll the leaves. Slice fine and add to the tomato puree.

Remove the loaf pan from the roasting pan; let cool 5 minutes. Slide the blade of a knife around the terrine between the sides of the pan and the eggplant strips. Invert a serving platter over the terrine and quickly reverse the two. Cut the anchovy fillets in half lengthwise and use them to make a lattice pattern on top of the terrine. Place an olive half in the center of each lattice opening. Spoon the tomato coulis around the base of the terrine. Serve warm or cold.

SUPÉRIEURE

Filet de Veau en Croûte
LOIN OF VEAL IN PUFF PASTRY

———

SERVES 6

Beef or veal served *en croûte* is rarely encountered anymore in French restaurants—and what a pity. It is a spectacular main dish that harmoniously combines the taste of seasonings and meat. True, there is no room for last-minute improvisation. Here, both the veal and mushrooms must be cooked in advance and allowed to cool before being carefully wrapped in dough and baked. The results, however, are well worth the effort and guests are duly appreciative of the skill necessary to make it.

PUFF PASTRY
1½ cups all-purpose flour

¾ cup cake flour

2 teaspoons salt

⅔ to ¾ cup water

2 tablespoons unsalted butter, melted

14 tablespoons unsalted butter

1 egg, slightly beaten, for glazing

2 boneless veal loin roasts, 1½ pounds each, trimmed of excess fat and connective tissue

Salt and freshly ground pepper

2 tablespoons unsalted butter

DUXELLES
3 tablespoons unsalted butter

2 large shallots, chopped fine

10 ounces mushrooms, trimmed, cleaned, and chopped fine

Salt and freshly ground pepper

PAPRIKA CREAM SAUCE
1 tablespoon unsalted butter

1 large shallot, chopped fine

1 teaspoon paprika

1¼ cups Brown Veal Stock (page 71)

½ cup heavy cream

Watercress for garnish

Unsalted butter, softened, for baking sheet

Prepare the puff pastry: Use the above ingredients and follow the directions on pages 209–10 and technique photos on pages 542–43.

Preheat the oven to 400°.

Tie the roasts with several lengths of kitchen twine, so that they will hold their shape during cooking. Season with salt and pepper. Heat the butter in a roasting pan over high heat. Add the roasts and brown quickly on all sides. Transfer the pan to the oven and roast 25 minutes, turning the roasts from time to time. Transfer the roasts to a platter and let cool; then chill in the refrigerator. Discard the fat in the roasting pan but reserve the pan and the juices for the sauce.

Prepare the duxelles: Heat the butter in a frying pan over low heat. Add the shallots and cook until tender but not colored. Increase the heat to high and stir in the mushrooms. Season with salt and pepper and cook quickly until all the moisture has evaporated. Spread the mixture on a plate to cool, then transfer to the refrigerator to chill.

(continued)

Filet de Veau en Croûte (continued)

Dust a work surface with flour. Roll out the puff pastry dough to a rectangle about ⅛ inch thick and several inches longer than the roasts. Cut the dough into 2 rectangles, each wide enough to wrap 1 roast. Spread a thin layer of cold duxelles in the center of each dough rectangle, over an area about the size of a veal roast. Remove the twine from the veal. Place each roast on the duxelles and coat with the remaining duxelles. Brush the long sides of the dough rectangles with a border of egg glaze and fold them up to enclose the roasts. The edges must not overlap by more than 1½ inches; trim off any excess and reserve. Gently press the seams together with the rolling pin to seal. Roll out the end flaps of dough ¹⁄₁₆ inch thick. Brush the flaps with egg glaze and fold up to cover the ends of the roast. The flaps should overlap the dough only slightly; trim off any excess and reserve. Gently press the seams together with the rolling pin to seal. Brush off any excess flour.

Lightly brush a baking sheet with the softened butter and sprinkle it with cold water.

Place the dough packages on the baking sheet, seam sides down. Brush with egg glaze. Cut the reserved dough scraps into small leaves or geometric shapes and arrange them decoratively on the dough packages. Brush with egg glaze. Make a small hole in the top of the dough packages with a knife to let the steam escape. Bake at 400° until the pastry is crisp and golden, at least 30 minutes.

While the veal is cooking, prepare the paprika cream sauce: Heat the butter over medium heat in the same roasting pan used to cook the veal. Add the shallot and cook until soft but not colored. Add the paprika, veal stock, and cream and cook, scraping the bottom of the pan with a whisk to release any cooked particles, until reduced by one-half. Skim off any fat. Taste and adjust seasonings. Strain through a fine strainer into a small saucepan. Keep warm in a shallow pan of hot water.

To serve, transfer the roasts to a serving platter. Garnish the platter with watercress and serve the sauce in a sauceboat on the side. Serve with Pommes à l'Anglaise (page 50), Carottes Vichy (page 102), or a tossed green salad.

Nougat Glacé
CHILLED NOUGAT MOUSSE

SERVES 6

Nougat is an ancient Mediterranean candy made from honey, sugar, and dried fruits. It is normally eaten alone but in recent years chefs have discovered that it can be combined with cream and meringue and chilled to make a delicious dessert. Le Cordon Bleu's nougat mousse is not made with a true nougat but with nougatine, a caramelized mixture of butter, sugar, and almonds. When the frozen mousse is sliced and served surrounded by a bright red raspberry sauce and topped with a few sprigs of mint, the candied fruits in it shine like glowing jewels.

NOUGATINE

1 1/2 tablespoons unsalted butter

2/3 cup sugar

1 1/4 cups chopped blanched
   almonds

8 ounces mixed candied fruits,
   diced fine

1/2 cup rum

2 cups heavy cream

FRENCH MERINGUE

3 egg whites

1 1/3 cups sugar

RASPBERRY COULIS

1 1/4 cups raspberries

1/4 cup confectioner's sugar

Mint leaves for garnish

Oil for baking sheet
   and loaf pans

EQUIPMENT: Two 7-by-3-by-2 1/2-inch loaf pans

Chill a bowl for the whipped cream.

Prepare the nougatine: Brush a baking sheet with the oil. Melt the butter in a saucepan over medium heat. Add the sugar and cook, stirring occasionally with a wooden spoon, until golden. (Do not stir too often or the mixture will crystallize.) Watch carefully, as the sugar burns easily. Add the almonds and cook, stirring constantly, until golden brown. Spread the mixture evenly over the baking sheet with the spatula. Let cool until hardened. Break the nougatine into pieces and wrap in a dish towel. Crush coarsely with a rolling pin but do not reduce to a powder.

Combine the chopped candied fruits and rum in a bowl and let macerate until needed.

Put the cream in the chilled bowl and beat with a whisk or electric mixer until stiff peaks form and the cream clings to the whisk or beater; set aside.

Prepare the French meringue: Beat the egg whites with a whisk or electric mixer until stiff peaks form. Gradually beat in about one-third of the sugar and then continue beating until stiff peaks form again and the meringue is glossy and smooth.

Put the bowl of meringue over a larger bowl of crushed ice. Fold in the remaining sugar with a wooden spoon or spatula. Fold in the whipped cream and crushed nougatine. Drain and fold in the candied fruit. Let the mixture rest 15 minutes to chill.

Brush the loaf pans with the oil and line the bottom of each with parchment paper. Fill with the nougat mixture and smooth the surface with a metal spatula. Freeze until firm, 2 to 3 hours.

Prepare the raspberry coulis: Reserve 6 perfect raspberries for garnish. Puree the remainder in a food mill or food processor. Strain the puree and whisk in the sugar. Refrigerate until needed.

To serve, run the blade of a small knife around the edge of the nougat mousses. Dip the base of each loaf pan briefly in hot water and then invert the mousses onto a platter. Spoon the raspberry coulis around the bases and decorate the top of each with the reserved berries and mint leaves. Serve immediately.

LESSON 70

Feuilletés d'Oeufs Brouillés aux Asperges
FRENCH SCRAMBLED EGGS IN PUFF PASTRY
WITH ASPARAGUS

—

Homard à l'Américaine
LOBSTER, AMERICAN STYLE

—

Gâteau à l'Ananas Singapour
PINEAPPLE CAKE

Feuilletés d'Oeufs Brouillés aux Asperges

FRENCH SCRAMBLED EGGS IN PUFF PASTRY WITH ASPARAGUS

———

SERVES 6

Scrambled eggs and green asparagus seem meant for each other. At Le Cordon Bleu, the creamy eggs and the emerald-tipped asparagus are served as a first course tucked inside perfect rounds of crisp puff pastry. There is only one problem with this delightful dish—what wine to serve with it. A white wine, no doubt, but since asparagus is notoriously hard to marry with wines the meal might have to begin with water—or maybe Champagne.

PUFF PASTRY
1½ cups all-purpose flour
¾ cup cake flour
1 teaspoon salt
⅔ to ¾ cup water
2 tablespoons unsalted butter, melted
14 tablespoons unsalted butter
1 egg, lightly beaten, for glazing

36 green asparagus stalks
Salt
12 eggs
⅔ cup crème fraîche or heavy cream
Freshly ground pepper
4 tablespoons unsalted butter

Unsalted butter, softened, for baking sheets

Prepare the puff pastry: Use the above ingredients and follow the directions on pages 209–10 and technique photos on pages 542–43.

Preheat the oven to 425°. Lightly brush 2 baking sheets with the softened butter and sprinkle with cold water.

Prepare the feuilletés: Dust a work surface lightly with flour. Roll out the puff pastry about 3/16 inch thick. Cut into twelve 5-inch rounds. Transfer the rounds to the baking sheets. Brush the surfaces with the egg glaze, but be careful not to let the egg run over the sides of the dough. Bake until the pastry is crisp and golden, at least 20 minutes. Split each pastry round in half horizontally. Cover with aluminum foil to keep warm.

Meantime, snap off and discard the tough ends of the asparagus. Starting 1 inch below the tip, peel each stalk with a vegetable peeler. Tie the asparagus into several bundles with kitchen twine. Bring a large saucepan of salted water to the boil. Add the asparagus and cook over high heat until tender, 10 to 12 minutes. Drain. Cut off the tips to a length of 2 inches. Slice the stalks ¼ inch thick. Put the tips in a buttered dish and cover to keep warm; set the sliced stalks aside separately.

Prepare the scrambled eggs (see technique photos on page 522): Break the eggs into a bowl. Add the cream and whisk until blended. Season with salt and pepper. Heat the butter in a medium frying pan over low heat. Add the egg mixture and cook, stirring constantly with a wooden spoon or whisk, until the eggs begin to thicken. Stir in the sliced asparagus stalks and continue cooking, stirring constantly, until the eggs have thickened but are very creamy and smooth.

To serve, place a pastry bottom on each of 6 serving plates. Spoon a portion of the eggs onto the center of it. Arrange the reserved asparagus tips on the eggs, like the spokes of a wheel. Top with a pastry "lid," tipped slightly backward, like the half-open lid of a box. Serve immediately.

Homard à l'Américaine
LOBSTER, AMERICAN STYLE

SERVES 6

Many French chefs refuse to call this dish *Homard à l'Américaine*, claiming that its real name is *Homard à l'Armoricaine*. (*Armor* was the Celtic name for Brittany, the source of most lobsters in France; hence these chefs are suggesting that the lobster is prepared the Breton way rather than American style.) To complicate matters, early versions of the recipe are sometimes called *à la provençale*. A compromise version of this dish's origin describes it as the brainchild of a certain Pierre Fraisse (a native of Provence), who, after working as a cook in Chicago, returned to Paris, opened his own restaurant, and created a dish using New World ingredients (tomatoes and cayenne). In the end, when all is said and done, no one really knows who invented the dish or why.

2 live lobsters, 3 pounds each

SAUCE "À L'AMÉRICAINE"
1/4 cup olive oil
1 medium onion, diced fine
4 ounces shallots, chopped fine
1 large carrot, diced fine
2 tablespoons chopped fresh tarragon or 2 teaspoons dried
2 tablespoons chopped fresh chervil
2 tablespoons chopped parsley
2 cloves garlic, chopped

2 tablespoons tomato paste
1 1/2 pounds tomatoes, peeled, seeded, and chopped (page 31)
1/2 cup cognac
1 Bouquet Garni (page 20)
2 cups dry white wine
4 cups Fish Stock (page 181)
Salt and freshly ground pepper
Pinch cayenne pepper
4 tablespoons unsalted butter, softened

To kill the lobster quickly, place it with the back facing up on a work surface. Use a dish towel to hold the lobster firmly at the back of the head. Insert the point of a heavy, sharp knife into the center of the head, just between the eyes and press down until the knife hits the work surface. Cut the head from the body and then cut the head lengthwise into 2 pieces. Save as much of the liquid as possible. Remove the green tomalley and any black coral and set aside with the liquid for the sauce. Discard the sac inside the head, and the intestines. Twist off the claws and legs. Do not shell the tail meat; cut the tail into 2-inch sections.

Prepare the sauce: Heat the oil in a large heavy-bottomed frying pan over high heat until very hot. Add the lobster tails, claws, legs and heads and sauté 1 to 2 minutes on all sides. Remove all the lobster pieces except the legs; set aside and keep warm. Reduce the heat to medium. Add the onion, shallots, carrot and 1 tablespoon each of the tarragon, chervil and parsley and cook until soft but not colored. Add the garlic and tomato paste and stir for a few seconds to mix well. Stir in the tomatoes. Return the lobster pieces to the pan, along with the cognac, bouquet garni, wine, and fish stock. If the lobster is not completely submerged in liquid, add a little water. Season with salt, pepper and the cayenne. Raise the heat to high and bring to a boil. Then reduce the heat and simmer for about 15 minutes.

Remove the lobster tails, claws and heads from the pan with a slotted spoon. Set aside and cover with aluminum foil to keep warm. Continue simmering the sauce for 10 minutes longer. Then strain the sauce into a small saucepan, pressing down on the solids to extract as much liquid as possible; discard the solids. Chop the tomalley and coral and mix with the softened butter; whisk in the reserved liquid from the lobster. Whisk this mixture little by little into the sauce and simmer for 2 to 3 more minutes. Keep the sauce warm over a pan of hot water.

To serve, remove the tail meat from the shell and slice into rounds about ³/₄ inch thick (these are known as "medallions" of lobster). Crack open the claws with a hammer and remove the flesh. Arrange the lobsters on a long serving platter, with the heads at either end, the claw meat on either side of the heads, and the tail-meat medallions overlapping down the center of the platter. Spoon a little of the sauce over the lobsters and sprinkle with the remaining chopped herbs. (Or, if you like, the lobster tails may be presented in their shells.) Serve with plain boiled rice and the remaining sauce in a sauceboat on the side.

Gâteau à l'Ananas Singapour
PINEAPPLE CAKE

SERVES 6

This is more than a cake that tastes of pineapple. It actually looks like a pineapple, leaves and all. The trick is to pipe dollops of Italian meringue over a pineapple-filled génoise and bake it just long enough to brown. As a finishing touch, thin strips of bright green candied angelica are made to look like leaves growing out of the end of the pineapple—a dramatic dessert as exotic as the city for which it is named.

(continued)

Gâteau à l'Ananas Singapour (continued)

GÉNOISE

3 eggs (room temperature)

¹/₂ cup sugar

³/₄ cup sifted all-purpose flour

1 teaspoon vanilla extract

3 tablespoons unsalted butter, melted and cooled

PINEAPPLE FILLING

1 pound fresh or drained, canned pineapple

¹/₃ cup sugar

KIRSCH SYRUP

¹/₄ cup water

¹/₂ cup sugar

2 tablespoons kirsch

ITALIAN MERINGUE

²/₃ cup sugar

¹/₃ cup water

3 egg whites (room temperature)

¹/₂ cup chopped blanched almonds

¹/₄ cup Apricot Glaze (page 62)

2 ounces angelica

Confectioner's sugar for dusting

EQUIPMENT: Pastry bag, medium star pastry tip

Prepare the génoise: Use the above ingredients and follow the directions on page 176, folding in the melted butter at the end. Let cool.

Prepare the pineapple filling: Puree the pineapple in a food processor, or chop very fine. Add the sugar and stir to dissolve; set aside.

Prepare the syrup: Combine the water and sugar in a saucepan. Bring to a boil over low heat, stirring to dissolve the sugar. Boil 1 to 2 minutes. Remove from the heat. Cool to lukewarm and add the kirsch.

Prepare the Italian meringue, using the above ingredients and following the directions on pages 293–94.

Preheat the oven to 425°. Toast the almonds on a baking sheet until golden.

Cut the cooled cake horizontally into thirds with a long serrated knife. Place the bottom third of the cake, cut side up, on a baking sheet. Brush the surface with kirsch syrup. Spread with half of the pineapple filling. Repeat with a second layer of syrup-soaked cake and pineapple filling. Cover with the remaining layer of cake, cut side down, and brush with the kirsch syrup.

Use a spatula to cover the entire surface of cake smoothly with about half of the meringue. Fit the pastry bag with the medium star tip and fill it with the remaining meringue. Trace the outline of the body of a pineapple (leave room at one end for angelica "leaves") on the top of the cake with the tip of a knife. Fill the outline with a mound of piped meringue to represent a pineapple half. Then pipe little dollops of meringue over the "pineapple" to represent the raised skin. Sift confectioner's sugar over the top. Bake the cake until the meringue is dry and lightly colored.

Heat the apricot glaze over low heat, adding 1 tablespoon of water if it is too thick. Remove the cake from oven and brush the sides with very hot glaze. Gently press the toasted almonds onto the side of the cake.

Cut the angelica into narrow strips, and cut the end of each strip on an angle to form a point. Arrange the angelica strips at the top end of the meringue pineapple, pointed ends pointing outward and fanned out to represent the leaves. Use a wide spatula to transfer the cake to a platter; refrigerate. Serve cold.

Pâtes Fraîches aux Fruits de Mer
FRESH PASTA WITH SEAFOOD

Tournedos Lavallière
BEEF TENDERLOINS WITH BORDELAISE SAUCE, ARTICHOKES, AND ASPARAGUS

Blanc-Manger aux Pêches
PEACH BLANCMANGE

Pâtes Fraîches aux Fruits de Mer
FRESH PASTA WITH SEAFOOD

SERVES 6

Pasta, like potatoes or rice, generally accompanies meat or fish in France. Once disdained by French chefs, it has risen in popularity and today can be found on the menus of better restaurants throughout the country.

PASTA DOUGH
2 cups all-purpose flour
3 egg yolks
3 tablespoons vegetable oil
1/4 teaspoon salt
5 to 6 tablespoons cold water

2 1/2 pounds mussels
3 tablespoons unsalted butter
2 large shallots, chopped fine
1/2 cup dry white wine
1 tablespoon chopped parsley

Freshly ground pepper
1/4 cup olive oil
3 cloves garlic, chopped fine
3/4 pound tomatoes, peeled, seeded, and diced (page 31)
8 sea scallops, cut in thirds
1/4 pound small cooked shrimp
1 tablespoon chopped parsley
Salt
2 tablespoons unsalted butter
Parsley leaves for garnish

Prepare the pasta dough: Use the above ingredients and follow the directions on page 199.

(continued)

Pâtes Fraîches aux Fruits de Mer (continued)

Clean the mussels (pages 39–40). Heat the butter in a large saucepan over medium heat. Add the shallots and cook until soft but not colored. Add the wine and parsley and bring to a boil. Add the mussels and season with pepper. Cover and cook, shaking the pan once or twice to rotate the mussels and ensure even cooking, until the shells open, about 6 minutes. Remove the mussels with a slotted spoon and set aside. Strain the liquid through a fine strainer lined with a damp kitchen towel into a bowl to remove the sand. Let the mussels cool and then remove from the shells; discard the shells.

Prepare the sauce: Warm 3 tablespoons of the olive oil in a saucepan over low heat. Add the garlic and cook until soft but not colored. Add the tomatoes and the strained cooking liquid from the mussels. Cover and simmer 20 minutes. Add the scallops, shrimp and mussels to the sauce. Bring just to a boil, then remove the pan from the heat. Season to taste with salt and pepper and add the chopped parsley. Cover to keep warm.

Bring a large saucepan of salted water and the remaining tablespoon of olive oil to a boil. Add the pasta and cook until tender, 3 to 5 minutes. Drain well. Add the butter to the saucepan and melt over low heat. Add the drained pasta and toss with the butter. Transfer to a serving platter. Rewarm the seafood sauce if necessary and pour it over the pasta. Serve garnished with parsley leaves.

Tournedos Lavallière

BEEF TENDERLOINS WITH BORDELAISE SAUCE, ARTICHOKES, AND ASPARAGUS

SERVES 6

Some say this dish was named in honor of the Duchesse de la Vallière, a favorite of Louis XIV. Perhaps the garnish of artichokes and asparagus (long considered aristocratic vegetables) explains the allusion, but since beef tenderloin steaks did not become popular in France until the mid-nineteenth century, *tournedos Lavallière* was certainly created long after the Duchess's hour of glory had passed.

From a strictly culinary point of view, this preparation demands perfect timing and the mastery of several techniques: paring, shaping, and cooking artichoke bottoms and château potatoes; simmering a spicy bordelaise; and a last-minute searing of the tenderloin steaks.

(continued)

Tournedos Lavallière (continued)

DEMI-GLACE SAUCE

2 tablespoons unsalted butter

1 onion, chopped fine

1 carrot, chopped fine

1 leek (white part only)
chopped fine

2 small stalks celery, chopped fine

1 tablespoon all-purpose flour

1 tablespoon tomato paste

3 tomatoes, quartered

1 clove garlic, crushed

1/2 cup dry white wine

3/4 cup Brown Veal Stock
(page 71)

1 Bouquet Garni (page 20)

Salt and freshly ground pepper

BORDELAISE SAUCE

2 tablespoons unsalted butter

2 shallots, chopped fine

10 peppercorns, crushed

1/2 cup dry red wine
(preferably Bordeaux)

2 sprigs fresh thyme or
1/4 teaspoon dried

1 1/4 cups Demi-Glace Sauce
(see above)

ARTICHOKE BOTTOMS

2 lemons

6 artichokes

Salt

2 tablespoons vegetable oil

CHÂTEAU POTATOES

12 waxy potatoes (red or white)

1 tablespoon vegetable oil

2 tablespoons unsalted butter

Salt and freshly ground pepper

1/2 red bell pepper,
cut into julienne

CROUTONS

6 slices firm white bread

3 tablespoons melted butter

1 1/4 pounds green asparagus stalks

6 beef tenderloin steaks,
5 ounces each

1 tablespoon unsalted butter

1 tablespoon vegetable oil

Salt and freshly ground pepper

2 tablespoons fresh chervil or
parsley, chopped fine

Unsalted butter, melted,
for asparagus

Unsalted butter for
parchment paper

Prepare the demi-glace sauce: Melt butter in a heavy-bottomed saucepan over medium heat. Add the onion, carrot, leek and celery and cook until tender but not colored. Stir in flour and tomato paste. Add the tomatoes, garlic, white wine, veal stock and bouquet garni. Season with salt and pepper. Cover with buttered parchment paper and bring to a boil. Reduce heat and simmer slowly, stirring occasionally for about 30 minutes. Strain into a saucepan; discard solids. Cover to keep warm.

Prepare the bordelaise sauce: Heat the butter in a small frying pan over medium heat. Add the shallots and cook until soft but not colored. Add the peppercorns, wine and thyme and cook over medium heat until most of the liquid has evaporated. Stir in 1 1/4 cups demi-glace sauce and cook until the sauce has reduced by about one-third. Strain. Taste and adjust seasonings. Cover and set aside in a saucepan of hot water. While the sauce is cooking, prepare and cook the artichoke bottoms (page 30 and technique photos on pages 520–521) and set them aside in the cooking liquid to keep warm.

Preheat the over to 425°.

Prepare the potatoes: Peel and turn the potatoes so that they are about ½ inch longer and thicker than Pommes à l'Anglaise (page 50 and technique photos on page 520). Put in a saucepan with cold salted water to cover. Bring to a boil and cook for about 3 minutes; drain.

Heat the oil in an ovenproof frying pan over medium heat. Add the potatoes and shake the pan to coat them with oil. Add the butter, season with salt and pepper, and cook over medium heat until golden brown on all sides. Transfer to the oven and roast, shaking the pan occasionally to rotate and evenly brown the potatoes, until tender, about 20 minutes.

While the potatoes are cooking, bring a small saucepan of salted water to a boil. Add the red pepper and blanch 5 minutes. Drain, refresh under cold running water, and drain again; set aside.

Prepare the croutons: Use a round cookie cutter of approximately the same diameter as the steaks to stamp out 6 rounds of bread. Brush both sides with melted butter and transfer to a baking sheet. Bake in the 425° oven until golden, about 8 minutes. Set aside in a warm place.

Snap off and discard the tough ends of the asparagus. Starting one inch below the tip, peel each stalk with a vegetable peeler. Tie the asparagus into several even bundles with kitchen twine. Bring a large saucepan of salted water to the boil. Add the asparagus and cook over high heat until tender, 10 to 12 minutes. Drain and refresh in cold water, taking care not to break off the tips. Drain again. Set aside in a buttered dish and cover to keep warm.

Tie a length of kitchen twine around each beef tenderloin steak to hold the shape during cooking. Heat the butter and the oil in a large frying pan over high heat. Season the steaks on both sides with salt and pepper and sear on each side. Continue cooking until done as desired (see page 129).

To serve, place the croutons on a platter and top each with a steak. Rewarm the sauce, if necessary, and spoon a little onto the platter until almost even with the tops of the croutons. Arrange the artichoke bottoms around the steaks. Spoon 1 or 2 tablespoons of the sauce onto each.

Remove and discard the twine from the asparagus bundles. Cut the asparagus into 2½-inch lengths and brush with melted butter. Put a bundle of 3 or 4 asparagus spears in each artichoke bottom and place a strip of red pepper across to resemble a string. Place 2 potatoes between each artichoke and sprinkle a little chopped chervil over the potatoes. Serve the remaining sauce in a sauceboat on the side.

Blanc-Manger aux Pêches
PEACH BLANCMANGE

SERVES 6

Recipes for *blanc-manger* ("white food") appear in the earliest French cookbooks known, and it has been served in one form or another continuously in France for over six hundred years. The whiteness referred to in its name is generally due to the presence of almonds (in the form of almond cream or almond milk) among its ingredients.

4 peaches
1 cup water
1 cup sugar
2 tablespoons maraschino liqueur

GÉNOISE
3 eggs (room temperature)
1/2 cup sugar
3/4 cup sifted all-purpose flour
1 teaspoon vanilla extract

ALMOND FILLING
1 envelope powdered gelatin
   (1/4 ounce)
2 tablespoons cold water

1 cup milk
1/2 cup sugar
1 cup fine-ground almonds
1 cup heavy cream
2 tablespoons maraschino liqueur

STRAWBERRY COULIS
3/4 pint basket strawberries
1/4 cup confectioner's sugar
1 teaspoon lemon juice

Unsalted butter, softened
   and flour for cake pan

EQUIPMENT: 9-inch springform cake pan

Chill a mixing bowl for the whipped cream. Skin the peaches (page 9).

Combine the water and sugar in a saucepan. Bring to a boil over low heat, stirring to dissolve the sugar. Reduce the heat, add the liqueur and peaches, and simmer until the fruit is tender; about 20 minutes. Transfer the peaches to a rack and let cool completely. Then cut the peaches in half and remove the pits; refrigerate. Reserve the poaching syrup.

Prepare the génoise: Use the above ingredients and follow the directions on page 176, but bake 15 to 20 minutes. Let cool.

Prepare the filling: Sprinkle the gelatin over the water in a small bowl and let stand until softened, about 5 minutes. Combine the milk and 1/4 cup of the sugar in a saucepan and bring to a boil. Remove from heat, stir in the almonds, and let stand 30 minutes to infuse. Strain. Return to a simmer and then remove from the heat. Add the softened gelatin and stir to blend well. Let cool, stirring occasionally, until the mixture begins to thicken.

Meanwhile, trim the top and bottom from the génoise to obtain a round about 1 inch thick; discard the trimmings. Set the ring of the springform pan on top of the génoise round and trim the génoise to the diameter of the ring with a sharp knife; discard the trimmings. Fit the génoise round into the ring of the springform pan (it must fit tight). Brush with the reserved peach syrup and top with a layer of peach halves, rounded sides up.

Combine the cream, the remaining 1/4 cup sugar and the maraschino liqueur in the chilled bowl and beat with a whisk or electric mixer until stiff peaks form and the cream clings to the whisk or beater. When the almond mixture has begun to thicken, fold in the whipped cream. Pour over the peaches and smooth the surface. Refrigerate until firm, about 5 hours.

Prepare the strawberry coulis: Puree the strawberries in a food mill or food processor. Strain to remove the seeds. Whisk in the confectioner's sugar and lemon juice; refrigerate.

To serve, remove the ring from the blancmange and transfer to a round serving platter. Serve the coulis in a sauceboat on the side.

LESSON 72

Omelette Joli Coeur

OMELET STUFFED WITH SPINACH AND CRAYFISH

Blanquette de Lotte aux Petits Légumes

MONKFISH IN WHITE-WINE CREAM SAUCE
WITH VEGETABLES

Savarin aux Kiwis et aux Fraises

RUM SAVARIN WITH KIWIS AND STRAWBERRIES

Omelette Joli Coeur

OMELET STUFFED WITH SPINACH AND CRAYFISH

SERVES 6

A *joli coeur* is a "charmer" in French and this omelet, filled with spinach, served with crayfish sauce, garnished with the crayfish tails and anchovies, has charmed students at Le Cordon Bleu for years.

24 oil-packed anchovy fillets,
    drained
1 cup milk
24 live freshwater crayfish
    (see Note on page 373), or
    whole frozen crayfish, defrosted
Salt and freshly ground pepper

CRAYFISH SAUCE
Crayfish shells and heads
    (see above)
6 tablespoons unsalted butter
1 carrot, chopped fine
1 leek (white part only),
    chopped fine
1 stalk celery, chopped fine
1 small onion, chopped fine
2 tablespoons chopped fresh basil
4 garlic cloves, chopped fine

1 tablespoon tomato paste
1/4 cup cognac
2/3 cup dry white wine
4 medium tomatoes, quartered
3 tablespoons crème fraîche or
    heavy cream
Salt
Cayenne pepper

1 pound fresh spinach
10 tablespoons unsalted butter
1 tablespoon vegetable oil
12 eggs

Unsalted butter, melted, for
    serving platter and omelets

EQUIPMENT: 8-inch frying pan (preferably nonstick)

Put the anchovy fillets into a bowl. Cover with the milk and let soak until needed.

Shell the crayfish; reserve the shells and heads for the sauce. Season the tails with salt and pepper and set aside.

Prepare the sauce: Put the crayfish shells and heads in a large saucepan and crush with a pestle. Add 2 tablespoons of the butter and melt over low heat. Add the carrot, leek, celery, onion, basil, garlic, and tomato paste. Cover and cook gently until the vegetables are tender. Add the cognac and carefully light with a match. When the flames die, add the white wine and tomatoes. Bring to a boil and cook 1 to 2 minutes. Add enough water to barely cover everything in the saucepan and return to a boil. Cover with a round of buttered parchment paper; reduce the heat and simmer 15 to 20 minutes. Strain, pressing down on the solids to extract as much liquid as possible; discard the solids. Return the liquid to the saucepan. Whisk in the crème fraîche and reduce over medium heat until the sauce thickens and coats the back of a spoon. Season to taste with salt and cayenne. Keep warm over a saucepan of hot water.

While the sauce is cooking, stem the spinach and rinse in several changes of water. Blanch 1 to 2 minutes in a large saucepan of boiling salted water. Drain, refresh under cold running water, and drain again. Squeeze out as much water as possible and coarsely chop.

Heat 1 tablespoon of butter and the oil in a frying pan over high heat. Add the spinach and sauté until all moisture has evaporated. Season to taste with salt and pepper. Remove the spinach to a bowl and cover to keep warm.

Heat 1 tablespoon of butter in the same frying pan over high heat. Add the crayfish tails and sauté 1 to 2 minutes. Season with salt and pepper. Set aside 8 crayfish tails for garnish, and stir the remaining 16 into the spinach. Set aside 6 whole anchovy fillets for garnish; coarsely chop the remainder and stir into the spinach mixture. Mix well.

Prepare the omelets (see technique photos on page 522): Brush a large oval serving platter with butter. Break the eggs into a bowl. Season with salt and pepper and beat lightly with a fork to blend. Heat 3 tablespoons of the butter in the nonstick frying pan over medium heat. Pour in half the eggs and cook gently, stirring constantly with a wooden spoon. (If the bottom of the omelet browns too quickly, lower the heat.) When the eggs begin to set but are still soft on top, spoon one-quarter of the spinach mixture over the center third of the omelet. Then, use a spatula to fold the edge of the omelet that is closest to the handle in toward the center (ideally you will be folding the omelet into thirds). Lift up the folded edge and slide 1 tablespoon of butter under it. Then, with your free hand, tap the handle of the pan sharply so that the far edge of the omelet slides up the side of the pan. Fold this edge in towards the center and continue cooking until the omelet is very lightly browned on the bottom, about 2 minutes. Hold the buttered platter with one hand, grasp the handle of the pan in the palm of the other, and turn the omelet out, seam side down, onto one half of the platter. Shape into an even form with a wooden spoon. Cut the omelet open lengthwise and spoon in another one-quarter portion of spinach filling. Arrange 4 of the reserved crayfish tails on top. Roll up 3 whole anchovy fillets and place in between the crayfish tails. Brush the surface of the omelet with a little melted butter. Cover with aluminum foil to keep warm. Repeat for the second omelet.

To serve, whisk the remaining 4 tablespoons of butter, little by little, into the sauce. Spoon around the omelets and serve immediately.

Blanquette de Lotte aux Petits Légumes

MONKFISH IN WHITE-WINE CREAM SAUCE WITH VEGETABLES

SERVES 6

Traditionally only veal was served in the white sauce thickened with cream and egg yolks that characterizes a *blanquette*. Here, in a modern variation on that classic preparation, firm-fleshed monkfish is substituted for meat. The traditional onion and mushroom garnish has also been enlarged here to include a whole range of vegetables that enhance both the dish's appearance and its taste.

VEGETABLE GARNISH	*2 1/2 pounds monkfish fillets*
6 ounces carrots	*6 tablespoons unsalted butter*
6 ounces turnips	*1 large shallot, chopped fine*
6 ounces green beans	*5 tablespoons all-purpose flour*
Salt	*1 cup dry white wine*
6 ounces shelled green peas	*1 Bouquet Garni (page 20)*
24 pearl onions, peeled	*Salt and freshly ground pepper*
4 tablespoons unsalted butter	*2 egg yolks*
Freshly ground pepper	*1 cup heavy cream*
6 ounces button or quartered large mushrooms, trimmed, rinsed, and dried	*Chervil or parsley leaves for garnish*

Prepare the vegetable garnish: Cut the carrots and turnips into sticks ("bâtonnets") 1 1/2 inches long and 1/4 inch wide; set aside. Snap the ends off the beans and cut into 1 1/2-inch lengths. Cook the beans in a saucepan of boiling salted water until crisp-tender, about 10 minutes. Drain, refresh under cold running water and drain again; set aside. Cook the peas with the pearl onions in a saucepan of boiling salted water for 8 minutes. Drain, refresh under cold running water, and drain again; set aside.

Heat 2 tablespoons of the butter in a frying pan over medium heat. Add the carrots and cook 8 to 10 minutes. Add the turnips and cook until tender, about 3 minutes longer. Season to taste with salt and pepper. Remove the pan from the heat and stir in the beans, peas and pearl onions; set aside and cover to keep warm. Heat the remaining 2 tablespoons butter in a frying pan over high heat. Add the mushrooms and cook quickly until all the moisture has evaporated; set aside with the vegetables.

Cut the monkfish into 2-inch squares. Heat 2 tablespoons of the butter in a large frying pan over high heat. Add the fish and sauté until golden brown on both sides. Remove to a platter with a slotted spoon; cover to keep warm. Reduce the heat to medium. Add the remaining 4 tablespoons butter and the chopped shallot and cook until soft but not colored. Stir in the flour and cook 2 minutes without coloring. Add the wine and bring to a boil. Return the fish to the pan along with any accumulated juices. Add the bouquet garni and enough water to come to the level of the fish. Season with salt and pepper. Reduce the heat and simmer 10 minutes. Remove the fish with a slotted spoon and set aside. Continue cooking the sauce over a very low heat for 20 more minutes to remove the acidity of the wine. Remove the bouquet garni.

Whisk the egg yolks with the cream in a small bowl. Add a little of the hot sauce and whisk until smooth. Return to the saucepan and cook over very low heat until the sauce has thickened. Do not allow to boil. Return the fish to the pan along with the cooked vegetables and simmer until warmed through, about 2 minutes. Transfer to a deep dish and serve, garnished with chervil leaves.

Savarin aux Kiwis et aux Fraises
RUM SAVARIN WITH KIWIS AND STRAWBERRIES

SERVES 6

A savarin is a ring-shaped cake that is generally brushed with a rum-flavored sugar syrup and served with Chantilly cream. It was named in honor of the famous gastronome Jean-Anthelme Brillat-Savarin (1755–1826) and has been popular in France since its creation more than 150 years ago.

SAVARIN
1 cup all-purpose flour
1/4 ounce fresh yeast or
 3/4 teaspoon dried yeast
1/3 cup warm milk
2 eggs (room temperature)
5 tablespoons unsalted butter, softened
Pinch salt
1 tablespoon sugar

SYRUP
1 cup sugar
3/4 cup water
1 teaspoon vanilla extract
1/4 cup dark rum
3/4 cup Apricot Glaze (page 62)

2 kiwifruit, peeled and sliced thin
1/2 pint basket small fresh strawberries, hulled and halved

CHANTILLY CREAM
1 1/4 cups heavy cream
3 tablespoons confectioner's sugar
1 teaspoon vanilla extract

Unsalted butter, softened, for savarin mold

EQUIPMENT: 8-inch savarin mold, pastry bag, medium star pastry tip

Brush the savarin mold with the softened butter.

Prepare the savarin: Sift the flour into a bowl. Make a well in the center of the flour and crumble in the yeast. Pour the warm milk over the yeast and stir to dissolve. Break the eggs into the well. Gradually draw in the flour with your hand and mix to a soft dough. Work the dough for 3 minutes by slapping it against the sides of the bowl; it will be quite soft and sticky. Cover the bowl with a damp cloth and let rise in a warm place until doubled in volume, about 45 minutes.

Preheat the oven to 375°.

Pound the butter until very soft. Then mix the softened butter, salt and sugar into the dough. Work the dough for about 5 minutes by lifting it up with the fingertips of both hands and then slapping it back into the bowl. (Use a scraper as needed to gather the dough into a ball.) Fit the dough into the savarin mold. Cover with a damp towel and let rest 15 minutes. Then bake until risen and lightly browned, 25 to 30 minutes. Unmold onto a cake rack to cool.

Prepare the syrup: Combine the sugar and water in a saucepan. Bring to a boil over low heat, stirring to dissolve the sugar. Cook 1 to 2 minutes. Remove from the heat and cool to lukewarm. Add the vanilla and rum.

Brush the cooled savarin with the syrup until it has absorbed as much of the syrup as possible. Place the soaked savarin on a round serving platter.

Heat the apricot glaze to lukewarm, adding a little water if the glaze is too thick. Brush the glaze over the savarin and decorate the top and sides with kiwi slices and strawberry halves.

Prepare the Chantilly cream: Use the above ingredients and follow the directions on page 21. Fit the pastry bag with the medium star tip and fill it with the cream. Pipe most of the cream into the center of the savarin and then pipe a ring around the base. Decorate the top of the savarin with piped rosettes. Serve chilled.

KNEADING SAVARIN AND OTHER SOFT DOUGHS

The soft, loose doughs used to make rich French yeast breads such as savarins or brioches must be kneaded quite differently from a stiff bread dough. While a stiff dough is kneaded by pushing and turning on a board, a soft dough is worked by being gathered up into a loose ball with a pastry scraper, then picked up with the fingertips of both hands and slapped back down into the bowl. The process will feel quite messy to begin with, but as you work the dough it will become more elastic and less sticky, until finally you can form it into a smooth, cohesive ball.

LESSON 73

Pâté en Croûte

VEAL AND PORK PÂTÉ IN A PUFF
PASTRY CRUST

---

*Filets de Saint Pierre en
Habit Vert à l'Oursinade*

JOHN DORY FILLETS BRAISED IN LETTUCE

Mousse Créole

PINEAPPLE MOUSSE

Pâté en Croûte

VEAL AND PORK PÂTÉ IN A PUFF PASTRY CRUST

SERVES 6

Once all pâtés were *en croûte*, that is, baked in pastry. A pâté baked without pastry was called a *pâté en pot*, potted meat, but today things have changed. Now most pâtés have lost their pastry crust and the word simply designates a baked paste made of meat, fish, or vegetables.

At Le Cordon Bleu students still learn how to make the classic *pâté en croûte* described below. It requires patience and attention to detail and is best prepared at least two or three days in advance to allow the flavor of the meat filling to mature before serving.

PUFF PASTRY

1½ cups all-purpose flour

¾ cup cake flour

1 teaspoon salt

⅔ to ¾ cup water

2 tablespoons unsalted butter, melted

14 tablespoons unsalted butter

MARINADE

½ cup dry white wine

½ cup Madeira wine

¼ cup cognac

6 ounces veal, diced

6 ounces ham, diced

5 ounces slab bacon, diced

PÂTE À PÂTÉ

3¾ cups all-purpose flour

2 teaspoons salt

3 tablespoons water

2 tablespoons vegetable oil

2 eggs

½ pound unsalted butter

1 egg, lightly beaten, for glazing

FORCEMEAT

1 pound lean ground veal

1 pound lean ground pork

¾ pound ground pork fat

¼ pound ground chicken livers

2 eggs

1 black truffle, chopped coarse

¼ cup dry white wine

2 tablespoons cognac

1 tablespoon salt

Cayenne pepper

Freshly grated nutmeg

ASPIC

4 cups Chicken Stock (page 12)

1 carrot, chopped

1 small onion, chopped

1 tomato

1 stalk celery

½ pound lean ground beef

3 egg whites

1 tablespoon chopped fresh chervil

1 tablespoon chopped fresh tarragon

1 tablespoon chopped parsley

1 tablespoon fresh thyme leaves

3 packages (¼ ounce each) powdered gelatin (about 3 tablespoons)

6 tablespoons cold water

Unsalted butter, softened, for baking sheet

EQUIPMENT: Hinged pâté mold (10 by 2³/₄ inch rectangular, or 10 by 5¹/₂ inch oval) or 8-inch springform pan

Day 1:

Prepare the puff pastry: Use the above ingredients and follow the directions on pages 209–10 and technique photos on pages 542–43.

Prepare the marinade: Combine all the ingredients in a bowl. Add the veal, ham and bacon and marinate at least 2 hours or overnight.

Prepare a pâte à pâté just as you would a pâte brisée (pages 37–38 and technique photos on page 540), using the above ingredients. Add the oil to the well with the water.

Prepare the forcemeat: Combine the ground veal, pork, pork fat and chicken livers in a bowl and mix well. Stir in the eggs, the marinated meat and the marinade. Add the truffle, white wine and cognac. Season with salt, cayenne pepper and a pinch of nutmeg. To taste for seasoning, fry a small patty of the mixture over medium heat. Taste and adjust seasonings as necessary.

Preheat the oven to 425°. Brush a baking sheet with the softened butter and set the pâté mold on it.

Dust a work surface with flour. Roll out the pâte à pâté dough to a rectangle about ¹/₈ inch thick, and large enough to line the bottom and sides of the pâté mold. Loosely roll up the dough onto a rolling pin and then unroll it over the mold. Press the dough into the corners of the mold without stretching it. Leave an overhang of about 1 inch and trim the excess.

Fill the dough-lined mold with the forcemeat, mounding the top slightly. Brush the forcemeat with egg glaze. Fold the pâté dough up over the stuffing and brush the dough with egg glaze.

On the floured working surface, roll out the puff pastry to a thickness of about ³/₁₆ inch. Roll it up on the rolling pin and then unroll it over the mold. Trim off the overhanging dough with scissors. Brush with egg glaze. Use a small knife to make a design on the top (see "Pithiviers," page 232, and technique photo on page 546). Cut a ¹/₂-inch hole in the center of the top (or cut 2 holes at either end if using a rectangular mold). Then roll up a cylinder of aluminum foil, about 2 inches long and the same diameter as the hole(s) and insert it into the hole. (This is the "chimney"—it lets steam escape during cooking.) Bake the pâté for about 2 hours, reducing the oven temperature to 300° after 10 to 15 minutes when the puff pastry has risen. If the pastry browns too much, cover it with a piece of aluminum foil to protect it. The pâté is cooked when a blade inserted into the center is warm and clean when withdrawn. Remove from the oven and cool in the mold on a rack. Refrigerate.

Day 2:

Prepare the aspic: First, clarify the stock, using the above ingredients and following the directions on page 267. While the stock is clarifying, sprinkle the gelatin over the water and let stand until softened, about 5 minutes. Five to 10 minutes before the end of clarification add the gelatin to the stock through the hole in the soft crust. Simmer 5 to 10 minutes and then strain as you would for a consommé.

Set the bowl of clarified stock over a larger bowl of crushed ice and cool, stirring occasionally with a wooden spoon. The stock will begin to thicken and gel as it cools. Watch the aspic carefully—when it becomes syrupy but not yet set, use a small ladle to pour about one-quarter of the aspic into the molded pâté through the hole(s) on top. (A funnel placed in the holes will make pouring easier.) Refrigerate about 10 minutes to set the aspic. Remove the bowl of aspic from the ice so that it will not gel completely. If the aspic does gel before you're ready to use it again, warm it over a bowl of warm water until it reliquifies. Then chill again until syrupy as described above. The aspic should be chilled to the point of setting each time before you use it. Remove the pâté from the refrigerator and repeat this process 3 more times until completely filled.

Chill thoroughly before serving. Unmold and serve with cornichons.

ASPIC

An aspic is a chilled, clarified stock that has solidified to a jelly, either because of the natural gelatin in the stock or because gelatin has been added. Aspics are used to coat and decorate foods (usually for buffets or banquets), in pâtés to fill the space formed during cooking when the pastry expands and the pâté shrinks (Pâté en Croûte, above), or to bind foods layered in molds (Oeufs en Gelée aux Crevettes, page 450).

Veal and poultry stocks often contain enough gelatin to set naturally. Otherwise, you can make a gelatinous stock by adding ingredients that are rich in gelatin, such as calf's feet, veal shank, or pork rind. (This is obviously not practical in a fish stock, so gelatin is nearly always added to make a fish aspic.) Once made, the stock must be clarified, as for a consommé (page 267). Soften the gelatin and add it through the chimney in the soft crust of the clarification five to ten minutes before the clarification is finished. Then strain the stock as for a consommé. Aspic is sometimes poured warm or at room temperature and then chilled to set. More often, however, and certainly in cases in which it is used to coat foods, it is chilled over ice until just on the point of setting before it is used.

Filets de Saint Pierre en Habit Vert à l'Oursinade

JOHN DORY FILLETS BRAISED IN LETTUCE

SERVES 6

John Dory is a firm, fine-textured whitefish, highly valued in France. Legend has it that the dark spot on each side of its body is a fingerprint left by St. Peter when he pulled the fish out of his net (which is why the fish is called "Saint Pierre" in French). If John Dory is unavailable, brill or tilapia, a tropical fish that is farm-raised in America, is a good substitute.

Note: At Le Cordon Bleu, John Dory is served with a foamy butter sauce flavored with the roe of two spiny sea urchins. Unfortunately, sea urchins are rarely sold in the United States and there is no real substitute for their pungent taste.

6 John Dory fillets
  (about 3¹/₂ pounds)
12 large leaves lettuce or chard
Salt
1 red bell pepper, cut into julienne
  (see technique photo 519)
36 green asparagus stalks
5 tablespoons unsalted butter
1 small carrot, diced fine
1 small onion, chopped fine
1 leek (white part only),
  chopped fine
1 stalk celery, diced fine
1 clove garlic, chopped
1 sprig fresh thyme or
  ¹/₄ teaspoon dried
Freshly ground pepper
¹/₂ cup dry white wine

BEURRE BLANC SAUCE
2 shallots, chopped fine
³/₄ cup dry white wine
2 tablespoons white-wine vinegar
1 sprig fresh thyme or
  ¹/₄ teaspoon dried
1 bay leaf
¹/₂ cup crème fraîche or
  heavy cream
¹/₂ pound unsalted butter, softened
Roe from 2 sea urchins, strained
  through a fine sieve (optional)
Few drops lemon juice
Salt and freshly ground pepper
1 tablespoon chervil or parsley
  leaves for garnish

Unsalted butter, melted,
  for asparagus

Cut each fish fillet into 2 pieces, approximately 4 inches long. Set aside.

Rinse the lettuce and blanch in a large saucepan of boiling salted water for 3 seconds. Remove the leaves with a slotted spoon. Drain and refresh under cold running water; drain again. Spread the lettuce on a dish towel or paper towel to dry.

Put the red pepper julienne in a saucepan with cold salted water to cover. Bring to a boil and cook 8 minutes. Drain, refresh under cold running water, and drain again; set aside.

(continued)

Filets de Saint Pierre en Habit Vert à l'Oursinade (continued)

Snap off and discard the tough ends of the asparagus. Starting 1 inch below the tip, peel each stalk with a vegetable peeler. Tie the asparagus into several even bundles with kitchen twine. Bring a large saucepan of salted water to the boil. Add the asparagus and cook over high heat until tender, 10 to 12 minutes. Drain and refresh in cold water, taking care not to break off the tips. Drain again. Cut each stalk into 3-inch lengths. Set aside in a buttered dish to keep warm.

Preheat the oven to 425°.

Heat 3 tablespoons of the butter in a large ovenproof frying pan over medium heat. Add the carrot, leek, onion and celery and cook until soft but not colored. Add the garlic and thyme leaves. Season with salt and pepper. Cover and cook until the garlic is soft.

Spread the blanched lettuce leaves out on a work surface. Center a piece of fish on each lettuce leaf. Season with salt and pepper. Fold the lettuce leaves around the fish to make 12 small packages. Put the packages, seam side down, in a single layer on top of the cooked vegetables. Add the wine and cover with a piece of buttered parchment paper. Bring quickly to a boil on top of the stove. Transfer to the oven and cook 5 minutes. Remove from the oven; cover to keep warm.

Prepare the sauce: Combine the shallots, wine, vinegar, thyme, and bay leaf in a small heavy-bottomed saucepan. Cook over medium heat until the liquid has evaporated. Remove the bay leaf and thyme. Whisk in the cream. Reduce the heat and simmer until the liquid has reduced by one-half. Remove from the heat and whisk in the butter, little by little. Whisk in the sea urchin roe, if using. Season to taste with a few drops of lemon juice and salt and pepper. Keep warm off the heat over a saucepan of hot water.

To serve, spoon some of the sauce over the bottom of a serving platter. Arrange the fish packages on top of the sauce. Arrange the asparagus in bundles of 6 around the platter and brush each bundle with melted butter. Place a piece of the red pepper julienne around the middle of each bundle, to represent a string. Garnish the fish with the remaining red pepper and chervil leaves. Serve the remaining sauce in a sauceboat on the side.

Mousse Créole
PINEAPPLE MOUSSE

—

SERVES 6

Rum or pineapple inevitably figures in "Creole" desserts in France—here we have both. The mousse is based on a pineapple sabayon lightened with a Swiss meringue. Before serving, the mousse is decorated with pieces of fresh pineapple, fresh strawberries, and whipped cream—a Parisian vision of a tropical Caribbean dessert.

1 small fresh pineapple
5 tablespoons dark rum
7 strawberries
6 egg yolks
1/4 cup sugar
Juice of 1/2 lemon, strained

SWISS MERINGUE
3 egg whites
3/4 cup sugar

1 1/4 cups heavy cream

CHANTILLY CREAM
1 cup heavy cream
2 tablespoons confectioner's sugar
1 teaspoon vanilla extract

EQUIPMENT: Pastry bag, medium star pastry tip

Using a long, serrated knife, cut the top and then the skin off the pineapple. Cut the flesh into 1/4-inch rounds. Remove the central core of each slice with a round cookie cutter. Cut 3 of the slices in half and put into a bowl. Sprinkle with 2 tablespoons of the rum and set aside to macerate. Coarsely chop the remaining pineapple and puree in a food mill or food processor. Strain through a fine strainer to extract the juice; discard the pulp. (You should have about 3/4 cup juice.)

Put the strawberries in another bowl. Sprinkle with 1 tablespoon rum and set aside to macerate.

Chill a mixing bowl for the whipped cream and a wide shallow serving bowl.

Prepare a sabayon: Bring 2 to 3 inches of water to a simmer in a large saucepan. Combine the egg yolks, sugar, lemon, pineapple juice and the remaining 2 tablespoons rum in a heatproof bowl and beat with a whisk or electric mixer until pale yellow and foamy. Set the bowl over the simmering water so that the bottom of the bowl does not touch the water. Continue beating until the mixture becomes thick and creamy and increases in volume, and the whisk or beater leaves a clear trail on the bottom of the bowl. Test the temperature of the sabayon occasionally with a finger: If it feels hotter than just tepid (the temperature should not exceed 80°), remove from the heat, beating continuously until slightly cooled. Then return to the heat and finish cooking as described. Remove from the heat and beat until cool. The cooled sabayon should be thick enough to form a ribbon when it falls from the whisk.

Prepare the Swiss meringue: Half-fill a large bowl with crushed ice and a little water. Bring 2 to 3 inches of water to a simmer in a saucepan. Put the egg whites and sugar in a heatproof bowl and beat 5 to 6 minutes until frothy. Set the bowl over the simmering water so that the bottom of the bowl does not touch the water. Beat the mixture over heat until soft peaks form. Remove the bowl from the heat and set it over the crushed ice. Continue beating until stiff peaks form and the meringue is cooled, smooth and shiny.

Put the 1 1/4 cups cream in the chilled bowl and beat with a whisk or electric mixer until stiff peaks form and the cream clings to the whisk or beater. Fold into the cooled sabayon. Then fold the sabayon mixture into the Swiss meringue and mound the mousse in the chilled serving bowl; smooth the top with a spatula. With the tip of a vegetable peeler, trace thin curved lines on the surface, starting at the center of the mound and radiating out to the edge like the spokes of a wheel. Refrigerate until firm, 4 to 5 hours.

Not more than 1 hour before serving, prepare the Chantilly cream: Use the above ingredients and follow the directions on page 21. Fit the pastry bag with the medium star tip and fill it with the cream; refrigerate until serving time.

To serve, decorate the mousse with the macerated pineapple halves. Pipe a rosette of Chantilly cream in the center of each, and top each rosette with a strawberry. Serve chilled, with the remaining Chantilly cream in a bowl on the side.

SWISS MERINGUE

Swiss meringue, made by beating egg whites and sugar to stiff peaks over heat and then beating off the heat until cool, is the hardiest of the three meringues used in French cooking. Like Italian meringue (page 294), it is very stable; it may be stored for up to a week without losing volume. Swiss and Italian meringues may be used interchangeably.

LESSON 74

Velouté Du Barry
CREAM OF CAULIFLOWER SOUP

Riz de Veau en Cocotte Grand-Mère
BRAISED SWEETBREADS

Tarte Feuilletée aux Fruits
PUFF PASTRY TART WITH FRESH FRUIT

Velouté Du Barry
CREAM OF CAULIFLOWER SOUP

SERVES 6

Little did the mistress of Louis XV suspect her name would be linked with a humble vegetable—cauliflower. Yet today, any dish *à la Du Barry* necessarily includes cauliflower. Here, it is used to make soup that is thickened with a roux and bound with egg yolk and cream; the results are a velvety texture *(velouté)* that would have done honor to the royal table.

1 small cauliflower
2 tablespoons white vinegar
2 tablespoons unsalted butter
1 large leek (white part only), chopped fine
1 large onion, chopped fine
1/4 cup rice flour
6 cups Chicken Stock (page 12) or water

Salt and freshly ground pepper
6 slices firm white bread, crusts removed
1 egg yolk
1 cup crème fraîche or heavy cream
Chervil or parsley leaves for garnish

Trim the outer leaves from the cauliflower. Break the head into small florets and soak 5 minutes in a large bowl of water with the vinegar added. Drain.

(continued)

Velouté Du Barry (continued)

Heat the butter in a medium saucepan over medium heat. Add the leek and onion and cook until soft but not colored. Stir in the rice flour and cook 2 minutes, stirring frequently. Add the stock or water along with all but 1 cup of the cauliflower florets. Season with salt and pepper. Bring to a boil, reduce the heat, cover and simmer 25 to 30 minutes.

Preheat the oven to 375°.

Prepare the croutons: Cut the bread into ¼-inch cubes. Toast in the oven on a baking sheet until golden; set aside.

Bring a saucepan of salted water to a boil. Add the reserved 1 cup cauliflower florets and boil rapidly for 5 minutes. Drain, refresh under cold running water and drain again. Set aside.

Puree the soup in a food mill or food processor. Strain into a saucepan, pressing down on the solids to extract all of the liquid; discard the solids. Bring the soup to a boil and then reduce to a simmer. Combine the egg yolk and cream in a small bowl and whisk until smooth. Whisk a little of the hot soup into the egg-cream mixture and then return to the soup. Warm gently, stirring constantly, but do not allow to boil because the egg yolk will curdle.

To serve, put the reserved cooked cauliflower in the bottom of a soup tureen. Pour the soup over. Sprinkle with chervil leaves and serve the croutons alongside.

Riz de Veau en Cocotte Grand-Mère

BRAISED SWEETBREADS

SERVES 6

Most dishes *en cocotte* call for cooking meat or poultry together with a vegetable garnish in a cast-iron casserole *(cocotte)*. At Le Cordon Bleu, delicate veal sweetbreads are indeed braised *"en cocotte"* but they are cooked separately from their *garniture grand-mère* (literally "grandmother's garnish") of onions, potatoes, mushrooms, and bacon. Sweetbreads cooked this way could, in fact, be garnished with other vegetables—spinach for example—but the dish could no longer be said to evoke the homey flavors associated with French grandmothers.

6 veal sweetbreads, about
   7 ounces each
3 tablespoons unsalted butter
2 medium onions, diced fine
2 medium carrots, diced fine
1 clove garlic, chopped fine
¼ cup dry white wine

¾ cup Brown Veal Stock
   (page 71)
1 bay leaf
1 sprig fresh thyme or
   ¼ teaspoon dried
Salt and freshly ground pepper

GARNISH

2 pounds small waxy potatoes
   (red or white)
Salt
7 tablespoons unsalted butter
2 tablespoons vegetable oil
30 pearl onions
1 tablespoon sugar

1 pound mushrooms, trimmed,
   rinsed, dried, and quartered
Freshly ground pepper
6 ounces slab bacon,
   sliced ¼ inch thick

Parsley leaves for garnish
Unsalted butter for
   parchment paper

Soak the sweetbreads in a bowl of cold water for at least 2 hours to remove the impurities; drain. Put them into a saucepan with fresh cold water to cover. Bring to a boil and blanch 2 to 3 minutes. Drain, refresh under cold running water and drain again. Pull off the fat and ducts and then use a small sharp knife to carefully remove the membrane that covers the sweetbreads (see technique photos on page 534).

Preheat the oven to 400°.

Heat the butter in a heavy-bottomed, ovenproof casserole over medium heat. Add the onions, carrots, and garlic and cook until soft and lightly colored. Place the sweetbreads on top of the vegetables. Add the white wine, veal stock, bay leaf, and thyme. Season with salt and pepper. Bring to a boil, cover with a piece of buttered parchment paper and transfer to the oven. Cook, basting every 10 minutes, until the juices run clear when the sweetbreads are pierced with the point of a knife, about 40 minutes.

While the sweetbreads are cooking, prepare the garnish: Peel and turn the potatoes into small ovals (pommes cocotte, page 50, and technique photo on page 520). Put the potatoes in a medium saucepan with cold salted water to cover. Bring to a boil and cook 3 minutes; drain. Heat 3

tablespoons of the butter and 1 tablespoon of the oil in an ovenproof frying pan over medium heat. Add the potatoes and sauté until golden brown on all sides. Season with salt. Transfer to the oven and cook until tender, about 20 minutes. Set aside.

Glaze the pearl onions with 1 tablespoon butter, a pinch of salt and 1 tablespoon of sugar (page 165). Set aside.

Heat 1 tablespoon of the butter in a medium frying pan over high heat. Add the mushrooms and cook until all the moisture has evaporated. Season to taste with salt and pepper. Set aside.

Cut the bacon into lardons, and blanch and drain following the directions on page 46. Heat the remaining tablespoon of oil in a small frying pan over medium heat. Add the lardons and cook until crisp and golden. Set aside.

To serve, heat the remaining 2 tablespoons butter in a large frying pan over medium heat. Add the potatoes, onions, mushrooms and bacon and cook gently until warmed through. Arrange the sweetbreads in a deep serving dish. Strain the cooking juices over the sweetbreads; discard the braising vegetables. Spoon the garnish around the sweetbreads and garnish with parsley.

Tarte Feuilletée aux Fruits
PUFF PASTRY TART WITH FRESH FRUIT

SERVES 6

This recipe can be used as a model for any number of fresh fruit tarts. Either choose a mixture of colorful seasonal fruits or use only one, and flavor the pastry cream according to your taste (try Cointreau with oranges and strawberries, raspberry brandy with a raspberry tart, or pear brandy with a fresh pear tart).

The pastry cream should be prepared ahead of time and the pastry baked in advance, but the tart should never be assembled more than a couple of hours before serving.

PUFF PASTRY
1 1/2 cups all-purpose flour
3/4 cup cake flour
1 teaspoon salt
2/3 to 3/4 cup water
2 tablespoons unsalted butter, melted
14 tablespoons (7 ounces) unsalted butter
1 egg, lightly beaten, for glazing

PASTRY CREAM
1 1/4 cups milk
1 teaspoon vanilla extract
3 egg yolks
6 tablespoons sugar
3 tablespoons all-purpose flour
3 tablespoons cornstarch
2 tablespoons kirsch
2 tablespoons unsalted butter, softened

3 kiwifruit

3/4 pint basket strawberries

2 nectarines

2 pears

Juice of 1/2 lemon, strained

RED CURRANT GLAZE

6 ounces red currant jelly

1 tablespoon kirsch

Unsalted butter, softened,
for baking sheet

EQUIPMENT: Pastry bag, medium star pastry tip

Prepare the puff pastry: Use the above ingredients and follow the directions on pages 209–10 and technique photos on pages 542–43.

Prepare the pastry cream: Use the above ingredients and follow the directions on page 183, reserving the kirsch and butter.

Preheat the oven to 400°. Lightly brush a baking sheet with the softened butter and sprinkle it with cold water.

Cut out an 8-by-8-inch square of cardboard.

Dust a work surface with flour. Roll out two-thirds of the puff pastry dough, about 1/8 inch thick. Loosely roll the dough up onto the rolling pin and unroll it over the baking sheet. Lay the cardboard square on top of the dough and trim the dough to a square 3/8 inch larger than the cardboard. Prick the dough all over with a fork. Roll out the remaining one-third of the pastry 1/8 inch thick. Using the cardboard square as a guide, cut out a band 8 inches long and 4 inches wide and then cut it lengthwise into four 1-inch-wide strips. Brush the dough square with a 1-inch border of egg glaze. (Be careful not to let the glaze run over the sides, or the pastry will not rise evenly.) Arrange the strips on the glazed borders, trimming them at each corner to prevent overlapping. Brush all over with the egg glaze. Lightly trace decorative lines on the strips with a fork. Use the back of a paring knife to make shallow indentations at 1/4-inch intervals along the outside edges of the bands of dough for decoration (this is known as *chiqueter;* see photo 4 on page 545). Bake until the pastry rises and is golden brown, 25 to 35 minutes. Cool on a rack.

Put the cooled pastry cream in a bowl and whisk until smooth. Add the reserved kirsch and softened butter and whisk until smooth. Fit the pastry bag with the medium star tip and fill it with the pastry cream; refrigerate until serving time.

Prepare the fruit: Peel the kiwifruit and slice into 3/8-inch-thick rounds. Rinse, dry, and hull the strawberries; cut the large ones in half lengthwise. Cut the unpeeled nectarines into sections 3/8 inch wide. Cut the unpeeled pears in half, remove the cores and hard fibers, and slice crosswise 3/8 inch thick. Toss the pears with the lemon juice to prevent discoloration.

Pipe the pastry cream over the bottom of the cooled pastry shell. Arrange the fruit in alternating rows of colors on top.

Prepare the red current glaze: Put the red currant jelly in a saucepan and melt over low heat. Add the kirsch and thin with a little warm water, if necessary. Whisk until the glaze is smooth. Use a pastry brush to pat the fruit with the glaze; transfer to a serving platter and serve chilled or at room temperature.

Paupiettes de Sole Béatrice
ROLLED SOLE FILLETS WITH
SHRIMP AND MUSHROOMS

Steak Mirabeau
BEEF TENDERLOIN STEAKS WITH
ANCHOVY BUTTER

Vacherin Glacé aux Framboises
VACHERIN FILLED WITH RASPBERRY SORBET

Paupiettes de Sole Béatrice
ROLLED SOLE FILLETS WITH SHRIMP AND MUSHROOMS

SERVES 6

Paupiettes are normally made by wrapping thin scallops of veal around a meaty stuffing and braising them with an aromatic mixture of vegetables and wine. At Le Cordon Bleu, sole fillets are rolled into tight little bundles that resemble *paupiettes* and served with a cream-rich shrimp sauce and thin-sliced truffles—the result is a striking first course with a memorable taste.

2 large sole or 8 sole fillets, with
   bones and heads for stock

FISH STOCK
Bones from 2 large sole
   (see above)
2 tablespoons unsalted butter
3 shallots, chopped
1 onion, chopped
1 stalk celery, chopped
1 leek (white part only), chopped

Bouquet Garni (page 20)
10 peppercorns
1 cup dry white wine
Water

16 medium mushrooms, trimmed,
   rinsed, and dried
Salt and freshly ground pepper
Juice of ¹/₂ lemon, strained
¹/₂ cup dry white wine
2 tablespoons unsalted butter

SHRIMP SAUCE
2 tablespoons unsalted butter
3 tablespoons all-purpose flour
2 cups cooled Fish Stock
 (see above)
Salt and freshly ground pepper
Sliced mushroom stems (see above)
1/2 pound shelled, cooked shrimp
2 egg yolks
1/4 cup heavy cream or
 crème fraîche

8 large shelled cooked shrimp
8 thin slices black truffle

Unsalted butter for frying pan
Unsalted butter, melted, for
 parchment paper and shrimp

If using whole fish, skin the sole on both sides; gut the sole and trim the tail and fins (see directions page 65 and technique photos on 527).

Fillet the sole (see technique photos on page 527): Place the sole on a work surface, with the tail facing toward you. With a flexible filleting knife, cut down the length of the backbone from head to tail. Then, holding the knife almost flat, insert the blade between the flesh and rib bones on one side of the backbone. Slide the blade along the length of the fillet to lift it from the rib bones. Hold the blade flat against the bones so that you lose as little flesh as possible. Remove the fillet. Repeat for the second fillet. Turn the sole over and repeat the operation to remove the two fillets on the other side. Repeat for the second sole. Reserve the bones for the stock. Soak the fillets in a bowl of cold water to remove any traces of blood.

Meanwhile, prepare the fish stock: Cut out and discard the entrails from the fish bones. Rinse the bones under cold running water and drain. Cut the backbones into several pieces. Melt the butter in a large saucepan over medium heat. Add the bones, the chopped shallots, onion, celery and leek and cook until the vegetables are soft but not colored, about 5 minutes. Add the bouquet garni, peppercorns and wine and bring to a boil. Cook 3 to 5 minutes. Add enough water to cover the contents of the saucepan. Bring to a boil, cover, reduce the heat and simmer for 20 minutes. Strain the stock through a fine strainer lined with cheesecloth, pressing down on the solids to extract all the liquid; discard the solids. Let cool.

Prepare the mushrooms: Cut off the mushroom stems just below the caps. Slice the stems lengthwise into strips and set aside for the shrimp sauce. Place the mushroom caps in a small frying pan and season with salt and pepper. Add the lemon juice, white wine and water to barely cover. Add the butter and cover with a buttered round of parchment paper. Bring to a boil, then reduce the heat and simmer 10 minutes. Drain; cover to keep warm.

Prepare the shrimp sauce: Melt the butter in a saucepan over medium heat. Whisk in the flour, and cook until foamy but not colored. Slowly whisk in the 2 cups cooled fish stock. Season with salt and pepper. Add the reserved mushroom stems and whisk until the sauce comes to a boil. Reduce the heat to low and simmer 10 minutes. Chop one-third of the shelled shrimp and add it to the sauce; continue cooking 5 minutes longer. Remove the sauce from the heat and strain into a saucepan, pressing down on the solids to extract all of the liquid; discard the solids. Taste and adjust seasonings. Keep the sauce warm over a saucepan of hot water.

Preheat the oven to 400°.

Remove the sole fillets from the water. Drain and pat dry with paper towels. Put the fillets, skinned side up, on a flat work surface. Score the flesh, lightly, on the diagonal to prevent the fillets from curling during cooking. Flatten the fillets with the back of a large-bladed knife, taking care not to tear the flesh. Season with salt and pepper. Roll up each fillet like a jelly roll and secure with toothpicks (these are "paupiettes"). Brush a frying pan with butter and stand the paupiettes of sole in it.

Add the remaining fish stock to the pan and water as needed to cover the fish. Cover with a round of buttered parchment paper. Bring to a boil, then reduce the heat and simmer for about 3 minutes. Remove the paupiettes with a slotted spoon; cover with aluminum foil to keep warm. Discard the cooking liquid or reserve for another use.

Finish the sauce: Whisk together the cream and egg yolk in a small bowl. Whisk in a little of the shrimp sauce. Return the mixture to the saucepan and whisk continuously over medium heat until warm; do not boil. Add the remaining shrimp. Remove the sauce from the heat and keep warm in a saucepan of hot water.

Put the 8 large shrimp on a baking sheet. Brush with melted butter and heat in the oven for a few minutes until just warmed through.

To serve, coat the bottom of a serving platter with a little sauce. Remove the toothpicks from the paupiettes and cut in half crosswise. Arrange in a circle on the platter and coat with a little sauce. Top every other roll with a mushroom cap and the remainder with truffle slices. Put the 8 remaining mushroom caps in the center of the platter and top with the large shrimp. Serve any remaining sauce in a sauceboat on the side.

Steak Mirabeau

BEEF TENDERLOIN STEAKS WITH ANCHOVY BUTTER

SERVES 6

Did the eighteenth-century French politician Mirabeau have a penchant for olives and anchovies or was it his brother, who loved to eat and was nicknamed "barrel belly" by his contemporaries? No one knows, but today any time steak is served crisscrossed with anchovies, dotted with olives, and spread with an anchovy butter, the Mirabeau family name resounds in dining rooms throughout France.

6 tenderloin steaks, 6 ounces each
Vegetable oil
Freshly ground pepper
18 oil-packed anchovy fillets,
  drained
6 green olives, pitted

MIRABEAU BUTTER
15 oil-packed anchovy fillets,
  drained
8 tablespoons unsalted butter,
  softened

3 large onions
Salt
1 tablespoon fine-chopped parsley
Milk
6 medium tomatoes
2 tablespoons unsalted butter
1 cup all-purpose flour

Bunch watercress for garnish
Oil for deep frying

Lightly rub the steaks with oil and freshly ground pepper; set aside.

Wrap 1 anchovy fillet around each olive. Cut the remaining 12 anchovies in half lengthwise; set aside for garnish.

Prepare the Mirabeau butter: Roughly chop the anchovy fillets. Push them through a fine sieve with the back of a wooden spoon, or mash to a paste with a fork. Mix the pureed anchovies with the softened butter. Transfer to a piece of parchment paper and roll up into a cylinder about 3/4 to 1 inch in diameter. Twist the paper at both ends to seal; freeze.

Slice the onions 1/4 inch thick and separate into rings (see technique photo on page 520). Put the onion rings into a flat container, season with salt and pepper and sprinkle with parsley. Add milk to cover and let macerate about 20 minutes.

Heat the oil to 360° in a deep-fat fryer or deep, heavy saucepan. (It is important that the container be no more than one-third full of oil.)

Drain the onion rings and pat dry with paper towels. Toss the onion rings in the flour to lightly coat. Fry 6 to 8 rings at a time in the hot oil, turning them occasionally, until golden. (The rings will rise to the surface of the oil if the temperature is correct.) Remove with a slotted spoon. Drain on paper towels; cover to keep warm.

Preheat the oven to 400°. Rinse and dry the tomatoes. Remove the stems with the point of a small knife and make a small incision in the shape of a cross on the bottoms. Place the tomatoes, bottoms up, on a baking sheet. Season with salt and pepper and dot each with 1 teaspoon of butter. Bake 10 to 15 minutes. Set aside; cover to keep warm.

Preheat a grill or grill pan, or heat a little oil in a heavy frying pan over high heat. Brush the steaks with oil and season with salt and pepper. Sear the steaks on each side. (If using a grill or grill pan, make the traditional lattice design by giving each steak a 90° turn after 1 or 2 minutes of cooking.) Turn the steaks with a wide spatula or tongs rather than with a fork; a fork would pierce the meat and allow the juices to escape. Continue cooking until done as desired (see page 129).

To serve, transfer the steaks to a serving platter. Lay 4 anchovy strips on top of each steak, in a lattice design. Top each steak with a 1/4-inch slice of Mirabeau butter. Top the butter with an anchovy-wrapped olive and surround the steaks with onion rings. Decorate one side of the platter with watercress and the other side with the baked tomatoes.

Vacherin Glacé aux Framboises
VACHERIN FILLED WITH RASPBERRY SORBET

SERVES 6

A vacherin is either a soft cheese or a frozen dessert. The former is much older than the latter, which seems to have been created around the turn of the century. At first it was made by filling a meringue shell with Chantilly cream but soon ice cream or sorbet and fresh fruit was added, all of which are now standard parts of this dessert.

Such an abbreviated description hardly hints at the complexities involved in making a frozen vacherin. The meringue shell is baked twice (first in its component parts and then a second time after being glued together with meringue), each time for eight to twelve hours. Of course, the sorbet must be made and frozen before assembling the dessert, so no one should envisage making a vacherin unless they can begin preparing it at least two days before it is served.

FRENCH MERINGUE
8 egg whites (room temperature)
3³/4 cups sifted confectioner's sugar

RASPBERRY SORBET
4 cups raspberries
Juice of ¹/2 lemon
2¹/4 cups confectioner's sugar

CHANTILLY CREAM
  (OPTIONAL)
¹/2 cup heavy cream
1 tablespoon confectioner's sugar
¹/2 teaspoon vanilla extract

Confectioner's sugar for dusting
Mint leaves for garnish

Unsalted butter, softened,
  for baking sheets

All-purpose flour for baking sheets

EQUIPMENT: Ice cream maker, pastry bag, ³/4-inch plain pastry tip, medium star pastry tip, ³/8-inch star pastry tip

Day 1:

Preheat the oven to 400°. Brush 2 heavy baking sheets with the softened butter. Dust with flour and tap off the excess. Use an 8-inch round vol-au-vent cutter or cake pan to trace one 8-inch circle on the first baking sheet and two 8-inch circles on the second sheet (see technique photo 1 on page 551).

Prepare half of the meringue: Beat 4 egg whites with a whisk or electric mixer until soft peaks form. Beat in 2 tablespoons of the sugar and continue beating until stiff peaks form. Gradually beat in the remaining 1¾ cups sugar and continue beating until stiff peaks form and the meringue is smooth and glossy. Fit the pastry bag with the plain tip and fill with meringue.

First, make the base of the vacherin on the baking sheet on which 1 circle is traced (see technique photos 2 and 3): Starting at the center of the circle and working outward in a spiral, pipe the meringue to fill the circle. (The meringue should be about ¾ inch thick.) Then, make the sides of the vacherin (see technique photos 4 and 5): Pipe a ring of meringue over just the outline of one of the 2 circles on the second baking sheet. Then pipe another ring inside of and touching the first. Repeat for the second circle. The finished double rings should be about ¾ inch thick and 1 inch wide.

Sift confectioner's sugar generously over the meringues. Transfer the baking sheets to the oven and immediately lower the temperature to 210°. Bake without coloring until the meringues are crisp and completely dry, 8

to 12 hours (or overnight, if possible). Carefully transfer to a rack with a metal spatula; let cool. Store in a cool dry place until needed.

Day 2:

Preheat the oven to 400°. Brush a heavy baking sheet with butter. Dust with flour and tap off the excess. Put the cooked meringue base in the center of the baking sheet and top with the 2 meringue circles, to form a basket.

Prepare the second half of the meringue with the remaining egg whites and confectioner's sugar. Use about half the meringue to spread a thick, even layer over the inside and outside of the meringue basket. Then fit the pastry bag with the medium star tip and fill with the remaining meringue. Decorate as shown in the photo.

Transfer the meringue shell to the oven and immediately lower the temperature to 210°. Bake without coloring until the meringue is crisp and completely dry, 8 to 12 hours (overnight if possible).

Prepare the raspberry sorbet: Chill a bowl in the freezer. Reserve several whole raspberries for decoration. Puree the remainder in a food mill or food processor. Strain through a fine strainer to remove the seeds. Add the lemon juice to the puree and sift in the confectioner's sugar. Mix well. Pour into an ice cream maker and freeze according to the manufacturer's instructions. Transfer to the chilled bowl and freeze until firm, at least 1 hour.

One hour before serving, chill the meringue shell in the freezer.

To serve, fill the chilled shell with scoops of sorbet, mounded into a dome. (Use an ice cream scoop and dip it into cold water after each use.) Decorate with mint leaves and fresh raspberries. If desired, prepare the Chantilly cream, using the above ingredients and following the directions on page 428. Fit the pastry bag with the 3/8-inch star tip and fill it with the cream. Pipe rosettes of cream in between the scoops of sorbet. Serve immediately.

LESSON 76

Pâté de Saumon Chaud en Croûte
HOT SALMON PÂTÉ IN PASTRY

—

Canette au Muscadet et aux Raisins
ROAST DUCKLING WITH MUSCADET
WINE SAUCE AND GRAPES

—

Omelette Soufflée Sucrée
SOUFFLÉED ORANGE DESSERT OMELET

Pâté de Saumon Chaud en Croûte
HOT SALMON PÂTÉ IN PASTRY

SERVES 6

Recipes for hot salmon pâté can be found in French cookbooks as early as the eighteenth century. At that time, however, slices of salmon were simply baked in pastry with a little butter and seasoning. Times have changed, and today both whole salmon fillets and a delicate pike *mousseline* are used as a filling. Serving the pâté with a rich *beurre blanc* is another modern touch. The sauce should be spooned around, not over, the slices of pâté to discreetly complement the pâté's taste without causing the pastry to become soggy.

PÂTE BRISÉE

1 1/2 cups all-purpose flour
3/4 cup cake flour
3 eggs
1/2 teaspoon salt
10 tablespoons unsalted butter
1 egg, lightly beaten, for glazing

1 1/4 pounds salmon fillets, skinned
Salt and freshly ground pepper
1/4 cup vegetable oil
1 tablespoon each chopped fresh
   chives and chervil

PIKE MOUSSELINE

1 1/4 pounds pike fillet
Salt and freshly ground pepper
1 egg white
1/2 cup crème fraîche or
   heavy cream

BEURRE BLANC SAUCE

2 shallots, chopped fine
3/4 cup dry white wine
2 tablespoons white-wine vinegar
Freshly ground pepper
1 sprig fresh thyme or
   1/4 teaspoon dried
1 bay leaf
1/2 cup crème fraîche or
   heavy cream
1/2 pound unsalted butter,
   softened
Lemon juice
Salt

EQUIPMENT: 9-inch springform pan

Prepare the pâte brisée: Use the above ingredients and follow the directions on pages 37–38 and technique photos on page 540.

Chill a bowl for the mousseline.

Working from tail to head, run your fingers along the surface of the salmon fillets to detect any small bones; remove them. Cut the fillets into thin slices. Put the slices in a shallow dish, season with salt and pepper, drizzle with oil and sprinkle with the chopped herbs. Marinate 20 minutes, then turn the slices and marinate 20 minutes longer.

While the salmon marinates, prepare the pike mousseline: Use the above ingredients and follow the directions on page 278. Chill.

Preheat the oven to 375°.

Dust a work surface with flour. Roll out two-thirds of the dough to a large circle about ⅛ inch thick. Roll the dough up onto the rolling pin and unroll it loosely over the springform pan. Gently press it into the bottom and up the sides of the pan, leaving an overhang of about 1 inch.

Spread one-half of the chilled mousseline evenly over the bottom of the dough-lined pan. Drain the salmon and arrange the slices in an even layer on top of the mousseline. Cover with the remaining mousseline and smooth the surface with a wet spatula.

Roll out the remaining dough to a 10-inch round about ⅛ inch thick. Brush the overhanging dough with the egg glaze and place the dough round on top of the pâté. Press the edges together to seal and trim the excess. Brush with the egg glaze. Make a hole, about ½ inch in diameter, in the center of the top to let the steam escape. Bake until a skewer inserted in the center of the pâté is warm to the touch when withdrawn, about 1 hour and 15 minutes. If the crust browns too much during cooking, cover with aluminum foil. Let the pâté cool on a rack for about 15 minutes before serving.

Prepare the beurre blanc sauce: Combine the shallots, wine, vinegar, pepper, thyme and bay leaf in a small, heavy-bottomed saucepan. Cook over medium heat until the liquid has evaporated. Whisk in the cream. Reduce the heat and simmer until reduced by half. Remove from the heat and whisk in the butter, little by little. Strain. Season to taste with a few drops of lemon juice and salt and pepper.

Keep the sauce warm off the heat in a saucepan of hot water.

To serve, unmold the pâté, taking care not to break the crust, and transfer to a doily-lined serving platter. Serve the beurre blanc in a sauce-boat on the side.

Canette au Muscadet et aux Raisins

ROAST DUCKLING WITH MUSCADET WINE SAUCE AND GRAPES

———

SERVES 6

The sweet taste of grapes and the slightly tart taste of apples might be a classic combination with duck, but by reducing the apples to a creamy rich puree, wrapping the puree in miniature crêpes, and using the grapes to flavor the sauce, this dish acquires a modern look and taste, with the three flavors juxtaposed on each plate in a culinary medley.

CRÊPE BATTER
1/2 cup all-purpose flour
Pinch salt
1 egg
3/4 cup milk
2 tablespoons unsalted butter,
  melted and cooled
2 tablespoons each chopped fresh
  chervil and chives

60 white grapes,
  preferably Muscat
1 cup dry white wine,
  preferably muscadet

APPLE PUREE
1 pound apples
2 tablespoons butter
2 tablespoons Calvados or
  domestic apple brandy
2 tablespoons crème fraîche or
  heavy cream

2 ducklings, about 3 pounds each,
  or 1 five-pound duck
Salt and freshly ground pepper
3 branches fresh thyme or
  1/2 teaspoon dried
3 bay leaves
2 tablespoons unsalted butter
1 large carrot, diced
1 onion, chopped
2 cloves garlic, crushed
6 small apples
4 tablespoons unsalted butter,
  melted
2 tablespoons sugar
2 tablespoons all-purpose flour
6 chives, blanched in boiling
  water for 1 to 2 minutes
Chervil or parsley leaves
  for garnish

Unsalted butter, softened, for
  baking sheet and crêpe pans

EQUIPMENT: 5-inch crêpe pans

Make the crêpe batter: Use the above ingredients and follow the directions on page 23, adding the chopped herbs at the end. Let rest 30 minutes at room temperature. Then cook the crêpes (page 23). Set 6 aside on a plate and cover with foil. Freeze or reserve the rest for another use.

Peel the grapes with a small knife and put them into a bowl with 1/2 cup of the wine. Let macerate until needed. (The wine will flavor the grapes and prevent them from discoloring.)

Prepare the apple puree: Peel, core, and dice the apples. Heat the butter in a frying pan over low heat. Add the diced apples and cook, stirring occasionally, until soft, 15 to 20 minutes. Add the Calvados and cream and continue cooking until the mixture has reduced to a thick puree. Remove from the heat. Cover to keep warm.

Preheat the oven to 425°.

Prepare the ducklings (or duck): Cut off the wing tips and set aside with the necks. Cut out the fat glands at the base of the tails with the point of a small knife. Cut out the wishbones to facilitate carving (page 76 and technique photos on page 531). Rinse the ducks inside and out with cold water and pat dry with paper towels. Season the cavities with salt and pepper and add the thyme and bay leaves. Truss as you would a chicken (see directions on page 6 and technique photos on page 530). Rub each duckling with 1 tablespoon butter (or a large duck with 2 tablespoons butter) and season all over with salt and pepper. Place in a roasting pan along with the wing tips and necks and transfer to the oven. Reduce the oven heat to 350° and roast the ducklings for 15 minutes, basting frequently, and turning occasionally to color evenly. Add the carrot, onion and garlic and continue cooking, basting frequently, until the juices run clear when the thigh is pierced with a skewer, 25 to 30 minutes longer. (Or roast a large duck at 400°: Roast on one side for 25 minutes, add the vegetables, turn onto the other side and roast for 25 more minutes. Then turn the duck breast side up and continue cooking 25 to 35 minutes longer.)

While the ducklings are roasting, peel and core the 6 apples. Pare them to about 2 inches in diameter. Place on a buttered baking sheet and brush with the melted butter. Bake 10 minutes at 350°. Sprinkle with the sugar and continue to bake until the apples are tender and slightly caramelized, 5 to 10 minutes longer. Set aside; cover with aluminum foil to keep warm.

When they are cooked, remove the ducklings to a cutting board. Reserve the roasting pan with the vegetables. Cut the legs and breasts off each duckling and cover with foil to keep warm. Crush the carcasses with a large knife or cleaver and set aside.

Increase the oven temperature to 400°.

Prepare the sauce: Discard the fat in the roasting pan. Place the pan over medium heat and cook the vegetables until well browned. Sprinkle with the flour and stir well. Stir in the remaining ½ cup muscadet. Bring to a boil, reduce the heat and simmer 2 to 3 minutes. Add 1 cup water. Transfer to a large saucepan, add the crushed duckling carcasses and simmer until the sauce has reduced by half. Strain into a smaller saucepan, pressing down on the solids to extract all the liquid; discard the solids. Return the sauce to the heat, bring to a simmer and skim the fat from the surface. Taste and adjust seasonings. Drain and add the grapes. Keep warm over low heat. (Do not allow to boil.)

To serve, rewarm the foil-wrapped crêpes in a low oven and the apple puree over low heat. Place a spoonful of apple puree in the center of each crêpe and draw up the edges to form a little purse. Secure each with a blanched chive.

Cut the breasts into thin slices and arrange the duckling pieces on a long serving platter. (If using a large duck, cut the legs into 2 pieces at the joint.) Lift the grapes from the sauce with a slotted spoon and scatter over and around the duckling. Place the crêpe purses around the platter and then place a baked apple in between each. Place a grape and a chervil leaf on each apple. Coat the duckling and grapes around it with the sauce. Garnish with a few chervil leaves. (For individual serving, see photo on page 431.)

Omelette Soufflée Sucrée
SOUFFLÉED ORANGE DESSERT OMELET

SERVES 6

A souffléd omelet is neither an omelet nor a soufflé but has elements of both. Stiffly beaten egg whites are added to egg yolks and sugar, then baked to produce an airy dessert. The omelet can be flavored in various ways (orange or lemon peel, vanilla, rum, and so on) and served simply as it comes from the oven, but at Le Cordon Bleu we often serve it flaming, garnished with orange slices and cherries for color.

3 oranges	1/4 cup Cointreau
4 egg yolks	4 egg whites
3/4 cup granulated sugar	Confectioner's sugar for dusting
1 1/2 ounces candied orange peel, chopped fine	2 tablespoons cognac
	12 glacé cherries

Preheat the oven to 375°.

Prepare 6 fluted orange slices: Follow the directions on page 9. Cut the slices in half.

Whisk the egg yolks and 1/2 cup of the granulated sugar in a bowl until pale yellow and creamy. Mix in the chopped orange peel and 1 tablespoon of the Cointreau. Beat the egg whites with a whisk or electric mixer until stiff peaks form. Beat in the remaining 1/4 cup granulated sugar, little by little, and continue beating until stiff peaks form again and the meringue is glossy and smooth.

Whisk about a third of the beaten whites into the sugar-yolk mixture. Fold in the remainder with a wooden spoon.

Mound the mixture onto a long, ovenproof serving platter and smooth the surface with a spatula. Draw shallow lines lengthwise along the top of the omelet with the back of a knife blade. Score the sides with slanting lines. Sift confectioner's sugar over the top. Lower the oven temperature to 300° and bake until golden brown and puffed, 8 to 10 minutes.

While the omelet is cooking, heat the remaining 3 tablespoons Cointreau and the cognac in a small saucepan.

To serve, arrange the orange slices around the hot omelet and place a cherry on top of each. At the table light the hot liquor with a match and pour it flaming over the omelet.

*Chaussons d'Écrevisses,
Sauce Nantua*

PUFF PASTRY TURNOVERS WITH
CRAYFISH AND NANTUA SAUCE

———

Longe de Veau du Presbytère

STUFFED LOIN OF VEAL WITH ARTICHOKES

———

Entremets Cordon Bleu

CORDON BLEU CHOCOLATE CAKE
WITH ORANGE SORBET

Chaussons d'Écrevisses, Sauce Nantua

PUFF PASTRY TURNOVERS WITH
CRAYFISH AND NANTUA SAUCE

———

SERVES 6

In French, a *chausson* is either a slipper or a small sock. It is also the name of a popular apple-filled pastry every French school child adores—a *chausson au pommes*. Few people realize that up until relatively recently *chaussons* were also made using fish or meat. The Cordon Bleu has preserved that tradition, and this crayfish-filled pastry demonstrates just how attractive such a savory starter can be. It is served with a crayfish-based sauce named after Nantua, a small village not far from the Swiss border in southeastern France where this sauce was created. The beautiful pink color of the sauce is produced by the shells, which turn bright red when cooked.

Today, crayfish dishes and sauces are rarely encountered on French menus because, alas, they are disappearing from rivers throughout the country. Two salt-water crustaceans, shrimp and *langoustines*, have progressively replaced them in many preparations, so if crayfish are unavailable, the tail meat of either of these could be used for filling the *chausson* and the shells for making the sauce.

(continued)

Chaussons d'Écrevisses, Sauce Nantua (continued)

PUFF PASTRY

2 cups all-purpose flour

1 cup cake flour

1 teaspoon salt

1 cup cold water

3 tablespoons melted butter

20 tablespoons unsalted butter

1 egg, lightly beaten, for glazing

NANTUA SAUCE

18 freshwater crayfish in the shell
  (see Note on page 373)

Salt and freshly ground pepper

6 tablespoons unsalted butter

1 small carrot, diced fine

1 small onion, diced fine

4 shallots, diced fine

1 sprig thyme

1 bay leaf

Cayenne pepper

1/4 cup cognac

4 medium tomatoes, peeled,
  seeded, and diced (page 31)

1 tablespoon tomato paste

1 1/4 cups white wine

1/2 cup crème fraîche

3 tablespoons unsalted butter

3 carrots, cut into julienne
  (see technique photo page 519)

1/2 pound mushrooms, trimmed,
  cleaned, and cut into julienne

Salt and freshly ground pepper

1 tablespoon olive oil

1 bunch parsley for garnish

Unsalted butter, softened,
  for baking sheet

Prepare the puff pastry: Use the above ingredients and follow the directions on pages 209–10 and technique photos on pages 542–43.

Prepare the sauce: Shell the crayfish. Season the tails with salt and pepper and set aside. Put the shells and heads in a large frying pan and crush with a pestle. Add the butter and melt over low heat. Add the diced vegetables, thyme and bay leaf and season with salt and a pinch of cayenne pepper. Cover and cook gently for a few minutes until the vegetables are tender. Add the cognac and light with a match. When the flames die, add the tomatoes and tomato paste. Stir in the wine and bring to a boil. Then lower the heat and simmer, stirring occasionally, until reduced to about 1/2 cup.

Prepare the filling: Melt 1 tablespoon of the butter in a medium frying pan. Add the julienned carrot and cook, stirring occasionally, until just tender, about 5 minutes. Drain; set aside in a bowl. Heat 2 tablespoons butter in the same pan over high heat. Add the mushrooms and cook quickly until all the moisture has evaporated. Add to the bowl with the carrots. Season.

Heat the olive oil in the same pan over high heat until sizzling hot. Add the crayfish tails and sauté for 1 to 2 minutes. Remove from the heat.

Finish the sauce: Strain through a fine strainer, pressing down on the solids with the back of a spoon to extract all the liquid; discard the solids. Return sauce to the frying pan and whisk in cream. Reduce over medium heat until the sauce thickens and coats the back of a spoon. Adjust seasonings.

Preheat the oven to 425°.

Assemble the turnovers: Dust a work surface with flour. Roll out the puff pastry dough about 1/8 inch thick. Cut out 6 rounds of dough, each about 7 inches in diameter. Prick all over with a fork. Brush each with a 1-inch border of egg glaze. Be careful not to let the egg run over the sides of the dough. Place 2 tablespoons of the carrot-mushroom mixture on the bottom half of each round. Top each with 3 crayfish tails and spoon a little sauce over. Fold the top halves of the rounds down to enclose the filling. Gently press the edges together to seal. Use the back of a knife blade to make shallow indentations at ¼-inch intervals around the rounded edges.

Lightly brush a baking sheet with butter and sprinkle with water. Transfer turnovers to the baking sheet and brush with egg glaze. Reduce oven temperature to 375°; bake turnovers until puffed and golden, about 35 minutes.

To serve, arrange the turnovers on a serving platter and garnish with the parsley. Serve any remaining sauce in a sauceboat on the side.

Longe de Veau du Presbytère
STUFFED LOIN OF VEAL WITH ARTICHOKES

SERVES 6

Clergymen have a reputation for being gourmets in France, and this stuffed loin of veal is described in French as being "from the Presbytery." The veal is boned, then stuffed with a mixture of ham, kidney, truffles, tongue, cream, and bell pepper and served with artichoke bottoms filled with mushrooms. A combination that would do honor to any bishop's table.

3½-pound boneless loin of veal
Salt and freshly ground pepper

STUFFING
¼ pound lean ground veal
¼ pound lean ground pork
Salt and freshly ground pepper
1 egg white, lightly beaten
1 tablespoon crème fraîche or
   heavy cream
1 small veal kidney
4 tablespoons unsalted butter
½ red bell pepper,
   cut into julienne
   (technique photo page 519)
2 ounces prosciutto,
   cut into julienne
2 ounces sliced beef tongue,
   cut into julienne
1 ounce black truffles, chopped
   (optional)

5 tablespoons unsalted butter
1 tablespoon vegetable oil
2 carrots, chopped coarse
2 large onions, chopped coarse

ARTICHOKE BOTTOMS
2 lemons
6 artichokes
Salt
2 tablespoons vegetable oil

1 pound mushrooms, trimmed,
   rinsed, dried, and sliced fine
½ cup plus 2 tablespoons crème
   fraîche or heavy cream
½ cup Brown Veal Stock
   (page 71)
¼ cup dry white wine
1 tablespoon finely chopped chervil
1 bunch watercress for garnish

Trim the veal of excess fat and connective tissues. Set the trimmings aside. Butterfly the veal: Place the veal on a work surface. Make a horizontal cut along the length of the loin to within one inch of the other side. Open up the loin like a book. Season the interior with salt and pepper; set aside.

Prepare the stuffing: Put the ground veal and pork in a bowl and set the bowl over a larger bowl of crushed ice. Season with salt and pepper. Gradually add the egg white, beating vigorously in a backward-to-forward motion with a wooden spoon. Add the cream in the same way. Spread this mixture over the veal to within $1/2$ inch of the edges.

Trim the kidney of all nerve fibers and membrane. Heat 2 tablespoons of the butter in a frying pan over high heat. Add the kidney and brown lightly on both sides. Remove the pan from the heat; let the kidney cool in the pan. Heat the remaining 2 tablespoons of butter in a small frying pan over low heat. Add the red pepper, cover and cook 10 minutes. Scatter the pepper, prosciutto, tongue, and truffle, if using, over the stuffing. Place the whole kidney in the center. Roll up the veal and tie with kitchen twine in 4 or 5 places. Season with salt and pepper.

Preheat the oven to 425°.

Heat 3 tablespoons of the butter and 1 tablespoon of oil in a roasting pan over high heat. Add the veal and brown quickly on all sides. Add the carrots, onions, and veal trimmings. Transfer to the oven and roast 45 minutes.

While the roast is cooking, prepare and cook the artichoke bottoms (see directions on page 30 and technique photos on pages 520–21). Let stand in the cooking liquid, off the heat, until serving time.

Heat the remaining 2 tablespoons of butter in a frying pan over high heat. Add the mushrooms and cook until all the moisture has evaporated. Stir in the 2 tablespoons cream and season to taste with salt and pepper. Cover to keep warm.

Reduce the veal stock by half in a small saucepan over medium heat; set aside.

After the veal has cooked 45 minutes, remove it to a platter. Reduce the oven temperature to 375°. Discard the fat in the roasting pan, add the wine and deglaze, scraping the bottom of the pan with a wooden spoon to release any cooked particles. Whisk in the remaining $1/2$ cup cream and the reduced brown stock. Return the loin to the pan, place again in the oven, and cook, basting frequently, about 15 minutes longer.

When the meat is cooked, set it aside on a platter; cover with aluminum foil to keep warm. Strain the sauce, pressing down on the solids to extract all the liquid; discard the solids.

To serve, remove and discard the twine from the veal. Slice the veal $1/8$ inch thick and arrange overlapping slices on a serving platter. Fill the artichoke bottoms with the mushrooms and sprinkle with chervil; arrange around the meat. Put a small bunch of watercress at either end of the platter. Spoon a little sauce over the meat and serve the remainder in a sauceboat on the side.

Entremets Cordon Bleu
CORDON BLEU CHOCOLATE CAKE
WITH ORANGE SORBET

SERVES 6

Le Cordon Bleu has attached its name to very few desserts—it proudly does so with this one. A chocolate génoise is filled with chocolate pastry cream, decorated with bands of confectioner's sugar, and served with freshly frozen orange sorbet. Making the elements just cited, as well as assembling and decorating the cake, demonstrates the skills one expects of a real Cordon Bleu.

CHOCOLATE GÉNOISE

3 eggs (room temperature)
1/2 cup sugar
1/2 cup sifted all-purpose flour
3 tablespoons cocoa powder, sifted

ORANGE SORBET

Juice of 10 oranges, strained
2 cups confectioner's sugar

CHOCOLATE PASTRY CREAM

*4 ounces semisweet chocolate,
    cut into small pieces*
2 cups milk
4 egg yolks
1/2 cup sugar
*3 tablespoons sifted all-purpose
    flour*
3 tablespoons cornstarch

COGNAC SUGAR SYRUP

3 tablespoons sugar
2/3 cup water
1 tablespoon cognac

*13 tablespoons unsalted butter,
    softened*
3 tablespoons cocoa powder, sifted
Cocoa powder for dusting
Confectioner's sugar for dusting
Mint leaves for garnish

*Unsalted butter, softened, for
    cake pan and pastry cream*

EQUIPMENT: 8-inch round cake pan, ice cream

Prepare the chocolate génoise: Use the above ingredients and follow the directions on page 176, adding the cocoa along with the flour. Let cool.

Chill a bowl in the freezer for the sorbet.

Prepare the sorbet: Combine the orange juice and the sugar in a bowl. Whisk well to dissolve the sugar. Pour into an ice cream maker and freeze according to the manufacturer's instructions. Transfer to the chilled bowl and freeze until firm, about 1 hour.

Prepare the chocolate pastry cream: Bring 2 to 3 inches of water to a simmer in a saucepan. Put the chocolate into a heatproof bowl and set it over the pan of simmering water. Let stand, without stirring, until completely melted.

Bring the milk to a boil in a heavy-bottomed saucepan; remove from the heat. Combine the egg yolks and sugar in a heatproof bowl and whisk until thick and pale yellow in color. Whisk in the flour and cornstarch. Whisk

the hot milk into the melted chocolate. Then whisk the chocolate-flavored milk into the egg mixture and return to the saucepan. Bring to a boil over medium heat, whisking constantly. Reduce the heat and simmer 5 minutes, whisking constantly to reach all parts of the pan. Spread the cream in a shallow dish and rub the top with the softened butter to prevent a skin from forming. Let cool. Reserve the softened butter and cocoa powder.

Prepare the syrup: Combine the sugar and water in a small saucepan. Bring to a boil over low heat, stirring to dissolve the sugar. Boil 1 to 2 minutes. Remove from the heat and add the cognac.

Cut the cooled chocolate génoise horizontally into three layers. Brush the cut side of each layer lightly with the syrup.

Put the cooled pastry cream in a bowl and whisk until smooth. Add the reserved butter, little by little, whisking well after each addition. Whisk in the reserved cocoa powder.

Assemble the cake: Place the bottom layer of génoise on a platter. Spread one-third of the pastry cream evenly over the génoise with a metal spatula. Top with the second layer of génoise and spread with half the remaining cream. Top with the remaining layer of génoise. Spread the remaining cream over the sides and top of the cake. Sift cocoa powder over the top. Cut out 4 strips of cardboard, ½ inch wide and 8 inches long. Lay the strips at regular intervals diagonally across the top of the cake. Sift confectioner's sugar over the top; then carefully remove the cardboard strips. (For an alternate design, cut out 8 strips of cardboard about 1 inch wide and make a lattice design as shown on the whole cake in the photo.)

To serve, use 2 spatulas, one on either side, to transfer the cake to a doily-lined platter. Mound scoops of sorbet into a footed serving dish and garnish with mint leaves. Serve alongside the cake.

LESSON 78

Velouté Agnès Sorel
CREAM OF CHICKEN SOUP AGNÈS SOREL

Suprêmes de Pintadeaux aux Écrevisses et Pois Gourmands
BREAST OF GUINEA HEN WITH
CRAYFISH AND SUGAR SNAP PEAS

Glace au Chocolat, Poires et Sabayon
CHOCOLATE ICE CREAM WITH
POACHED PEARS AND SABAYON SAUCE

Velouté Agnès Sorel
CREAM OF CHICKEN SOUP AGNÈS SOREL

SERVES 6

Agnès Sorel (1422–1450) was a favorite of Charles VII of France. Several dishes have been named in her honor, most of which contain chicken and a garnish that includes ham or tongue. The whiteness of these dishes echoes Agnès's purity, and the red the blushing beauty of "Dame Sorel."

3¹/2-pound chicken
2 carrots, chopped
1 large onion, studded with
   2 cloves
Bouquet Garni (page 20)
12 cups water
Salt
¹/2 pound large mushrooms,
   rinsed and dried

2 tablespoons unsalted butter
Freshly ground pepper
5 ounces cooked beef tongue or ham
2 egg yolks
²/3 cup heavy cream
Chervil or parsley for garnish

Truss the chicken (see directions on page 6 and technique photos on page 530). Put it in a soup kettle or Dutch oven with the carrots, onion and bouquet garni. Add the water and a pinch of salt. Bring to a boil and cook over medium heat for 30 minutes, skimming the fat that rises to the surface. Transfer the chicken to a platter, cover with a damp cloth to prevent it from drying out, and let cool. Line a strainer with a clean wet dish towel and strain the stock. Measure out 6 cups of stock (refrigerate the remainder for another use); cover to keep warm.

Remove and discard the mushroom stems as well as the dark parts of the mushroom caps. Slice the caps fine and cut into julienne (see technique photo on page 519). Heat the butter in a frying pan over high heat and cook the mushrooms quickly until the moisture has evaporated. Season to taste with salt and pepper. Set aside.

Cut the sliced tongue into julienne the same size as the mushrooms. When the chicken is cool, peel off the skin and carefully remove the two breasts; remove any bones. Cut the breasts into slices and then into julienne the same size as the mushrooms and tongue. Wrap and refrigerate the remaining chicken for other preparations, such as croquettes, salads or sandwiches.

Whisk the egg yolks and cream in a large bowl. Whisk in 1 cup of the warm chicken stock and then whisk in the remaining 5 cups. Pour the mixture into a saucepan and stir with a wooden spoon over medium heat until the soup thickens enough to coat the back of the spoon. (Do not let the soup boil or it will curdle.) Add the julienne of mushrooms, tongue and chicken. Heat for a few minutes, then taste and adjust seasonings. Serve the hot soup in a soup tureen sprinkled with chervil or parsley.

Suprêmes de Pintadeaux aux Écrevisses et Pois Gourmands
BREAST OF GUINEA HEN WITH CRAYFISH AND SUGAR SNAP PEAS

SERVES 6

Fish and meat are rarely combined in French cooking, although chicken and crayfish are a classic combination dating back to the seventeenth century. This is a modern variation on that classic theme. Here light and dark meat of a guinea hen are cooked separately, served with a creamy crayfish sauce, and garnished with a relatively new addition to the French vegetable garden—tender edible-pod peas boiled just until tender and flavored with a dab of fresh butter.

(continued)

Suprêmes de Pintadeaux aux Écrevisses et Pois Gourmands (continued)

3 young guinea hens
Salt and freshly ground pepper

GUINEA HEN STOCK

Guinea hen carcasses and wing
   tips (see above)
4 tablespoons unsalted butter
1 medium carrot, diced fine
1 medium onion, diced fine
1 clove garlic, crushed
1 tablespoon all-purpose flour
1/2 cup dry white wine
1 cup Brown Veal Stock
   (page 71)
1 Bouquet Garni (page 20)
Salt and freshly ground pepper

CRAYFISH STOCK

24 live freshwater crayfish
   (see Note page 373), or
   whole frozen crayfish, defrosted
7 tablespoons unsalted butter
1 medium carrot, diced fine
1 medium onion, diced fine
2 shallots, chopped fine
2 tablespoons cognac
1 tablespoon tomato paste
1 cup dry white wine
1 clove garlic, crushed
1 sprig thyme or 1/4 teaspoon dried
Bay leaf
Cayenne pepper
Salt

1/2 cup crème fraîche or
   heavy cream
1 pound sugar snap or other
   edible-pod peas
6 tablespoons unsalted butter
Chervil leaves for garnish

Cut the guinea hen into serving pieces just as for a chicken (see directions on page 6 and technique photos on pages 530–31). Reserve the carcasses and wing tips. Rub the breasts with salt and pepper. Bone the legs and dice the flesh. Set the breasts and leg meat aside.

Prepare the guinea hen stock: Coarsely chop the reserved carcasses with a large knife or cleaver. Heat the butter in a large frying pan over medium heat. Add the chopped carcasses and wing tips and cook 2 minutes. Add the carrot, onion, and garlic and cook gently for about 5 minutes. Stir in the flour and cook for about 2 minutes. Add the wine, bring to a boil and cook 2 to 3 minutes. Add the veal stock and bouquet garni and season with salt and pepper. Cover and cook over low heat for 20 minutes.

Meanwhile, prepare the crayfish stock: Twist the middle tail fin of each crayfish gently and pull it carefully to withdraw the intestines. Heat the butter in another large, deep frying pan over high heat. Add the crayfish. When the crayfish start to color, reduce the heat to medium, add the carrot, onion and shallots and cook gently until the vegetables are tender but not colored. Add the cognac and carefully light it with a match. When the flames die, stir in the tomato paste and cook 2 minutes. Add the wine along with the garlic, thyme, bay leaf and a pinch of cayenne. Season with salt. Bring to a boil and cook 3 minutes. Remove the crayfish; set aside and cover to keep warm. Cook the stock 15 more minutes over medium heat. Add the guinea hen stock and cook 2 more minutes. Strain, pressing down on the solids with the back of a spoon to extract all the liquid; discard the solids. Return the strained sauce to the pan, add the cream and cook over low heat until reduced by one-half.

Rinse and drain the sugar snap peas. Snap off the ends to remove any strings. Cook in a large saucepan of boiling salted water until crisp-tender, about 5 minutes. Drain. Return the peas to the saucepan and toss with 2 tablespoons of the butter. Season to taste with salt and pepper. Cover to keep warm.

Heat 3 tablespoons of the butter in a large frying pan over high heat. Add the guinea hen breasts and cook until golden brown on both sides. Discard the fat in the pan; reserve the pan. Add the breasts to the sauce and simmer gently over low heat until the breasts are cooked through, about 10 minutes.

Heat the remaining tablespoon of butter in the reserved frying pan over high heat. Season the diced leg meat with salt and pepper and sauté until golden brown. Remove from the pan and set aside. Add a little of the sauce to the pan and deglaze, scraping the bottom of the pan with a wooden spoon to release the cooked particles. Add the deglazing juices to the sauce.

To serve, mound the sautéed leg meat in the center of a serving platter. Arrange the breasts around the leg meat. Put the peas around the edge of the platter. Place the crayfish on top of the peas, claws pointing outward. Spoon a little sauce over the breasts and garnish with chervil leaves. Serve the remaining sauce in a sauceboat on the side.

Glace au Chocolat, Poires et Sabayon
CHOCOLATE ICE CREAM WITH POACHED PEARS AND SABAYON SAUCE

SERVES 6

Not all ice cream comes in scoops. In France, most elegant ice cream desserts are molded and sliced at the table. At Le Cordon Bleu, chocolate ice cream is presented this way surrounded by freshly poached pears and served with pear-flavored sabayon. The flavor of the fruit harmonizes perfectly with that of the ice cream and the sauce perfectly mediates their tastes.

CHOCOLATE ICE CREAM

CRÈME ANGLAISE:
    3 cups milk
    1½ teaspoons vanilla extract
    6 egg yolks
    ¾ cup sugar
    6 tablespoons cocoa

    6 medium pears
    1 lemon, halved

SUGAR SYRUP
    4 cups water
    2⅔ cups sugar
    1 teaspoon vanilla extract

SABAYON
    4 egg yolks
    5 tablespoons sugar
    ¼ cup Poire William liquor,
        domestic pear brandy,
        or white rum
    1 cup dry white wine
    1 teaspoon cornstarch

    ½ cup heavy cream

EQUIPMENT: Ice cream maker, 4-cup ice cream mold

Chill a mixing bowl for the whipped cream and an ice cream mold in the freezer.

Prepare the chocolate ice cream: First, make a crème anglaise, using the above ingredients and following the directions on page 35. Then put the cocoa power into a heatproof bowl and gradually whisk in the hot crème anglaise. Set the bowl over a larger bowl of crushed ice to cool. Stir from time to time to keep a skin from forming. When cool, pour into an ice cream maker and freeze according to the manufacturer's instructions. Pack the ice cream into the chilled mold and freeze until firm, at least 1 hour.

Peel the pears and cut in half lengthwise. Remove the cores and hard fibers. Rub with the cut side of a lemon to prevent darkening.

Prepare the syrup: Combine the water, sugar and vanilla in a large saucepan. Bring to a boil over low heat, stirring to dissolve the sugar. Boil 1 to 2 minutes. Add the pears and one-half of the lemon. Reduce the heat, cover, and poach until tender, 15 to 20 minutes. Remove from the heat and let cool in the syrup. Remove the pears with a slotted spoon and drain on paper towels; set aside to cool.

Prepare the sauce: First make a sabayon, using the above ingredients and following the directions on page 115. Beat until cool. Sift over and fold in the cornstarch (this will "hold" the sabayon and make it more stable).

Then, beat the cream in the chilled bowl with a whisk or electric mixer until stiff peaks form and the cream clings to the whisk or beater. Fold the cooled sabayon into the whipped cream.

To serve, unmold the ice cream: Dip the mold into hot water for a few seconds. Then invert a platter over the mold and quickly reverse the two. Stand the pear halves around the molded ice cream, rounded sides out. Serve the sauce in a sauceboat on the side.

Oeufs en Gelée aux Crevettes
MOLDED EGGS AND SHRIMP IN ASPIC

———

Civet de Lapin à la Française
RABBIT STEW WITH RED WINE

———

Tulipes aux Trois Fruits Rouges
TULIPS WITH FRESH RED BERRIES

Oeufs en Gelée aux Crevettes
MOLDED EGGS AND SHRIMP IN ASPIC

———

SERVES 6

Eggs in aspic come in many forms in France. The most common is simply made by molding poached eggs in ramekins lined with a thin slice of cooked ham or smoked salmon. At Le Cordon Bleu our chef developed a multi-colored version of this traditional starter by arranging a layer of shrimp in the mold, setting a poached egg on top, and finishing with a little freshly chopped tomato. When turned out, the eggs are plump and white under a "flower" of shrimp, nestling on a bright red bed of tomato with an appetizing shine inside their transparent aspic casing.

ASPIC
6 cups Chicken Stock (page 12)
6 ounces lean ground beef
1 leek (green part only), chopped
1 tablespoon chopped chervil or
    parsley
Salt and freshly ground pepper

2 egg whites
4 packages (1/4 ounce each)
    powdered gelatin
    (about 4 tablespoons)
1/4 cup cold water
1/4 cup port wine

12 eggs
6 tablespoons white vinegar
Chervil or parsley leaves
60 small shrimp, cooked
    and shelled

1 medium tomato, peeled, seeded,
    and diced (page 31),
    and well drained
1 head Boston lettuce

EQUIPMENT: 12 half-cup oval molds

Chill the molds.

Prepare the aspic: First clarify the stock, using the ground beef, leek, chervil, salt, pepper, and egg whites and following the directions on page 267. While the stock is clarifying, sprinkle the gelatin over the water and let stand until softened, about 5 minutes. Five to 10 minutes before the end of the cooking time, add the gelatin to the stock through the hole in the soft crust. Simmer 5 to 10 minutes and then strain as indicated for a consommé (page 268). Cool to tepid and add the port.

Set the bowl of clarified stock over a larger bowl of crushed ice and cool, stirring occasionally with a wooden spoon. The stock will begin to thicken and gel as it cools. Watch the aspic carefully and when it becomes syrupy but not yet set, pour some into each mold to the depth of about ⅛ inch. Transfer the molds to the refrigerator and chill until firm, about 15 minutes. Remove the bowl of aspic from the ice so that it will not gel completely. If it does gel before you are ready to use it again, put it over a bowl of warm water until it reliquifies. Then chill again until syrupy as described above. The aspic should be chilled to the point of setting each time you use it.

Poach the eggs: Bring 8 cups water to a boil in a large frying pan. Add the vinegar and then reduce the heat to maintain the water at a slow simmer. Fill a bowl with cold water. Break an egg into a cup and slide it gently into the pan, gathering the white around the yolk with a slotted spoon. Repeat with 1 or 2 more eggs, depending on the size of your pan (the eggs must not be crowded and the water must maintain a gentle simmer). Poach until the whites are firm and the yolks are still soft to the touch, about 3 minutes. Transfer the poached eggs to the bowl of cold water. Repeat to poach all the eggs. Remove the eggs from the water and drain on paper towels. Trim the eggs into oval shapes. Chill in refrigerator.

Remove the molds from the refrigerator when the aspic has set, and place 1 chervil leaf in the center of each aspic layer. Arrange 5 shrimp around each leaf, fanned out to resemble a flower. Set a chilled poached egg on top. Carefully spoon enough aspic into each mold to surround and barely cover the eggs. Return the molds to the refrigerator for about 15 minutes to set the aspic. Then sprinkle each with a little tomato and cover with a final layer of aspic. Chill for at least 1 hour. Reserve and chill any remaining aspic for garnish.

To serve, dip the blade of a small knife in hot water. Dry it and slide the warm blade around the edge of each mold. Invert the molds onto a round platter. Garnish with chervil leaves. Arrange lettuce leaves around the platter. Chop any remaining aspic and sprinkle it between the eggs.

Civet de Lapin à la Française
RABBIT STEW WITH RED WINE

———

SERVES 6

A French *civet* is normally a winter dish made with hare. It is cooked in red wine and the sauce is traditionally thickened with the animal's blood, which gives the *civet* its characteristic color and taste. A simpler year-round *civet* can be made with rabbit, marinated overnight in an aromatic mixture of wine, garlic, and peppercorns. Even without the blood, this stew has a mildly gamy taste and is best served with a rich red wine either from Burgundy or the Côtes du Rhône.

3³/₄-pound rabbit

MARINADE
1 medium carrot, sliced
1 medium onion, sliced
2 cloves garlic, crushed
2 whole cloves
20 peppercorns
1 Bouquet Garni (page 20)
4 cups dry red wine
3 tablespoons cognac
1 tablespoon vegetable oil

7 tablespoons unsalted butter
3 tablespoons all-purpose flour
Salt and freshly ground pepper
2 pounds waxy potatoes
   (red or white)
36 pearl onions
1 tablespoon sugar
5 ounces slab bacon, sliced
   ¹/₄ inch thick
1 tablespoon vegetable oil
¹/₂ pound button or large,
   quartered mushrooms, trimmed,
   rinsed and dried

CROUTONS
3 slices firm white bread,
   crusts removed
2 tablespoons unsalted butter,
   melted
3 tablespoons chopped parsley

Cut the rabbit into serving pieces (see recipe on page 198 and technique photos on page 534). Put the pieces into a nonaluminum container with all of the marinade ingredients except the oil; drizzle the oil over the top. Let the rabbit marinate for at least 12 hours, or overnight.

Preheat the oven to 425°.

Remove the rabbit pieces from the marinade and pat dry with paper towels. Strain the marinade; reserve the liquid and the vegetables separately. Heat 3 tablespoons of the butter in a heavy oven-proof casserole over high heat. Add the rabbit pieces and cook until golden brown on all sides. Transfer to a shallow dish. Add the marinated vegetables to the pan and cook over high heat until lightly browned. Stir in the flour and cook 1 minute. Whisk in the marinade and bring to a boil. Reduce the heat and simmer 2 minutes, stirring occasionally. Return the rabbit to the pan, season with salt and pepper and cook in the oven until tender when pierced with a knife, about 45 minutes.

Meanwhile, turn and boil the potatoes à l'anglaise (see recipe on page 50 and technique photos on page 520). Meanwhile, keep warm in the cooking liquid.

Peel and glaze the pearl onions with 1 tablespoon of the butter, a pinch of salt and the sugar (page 165). Cover to keep warm.

Cut the bacon into lardons; blanch and drain (page 46). Heat 1 tablespoon oil and 2 tablespoons of the butter in a frying pan over high heat. Add the blanched lardons and cook until crisp and golden. Drain and add to the pan with the onions.

Heat 2 tablespoons of the butter in the pan used for the lardons. Add the mushrooms and cook over high heat until the moisture has evaporated and the mushrooms are golden. Add to the pan with the onions and the lardons.

Prepare the croutons: Cut each slice of bread in half to form 2 triangles. Brush each triangle on both sides with melted butter and arrange on a baking sheet. Toast in the 425° oven until golden; set aside.

When the rabbit is tender, remove from the oven. Transfer the rabbit pieces to a bowl. Strain the cooking liquid, pressing down on the solids to extract the liquid; discard the solids. Return the strained liquid to the casserole, bring to a boil, and reduce over medium heat until thickened. Return the rabbit, along with the onions, lardons and mushrooms to the casserole and simmer 5 minutes, stirring occasionally. Taste and adjust seasonings.

To serve, transfer the rabbit, onions, lardons, and mushrooms to a large serving platter with a slotted spoon. Dip one end of each crouton into the sauce and then into the chopped parsley and arrange around the edge of the platter. Spoon the sauce over the rabbit and vegetables. Serve with the boiled potatoes.

Tulipes aux Trois Fruits Rouges
TULIPS WITH FRESH RED BERRIES

SERVES 6

No, the French don't eat tulips for dessert. The "tulips" referred to in the title of this recipe are delicious waferlike cups made by molding thin rounds of pastry as soon as they come from the oven. They can be filled simply with fresh fruit and Chantilly cream or with a mixture of ice cream, sorbet, and fresh fruit.

Making the tulips requires a certain amount of dexterity, and the chef must work quickly; otherwise the pastry becomes brittle and can no longer be shaped into a cup as described below. Once they are made, however, they keep well if protected from humidity. The most difficult part of this dessert, the tulips, can therefore be prepared in advance and simply filled and served at the very last minute.

(continued)

Tulipes aux Trois Fruits Rouges (continued)

TULIP BATTER

4 tablespoons unsalted butter,
    softened
6 tablespoons confectioner's sugar
2 egg whites (room temperature)
5 tablespoons sifted all-purpose
    flour
1 teaspoon vanilla extract

CHANTILLY CREAM

2/3 cup heavy cream
1 tablespoon confectioner's sugar
1 teaspoon vanilla extract

1/2 pint basket strawberries
1 cup red currants
1 cup raspberries
1/4 cup sugar

Unsalted butter, softened,
    for baking sheet

EQUIPMENT: 4 small brioche molds or custard cups, pastry bag, small star pastry tip

Preheat the oven to 400°. Brush a baking sheet with the softened butter.

Prepare the tulip batter: Beat the softened butter with a whisk or electric mixer until creamy. Add the confectioner's sugar and beat until well blended. Lightly whisk the egg whites in a bowl and then whisk them gradually into the butter-sugar mixture. Add the sifted flour and vanilla and whisk just until blended; do not overmix. Let the batter rest 30 minutes.

Have ready the 4 brioche molds or custard cups for shaping the tulips.

Spoon 1 tablespoon of batter onto the baking sheet. Dip a spoon into cold water and use the back of the spoon to spread the mound of batter into a round about 5 inches in diameter. Repeat to make another tulip on the baking sheet (see technique photo 1 on page 550).

Reduce the oven temperature to 350° and bake the tulips until golden brown, about 5 minutes. Shape the tulips: (They must be shaped while still hot, before hardening.) Open the oven door and pull the baking sheet halfway out. Starting with the more colored, remove the tulips one at a time with a metal spatula and press each into a mold to form a cookie "dish" with a flat bottom. Then place a second mold over the cookie, inside the first, and press gently to shape (see technique photo 2). (This will permit the tulip to stand by itself when cool.) If the tulips cool and become too brittle to shape, return to the oven for 30 seconds to soften. Let cool in the molds for 2 minutes. Then carefully remove from the molds, and set aside. Raise the oven temperature to 400° and repeat until the batter is finished. Scrape and rebutter the baking sheet in between each batch so that the tulips don't stick. Reduce the oven temperature to 350° immediately after you put each new batch of tulips in the oven.

Not more than 1 hour before serving, prepare the Chantilly cream: Use the above ingredients and follow the directions on page 21. Fit the pastry bag with the small star tip and fill with the cream; refrigerate until serving time.

To serve, rinse, dry, and hull the strawberries. Rinse, dry, and stem the red currants. Combine the strawberries, red currants, and raspberries in a bowl and toss with sugar. Place a tulip on each of 6 dessert plates. Divide the fruit evenly among the tulips and decorate with rosettes of Chantilly cream.

Salade de Navets au Haddock

WARM SALAD OF SMOKED HADDOCK AND TURNIPS

———

Noisettes d'Agneau au Thyme, Tian Provençal

LAMB MEDALLIONS WITH THYME AND
A PROVENÇAL GRATIN

———

Bavarois aux Fruits de la Passion

PASSION FRUIT BAVARIAN

Salade de Navets au Haddock
WARM SALAD OF SMOKED HADDOCK AND TURNIPS

SERVES 6

Haddock, a member of the cod family, is sold fresh in many parts of the world—but rarely in France. There it is almost always smoked, and many a tourist who has ordered what the French simply call *haddock* has been surprised at being served golden smoked haddock (the fresh fish is called *aiglefin*).

Traditionally a main course served simply with a little melted butter, smoked haddock frequently appears as a starter nowadays—most often in one of the many *salades tièdes* (warm salads) so popular with young French chefs.

2 pounds smoked haddock
4 cups cold milk
2 pounds small turnips
Salt
Juice of 2 lemons, strained

VINAIGRETTE
1 teaspoon Dijon mustard
3 tablespoons lemon juice,
 strained
Salt and freshly ground pepper
9 tablespoons vegetable oil
2 tablespoons combined chopped
 chervil, chives, and tarragon
 (optional)

LEMON BUTTER
2 tablespoons lemon juice,
 strained
Salt
White pepper
7 tablespoons unsalted butter

2 tomatoes, peeled, seeded,
 and diced (page 31)
Chives and chervil or parsley
 leaves for garnish

Put the haddock in a shallow dish and cover with 2 cups of the milk. Let soak 3 to 4 hours to reduce the strong, smoked flavor of the fish. Pour off and discard the milk. Place the fish in a saucepan. Add the remaining 2 cups milk and 2 cups cold water. Cover and bring to a boil over medium heat. Reduce the heat and simmer 2 minutes. Skim off any foam that rises to the surface. Remove from the heat and let the haddock cool in the cooking liquid.

While the haddock cools, cut off and discard the tops and bottoms of the turnips. Trim the turnips to equal sizes with a round cookie cutter and then slice about ⅛ inch thick. Put the slices in a bowl and season with salt and the lemon juice. Let macerate for about 20 minutes.

Prepare the vinaigrette: Whisk together the mustard, lemon juice and salt and pepper to taste. Whisk in the oil and then 1 tablespoon of the herbs, if using.

Prepare the lemon butter: Combine the lemon juice, salt and pepper in a bowl. Melt the butter and then whisk into the lemon juice. Keep warm off the heat over a saucepan of hot water.

(continued)

Salade de Navets au Haddock (continued)

When cool, remove the haddock from the milk and drain on paper towels. Drain the sliced turnips in a colander. Transfer to a bowl and toss with the vinaigrette.

To serve, flake the haddock and arrange it down the center of a long serving platter. Arrange a crown of overlapping slices of turnip around the haddock. Pour the warm lemon butter over the fish and sprinkle the diced tomato in a line down the haddock. Sprinkle the remaining chopped herbs over the salad and garnish with chives and chervil leaves. (For individual serving, see photo on page 456.)

Noisettes d'Agneau au Thyme, Tian Provençal

LAMB MEDALLIONS WITH THYME AND A PROVENÇAL GRATIN

SERVES 6

This dish combines the flavors frequently associated with the south of France: olive oil, garlic, tomatoes, thyme, eggplant, zucchini, and lamb. Traditionally the vegetables are baked in a rectangular earthenware dish called a *tian*, but they can easily be prepared, as described below, in an ordinary cake pan when this specifically provençal utensil is lacking.

PROVENÇAL VEGETABLE TIAN
3 medium eggplants
Salt
1¹/₂ pounds zucchini, diced fine
8–10 tablespoons olive oil
2 medium onions, chopped fine
3 cloves garlic, chopped fine
Freshly ground pepper
1 tablespoon chopped fresh mint
1 large shallot, chopped fine
1¹/₂ pounds tomatoes, peeled, seeded, and diced (page 31)

1 saddle of lamb, boned and split to yield 2 loins and 2 tenderloins, about 2¹/₂ to 3 pounds (see technique photos 1 to 4 on page 538)
4 sprigs fresh thyme or ¹/₂ teaspoon dried
Mint leaves for garnish

Vegetable oil for frying eggplant, zucchini, and noisettes
Unsalted butter, softened, for cake pan and parchment paper

EQUIPMENT: 8-inch round cake pan

Prepare the tian: Peel the eggplants lengthwise with a vegetable peeler, in long strips. Trim the strips to about ¹/₄ inch wide. Blanch the strips in a saucepan of boiling salted water for about 3 minutes; drain well.

Line a rack with paper towels. Cut the eggplants lengthwise into ¹/₈-inch-thick slices. Heat 3 tablespoons oil in a large, nonstick frying pan over high heat. Add several slices of eggplant and sauté until tender but not colored. Transfer to the rack and season with salt. Repeat to cook all the eggplant slices. Add a little more oil to the pan, if necessary, and then add the diced zucchini. Cook rapidly over high heat until tender. Drain on paper towels.

Heat 2 tablespoons of the olive oil in another frying pan over low heat. Add the onions and cook until tender but not colored. Add the garlic and cook 1 minute without coloring. Season with salt and pepper. Stir in the chopped mint and cooked zucchini and cook 5 minutes longer.

Preheat the oven to 425°.

Lightly brush the cake pan with the softened butter. Line the bottom with a round of parchment paper and lightly butter it.

Assemble the tian: Arrange the blanched strips of eggplant, shiny side down, over the bottom of the cake pan in a large lattice pattern. Line the bottom and sides of the pan with fried eggplant slices. Fill the pan with the zucchini mixture, packing it down tightly. Cover with the remaining eggplant slices. Put the cake pan into a large roasting pan and pour in hot water to come halfway up the sides of the cake pan. Bring to a simmer on top of the stove, then transfer to the oven and bake for 25 minutes.

While the tian is baking, heat the remaining 3 tablespoons olive oil in a frying pan. Add the shallot and cook until tender but not colored. Add the tomatoes, season to taste and cook slowly until moisture has evaporated.

When the tian is cooked, unmold it: Invert a serving platter over the cake pan and quickly reverse the two. Remove the paper. Fill the spaces between the lattice with the cooked tomato mixture. Garnish with mint.

Prepare the lamb medallions (see technique photos 5 to 7 on page 538): Slice each loin into 6 rounds, each about 1¼ inches thick. Flatten each medallion slightly with the side of a knife. Slice each tenderloin into 3 equal pieces or tie the 2 tenderloins together in 4 places with kitchen twine and cut into 3 or 4 slices. Brush all the medallions lightly on both sides with oil and season with salt and pepper. Sprinkle with crumbled thyme leaves and press to adhere.

Heat a little oil in a large frying pan over high heat. When very hot, add the medallions and cook until browned and medium rare, about 2 minutes each side. Arrange medallions around the terrine and serve.

Bavarois aux Fruits de la Passion
PASSION FRUIT BAVARIAN

SERVES 6

As in a classic charlotte, bavarian cream is molded inside a ring of cakey pastry. Here, slices of jelly roll replace the traditional ladyfingers and a simple cake pan is used instead of the high-sided charlotte mold. The result is a spectacular "cake" with a multicolored exterior.

(continued)

Bavarois aux Fruits de la Passion (continued)

SPONGE CAKE

4 eggs (room temperature)

1/2 cup sugar

1/2 cup sifted all-purpose flour

6 tablespoons passion fruit jam

*Unsalted butter, softened,
    for jelly roll pan*

Flour for jelly roll pan

PASSION FRUIT BAVARIAN
CREAM

*1 envelope powdered gelatin
    (1/4 ounce)*

2 tablespoons cold water

*1/2 cup plus 2 tablespoons
    passion fruit jam*

1 cup passion fruit juice

3/4 cup heavy cream

EQUIPMENT: 15-by-10-by-1-inch jelly roll pan, 8-inch round cake pan

Preheat the oven to 375°. Brush the jelly roll pan generously with the softened butter. Line with parchment paper and brush the paper with butter. Dust with flour and tap out the excess.

Chill a mixing bowl for the whipped cream.

Prepare the cake: Beat the eggs and sugar with a whisk or an electric mixer until pale and creamy and doubled in volume. Gently fold in the flour. Pour the batter onto the jelly roll pan and smooth with a spatula. Bake 10 minutes. Lay a damp dish towel on a work surface with one of the long sides facing you. Turn the cake out onto the dish towel and peel off the paper. Trim any crisp edges with a long serrated knife. Spread the cake with the 6 tablespoons jam and roll it up. Wrap it in the damp dish towel and refrigerate for at least 2 hours.

Prepare the bavarian cream: Sprinkle the gelatin over the water and let stand until softened, about 5 minutes. Stir together the jam and the juice in a small saucepan over low heat until blended and warm. Add the gelatin and stir to dissolve. Transfer to a bowl and let cool to lukewarm.

Beat the cream in the chilled mixing bowl with a whisk or electric mixer until stiff peaks form and the cream clings to the whisk or beater. Mix about one-third of the whipped cream into the lukewarm passion fruit mixture. Then fold this mixture into the remaining whipped cream with a wooden spatula.

Line the bottom of the cake pan with parchment paper. Cut the cooled jelly roll into slices 1/4 inch thick. Line the bottom and the sides of the cake pan with the slices. Fill the pan with the bavarian cream and smooth the surface. Cover with parchment paper and refrigerate for at least 12 hours. If necessary, trim the cake so it is level with the top of the cream. Unmold onto a round dessert platter and remove the paper. Serve with a rum-flavored crème anglaise (page 352) if you wish.

LESSON 81

Potage Ambassadeur
SPLIT PEA SOUP WITH BACON,
SORREL, AND LETTUCE

Feuilletés de Saumon
aux Asperges
PUFF PASTRY SHELLS WITH SALMON AND ASPARAGUS
AND A LEMON BUTTER SAUCE

Concorde
CHOCOLATE MERINGUE CAKE FILLED WITH
CHOCOLATE MOUSSE

Potage Ambassadeur
SPLIT PEA SOUP WITH BACON, SORREL, AND LETTUCE

SERVES 6

Split peas are a popular winter vegetable in France. They are either made into soup or served as a puree, generally with pork or pork products. This is a particularly refined split pea soup that includes a little rice (cooked separately) for added texture, sorrel for a touch of acidity, and lettuce, which contributes a light, fresh taste to the whole.

2 cups dried split peas
4 tablespoons unsalted butter
1 large carrot, chopped fine
1 large onion, chopped fine
3 ounces slab bacon, chopped fine
2 leeks (white part only)
    chopped fine
1 clove garlic, crushed
4 cups Chicken Stock (page 12)
1 Bouquet Garni (page 20)

1/4 cup short-grain rice
Salt
1/3 cup heavy cream
Freshly ground pepper
3 ounces sorrel, cut into chiffonade
    (page 8 and technique
    photo page 520)
3 ounces lettuce, cut into
    chiffonade
Small bunch chervil or parsley
    for garnish

Soak the split peas overnight in cold water to cover. Drain.

Melt 2 tablespoons of the butter in a large saucepan over low heat. Add the carrot, onion, bacon, leeks and garlic and cook, stirring occasionally, until the vegetables are soft but not colored. Add the drained peas and the chicken stock. Bring to a boil, then reduce the heat, add the bouquet garni and simmer for 40 minutes.

Meanwhile, cook the rice in 1 cup boiling salted water until tender, about 20 minutes. Drain and set aside.

Puree the soup in a food mill or food processor. Return to the saucepan and add the cream. Bring to a boil and then add the rice. Taste and adjust the seasonings.

Heat the remaining 2 tablespoons of butter in a saucepan over low heat. Add the sorrel and lettuce and cook until the moisture has evaporated. Pour the hot soup into a tureen and add the cooked sorrel and lettuce. Serve sprinkled with chervil leaves.

Feuilletés de Saumon aux Asperges

PUFF PASTRY SHELLS WITH SALMON AND ASPARAGUS AND A LEMON BUTTER SAUCE

SERVES 6

This combination of pastry, vegetables, and fish is a typically modern creation in which each element is prepared separately. The vegetables are an integral part of the dish, rather than simply a garnish, and the sauce is the essence of simplicity (butter is whisked into lemon juice, seasoned, and served). In all, this is the sort of "light" French cooking that many young chefs prefer.

PUFF PASTRY

1¹/₂ cups all-purpose flour
³/₄ cup cake flour
²/₃ to ³/₄ cup water
1 teaspoon salt
2 tablespoons unsalted butter, melted
14 tablespoons unsalted butter
1 egg, slightly beaten, for glazing

1¹/₂ pounds fresh spinach
2 tablespoons unsalted butter
Salt and freshly ground pepper
1 pound green asparagus stalks

LEMON BUTTER SAUCE

14 tablespoons unsalted butter
3 tablespoons lemon juice, strained
Salt
White pepper

1¹/₂ pounds boneless salmon fillet

1 tablespoon unsalted butter
Small bunch chives, chopped

Unsalted butter, softened, for baking sheet

Prepare the puff pastry: Use the above ingredients and follow the directions on pages 209–10 and technique photos on pages 542–43.

Preheat the oven to 450°. Lightly brush a baking sheet with the softened butter. Sprinkle it with water; set aside.

Prepare the feuilletés (see technique photos on page 544): Dust a work surface with flour. Roll out the puff pastry dough about ¹/₈ inch thick and cut into 6 rectangles, 4 inches long by 2¹/₂ inches wide. Or, use an oval cutter of approximately the same dimensions, if available. Transfer the shapes to the baking sheet with a metal spatula. Brush the tops with egg glaze. Be careful not to let the egg drip over the edges of the dough, or it will not rise evenly. Refrigerate for 10 minutes. When chilled, brush again with egg glaze and bake until puffed and golden, about 25 minutes. Let cool.

While the pastry is baking, cut the salmon into scallops: Working from tail to head, run your fingers along the surface of the salmon fillets to detect any small bones; remove them. Holding the knife at a shallow angle to the fish, cut the salmon into 6 equal portions, or scallops (see technique photo on page 525). Set salmon aside.

Stem the spinach and rinse in several changes of water. Then coarsely chop it. Melt 2 tablespoons of the butter in a saucepan over medium heat, add the spinach, and cook, stirring frequently, until the moisture has evaporated. Season to taste with salt and pepper; cover to keep warm.

Snap off and discard the tough ends of the asparagus. Starting 1 inch below the tip, peel each stalk with a vegetable peeler. Tie the asparagus into several even bundles with kitchen twine. Bring a large saucepan of salted water to the boil. Add the asparagus and cook over high heat until tender, 10 to 12 minutes. Drain and cover to keep warm.

Prepare the lemon butter sauce: Cut the butter into small pieces. Bring the lemon juice to a boil in a small saucepan and reduce by one-half. Whisk in the butter little by little until the sauce is creamy. Season to taste with salt and white pepper; keep warm off the heat in a saucepan of hot water.

Cook the salmon: Season both sides of each scallop with salt and pepper. Heat 1 tablespoon of butter in a large frying pan over medium heat. Add the salmon and sauté until lightly cooked, 2 to 3 minutes each side.

To serve, cut each pastry rectangle in half horizontally. Place the bases on 6 serving plates. Make a bed of spinach on each pastry base and top with a piece of salmon. Arrange the asparagus spears on the plates. Pour the hot lemon butter over the salmon and asparagus. Sprinkle with chives. Top with the remaining puff pastry halves, tipped slightly backwards to resemble the half-open lid of box. Serve immediately.

Concorde

CHOCOLATE MERINGUE CAKE FILLED WITH CHOCOLATE MOUSSE

SERVES 6

A Parisian pastry chef is said to have invented this cake in the early 1970s. His idea? Use chocolate mousse instead of a pastry cream or buttercream as a filling and use chocolate meringue instead of a génoise or sponge cake to create a layered dessert. The crisp meringue and the velvety mousse proved to be perfect companions, and today his creation is a "classic" that can be found in pastry shops throughout the country.

CHOCOLATE MERINGUE
1 cup confectioner's sugar
6 tablespoons cocoa powder
5 egg whites
³/₄ cup granulated sugar
¹/₂ teaspoon vanilla extract

CHOCOLATE MOUSSE
3¹/₂ ounces semisweet chocolate,
  cut into small pieces
4 tablespoons unsalted butter
5 tablespoons granulated sugar
2 egg yolks
4 egg whites

Confectioner's sugar for dusting

Unsalted butter, softened,
  for baking sheet

EQUIPMENT: Pastry bag, large plain pastry tip, medium plain pastry tip

Preheat the oven to 200°.

Lightly brush 2 baking sheets with the softened butter and cover with parchment paper. Cut an oval pattern, about 8 inches long and 5 inches wide, from a thin piece of cardboard. Use the pattern to trace 2 ovals on 1 baking sheet and 1 oval on the second. Leave one-half of the second baking sheet free for piping strips of meringue.

Prepare the chocolate meringue: Sift together the confectioner's sugar and the cocoa powder. Beat the egg whites with a whisk or electric mixer until soft peaks form. Gradually beat in the granulated sugar and then continue beating until stiff peaks form again and the meringue is glossy and smooth. Fold in the confectioner's sugar, cocoa and vanilla with a wooden spoon. Fit a pastry bag with the large plain tip and fill with the meringue. Pipe the meringue to fill each traced oval, starting in the centers and working outward in a spiral. Fit another pastry bag with the medium plain tip and fill with the remaining meringue. Pipe long thin strips on the second baking sheet, leaving about 1 inch in between each. Bake until the meringue is crisp and thoroughly dry, at least 2 hours. Cool and carefully peel off the paper; trim the ovals to equal sizes.

Prepare the chocolate mousse: Bring 2 to 3 inches of water to a simmer in a saucepan. Combine the chocolate, butter and 3 tablespoons of the sugar in a heatproof bowl and set it over the simmering water. Let stand, without stirring, until the chocolate has completely melted. Remove from the heat and stir in the egg yolks with a wooden spoon. Beat the egg whites with a whisk or electric mixer until stiff peaks form. Gradually beat in the remaining tablespoons of sugar and continue beating until stiff peaks form and the meringue is glossy and smooth. Whisk about one-third of the egg whites into the chocolate mixture. Gently fold this into the remaining egg whites with a wooden spoon.

Assemble the concorde: Spread a thin layer of mousse over 1 meringue oval with a metal spatula. Place a second oval on top and spread it with a thin layer of mousse. Top with the third meringue and spread the top and sides of the concorde with the remaining mousse. Carefully cut the meringue strips into 1-inch lengths with a serrated knife and use them to decorate the top and sides of the concorde. Sift confectioner's sugar over the top.

Cover and refrigerate for 2 hours before serving.

LESSON 82

Bouchées aux Crevettes
PUFF PASTRY SHELLS FILLED WITH
SHRIMP AND MUSHROOMS

—

Noisettes de Chevreuil, Grand Veneur
MEDALLIONS OF VENISON, HUNTER STYLE

—

Glace au Crème de Marrons
CHESTNUT ICE CREAM

Bouchées aux Crevettes
PUFF PASTRY SHELLS FILLED WITH SHRIMP
AND MUSHROOMS

—

SERVES 6

Bouchées are literally "mouthfuls" of puff pastry filled with meat or fish in a creamy sauce (a *vol-au-vent* is a larger version of the same preparation). Large or small, they are made by baking two rounds of puff pastry, one on top of the other, hollowing out any undercooked dough from the center, and filling the flaky wells with a savory mixture. *Bouchées* can be baked in advance but should always be warmed in the oven and filled just before serving.

Note: Shrimp are often sold already boiled in France. If using fresh shrimp, boil in salted water until they turn red, drain and allow to cool, then use as described in the recipe.

(continued)

Bouchées aux Crevettes (continued)

PUFF PASTRY

3 cups all-purpose flour

1¹/₂ cups cake flour

2 teaspoons salt

1¹/₃–1¹/₂ cups cold water

4 tablespoons unsalted butter, melted

28 ounces unsalted butter

1 egg, slightly beaten, for glazing

SHRIMP AND MUSHROOM SAUCE

3 tablespoons unsalted butter

3 tablespoons all-purpose flour

1³/₄ cups cold milk

Salt and freshly ground pepper

²/₃ cup crème fraîche or heavy cream

5 ounces mushrooms, trimmed, rinsed, dried, and chopped fine

1³/₄ pounds small cooked shrimp

3 tablespoons cognac

Pinch of paprika

Chervil or parsley for garnish

Unsalted butter, softened, for baking sheet

Prepare the puff pastry: Use the above ingredients and follow the directions on pages 209–10 and technique photos on pages 542–43.

Preheat the oven to 425°. Lightly brush a baking sheet with the softened butter and sprinkle it with cold water.

Prepare the bouchées (see technique photos on page 545): Dust a work surface with flour. Roll out the puff pastry dough ¹/₈ inch thick. Use a fluted 4-inch cookie cutter to stamp out 12 rounds of dough. Transfer 6 of the rounds to the baking sheet. Prick all over with a fork and brush lightly with egg glaze. Be careful not to let the glaze run over the edges of the dough or it will not rise evenly.

Cut out the centers of the remaining 6 rounds with a fluted 3-inch cookie cutter and discard. Place the rings on top of the glazed rounds and press them gently to seal. Brush the rings lightly with egg glaze. (Do not let it run over the edges of the dough.) Bake until puffed and golden, about 30 minutes.

When the bouchées are cooked, use a small spoon to remove the soft pastry from the center of each; discard. Set the bouchées aside and keep warm.

Prepare the sauce: Melt 2 tablespoons of the butter in a saucepan over medium heat. Remove from the heat and whisk in the flour. Return to the heat and cook, whisking, 2 or 3 minutes without coloring. Add the milk and continue whisking, until blended and thickened. Season to taste with salt and pepper. Add the cream, bring to a boil and cook 1 minute. Keep the sauce warm over a pan of simmering water.

Heat the remaining tablespoon butter in a small frying pan over high heat. Add the mushrooms and cook quickly until all moisture has evaporated. Stir in the shrimp. Add the cognac and light carefully with a match. When the flames die, add the shrimp and mushrooms to the sauce. Season with paprika.

To serve, place the pastry shells on a serving platter. Spoon the sauce into the pastry shells and garnish each with a sprig of chervil.

Noisettes de Chevreuil, Grand Veneur
MEDALLIONS OF VENISON, HUNTER STYLE

SERVES 6

You needn't be a *grand veneur* (a noble huntsman) to enjoy this dish. Tender venison is cooked only a few minutes, then served with a carefully simmered red wine sauce and surrounded by little tartlets filled with a vegetable puree (chestnut or celery root).

Note: This dish must be begun the day before it is served: prepare the marinade and pastry on the first day and cook the venison, sauce, and garnish on the second.

3¹/₂ pounds tenderloin of venison

MARINADE
1 medium onion, chopped
1 medium carrot, chopped
2 cloves garlic, lightly crushed
2 whole cloves
1 stalk celery, chopped
1 sprig fresh thyme or
    ¹/₄ teaspoon dried
Bay leaf
20 peppercorns, crushed
2 tablespoons red-wine vinegar
3 tablespoons cognac
1 bottle (750 ml.) dry red wine
Salt
2 tablespoons vegetable oil

PÂTE BRISÉE
1 cup all-purpose flour
¹/₂ cup cake flour
Salt
1 egg
1 tablespoon water
7 tablespoons unsalted butter
1 egg, slightly beaten, for glazing

4 tablespoons vegetable oil
9 tablespoons unsalted butter
1¹/₄ pounds celery root
1 lemon, halved
Salt
¹/₂ cup crème fraîche or
    heavy cream
Freshly ground pepper
³/₄ pound canned, unsweetened
    whole chestnuts
6 small Golden Delicious apples
4 tablespoons unsalted butter,
    melted
1 cup whole cranberries in syrup

GRAND VENEUR SAUCE
Marinade (see above)
2 tablespoons sugar
2 tablespoons red-wine vinegar
2 tablespoons unsalted butter
¹/₂ cup red currant jelly

Chervil or parsley sprigs
    for garnish

EQUIPMENT: Twelve 2-by-4³/₄-inch fluted, oval tartlet molds

Trim the venison tenderloin of all fat and connective tissue. Reserve the trimmings. Tie the tenderloin with kitchen twine at 2-inch intervals. Wrap in plastic wrap and refrigerate until needed.

(continued)

Noisettes de Chevreuil, Grand Veneur (continued)

Prepare the marinade: Combine all of the ingredients except the oil in a large, shallow nonaluminum container. Add the venison trimmings. Sprinkle the surface with the oil. Cover with a dish towel and set aside to marinate 12 hours. (This marinade will form the base of the sauce.)

Prepare the pâte brisée. Use the above ingredients and follow the instructions on pages 37–38 and technique photos on page 540.

Strain the marinade, reserving the liquid. Pat the vegetables and venison trimmings dry with paper towels. Heat 2 tablespoons of the oil and 1 tablespoon of the butter in a frying pan over medium heat. Add the venison trimmings and sauté until lightly browned; remove from the pan and set aside. Discard the fat from the pan. Add 1 more tablespoon each butter and oil to the same pan and heat. Add the vegetables and sauté until lightly browned, 5 to 10 minutes. Return the venison trimmings to the pan and add the reserved marinade liquid. Bring to a boil, then reduce the heat and simmer gently for 2 hours, skimming the foam that rises to the surface. (The liquid will reduce as it cooks.)

Preheat the oven to 400°.

Dust a work surface with flour. Roll out dough about ⅛ inch thick and stamp out 12 ovals of dough the same shape as the molds, but at least ½ inch larger. Line the molds and blind bake (pages 38–39 and technique photos on page 541). Let cool slightly, remove from molds and cool completely.

Prepare a celery root puree: Peel the celery root. Rinse in cold water, drain and dry with paper towels. Cut into chunks and rub with the cut side of a lemon to prevent darkening. Cook in a large saucepan of boiling salted water until tender, about 20 minutes. Drain. Puree in a food mill or food processor. Return to the saucepan and whisk in ¼ cup of the cream and 3 tablespoons butter. Season to taste with salt and pepper. Keep warm.

Prepare the chestnut puree: Warm the chestnuts in a saucepan over medium heat. Drain. Puree in a food mill or food processor and return to the saucepan. Whisk in the remaining ¼ cup cream and 3 tablespoons of the butter. Season to taste with salt and pepper. Keep warm over a saucepan of hot water.

Peel and core the apples. If the apples are large, pare to about 2 inches in diameter. Put in a baking dish and brush with some of the melted butter. Reserve the remaining butter to brush tartlet molds. Bake at 400° until tender, about 25 minutes. Set aside; cover with aluminum foil to keep warm.

Prepare the sauce: After the marinade has simmered 2 hours, strain it into a saucepan, pressing down on the solids to extract all the liquid; discard the solids. Bring to a boil, then reduce the heat and simmer until the liquid thickens enough to coat the back of a spoon.

Then, make a caramel: Combine the sugar, vinegar and butter in a small, heavy-bottomed saucepan. Cook over medium heat until the butter and sugar melt and caramelize to a light amber color. Remove from the heat and immediately pour in a little of the reduced marinade to stop further caramelization. Be careful; the mixture will sputter. When it stops sputtering, return the saucepan to the heat and whisk well to blend. Simmer 5 minutes. Add the mixture to the reduced marinating liquid.

In the saucepan used to make the caramel, stir the jelly over low heat until dissolved. Whisk in a little of the sauce and then return the mixture to the pan with the sauce. Taste and adjust seasonings.

Warm the cranberries in a small saucepan over low heat.

To serve, preheat the oven to 200°.

Mound the warm chestnut puree into 6 of the oval tartlets. Mound the celery root puree into the remaining 6 tartlets. Place on a baking sheet and transfer to the oven to keep warm.

Slice the venison tenderloin into rounds or medallions, about 1¼ inches thick. Brush the noisettes on both sides with oil and season with pepper. Heat 1 tablespoon oil and 1 tablespoon butter in a heavy or nonstick frying pan over high heat. Add the venison medallions and cook until evenly browned, about 3 minutes on each side. Transfer to a serving platter. Discard the fat from the pan, add a little of the sauce and deglaze, scraping the bottom of the pan with a wooden spoon to release any cooked particles. Stir these pan juices into the sauce.

Spoon a little sauce over the medallions. Brush the warmed tartlets with the remaining melted butter and arrange around the venison. Brush the apples with melted butter and place one in between every other tartlet. Drain the cranberries and place a spoonful on top of each apple. Garnish with chervil or parsley. Serve the remaining sauce in a sauceboat on the side.

Glace au Crème de Marrons
CHESTNUT ICE CREAM

SERVES 4

Parisians love roasted chestnuts, and vendors sell them in the winter on busy street corners throughout the city. Young and old alike also relish a dessert made by serving sweet chestnut cream with a heavy cream topping. At Le Cordon Bleu, students enjoy chestnuts in yet another guise—churned into ice cream, molded, and served with candied violets and Chantilly cream.

CHESTNUT ICE CREAM
1¾ cups milk
2 teaspoons vanilla extract
3 egg yolks
3 tablespoons sugar
½ pound canned sweetened
    chestnut puree

CHANTILLY CREAM
¾ cup heavy cream
1 teaspoon vanilla extract
1 tablespoon sugar

Candied violets for decoration

EQUIPMENT: Ice cream maker, pastry bag, medium star pastry tip

Chill a shallow rounded bowl (about 4-cup capacity), in the freezer for the ice cream, a bowl for the whipped cream, and a serving platter.

(continued)

Glace au Crème de Marrons (continued)

Prepare the ice cream: Put the milk and the vanilla in a heavy-bottomed saucepan and bring to a boil. Combine the egg yolks and sugar in a heat-proof bowl and beat until thick and pale yellow in color. Gradually whisk in the hot milk. Return the mixture to the saucepan and cook over low heat, stirring constantly with a wooden spoon, until thickened enough to coat the back of a spoon. Do not boil. Test the consistency of the cream by drawing a finger across the back of the spoon: it should leave a clear trail. Strain into a bowl; let cool to room temperature, stirring occasionally to prevent a skin from forming. Whisk in the chestnut puree, little by little, until well blended. Pour into an ice cream maker and freeze according to the manufacturer's instructions. Transfer to the chilled bowl and smooth the surface with a spatula. Freeze until firm, about 1 hour.

Not more than one hour before serving, prepare the Chantilly cream: Beat the heavy cream in the chilled bowl over crushed ice. When it begins to stiffen, add the vanilla and sugar and continue beating until stiff peaks form and the cream clings to the whisk or beater. Fit the pastry bag with a medium star tip, and fill with the cream; refrigeraté until serving time.

To serve, unmold the ice cream: Dip the bowl of ice cream in hot water for a few seconds. Put the chilled serving platter over the top of the bowl and quickly invert the two. Remove the bowl. Pipe small rosettes of Chantilly cream all over the surface of the ice cream and decorate with the candied violets. Serve immediately.

Oeufs Moulés Bragance
BAKED EGGS WITH BÉARNAISE SAUCE

———

*Épaule d'Agneau
Farcie Provençale*
STUFFED LAMB SHOULDER PROVENÇALE

———

Pêches Cussy
BAKED PEACHES WITH MERINGUE

Oeufs Moulés Bragance
BAKED EGGS WITH BÉARNAISE SAUCE

SERVES 6

Bragance (Bragança) is a Portuguese town and the home of a dynasty of Portuguese kings. Not surprisingly, therefore, this preparation evokes a typically Portuguese combination of tastes—eggs and tomatoes. Perhaps it has Portuguese origins; nonetheless this recipe remains resolutely French.

3 medium tomatoes
Salt and freshly ground pepper
2 tablespoons vegetable oil

BÉARNAISE SAUCE
4 peppercorns, crushed
1 large shallot, chopped fine
2 tablespoons chopped tarragon
2 tablespoons wine vinegar
¼ cup white wine
2 egg yolks
2 tablespoons water
8 ounces unsalted butter, clarified (page 94) and cooled
1 tablespoon each chopped fresh chervil and tarragon
Salt and cayenne pepper
6 eggs

1 tablespoon chervil or parsley leaves
Parsley sprigs for garnish

Unsalted butter, softened, for baking sheet and molds

EQUIPMENT: Six 6-ounce oval molds or ramekins

Preheat the oven to 400°. Lightly brush a baking sheet with the softened butter. Cut the tomatoes in half crosswise. Scrape out seeds, season with salt; and turn the halves upside down on a rack to drain for a few minutes. Season the cut sides with pepper, put them, cut side down, on the baking sheet and drizzle with the oil. Bake until tender, about 10 minutes.

Prepare the béarnaise sauce: Use the above ingredients and follow the directions on page 252. Set aside off the heat over a saucepan of hot water.

Lightly brush the molds with softened butter. Sprinkle with salt and pepper and place in a roasting pan. Break 1 egg into each mold. Add hot water to the pan to come halfway up the sides of the molds. Set roasting pan on the heat and bring the water to a simmer. Transfer to the oven and bake 3 minutes. Remove molds from the pan; cool briefly.

To serve, arrange the tomatoes, cut sides up, on a large serving platter. Then unmold the eggs by running the blade of a small knife around the inside of each mold. Invert a small plate over each mold and reverse the two quickly. With a spatula, carefully place one egg on top of each tomato. Spoon the béarnaise sauce over. Garnish with chervil and parsley.

Épaule d'Agneau Farcie Provençale

STUFFED LAMB SHOULDER PROVENÇALE

SERVES 6

Few things are as hard to carve as a shoulder of lamb roasted on the bone. Anyone who has ever tried understands why this cut is generally boned, rolled, and tied before roasting. In Provence, the meat is spread with an aromatic mixture of olives, bread, garlic, and eggs before rolling; the result is a simple and delicious stuffed roast. At Le Cordon Bleu the shoulder is served with a garnish of bacon, carrot, onions, and baked tomatoes.

4- to 5-pound shoulder of lamb

STUFFING
1¼ cups fresh white bread crumbs
2 teaspoons each chopped fresh parsley, tarragon, and chervil
2 cloves garlic, chopped fine
2 eggs, lightly beaten
Salt and freshly ground pepper

2 ounces pitted black olives (preferably Niçoise or Kalamata)
7 tablespoons unsalted butter
5 carrots
3 medium tomatoes, chopped coarse
1 medium onion, chopped
1 stalk celery, chopped coarse
1 Bouquet Garni (page 20)
1 cup dry white wine
Salt and freshly ground pepper
½ pound slab bacon, sliced ¼ inch thick
½ pound pearl onions, peeled
1 tablespoon sugar

TOMATES PROVENÇALES
3 medium tomatoes
5 tablespoons unsalted butter, softened
5 cloves garlic, chopped fine
3 tablespoons chopped parsley
½ cup fresh white bread crumbs
Salt and freshly ground pepper

Watercress and parsley leaves for garnish

Olive oil for drizzling
Unsalted butter, softened, for baking sheet

Bone the lamb shoulder (see technique photos on page 536): Place the shoulder, fat side up, on a work surface. Use a boning knife to remove the skin, or fell, and excess fat. Then turn the shoulder fat side down. Make an incision in the large end of the shoulder opposite the shank bone and locate the flat, triangle-shaped blade bone. Cut and scrape the meat from around this bone up to and around the joint. Cut through the joint. Scrape the meat from around the underside of the joint and part of the way down the underside of the blade bone. Then take hold of the joint and pull the blade bone sharply toward you to free the bone from the meat. Make an incision along the length of the arm bone to expose it and then cut and scrape the meat from around the bone. Cut and scrape around the shank bone and joint to free the bone from the meat and then remove the arm and shank bones in 1 piece.

Preheat the oven to 425°.

Prepare the stuffing: Combine the bread crumbs, the herbs, the chopped garlic and the eggs in a bowl. Season with salt and pepper and mix well.

Stuff the shoulder (see technique photos on page 537): Open out the shoulder, skinned side down, on a work surface. Butterfly the shoulder by making a horizontal cut about three-quarters of the way through the thick muscle and open out the top flap. Spread the stuffing over the meat to within ½ inch of the edges. Place the olives in a line down the center of the stuffing. Tightly roll up the lamb so that the olives run the length of the roast and tie in several places with kitchen twine. Melt 4 tablespoons of the butter in a roasting pan over medium heat. Add the lamb and brown on all sides. Chop 1 of the carrots and add it to the pan along with the tomatoes, onion, and celery. Cook, stirring, about 2 minutes, until the vegetables are well coated with butter. Add the bouquet garni and wine. Season with salt and pepper and bring to a simmer. Transfer to the oven and cook, basting occasionally, until cooked to medium, 50 to 60 minutes. Transfer the lamb to a platter and cover with foil. Let rest for about 15 minutes. Set the roasting pan aside for the sauce.

While the lamb is cooking, cut the slab bacon into lardons and blanch them (page 46). Heat 2 tablespoons of the butter in a frying pan over high heat. Add the blanched lardons and sauté until crisp and golden; set aside.

Turn the 4 remaining carrots into small ovals (see page 50 and technique photo on page 520). Put them in a saucepan with cold salted water to cover. Bring to a boil and cook until tender, 10 to 15 minutes. Drain and then add to the pan with the lardons. Cover to keep warm.

Glaze the pearl onions using the remaining 1 tablespoon of butter, the sugar, and a pinch of salt (page 165). Add to the pan with the lardons and carrots; cover to keep warm.

When the lamb is cooked prepare the tomatoes: Reduce the oven temperature to 375°. Cut the tomatoes in half crosswise. Scrape out the seeds and juice, and drain upside down on a wire rack. Combine the butter, chopped garlic, parsley, bread crumbs, and salt and pepper in a bowl and work to a paste with a fork. Fill the tomato halves with this mixture. Lightly brush a baking sheet with the softened butter. Put the tomatoes, cut side up, on the baking sheet, and drizzle with a little olive oil. Bake until the tomatoes are tender and the filling is golden brown, 15 to 20 minutes.

Meantime, prepare the sauce: Skim the fat from the pan juices in the roasting pan. Set the pan over high heat, bring the juices to a boil and cook for a few minutes to reduce. Strain into a small saucepan, pressing down on the solids with the back of a spoon to extract all the liquid; discard the solids.

To serve, warm the garnish of carrots, lardons and onions in the covered pan over low heat. Remove and discard the twine from the lamb. Slice the meat about ¼ inch thick and arrange overlapping slices on a long serving platter. Spoon the garnish around the lamb. Arrange the tomatoes around the platter. Garnish the platter with small bunches of watercress and parsley leaves. Spoon a little sauce over the lamb and present the remaining sauce in a sauceboat on the side.

Pêches Cussy
BAKED PEACHES WITH MERINGUE

SERVES 6

This splendid peach and apricot creation is named in honor of the Marquis de Cussy (1766–1837), one of Brillat-Savarin's contemporaries and a famous gourmet. He was a great promoter of the "modern" cooking of his day and is said to have eaten his meals without speaking a word until dessert arrived, when he would suddenly become talkative and begin proffering witty opinions upon everything and all. In addition to this dessert, several savory garnishes have also been named for this once prominent champion of fine food.

2 ounces mixed candied fruit, chopped fine
¼ cup kirsch
3 very ripe peaches, peeled (page 9), or 6 canned peach halves
12 ladyfingers (page 118)

APRICOT SAUCE
1½ pounds fresh apricots, or canned apricot halves
2 tablespoons kirsch
¼ cup water
Juice of ½ lemon, strained

ITALIAN MERINGUE
3 egg whites
1 cup sugar
¼ cup water

Confectioner's sugar for dusting

EQUIPMENT: 9-by-13-inch ovenproof serving dish, pastry bag, medium star pastry tip

Put the candied fruit in a bowl and sprinkle with 2 tablespoons of the kirsch. Set aside to macerate.

Cut the peaches in half and remove the pits.

(continued)

Pêches Cussy (continued)

Line the bottom of the ovenproof serving dish with ladyfingers and brush with the remaining 2 tablespoons kirsch. Sprinkle with the candied fruit. Arrange the peach halves on top, rounded sides up (there will be space between the peaches).

Prepare the apricot sauce: Use the above ingredients and follow the directions on page 62; refrigerate.

Preheat the oven to 400°.

Prepare the Italian meringue: Use the above ingredients and follow the directions on pages 293–94.

Fit the pastry bag with the medium star tip and fill with the meringue. Pipe rosettes of meringue in the spaces between the peach halves, over the exposed ladyfingers. Do not pipe meringue over the peaches. Dust the meringue with confectioner's sugar. Bake until the meringue is dry and lightly browned, 10 to 15 minutes.

Serve warm or cold with the apricot sauce.

LESSON 84

Terrine de Mer à la Gelée de Safran
SEAFOOD TERRINE IN SAFFRON ASPIC

—

Beuchelle Angevine
SWEETBREADS WITH VEAL KIDNEYS
AND OYSTER MUSHROOMS

—

Crêpes Suzette
CRÊPES SUZETTE

Terrine de Mer à la Gelée de Safran

SEAFOOD TERRINE IN SAFFRON ASPIC

SERVES 6

This could be called a bouillabaisse *en terrine*. Indeed, this modern creation cleverly combines the flavors found in that famous soup to make a cold first course. A firm-fleshed fish, like monkfish, along with a flaky-fleshed fish, like red mullet, plus scallops and langoustines or shrimp are each poached separately before being molded together to make the terrine. The aromatic aspic that surrounds the fish is flavored with saffron and, like a bouillabaisse, the terrine is served with a *rouille*, a spicy rust-colored sauce.

2 red mullet, 6 ounces each,
   or 6 to 8 ounces red or
   yellowtail snapper fillet,
   with bones for stock
14 ounces monkfish fillet
1/4 pound sea scallops
9 langoustines (see page 114)
   or large shrimp

MARINADE
4 cloves garlic, peeled and
   lightly crushed
1/2 bunch basil, chopped coarse
2 shallots, chopped fine
Salt and freshly ground pepper
2 tablespoons olive oil

FISH STOCK
2 pounds whiting
Reserved bones from mullet
   (see above)
1 small leek (white part only),
   sliced fine
1 small stalk celery
Parsley stems
1 clove garlic, peeled
1 onion, chopped
1 cup dry white wine
5 cups water

SAFFRON ASPIC
3 envelopes powdered gelatin
   (1/4 ounce each)
6 tablespoons cold water
3 cups fish stock (see above)
1/2 small bulb fennel, chopped fine
1 leek (green part only),
   chopped fine
1 branch dill
Salt and freshly ground pepper
1/2 bunch chervil or parsley
3 egg whites
1 pinch saffron

ROUILLE
1 small baking potato, peeled
   and quartered
2 pinches saffron
1/2 red bell pepper
3 cloves garlic, peeled
1 egg yolk
Pinch cayenne pepper
1/2 cup vegetable oil
1/2 cup olive oil
1/2 teaspoon tomato paste

Lettuce leaves for garnish
2 small tomatoes, peeled, seeded,
   and diced (page 31)

EQUIPMENT: 11-by-4 1/4-by-3 1/4-inch rectangular terrine mold

Prepare the seafood: Scale, clean and fillet the red mullet, if using (see directions on pages 32 and 75 and technique photos on pages 524–25) but do not remove the skin; it will add color to the terrine. Reserve the bones for the stock. Run your fingers over the fillets to detect and remove all small bones. Trim the monkfish fillet and cut into long strips 3/8 inch wide. Pull off and discard the small muscle attached to each scallop. Slice the scallops crosswise into 3 or 4 rounds, depending on the size. Shell the langoustines (see technique photos on page 523) or shrimp. Discard the carcasses and set the tails aside. Put all the prepared seafood into a large, shallow dish, keeping each variety separate. Sprinkle with the marinade ingredients and let marinate for 1 hour, turning occasionally.

Prepare the fish stock as described on page 181, reserving the leek green for the aspic. Strain into a large frying pan and heat to simmering. Keeping each variety separate, drain the marinated seafood and pat dry with paper towels. Poach each variety separately in the simmering stock until tender but firm: about 1 minute for the scallops, 2 minutes for the langoustines or shrimp; 1 minute for the mullet; 2 minutes for the monkfish. Remove with a slotted spoon. Drain well and pat dry with paper towels. Let cool.

While the seafood is cooling, prepare the aspic: Sprinkle the gelatin over the water and let stand to soften, about 5 minutes. Measure 3 cups fish stock into a saucepan (add a little water to make up the 3 cups, if necessary) and bring to a boil. Put the fennel, leek green, dill, salt and pepper into a bowl. Coarsely chop half the chervil, reserving the remainder for garnish, and add it to the bowl along with the egg whites. Stir in a little of the hot fish stock. Return the mixture to the saucepan and bring to a boil over medium heat, whisking and scraping the bottom of the pan to make sure that nothing sticks. Stop whisking once the mixture boils. Reduce the heat and simmer for 30 minutes to clarify the stock. As the mixture simmers, the egg whites will form a soft crust on top of the stock through which the impurities will rise and be filtered. (If there is no natural break in the crust through which the stock can bubble up, gently clear a hole or "chimney" with a ladle.)

Five to 10 minutes before the end of cooking, add the gelatin and saffron through the hole in the soft crust. Simmer 5 to 10 more minutes, and then strain as for consommé (page 268).

Assemble the terrine: Arrange the cold, drained seafood in layers in the terrine, starting with the red mullet fillets, skin side down on the bottom. Pour over the warm aspic, to just cover the seafood. Refrigerate until completely firm, at least 2 hours.

While the terrine is chilling, prepare the rouille sauce: Use the above ingredients and follow the instructions on page 111.

To serve, line a serving platter with lettuce leaves. Dip the terrine mold into hot water for 5 seconds and then turn it out onto the center of the platter. Garnish with the remaining chervil leaves and the diced tomatoes. Serve the rouille sauce in a sauceboat on the side.

Beuchelle Angevine
SWEETBREADS WITH VEAL KIDNEYS AND
OYSTER MUSHROOMS

SERVES 6

Beuchelle is the name of a dish made with sweetbreads and kidneys throughout the Loire valley. Both ingredients are delicacies in France, but they are very rarely served together. In the Loire, they are cooked separately, then combined at the last minute and served with a sauce made almost exclusively with cream. This dish, which often includes mushrooms as well, is made with oyster mushrooms at Le Cordon Bleu, though fresh chanterelles or even button mushrooms might be used instead.

2 veal sweetbreads
2 veal kidneys
5 tablespoons unsalted butter
2 tablespoons vegetable oil
Salt and freshly ground pepper
2 shallots, chopped fine

1 pound oyster mushrooms,
*   trimmed, rinsed, and dried*
¼ cup cognac
1 cup crème fraîche or
*   heavy cream*
1 tablespoon chopped parsley

Soak the sweetbreads in cold water to cover for at least 2 hours.

Meanwhile, use the point of a small knife to remove the outer membrane from the kidneys. Cut away the fatty tissue from the interior; set the kidneys aside. Preheat the oven to 375°.

Drain the sweetbreads and put them into a saucepan with fresh cold water to cover. Bring to a boil and blanch 2 to 3 minutes. Drain, refresh under cold running water and drain again. Pull off the ducts and fat and use a small sharp knife to carefully remove the outside membrane (see technique photos on page 534). Dry thoroughly with paper towels. Heat 2 tablespoons of the butter and 1 tablespoon of the oil in an ovenproof frying pan over medium heat. Add the sweetbreads and cook until lightly browned on all sides. Season with salt and pepper. Cover with a round of buttered parchment paper. Transfer to the oven and bake until tender and the juices run clear when the blade of a knife is inserted into the thickest part of the sweetbreads, about 40 minutes. Remove from the oven and set aside. Reserve any pan juices.

When the sweetbreads are cooked, melt 2 tablespoons of the butter in a frying pan over medium heat. Add the shallots and cook until tender but not colored. Increase the heat to high, add the mushrooms and cook until tender and all the moisture has evaporated. Season to taste.

Season the kidneys with salt and pepper. Heat the remaining tablespoon of oil and butter in a frying pan over high heat. Add the kidneys and cook until browned on all sides. The interior of the kidneys should remain slightly pink. Remove from the pan; cover to keep warm. Discard the fat in the pan, add the cognac and deglaze, scraping the bottom of the pan with a whisk to release the cooked particles.

Add the cream and any cooking juices from the sweetbreads. Reduce until the sauce thickens enough to coat the back of a spoon. Taste and adjust seasonings. Add the mushrooms to the sauce.

To serve, slice the kidneys and sweetbreads about 1/2 inch thick. Place alternating slices of each on a serving platter, making them overlap. Spoon the sauce over and serve sprinkled with chopped parsley.

Crêpes Suzette
CRÊPES SUZETTE

SERVES 6

Who has never heard of crêpes Suzette? It is the archetype of the flaming crêpe dessert that was once the emblem of *grande cuisine* around the world. Some say the dish was created by Escoffier, who served crêpes with an orange-flavored butter around the turn of the century, but the dessert truly gained popularity when a French chef working for the Rockefeller family decided to have the crêpes flaming as they were brought to the table. Though some purists might object, it was then that crêpes Suzette were truly born.

CRÊPE BATTER
1 cup sifted all-purpose flour
1 teaspoon sugar
1/2 teaspoon salt
grated zest of 1 orange
2 eggs, beaten
1 cup milk
3 tablespoons unsalted butter, melted
1 teaspoon vanilla extract

ORANGE BUTTER
4 tablespoons unsalted butter, softened
Zest of 1 orange, grated fine
2/3 cup confectioner's sugar
3 tablespoons Cointreau

3 tablespoons cognac
3 tablespoons Cointreau

Unsalted butter, melted, for platter and cooking crêpes

EQUIPMENT: Two 5-inch crêpe pans

Prepare the crêpe batter: Use the above ingredients and follow the directions on page 23, adding the orange zest to the dry ingredients.

While the crêpe batter is resting, prepare the orange butter: Combine the butter, orange zest, confectioner's sugar and Cointreau and beat well.

Cook the crêpes as described on page 23.

Preheat the oven to 350°. Brush a serving platter with the melted butter.

Put 1 teaspoon of orange butter in the center of each crêpe. Fold the crêpes in half and then into quarters. Arrange rows of overlapping crêpes on the platter. Brush with the remaining orange butter. Warm in the oven for several minutes, until hot.

To serve, heat the cognac and Cointreau in a small saucepan over low heat. At the table light the hot liquor with a match and pour it flaming over the hot crêpes.

Lapin en Gelée au Romarin

TERRINE OF RABBIT IN ROSEMARY ASPIC

———

Saumon au Champagne

SALMON IN CHAMPAGNE SAUCE

———

Feuillantines aux Framboises, Coulis de Framboise

COOKIE WAFERS LAYERED WITH
RASPBERRIES AND CHANTILLY CREAM

Lapin en Gelée au Romarin
TERRINE OF RABBIT IN ROSEMARY ASPIC

———

SERVES 6

Rosemary is a pungent herb that should always be used fresh (dried rosemary loses much of its "sweetness" and has an almost musky taste). In this recipe, the delicate taste of rosemary infuses the *court bouillon* that the rabbit is cooked in. The liquid is clarified to make a transparent aspic, poured over the rabbit, and refrigerated to make the *gelée*. The terrine is served with a sweet and sour onion relish—a modern substitute for the vinegary *cornichon* pickles that traditionally accompany terrines in France.

3¹/₂-pound rabbit

COURT BOUILLON
¹/₂ bunch fresh rosemary
1 onion, sliced
1 carrot, sliced
1 stalk celery, sliced

4 sprigs fresh thyme or
    ¹/₂ teaspoon dried
1 bay leaf
3 cloves garlic, peeled and halved
Salt and freshly ground pepper

ROSEMARY ASPIC

2 envelopes powdered gelatin
  (¹/₄ ounce each)
¹/₄ cup cold water
Court Bouillon (see above)
¹/₂ pound lean ground beef
1 leek (white part only),
  chopped fine
1 stalk celery, chopped fine
1 tablespoon chopped fresh chervil
  or parsley
4 egg whites
Salt and freshly ground pepper

ONION RELISH

4 tablespoons unsalted butter
1 pound onions, sliced thin
6 tablespoons sugar
¹/₂ cup wine vinegar
Salt and freshly ground pepper

Chervil or parsley leaves
  for garnish

EQUIPMENT: 11-by-4¹/₄-by-3¹/₄-inch rectangular terrine mold

Cut the rabbit into 6 pieces: Remove the fore and hind legs, and cut the saddle into 2 pieces.

Combine the rabbit and the court bouillon ingredients in a large saucepan. Add water to cover. Bring to a boil, reduce the heat and simmer gently until the rabbit is very tender and beginning to fall off the bone, about 2 hours.

Lift the rabbit pieces from the court bouillon with a slotted spoon; set the court bouillon aside to cool. Remove the rabbit meat from the bones. Shred and pack into the terrine mold.

Prepare the rosemary aspic: First, sprinkle the gelatin over the water and let stand to soften. Then, clarify the court bouillon: Skim the fat from the court bouillon. Put the beef, leek, celery, chervil, and egg whites in a bowl and mix well. Season with salt and pepper. Strain 4 cups of the court bouillon into the bowl and mix well. Pour into a medium saucepan. Bring to a boil over medium heat, whisking and scraping the bottom of the saucepan to make sure that nothing sticks. Stop whisking once the mixture boils. Reduce the heat and simmer for about 35 minutes to clarify the stock. As the mixture simmers, the egg whites will form a soft crust on top of the stock through which the impurities will rise and be filtered. (If there is no natural break in the crust through which the stock can bubble up, clear a hole or "chimney" with the ladle.)

Five to 10 minutes before the end of cooking, add the softened gelatin through the hole in the soft crust; simmer 5 to 10 more minutes and then strain as for consommé (page 268).

Pour warm aspic to cover the shredded rabbit meat in the terrine mold. Refrigerate for about 12 hours. Pour the remaining aspic into a shallow flat container and refrigerate until set.

Prepare the onion relish: Heat the butter in a frying pan over medium heat. Add the onions and cook, stirring frequently, until soft and golden. Add the sugar and the vinegar and season with salt and pepper. Cook over low heat for about 30 minutes, stirring frequently. Remove from heat and let cool to room temperature.

(continued)

Unmold the terrine: Dip a small knife into hot water and slide it around the inside of the terrine. Invert an oval platter on top of the terrine and quickly reverse the two. Remove the terrine mold.

To serve, cut 3 or 4 slices from the terrine and overlap them on the platter in front of the uncut terrine. Roughly dice the reserved aspic and scatter it around the terrine. Garnish with chervil leaves. Put a spoonful of onion relish at either end of the platter. Serve the remainder in a small bowl on the side.

Saumon au Champagne

SALMON IN CHAMPAGNE SAUCE

SERVES 6

Everyone knows that Champagne is a festive drink but few people realize that its bubbles and slight acidity make it perfect for sauces as well. Indeed, in the eighteenth century, Champagne was the wine most frequently called for by famous chefs in their cookbooks, and today it still adds its distinctive flavor to several fish dishes.

Chefs at Le Cordon Bleu have found that fresh salmon and Champagne make a heavenly combination. In this recipe, Champagne is used for both cooking the fish and making the sauce—an extravagance, perhaps, but one well worth the expense.

5 tablespoons unsalted butter	*1 Bouquet Garni (page 20)*
1 medium onion, sliced thin	*Salt and freshly ground pepper*
1 carrot, sliced thin	*6 salmon steaks, 8 ounces each*
1 pound whiting (on the bone) or other lean white fish, cleaned and sliced	*1 large shallot, chopped fine*
	2½ tablespoons all-purpose flour
1 bottle Champagne (about 3 cups)	*1 egg yolk*
3¾ cups water	*⅓ cup crème fraîche or heavy cream*

Prepare a fish stock: Melt 1½ tablespoons of the butter in a large saucepan over low heat. Add the onion, carrot, and whiting and cook for several minutes without coloring, stirring well to coat with butter. Add 2 cups each of the Champagne and water, the bouquet garni, a pinch of salt, and pepper. Bring to a boil and skim the froth that rises to the surface. Reduce the heat and simmer 20 minutes. Strain into a saucepan.

Preheat the oven to 425°.

Wipe the salmon steaks with paper towels. Butter a roasting pan with 1½ tablespoons of the butter and sprinkle with the chopped shallot, salt, and pepper. Place the salmon steaks in the roasting pan and season with salt and pepper. Add the remaining Champagne and 2¾ cups water to the pan. Cover with a piece of buttered parchment paper and bake until the salmon is tender and the point of a knife easily enters the flesh, 12 to 15 minutes. Remove the steaks from the pan and drain on paper towels. Remove the skin and backbones. Transfer to a serving dish; cover to keep warm.

Prepare the sauce: Strain the cooking liquid into the saucepan with the fish stock. Cook over high heat until reduced to 2 cups. Melt the remaining 2 tablespoons butter in a separate saucepan. Remove from the heat and whisk in the flour. Return to the heat and cook for about 2 minutes, whisking constantly to prevent coloring. Whisk in the 2 cups of reduced fish stock mixture off the heat. Then return to the heat, and bring the sauce to a boil, whisking constantly. Reduce the heat and simmer 10 minutes. Taste and adjust seasonings.

Whisk the egg yolk with the cream in a small bowl. Whisk in a little of the hot sauce. Return the mixture to the saucepan, whisking constantly, and simmer for 1 minute.

Spoon the sauce over the salmon steaks and serve with Pommes à l'Anglaise (page 50), if desired.

Feuillantines aux Framboises, Coulis de Framboise

COOKIE WAFERS LAYERED WITH RASPBERRIES AND CHANTILLY CREAM

SERVES 6

Traditionally a *feuillantine* is a small rectangle of puff pastry simply served sprinkled with a little confectioner's sugar. Today the term is also applied to thin wafers of virtually any type of pastry arranged in successive layers with a filling of fresh fruit and Chantilly cream. Once the technique of making the wafers has been mastered, nothing could be simpler than these fresh fruit desserts.

Note: The wafers may be made ahead of time and stored up to 1 week in an airtight container. If raspberries are not available, equal amounts of fresh strawberries, peaches, or blueberries could be used for filling the pastries and making the sauce.

(continued)

Feuillantines aux Framboises, Coulis de Framboise (continued)

WAFER BATTER

5 tablespoons unsalted butter,
  softened
1 cup confectioner's sugar
¹/₂ cup sifted all-purpose flour
¹/₄ cup sifted cake flour
1 teaspoon vanilla extract
3 egg whites

RASPBERRY COULIS

2 cups fresh raspberries
¹/₃ cup confectioner's sugar

CHANTILLY CREAM

2 cups heavy cream
6 tablespoons confectioner's sugar
1 teaspoon vanilla extract

1 cup raspberries
Mint leaves for garnish

Unsalted butter, softened,
  for baking sheet

EQUIPMENT: Pastry bag, large plain pastry tip, medium star pastry tip

Preheat the oven to 350°. Brush 2 baking sheets well with the softened butter.

Prepare the wafer batter: Combine the butter and sugar in a bowl and beat with a whisk or an electric mixer until light and creamy. Add the sifted flours and vanilla and beat well. Whisk the egg whites lightly in another bowl and whisk them into the batter. Fit the pastry bag with the large plain tip and fill with the batter. Pipe nine 1-inch mounds, 3 inches apart, on each baking sheet. Tap the bottom of the baking sheets hard on a flat surface to flatten and spread the mixture. Bake the wafers until golden and crisp, 5 to 8 minutes. Transfer the warm wafers to a wire rack with a metal spatula; let cool.

Prepare the raspberry coulis: Puree the raspberries in a food mill or food processor. Strain through a fine strainer to remove seeds. Whisk in the confectioner's sugar. Chill.

Not more than 1 hour before serving, prepare the Chantilly cream: Use the above ingredients and follow the directions on page 21. Fit the pastry bag with the medium star tip and fill it with the Chantilly cream. Refrigerate until serving time.

To serve, spread 6 of the wafers in a single layer on a serving platter. Cover with rosettes of Chantilly cream. Put a raspberry in the center of each rosette and top each wafer lightly with another wafer. Make a second layer of cream and raspberries and top with a third wafer. Pipe 1 cream rosette on the center of each and decorate each rosette with a raspberry and a small sprig of mint. Spoon the raspberry coulis around the feuillantines.

LESSON 86

Courgettes et Tomates Farcies
STUFFED ZUCCHINI AND TOMATOES

—

Filet de Boeuf en Croûte, Sauce Périgueux
BEEF TENDERLOIN IN PUFF PASTRY
WITH PÉRIGUEUX SAUCE

—

Glace aux Pruneaux et à l'Armagnac
PRUNE ARMAGNAC ICE CREAM

Courgettes et Tomates Farcies

STUFFED ZUCCHINI AND TOMATOES

SERVES 6

When one thinks of stuffed vegetables in France, cabbage, zucchini, or tomatoes most quickly come to mind. The latter two are often prepared together since the basic filling for them is the same.

The filling can be seasoned to taste and may include tarragon, chives, or basil when these fresh herbs are available. Serve the zucchini and tomatoes hot or cold as a starter for six or main dish for three.

3 medium zucchini
Salt
6 medium tomatoes

STUFFING
4 slices firm white bread, crusts removed
1½ cups milk
2 tablespoons unsalted butter
9 shallots, chopped fine
1 pound sausage meat
2 eggs, lightly beaten
2 cloves garlic, chopped fine
Pinch allspice

2 tablespoons unsalted butter
1 tablespoon vegetable oil
1 medium onion, diced fine
2 medium carrots, diced fine
1 large leek (white part only), chopped fine
1 stalk celery, diced fine
2 tablespoons tomato paste
2 cloves garlic, crushed
Freshly ground pepper
1 cup dry white wine
Bouquet Garni (page 20)
2 tablespoons grated Parmesan cheese
Watercress or parsley for garnish

Cut off the ends of the zucchini and trim the stems; reserve. Cut the zucchini crosswise into 2½-inch lengths. Scoop out the flesh with a melon baller or small spoon, leaving a ¼-inch wall of flesh around the sides and over the bases to make small "barrels." Sprinkle the interiors with salt. Invert on a rack for 15 minutes to drain some of the moisture. Chop the scooped-out flesh and set aside.

Slice the top third from the tomatoes; reserve. Scrape out and discard the seeds. Scoop out the flesh with a teaspoon, leaving a ⅜-inch wall of flesh. Sprinkle the interiors with salt. Invert on a rack to drain some of the moisture. Chop the flesh and set aside.

While the vegetables are draining, prepare the stuffing: Soak the bread slices in the milk; set aside. Heat the butter in a frying pan over medium heat. Add the shallots and cook until soft but not colored. Add the sausage meat and cook, stirring often, for 5 minutes. Squeeze out the bread and discard the milk. Remove the pan from the heat. Mix in the bread. Gradually stir in the eggs and mix in the garlic and allspice.

Bring a saucepan of salted water to a boil. Add the zucchini "barrels" and ends to the pan, open ends down, and blanch for about 5 minutes. Remove with a slotted spoon. Drain on a rack, open ends down.

Heat the butter and the oil in a frying pan over medium heat. Add the onion, carrots, leek and celery and cook until soft but not colored, 5 to 8 minutes. Stir in the tomato paste and garlic. Season with salt and pepper. Add the wine and bouquet garni. Bring to a boil, reduce the heat and simmer 5 minutes. Spread over the bottom of a roasting pan; set aside.

Preheat the oven to 400°.

Stuff the vegetables: Divide the stuffing in half. Add the chopped tomato to one half and the chopped zucchini to the other. Mix well. Mound the tomato-flavored stuffing into the tomatoes and the other into the zucchini. Sprinkle with Parmesan cheese. Set the reserved tops on the tomatoes and top as many zucchini "barrels" as possible with the zucchini ends. Place the stuffed tomatoes and zucchini on top of the cooked vegetables in the roasting pan. Reduce the oven temperature to 375° and cook, basting often with the juices, for 40 to 45 minutes.

To serve, transfer the stuffed vegetables to a serving platter. Strain the cooking liquid, pressing down on the solids with the back of a wooden spoon to extract all the liquid; discard the solids. If the sauce is too thin, cook over medium heat until reduced and slightly thickened. Spoon a little sauce over the vegetables. Garnish the platter with watercress or parsley.

Filet de Boeuf en Croûte, Sauce Périgueux

BEEF TENDERLOIN IN PUFF PASTRY WITH PÉRIGUEUX SAUCE

SERVES 6

Beef Wellington is not French . . . but *filet de boeuf en croûte* is. The French dish was a favorite of the Duke of Wellington and his name is now associated with it throughout the world. This Cordon Bleu version of that famous recipe is served with a truffle-flavored sauce named for the town of Périgueux in southwest France, a large truffle-producing area. It also includes another specialty, a little diced *foie gras*, though this is optional.

The *foie gras* and truffles should be used fresh whenever possible, though good-quality canned products make acceptable substitutes in this case.

PUFF PASTRY
1 1/2 cups all-purpose flour
3/4 cup cake flour
2 teaspoons salt
2/3 to 3/4 cup water

2 tablespoons unsalted butter, melted
14 tablespoons (7 ounces) unsalted butter
1 egg, lightly beaten, for glazing

3¹/₂-pound beef tenderloin
Salt and freshly ground pepper
3 tablespoons unsalted butter
1 large carrot, sliced
1 large onion, quartered

1 bunch watercress for garnish

Unsalted butter, softened,
* for baking sheet*

PÉRIGUEUX SAUCE
¹/₄ cup port wine
2 tablespoons cognac
1¹/₄ cups Brown Veal Stock
* (page 71)*
1 tablespoon chopped black truffles
2 ounces cooked foie gras, or
* good-quality foie gras mousse,*
* diced fine*

Prepare the puff pastry: Use the above ingredients and follow the directions on pages 209–10 and technique photos pages 542–43.

Preheat the oven to 475°. Trim all fat and connective tissue from the tenderloin. Reserve the trimmings. Fold the thin tail end underneath the tenderloin and tie the meat with kitchen twine in 4 or 5 places so it will hold its shape during cooking. Season with salt and pepper.

Heat the butter in a roasting pan over high heat. Add the beef and brown on all sides. Place the trimmings under the beef, add the carrot and onion and roast 20 minutes. Remove the beef from the roasting pan and set aside to cool. Then refrigerate. Return the pan of trimmings and vegetables to the oven and roast until well browned, 10 to 15 minutes.

When the meat is chilled, wrap it in puff pastry (see technique photos on page 547). Dust a work surface with flour. Roll out the puff pastry dough to a rectangle ¹/₈ inch thick and several inches longer than the tenderloin. Trim the edges. Remove and discard the twine from the beef and place it in the center of the dough rectangle. Brush the exposed dough with egg glaze and fold up the long sides of the dough to enclose the tenderloin. The edges must not overlap more than 1¹/₂ inches; trim off the excess and reserve. Gently roll the rolling pin over the seam to seal. Roll out the end flaps of dough ¹/₁₆ inch thick. Brush the flaps with egg glaze and fold up over the dough package. Gently press the seams together with the rolling pin to seal. Brush off any excess flour.

Lightly brush a baking sheet with butter; sprinkle with cold water.

Transfer the dough-covered beef to the baking sheet, seam side down. Brush with egg glaze. Make a small hole in the top of the dough package with a pastry tip to allow steam to escape. Then roll a small piece of aluminum foil into a short cylinder and insert it into the hole. Cut long strips, about ¹/₄ inch wide, from the reserved dough and lay them diagonally over the surface. Lay other strips across the first set to form a diamond pattern. Brush all over with egg glaze. Chill for 30 minutes. Meanwhile, preheat oven to 400°.

Remove the dough-covered beef from the refrigerator and brush again with egg glaze. Transfer to the oven and bake until the pastry is crisp and golden, 45 to 50 minutes.

While the beef is cooking, prepare the Périgueux sauce: Set the reserved roasting pan on the heat. Bring to a boil and skim off any fat. Add the port and cognac and deglaze, scraping the bottom of the pan with a whisk to release any cooked particles. Pour the contents of the roasting pan into a small saucepan and add the veal stock. Cook over medium heat until reduced by about one-quarter. Strain, pressing down on the solids to extract all the liquid; discard the solids. Add the truffles (and the juice, if using canned) and heat to simmering. Add the foie gras off the heat just before serving.

To serve, transfer the beef to a serving platter. Garnish both ends of the platter with watercress. Serve the Périgueux sauce on the side.

Glace aux Pruneaux et à l'Armagnac

PRUNE ARMAGNAC ICE CREAM

SERVES 6

S weet, plump prunes from the city of Agen are a delicacy that rivals the best dried pears, peaches, or apricots. Not far from where they are produced, Armagnac, a famous brandy, is also made. Here they are combined to make a rich ice cream scented with a pinch of tea.

6 prunes, pitted, for garnish
2 tablespoons Armagnac

SUGAR SYRUP
1 cup water
Pinch Ceylon tea
3 tablespoons sugar
1/4 cup Armagnac

7 ounces prunes (1 cup), pitted

CRÈME ANGLAISE
2 cups milk
1 teaspoon vanilla extract
4 egg yolks
2/3 cup sugar

1/4 cup Armagnac

EQUIPMENT: Ice cream maker

Chill a bowl and 6 dessert glasses in the freezer.

Macerate the 6 prunes in 2 tablespoons Armagnac. Set aside for garnish.

Prepare the syrup: Bring the water to a boil in a saucepan. Add the tea and let infuse off the heat for about 15 minutes. Strain 1/2 cup of the tea into another saucepan and discard the rest. Add the sugar and Armagnac to the infusion. Bring to a boil over medium heat, stirring to dissolve the sugar. Add the 7 ounces pitted prunes, cover with parchment paper and simmer 15 minutes. Remove from the heat and let the prunes cool in the syrup. When cool, remove and quarter the prunes, then return them to the syrup.

Prepare the crème anglaise (page 35); let cool. Pour into an ice cream maker and freeze according to the manufacturer's instructions. Five to 10 minutes before the ice cream is finished, add the prunes along with the syrup. Transfer to the chilled bowl and freeze until firm, at least 1 hour.

To serve, place 2 scoops of ice cream into each dessert glass. Top each with an Armagnac-soaked prune and spoon over remaining Armagnac.

LESSON 87

Pain d'Épinards à la Romaine
SPINACH TERRINE WITH FRESH TOMATO SAUCE

Selle d'Agneau Rôti
ROAST SADDLE OF LAMB

Gratin Dauphinois
POTATO GRATIN WITH GARLIC AND CREAM

Feuilletés aux Poires Chauds au Sabayon
WARM PEARS IN PUFF PASTRY WITH SABAYON

Pain d'Épinards à la Romaine

SPINACH TERRINE WITH FRESH TOMATO SAUCE

SERVES 6

In French, this vegetable terrine is said to be *à la romaine,* literally, "Roman style." In culinary terms, this most often means that a dish includes anchovies, a green vegetable (in this case spinach), and eggs; however, the methods used for making the terrine and most of the other ingredients are resolutely modern and French.

2 pounds spinach
Salt
7 tablespoons butter

BÉCHAMEL SAUCE
1 tablespoon unsalted butter
2 tablespoons all-purpose flour
3/4 cup milk
Salt and freshly ground pepper
4 eggs, lightly beaten

8 oil-packed anchovy fillets,
* drained and chopped coarse*
Freshly ground pepper

TOMATO SAUCE
2 tablespoons olive oil
1 onion, chopped fine
2 cloves garlic, chopped fine
1 pound tomatoes, peeled,
* seeded, and diced (page 31)*
2 tablespoons chopped fresh basil

Unsalted butter for bread pans
* and parchment paper*

EQUIPMENT: Two 4 1/2-by-8 1/2-by-2 1/2-inch loaf pans

Preheat the oven to 400°.

Brush the loaf pans with the softened butter. Line the bottoms with parchment paper and brush the paper with butter.

Stem the spinach and rinse in several changes of water; drain. Blanch the spinach in a large saucepan of boiling salted water for 2 minutes; drain well. Choose several of the best leaves and spread them out flat on a dish towel; pat dry. Use these leaves to line the loaf pans so that they overhang the sides by a few inches. Reserve a few to cover the filled pans. Squeeze the remaining spinach to remove excess water and coarsely chop.

Prepare the béchamel sauce: Use the above ingredients and follow the directions on page 18. Remove from the heat and gradually whisk in the eggs. Return the pan to the heat and cook for 1 minute, stirring constantly. Add the chopped spinach and anchovies. Season with pepper. Pour the mixture into the lined loaf pans and cover with the reserved spinach leaves. Cover the pans with buttered parchment paper and put them into a roasting pan. Pour hot water into the roasting pan to come halfway up the sides of the loaf pans and bring to a simmer on top of the stove. Transfer to the oven and cook until a knife blade inserted in the center of a loaf comes out clean, about 30 minutes.

While the terrines are cooking, prepare the tomato sauce: Heat the olive oil in a medium skillet over medium heat. Add the onion and cook until soft but not colored. Add the garlic and cook 1 minute. Stir in the tomatoes. Cover and cook, stirring occasionally, 15 to 20 minutes. Stir in the basil and then puree the sauce in a food processor or food mill and return to the pan. If too thin, cook over medium heat until reduced and slightly thickened.

To serve, unmold the pans onto a long serving platter. Remove the parchment paper. Spoon a little sauce around the terrines and serve the remainder in a sauceboat on the side. Serve the terrines hot or cold.

Selle d'Agneau Rôti
ROAST SADDLE OF LAMB

SERVES 6

Meat roasted on the bone is generally more flavorful than boned roasts, and a roast saddle of lamb can rival the best *gigot* (leg of lamb). In France, roast lamb is always served rare—cooked in a very hot oven and left to rest before serving, the meat should be tender, juicy, and an even pink color throughout when served.

Few roasts are simpler to prepare than this one, and if the pan juices are carefully boiled down and degreased, the sauce discreetly intensifies the taste of the lamb.

4-pound saddle of lamb
Salt and freshly ground pepper
Several sprigs fresh thyme or
 ¹/₂ teaspoon dried
2 tablespoons unsalted butter
2 tablespoons vegetable oil

2 medium carrots, quartered
2 medium onions, quartered
2 cloves garlic, crushed
1 bay leaf
Watercress for garnish

Preheat the oven to 475°. Prepare the saddle of lamb (see technique photos on page 537): Place the saddle, fat side up, on a work surface. Trim a 3-to-4-inch strip from the ends of both flaps. Carefully remove and discard the fine layer of skin, called the fell, that covers the outside of the saddle.

Trim some of the excess fat from the saddle. Turn the saddle fat side down and remove the nerve that runs down the length of the meat and the excess fat. Season the underside with salt, pepper and thyme. Roll each flap in towards the backbone. Tie the roast at even intervals with kitchen twine. Rub with the butter and oil, and season with salt and pepper. Put the lamb and trimmings in a roasting pan and roast 15 minutes. Add the carrots, onions, garlic, and bay leaf to the pan and continue roasting about 20 more minutes.

When the lamb is cooked, transfer to a platter. Cover with aluminum foil to keep warm. Discard the fat and set the pan over high heat. Add

1¼ cups of water, bring to a boil and deglaze, scraping the bottom of the pan with a wooden spoon. Then reduce heat and simmer 10 minutes to reduce. Strain the juices, and skim any fat from the surface.

To serve, remove and discard the twine from the roast. Put it in the center of a large serving platter, and garnish the platter with watercress. Rewarm the juices, if necessary, and serve in a sauceboat on the side. Serve with Gratin Dauphinois, below.

Gratin Dauphinois
POTATO GRATIN WITH GARLIC AND CREAM

SERVES 6

The Dauphiné is a mountainous region near the French-Italian border. Its most famous dish is this creamy potato gratin, which is now served in restaurants throughout France. Potatoes are first cooked in milk and then baked in thick heavy cream with a simple seasoning of salt, pepper, nutmeg, and a little garlic. At Le Cordon Bleu, grated Gruyère is sprinkled over the potatoes to give the dish a crisp surface.

Note: This gratin can be cooked well in advance of serving and reheated at the last minute. The cheese can also be omitted, if desired, without compromising taste.

6 cups milk
Salt
Freshly grated nutmeg
1 Bouquet Garni (page 20)
2½ pounds baking potatoes
Freshly ground pepper
2 cloves garlic

⅔ cup heavy cream
4 ounces grated Gruyère cheese (about 1 cup)

Unsalted butter, softened, for gratin dish

EQUIPMENT: 9-by-13-inch gratin dish

Bring the milk to a boil in a large saucepan. Add salt, nutmeg, and bouquet garni.

Peel and slice the potatoes about ⅛ inch thick. Put the sliced potatoes into the boiling milk. Return the milk to a boil, reduce the heat, and simmer 10 to 15 minutes. Stir gently from time to time with a slotted spoon to prevent the potatoes from sticking to the bottom of pan (be careful not to break the potatoes). Drain; discard the milk.

Preheat the oven to 400°.

Slice the garlic cloves in half. Rub the interior of the gratin dish well with the cut garlic. Brush the dish well with the softened butter. Layer the potatoes in the gratin dish, seasoning each layer with salt and pepper. Bring the heavy cream to a boil and pour it over the potatoes. Sprinkle with the grated cheese and bake 40 minutes.

Feuilletés aux Poires Chauds au Sabayon

WARM PEARS IN PUFF PASTRY WITH SABAYON

―――

SERVES 6

These elegant little pastries are a cross between a classic *bouchée* and a simple fruit tartlet. Puff pastry is folded and cut to produce layered borders that rise to create pastry shells. The pastry is hollowed out after baking, filled with a poached pear and served with a pear-flavored sabayon.

Note: Poach the pears and bake the pastry ahead of time but make the sauce and assemble the dessert just before serving.

PUFF PASTRY
1½ cups all-purpose flour
¾ cup cake flour
1 teaspoon salt
⅔ to ¾ cup water
2 tablespoons unsalted butter, melted
14 tablespoons unsalted butter
1 egg, lightly beaten, for glazing

SUGAR SYRUP
½ lemon
4 cups water
2⅔ cups sugar
1 teaspoon vanilla extract

6 ripe medium pears
½ lemon

SABAYON
4 egg yolks
⅔ cup sugar
1 cup pear poaching liquid (see above)
¼ cup Poire William or domestic pear brandy
1 teaspoon cornstarch

6 mint leaves for garnish

Unsalted butter, softened, for baking sheet

Prepare the puff pastry: Use the above ingredients and follow the directions on pages 209–10 and technique photos pages 542–43.

Prepare the syrup: Cut the lemon half in two and put into a saucepan with the water, sugar, and vanilla. Bring to a boil over medium heat, stirring to dissolve the sugar. Boil 1 to 2 minutes. Remove from the heat and set aside.

Peel the pears, leaving the stems intact. Insert a vegetable peeler into the base of each pear, to the depth of about 1 inch. Gently twist and pull out the core. Rub the pears with the cut side of the lemon to prevent darkening. Add the pears to the warm syrup and cover with parchment paper. Bring to a boil, reduce the heat and poach until the pears are tender, 10 to 15 minutes. Remove from heat and let stand in the poaching liquid.

(continued)

Feuilletés aux Poires Chauds au Sabayon (continued)

Preheat the oven to 400°. Brush a baking sheet with the softened butter and sprinkle with cold water.

Prepare the feuilletés (see technique photos on page 544): Dust a work surface with flour. Roll out the puff pastry dough to a rectangle about 1/8 inch thick. Trim the dough to a 10-by-15-inch rectangle. Cut the rectangle into two even strips 5 inches wide and 15 inches long. Cut each band into three 5-inch squares. Fold each square in two to form a triangle. Arrange one dough triangle on the work surface with the base towards you. Starting about 1/2 inch in from the left side, cut up toward the top of the triangle, stopping about 1/2 inch from the top. Repeat on the right side. Unfold the dough square and brush the edges of the inner square lightly with egg glaze. Lift the two outside cut corners, pass one corner under the other and then fold each over flat to meet the corners at the opposite sides. Brush off any excess flour. Repeat with the remaining dough triangles. Brush the edges of the feuilletés with egg glaze, but do not let the glaze run down the sides or the dough will rise unevenly. Prick the bottoms all over with a fork. Transfer to the baking sheet. Bake until puffed and golden, 35 to 45 minutes. Let cool on a cake rack.

Drain the pears; reserve the poaching liquid.

Prepare the sabayon: Bring 2 to 3 inches of water to a simmer in a saucepan. Combine the egg yolks and sugar in a large heatproof bowl and beat with a whisk or electric mixer until pale yellow and foamy. Whisk in 1 cup of the lukewarm pear poaching liquid and the Poire William. Set the bowl over the simmering water so that the bottom does not touch the water. Continue beating until the mixture becomes thick and creamy and increases in volume, and the whisk or beater leaves a clear trail on the bottom of the bowl. Test the temperature of the sabayon occasionally with a finger: If it feels hotter than just tepid (the temperature should not exceed 80°), remove from the heat and continue to beat until slightly cooled. Then return to the heat and continue cooking as described. Remove from the heat and sift in 1 teaspoon of cornstarch to "hold" the sabayon. Whisk or beat to blend.

To serve, reheat the feuilletés, if necessary. Cut out and remove the center of each case with a small knife. Scrape out and discard any uncooked pastry. Transfer to a doily-lined platter. Stand a pear in each feuilleté and spoon a little of the hot sabayon over each. Decorate the top of each pear with a mint leaf. Serve the remaining sabayon in a sauceboat on the side.

LESSON 88

Sorbet de Tomates au Basilic
TOMATO SORBET WITH BASIL AND VODKA

—

Loup de Mer Farci Marseillaise
STUFFED SEA BASS, MARSEILLE STYLE

—

Tartelettes aux Fraises
STRAWBERRY TARTLETS

Sorbet de Tomates au Basilic
TOMATO SORBET WITH BASIL AND VODKA

—

SERVES 6

The French travel more and more these days, and one of the exotic tastes some have acquired is for American cocktails like the Bloody Mary. The classic vodka and tomato mixture inspired one of the chefs at Le Cordon Bleu to create this refreshing first course.

2 pounds tomatoes, peeled, seeded, and diced (page 31)
1 tablespoon tomato paste
Salt

2 teaspoons confectioner's sugar
10 drops Tabasco
6 teaspoons vodka
Fresh basil leaves for garnish

EQUIPMENT: Ice cream maker

Chill a bowl and 6 champagne glasses in the freezer.

Puree the tomatoes in a food mill or food processor. Add the tomato paste, salt, sugar, Tabasco and 4 teaspoons vodka. Mix well. Pour into the ice cream maker and freeze according to the manufacturer's instructions. Transfer to the chilled bowl and freeze until firm, about 1 hour. Serve sprinkled with a little vodka and garnished with basil leaves in the chilled champagne glasses or individual glass bowls, if you like.

Loup de Mer Farci Marseillaise

STUFFED SEA BASS, MARSEILLE STYLE

SERVES 6

Tomatoes and Marseille are inextricably linked. This dish acknowledges that association by surrounding a beautifully stuffed fish with a bright red tomato sauce, nevertheless revealing its *grande cuisine* origins by lightly coating just the fish with a rich *beurre blanc* as well. The result is a spectacular creation that harmonizes a North-meets-South medley of tastes.

4-pound sea bass or striped bass
Salt and freshly ground pepper

SALMON MOUSSELINE

¹/₂ small red bell pepper, diced fine
¹/₂ small green bell pepper, diced fine
Salt
³/₄ pound fresh salmon fillet, skinned
2 egg whites
¹/₂ cup crème fraîche or heavy cream
Fresh ground pepper

TOMATO SAUCE

¹/₄ cup olive oil
1 medium onion, chopped fine
2 cloves garlic, chopped fine
1 pound tomatoes, peeled, seeded, and diced (page 31)
Pinch of sugar
Salt and freshly ground pepper

4 bulbs fennel
3 tablespoons unsalted butter
3 shallots, chopped fine
1¹/₄ cups dry white wine

BEURRE BLANC SAUCE II
Cooking liquid from sea bass
2 tablespoons white-wine vinegar
1/2 cup crème fraîche or
　　heavy cream
1/2 pound unsalted butter, softened
1 tablespoon chopped fresh dill

2 tablespoons olive oil
Sprigs of dill for garnish
1 tablespoon chopped fresh dill

Clean the sea bass and trim the tail (page 32 and technique photos on page 524). Then remove the backbone to create a boneless cavity for the stuffing (page 236 and technique photos on page 526). Season the cavity with salt and pepper; set aside.

Make the salmon mousseline: Chill a mixing bowl. Put the diced red and green peppers in a saucepan with cold salted water to cover. Bring to a boil and blanch 2 to 3 minutes. Drain, refresh under cold running water and drain again. Set aside to dry on paper towels. Moving from tail to head, run your fingers over the surface of the salmon, to detect any small bones; remove them. Pass the fillet through a meat grinder fitted with the finest blade or puree in a food processor. Work the puree through a fine sieve to eliminate any remaining bones and tough fibers. Put the puree in the chilled bowl and set it over a larger bowl of crushed ice. Season with salt and pepper. Whisk the egg whites until foamy and add little by little to the pureed salmon, beating vigorously with a wooden spoon in a forward-to-backward motion until the mixture is well blended, smooth and slightly thickened. Add the cream in the same way, beating well after each addition. The mousseline should have a firm texture. Season with salt and pepper. Stir in the diced peppers. Refrigerate until needed.

Prepare the tomato sauce: Heat the olive oil in a medium frying pan over medium heat. Add the onion and cook until soft but not colored. Add the garlic and cook 1 minute. Stir in the tomatoes and sugar, season with salt and pepper, and cook 15 minutes, stirring occasionally. Puree in a food mill or food processor and then return to the pan. If the sauce is very thin, cook over medium heat until reduced and thickened. Set aside.

Remove and discard the tough outer leaves from the fennel. Cut the bulbs in half lengthwise. Cook in a saucepan of boiling salted water until tender, about 20 minutes. Drain; set aside.

Preheat the oven to 400°. Brush a roasting pan with the 3 tablespoons of butter. Sprinkle with the shallots, salt and pepper.

Stuff the sea bass with the salmon mousseline; be careful not to pack it too tightly as the mousseline will expand during cooking. Gently press the two sides of the fish together to close the opening. Place the fish on its side in the roasting pan. Add the wine, and cover with a piece of buttered parchment paper to prevent the fish from drying out during cooking. Bring to a boil over high heat, transfer to the oven and bake until the point of a small knife enters the flesh easily, about 30 minutes. Transfer the fish from the roasting pan to a serving platter with 2 spatulas. Carefully remove the skin by scraping and peeling it off with a sharp knife. Cover the fish with a piece of buttered parchment paper while you make the sauce.

Prepare the beurre blanc sauce: Strain the fish cooking liquid into a small heavy-bottomed saucepan. Add the vinegar and cook over medium heat until the liquid has reduced to a thick syrup. Whisk in the cream, reduce the heat to low and cook until reduced by one-half. Remove from the heat and whisk in the softened butter little by little. Add the dill. Taste and adjust seasonings. Keep the sauce warm off the heat, over a pan of hot water.

Cut any large pieces of fennel in half. Heat the olive oil in a frying pan over medium heat. Add the fennel and warm it quickly in the hot oil without coloring. Turn it carefully so that the pieces do not fall apart.

To serve, remove the parchment paper from the fish. Blot up any juices on the platter with paper towels. Spoon the beurre blanc sauce over just the body of the fish, leaving the head unsauced. Place the fennel at either end of the platter and garnish with sprigs of dill. Spoon the tomato sauce onto the platter on either side of the fish and in between the fennel. Serve sprinkled with the chopped dill.

Tartelettes aux Fraises
STRAWBERRY TARTLETS

SERVES 6

Everyone loves strawberries and cream; here they are served in a sweet pastry shell and brushed with a glaze of raspberry jam and kirsch. The simplicity and freshness of this dessert make it the perfect finish to an elegant meal.

Note: Other fresh fruit tartlets may also be prepared following the directions given here.

The pastry can be baked in advance, but always fill the pastry shells at the very last minute; otherwise they risk being soggy when served.

PÂTE BRISÉE SUCRÉE
1¹/₃ cups all-purpose flour
²/₃ cup cake flour
³/₄ cup confectioner's sugar
1 egg
11 tablespoons unsalted butter
1 egg, lightly beaten, for glazing

1¹/₂ pint baskets strawberries

RASPBERRY GLAZE
*6 ounces raspberry jam
(a generous ¹/₂ cup)*
1 tablespoon kirsch

CHANTILLY CREAM
1¹/₄ cups heavy cream
¹/₄ cup confectioner's sugar
1 teaspoon vanilla extract

EQUIPMENT: 24 tartlet molds 3 inches round, pastry bag, medium star pastry tip

Prepare the pâte sucrée as you would a pate brisée (pages 37–38 and technique photos on page 540), but sift the flours with the sugar.

Line and blind bake the tartlet molds (see technique photos on page 541). Dust a work surface with flour. Roll out the dough about ⅛ inch thick and cut out 12 rounds with a 4-inch fluted cookie cutter. Make a small ball of dough from the scraps. Dip it in flour and use it to gently press the dough rounds into the bottoms and sides of the molds. Be careful not to stretch the dough as it will shrink somewhat during cooking. The dough should extend slightly above the rim of the molds. Refrigerate 30 minutes.

Preheat the oven to 400°.

Remove the tartlet molds from the refrigerator. Lightly prick the bottom of each with a fork. Place a smaller mold inside each to prevent the pastry from rising and deforming during cooking, or line with a round of parchment paper and fill with dried beans (see directions on pages 37–38 and technique photo 6 on page 541). Bake 10 minutes. Remove the smaller molds, brush the interior of each pastry shell with egg glaze and bake 5 minutes longer. Remove from oven and let cool slightly. Then remove the shells from the molds and let cool completely on a rack.

Rinse, drain and hull the strawberries. Pat dry on paper towels.

Prepare the raspberry glaze: Work the jam through a fine strainer with the back of a spoon to remove the seeds. Add the kirsch and whisk until smooth. The glaze should be liquid enough to brush easily over the fruit; add a little water if necessary.

Not more than 1 hour before serving, prepare the Chantilly cream (page 21). Fit the pastry bag with the medium star tip and fill it with the Chantilly cream; refrigerate until needed.

Assemble the tartlets: Put the shells on a doily-lined serving platter. Pipe the Chantilly cream into the shells, reserving a little for final decoration. Carefully arrange the strawberries on top. Brush with the glaze. Decorate the top of each tartlet with a rosette of Chantilly cream. Serve immediately.

LESSON 89

Fonds d'Artichauts Cussy

ARTICHOKES WITH FOIE GRAS AND TRUFFLES

———

Raie à l'Embeurée de Chou

SKATE WINGS WITH CAPER SAUCE AND
GREEN CABBAGE COMPOTE

———

Le Saint-Honoré

SAINT-HONORÉ CAKE

Fonds d'Artichauts Cussy

ARTICHOKES WITH FOIE GRAS AND TRUFFLES

———

SERVES 6

France imports more artichokes than any other country in Europe because its own production can't keep up with the demand. The province of Brittany produces more than half of all the French artichokes grown (the rest are grown near the Mediterranean coast).

Artichokes can be purchased all year long but they are most plentiful during the summer and fall, or "artichoke season" in France; at other times of the year they are imported from Italy and Spain. They are most frequently eaten simply boiled and served with a vinaigrette. Fresh artichoke bottoms are a special treat and are more likely to be served in restaurants than at home. Chefs stuff them with either meat or fish to make attractive starters that can be eaten either hot or cold.

This is a classic recipe named in honor of a famous French gastronome, the Marquis de Cussy, who was a contemporary of Brillat-Savarin. It calls for filling artichoke bottoms with a rich mixture of *foie gras* and truffles and spooning over a creamy *velouté*. Originally, equal weights of *foie gras* and truffles were used in the stuffing, and the artichoke bottoms were breaded and deep-fried; modern chefs prefer boiling to frying and find that the *foie gras* filling is sufficiently "rich" with a single black truffle to enliven its taste.

(continued)

Fonds d'Artichauts Cussy (continued)

ARTICHOKE BOTTOMS
1 lemon
6 artichokes
Salt
2 tablespoons vegetable oil

VELOUTÉ SAUCE
2¹/₂ tablespoons unsalted butter
¹/₄ cup all-purpose flour
1¹/₄ cups Chicken Stock (page 12)
³/₄ cup crème fraîche
3 egg yolks
Salt
Cayenne pepper

7-ounce can of good-quality
foie gras mousse
1 black truffle, chopped

Unsalted butter, softened,
for baking sheet

EQUIPMENT: Pastry bag, large star pastry tip

Prepare and cook the artichoke bottoms (page 30 and technique photos on pages 520–21). Set aside in cooking liquid to keep warm.

Make the velouté sauce: Melt the butter in a saucepan over low heat. Stir in the flour and cook 2 minutes without coloring. Whisk in the cold chicken stock. Bring to a boil, then reduce the heat and simmer, whisking constantly, for about 10 minutes. Whisk together the cream and egg yolks in a small bowl. Whisk in a little of the hot sauce and then return the mixture to the saucepan. Season to taste with salt and cayenne. Simmer over low heat for 1 minute, whisking constantly. Set aside.

Preheat the broiler. Brush a baking sheet with the softened butter.

Drain the artichoke bottoms.

Mash the foie gras mousse with a fork. Mix in the chopped truffle. Fit the pastry bag with the large star tip and fill with the foie gras mixture. Put the cooked artichoke bottoms on the baking sheet and pipe the foie gras mixture into each. Spoon a little of the sauce over each and broil until golden. Serve warm.

Raie à l'Embeurée de Chou
SKATE WINGS WITH CAPER SAUCE AND
GREEN CABBAGE COMPOTE

———

SERVES 6

Skate has long been a popular fish in France. It was one of the few salt-water fish that kept well enough to be sent to the most isolated inland cities. Traditionally, it is served with nut brown butter to which a little vinegar and capers have been added. This recipe echoes that tradition by the use of capers in the sauce but is otherwise unashamedly modern, both in its use of a simple cream sauce and because the fish is served with slowly simmered cabbage—a deliciously unorthodox garnish for fish.

3¹/2 pounds skate wings	*2 medium carrots*
CABBAGE COMPOTE	*Salt*
1 head green cabbage, about	*2 tablespoons unsalted butter*
* 3¹/2 pounds*	*1 tablespoon peppercorns*
Salt	*1 Bouquet Garni (page 20)*
5 ounces bacon, sliced	*1 onion, sliced*
* ¹/4 inch thick*	*1 clove garlic*
7 tablespoons unsalted butter	*¹/2 cup wine vinegar*
1 onion, chopped	*²/3 cup crème fraîche*
1 clove garlic, chopped	* or heavy cream*
Freshly ground pepper	*6 tablespoons capers*
¹/4 cup wine vinegar	*Chervil or parsley for garnish*

If the skate wings are large, cut them into three or four pieces of approximately equal size. Soak under cold running water for 30 minutes.

Meanwhile, prepare the cabbage compote: Remove and discard the tough outer leaves of the cabbage. Cut the cabbage in half and cut out the core. Then cut the cabbage into wedges. Bring a saucepan of salted water to a boil. Add the cabbage and cook 10 minutes. Drain, refresh under cold running water and drain again. Squeeze to remove as much moisture as possible. Coarsely chop and set aside in a colander.

Cut the bacon into "lardons"; blanch and drain (page 46).

Heat the 7 tablespoons butter in a large frying pan over high heat. Add the lardons and cook until crisp and golden. Remove with a slotted spoon and set aside. Reduce the heat to low. Add the onion to the pan and cook until soft but not colored. Stir in the garlic and cook 1 minute. Return the lardons to the pan along with the blanched cabbage and stir to coat well with the butter. Season with salt and pepper, add the vinegar and bring to a boil. Reduce the heat to low, cover, and cook, stirring occasionally, until the cabbage is very soft. (Add a little water if the cabbage begins to stick.) When the cabbage is cooked, remove the lid and continue cooking until all the liquid has evaporated. Taste and adjust seasonings.

While the compote is cooking, peel the carrots. Score lengthwise with a zester at even intervals and then slice about ¹/4 inch thick. Put the carrots in a saucepan with cold, salted water to cover. Bring to a boil and cook until crisp-tender. Drain, refresh under cold running water and drain again. Return the carrots to the saucepan and toss with butter to prevent them from drying out. Cover to keep warm.

Drain the skate wings and put them into a large saucepan. Add the peppercorns, bouquet garni, onion, garlic, vinegar, salt and cold water to barely cover. Bring to a boil, reduce the heat and poach at a simmer for 15 minutes. Remove the pan from heat and let the skate stand in the poaching liquid while you prepare the sauce.

(continued)

Bring the cream to a boil in a saucepan. Season with pepper and reduce until slightly thickened. Add the capers. Taste and adjust seasonings.

To serve, remove skate from the poaching liquid. Carefully peel off the skin while still warm. Transfer to a serving platter. Arrange 6 mounds of cabbage compote around the skate and garnish each with carrot slices. Spoon the sauce over the skate and garnish with chervil leaves.

Le Saint-Honoré
SAINT-HONORÉ CAKE

SERVES 6 TO 8

Saint-Honoré is both the name of a fashionable street not far from the Champs Élysées and that of the patron saint of bakers. Some speculate that this elaborate dessert was named in honor of the latter while others claim it was simply the creation of a baker who had his shop on the Faubourg Saint-Honoré.

The pastry was originally filled with Chantilly cream. Later a pastry cream combined with Italian meringue took its place. Today at Le Cordon Bleu the cake is filled with a *crème Chiboust*, essentially a classic pastry cream to which a little gelatin and beaten egg whites have been added.

Note: The cake cannot be assembled too far in advance but should be refrigerated for a good 30 to 45 minutes once it has been filled with the cream and before serving.

PÂTE BRISÉE SUCRÉE

1 cup all-purpose flour

1/2 cup cake flour

1 egg

Pinch of salt

3 tablespoons sugar

1 tablespoon water

1 teaspoon vanilla extract

7 tablespoons unsalted butter

CHOUX PASTRY

1 cup water

3/4 teaspoon salt

3/4 teaspoon sugar

1/4 pound unsalted butter

1 1/4 cups all-purpose flour

4 egg yolks

1 egg, lightly beaten, for glazing

CARAMEL

3/4 cup sugar

1/3 cup water

CHIBOUST PASTRY CREAM

1 package powdered gelatin
 (1/4 ounce)

2 tablespoons water

1 cup milk

1 teaspoon vanilla extract

4 egg yolks

2/3 cup sugar

1/4 cup all-purpose flour

4 egg whites

Unsalted butter, softened,
 for baking sheets

Vegetable oil for baking sheets

EQUIPMENT: Pastry bag, medium plain pastry tip, medium star pastry tip

Lightly brush 2 baking sheets with the softened butter.

Prepare the pâte brisée sucrée just as you would a pâte brisée (pages 37–38 and technique photos on page 540) but add the sugar and vanilla to the well with the egg, salt, and water.

Dust a work surface with flour. Roll out the dough about 1/8 inch thick. Cut out a round 10 inches in diameter and transfer to one of the baking sheets. (This will be the base of the pastry.) Refrigerate.

Preheat the oven to 350°.

Prepare the choux pastry: Use the above ingredients and follow the directions on page 43. Fit a pastry bag with the plain tip and fill with the choux pastry. Brush the pâte sucrée base with egg glaze and pipe a circle of choux pastry around the edge of it. Pipe a second circle inside and touching the first. Then pipe a 1-inch mound of choux pastry in the center of the base. Brush the choux pastry with egg glaze. Bake until the choux is puffed and golden brown (including the interiors of any small cracks), about 30 minutes. Do not open the oven during the first 15 minutes of cooking or the choux will not rise. Let cool on a rack.

Fill the pastry bag with some of the choux pastry. Pipe 1-inch mounds on the second baking sheet, each about 2 inches apart. Brush each with egg glaze. Gently flatten the top of each mound with the back of a fork dipped in egg glaze. Bake until the choux have at least doubled in volume, are golden brown (including the interiors of any small cracks), and sound hollow when tapped, about 25 minutes. (Do not open the oven door during the first 15 minutes of cooking.) Let cool on a rack.

Prepare the caramel: Combine the sugar and water in a small saucepan and bring to a boil over low heat, stirring to dissolve the sugar. Boil, without stirring, until mixture turns a caramel color. Remove pan from heat and immediately dip the bottom into cold water to stop caramelization.

Assemble the pastry base: Lightly oil a baking sheet. Carefully dip the top of each choux puff into the hot caramel to lightly coat it and put them on the baking sheet, caramel-side down. Let stand until the caramel hardens. Then, turn the choux over and dip the bottoms into the caramel to attach them to the choux ring of the pastry base; place about 3/4 inch apart. If the caramel hardens while you are working, rewarm gently over low heat until liquid.

Prepare the Chiboust pastry cream: Sprinkle the gelatin over the water and let stand until softened, about 5 minutes. Bring the milk and vanilla to a boil in a heavy-bottomed saucepan; remove from heat. Combine the egg yolks and sugar in a bowl and whisk until thick and pale yellow. Whisk in the flour. Gradually whisk in the hot milk and return the mixture to the saucepan. Bring to a boil over medium heat, whisking vigorously, and then reduce the heat and simmer 5 minutes, whisking constantly to reach all parts of the pan. Remove from the heat and whisk in the softened gelatin. Beat the egg whites until stiff peaks form. Stir one-third of the egg whites into the hot pastry cream with a whisk, then gently fold in the rest.

Fit the pastry bag with the medium star tip and fill with the pastry cream. Pipe the cream decoratively over the bottom of the pastry ring. Then pipe a large rosette of cream between each choux puff. Chill before serving.

LESSON 90

Salade de Sandre aux Pleurottes
WARM SALAD OF YELLOW PIKE
AND OYSTER MUSHROOMS

———

*Oie Farcie aux Marrons
et aux Pommes*
GOOSE STUFFED WITH CHESTNUTS AND APPLES

———

Omelette Norvégienne
BAKED ALASKA

Salade de Sandre aux Pleurottes
WARM SALAD OF YELLOW PIKE
AND OYSTER MUSHROOMS

———

SERVES 6

This is the sort of typically modern first course that fine restaurants are offering in France today. Fish, traditionally served with cream or butter sauces, is here presented warm on a bed of lettuce, with green beans, mushrooms, and a sprinkling of vegetables cut into thin matchsticks *(julienne)*. The whole is seasoned with an aromatic vinaigrette to which a little cream has been added. The result is a mouth-watering array of colors, tastes, and textures all on the same plate.

Note: If yellow pike (also called walleye or pike perch) is unavailable, any firm-fleshed whitefish may be used instead.

2-pound yellow pike
Salt and freshly ground pepper
2 shallots, chopped fine
4 tablespoons unsalted butter
1 carrot, cut into julienne
  (see technique photo 519)
1 leek (white part only),
  cut into julienne
1 small turnip, cut into julienne
1 pound oyster mushrooms,
  trimmed, rinsed, and dried
6 ounces green beans, trimmed
1 head radicchio or
  red leaf lettuce

VINAIGRETTE

2 tablespoons sherry vinegar
Salt and freshly ground pepper
1 small shallot, chopped fine
1/4 cup peanut or vegetable oil
3 tablespoons olive oil

2 tablespoons crème fraîche or
  heavy cream
Chervil or parsley for garnish

Unsalted butter for baking sheet

Clean the pike (page 32 and technique photos on page 524) and then fillet it (page 75 and technique photos on page 525). Cut the fillets diagonally into strips about 1/2 inch thick. Brush a baking sheet with the softened butter. Sprinkle with salt, pepper and half of the chopped shallots. Spread the fish strips in a single layer over the baking sheet.

Heat 1 tablespoon of butter in a small pan over medium heat. Add the julienned vegetables and cook until crisp-tender; set aside and cover to keep warm. Heat the remaining 3 tablespoons of butter in a frying pan over low heat. Add the remaining shallots and cook gently until soft but not colored. Raise the heat to high, add the mushrooms and cook quickly until all the moisture has evaporated. Set aside; cover to keep warm.

Cut the beans into 2-inch pieces. Cook in boiling salted water until crisp-tender. Drain, refresh under cold running water and drain again.

Rinse and spin the lettuce dry.

Prepare the vinaigrette: Combine the vinegar, salt, pepper and shallot in a bowl. Whisk in the oils.

To serve, preheat the broiler. Arrange the lettuce in a ring on a large serving platter. Toss the beans with one-third of the vinaigrette and arrange in a ring inside the lettuce. Place a bed of mushrooms in the center of the platter.

Broil the fish strips for 4 minutes. Transfer to the bed of mushrooms with a spatula. Whisk the cream with the remaining vinaigrette and spoon over the fish. Sprinkle with the julienned vegetables. Serve decorated with sprigs of chervil.

Oie Farcie aux Marrons et aux Pommes

GOOSE STUFFED WITH CHESTNUTS AND APPLES

SERVES 6

As Christmas approaches, geese appear in poultry shops throughout Paris, although in recent years the turkey has all but taken its place. Indeed, in France, both birds tend to be prepared in much the same way: they are stuffed with a pork and chestnut dressing and served simply with the pan juices as a sauce.

Goose, like duck, is often served with fruit, and the French are discovering that American cranberries (sold fresh in Paris at Christmastime) nicely complement the taste of this traditional roast. Here is how the Christmas goose is roasted and served at Le Cordon Bleu in Paris.

8-pound goose
Salt and freshly ground pepper
2¹/₂ pounds small Golden
*   Delicious apples*
15 tablespoons unsalted butter
1¹/₂ pounds chipolata sausages
18 ounces chestnuts, canned
Pinch cinnamon

1 medium carrot, quartered
1 medium onion, quartered
1 stalk celery, cut crosswise
*   into thirds*
¹/₂ lemon
3 tablespoons melted butter
¹/₂ cup white wine
1 can (16 ounces) whole
*   cranberries in syrup*
¹/₂ bunch watercress for garnish

Rinse the goose inside and out under cold water and pat dry with paper towels. Remove the wing tips at the second joint and reserve, along with the neck and gizzard. Sprinkle all over with salt and pepper.

Prepare the stuffing: Reserve 6 apples for the garnish. Peel, core and quarter the rest. Heat 4 tablespoons of the butter in a frying pan over medium heat. Add the quartered apples and cook, stirring frequently, until tender, about 15 minutes. While the apples are cooking, put the sausages in a medium saucepan with cold water to cover. Bring to a boil and cook for 1 minute; drain. Heat 2 tablespoons of the butter in a frying pan over medium heat. Reserve half the sausages for garnish and sauté the rest until lightly browned, 2 to 3 minutes. Remove from the pan with a slotted spoon. Roughly chop the cooked apples and the sautéed sausages and combine in a bowl. Drain the chestnuts; reserve half for garnish and crumble the rest into the bowl with the apples and sausages. Season with salt, pepper and a pinch of cinnamon and mix carefully.

Preheat the oven to 425°.

Spoon the stuffing into the body cavity of the goose. Sew the opening closed with kitchen twine and a trussing needle. Truss the goose, just as you would a chicken (page 6 and technique photos on page 530).

Heat 4 tablespoons of the butter in a roasting pan over medium heat.

(continued)

SUPÉRIEURE

Oie Farcie aux Marrons et aux Pommes (continued)

Add the goose and brown it on all sides. Add the carrot, onion, celery and the reserved neck, wing tips and gizzard. Roast until the juices run clear when the thigh is pierced with a skewer, about 2 hours. Cover the goose with aluminum foil once it has browned. Baste frequently with the pan drippings to prevent the meat from drying out.

While the goose is roasting, peel the 6 reserved apples and trim them to equal sizes (see photo). Hollow out the centers with a vegetable peeler or melon baller, without piercing the sides or bottom of the apples. Rub the apples with the cut side of the lemon to prevent darkening. Put them on a baking sheet and brush with the melted butter. Set aside.

When the goose is cooked, transfer it to a platter; reserve the roasting pan with the juices. Cover the goose with aluminum foil and let rest in a warm place for about 15 minutes.

Reduce the oven temperature to 400° and bake the apples until tender, 15 to 20 minutes.

While the apples are cooking, prepare the sauce: Discard the fat in the roasting pan and add the wine. Bring to a boil over high heat and deglaze the pan, scraping the bottom to release the cooked particles. Strain into a small saucepan. Return to a boil, then reduce the heat and simmer, skimming off any fat that rises to the surface, until slightly reduced, about 5 minutes. Off the heat, whisk in 2 tablespoons of butter, little by little. Keep the sauce hot over a saucepan of hot water.

While the sauce is cooking, prepare the garnish: Heat 2 tablespoons of the butter in a frying pan over medium heat. Add the reserved chestnuts and cook 10 minutes, stirring gently so as not to break them. Meanwhile, heat 1 tablespoon of the butter in another frying pan over medium heat. Add the reserved sausages and brown 5 minutes. Warm the cranberries in their juice in a small saucepan over low heat.

To serve, remove the trussing twine from the goose. Transfer to a serving platter. Spoon cranberries into the hollowed-out centers of the cooked apples. Arrange the filled apples, sausages and chestnuts around the goose. Garnish the platter with watercress. Serve sauce in a sauceboat.

Omelette Norvégienne
BAKED ALASKA

—

SERVES 6

The French laugh when they learn that Americans call this a baked Alaska—they call it a Norwegian omelet! Its popularity dates from the nineteenth century when, some claim, a Chinese chef brought it to France.

Restaurants often accentuate the festive appearance of a baked Alaska by planting sparklers in it or pouring flaming brandy over it before serving, but with or without such eye-catching additions, this legendary combination of hot and cold is always spectacular.

GÉNOISE

3 eggs (room temperature)
1/2 cup sugar
3/4 cup all-purpose flour

ICE CREAM

2 cups milk
1 teaspoon vanilla extract
4 egg yolks
1/2 cup sugar

SUGAR SYRUP

1/4 cup water
1/4 cup sugar
2 tablespoons kirsch

FRENCH MERINGUE

*1/3 cup plus 2 tablespoons
 granulated sugar*
1/2 cup confectioner's sugar
3 egg whites

2 egg yolks, lightly beaten
1/2 cup slivered almonds
2 tablespoons confectioner's sugar

EQUIPMENT: Pastry bag, medium star pastry tip

Chill a mixing bowl in the freezer for the ice cream.

Prepare the génoise: Use the above ingredients and follow the directions on page 176. Remove from the cake pan and let cool on a rack.

Prepare the ice cream: First, make a crème anglaise, using the milk, vanilla, egg yolks, and sugar (page 35). Cool. Pour into an ice-cream maker and freeze according to the manufacturer's instructions. Transfer to the chilled bowl and freeze until firm, about 1 hour.

Prepare the syrup: Combine the water and sugar in a small saucepan. Bring to a boil over low heat, stirring to dissolve the sugar. Boil 1 to 2 minutes. Add the kirsch off the heat and set aside.

Cut the génoise crosswise into 2 rounds, each about 1/2 inch thick. Trim each to a square. Put the 2 squares side by side (to make a rectangle) on an oval heat-proof serving platter. Trim the edges to fit the platter. Brush the génoise with the syrup until well soaked. Freeze for about 1 hour.

Mound the ice cream on the frozen génoise with a metal spatula. Freeze for at least 1 hour. (At this stage, the baked Alaska may be stored in the freezer for several days, covered with plastic wrap.)

Preheat the broiler.

Prepare the meringue: Sift together the 1/3 cup granulated sugar and the confectioner's sugar; set aside. Beat the egg whites with a whisk or electric mixer until stiff. Gradually beat in the 2 tablespoons granulated sugar and continue beating until stiff peaks form again. Beat in the mixed sugars, slowly and gradually, until stiff peaks form again and the meringue is glossy. Whisk in the egg yolks.

Use a metal spatula to coat the baked Alaska thickly and evenly with half of the meringue mixture. Fit the pastry bag with the medium star tip and fill it with the remaining meringue. Decorate the baked Alaska with spirals and rosettes. Sprinkle with almonds and confectioner's sugar.

Broil the cake on an oven rack in the middle of the oven until lightly colored, 3 to 5 minutes. (Watch carefully—the meringue burns easily.) Serve immediately.

ILLUSTRATED TECHNIQUES

VEGETABLES

SLICING
Use the fingers of the hand not holding the knife to guide the knife to cut thin, even slices.

DICING
1 Peel the carrot and slice it vertically.

2 Cut the slices into strips.

3 Cut the strips into small squares for "brunoise."

4 Vegetables may be cut into larger dice depending upon the desired use.

JULIENNE
Cut the vegetables crosswise into 2-inch pieces. Cut the pieces vertically into thin slices and then cut the slices into matchstick pieces.

DICING ONIONS
1 Peel and cut in half through the root end. Place the halves cut side down and cut thin vertical slices up to but not through the root end.

2 Holding the knife flat, cut thin horizontal slices up to but not through the root end.

3 Then cut crosswise into dice.

ONION RINGS
Peel the onion and cut crosswise into slices. Separate the slices into rings.

CHIFFONADE
Stack the leaves one on top of the other and roll tightly into a cylinder. Then cut the cylinder crosswise into thin slices.

BOUQUET GARNI
Lay the bay leaf, thyme, parsley, and celery on 1 piece of leek leaf. Cover with another piece of leek and tie securely with kitchen twine.

TURNING VEGETABLES
Cut tubular vegetables into 2-inch lengths and round vegetables into chunks of about the same length and about 1½ inches wide. Pare down the sides of the pieces, shaping them into small barrel shapes with 7 faces.

PREPARING POTATOES
Potatoes may be cut into balls for pommes parisiennes (page 135); into thin, latticed slices for pommes gaufrettes; into thin rounds for pommes chip; into thick sticks for pommes pont neuf (page 253); into ¼-inch-thick sticks for pommes frites; into julienne for pommes allumettes; into a very fine julienne for pommes pailles; or they may be turned (page 50).

ARTICHOKE BOTTOMS
1 Snap off the stem of the artichoke.

2 Cut off and discard the bottom leaves, using a sharp knife.

3 Continue cutting the leaves until you reach the soft inner core.

4 Cut off the top of the artichoke, leaving the bottom about 1 inch high.

5 Trim the artichoke bottom to remove all the tough outer green parts so that it has a round regular shape and a smooth edge.

6 Rub the bottom well with the cut edge of a lemon to prevent it from darkening.

HOLLOWING OUT A PINEAPPLE

1 Trim the pineapple. Insert a long, thin knife vertically, and about ¼ inch in from the rind, through the top and just short of the base of the pineapple. Cut all around the inside of the rind with an up-and-down sawing motion to release the flesh without cutting through the base.

2 Remove the knife and reinsert the blade horizontally into the base of the fruit, ½ inch up from the bottom, pushing the knife tip almost through to the opposite side. Swivel the blade to the left to release half of the base of the pineapple.

3 Remove the knife and turn it over so that the blade faces in the opposite direction, and repeat the operation to release the other half of the base.

4 Use the knife to push the flesh up and out of the rind.

PREPARING FRENCH SCRAMBLED EGGS

1 Whisk the eggs with the cream. Melt butter in frying pan over low heat.

2 Add the egg mixture and cook, stirring constantly with a wooden spoon.

3 Cook just until the eggs have thickened but are very creamy and smooth.

PREPARING OMELETS

1 Heat the butter in a small frying pan over medium heat.

2 Add the eggs and cook gently, stirring with a wooden spoon.

3 When the eggs are set but still soft on top, fold the omelet with a spatula.

4 Fold the edge of the omelet that is closest to the handle in toward the center.

5 Tap handle of pan sharply; the far edge of the omelet will slide up the side of the pan.

6 Fold edge in toward center; continue cooking until bottom is lightly browned.

7 Grasp the handle of the pan and turn omelet out, seam-side down, onto the plate.

8 Pour over or brush the omelet with any butter remaining in the pan.

SHUCKING OYSTERS

1 Hold the oyster in your hand on a folded cloth with the rounded shell facing down and the pointed, hinged end facing toward you.

2 Insert a small knife between the two shells near the hinge and twist slightly to open the shells.

3 Slide the knife along the upper shell to sever the small muscle that connects the oyster to it.

SHELLING LANGOUSTINES

Langoustines are called scampi in Italian, but are not the same as the large shrimp often sold as scampi in the United States. They look more like small lobsters than shrimp. Only the tail meat is eaten.

1 Twist off the tails.

2 Then peel off the shells.

CLEANING ROUNDFISH

1 Cut off the fins behind the head with kitchen scissors.

2 Cut off fins on the belly.

3 Cut off all the remaining fins.

4 Working from tail to head, against the direction in which the scales lie, scrape the back of a knife blade along the skin to remove the scales.

5 Pull or cut out the gills.

6 To gut the fish, make a small incision in the belly just behind the head and pull out the entrails.

CUTTING ROUNDFISH INTO SLICES OR STEAKS

Use a heavy knife to cut the fish into slices through the backbone. (With larger fish such as salmon, these slices are called "steaks.")

FILLETING ROUNDFISH

1 Place your free hand on the fish to steady it and cut along the length of the backbone from head to tail. Then cut crosswise, down to the bone, above the tail.

2 Holding the blade of the knife flat, slide it along the length of the backbone and ribs to detach the fillet in one piece. Make a curved cut down to the bone behind the head to release the fillet.

3 Turn the fish over so that the tail points away from you. To remove the second fillet, first make a curved cut down to the bone behind the head.

4 Then cut crosswise, down to the bone, above the tail and cut along the length of the backbone from tail to head.

5 Finally, slide the knife along the backbone and ribs to detach the fillet.

ROUNDFISH FILLETS

SKINNING
Lay one fillet, skin side down, on a work surface. Grasp the fillet firmly at the tail end and, holding the knife blade flat, work it in between the flesh and skin and slide it down the length of the fillet to remove the skin.

ESCALOPES
Starting at the tail end of the fillet and holding the blade of the knife at a slight angle, cut the fillet diagonally into very thin slices.

BONING A ROUNDFISH FOR STUFFING

1 Make a shallow incision down the length of both sides of the backbone. Holding the blade against one side of the backbone, insert the blade down into the body, being careful not to pierce the skin of the stomach. Then, working from head to tail, slide the blade along the rib bones to lift the flesh, without cutting through the tail end.

2 Turn the fish over and insert the knife blade into the body on the other side of the backbone. Then slide the blade along the rib bones to lift the second fillet without cutting through the belly or the tail end.

3 To remove the backbone, cut it twice, behind the head and as close to the tail as possible. Pull out the backbone and the entrails.

CLEANING AND GUTTING FLATFISH

1 Cut the tail fin straight across, leaving it about ½ inch long.

2 Cut along one side of the fish to remove the fins.

3 Turn the fish and cut off fins on the other side.

4 Make a shallow cut across the tail fin and scrape up about ¼ inch of black skin.

5 Pull the skin sharply toward the head of the fish.

6 Scrape the back of a knife blade along the white skin to remove the scales.

7 Lay the fish, skin side down. Make a 3-inch incision behind the head and pull out the entrails.

8 Cut out the gills with kitchen scissors.

FILLETING FLATFISH

1 Cut along the backbone. Slide the knife along length of one fillet to lift from rib; repeat for second fillet.

2 Turn the fish over and repeat to remove the remaining 2 fillets.

BONING A FLATFISH FOR STUFFING

1 Cut along both sides of the fish to remove the fins. Trim the tail straight across.

2 Lay the fish black skin up. Slide knife under the skin just behind the head and free a flap of skin across the width of the fish.

3 Lift the flap with your free hand and gently pull it at the same time that you scrape the underside to completely remove the skin.

4 Cut down the length of the backbone. Then slide the blade between the flesh and rib bones on one side of the backbone to lift it from the rib bones.

5 Repeat on the other side of the backbone to completely expose the ribs. Do not cut completely through the outer edge of the fish.

6 Slide the knife under the ribs and backbone to begin to detach them from the flesh.

7 Cut the backbone just behind the head with kitchen scissors.

8 Then cut all the way around the outer edges of the ribs with scissors.

9 Slide the knife underneath ribs and backbone to free them from the flesh.

10 Then cut the backbone at the tail end; remove it.

11 You have now created a boneless pocket for stuffing.

CLEANING A CHICKEN

1 Lay the chicken breast side up on a work surface. Cut off the wing tips with a large, heavy knife.

2 Cut off the feet.

3 Turn the chicken over. **Pull the skin of the neck tight against the neck with one hand and then cut down the back of the neck skin.**

4 Pull the skin away from the neck and cut the skin just below the head.

5 Cut off the neck where it joins the body, leaving the skin intact. Cut off the head.

6 **Turn the chicken breast side up. Put your second finger into the neck end and work it around the cavity to detach and pull out the lungs.**

7 Turn the chicken around. Lift the legs and make a crosswise incision above the tail to enlarge the opening of the cavity.

8 Reach one hand into the cavity and pull out the innards (be careful not to break the green **gallbladder** attached to the liver).

9 **Cut the gallbladder carefully from the liver and set the liver aside. Discard the gallbladder along with the lungs, heart, and gizzard.**

TRUSSING A CHICKEN

1 Pass a long piece of kitchen twine underneath the tail. Bring the ends of the twine up around each leg and cross the ends over the top.

2 Bring twine under drumsticks and pull both ends to pull legs together. Then draw the ends of the twine along either side of the chicken and over the wing joints.

3 Turn the chicken onto its breast, cross the twine over the neck skin, and tighten to pull the wings to the body.

4 Tie securely.

5 Return the chicken to its back; it is now ready to cook.

CUTTING A CHICKEN INTO 6 SERVING PIECES

1 Lay the chicken flat on its back on a work surface. To remove the legs, pull one leg away from the body and cut down to the leg joint.

2 Twist the leg to break the joint and cut through the joint to separate the leg from the body. Repeat to remove the second leg.

3 On each leg, cut off the small bit of leg remaining below the drumstick at the joint.

4 Cut each leg in 2 pieces at the joint between thigh and drumstick.

5 Cut the breast in half lengthwise through the breast and back bones.

6 Cut the rib and back bones from the 2 halves of the breast.

PREPARING A DUCK: REMOVING THE BREAST

1 Pull up the skin around the opening of the neck cavity and scrape along both sides of the opening to expose the V-shaped wishbone.

2 Hook your finger behind the bone and give it a sharp tug to remove it in one piece.

3 Cut down one side of the breastbone and then cut and scrape along the ribs to release one half of the breast. Repeat on the other side.

4 Then cut along the bottom edge of each half of the breast, above the wing bones and legs, to remove the breast halves from the carcass.

PREPARING SQUAB

1 Cut off the neck and wing tips.

2 Cut the squab in half lengthwise.

3 The cut is made through the breast and back bones.

PREPARING SQUAB PAPILLOTES

1 Place a squab half, cut side down, on the lower half of a parchment rectangle and spoon the duxelles mixture on top of the squab.

2 Brush a ¼-inch border of beaten egg white along the edges of the lower half of the rectangle. Fold the upper half of the rectangle over the squab.

3 Brush all but the folded edge with a ¼-inch border of beaten egg white. Turn up the bottom edge two or three times and press to seal.

4 Turn the side edges in two or three times each.

5 Press the edges to seal.

BONING A RABBIT WHOLE FOR STUFFING

1 Cut off the tips of the fore and hind legs and remove the kidneys and liver.

2 Cut one foreleg off at the joint.

3 Cut off the other foreleg.

4 Working on insides of forelegs, cut along length of the bones to expose them, then cut away flesh in one piece.

5 Working on insides of hind legs, cut along the length of the thigh and leg bones, then scrape to release them. Cut

through the hip joint to remove the leg bones in one piece. Repeat to bone the second hind leg.

6 Cut along the length of one side of the backbone to release the fillet.

7 Repeat with the fillet on the other side.

8 Working at the tail end, carefully cut underneath the backbone to release it.

9 Then, moving toward the rib cage and taking care not to pierce the thin skin, continue to cut and scrape the flesh from the backbone.

10 Cut and scrape away the flesh from around and underneath the rib cage and then remove both backbone and rib cage.

11 The rabbit is boned and ready for stuffing.

CUTTING A RABBIT INTO SERVING PIECES

1 With a large, heavy knife trim the ends of the front and hind legs.

2 Cut off the front and hind legs at the joints. Cut the hind legs into two pieces at the joint and the body into three equal sections. Cut the rib section in half through the breast and back bones and then cut each half in half again.

CLEANING SWEETBREADS

1 Blanch the sweetbreads and then pull off the fat and ducts.

2 Remove the thin outer membrane with the point of a small knife.

BONING A LEG OF LAMB FOR STEW

1 Lay the leg, fat side up, on a work surface and trim off the skin, fat, and connective tissue.

2 Turn the leg over. Cut down the length of the upper leg to expose the bone. Cut and scrape to free it from the meat.

3 Then cut from the joint down the shank bone to expose the bone. Cut and scrape around the bone to free the meat. Remove the bones in one piece.

4 Cut the meat into 1½-inch cubes.

BONING A LAMB SHOULDER

1 Place the shoulder fat side up on a work surface. Use a boning knife to trim.

2 Remove the skin and excess fat.

3 Turn the shoulder over. Make a long incision in the meat opposite the shank bone and locate the flat, triangle-shaped blade bone. Cut and scrape from around the blade bone up to and around the joint. Cut through the joint.

4 Scrape the meat from around the underside of the joint and part of the way down the underside of the blade bone.

5 Then take hold of the joint and pull the blade bone sharply toward you to free it from the meat.

6 Make an incision along the length of the arm bone to expose it and then cut and scrape the meat from around the bone.

7 Cut and scrape around the shank bone and joint to free the bone from the meat.

8 Then remove the arm and shank bones in one piece.

STUFFING A BONED LAMB SHOULDER

1 First butterfly the shoulder: Make a horizontal cut about three quarters of the way through the thick muscle and open out the top flap.

2 Spread the meat with the stuffing and place the olives in a row down the center of the stuffing.

3 Tightly roll the shoulder and tie with a length of kitchen twine.

PREPARING A SADDLE OF LAMB FOR ROASTING

1 Place the saddle fat side up on a work surface. Use a boning knife to trim a 3-to-4-inch strip from the ends of both flaps.

2 Remove the skin and excess fat from the saddle.

3 Turn the saddle over and remove the nerve that runs down the length of the saddle. Remove the excess fat.

4 Roll each flap in toward the backbone and tie at even intervals with kitchen twine.

BONING A SADDLE OF LAMB AND PREPARING MEDALLIONS

1 Lay the saddle fat side down on a work surface and cut off the flaps with a boning knife.

2 Holding the knife close to the bone, cut and scrape down both sides of the backbone to release the 2 slender tenderloins.

3 Turn the saddle fat side up. Holding the knife flat against the bone, cut and scrape down both sides of the backbone to release the eye meat.

4 Strip off the fat and silverskin from the eye meat.

5 Use a large knife to cut each strip of eye meat into 6 medallions, each about 1¼ inch thick.

6 Flatten each medallion slightly with the side of the knife.

7 Tie the 2 tenderloins together in 4 places with kitchen twine and then cut into 3 or 4 slices. Alternatively, slice each tenderloin into 3 equal pieces.

PREPARING A RACK OF LAMB

1 Use a boning knife to remove the flat piece of cartilage that lies at one end of the rack.

2 Remove the skin and all but ½ inch of fat from the rack.

3 Lay the rack fat side down on the work surface. Cut off the yellow strip of connective tissue that lies underneath the backbone.

4 Set the rack on one end and cut off the chine bone (backbone) with a heavy chef's knife or cleaver.

5 Place the rack, fat side down, on a work surface and score a line along the rib bones, about 2 inches in from the tips.

6 Then cut along the edge of each rib, down to the scored line.

7 Cut out the meat between the bones.

8 Turn the rack over, fat side up, and repeat step 5. Remove the fat and meat above the line, in one piece, to expose the rib bones.

9 Scrape carefully around the exposed rib bones to clean them of all meat and connective tissue.

PREPARING PÂTE BRISÉE AND PÂTE SUCRÉE

1 Combine the flours in a mound on a cool work surface. Make a well in the center and put in egg, water, salt, and butter (plus sugar and vanilla for pâte sucrée).

2 Move the butter to one side and combine the egg, water, and salt (plus sugar and vanilla if using) with the fingertips of one hand.

3 Work the butter into the wet ingredients until well blended.

4 Gradually cut in the flour with a plastic pastry scraper.

5 Continue until the dough holds together.

6 Then push bits of dough away from you, smearing across the work surface to blend into a smooth dough.

7 Scrape the dough up into a ball. Flatten it into a disk and dust lightly with flour. Chill 30 minutes.

LINING AND BLIND BAKING TART SHELLS

1 Dust a work surface with flour. Roll out the dough to a round about ⅛ inch thick.

2 Fold the dough round in half and unfold it over the tart pan.

3 Gently press the dough into the pan with your fingers or with a ball of dough.

4 With the thumb and index fingers of one hand, mold a ¼-inch horizontal lip around the inside of the rim. Then roll the rolling pin over the rim to cut off the excess dough.

5 Push the lip up so that it extends about ¼ inch above the pan, and then pinch into a decorative shape with pastry pinchers or your fingers. Prick the bottom with a fork and refrigerate.

6 Cut out a round of parchment paper a few inches larger than the tart pan and fit it over the dough. Fill the center with weights and bake until the edges begin to brown, about 15 minutes.

LINING AND BLIND BAKING TARTLET MOLDS

1 Roll out dough about ⅛ inch thick and cut out the desired shape. Line the molds, chill, and prick with a fork.

2 Put a smaller mold inside each to prevent the pastry from rising and deforming during cooking. Bake 10 minutes.

PREPARING PÂTE FEUILLETÉE

1 Combine the flours in a mound on a cool work surface and make a well in the center. Add the salt, water, and melted butter to the well.

2 Mix with your fingers until the salt dissolves.

3 Then use a plastic pastry scraper to pull the flour into the well and mix until blended, adding the remaining water if the dough is dry.

4 Work the dough into a sticky ball with the pastry scraper.

5 Make an X-shaped incision on top of the dough, wrap in lightly floured parchment paper, and refrigerate for about 30 minutes.

6 Sandwich the remaining butter between 2 sheets of parchment paper and tap with a rolling pin until softened. Form the butter into a square about ¾ inch thick. Set the ball of dough on a lightly floured work surface and flatten slightly with the palm of your hand. Then press the rolling pin into the top edge of the dough and roll out an "arm." Give the dough a quarter turn and roll out another "arm." Continue to turn and roll twice more until the dough is in the shape of a cross. It should be mounded in the center, tapering out to the four arms (see above).

7 Place the square of butter on the mounded center of the dough and fold in the arms, stretching the dough slightly as needed to completely seal in the butter.

8 After lightly tapping the top of the dough with a rolling pin to seal the edges, roll out the dough to a long rectangle.

9 The edges should be even and straight.

10 Fold the bottom third of the rectangle up toward the center, carefully aligning the edges, and brush off any flour.

11 Fold the top third down to make a neat square and brush off any flour.

12 You will have a neat square with the fold on the bottom.

13 Give the square a quarter turn to the left.

14 The fold should be at the side.

15 Roll the dough out again to a rectangle.

16 Fold again into thirds. Gently press 2 fingertips into the dough to indicate the 2 turns have been completed.

17 Wrap and refrigerate 30 minutes. Give the pastry 2 more turns and then refrigerate 30 minutes before completing the final 2 turns.

PREPARING PASTRY "BANDES" FOR FRUIT TARTS

1 Roll out puff pastry dough ⅛ inch thick. Trim the edges, then cut a 12- by 5½-inch rectangle and 2 strips of pastry, each 12 inches long and ½ inch wide.

2 Transfer the rectangle to a baking sheet and prick with a fork. Brush egg glaze along the 2 long edges, then lay the pastry strips over the glazed borders, 1/16 inch in from the edges.

3 Use the back of a paring knife to make shallow indentations at ¼-inch intervals along the sides of the dough for decoration. Brush the pastry strips with egg glaze.

PREPARING FEUILLETÉS

(Puff pastry cases, or feuilletés, may be prepared in a variety of shapes. The following shape is a bit more complicated than some.)

1 Roll out puff pastry dough about ⅛ inch thick, then cut into 5-inch squares. Fold each square in two to form a triangle.

2 Starting about ½ inch in from the left side, cut up to within ½ inch of the top of the triangle. Repeat on the right side.

3 Unfold the dough square and brush the edges of the inner square lightly with egg glaze.

4 Lift the two outside cut corners, pass one corner under the other and then fold each over flat to meet the corners at the opposite sides.

5 Brush the edges of the pastry cases with egg glaze.

6 Prick the bottoms all over with a fork.

PREPARING RECTANGULAR FEUILLETÉS

1 On a lightly floured work surface, roll out the dough ⅛ inch thick and cut it into six rectangles.

2 Transfer the rectangles to a baking sheet with a metal spatula.

3 Brush each with egg glaze (be careful not to let the glaze run over the edges of the dough or the feuilletés will not rise evenly).

4 If you like, decorate the feuilletés by making shallow indentations at ¼-inch intervals along the outside edges with the back of a knife.

5 Lightly trace decorative lines on the tops of the feuilletés.

PREPARING BOUCHÉES

1 Roll out puff pastry dough and stamp into rounds ⅛ inch thick. Transfer half the rounds to a baking sheet; remove centers of remaining rounds with a smaller cutter.

2 Prick the rounds on the baking sheet and brush with egg glaze. Place the cutout rings on top of the glazed rounds, pressing gently to adhere.

PREPARING PITHIVIERS

1 Divide the dough in half. On a lightly floured work surface, roll out one half about 1/8 inch thick; set aside. Roll out the remaining dough 1/8 inch thick (see above) and place it on a baking sheet.

2 Brush the dough with a 2-inch circular border of egg glaze.

3 Pipe or mound the cream in the center of the dough to within 1/4 inch of the glaze.

4 Lay the second piece of dough over the filling. Press the edges together to seal.

5 Using an 8-inch vol-au-vent cutter as a guide, cut a scalloped edge with the point of a small knife.

6 Brush the surface with egg glaze, but do not let the glaze run over the sides or the pastry will rise unevenly.

7 Use a knife to trace shallow, curved lines radiating from the center of the pastry out to the edge, like the spokes of a wheel.

WRAPPING A BEEF TENDERLOIN IN PUFF PASTRY

1 Roll out puff pastry dough to a rectangle ⅛ inch thick. Place the cooled tenderloin in the center of the dough rectangle. Brush the exposed dough with egg glaze.

2 Fold up the long sides of the dough to enclose the tenderloin.

3 Gently roll the rolling pin over the seam to seal. Roll out the end flaps of dough ¹⁄₁₆ inch thick.

4 Brush the flaps with egg glaze and fold up over the dough package. Press the seams together to seal. Brush off any excess flour.

5 Transfer the dough-covered beef to a baking sheet, seam-side down, and brush with egg glaze.

6 Make a small hole in the top of the dough package with a pastry tip to allow steam to escape. Insert a short cylinder of foil into the hole.

7 Cut long strips about ¼ inch wide from the reserved dough and lay them over the surface in a diamond pattern. Brush with egg glaze, chill, then glaze again.

PREPARING PÂTE À CHOUX

1 Combine water, butter, and salt in a saucepan and cook until butter melts and water boils.

2 Remove from the heat and add the flour all at once.

3 Beat with a wooden spoon until a thick dough forms. Stir over low heat until dough pulls away from pan.

4 Beat in the first 2 eggs, one at a time, beating until thoroughly blended after each addition.

5 Then lightly beat the third egg in a small bowl and add it little by little.

6 Add just enough egg for the dough to become smooth and shiny and fall slowly from the spoon in a point

PIPING PÂTE À CHOUX

PROFITEROLES
1 Using a plain ½-inch tip, pipe small mounds of dough on a baking sheet.

2 Brush each choux with egg glaze.

3 Flatten each slightly with a fork dipped in water.

SWANS
With a medium plain tip, pipe teardrop shapes on baking sheet; with a small plain tip pipe S-shaped figures.

PIPING LADYFINGERS

1 Using a pastry bag fitted with a large plain tip, pipe strips of batter 5 inches long and ¾ inch wide diagonally onto the baking sheet.

2 Sprinkle half of the confectioner's sugar over the ladyfingers; wait 5 minutes and sprinkle with the remaining sugar.

LINING A CHARLOTTE MOLD WITH LADYFINGERS

1 First line the bottom of the mold: Cut 6 to 8 ladyfingers in half crosswise and trim each half to a V-shape (each piece will resemble a daisy petal). Turn the mold upside down and arrange the shaped ladyfingers on the bottom to form a flower pattern.
Then use a small round cookie cutter to cut out a circle in the center of the flower. Use the same cutter to cut a neat round piece from another ladyfinger and place it in the center of the flower (see above).
Invert a plate over the ladyfinger flower and turn the mold and plate right side up. Re-form the flower, rounded side facing down, in the bottom of the charlotte mold.

2 Then line the sides of the mold: Square off one end of each of about 14 ladyfingers, leaving them long enough to extend above the rim of the mold. Trim the sides slightly and fit tightly around the inside of the mold, rounded ends up.

LINING A MOLD FOR CHARLOTTE AUX POMMES

1 Trim the crusts from the bread and trim the bread to 4-inch squares. Cut 6 of the slices in half to make 12 rectangles. Cut the remaining slices in half diagonally and then in half again to make small triangles. Turn the mold upside down and arrange the triangles on it like the pieces of a pie, to cover the bottom.

2 Remove the triangles and turn the mold over. Brush both sides of all of the bread pieces with clarified butter and fit the triangles into the bottom of the mold. Then arrange the rectangles around the inside so that they overlap generously. The bread should extend slightly above the rim of the mold.

PREPARING TULIPS

1 Have ready 4 brioche molds or custard cups for shaping the tulips. Spoon 1 tablespoon of batter on the baking sheet. Dip a spoon into cold water and use the back of the spoon to spread the mound of batter into a round about 5 inches in diameter. Repeat to make another cookie.

2 Bake the tulips until golden brown, about 5 minutes. Then open the oven door and pull the baking sheet halfway out. Starting with the most colored, remove the tulips one at a time with a metal spatula and press each into a mold. Then place a second mold over the cookie, inside the first mold, and press gently to shape.

PREPARING TILES

1 Spoon small spoonfuls of batter about 4 inches apart on a buttered baking sheet. Flatten each to a 2-inch round.

2 After baking until evenly golden, remove the tiles one at a time and drape them over a rolling pin to shape them.

PIPING MERINGUE

FOR VACHERIN
1 Trace an 8-inch circle on the baking sheet with a vol-au-vent cutter or 8-inch cake pan.

2 Pipe meringue into the circle, starting at the center and working outward in a spiral.

3 Continue piping the meringue to completely fill the circle.

4 Trace two 8-inch circles on a second baking sheet and outline each with a ring of meringue.

5 Then pipe a second ring of meringue just inside of and touching each of the first 2 rings.

FOR BASKETS
Trace 4-inch circles on a parchment-covered baking sheet. Fill a pastry bag fitted with a medium plain tip with meringue. Starting at the center of each circle and working outward in a spiral, pipe the meringue to fill each circle on the baking sheet. Then using a pastry bag fitted with a medium star tip, pipe a raised, spiral border around the edge of each meringue round.

PREPARING CRÈME ANGLAISE

1 Combine the egg yolks and sugar in a heatproof bowl.

2 Whisk until thick and pale yellow.

3 The mixture should form a ribbon when the whisk is lifted from the bowl.

4 Gradually whisk in half of the hot milk and then add the remainder all at once. Stir constantly over low heat.

5 The custard should be thick enough to leave a clear trail when a finger is drawn across the back of the spoon.

PREPARING CHOCOLATE CURLS

1 Melt the chocolate and beat with a spoon until smooth and shiny.

2 Pour the chocolate onto a flat surface.

3 Spread about ⅛ inch thick with a metal spatula. Let cool until firm but not brittle.

4 Then hold the blade of a knife at an angle and scrape up curls of chocolate.

ACKNOWLEDGMENTS

Le Cordon Bleu would like to acknowledge all those people who helped in the realization of this work:

Le Cordon Bleu's team of chefs: Didier Beauclair, Michel Besnard, Jean-Claude Boucheret, Christian Georges, Patrick Lebouc, Jackie Martin, Patrick Martin, Alexandre Petroff, Roger Simon, Rene Sourdeix, Patrick Terrien, Alain Villiers.

The writing, translating, and organizational team: Mena Bartley, Susanne Haase, Drayton Nutall, Anne de Perignon, Charlotte Turgeon, Gregory Usher.

The people who helped to test each and every recipe: Francine Ades, Kaya Baudinette, Janice Calendar, Judith Elson, Kathleen de Fouchier, Joanne Gates, Barbara Graham, Jack Hasey, Margaret Kirby, Patricia Kreuzburg, Shirley Lui, Merry McCabe, Carol Wagner, David Wilson, Colleen Wohlforth.

The administrative back-up: Catherine Baschet, Antonella Boudet, Thierry Chaunu, Cecile Cointreau, Patrice de Jeu, Catherine del Pozzo, Caroline Delrieu, Valerie Follet, Michel Grelet, Harold Israel, Laurence Legris, Anne Leroy, Norbert Leuret, Florence Maigret, Bernard Mouro, Agnes Poissonnier, Setsuko Shoai-Therani, Beatrice Tabeling.

The photography: Christian Délu, Pierre Ginet.

And last but not least, André Cointreau, president of Le Cordon Bleu, wishes to thank Robyn Cahill, who has been a guiding force behind this project.

LE CORDON BLEU WORLDWIDE

France

LE CORDON BLEU
Ecole de Cuisine et de Pâtisserie
8, rue Léon Delhomme
75015 Paris France

Telephone: 33 (1) 48.56.06.06
Fax: 33 (1) 48.56.03.96

England

LE CORDON BLEU
Ecole de Cuisine et de Pâtisserie
114 Marylebone Lane
London W1M 6HH England

Telephone: 44 (71) 935-3503
Fax: 44 (71) 935-7621

Canada

LE CORDON BLEU PARIS COOKING SCHOOL
Suite 400
1390 Prince of Wales Drive
Ottawa, Ontario
Canada K2C 3N6

Telephone: (613) 224-8603
Fax: (613) 224-9966

INDEX